A New Edition of
HEALTH AND SAFETY FOR YOU
Wellness from Webster/McGraw-Hill

Health and Safety for You has it all. This new edition, revised to keep pace with the fast-changing field of health, was designed with teachers and students in mind. Here are some highlights:

An Active Approach to Wellness
The wellness orientation of health begins in the first chapter (page 3) and continues throughout the book—both motivation and information help teenagers make positive health decisions for today and for the long term.

Current Health Topics
Today's serious health concerns are all here—stress (page 66), cancer prevention (page 132), sexually transmitted diseases (page 266), nutrition (page 288), smoking (page 232), alcohol (page 242), and drug abuse (page 252).

Solid Content
The foundation of effective health education is solid content on body systems. Unit 5 (beginning on page 141) treats all these important areas.

Self-Care and Emergencies
The latest in practical health information is covered—emergency procedures and other self-care aspects of health and wellness, including CPR (page 361), first aid (page 351), the Heimlich maneuver (page 367), poisoning (page 352), and being a health consumer (page 384).

Solid Educational Features
Each chapter is reinforced with seven features to support learning. The Preface on page iv describes them all.

A Beautiful Book
The book features photographs and illustrations that are as functional as they are colorful—thumb through the book and see the appeal.

The Teacher's Manual
The Teacher's Manual contains teacher notes, answers to chapter questions, reproducible student activity and resource sheets, chapter and unit tests, and test answers.

HEALTH AND SAFETY FOR YOU

Sixth Edition

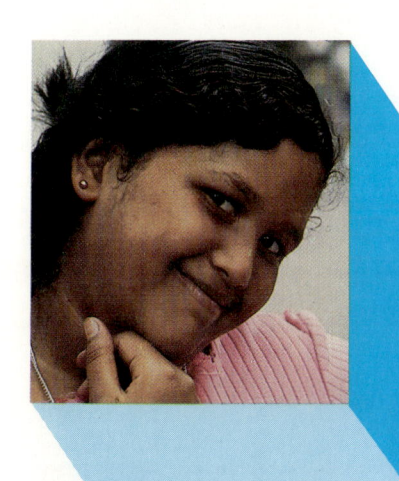

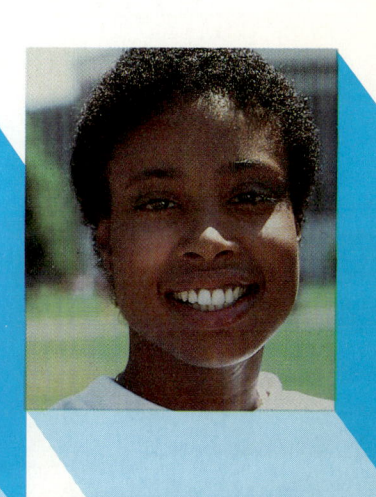

WEBSTER DIVISION/McGRAW-HILL BOOK COMPANY

New York　St. Louis　San Francisco　Auckland　Bogotá　Guatemala
Hamburg　Johannesburg　Lisbon　London　Madrid　Mexico　Montreal　New Delhi
Panama　Paris　San Juan　São Paulo　Singapore　Sydney　Tokyo　Toronto

Editor: Martha O'Neill
Editorial Assistant: Nancy Hernandez
Coordinating Editor: Caroline Levine
Production Supervisor: Salvador Gonzales
Photo Editing Manager: Rosemary O'Connell

Editorial Consultant: Lois Kierstead-Lapid
Page Layout: Bo Lam
Artists: Helen Li, Joel Snyder, Lorna Tomei, Vicki Vebell
Medical Illustrations: Lou Barlow
Cover: Edward Lettau/Photo Researchers; Blaise Zito, Associates, Inc.

Anatomical Drawings: Lou Barlow

This book was set in 11 point Baskerville by
 Lehigh/ROCAPPI
The color separation was done by
 Lehigh/Electronic Color, Inc.

Library of Congress Cataloging in Publication Data

Tsumura, Ted K.
 Health and safety for you.

Rev. ed. of: Health and safety for you / Harold Sheely Diehl et al. 5th ed. c1980.
 Includes index.
 SUMMARY: An introduction to anatomy, physiology, mental and physical health, preventive medicine, environment and heredity, safety, drugs, nutrition, human sexuality, and health careers.
 1. Health—Juvenile literature. [1. Health]
I. Jones, Lorraine Henke. II. Bonekemper, Thomas W. III. Diehl, Harold Sheely, date. Health and safety for you. IV. Title.
RA777.T77   1984   613   82-24878
 ISBN 0-07-065378-X

Copyright © 1984, 1980, 1975, 1969, 1964, 1961, 1957 by McGraw-Hill, Inc. Copyright 1954 by McGraw-Hill, Inc. Copyright renewed 1982 by Anita D. Laton. All rights reserved. Printed in the United States of America. Except as permitted under the Copyright Act of 1976, no part of this publication may be reproduced or distributed in any form or by any means, or stored in a data base or retrieval system, without the prior written permission of the publisher.

6 7 8 9 10 DOWDOW 92 91 90 89 88 87 86

The Authors

TED K. TSUMURA teaches health at George Washington High School in Denver, Colorado. He holds a doctorate in Health Education and has twenty years of experience as a high school teacher. In 1976, he was named Colorado Teacher of the Year and was runner-up for the National Teacher of the Year Award. He is also a member of the Advisory Board of the Colorado Department of Health Neonatal Screening for Genetic Disorders. He is a coauthor of a textbook for high school biology students. He is past president of the Colorado Biology Teachers' Association.

LORRAINE HENKE JONES is assistant professor of nursing at Ball State University in Indiana. Formerly, she was a teacher and health education specialist for Prince George's County Public Schools, Maryland. She holds a master's degree in both nursing and health education. She is also a member of Sigma Theta Tau (the national honor society of nursing) and Eta Sigma Gamma (the national professional health science honorary). She has written articles for health education and nursing journals. In addition, the American National Red Cross and the Agency for Instructional Television have published health and safety programs that she helped to write.

THOMAS W. BONEKEMPER is assistant professor of medicine at Hahnemann University School of Medicine in Philadelphia. Prior to pursuing his medical career, he taught health education at the secondary level. He is a diplomate of the American Board of Internal Medicine and a member of the American Society of Internal Medicine. As a physician, his special interests are patient education and preventive medicine.

Preface
A Modern Textbook, with a Comprehensive Scope

Health and Safety for You is a comprehensive textbook that will help you to learn about *total health*—physical, mental, and social well-being. Its focus is on *wellness* and *preventive health and safety measures.* It encourages you, the student, to choose responsible health behaviors right now to improve and safeguard your health.

Highlights

- *Up-to-date content* features current, simple, direct explanations that allow you to make intelligent decisions about health behavior. You will learn how your body works, how to prevent disease, and how and where to get treatment if necessary.
- *Readable text* has many subject headings that organize the content for you and allow easy reference.
- *Colorful photographs and illustrations* bring the text to life. They show how your body works and help you to learn by letting you see facts and ideas for yourself.
- *Easy-to-read captions* focus your attention on the important ideas in each chapter. They help you to understand the more complex information.
- *Introductory "Do you know" questions* at the beginning of each chapter guide your learning. They alert you to the key concepts within each chapter.
- *Effective chapter summaries* in the form of "Main Ideas" and "Key Words" allow you to review and evaluate what you have learned. Important key words are defined in the glossary. Pronunciations are included.
- *Discussion* is encouraged beyond the scope of each chapter in the section called "Something to think about." This section features the latest health topics and covers controversial health research.
- *Active learning* is stimulated in the section called "Extend Your Knowledge." This section engages you in independent research, interviewing, and community participation.
- *Information on the latest health careers* offers you the chance to consider future opportunities in the field of health service.

Contents

Unit 1   Active Body

1. Health and Wellness   2
   Health in the twentieth century
   Prevention
   Health inventory

2. Basis of Movement   10
   The skeletal support
   Muscles in motion

3. Keeping Fit through Sports and Recreation   24
   The importance of exercising
   Knowing your limitations
   What you should do about injuries

Unit 2   Understanding Yourself

4. Emotional Needs and Mature Personality   42
   Emotional needs
   Mature personality
   Developing maturity in the teen years

5. Emotions and Mental Health   54
   Anger and hostility
   Fear and anxiety
   Defense mechanisms
   Mental illness
   A self-check on your mental health

6. Living with Stress   66
   The stress response
   Is stress harmful?
   Coping with stress

Unit 3   Human Sexuality

7. Human Reproduction   78
   The male reproductive system
   The female reproductive system
   The beginning of life
   Birth
   Multiple births
   Prenatal care

8. **Family Life** 92
   Family relationships
   Dating
   Marriage
   Family planning
   Sexual attitudes and behaviors

Unit 4   Environment and Heredity

9. **From Generation to Generation** 108
   What are genes?
   Genetics in medicine

10. **Environmental Hazards** 120
    Air pollution
    Water pollution
    Noise pollution
    Radiation pollution

11. **Cancer Prevention** 132
    What is cancer?
    What is a tumor?
    How does cancer spread?
    What causes cancer?
    Prevention of cancer
    Treatment of cancer
    Cancer quacks
    The future

Unit 5   Functioning Body

12. **Coordination and Control** 142
    Your nervous system
    Transmitting a message
    Acting upon a message
    The central nervous system
    Disorders of the nervous system
    Taking care of your nervous system

13. **Eye and Ear Care** 154
    Structure and protection of the eye
    Visual problems
    Education of blind and visually handicapped people
    Protection and structure of the ear
    Hearing disorders
    Education of the deaf

14. Transport System   170
    Your blood
    The role of lymph
    Your heart
    Heart disease
    Taking care of your circulatory system

15. Respiration   188
    Respiratory tract
    Breathing and respiration
    Air pressure and oxygen
    Respiratory disorders
    Taking care of your respiratory system

16. Skin and Hair: Your Protective Covering   200
    Skin structure
    Functions of the skin
    Skin problems
    Your hair and nails
    Care of the hair

17. Regulators of Your Body   210
    Pituitary gland
    Thyroid gland
    Parathyroid glands
    Islands of Langerhans
    Adrenal glands
    Gonads
    Pineal and thymus glands
    Taking care of your endocrine system

18. Healthy Teeth   220
    Your teeth
    Care of the teeth
    Cleaning the teeth
    Dental problems
    Dental health

Unit 6 Social Drugs

19. Use of Tobacco   232
    Substances in tobacco smoke
    Effects of smoking on the body
    Smoking and disease
    Involuntary smoking
    The smoking habit

vii

20. Use of Alcohol   **242**
   Alcoholic beverages
   Misuse of alcohol
   Help for the problem drinker

21. Drugs: Use and Abuse   **252**
   Drugs for health
   Some reasons why people use psychoactive drugs
   Commonly abused drugs

Unit 7   Preventing Communicable Diseases

22. Sexually Transmitted Diseases   **266**
   Types of STDs
   Preventing STDs

23. The Common Cold and Other Miseries   **272**
   Pathogens
   Infectious diseases
   Common infectious diseases
   Preventing infectious diseases

24. Immunizations   **280**
   Active immunity
   Passive immunity
   Responsibility and immunity

Unit 8   Food, Diet, and Digestion

25. Nutritional Needs   **288**
   Using the Daily Food Guide
   Nutrients
   Basal metabolic rate

26. Snacks and Special Diets   **302**
   Snacking
   Weight control
   Special diets

27. Nutrition, Labels, and the Consumer   **316**
   Food labeling
   Food additives: Are they all necessary?
   Are health foods nourishing?
   What are open dating and unit pricing?

28. Digestion and Elimination   326
    The digestive tract
    Elimination of wastes
    More about the digestive system

Unit 9   Safety and Emergency Care

29. Personal Safety   342
    Automobile accidents
    Motorcycle accidents
    Bicycle accidents
    Accident prevention

30. Basic First Aid   350
    First aid
    Everyday emergencies

31. Cardiopulmonary Resuscitation (CPR)   360
    Prevention of sudden death
    The A-B-C steps of cardiopulmonary resuscitation
    Choking

Unit 10   Health Careers and Services

32. Selecting Health Care   372
    Medical care
    The medicine show

33. Self-care and the Health Consumer   384
    The health consumer
    Self-care
    Can some medicines be harmful to you?

34. Health in the United States   396
    History of our healthy nation
    Health services
    A special health organization
    Toward better health for everyone

35. Health Careers for You   406
    Health service—one of the fastest growing areas of employment
    How should you prepare for a health career?

Unit 1

CHAPTERS:

1 Health and Wellness
2 Basis of Movement
3 Keeping Fit through Sports and Recreation

Active Body

Chapter 1

Do you know . . .

- what *health* and *wellness* mean?
- how your body is changing, and what you can expect from it in the future?
- what preventive health habits are?
- why everyone does not take preventive health measures?
- how to take an inventory of your own health?

Health and Wellness

Would you say that you are a healthy person?

>Terry: "Sure, I haven't had a cold or the flu in two years."
>Pauline: "My knees don't hurt when I jog now. It's easy for me to run 40 minutes a day."
>Ross: "I'm healthy until hay fever season—then I feel terrible."

These teenagers are talking about the way their bodies function. Terry keeps track of past illnesses. Pauline is aware of how her body is presently performing and changing. Ross knows what to expect of his body at certain times in the future.

Health in the twentieth century

Knowing how your body has performed, how it is changing, and what to expect of it is important to being healthy. But today, there is more to health than that. The World Health Organization defines *health* as:

>A state of complete physical, mental, and social well-being, and not merely the absence of disease or infirmity.

In other words, being free from physical problems does not necessarily mean that you are healthy. Mental well-being and social well-being must be considered, too. Can you be depressed and still be healthy? Can you be healthy if you are often in trouble with the law? Read the World Health Organization definition again. Is it realistic? Is there ever a time when you experience complete physical, mental, and social well-being?

The World Health Organization decided on its definition in 1947. During this century, the leading causes of death changed in the United States and in other developed countries. Look at the table on page 4. In 1900, at the beginning of the century, the leading causes of death were pneumonia, influenza, and tuberculosis. These are diseases caused by bacteria and viruses. They are known as infectious diseases because they can spread when conditions are favorable for bacteria and viruses to grow.

Medical research in the twentieth century found a way to prevent and control infectious killers. New sanitation laws and better drugs meant that people could avoid these illnesses, or be cured of them. By 1979, more than three-fourths of the way through the century, the leading causes of death were different. People were more free of infectious disease. They lived a longer time and were now becoming victims of noninfectious diseases: heart attacks, cancer, high blood pressure, and strokes. Most evidence shows that these diseases are *not* spread by bacteria and viruses. They are diseases that often take place later in life. And they are influenced by a lifetime of day-to-day health habits. This has led to new ideas about what health means. The term *wellness* is often used to describe a broader view of good health. Wellness includes not only physical well-being but also emotional, social, and intellectual fitness as well.

In the 1980s, medical researchers are finding new ways to control some of these noninfectious killer diseases. More importantly, they are finding that these diseases can be prevented.

Mental and social well-being

When was the last time you felt good about yourself? Can you really enjoy another person? Are you able to handle normal disappointments? The answers have to do with your mental and social well-being.

In the first part of the twentieth century, the behavioral sciences of psychology and sociology had just begun serious research. By the time of the World Health definition, health professionals and the public were taking psychological and sociological findings seriously. It seemed as if mental and social ills could be successfully prevented and treated. Well-being also could be called a state of mind, not just a state of the body.

Of course, mental health and physical health are closely connected. Can you experience mental and social well-being during a painful ear infection? Is your attitude about yourself any different during a period in your life when you have acne?

Or can you experience physical well-being when you are constantly under mental or social tension—involved in an ongoing battle with your

Since 1900, the leading causes of death have changed. People are now more free of diseases that are spread by bacteria and viruses. Now they are becoming victims of heart attacks, high blood pressure, cancer, and strokes. Can you think of reasons for this change?

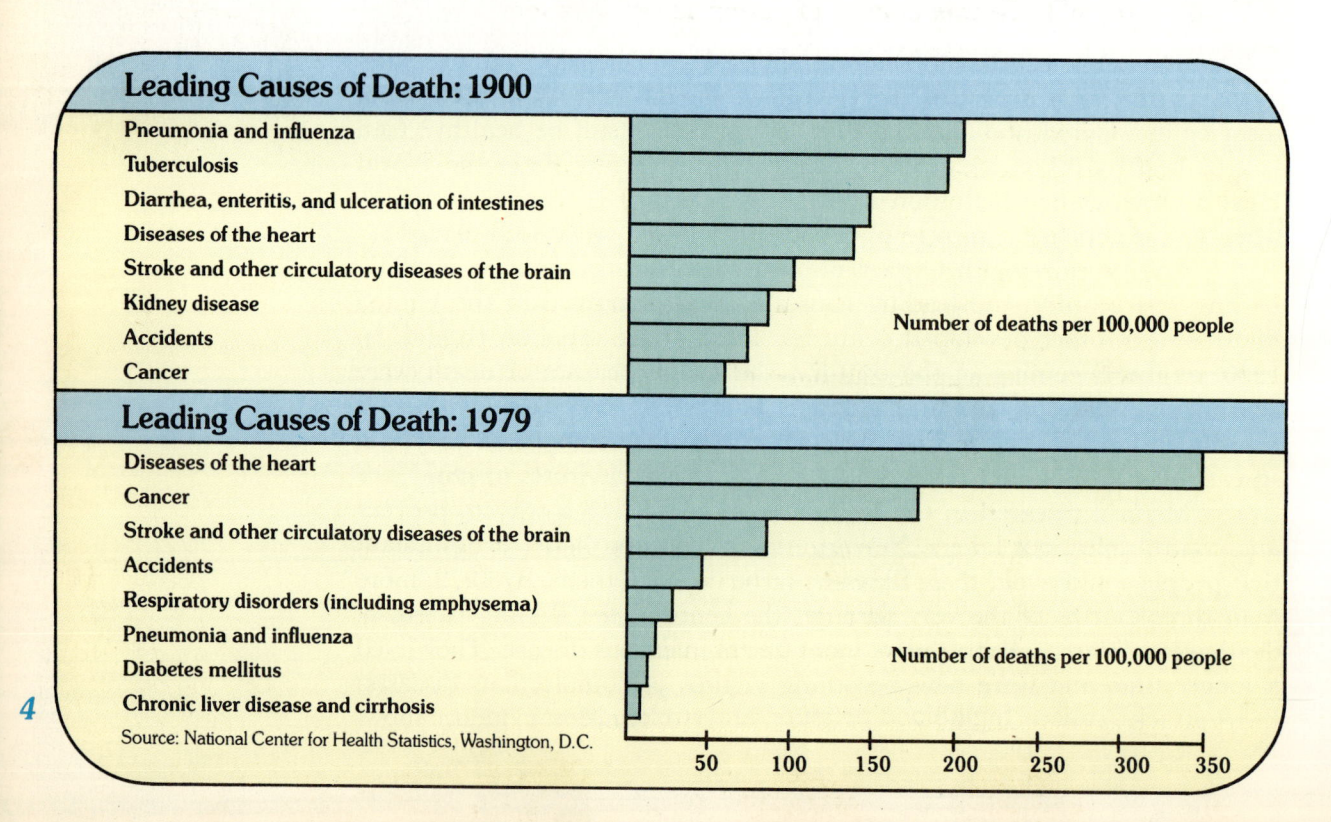

Leading Causes of Death: 1900
- Pneumonia and influenza
- Tuberculosis
- Diarrhea, enteritis, and ulceration of intestines
- Diseases of the heart
- Stroke and other circulatory diseases of the brain
- Kidney disease
- Accidents
- Cancer

Number of deaths per 100,000 people

Leading Causes of Death: 1979
- Diseases of the heart
- Cancer
- Stroke and other circulatory diseases of the brain
- Accidents
- Respiratory disorders (including emphysema)
- Pneumonia and influenza
- Diabetes mellitus
- Chronic liver disease and cirrhosis

Number of deaths per 100,000 people

Source: National Center for Health Statistics, Washington, D.C.

50 100 150 200 250 300 350

parents, for example? When you think about it, it is almost impossible to separate mental and social health from physical health.

Prevention

Can you predict how healthy you will be in the year 2000? Do you know how healthy you will be when you reach 35? Can you tell how healthy you will be next year, or even a week from now?

While you cannot predict the future with certainty, you can get an idea of what your chances are for good health. Is there a new, miracle method of diagnosis to tell you this? No. You can tell yourself by reviewing your own day-to-day health habits. If the health habits you practice *right now* are preventive ones, you have a better chance of avoiding or postponing illness and injury.

It seems so simple. Why doesn't everyone practice preventive health habits? Medical research has linked lung cancer and heart disease to cigarette smoking. Why don't people stop smoking? Safety belts can prevent needless deaths during an automobile accident. Why doesn't everyone wear a safety belt while riding in an automobile or driving?

In the 1960s, the United States Public Health Service tried to find out why people do or do not take actions that prevent illness and injury. They found that people will take preventive action if:

1. **they see the health problem as one which has a good chance of affecting them.**
2. **they think that there would be serious consequences if the problem did affect them.**
3. **they believe there is a course of action that can reduce the threat.**
4. **they believe this course of action is reasonable.***

Good health in later life depends in part on your health behavior right now.

In other words:
- if you believe that it is possible for you to become involved in an automobile accident;
- if you think that it is possible for that accident to result in injury or death to you;
- if you believe that safety belts can reduce injuries and death in automobile accidents;
- if you find that snapping on your safety belt is really not such a chore . . .

then you will probably get in the habit of fastening your safety belt each time you ride in an automobile.

You know, of course, that not everyone takes preventive health measures. People's information, lack of information, and attitudes vary a great deal. Suppose that you interview five people. You tell each person that he or she is 25 pounds overweight. You also tell each person that overweight increases the chances of heart disease. Then you ask each person the four questions that decide preventive behavior. Their responses are on page 6. Take a look at them now.

* Adapted from "What Research in Motivation Suggests for Public Health," by Irwin M. Rosenstock, in the *American Journal of Public Health* (March 1960).

Question	Ray	Anne	Cheryl	Max	Sue
Do you think you have a chance of having heart disease?	Probably. My grandparents were both overweight, and they both died of heart disease.	I'm only 20. I can't imagine having a heart attack. It doesn't seem possible.	I'm not so worried about heart disease. I read that women don't get heart diseases as often as men do.	Yes. I guess my chances of heart disease are increased by overweight.	Yes. Overweight is a risk factor for the heart.
Do you think having heart disease would be serious?	Yes. It seems like it could be serious—even fatal.	Very serious. You would have to do something about overweight if you ever got heart disease.	Heart disease is serious for those people who get it.	It all depends. People recover from heart disease. I have a friend who had three heart attacks. So he takes it easy.	Yes. Heart disease is a leading cause of death in the United States.
Is there anything you can do about your weight to lower the risk of heart disease?	Probably not. Fat people and thin people get heart disease. There are many factors. Who can tell for sure?	Look, I'll cross that bridge when I come to it. I'm only 20!	I don't think my weight has anything to do with my own risk of heart disease. That's a problem men have. (End of interview.)	I can drop these extra pounds.	I could lose weight.
If there is something you can do, is it reasonable?	If your time is up, you go. Dieting is hard and it might not make any difference.	It's not reasonable to live in the future. You have to live in the present.		I want to lose some weight, but not because of heart disease. I'd like to lose it because I think I'd be more attractive if I were 25 pounds slimmer.	I probably won't. I hate to diet. I can't stick to a diet long enough to lose 25 pounds.

Excuses for lack of prevention

What does each person seem to be saying? If you look closely at these interviews, you will see some common excuses for not taking preventive measures:

- Ray believes it is all a matter of fate. He thinks there is nothing you can do to prevent disease and death.
- Anne feels she is too young to be concerned. She can't imagine a time when her health will show the effects of her long-term health habits.
- Cheryl thinks this is all someone else's problem. *She* doesn't have to worry about heart disease.
- Max might take some preventive measures—but for his own reasons. He is not so concerned about heart disease.
- Sue finds the preventive measures too difficult.

What do you think of each person's responses? What part do information and attitude play in these answers?

As a textbook, HEALTH AND SAFETY FOR YOU can provide you with information about your body: how it is constructed and how it functions. It can give you information about preventive health measures. It can explore the meanings of mental and social well-being. It can give you insights into new developments in health and medicine.

But, by itself, HEALTH AND SAFETY FOR YOU cannot make you a healthier person. It will be up to you to take the information you learn from this text and apply it to your own health behaviors.

But before you decide on your health behaviors, you will need to know where you stand. The following health inventory can help you take stock of your present well-being—physical, mental, and social.

Physical well-being

1. **Are you physically fit?**

    Physical fitness can be measured. In Chapter 3, you can participate in a fitness test. But before you move on, try the following inventory test. (If you have an injury, or your doctor has advised you not to participate in any physical activity, tell your teacher.)

    Sit and slowly reach for your toes. If you can reach 6 centimeters (about 2½ inches) beyond your toes, you are fairly flexible. If you can go beyond 16 centimeters (about 6½ inches), you are very flexible. How did you do? Most students range between 5 centimeters (about 2 inches) and 14 centimeters (about 6 inches).

2. **Are you feeding your body the required nutrients?** Think of everything you ate yesterday. Did you:
    - eat or drink at least four servings from the milk and cheese group: yogurt, milk, or cheese?
    - eat at least four servings of fruits and vegetables that are a good source of vitamins A or C?
    - eat at least four servings of bread and cereal products?

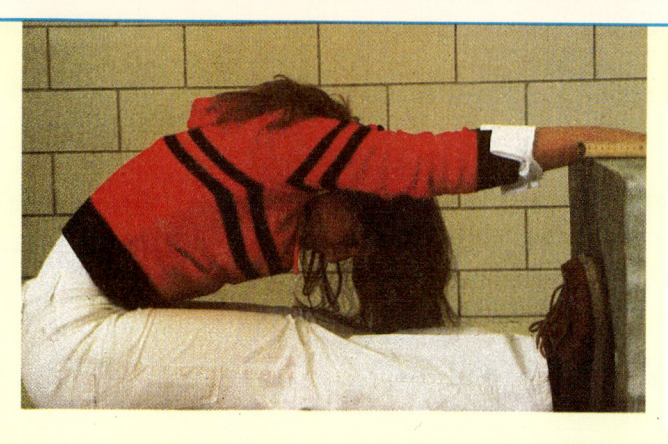

Try this physical health inventory test. Sit and slowly reach for your toes. If you can reach about 2½ inches beyond your toes, you are fairly flexible. How did you do?

- eat at least two servings of meat, poultry, fish, or beans?
- avoid junk foods?

3. Have you had your blood pressure taken within the last year?
4. Do you know if there are any substances that cause you to have contact dermatitis (redness and swelling of the skin)?
5. Do you brush and floss your teeth every day?
6. Do you know what symptoms would make you suspect that you had a sexually transmitted (venereal) disease?
7. How often do you take over-the-counter medications (laxatives, antacids, pain relievers, and so forth)?
8. Do you have a record of your inoculations? Do you know if you are still protected by these inoculations?
9. How many hours of sleep do you average at night?
10. Do you routinely do warm-up exercises before strenuous physical activity?
11. Do you know the first thing to do if you are burned?
12. Do you wear a safety belt while driving or riding in an automobile?
13. Do you know the seven warning signals of cancer?
14. Do you know how good your vision is?
15. Do you know how to spot medical quackery?

Mental and social well-being

1. Which need seems to cause you the most conflict: your need for dependence or your need for independence?
2. How do you fulfill your need to create?
3. Do you have sudden changes of mood for no clear reason?
4. Do you have a social relationship that you find satisfying?
5. How do you react when you deal with people who are different from you?
6. Name one goal that you have achieved.
7. Name three goals that you have set for yourself for the future.
8. Do you feel good about being the sex you are?
9. How do you relax when you are feeling the effects of stress?
10. Under what conditions would you seek professional help? Where would you go to find it?

Whether you could answer one or most of the questions, the inventory will have helped you learn more about yourself in a very different way. You owe it to yourself to know all you can about the complex person that you are. This book will help you to do that.

Do you realize that your telephone may be a health resource? *Tel-Med* is a service that offers over 1000 tape recordings on all sorts of health issues. You just pick up the phone, dial the Tel-Med number, state the title and number of the tape you would like to hear, and sit back and listen. The recordings vary in length from 3 to 5 minutes. They stress preventive measures, early warning signs of illness, and when or how to get medical help.

Look for leaflets about Tel-Med in the library, supermarket, or doctor's office. You may also call your county medical society to find out if this service is available in your area.

Something to think about . . .

Main Ideas

1. Health is a state of complete physical, mental, and social well-being.
2. Being free of physical problems does not always mean you are healthy.
3. Not everyone practices preventive health habits, because people's information, lack of information, and attitudes vary a great deal.
4. One common excuse for not taking preventive health measures is believing that a health issue is someone else's problem.

Extend Your Knowledge

1. Discuss the following statement with your class: "Health determines the quality of your life." Is this statement always true?
2. Interview ten people about whether or not they practice the following preventive health measures:
   a. using a safety belt
   b. flossing the teeth
   c. being aware of the seven warning signals of cancer
   d. feeding the body the required daily nutrients
   e. having the blood pressure checked at least once each year.

   What can you conclude about the answers you were given? How many people practice most of the preventive measures?
3. Keep a weekly diary as you use this health book. Include a list of the new health and safety habits you will add to those you already practice.

Chapter 2

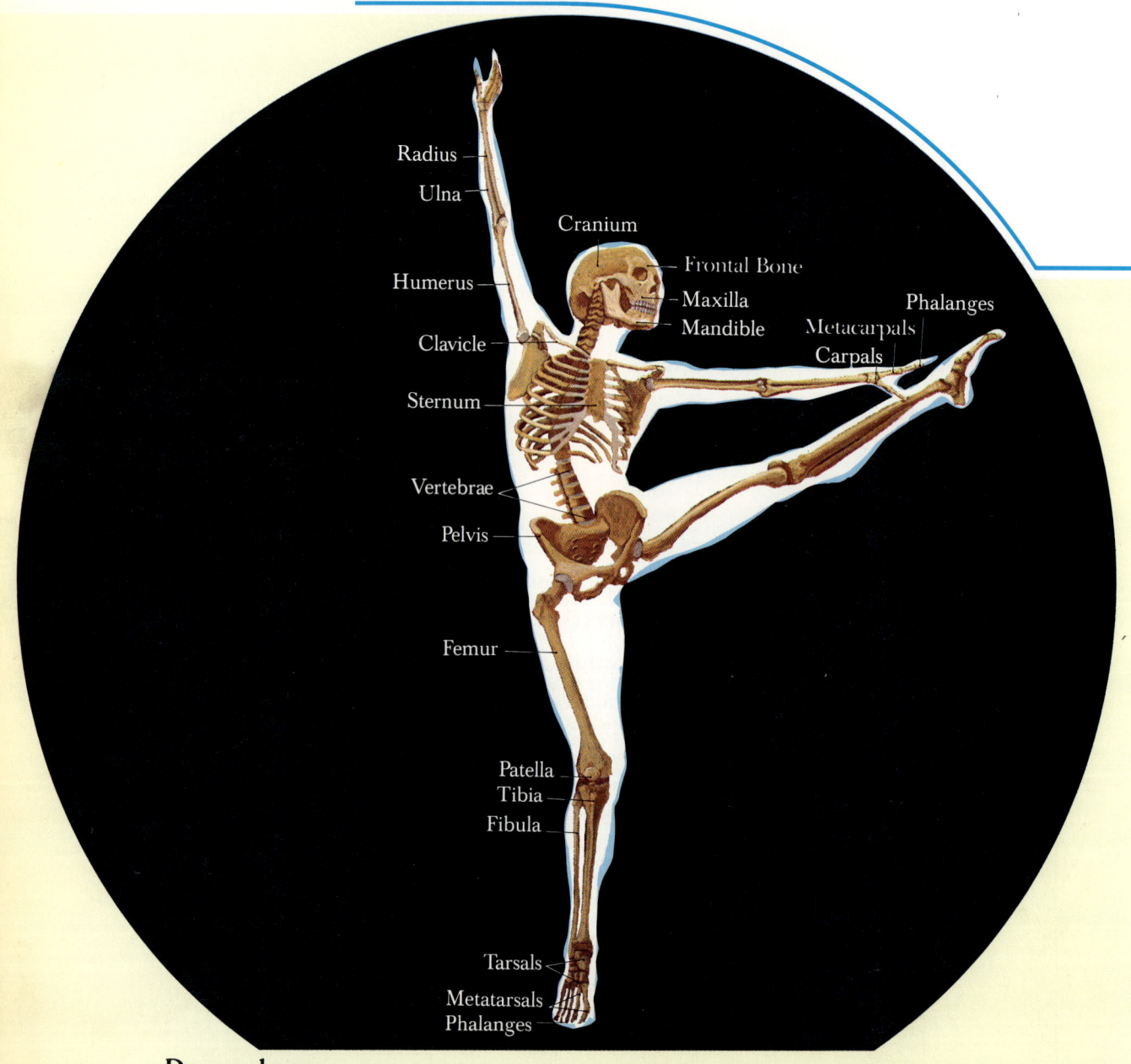

Skeleton diagram with labels: Radius, Ulna, Cranium, Frontal Bone, Humerus, Maxilla, Mandible, Phalanges, Clavicle, Metacarpals, Carpals, Sternum, Vertebrae, Pelvis, Femur, Patella, Tibia, Fibula, Tarsals, Metatarsals, Phalanges

Do you know . . .

- that broken bones can bleed?
- how the arches of the foot protect the body?
- that your muscles are made up of different colored fibers?
- whether or not heat is given off when muscles contract?
- why a warm-up before physical activity is important to prevent muscle injury?

Basis of Movement

In Chapter 1, you made some movements to test your physical fitness. The movements were made possible by muscles and bones. If your muscles are well-coordinated and the supporting bones are strong, you can make almost any movement with ease.

The skeletal support

Have you heard the expression "dry as a bone"? Actually, the bones in your body are not dry at all. They are living tissue, and they need blood and nourishment, just like other organs of the body.

You know that bones support the body and that muscles are attached to them. But did you know that most of the cells of the blood are formed inside the bone? A hollow area inside each bone contains special tissue called *bone marrow*. Red bone marrow produces red blood cells and three types of white blood cells. It also produces platelets that aid in the clotting of blood. Red bone marrow is found in all the bones of young children and in the breastbone, ribs, and backbone of adults.

The bones protect vital organs, such as the brain, heart, lungs, and spinal cord. Calcium and phosphorus are two of the minerals in the bone that make it hard and strong. Calcium is also important for other vital functions in the body. It helps muscles to contract, blood to clot, and nerves to carry impulses.

You are supported and protected by 206 bones. They differ greatly in size and shape. All of the bones are connected by tough, fibrous tissues called *ligaments*. The place where two or more bones are connected is called a *joint*. The ends of the bones in a joint are surrounded by *synovial fluid*. This fluid is like a lubricant and lets the ends of the bones move freely. When there is injury to a joint, too much fluid may be produced. This causes swelling and pain. It happens when an ankle or knee is injured, for example.

There are many types of joints in the skeleton.

Hinge joints permit back-and-forth movement. The joints of the fingers, knees, and elbows are hinge joints.

Shaft of Bone

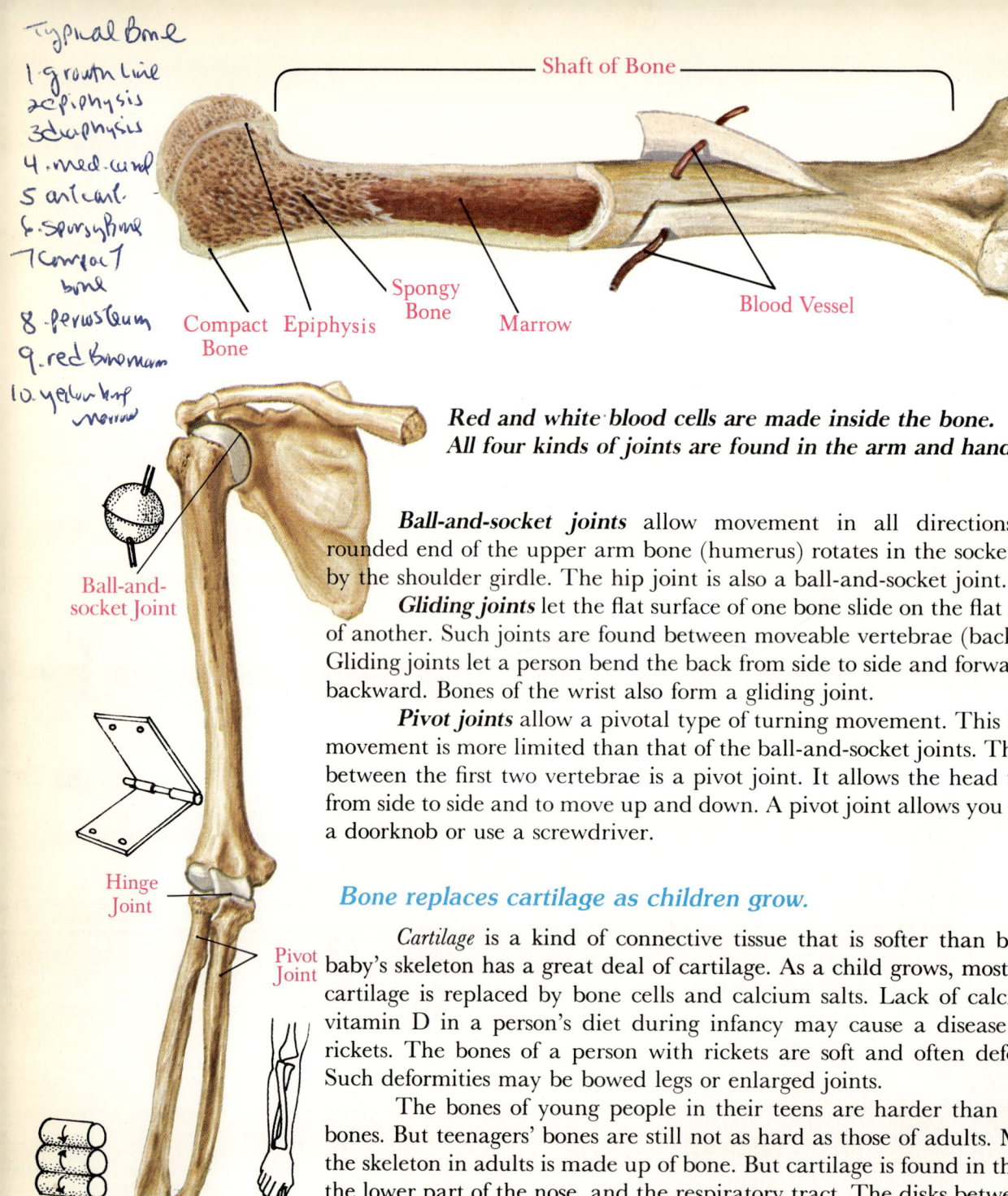

Compact Bone · Epiphysis · Spongy Bone · Marrow · Blood Vessel

Handwritten notes:
Typical Bone
1. growth line
2. epiphysis
3. diaphysis
4. med. canal
5. art. cart.
6. spongy bone
7. compact bone
8. periosteum
9. red bone marrow
10. yellow bone marrow

Ball-and-socket Joint
Hinge Joint
Pivot Joint
Gliding Joint
Hinge Joints

Red and white blood cells are made inside the bone.
All four kinds of joints are found in the arm and hand.

Ball-and-socket joints allow movement in all directions. The rounded end of the upper arm bone (humerus) rotates in the socket made by the shoulder girdle. The hip joint is also a ball-and-socket joint.

Gliding joints let the flat surface of one bone slide on the flat surface of another. Such joints are found between moveable vertebrae (backbone). Gliding joints let a person bend the back from side to side and forward and backward. Bones of the wrist also form a gliding joint.

Pivot joints allow a pivotal type of turning movement. This kind of movement is more limited than that of the ball-and-socket joints. The joint between the first two vertebrae is a pivot joint. It allows the head to turn from side to side and to move up and down. A pivot joint allows you to turn a doorknob or use a screwdriver.

Bone replaces cartilage as children grow.

Cartilage is a kind of connective tissue that is softer than bone. A baby's skeleton has a great deal of cartilage. As a child grows, most of this cartilage is replaced by bone cells and calcium salts. Lack of calcium or vitamin D in a person's diet during infancy may cause a disease called rickets. The bones of a person with rickets are soft and often deformed. Such deformities may be bowed legs or enlarged joints.

The bones of young people in their teens are harder than babies' bones. But teenagers' bones are still not as hard as those of adults. Most of the skeleton in adults is made up of bone. But cartilage is found in the ears, the lower part of the nose, and the respiratory tract. The disks between the vertebrae and the ends of long bones are also made of cartilage. This cartilage cushions and protects the end of the bone.

While a bone is being formed, tiny blood vessels called capillaries reach every part of the bone. Calcium salts harden the bone tissue, but tiny canals that contain blood vessels remain. Thanks to these small canals in the bones, there is a constant exchange of minerals between bone and blood. In this way, bone structure changes slowly all through life. If a bone breaks, bone cells in the area begin to build new bone tissues.

The more you use your bones, the stronger they will become.

The early astronauts returned to Earth with bones that had weakened. This weakening was due to weightlessness in space. In zero gravity, the muscles did not stimulate the bones. So the bones became weaker through a loss of calcium (*decalcification*). Do you know what would happen to your leg if it were in a cast and not able to move for months? Fortunately, a walking cast lets you put stress on a broken bone and helps the bone heal faster.

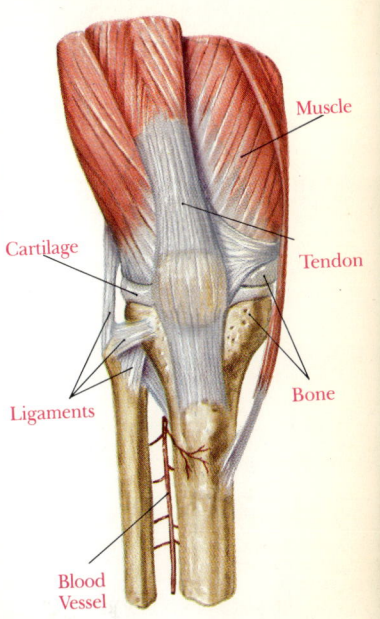

Some interesting points about the skeleton

The human skull is made up of the 8 flat bones of the *cranium* and the 14 bones of the face. The cranium holds the delicate human brain. A person's brain is not fully grown at birth. It can continue to grow because the 8 cranial bones are not joined together when the baby is born. The soft spaces between the bones are called *fontanels*. The fontanels let the baby's skull become smaller during its passage through the mother's narrow pelvic opening at birth. All the fontanels usually close between the third and twelfth month after birth. But if the fontanels close too early, the brain cannot grow and the child will be mentally retarded. This is called a *microcephalic* condition (*micro* = small/*cephalic* = headed).

Cerebrospinal fluid helps to protect the brain and spinal cord by acting as a cushion against blows to the head. But if this fluid becomes trapped inside the brain, the pressure will grow and cause the brain to push outward. This creates what is called a *hydrocephalic* condition (*hydro* = water/*cephalic* = headed). The fontanels may remain open because of the extra pressure.

Ligaments connect bones to joints. Tendons connect muscles to bones.

Skeletal difference between females and males

One major difference between a male skeleton and a female skeleton can be seen in the pelvic region. The female pelvis is wider and shallower. While the opening in a male pelvis is triangular, the opening of the female pelvis is almost oval. The special features of the female pelvis are important for childbearing.

Is there an advantage to having arches in the foot?

Humans are the only animals with arches. Do you run faster, jump higher, or land more gracefully with arches? The answer to this question is *no*. However, since you have arches, your body weight is spread evenly over the foot. Arches also provide the necessary support to let the foot be used as a lever when you stand on your toes. And after you jump, arches will help absorb the shock when you land. The curved arch of the foot also protects blood vessels and nerves.

Ligaments and muscles support the bones that form the foot's crosswise and lengthwise arches. To keep these arches from falling (a condition called flatfoot), it is important to exercise the muscles that support them. People who spend many hours standing should be aware of this problem.

Some people believe that wearing a copper bracelet can cure or relieve arthritis. This is not true. Can you think of other health "cures" that are supposed to stop disease?

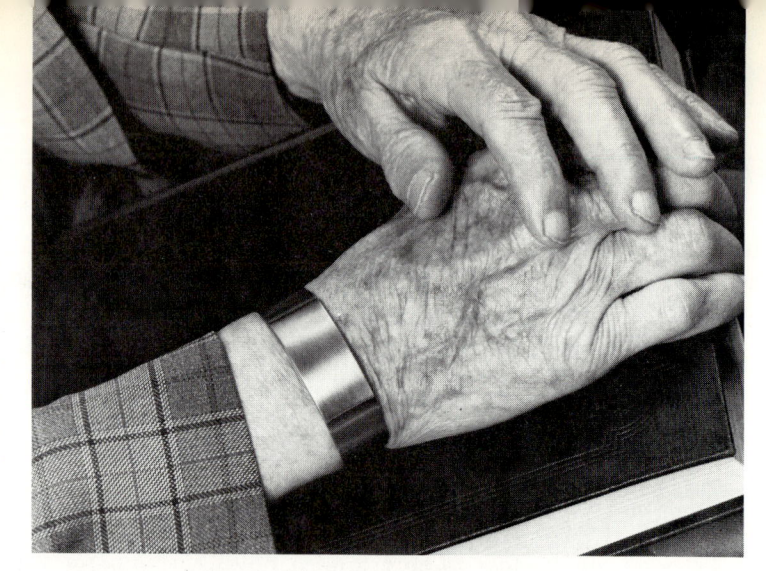

Is arthritis common only to older people?

Arthritis is a condition that causes the joints to swell and become painful. One form, called "stress" or traumatic arthritis, is common to young people. Young athletes often injure or irritate the same joint over and over again. They may find that the bones of the injured joint become thicker. The joint may become more and more painful and harder to move.

There are many other types of arthritis. The most common form is a "wear-and-tear" disease that chiefly affects older people. Another form, called rheumatoid arthritis, is the most severe kind. It usually strikes people between 20 and 50 years of age. Even children can get a form of this disease known as juvenile rheumatoid arthritis. Gout is a type of arthritis that mainly affects men.

People who have arthritis should be under the care of a physician. Physicians cannot cure all forms of arthritis. In fact, they do not know for sure what causes it. But doctors can prescribe drugs that bring some relief. Heat, massage, and other forms of physical therapy may help to lessen swelling, ease pain, and prevent crippling. Unfortunately, many arthritis sufferers fall victim to quacks who claim they can bring about "cures."

Arches spread body weight evenly over the foot. The shape of the arch differs from person to person. Do flat arches cause any problems?

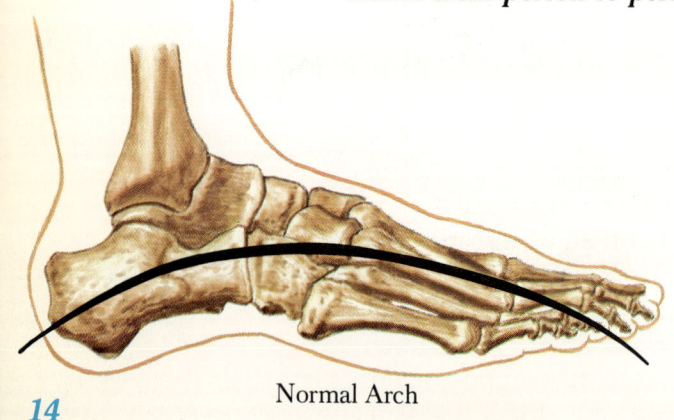

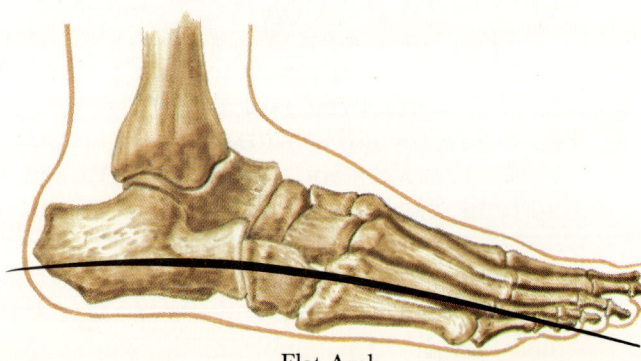

Normal Arch

Flat Arch

Bone surgery—a case history

With her airline ticket in hand, Julie calmly waited in line to enter the boarding area. The line moved quickly. Soon, Julie placed her suitcase on the belt and walked through the gates of the metal detector. She knew what was going to happen. The gates buzzed loudly, and the guard took Julie off to the side. She began to explain. The year before, Julie had been in a motorcycle accident. Because she was wearing a helmet, she lived. But her right arm and shoulder were badly injured. The right clavicle, the ball-and-socket joint, and the humerus were crushed. The doctors carefully cleaned the wound to prevent *osteomyelitis,* or bone infection. Then they used metal pins to join the bones together. The crushed ball-and-socket joint was replaced with an exact replica made from stainless steel. And some of Julie's crushed bone was repaired by using pieces of preserved bone from a bone bank.

Modern methods of bone surgery, such as the use of human-made replacement parts and transplants from a bone bank, made it possible for Julie to get back full use of her arm. She caused the metal detector to buzz when she walked through because her arm joint is made of stainless steel rather than bone. The guard checked Julie for any weapons and then let her through. She made her plane on time.

Muscles in motion

Before you buy a car, it is a good idea to test-drive it. You should be interested in its total performance. You will want to check the brakes, gears, and accelerating power. After the test drive, you may look at the parts under the hood to see how they fit together. Then, in case of a breakdown, you might know what to do.

In Chapter 1, you studied the performance of your body. You stretched, pulled, and jumped to test your motor functions. Now it is important for you to know something about the body parts that let you move, just in case something goes wrong.

There are over 600 muscles that move different parts of your body. Winking, chewing, breathing, and walking are just a few of the many movements that depend on muscles. Some muscles are made up of over 200,000 cells. Other muscles are small, having only a few hundred muscle cells. Muscle cells are long and can contract. They are also known as muscle fibers.

Each muscle is surrounded by blood vessels, nerves, and connective tissue. Many muscle fibers are grouped together by connective tissue to form a *fasciculus*. Many fasciculi form a muscle bundle—which works as a single muscle. The connective tissue that holds the muscle fibers together is usually longer than the fiber. This tissue extends to form the *tendon*. The tendon attaches the muscle to the bone.

The nerve that attaches to a muscle cell causes the muscle cell to contract. When a muscle contracts, it becomes shorter and thicker. The two ends of the muscle draw closer together. During muscle contraction, energy is given off as work and heat. When a muscle is not contracted, it is said to be relaxed.

Muscles never totally relax, even when a person is asleep. This slight, constant contraction of muscles is called muscle tone. A healthy muscle feels firm because of its tone. A muscle with poor tone feels soft and flabby. Good muscle tone helps the posture. It also aids circulation, diges-

Tiny groups of muscle fibers form a muscle bundle. There are three types of muscles. They allow for movement, digestion, and circulation.

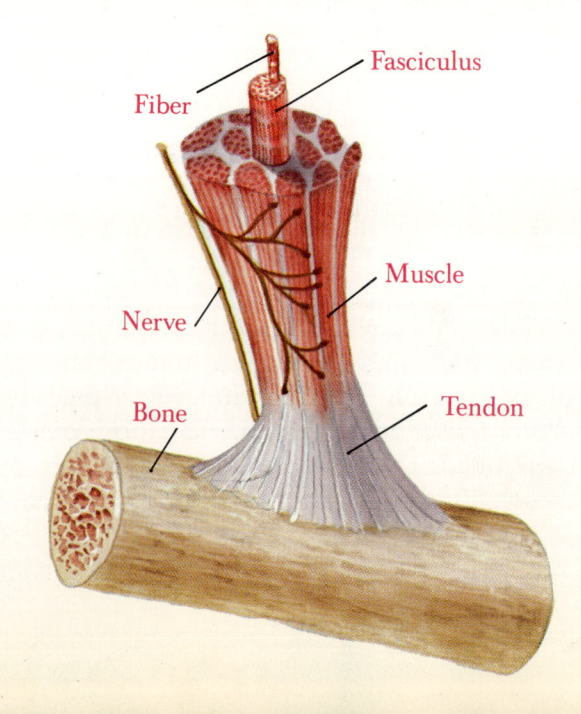

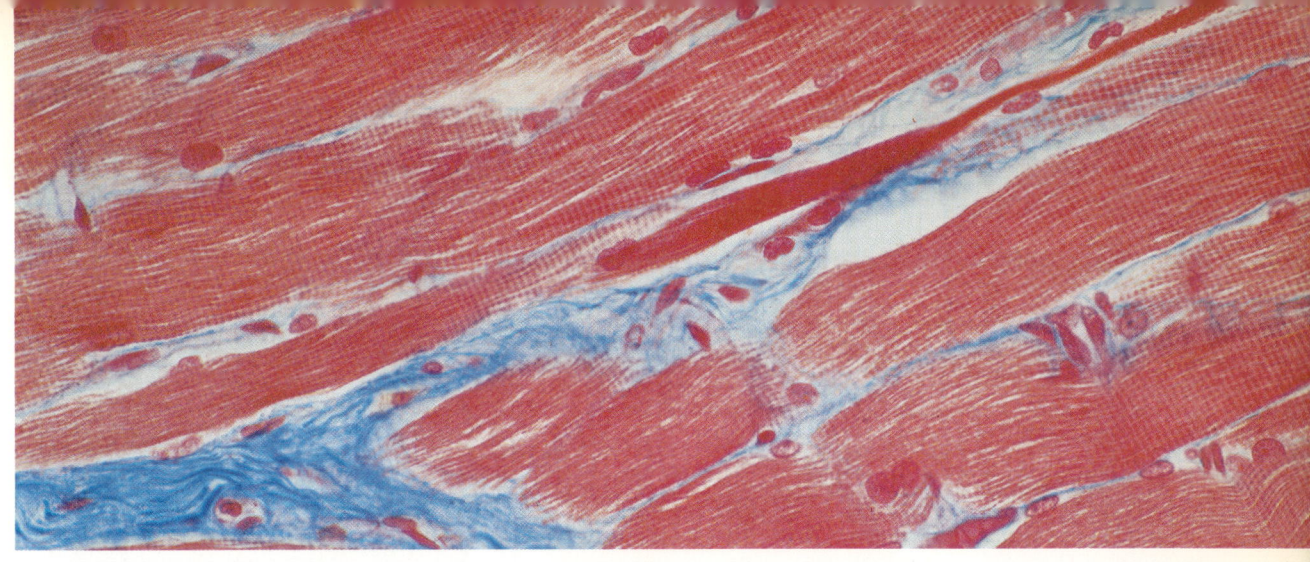

All muscle is made up of white and red muscle fibers. White muscle gives you bursts of energy for movement. Red muscle gives you endurance.

tion, and the elimination of wastes from the digestive tract. Good muscle tone is important in sports and in many other forms of physical activity. It is also important in keeping your body healthy.

There are three types of muscles.

Voluntary muscles. Skeletal muscles are all called voluntary muscles because a person can control their movements. They are also called striated muscles because they look striped, or striated, when seen under a microscope.

Involuntary muscles. The smooth muscles in the walls of the blood vessels, stomach, intestines, and other hollow tubes of the body are called involuntary muscles. A person cannot consciously control them. They are also called smooth muscles because they have no stripes, or striations. The smooth involuntary muscles are very strong, but they contract slowly. The nerves that attach to smooth muscle come from the part of the nervous system that controls involuntary action.

Cardiac muscle. The heart muscle, or cardiac muscle, looks very much like striated muscle under a microscope. Its fibers seem to be woven together. However, it is an involuntary muscle. Nerve impulses to the heart muscle may speed up or slow down its rate of contraction. During exercise, the heart muscle contracts faster and with more force than when the body is at rest.

General health and emotions such as excitement and worry affect the tone of all muscles—voluntary and involuntary.

Some interesting points about muscles

When we eat the meat of a chicken, cow, or pig, we are eating the muscles of these animals. In some animals, such as chickens and turkeys, we have a choice of eating white or dark meat. Scientists have found that dark and white meat are different colors because the dark meat has more of a red-colored protein called *myoglobin*. This protein is very much like the hemoglobin that gives red blood cells their color. Myoglobin supplies oxygen to the muscle cells.

Some muscles work in pairs to produce movements. When one contracts, the other relaxes. Look at the leg below for example.

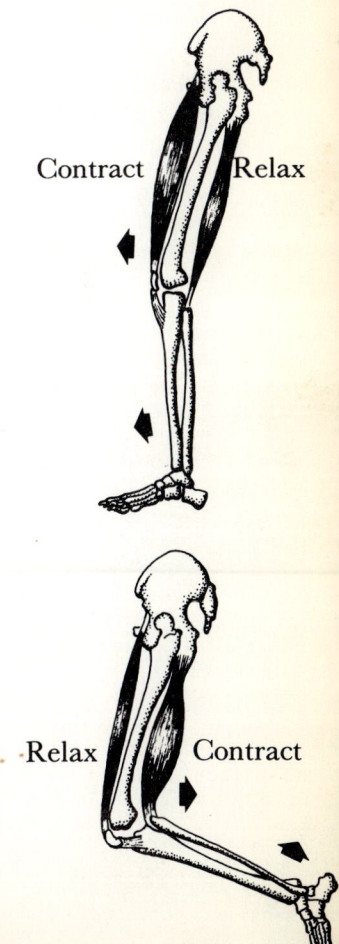

Contract   Relax

Relax   Contract

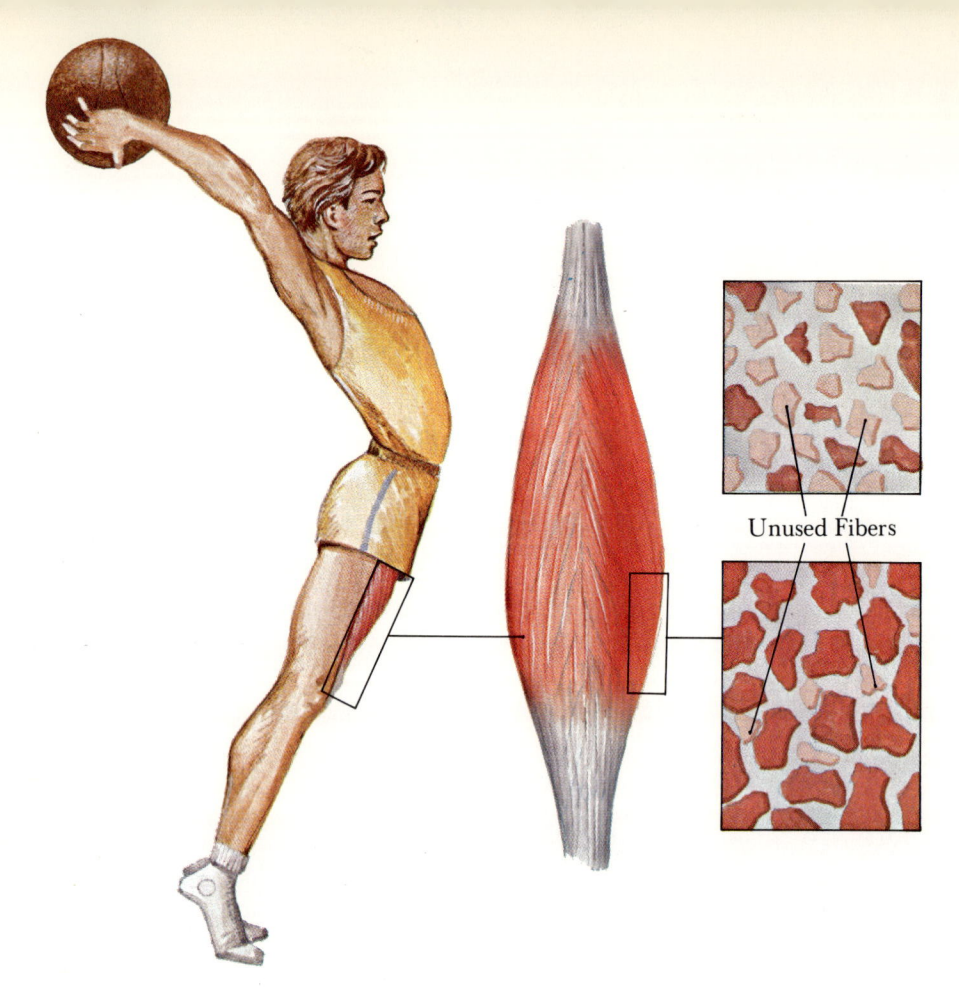

How do you make muscles stronger?
A) Make the muscle fibers larger.
B) Use more muscle fibers.
If you exercise regularly, the muscle fibers are made larger.

Unused Fibers

In your body, muscles are a mixture of red and white. If you were to examine a muscle, it would be hard to see the color difference with your naked eye. It has been estimated that the calf muscle has about 50 percent red and 50 percent white fibers. Not only do muscles have different amounts of myoglobin, but the nerve cells leading to the muscles are also different. Red muscle has a nerve that is small in diameter. This nerve is slow in carrying nerve impulses. But it is always carrying impulses, even when the muscle is at rest. White muscle has a nerve that is large, fast in carrying impulses, but not as active when the muscle is at rest.

Muscles also differ in the jobs they do. When you run 100 meters, or when you lift, push, or pull heavy objects, the white muscle is in action. But the white muscle, though powerful, cannot continue to exert force. It lacks endurance and will tire quickly. The red muscle has more staying power since it is always being stimulated by nerves. It helps you to keep good posture and to move gracefully. It will also endure cross-country or long-distance running.

The shoulder and arm muscles of a weight lifter are large because the diameter of each white muscle fiber increases with exercise. The red muscle fiber of a long-distance runner does not change in size. However, there are more blood vessels, myoglobin, and chemicals to give the runner continuous energy. With the blood flow increased, oxygen and nutrients can reach the red fibers more quickly and efficiently. This increases muscular endurance. Thus, white muscle gives you the burst of energy needed for powerful, short movements. But red muscle provides support and is useful for activities that need endurance. When you exercise, try to strengthen both red and white muscle. (Refer to Chapter 3 for information on developing the muscles.)

Women and girls do not have to worry about developing large, bulging muscles. For muscle growth like that of males, a male hormone called testosterone is needed. Most females do not have much testosterone in their bodies. Exercise will simply help to strengthen and tone their white muscle fibers and to make their red muscle fibers more efficient.

Sometimes an increase in muscle size is desirable. Large, strong muscles can be an advantage in sports such as football, wrestling, and gymnastics. It is not possible to grow new muscles where there were none before. But if the size of muscle cells is enlarged, the tissue will become larger. It may seem as if you have grown new muscles, but you have only enlarged the muscle cells you already had.

What can go wrong with the muscles?

Almost everyone has had aching muscles at one time or another. The most common causes of aching muscles are strains, too much stretching, or overuse of muscles that have not been used regularly. If you have not played volleyball for a season and then join in a volleyball tournament, your neck muscles may feel sore and stiff the next day. This condition is called sore muscles.

Whenever your muscles have been conditioned for a special kind of exercise, they are able to use up a substance called *lactic acid*. Lactic acid is normally produced by contracting muscles. However, if the muscles do a little more than usual, or if you change exercises and use different muscles, the lactic-acid level increases. The buildup of lactic acid and other waste materials irritates the muscles. This is felt as muscle soreness.

General warm-ups prepare the muscles, blood vessels, and heart for increased action.

Specific warm-ups stretch the muscles that are used in a certain activity. For what sport might this specific exercise be used?

How do you prevent muscle soreness?

To prevent soreness, a proper warm-up of the muscles is necessary. No matter how flexible you are, if the muscles are not warmed up before vigorous exercise, you may become sore. The purpose of a warm-up for a car engine is to let the working parts get enough lubrication. This stops the friction between parts. This is also true of your body. During your warm-up, the temperature of the body fluid and muscle will rise slightly. This will increase the need for chemicals that produce energy in the muscles. Warm-ups may vary with the type of activities involved. But it is a good idea to warm up as many parts of the body as possible.

Warm-ups can be divided into two types: general and specific.

General warm-ups are not related to the sport or activity in which you will be taking part. They include calisthenics that let you slowly stretch the muscles, tendons, and ligaments all over the body.

Specific warm-ups are closely related to the activity you will take part in. If the sport is volleyball, the specific warm-up should include the correct movements of the arms, the follow-through with the head, and other movements used in the game.

Both types of warm-ups allow the muscles to adapt to new physical demands. They also prepare the heart and blood vessels for vigorous action. Unfortunately, the heart is not 100 percent efficient. If it were, you could begin an activity without any warm-up, and your heart would be able to increase the volume of blood at once.

The amount of warm-up needed will change with the person, the temperature, and the type of activity. Some people are very flexible and have no difficulty with stretching exercises. Others are stiff. Also, on cold days, the body will take longer to warm up.

Why do you yawn?

Human beings yawn for the same reason cats and dogs do. A yawn helps circulate the blood carrying oxygen to the head. The next time you feel sleepy in a classroom, stretch your arms and your neck muscles and you may avoid yawning.

What is a hernia?

When any organ is pushed through the wall around it, the condition is called a *hernia*, or rupture. The most common hernia occurs when a part of the intestine is pushed through the wall of the abdomen. In men, there are two weak areas in this muscular wall in the groin. This is where most hernias occur. The navel is another place where many hernias happen. The muscles of the abdomen may be weakened. Strain may cause the intestine to push through the weak area.

A hernia should receive medical attention at once. The loop of intestine that comes from a hernia must be returned permanently to the abdominal cavity. It is important to stop interference with the blood supply to that part of the digestive tract. It is also important to let food pass through the injured part of the intestine.

Keeping the muscles of the abdomen in good condition will help prevent hernias. Young people, especially boys, should be careful about lifting very heavy objects. Not until boys are fully grown are their abdominal muscles fully developed and strong.

When you yawn, your muscles stretch to aid the flow of blood to the head.

Are you getting too much phosphorus in your diet?

Calcium and phosphorus are minerals that play an important role in contributing to the hardness of bone around the teeth and in other parts of the body. For this reason, it is very important that the balance of calcium and phosphorus be maintained. The recommended daily allowance of calcium and phosphorus is 1200 milligrams each. As you will see below, it is important to try not to exceed this allowance.

Since milk is a good source of both minerals, people who drink milk usually have an adequate calcium-phosphorus balance. Researchers are finding, however, that teenagers who switch from drinking milk to drinking soft drinks such as colas are upsetting the balance. A popular cola contains almost 70 milligrams of phosphorus per 340-gram (12-ounce) serving. The excess intake of phosphorus is thought to interfere with the absorption of calcium from the digestive system and thus cause weak bones. In addition to causing weak bones, the excess intake of phosphorus may contribute to poor development of the teeth.

To maintain the proper calcium-phosphorus balance, you should include milk or some other dairy product in your diet every day—and cut down on your intake of soft drinks.

Something to think about . . .

Main Ideas

1. Bones are living organs and have important jobs, such as mineral storage, blood formation, support, movement, and protection.
2. The ends of bones are held together by ligaments and are protected by cartilage and fluid.
3. Bones need physical stimulation in order to stay strong.
4. At birth, the cranium has soft spots called fontanels.
5. There are now many ways to correct skeletal injuries by surgery.
6. The three types of muscles allow for movement, digestion, and circulation.
7. Skeletal muscles are under voluntary control. Smooth muscles and the heart muscle are not under voluntary control.
8. The color of muscle depends on myoglobin and on the amount of nerve stimulation to the fibers.
9. General and specific warm-ups are important not only for skeletal muscles but also for the blood vessels and heart.
10. Muscles can develop weak spots and let internal organs push through. This is called a rupture, or hernia.

Key Words

arthritis	fontanel	microcephalic
bone marrow	hernia	myoglobin
cardiac muscle	hydrocephalic	osteomyelitis
cartilage	involuntary muscle	synovial fluid
cranium	joint	tendon
decalcification	lactic acid	voluntary muscle
fasciculus	ligament	

Apply Your Knowledge

1. Why is the skeleton called a living organ?
2. Name the specific bones, or group of bones, that protect the heart, brain, lungs, spinal cord, and eyes.
3. Give three reasons why calcium is important for your body.
4. What is the function of synovial fluid? Where is it found?
5. Explain the difference between a ligament and a tendon.
6. List the four major kinds of joints and describe the movement of each.
7. Describe how cartilage is slowly replaced by bone.
8. What is the advantage of having fontanels at birth?
9. What are the major differences between male and female skeletons?
10. Explain how flatfoot can happen.
11. Are there any advantages to having arches in the foot?
12. Can all forms of arthritis be cured? Explain.
13. How would a sprinter's thigh muscle compare in size to a long-distance runner's?
14. Name the three kinds of muscles. Where are they found? How are they controlled?
15. Why is it important to strengthen both red and white muscle?

Extend Your Knowledge

1. Explain what would happen to your radius and ulna bones and the surrounding muscles if you had to wear a cast on the lower arm for several months.
2. If you wanted to take part in an arm-wrestling contest, which muscle fiber—red or white—would you strengthen? What large muscle would you have to strengthen in order to be good at arm wrestling?
3. Give examples of general and specific warm-ups for these sports: football, basketball, track, volleyball, wrestling, swimming, skiing, gymnastics, and soccer.
4. Sheila was afraid that she would develop large, bulging muscles if she took part in active sports. What would you say to her if you were a coach?
5. The next time you yawn in a crowd or in class, check to see how many others copy you. Is yawning "catching"? Explain.

Chapter 3

Do you know . . .

- why exercise is good for your heart and muscles?
- whether or not you have good eye-hand coordination?
- how exercise affects blood pressure and pulse rate?
- that you shouldn't wait until you are thirsty to drink water?
- how to prevent shinsplints?

Keeping Fit through Sports and Recreation

Have you noticed that many people spend their free time jogging, biking, or playing tennis? Exercising lets you break away from daily routine or from boredom. It also keeps you physically fit. Keeping fit means more than simply exercising your muscles. You must also know how to prevent injuries to your muscles and how to keep your heart and blood vessels in top condition. Fitness is a part of wellness.

The importance of exercising

Your body is made for movement. The greatest value of exercise is that it helps to tone the muscles and strengthen the heart. If you understand what happens to your body when you exercise, you should be able to choose the activities that are best for you.

Warming up the engine

While you are asleep, most of your muscles are flexed rather than extended. When you are sitting at your desk, your knee, hip, and elbow joints are usually flexed. If your muscles remain in a flexed, or bent, position for a long time, they can temporarily shorten and become tighter. Thus, when you get up in the morning or stand after sitting for a long time, your body may be stiff and sluggish.

Before you do any fast-paced activities, it is always best to warm up your body. General and specific warm-ups are recommended for sports and recreational events. (See Chapter 2.) But even when you wake up in the morning, simple stretching movements can make you feel good.

Athletes have different physical abilities.

Karen and Sandy are both good athletes. They both enjoy competitive sports and recreational activities. Karen is flexible, agile, and well-coordinated. She also has good equilibrium (balance). Sandy is fast and strong and has great physical endurance. From the description of Karen and Sandy, can you decide who is the balance-beam star and who is the low-hurdle champ? Actually, both of these sports call for many of the same strengths. But some of Karen's and Sandy's strong points differ.

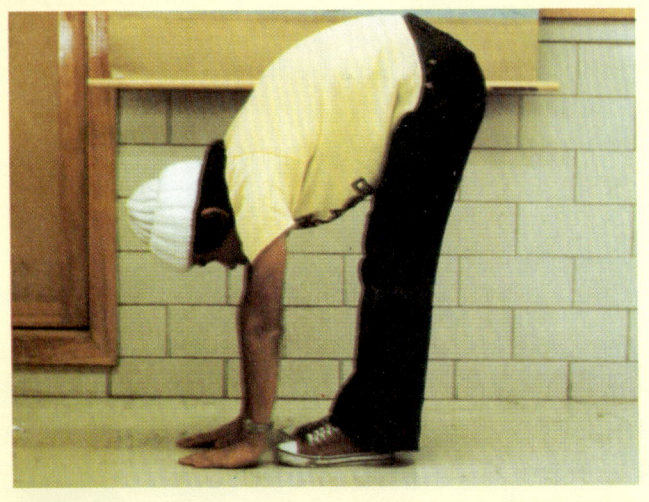

How flexible are you?
Can you do these things?

First: Standing with your feet together, bend down slowly. Touch your toes without bending your knees. Do not bounce up and down. *Second:* Start in the same position. Bend down slowly. Touch the floor with your fingers. *Third:* Bend down again. Try to touch your knuckles to the floor. *Fourth:* Touch your palms to the floor.

Touched toes _____ Fair
Touched floor _____ Good
Touched knuckles
  to floor _____ Very Good
Touched palms to floor Excellent

How is your eye-hand coordination?
You can find out.

Stand about 2 meters (about 6 feet) from a flat wall. Toss a tennis ball from your right hand, underhand, against the wall. Catch the ball with your left hand and quickly toss it back with that hand. Catch it with your right hand. Continue to do this for 30 seconds. Count the number of times you catch the ball.

25 _____ Fair
28 _____ Good
32 _____ Very Good
35 _____ Excellent

How is your balance?
Try this activity.

Stand on your toes with your heels together. Close your eyes and hold your arms straight out in front of you. Stay in this position for 30 seconds without shifting your feet or opening your eyes.

15 seconds _____ Fair
20 seconds _____ Good
25 seconds _____ Very Good
30 seconds _____ Excellent

Flexibility means being able to move the joints of the body easily and smoothly when you bend, twist, and stretch. The more flexible you are, the easier you can move in and out of various positions without injury.

Coordination means that your entire body is working smoothly. When you play tennis and your eyes follow the ball across the net, you may already be moving where you think the ball will be returned. When you first try to dribble a soccer ball with your feet, you might not do it with grace and ease. But your coordination usually improves with practice.

Equilibrium means that you can easily balance yourself if your body begins to sway or lean in one direction. Expert ice skaters can spin around 30 or more times at a blurring speed, and they are able to balance themselves during and after spinning. Bowlers, discus throwers, and gymnasts also need good equilibrium to perform gracefully and well.

Agility means that you can react quickly, with fast, sure movements. Springing to your feet and dodging easily from side to side are examples of being agile.

Speed is the measure of how fast your body parts can move. In order to run a 100-meter dash or to chase a tennis ball, you need speed. The legs, the arms, and other parts of the body can all move with speed.

Strength means being able to use the power of the muscles to lift, push, jump, or pull. Developing strong muscles also strengthens tendons, ligaments, and bones. You are less likely to be injured when your body is strong.

Endurance is the ability of your body to stand up to stress for long periods of time. Your body may be flexible, agile, speedy, strong, and well-coordinated. But you can still be physically unfit if you lack endurance. Muscles need oxygen. This oxygen is carried by the red blood cells that give nourishment to all parts of the body. You don't need much strength to move your arms through the water while swimming. But you do need endurance to swim the length of the pool six times. If you keep doing the same activity over a period of time, new blood vessels will be formed. These newly formed blood vessels will carry more nutrients and oxygen to the small muscle fibers that make up the larger muscle bundle. Thus, the more you swim, the better your muscles can endure long periods of movement.

It is your heart that chiefly determines your endurance. The heart itself is a muscle and has to be strong. How can you check to find out how much work your heart is doing? While you are in your chair, press two fingers of one hand on the wrist joint below the thumb of the other hand and feel your pulse. Count the number of beats for 30 seconds. Then multiply the number by two to get the rate for one minute. What is your pulse rate for one minute?

When you exercise more actively, your body needs more oxygen. So your heart muscle increases its rate of beating. This supplies the extra oxygen to the body muscles. Standing up and sitting down again does not take much effort. But if you repeated these movements 60 times, your muscles would need more oxygen. Therefore, your heart would have to work harder.

Find out how agile you are.

Draw a line on the floor. Stand along the side of it. As quickly as you can, jump from side to side over the line. Keep your feet together. Have someone time you for one minute. Count the number of times your feet touch the floor.

145 _____ Fair
160 _____ Good
175 _____ Very Good
185 _____ Excellent

How is your speed?

Try the following test.
Step one: Mark the chalkboard with a circle approximately 25 cm (10 in.) above your head.
Step two: Stand 25 cm (10 in.) away from the chalkboard with your side facing the board.
Step three: Spread your legs approximately 60 cm (2 ft.) apart.
Step four: Now touch the small circle with your hand closest to the chalkboard and quickly reach across and touch the foot on the side farthest from the chalkboard. Repeat the complete movement 10 times in the shortest time possible.

11 seconds _____ Fair
10 seconds _____ Good
9 seconds _____ Very Good
8 seconds _____ Excellent

Sit in your chair, and when the signal is given, stand and sit 60 times. After you have completed these movements, take your pulse rate for one minute. Now subtract your pulse rate while resting from the result after standing and sitting. How many more times did your heart have to beat to get oxygen to the working muscles of your body? The simple stand-and-sit test will probably not increase your pulse rate a great deal. But if you were to continue getting up and sitting down for ten minutes longer, your pulse rate might rise to 150 beats per minute or more. Activities that call for endurance help to strengthen your heart and improve your lung capacity. The sooner your heart returns to its normal resting rate after exercise, the better your endurance.

Researchers have found that, when young people exercise, their hearts should beat about 150 to 175 times per minute. If your heart rate does not reach 150 beats per minute while you are bowling, it might be wise to take on another sport as well. The heart can become stronger and work more efficiently only if you apply some degree of stress. After heavy exercise, such as a one-on-one basketball game, check your pulse for 30 seconds. Then multiply the number of beats by two to get your pulse rate per minute. If this rate is over 175, you might be overdoing the exercise. There has been too much stress, and you need to rest.

Don't be a once-a-week jogger or a weekend superstar. You should exercise at least three days a week, or once every other day. Regular exercise improves your endurance. If your exercise raises your heart rate to 150 beats per minute, 15 to 20 minutes of activity per day will be enough. If your heart rate is less than 150, you need to put in more days or longer hours of exercise.

When you exercise, your heart pumps more blood into circulation with each heartbeat than it does when you rest. This puts greater pressure on the walls of the arteries carrying the blood. Thus your blood pressure is increased. Blood usually travels at the rate of 17 meters (55 feet) per minute in the large arteries. But during vigorous exercise, the blood in the large arteries may travel at the rate of 137 meters (450 feet) per minute.

Eating just before or after exercising may cause stomach pains.

For an hour or two after you eat, a greater flow of blood is needed in your digestive tract. If you exercise soon after eating, digestion is interrupted. The extra supply of blood is taken away to fill the needs of the skeletal muscles. Something similar happens if you eat just after exercising. Then the extra supply of blood cannot be moved quickly away from the skeletal muscles to the stomach and intestines. In either case, stomach pains may result.

Aging and exercising

As people get older, they sometimes forget the importance of activity and exercise. They forget that the condition of the circulatory system is directly related to the amount and kind of exercise they get.

How strong are your legs? Test their strength.

First measure your height in centimeters. From a line on the floor, mark off a distance equal to your height. Stand behind the line. Bend your knees, swing your arms backward, and then jump. Measure how far you can jump.

Own height _____ Fair
5 cm (2 in.) beyond _____ Good
10 cm (4 in.) beyond _ Very Good
15 cm (6 in.) beyond __ Excellent

Do you have good endurance?

A 3-minute test will tell you. Use a sturdy chair or bench. Step up and down 30 times each minute. After exactly 3 minutes of stepping up and down, sit down and quickly find the pulse in your wrist. Count your pulse for 1 minute.

120–125 _____ Fair
95–115 _____ Good
85–90 _____ Very Good
75–80 _____ Excellent

For a time, British doctors were puzzled by the fact that bus drivers in London had a higher rate of heart attacks than bus conductors. When the doctors looked for reasons, they found that the bus drivers got little exercise. The bus conductors moved about as they went up and down the steps of the double-decker buses to collect tickets. Most people need more exercise than they get, especially older people who live and work indoors. A good exercise program and proper diet will help prevent heart attacks and problems with blood circulation.

The kind of exercise you do is not important. Swimming is just as good as stickball, and stickball is just as good as jogging. What matters is that you enjoy the exercise and keep doing it.

When you are young, you may enjoy strenuous sports such as basketball and football. But as you reach middle age, your heart and blood vessels will change. Then vigorous exercise may not always be wise. It can sometimes cause serious damage, especially if you have not been exercising regularly. Therefore, in addition to sports that you can enjoy in your youth, it is good to learn some "lifetime sport" that you can continue to do. Bowling, golf, cycling, hiking, jogging, and swimming are good lifetime sports. They give you pleasure and also improve your health.

Knowing your limitations

Most people need regular exercise in reasonable amounts. But before any person takes part in heavy physical work or exercise, a physician should check the condition of the heart. Most high schools and colleges require that all students have a physical exam to find out if they are in condition to join in physical-activity programs. Most schools also require medical supervision of sports events.

A person should feel better, rather than worse, just after exercise and for several hours afterwards. If the person feels exhausted, weak, or shaky, overexercising may be the problem.

A conditioning program is important for athletes.

Conditioning, or training, is a program of exercise, rest, and eating that athletes follow to get and stay in top physical condition. In conditioning, exercise must be regular. It should also be increased slowly, from day to day. How exercise affects a person's muscles, digestion, circulation, and sleep will show what that individual is able to do. Then, after the person has reached a level of maximum performance, the daily amount of exercise at that level should be kept up. Conditioning also includes regular periods for sleep and relaxation. A person in training needs the same kinds of foods that any healthy person does.

Water and salt requirement during exercise

Exercise usually makes a person perspire. The body can lose large amounts of water and salt through perspiration. These losses must be replaced, or cramps and nausea may result. On a warm day, a football player may lose as much as 4.5 kilograms (10 pounds) during a game. But the player may regain the lost weight by the following morning simply by drinking water. On a day when water is lost from the body through perspiration and is not replaced, the average amount of urine excreted is less. This urine is likely to be darker than usual. Water can also be lost through the kidneys and from the surface of the lungs.

If you are taking part in vigorous physical activities, your body may need water even if you are not thirsty. In fact, a large amount of water is lost through the skin even when you are not perspiring. In low humidity, when the air is dry, water loss from the skin and breathing organs is high. Also, drinking certain fluids that contain caffeine or alcohol can cause the body to lose water faster. You can prevent heat cramp, heat exhaustion, and heatstroke by drinking plenty of water before and during physical activity.

What you should do about injuries

CAUTION: SPORTS AND RECREATIONAL ACTIVITIES CAN BE INJURIOUS TO YOUR HEALTH. Injuries to the muscle and soft tissue are common among young people who take part in physical activities or active sports.

Muscle lameness happens when you overuse your muscles. It is similar to muscle soreness. But muscle soreness is caused by a buildup of waste products (lactic acid). Muscle lameness occurs when there is tearing of tiny muscle fibers that have been forced to contract under a heavy load or force. Since the muscle tissue is injured, the pain and stiffness may last for three to four days.

To prevent muscle lameness, it is a good idea to exercise with barbells or with weights strapped to the body or legs. Gradually increasing the weight will help to condition your muscles for the forceful movements needed in many sports. This kind of exercise is called weight training.

Athletes follow strict conditioning programs to stay in top physical shape.

Even on a cold day, active people perspire. Their bodies lose both water and salt.

Your body may need water even when you are not thirsty. Drink water before and during physical activities.

Very light exercise, gentle stretching, and heat, ointment, or light massage will help to speed up healing for muscle lameness. Resting the muscles for three to four days will also help.

A *pulled muscle* causes severe pain, and you will not be able to continue the exercise. In a pulled muscle, a large muscle bundle or a tendon that attaches muscle to bone may have torn or separated from the attachment points. Since the blood vessels of the muscle bundle are damaged, fast treatment by a physician may be needed. Again, lack of warm-up and too much force on a cold muscle are the major causes of damaged muscle. The injured muscle should be treated by putting on cold packs as soon as possible.

Certain kinds of muscle pulls are common to certain sports. In most cases, the injury happens where there is a fast and forceful movement. For example, the biceps and triceps of the upper arm are important muscles for throwing. So if you are a baseball pitcher, these are the muscles likeliest to be injured. If you are a tennis player, your calf muscles may be injured. These muscles give you the power to pull up your heels when you serve and to position yourself for the return. The calf muscle attaches to the Achilles' tendon, which is in turn attached to the heel bone. If you are a sprinter, you may injure the hamstring muscles at the back of the thigh.

A *charley horse* comes from a hard blow to the front part of the thigh. The muscle, blood vessels, nerves, and other soft tissues are damaged. If you told your friends that you had a contusion of the quadriceps femoris, they might not know you meant a charley horse.

For a charley horse, use treatments that stop internal bleeding as much as possible. Put ice or a cold pack on the injured area. The cold will

Know your limits! The right amount of exercise makes you feel better, not worse.

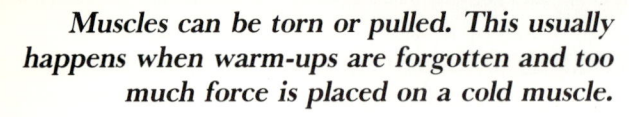

Muscles can be torn or pulled. This usually happens when warm-ups are forgotten and too much force is placed on a cold muscle.

Wear protective clothing to help prevent injuries.

cause the blood vessels to become narrow. That will lessen the bleeding. If you apply pressure to the area, the blood vessels will be squeezed. Therefore less blood will flow around the injured area. Also, raising the thigh will lower the blood flow through the arteries. This will increase the blood flow in the veins that lead away from the injury.

You should rest the injured leg as much as possible. Keep it in a horizontal position. If the charley horse is very bad, you should contact your doctor for further treatment. For a mild injury, heat can be applied to the area after two or three days. The heat will improve circulation and will help speed the healing. If you are involved in any contact sport, you could get a charley horse. Even football players with protective padding can get very bad muscle injuries.

Muscle cramps usually happen in muscles that must carry weight, such as the calf, hip, or thigh muscles. Cramps sometimes happen in a tired muscle during sleep, or in a muscle that has been working very hard. Sometimes cramps are caused by a light blow or strain on a tired muscle.

In a normal muscle bundle, some of the fibers are resting and some are contracting. However, during a cramp, almost all of the muscle fibers are contracting at the same time.

Stretching the muscle within the normal range of movement may help the cramping. Applying firm pressure while gently massaging the area may also help. The best way to avoid muscle cramps is to warm up properly and to take enough fluids before and after exercise. Wearing protective clothing, whenever possible, may also prevent serious muscle injury.

Sprains and dislocations are problems that have to do with the joints. In addition to muscle injuries, the joint between two bones may receive a sudden, forceful blow called a trauma. Also, if stress is put on a joint by twisting, stretching, or pounding, the ligament that joins the bones can weaken, tear, or be cut. These injuries are called *sprains*.

If you step off a curb wearing shoes with high heels, you could twist your ankle. Usually, when an ankle is sprained, blood vessels break and swelling takes place. Many athletes will sprain an ankle at one time or another. If the sprain is very bad, an X ray should be taken to make sure that no bones are broken.

Wrap the sprained area tightly to help close broken blood vessels. Then put on a cold pack every half hour. Keep it on for about 20 minutes at a time. This will slow the circulation. Don't leave the cold pack on too long. If you do, the joints could become stiff and painful. Also, prop the leg up for better circulation of fluids away from the injury. Then when the swelling lessens, 24 to 48 hours later, use heat on the injured area. The blood vessels will get larger and will carry more nourishment to the tissue. They will also help remove injured tissue from the sprain area.

Bones are held together at the joints by ligaments, tendons, and muscles. But, if enough force is applied, a bone may be pushed out of its socket. This painful injury is called a *dislocation*. Don't move the injured area. And allow no one but a doctor to treat the dislocation. There are many blood vessels, soft tissues, and nerves connected to the joint. So if you think your thumb is dislocated, for example, never have a friend or coach pull it "back into place."

Active people can get injured. Learn which injuries require a doctor's care.

Improving Your Skills through Sports and Recreational Activities

	Flex.	Coord.	Equil.	Agility	Speed	Strength	Endur.
Badminton	*	*		*	*		*
Ballet	*	*	*	*	*	*	*
Baseball		*		*	*		
Basketball		*	*	*			*
Bicycling					*		*
Bowling			*				
Boxing		*		*	*	*	*
Calisthenics	*	*	*	*			*
Canoeing						*	*
Diving	*	*		*			
Fencing		*	*	*	*		*
Figure skating	*	*		*	*		
Fishing		*					
Football				*	*		
Frisbee	*	*		*			
Golf		*					
Gymnastics	*	*	*			*	
Handball		*			*		*
Hiking							*
Hockey		*	*	*	*		*
Horseback riding			*				
Jogging							*
Judo	*			*	*	*	
Jumping rope		*		*			*
Karate	*	*		*	*		*
Lacrosse		*					*
Mt. climbing	*		*				*
Pool/Billiards		*					
Racquetball	*	*		*	*		*
Rowing						*	*
Scuba diving							
Skateboarding	*	*	*	*			
Skiing	*	*		*			*
Soccer	*	*		*	*		*
Softball		*			*		
Square dancing		*		*			
Swimming		*				*	*
Table tennis		*		*	*		
Tennis		*		*	*		*
Track and field					*		*
Volleyball	*			*	*		*
Waterskiing			*				
Wrestling	*			*	*	*	*
Weight training						*	
Yoga	*		*				

Shinsplints is a lower-leg pain that is felt by athletes who run on hard surfaces. It can happen to you if you run on a track or cross-country, or even if you jog down the street. It can also occur if you play tennis or basketball. What causes shinsplints? There are two theories. Both theories state that the partial separation of the muscle from its bone attachment is the main cause of shinsplints.

Fast treatment by your doctor is very important. The swelling must be stopped. And the injured muscle needs long periods of rest. Since shinsplints is painful, you should know how to avoid or prevent it.

1. Before you run, it is important to strengthen any weak muscles.
2. Try not to run on hard surfaces during warm-up and early training.
3. Make sure that your shoes fit well. Wear an extra pair of socks to help absorb the shock.
4. Learn the correct way to run or jog.
5. Always warm up enough, even if your muscles are toned and strong.

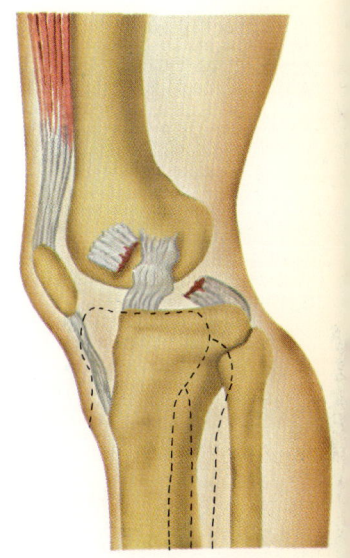

A dislocation is a bone pushed out of its socket. Don't move a person who has suffered a dislocation. Call a doctor at once.

Dislocated Knee

Something to think about . . .

Is concentration really important in sports? In a baseball game, a batter tries to hit a ball traveling 80 miles per hour, while the fans shout and cheer. Can the player concentrate? A golfer strikes at a ball moving 0 miles per hour. But the slightest cough from the gallery upsets the golfer's concentration. Is concentration different for every sport?

In every sport, a player needs some degree of mental preparation before making movements. Sometimes concentration is nothing more than breathing properly. At other times, it calls for a series of calculations. Some players think about such things as wind velocity, angle of slope, distance the ball must travel, and speed of the ball. Watch a high jumper concentrate before trying to jump several feet above his or her own height. What does the jumper think about?

Sometimes concentration is required to keep the mind from thinking about what the body is feeling. The Tibetan monks called Mohetangs were experts at this kind of concentration. These monks used to carry messages from monastery to monastery. They had to run long distances through rough country and at high altitudes. They are reported to have run up to 300 miles in just 30 hours. To maintain this amazing pace, they would gaze on a distant object and repeat their sacred mantra (prayer) over and over. By concentrating on their mantra, they lost awareness of physical pain, distance, and time.

The race will start in a few seconds. The athlete's body is prepared. Can his mind help him to run?

Uniting the body and mind in sports is essential for the development of the athlete. Many professional baseball players claim that after learning to concentrate, they can watch the ball coming toward them in slow motion. The noise made by the cheering crowds is no longer a reality to them.

Main Ideas

1. Your muscles are made for movement. When they don't move, they get weaker.
2. The most important muscle to strengthen is the heart.
3. Exercises that cause the heart to beat 150 to 175 times per minute are good for you.
4. Exercising on a full stomach may cause stomach pains.
5. Water lost during exercise must be replaced.
6. Most muscle injuries can be prevented.

Key Words

agility	endurance	pulled muscle
charley horse	equilibrium	shinsplints
conditioning	flexibility	speed
coordination	muscle cramps	sprain
dislocation	muscle lameness	strength

Apply Your Knowledge

1. Look at page 36. Choose one activity that seems to call for most of the skills listed.
2. Using the same chart, list five sports that can help you increase your endurance.
3. List some sports that call for a great deal of coordination.
4. Why should exercise be avoided just before and after eating?
5. What are the effects of exercise? Why do you feel tired after exercise?
6. What makes up a conditioning program?
7. Explain the differences between muscle lameness and muscle cramps.
8. How does a cold pack help a charley horse or a sprained ankle? Why should you prop up the injured area?
9. List some sports activities that call for a lot of flexibility.
10. Explain how shinsplints can be prevented.

Extend Your Knowledge

1. Plan a physical activity program you would enjoy for the entire year.
2. Are large, tall people as agile as small, short people? Explain.
3. Take your pulse for one minute just before you get out of bed. Then sit up and take the pulse again. Next, stand and take the pulse. Explain why the pulse rates are different.
4. Why are some people better coordinated than others?
5. Make a list of all the physical activities you do that cause your pulse rate to reach 150 beats per minute or more. Take your pulse after each activity.
6. Take the pulse of an athlete and a nonathlete in your class. Explain any difference in the pulse rate.
7. Invite one of the coaches to tell your class about the conditioning programs in your school.

Unit 2

CHAPTERS:

4 Emotional Needs and Mature Personality
5 Emotions and Mental Health
6 Living with Stress

Understanding Yourself

Chapter 4

Do you know . . .

- how emotions can affect your physical well-being?
- why conflict between a parent and child is likely to increase during most people's teen years?
- how to develop self-confidence?
- what it means to be mature?
- why you have sudden shifts of mood?

Emotional Needs and Mature Personality

Emotions are feelings. Everyone has them. As you grow, you learn to express or hide your feelings in various ways. The patterns and habits you adopt for handling your emotions form an important part of your developing personality—the combination of feelings, thoughts, and behavior that makes you different from all other people. Your success in finding ways to meet your own emotional needs determines whether or not you will reach adulthood with a mature, healthy personality.

Emotional needs

People have basic *emotional needs,* just as they have basic physical needs. Emotional needs must be satisfied if a person is to enjoy life and feel a sense of security. People who cannot satisfy their emotional needs may feel frustrated, lonely, or insecure. They may feel that they don't have a purpose, or a worthwhile place, in life.

Unmet emotional needs can make a person very unhappy or even emotionally sick. Sometimes, disturbed emotions can lead to physical illness. This happens when feelings are "transferred," or unconsciously given, to the body. The result may be aches, pains, or other physical problems. It is important to understand the causes of disturbed emotions or feelings. These problems almost always can be traced back to unmet emotional needs.

Love

The need to give and receive love and affection is very strong in all human beings. This need exists from the beginning to the end of life. Newborn babies respond to being held and cuddled, while children show a strong need to exchange affection with the family and friends. Adolescents have basically the same needs as children. But they also need the additional reassurance of belonging to a group. Young adults expand their need for loving relationships through dating, seeking a long-term partner, or planning and caring for a family. Adults need to go on giving and receiving love, and maintaining loving relationships. Finally, the need for love does not stop as a person grows older. Elderly adults continue to need loving relationships with people of all ages. Meeting this need is thought to add years to a person's life.

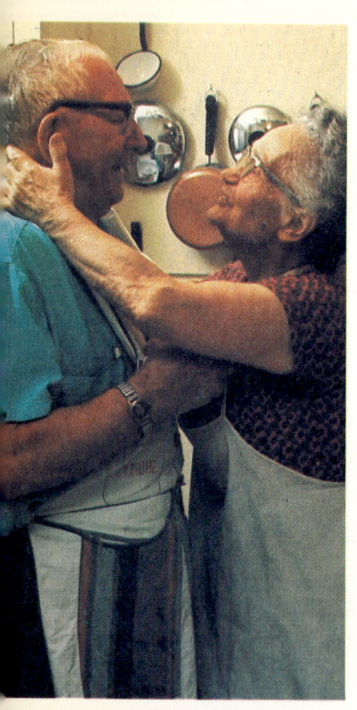

The need for love does not stop as a person gets older. Older adults need loving relationships with people of all ages. Meeting this need is thought to add years to a person's life.

A positive self-concept

Everyone needs to have a positive self-concept. *Self-concept* is a term used to describe how a person views herself or himself. People with a positive self-concept understand and accept their personalities, abilities, and shortcomings.

Having a positive self-concept includes self-respect—a feeling of personal worth. Getting respect from others is important, but holding yourself in high esteem is even more important. It takes hard and serious thought to know who you are and what you want to be. Then it takes courage to learn to be yourself, to let your words and actions reflect the person you are. You alone are responsible for forming your personal identity.

During the high school years, you will probably depend on your parents to satisfy many of your physical needs, such as food, clothing, and shelter. However, at the same time, you are learning to become an independent person. More and more, you think and act for yourself and make your own decisions. Your dependence and independence may cause problems between you and your parents. You may accept your dependence on them sometimes. But you may reject that dependence when it conflicts with your growing need for personal self-esteem. Through both conflicts and positive experiences, you will gain the judgment that will help you make choices as an independent person.

Personal achievement

Everyone has a strong need to succeed at something. For example, a child may get emotional satisfaction from completing a jigsaw puzzle or coloring a picture book. A young adult may feel satisfaction upon graduating from high school, finding a job, or being accepted by a college. Some people are "A" students. Some are athletes. Some achieve success in the fine arts, music, or theater. Others develop their abilities in fields such as business, education, social work, law, industrial arts, or medicine.

It is important for you to discover the areas in which you can feel a sense of achievement. One way you can find out a great deal about your own strengths is through aptitude tests. Another way is by talking to counselors or other adults who have special training in helping others to know themselves better. Or you can simply try new activities to see what you enjoy. Knowing your strongest points and how they can be put to use will help you to achieve.

The need to create

The need to create is probably one of the strongest emotional needs. Children satisfy this need by drawing, playing "make-believe," or building models, for example. Young people may paint, sew, play musical instruments, work imaginatively in a craft such as ceramics—or write poems or stories. Sometimes, young adults may build full-sized boats or may remodel cars. Coming up with a new solution to a problem is a way of being creative, as well.

Creating a home and a family of one's own is a common way to satisfy the need to create. Dating is an early expression of this need. For most people, dating and getting to know people of the other sex are preparations for choosing a long-term partner. In exploring close personal relationships, you discover the character and traits you like best in others. You are learning to build a meaningful relationship, and this is a creative act. At the same time, you will also be satisfying your need for love and a sense of belonging.

Philosophy of life

Everyone needs to have a purpose in life. Your philosophy of life includes your standards, your sense of values, and your idea of the direction in which you are growing. Even small children, in their own way, need to have a personal plan for living.

Your plan for living is likely to change and grow as you change and grow. But it is important that your philosophy of life fit you and also fit into the world in which you live. Take the time to think about your philosophy of life. Your plan will help you with many of the day-to-day decisions you have to make. Your philosophy may be affected by many things: family customs or standards, religion, ideas you have read, experiences you have been through, and personal beliefs.

What is personality? To people who study human behavior, *personality* means the total person: the thinking, acting, and feeling self that reacts to the world. Your individual traits make your personality different from anyone else's.

Development of personality

The family is one of the most important influences on personality. A child's first lessons in behavior and emotions are learned from parents. By the time the child is five years old, patterns of behavior and ways of reacting to different situations have been set up.

From the age of five until about the age of twelve, role models, especially parent models, are very important. Family relationships have a great impact on the kind of adult a child will become. If parents understand and accept their child, there is a very good chance that the child will develop a healthy personality. On the other hand, if parents often reject or punish a child without good reason, the child may grow up always expecting to be rejected or punished. The child may then become unsure and uncomfortable when relating to others.

During adolescence, family relationships continue to influence the growing personality. Adolescents feel a strong inner drive for freedom and independence. Also, their increased knowledge and exposure to other values lead them to question previously accepted values and advice from parents. This is often a difficult stage. The way a teenager and his or her parents handle the conflicts and strains of this period will greatly affect the young person's ability to form a mature personality.

Developing maturity

Maturity means full development. Maturity is not necessarily a characteristic of adulthood. Some adults are not mature in their actions and attitudes. And some high school students, and even younger people, show

Mature personality

Finding out what you are like is a major step toward maturity.

Why is belonging to a group important to most teenagers?

maturity in their behavior. Mature behavior is behavior that is appropriate for a person's age and stage of development. In general, maturity means having realistic goals, making wise decisions, practicing self-control, and accepting responsibility for your behavior.

Developing maturity in the teen years

The teenage years are an important stage in the process of maturing. For many people, this is a difficult and confusing time. It is normal for young people to change back and forth many times from being mature to acting immature at this stage. Adulthood holds the promise of greater freedom, but it demands greater responsibility, too.

"What am I like?" "What will I become?" Discovering the makeup of your personality and setting your life on course are major steps toward maturity. The options offered to teenagers can be upsetting. As one teenager summed it up, "When I began to realize all the decisions I had to make, I really got scared." The transition from the teenage years to adulthood is rarely a smooth process for anyone.

Understanding your feelings

Do you have sudden changes of mood for no clear reason? Do you feel impatient or "in a hurry" without knowing why? Are you easily bored by things you used to enjoy? These feelings can be expected during the teen years. You will probably have feelings like these again. But you may never again have as many different, strong, and confusing feelings as those you have during your teens.

Some of the causes of such feelings are physical. The hormones bringing about physical changes at this time also affect your feelings and attitudes. These changes take place at a fast rate. They can cause troublesome changes in your mood and in your feeling of well-being.

A big change is also taking place in your social relationships—your relationships with people. You are in the middle of building a different kind of relationship with the people around you, especially with your parents. At times, you or your parents, or all of you, may feel worried and tense about your new role. For example, you may be expected to take on more responsibility. At the same time, you are expected to continue to accept the rules that your parents have set down. Such double messages result in conflicts. Below are some uneasy feelings expressed by teenagers. How typical do you think these are?

"I wish I didn't have to depend on Mom and Dad for anything. Then I could do what I wanted, when I wanted . . ."
Barbara, age 14

"My parents are overprotective. They watch over me like a hawk . . ."
Diane, age 16

"I love my parents, but it seems as though I'm always arguing with them . . ."
Tom, age 16

"I'm old enough to take care of myself now, but my parents rarely let me stay out past 12:30 A.M. They say they can't fall asleep until they know I am back safely . . ."
Maria, age 17

By being more aware of the reasons why you feel as you do, you ought to be able to handle your feelings better. In the meantime, think about this statement by one young adult:

"I knew that I was mature when I was willing to ask for advice from my parents—and my parents talked to me as if I were an adult . . ."
Brian, age 23

You are also learning new ways of relating to people your own age. In addition, relationships change quickly during adolescence, since teenagers themselves are changing so quickly. For most people at this age, the need to belong makes relationships with other teenagers seem like the most important part of life. Being accepted can make you feel very happy. Being rejected can cause real pain. Have you ever shared these feelings?

First teenager: "I felt really good when they began to wait for me after school."

Second teenager: "I made up a story about something I had to do on that night so I wouldn't have to admit I wasn't invited to the party."

Developing self-confidence

Self-confidence—feeling secure in yourself—is a very valuable trait. It is one of the "prizes" of maturity. Like maturity itself, self-confidence is often earned through experience.

It is normal to think that others are more sure of themselves than you are. Your own doubts and insecurities seem much greater to you than anyone else's. But the fact is, everyone has self-doubts. How many times have you heard a friend say, "I was too embarrassed to ask," or "I just didn't have the nerve to try"? Many young people feel uncertain and fear failure. So they don't risk talking to people they want to know. They don't try out for the band, the school play, a team sport, or a job they would like to have. They may never find out what they have to offer. Remember that risking failure also means risking success. It is important to learn how to handle feelings of being unworthy and insecure. Sometimes these feelings can serve to make people try to better themselves.

There are many ways to increase your self-confidence. First, understand yourself. Know what your abilities are, and learn how to make the most of them. Then, from time to time, stop and think about yourself. Are you fulfilling your needs and goals? Are you using your abilities fully? If the answer is "yes," congratulate yourself! Next, use your energy to work on your strengths rather than to worry about your weaknesses. The more you build up your strengths, the more confidence you will have. Finally, check up on your inner appearance—your inner self—as often as you check up on your outward appearance. Remember the times when you like what you see.

Making responsible decisions

More and more often, you think and act for yourself. You are learning to make your own decisions. This is necessary. In the future, you will have to decide about such things as education, career, marriage, a place to live, and a personal lifestyle. For now, you must make decisions about school, social life, and family.

A *responsible decision* is one that is based upon personal standards and that causes the least possible harm to you or others. But knowing what a responsible decision is may not always be enough. You may have to pick from among several possible choices.

It is a good idea to have ready a set of steps to follow when making decisions. With a plan of action, you will be more likely to make a responsible long-run decision or a good day-to-day decision.

Expect that some of your decisions will be better than others. Everyone makes mistakes from time to time. When you do make the wrong choice, try not to spend too much time feeling sorry about it. Instead, learn to profit from mistakes.

Remember that many people are willing to help you with long-run decisions as well as with day-to-day situations that you have to handle. In addition to parents, teachers, school counselors, doctors, and clergy, free

> **A Guide For Making Responsible Decisions**
>
> 1. *Use available resources.* Ask yourself, "Where can I get some worthwhile help in making this decision?" This may mean talking over your feelings with a friend, parent, or counselor. Friends may seem the easiest choices for help, but they may be struggling with questions just like yours. Reading a book, going to a meeting, or having information mailed to you are also ways to get help.
>
> 2. *Explore the choices.* List, in your mind or on paper, all of your possible choices. Many times people do not consider all the options they have.
>
> 3. *Think about the results.* Think about each of your possible choices. Consider what might happen as a result of your decision. Then be sure you are willing to accept the consequences of your actions.

counseling services and telephone "hotlines" are available in almost every community. These services have been set up to help you, in case you need them.

Looking at your personality

To rate your personality, first try to measure yourself according to your own values. Do you measure up to your own standards for yourself? Then, try to see yourself as others see you. How do you think you appear to others?

Once you have named your desirable and undesirable traits, you can work to correct your weaknesses and to build up your strengths. You might like to check your characteristics against the following personality traits. Each is thought to be a desirable trait.

Do you measure up to your own standards for yourself? How do you think you appear to others?

There are many ways to build self-confidence. Understand yourself. Know what your abilities are. Learn how to make the most of your skills and talents.

Personality Traits*

1. **I feel comfortable about myself.**
   - I am not overcome by my emotions of fear, anger, love, jealousy, guilt, or worry.
   - I can take life's disappointments as they come.
   - I have a tolerant, easygoing attitude toward myself as well as toward others.
   - I can laugh at myself.
   - I neither think too much nor too little of my abilities.
   - I feel able to deal with most situations in my life without help.
   - I do my everyday tasks without complaining.
   - I enjoy spending some time alone in building or creating something, or reading, or just thinking.
   - I have developed a philosophy of life and a standard of values.

2. **I feel comfortable with other people.**
   - I am able to show a real and friendly interest in others.
   - I have personal relationships that are satisfying and lasting.
   - I like and trust my friends, and I can be sure that they like and trust me.
   - I respect the many differences I find among people.
   - I do not take advantage of others, nor do I allow others to take advantage of me.
   - I feel that I am part of a group.
   - I feel a sense of responsibility to my neighbors and to all people of the world.

3. **I can meet the demands of life.**
   - I do something about my problems as they happen.
   - I accept my responsibilities toward myself and other people, whether they are my friends or not.
   - I shape my environment whenever possible. I adjust to it whenever necessary.

- I make plans for the future and hope to reach my goals.
- I welcome new experiences and new ideas.
- I make use of my abilities and set realistic goals for myself.
- I put my best effort into whatever I do, and I get satisfaction from doing it.

*Adapted from *Mental Health Is 1, 2, 3* (New York: National Association for Mental Health).

Your feelings about another person are usually a response to personality. When you vote, when you choose a friend, or when you seek a life companion, for example, you will be acting on your judgment of personality.

To rate someone else's personality traits, use the traits suggested for measuring your own personality. Does the person feel comfortable about herself or himself? Does the person meet the demands of life? You must watch an individual in many different situations to learn how the person behaves.

Your opinion of someone else's personality should be based on all you can know. You should consider background, aims, wants, and the ways used to reach personal goals. In rating another person's personality, try to avoid the following kinds of mistakes in judgment!

Mistakes to Avoid in Rating Others' Personalities

1. *Drawing a conclusion from only one event.* The new girl who did not return your greeting on her first day in class may not be a snob. She was probably nervous. Perhaps she did not hear you. Give her a chance before you decide.

2. *Placing too much value on surface traits.* Sometimes young people make the mistake of thinking that someone has a good personality because the person is good-looking or dances well.

3. *Using a "personality test" from a magazine or newspaper.* These tests are very limited. They usually tell only a small part of the personality. However, carefully prepared tests given by a trained psychologist can often help in judging certain aspects of personality.

4. *Stereotyping.* People often expect others to have a certain kind of personality because of their body type, nationality, religion, or race. This kind of "prejudging," which we call stereotyping or prejudice, leads to many false ideas and wrong judgments. Remember that people are individuals. Personality is the whole person in relation to his or her environment.

Your hopes in relationships with others should be reasonable. Relationships with other people (including friends) are always mixtures of happiness and disappointment. Good friends accept this fact. Many times, you and your friends will have different views and may argue. To remain friends, you have to accept and respect the personality of the other person. This acceptance is a sign of mature behavior.

Something to think about . . .

Over the years, many people have tried to describe the "normal" adolescent. Anna Freud, a psychoanalyst, explained adolescent behavior in these words:

> I take it that it is normal for an adolescent to behave for a considerable length of time in an inconsistent and unpredictable manner; to fight impulses and to accept them; to ward them off successfully and to be overrun by them; to love his [or her] parents and to hate them; to revolt against them and to be dependent on them; to be deeply ashamed to acknowledge [her or] his mother before others and unexpectedly, to desire heart-to-heart talks with her; to thrive on imitation of and identification with others while searching unceasingly for his [or her] own identity; to be more idealistic, artistic, generous, and unselfish than [she or] he will ever be again, but also the opposite: self-centered, egotistic, calculating. Such fluctuations between extreme opposites would be deemed highly abnormal at any other time of life.*

* Anna Freud, *Psychoanalytic Study of the Child.* Reprinted by permission of International Universities Press, New York.

Main Ideas

1. **Emotional needs must be satisfied if a person is to enjoy life and feel a sense of security.**
2. **Among the most important emotional needs shared by all people are the need to give and receive love and affection; the need for a positive self-concept; the need to succeed at something; the need to create; and the need for a personal philosophy of life.**
3. **The process of building a new relationship with one's parents during the teenage years often leads to conflict and tension.**
4. **Self-confidence is often learned through experience.**
5. **An important aspect of mature behavior is the ability to accept and respect the personalities of others.**
6. **A healthy personality includes the ability to be comfortable with oneself and with others and the ability to meet the demands of life.**

Key Words

emotional needs
maturity
personality
responsible decision
self-concept

Apply Your Knowledge

1. List the five important emotional needs described in this chapter.
2. Describe what can happen—both emotionally and physically—to a person whose emotional needs are not met.
3. What emotional need do teenagers satisfy by forming small, close groups?
4. Explain why it is important to have a positive self-concept.
5. List three methods you can use to find the activities in which you are most likely to experience personal achievement.
6. What is maturity? Are all adults mature? What is mature behavior?
7. What are the physical and social reasons why teenagers sometimes experience rapid changes in feelings or moods?
8. How does taking risks increase self-confidence?
9. List three good steps to follow in order to make a responsible decision.
10. List four errors to avoid in rating the personalities of other people.

Extend Your Knowledge

1. Describe three activities you participate in frequently. Explain how each one adds to your sense of personal achievement.
2. Think of three people who are famous for work in creative fields (dance, music, painting, writing, theater, or fashion design, for example). Write a brief description of each person and her or his work. Then think of three people you know about (preferably among your own friends, family, or acquaintances) who satisfy their need to create in ways that are not usually called "art." Describe the creative work of these people.
3. Review the list of factors that might affect a philosophy of life. How have these influences affected your values and goals? Describe at least three specific examples.
4. Read a novel that describes a teenager growing up before the twentieth century. Report on the influences that helped shape that person's developing philosophy of life. Discuss the presence or absence of these influences in your life.
5. Review the list of errors to avoid in rating others' personalities. Describe a situation from your own past in which you made one of these errors. Do you think other people ever make these kinds of errors in judging you? Give an example of the kind of misjudgment you think has been made or might be made about you.

Chapter 5

Do you know . . .

- how to handle hostile feelings?
- how fear can help you?
- why you feel uncomfortable when you have done something wrong?
- why some people lie to themselves in trying to excuse their failures?
- how to do a self-check on your mental health?

Emotions and Mental Health

Most behavior is an attempt to satisfy basic emotional needs. Life would be simple if nothing stood in the way of meeting these needs. But usually there are obstacles to overcome. Such obstacles may be a challenge to you or a roadblock. If you cannot overcome them, your emotional needs cannot be met. Then you may become angry or hostile. Or you may feel fearful or anxious. Or you may use what are called "defense mechanisms." This chapter will look at some of these emotional responses. It will discuss what can be done about them. It will also explain how some of these responses can lead to emotional or mental problems.

Anger and hostility

Everyone is capable of becoming angry or hostile. At an early age, you learn how to control these strong emotions. You are also learning, as you grow older, when and how to put anger to use. For example, you may have allowed your grades to fall, so you do not get a reward you want, such as being listed on the honor roll. Your anger with yourself may make you work much harder to improve your grades.

Even anger toward others can be constructive. Suppose a classmate was left out of certain activities because the person was of a different race or had a handicap. Your anger may cause you to take a strong stand for what you believe is fair. Your action may persuade others to change their behavior.

Constructive ways to get rid of anger

Anger and hostility may build up in anyone. Many kinds of small conflicts and frustrations may cause this to happen. If it happens to you, you can usually get rid of *hostile feelings* by talking about the problem with someone who is not involved. However, it is sometimes not really a good idea to talk over the matter too soon with the person you are angry with. More anger, not less, may result. Sometimes, too, you may not feel like talking about the problem, or you may not be able to find the right person to talk to. Then it may be possible to relieve the hostility in another way. One good way is to work off the anger in a very demanding physical activity. Physical action will use the extra energy that builds up when you get angry. Then you will be able to think more clearly about why you felt the anger and how you can handle the situation that made you angry.

Physical exercise is not only fun, it is also a good way to drain off the extra energy that builds up when you get angry.

Later, if you talk over your feelings with the person who made you angry, remember to *attack the issue, not the person.* In other words, don't name-call or make nasty remarks. They get in the way and make it hard for the other person to understand the reasons why you got angry and the behavior you expect in the future. Did you ever notice how uncontrolled remarks have a way of bringing about future situations which are also out of your control? In the following two examples, who do you think makes the point best?

First teenager to younger sister: "You stupid brat! You broke my new record. You're always doing rotten things! You can never listen to any of my records again."

Second teenager to younger sister: "I'm very angry. You broke my new record and I was *really* looking forward to listening to it. Next time, ask me to put the records on the turntable."

Poor ways of relieving anger

Many ways of getting rid of hostility and anger are *antisocial.* That is, they work against other people and society. For example, Sal is "touchy" and gets into an argument easily. If you could read his mind, you would discover that he feels a need for more friends—a group to belong to. But for some reason, Sal thinks that this goal cannot be reached, and he has stopped trying. Frustration and loneliness cause him to be disagreeable and hostile toward the very people he wants as friends.

Rule breaking is a hostile act. Rules help you learn what is expected of you. Breaking a rule usually results in unwanted consequences. A student who breaks rules and upsets classes may be getting rid of anger. The emotion may have been the result of failure to achieve in school. Two things may help. First, the person can look for an area in which she or he can do well. Doing well in any area will increase positive feelings of self-worth. Second, the student can look for acceptable ways to relieve the built-up anger. For example, taking part in sports or talking out angry feelings can help.

It is not always wrong to challenge rules. Questioning—and even rebelling against—some rules is part of growing up. Intelligent challenging of rules you do not agree with takes courage. Conforming to or following rules because "everybody else is doing it" is easy.

Most criminal and delinquent acts are antisocial acts against a person, a group, or society as a whole. There is no single cause of such behavior. But anger and hostility are often the reasons behind law-breaking acts.

Fear and anxiety

Everyone has felt fear of one kind of another. Feeling afraid is normal. It helps a person get ready for what may happen next. There are two general types of fear—fear of the unknown and fear of the known.

Fear of the unknown

Almost everyone has at some time felt afraid of the unknown. Unexplained things may seem to threaten our safety or well-being. For example, a child may be very fearful of the loud noises at a fireworks display. But an older person knows that the explosions are under control.

To get rid of fears of the unknown, you should learn as much as possible about the world. Then, when the unknown becomes known, you can decide whether or not your fear is reasonable. Having an open mind also helps you to overcome fears of the unknown or unfamiliar. If you are willing to consider new ideas, you will find that the unknown can sometimes turn out to be exciting.

Fear of the known

Fears of the known can be either useful or harmful. Reasonable fears can get you ready to act. If you wake up in the middle of the night and smell smoke, you are wise to be fearful. You will check out the source of the smoke and perhaps avoid a tragedy.

Fear of thunder, on the other hand, is an unreasonable fear. Light and electricity (lightning) travel much faster than sound (thunder). When you hear thunder, lightning has already flashed. The danger is over. The damage, if any, has already been done.

It is hard for many people to tell the difference between reasonable and unreasonable fears. Learning the difference is an important part of growing.

Anxiety and worry

Anxiety is a sense of uneasiness and distress about the future. Anxiety and worry are forms of fear. People learn unreasonable worries in the same way they learn unreasonable fears. Some worries are reasonable and useful, however. For example, if you worry about failing a test, you may begin to study. A reasonable sense of worry leads to concern and positive action. So, worry can have a positive result.

Depression is one major kind of anxiety. Most people feel depressed at times. They may say they feel "blue" or "low." A depressed person thinks too much about worries, anxieties, frustrations, fears, or failures. Depression wipes out feelings of self-worth. So the first step in overcoming depression is to begin a constructive activity or project. If depression continues for a long period of time and cannot be explained, the depressed person may need to seek special help.

An understanding teacher, counselor, or school doctor or nurse can sometimes help a young person overcome depression. These people may also know about other sources of help. Deep and long-lasting depression can harm you. It can lead to serious mental or emotional illness.

A depressed person thinks too much about worries, fears, or failures. Most people feel depressed at times. The first step in overcoming depression is to get active. Do something!

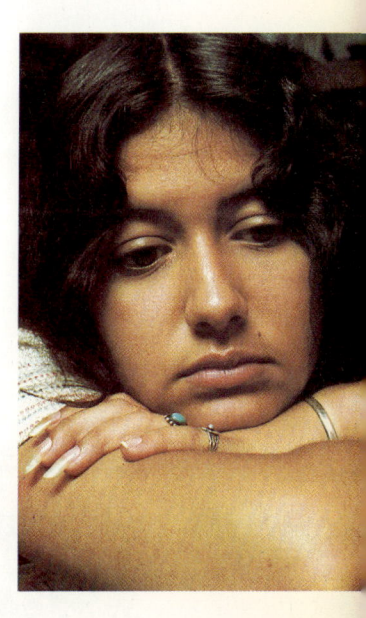

Guilt feelings are another major kind of anxiety. Your values are your ideas of what is right and wrong. You feel good, or have a clear conscience, when you do what you believe is right. You feel uncomfortable, or have a guilty conscience, when you have done something you believe is wrong. Guilt feelings can be constructive when they help you live up to your values. But if strong feelings of guilt last for a long time, they can lead to serious emotional disturbance. Extreme guilt feelings are a good reason for seeking help from those who are professionally trained.

Defense mechanisms

People sometimes use *defense mechanisms* to satisfy emotional needs. A defense mechanism helps someone relieve or avoid the pain of emotional conflict. It helps people "save face" in their own eyes and in the eyes of others. This may provide a false sense of security. But if problems become too much to handle, defenses may break down. This can cause severe emotional problems requiring professional treatment. Several different kinds of defense mechanisms are explained below.

Rationalization is a substitute reason for a failure or a mistake. People are often not aware that they are rationalizing. Rationalization can easily become a habit. It helps preserve self-respect for a time. But it is a way of sidestepping a problem and shifting the blame onto someone or something else. Only by learning to face failure honestly can a person work to overcome it and succeed.

Compensation is trying to provide substitutes for real or imagined shortcomings. Compensation can result in successful actions. For example, the person with too much stage fright to try out for the school play applies for the job of assistant director, and gets it.

Sometimes a person covers up a shortcoming with unacceptable behavior. Then poor compensation is being used. For example, a child who is physically smaller than others of the same age may unconsciously try to seem bigger and more important by bragging about his or her experiences.

Negativism is always saying "no" to the suggestions or instructions of others. Instead of attacking a problem directly, a negative person may do nothing or may do the opposite of what is suggested. The negativist refuses to try, perhaps out of a fear of failure. He or she passes up the chance to gain recognition or a sense of personal worth.

What defense mechanism might this person be using?

Identification consists of thinking that you are much like another person. Sometimes, for example, people mentally link themselves with a character in a film or television play. They experience what the character experiences and feel and think as the character feels and thinks. Sometimes identification is a way of fulfilling a wish. A person may wish to be just like someone else. Identification is easy to see in fans who act or dress just like the sports star or entertainer they most admire.

Occasional use of identification may help a person to satisfy a need for a role model. But, if used too much, this mechanism may cause a person to live in a dream world. In extreme cases, this pattern can be corrected only with special professional help.

Daydreaming is like identification. In daydreaming, a person substitutes a dream world for the real one. Daydreaming can be a normal and sometimes useful part of a creative life, if it is not carried too far. Some inventions and artistic masterpieces are the result of daydreams. Creative ideas, make-believe thoughts, or dreams can be acted upon and turned into real products or works of art.

Escape is running away when real or imagined defeat seems certain. When some people think they cannot face or solve a problem, they try to avoid it. A person who behaves in this way will gain little self-respect until the problem is faced in a direct way. There are several different escape mechanisms. *Repression* is an unconscious method of escape. A person pushes unwanted conflicts out of awareness. The person may even deny that there is any problem at all. *Suppression* is a conscious process of ignoring or avoiding an emotion. It is like closing the door to a room where something unpleasant is happening. *Regression* is living and behaving like a child. A person who does not have the courage or resources to face and solve a problem directly will sometimes go backward to a dependent position. This person may become more dependent, rather than less, on parents or others for support and for satisfaction of needs. *Conversion* takes place when a mental conflict is turned into a physical symptom. For example, a student who fears that he or she will not know what to say on a date may become so ill that it is impossible to go out. The pains and physical symptoms are real, not imagined. But the cause of the physical symptoms is mental conflict.

About one-fifth of all the hospital patients in the United States are people who are mentally ill. Many more people not in hospitals have mental or emotional disturbances severe enough to make their relationships with other people very difficult.

By learning about mental and emotional illnesses and their causes, you can better understand the principles of good mental health. Knowing about mental illness will also help you understand people who are undergoing treatment for mental or emotional disorders.

Causes of mental illness

The causes of mental illness may be physical, emotional, or both. Some are the result of changes in brain structure or in other parts of the

There are times when it is hard to be with others. Everyone needs some time alone. But for people with emotional or mental problems, being with others may be hard most or all of the time.

Mental illness

nervous system. These changes may be caused by disease, injury, or age. Mental illnesses may also be caused by changes in physical and chemical balances within the body. Still other mental disorders seem to have no physical cause. Such disorders are usually thought to result from the failure to satisfy emotional needs or to recover from emotional shock.

Degrees of mental illness

It is not always easy to know when a person is mentally ill. The behavior of a disturbed person often appears to be much like the behavior of a normal person. All people get upset from time to time and occasionally lose control over their emotions. In general, however, mentally healthy people are able to face the realities of life and act in a way to get greatest satisfaction. Mentally ill people use some of the same methods that normal people do to solve problems. But they may use them at the wrong time or carry them to extremes. And their goals are often unrealistic.

One common sign of mental disturbance is an inability to get along with other people. All of us find it hard at times to get along with others. This is normal. But for emotionally or mentally disturbed persons, it may be hard most or all of the time. It is not always easy to tell whether the difficulty is normal or is the symptom of a more serious disturbance. The changes from normal behavior to severe mental illness are not exact. Mental illness is a matter of degree, not a certain kind of behavior.

Kinds of mental illness

Most mental illnesses fall into three major categories: neurosis, psychosis, and psychosomatic disorder.

Neurosis is a mental disorder characterized by poor development of skills used to meet basic emotional needs. These poorly developed skills make relating to others more difficult. They also make a person vulnerable to emotional shocks. The shock might be losing a job, an action that brings on strong guilt feelings, or the sudden loss of a loved one.

One common type of neurotic illness is excessive fear or anxiety. Often the person cannot explain the fear. It is not unusual for a child to be afraid of the dark, but it is abnormal for an adult to experience this fear. Darkness may not be the cause of the fear. It may be that a deeply repressed fear is the real cause—a fear that the person is not aware of or cannot openly discuss.

Sometimes anxiety is unconsciously changed into physical disability. For example, an athlete's extreme worry about a pole-vault contest might result in leg paralysis. If no physical cause were present, the vaulter would be said to suffer from physical conversion of a mental anxiety. The person would not be conscious of this conversion.

Psychosis is a mental disorder in which a person is out of touch with reality at least part of the time. Because the person cannot adjust to the real world, he or she makes up a new world. The dream world may be a world filled with great anxiety. Or it may be a place where the person is a hero. But these feelings have no relation to real situations. Psychotics are usually not conscious of their behavior. They cannot tell the difference between the dream world and the real world.

Sometimes psychoses are caused by physical damage to the brain. These are called organic psychoses. Brain tumors, syphilis, alcohol and other drugs can cause this kind of psychosis.

Psychosomatic disorders are physical problems caused by emotional or psychological factors. Physicians believe that some cases of heart trouble, stomach ulcers, constipation, diarrhea, skin disorders, and other physical disorders are caused or made worse by mental and emotional disturbances. Psychosomatic disorders are real. The physical effects are just as damaging as the effects that result from physical illness.

Treating mental illness

The treatment of mental and emotional disturbances is called *psychotherapy*. Psychotherapy is practiced by a *therapist,* a person trained to help the mentally ill get well.

Therapists can guide patients, but they cannot force them to change. Psychotherapy helps people to help themselves. The situation is similar to a doctor's treatment of an overweight patient. The physician can suggest a diet and prescribe exercises. But it is up to the patient to do the rest of the job.

Psychotherapy is a slow process of learning about oneself. Working together, the patient and therapist search for reasons for the abnormal feelings and behavior. The patient expresses her or his feelings, dreams, and thoughts to the therapist. In time, better ways of meeting emotional needs are learned, and the patient is able to live more happily and fully.

Several kinds of specialists are trained to deal with emotional and mental health. Their goal is the same: to help the patient find acceptable ways of meeting emotional needs. The following are mental health specialists:

Even people with good mental health sometimes need help with an emotional problem. Treating problems early can prevent mental illness.

61

Mental Health Specialists

1. *Psychiatrist:* a physician holding a medical degree who has completed several years of treating mentally ill patients under the direction of a psychiatrist. A psychiatrist must pass tests to receive a license to practice in an office or hospital.
2. *Clinical psychologist:* an individual who has a doctoral degree in psychology. This person is trained in both theories and techniques of treatment of psychological problems. In most states, psychologists must also be licensed to practice.
3. *Psychiatric nurse:* a registered nurse with special training in caring for the mentally ill. These nurses are usually more closely involved in the daily lives of hospitalized patients than are other members of the hospital staff. Nurses' observations are very important to doctors. Their insights often influence a patient's treatment and response.
4. *Psychiatric social worker:* a specialist trained to work with a family, individual, or group to help them deal with problems that arise during a life crisis. This person also has a knowledge of community resources available to both patient and family.
5. *Occupational and recreational therapists:* specialists in helping patients to enjoy creative activities. Occupational therapists use various crafts to teach patients how to make things. Recreational therapists set up sports and social events.

Mental health specialists use several different kinds of therapy to help mentally ill patients. The kind of therapy used depends upon the individual patient.

Individual therapy, or face-to-face therapy, can be practiced by a psychiatrist, psychologist, or social worker in an office, hospital room, or any other setting. The patient usually talks with a therapist for about one hour. A regular schedule is usually followed—one or more times per week, for example. These sessions take place for weeks, months, or even years. Between interviews, the patient tries to change her or his behavior in the way agreed upon with the therapist.

Psychoanalysis is a special kind of psychotherapy. A psychoanalyst works with a person intensely over a long period of time (usually two to five years). The goal of this type of treatment is to help the patient to thoroughly understand *all* of his or her psychological makeup. The patient learns what is in the subconscious, what desires are suppressed, and the meaning of behavior since birth.

Drug therapy uses both tranquilizing and stimulating drugs to treat mental illnesses. Tranquilizing drugs are used to calm patients. Stimulating drugs do just the opposite. Scientists are not sure how all of these drugs work, but good results have been achieved in many cases.

Electric shock treatment must be carried out by an experienced psychiatrist. The patient is first given drugs to make sure the treatment will be painless. Then the patient is given an electric shock. This kind of treatment has been effective in relieving severe depression.

Group therapy is practiced by a therapist with several patients at the same time. The group members usually have emotional problems that are somewhat alike. The main focus is on how well the people communicate with each other.

Some people find that group therapy works better than individual therapy. One advantage is that you see that other people have emotional problems, too. This alone can help build self-confidence. Another advantage is that you learn from others in the group. Group members see how certain ways of communicating add to emotional imbalance. Also, group therapy costs less because the therapist works with more than one person at a time.

One sign of mental health is the ability to find satisfaction in relationships with others—friends, family, and coworkers.

One definition of mental health is the ability to face the real facts of life and achieve the greatest possible satisfaction. Below are some characteristics of the mentally healthy person. Using this list as a guide, do a self-check on your mental health. Make a note of those areas in which you think you need to improve. Think of ways you can make changes.

A self-check on your mental health

The Mentally Healthy Person

1. Accepts problems and conflicts and works through them to a satisfactory end.
2. Is able to love and to accept the love of others. Finds satisfaction in human relationships.
3. Can work and play cooperatively in give-and-take relationships.
4. Tries to understand the reasons for her or his own behavior and the behavior of others. Remembers that behavior is an effort to satisfy emotional and physical needs.
5. Uses defense mechanisms when effective, but does not depend upon them to solve all problems.

6. Has a standard of values that guides actions.
7. Is able to change or adjust behavior when necessary, but only if moral standards are maintained.
8. Has developed a philosophy of life that meets the demands of society, satisfies personal dreams and goals, and is within his or her capabilities.
9. Can control anger and hostility, as well as other emotions, and has learned harmless ways of getting rid of hostility.
10. Develops creative interests and abilities so that satisfaction can be found in doing things well.
11. Takes pride in being prepared to accept responsibility for ideas, feelings, and actions.

Something to think about . . .

Mental health specialists now think that some kinds of mental illness may be caused by allergies. They are convinced that some forms of psychoses, depression, or chronic fatigue result from eating a common food or from breathing an ordinary substance.

Dr. H. L. Newbold, a New York psychiatrist, is a leader in the new field of cerebral allergies. He has observed numerous cases in which household cleaning products or common foods, such as sugar, are at the root of mental illness.

The case of Dorothy L. is an example. Dorothy had been in a psychiatric hospital for five years. Her illness was a form of psychosis, a severe paralyzing schizophrenia. Dorothy was so out of touch with reality that she did not even remember how to use money. Dr. Newbold put Dorothy on a five-day fast to cleanse her body of all allergens. (An *allergen* is any substance that causes an allergic reaction.) During this period, Dorothy consumed only spring water. At the end of the five days, her system was free of allergens. The results were dramatic. She spoke her first complete sentence in five years, showed an awareness of her surroundings, and even smiled.

By carefully and systematically reintroducing certain substances into her system, Dr. Newbold was able to determine that Dorothy is seriously allergic to certain foods—one of which is sugar. To remain well, Dorothy will always have to avoid those foods.

Main Ideas

1. You usually have to overcome obstacles in order to meet your emotional needs. Each obstacle is a challenge.
2. A person who is angry can usually get rid of hostile feelings by talking about the problem.
3. It is sometimes difficult to tell the difference between reasonable and unreasonable fears.
4. Anxiety and worry are forms of fear.
5. A guilt feeling is the uncomfortable feeling you have when you have done something you believe is wrong.
6. Defense mechanisms sometimes give a false sense of security.

7. Mental illness is an extreme degree of emotional disturbance.
8. Mental health is the ability to face the real facts of life and adapt oneself in order to gain the greatest possible satisfaction.

Key Words

antisocial
anxiety
defense mechanism
drug therapy
electric shock treatment
group therapy
hostile feelings
individual therapy
neurosis
psychoanalysis
psychosis
psychosomatic disorder
psychotherapy
therapist

Apply Your Knowledge

1. What are some good ways of getting rid of anger and hostility?
2. Describe how you might help a friend who is feeling very angry.
3. Name three fears or worries about the unknown with which you are familiar.
4. How can fear of the known be useful?
5. What can you do about situations that produce guilt feelings? Give an example.
6. What is the purpose of a defense mechanism? How is it sometimes helpful? When can it cause severe emotional disturbance?
7. Explain how compensation can have wanted and unwanted results.
8. What methods are used by therapists in treating emotional problems?
9. List the differences between a psychiatrist and a psychologist.
10. In your own words, describe a mentally healthy person.

Extend Your Knowledge

1. From your own experience, give an example of being blocked in reaching a goal. Then suggest a good way to reach it.
2. Write a brief story in which the main character uses rationalization to cover up a failure.
3. Find out how your community helps people with mental disorders. (Ask nurses, physicians, church workers, social workers, and so forth.) Do you think your community has enough resources for this health problem? Explain your answer.
4. Plan a debate between members of your class on this statement: *It is more important to treat some criminals for their mental illness than to imprison them.* For the debate, find out how treatment of criminals has been improved and what further improvements are hoped for. Decide on your own point of view about the treatment of criminals and prepare to defend it.
5. Give a report on the role of occupational therapy in the treatment of mentally ill patients.

Chapter 6

Do you know . . .

- what a stress reaction is?
- that stress can be helpful?
- what distress is?
- how to cope with stress?

Living with Stress

Human beings face their problems and challenges in the mind. However, the mind does not operate alone. It works closely with the physical processes of the body. While you don't expect your stomach to solve a problem or to feel excited, you might pass on the problem or excitement to your stomach. The effect on the human body of physical and mental demands and pressures may be thought of as *stress.* Everyone experiences stress. In fact, a certain amount of stress is necessary to perform the daily tasks of your life. But too much stress—especially constant, unrelieved stress—can result in physical and mental illness.

The stress response is the body's way of reacting to any demand made on it. The stress response is a kind of alarm. Your body can produce a stress reaction in response to a crisis, to everyday situations, and to change.

The stress response

Stress—a response to crisis

Imagine this: a prehistoric woman is sitting outside her cave, enjoying the afternoon sunlight. Suddenly, from the corner of her eye, she sees the shadow of a leopard, crouched close to the ground. Instantly, her body reacts. Her heart beats quickly and her blood pressure rises. Hormones that aid muscle performance flood into her bloodstream. She starts to breathe rapidly, taking in more oxygen. Digestion is turned off at once, so that all her body energy can be used to fight off the attack, or to flee from it.

The woman has experienced a stress reaction. Her body processes spring into action, ready for fight or flight. This stress response helped our ancestors to survive in dangerous environments.

Thousands of years later, the stress response is the same for people who are reacting to a danger signal. For example, you are walking towards home late at night. The street is completely empty. You hear footsteps behind you and look over your shoulder. Three large figures are following you. You walk faster, and the footsteps quicken, too. You turn sharply at the next corner, but the figures follow you, more closely now. Your home is a mile away, so you walk rapidly to the door of the nearest house and ring the bell. No answer. No one is at home. The figures move to the doorstep where you are standing. At this point, your body would be experiencing the same stress reaction that occurred in your ancestors' bodies when they were threatened. Your body systems would be all set to fight or to flee.

Physical dangers are not the only demands that people face today. Your life is far more complicated than that of the cave dweller who was enjoying the sunshine. Suppose that you have a tough math course. To keep up, you should be doing the homework problems every night. You never seem to understand the problems well enough to do the homework. Class is confusing, too. As a result, your grade on the last test was terrible. Today, you walk into the classroom and the teacher asks the class to put away their books. She is going to give a "pop" quiz.

Probably, your body reacts with a surge of activity. Your pulse rate and breathing rate increase. Hormones rush into the bloodstream. Your temperature rises and you begin to perspire. Physically, you experience a stress reaction. Your body is all prepared to fight or to flee—but you can't. There is no physical danger from the math teacher or from a paper-and-pencil quiz. Besides, the rules of classroom behavior do not permit you to rush from the room.

What happens when your body experiences a stress reaction and then cannot use the physical responses that result? In the case of the math quiz, your body will absorb this quick surge of energy. In a very short time, the body will adjust to the stress situation and return to normal. If the demand made on the body by the stress was very strong, you might later experience a physical reaction such as indigestion or a headache.

Something that makes a demand on the body is known as a *stressor*. The leopard, the three figures, and the quiz are all stressors. In these examples, each of the stressors is a crisis situation.

Stress—a response to everyday situations

The math course itself can be a stressor, too. Each time you go to class or try to do your homework, you might experience low-level stress reactions. If your poor performance in math continues, you might experience unnoticeable stress symptoms even when you are not consciously thinking about the course. These low-level stress reactions are caused by worrying about math. They result in ongoing bodily changes that you probably don't notice—at first.

Everyone's life has some stress. In day-to-day situations, your body can handle normal stress. Even when stress continues, the body will react by demanding physical and mental rest. After rest, it is again ready to take on stress.

In fact, a certain amount of stress is necessary. The right amount for you depends on your individual physical and mental makeup. Alicia, for example, is always on the go. She participates in all sorts of clubs and organizations in school. Out of school, she competes year-round in sailing races. Keeping up with all her activities requires her to handle a great deal of physical and mental stress.

Mike, on the other hand, is more easygoing. He's not lazy at all. He spends time with his friends, works part-time at a record store, and keeps up with schoolwork. However, he would not be comfortable with Alicia's

Stress is your body's way of reacting to any demand made on it. The demand can be a crisis, a change in your life, or even an everyday situation. Everyone's life has some stress.

schedule. To him, that much stress would be harmful. This is sometimes called *distress*. His body and mind would begin to demand rest. Eventually, his body and mind would refuse to function properly until he got rest.

Both Alicia and Mike can give their top performance when the stress in their lives is at the best level for each of them.

Too little stress can be as undesirable as distress. Many older people in the United States find themselves in situations where they have too little stress in their lives. Low performance levels and physical and mental illness can result from too little stress.

Stress—a response to change

Life-changes are powerful stressors. When a baby changes from eating liquid foods to eating solid foods, the baby changes the way of eating. When a child enters school, the child must adjust to the fact that many of the needs of the group come first. In adolescence, young people must begin to develop adult attitudes or ideas about responsibility. They must learn to behave in a mature way. Falling in love, getting married, and becoming a parent are other examples of changes that involve new stresses in living.

The Life Change Scale shown on page 70 is based on the idea that even a happy event can cause stress if a lot of change is needed. The scale was made by Drs. T. H. Holmes and R. H. Rahe after surveying hundreds of people. People who took part in the survey were asked how much stress they experienced in getting used to a change in life's events. Marriage was given a value of 50 points; people were then asked to rate other events by how much adjustment each event called for, compared to marriage. For example, the scale shows that getting married (50 points) took twice as much adjustment as a change in a person's living conditions (25 points). Losing a spouse by death (100 points) seemed twice as hard for a person to adjust to as getting married. You may agree with some of the ratings. You may disagree with others. Think about why some events would cause more stress for you than other events.

A certain amount of stress is needed to help you achieve. The right amount of stress for you depends on your physical and mental makeup.

LIFE CHANGE SCALE

RANK	LIFE EVENT	MEAN VALUE
1	Death of spouse	100
2	Divorce	73
3	Marital separation	65
4	Jail term	63
5	Death of close family member	63
6	Personal injury or illness	53
7	Marriage	50
8	Fired at work	47
9	Marital reconciliation	45
10	Retirement	45
11	Change in health of family member	44
12	Pregnancy	40
13	Sex difficulties	39
14	Gain of new family member	39
15	Business readjustment	39
16	Change in financial state	38
17	Death of close friend	37
18	Change to different line of work	36
19	Change in number of arguments with spouse	35
20	Mortgage over $10,000	31
21	Foreclosure of mortgage or loan	30
22	Change in responsibilities at work	29
23	Son or daughter leaving home	29
24	Trouble with in-laws	29
25	Outstanding personal achievement	28
26	Wife to begin or stop work	26
27	Begin or end school	26
28	Change in living conditions	25
29	Revision of personal habits	24
30	Trouble with boss	23
31	Change in work hours or conditions	20
32	Change in residence	20
33	Change in schools	20
34	Change in recreation	19
35	Change in church activities	19
36	Change in social activities	18
37	Mortgage or loan less than $10,000	17
38	Change in sleeping habits	16
39	Change in number of family get-togethers	15
40	Change in eating habits	15
41	Vacation	13
42	Christmas	12
43	Minor violations of the law	11

Reprinted with permission from *Journal of Psychosomatic Research,* Vol. II, T.H. Holmes and R.H. Rahe, "The Social Readjustment Rating Scale," Copyright 1967, Pergamon Press Ltd.

Is stress harmful?

You probably have felt the effects of unrelieved stress in the form of stomachache, headache, diarrhea, or indigestion. In your body's attempt to adjust to stress, you may have found that your mouth became dry, that you got depressed or irritable, or that you lost your appetite or started to eat uncontrollably. These are common stress symptoms.

Researchers are finding that ongoing stress may have more effects on the body than the common stress symptoms show. New research is underway to find out to what degree stress over a long period of time is responsible for damage and diseases of major body systems:

Major Body System	Conditions Caused or Made Worse by Unrelieved Stress
cardiovascular system	heart attack, high blood pressure, migraine headache
digestive system	ulcers, colitis
skeletal-muscular system	backache, arthritis, being "accident-prone"

In addition, researchers have found that unrelieved stress can lower the body's resistance to ordinary infections—such as the common cold. It is known that a person who makes a high score on the stress scale (more than 100 points in 1 year) is likely to have more colds and minor illnesses than a person with a low score. Dr. Holmes found that people with a rating of 200 points for a given year almost always became ill as a result of too much stress.

Coping with stress

How do you keep your stress level at the proper point—where you can perform at your best as an active individual but avoid the harmful effects of stress?

Keep your body working for you, not against you. A healthy body makes you better able to adapt to the normal stresses of everyday life and helps you to weather the stresses caused by life changes. You probably already know the rules for maintaining the good health of your body. They are the simple rules that you have learned at home and in school for most of your life: eat a well-balanced diet, get enough sleep, and exercise regularly. You may get tired of hearing these rules. They may seem too familiar, too "goody-goody." But the fact is that these simple health practices keep you alive and functioning.

Know how to judge reality. Some situations can and must be changed. Some situations should be left alone. When to act and when to "let it pass" are judgments usually made on the basis of experience. You can make the most of the experience you are having by looking closely at your actions and the actions of others.

For instance, suppose you eat lunch with Fred. Every once in a while, Fred gets loud and rowdy. It seems funny to you at first, but then it becomes hard to take. Fortunately, you like Fred for a number of reasons, and his loud behavior doesn't happen that often. But today is "one of those days," and by lunchtime you're tired of it. Fred is causing you some stress. You have had a polite discussion once before about your reaction to his loudness. But Fred hasn't changed much as a result. Here's what you could do:

- Yell at Fred, call him a bigmouth, and tell him to shut up. You feel like doing this.
- Sit there and take it. You don't feel like doing this, but you think it might be wise.
- Finish your lunch and go to the library. Tell Fred you feel like being by yourself.

The reality of the situation is that you like Fred and want to be his friend despite his occasional outbursts. He hasn't changed his behavior and isn't likely to. Yelling will add stress because it will make you worry about hurting your friendship. Sitting and fuming will let the stress reactions build up in you. Simply removing yourself until things become more calm

The ability to make quick judgments under stress is a part of many jobs. A healthy body is needed to withstand the stress levels required for top performance.

is a realistic way to handle the situation. Tomorrow, Fred will be his old self again.

Try to spot stress and plan for it. If you know of a stressful situation that will soon occur, it will help to be prepared. Suppose you are afraid to give speeches and you have an oral report due next week. You know all about the stress reaction that you will experience when you stand in front of the class. You can:

- Prepare your report thoroughly, put it on note cards, and practice it in front of the mirror and in front of your family or friends.
- Get yourself ready to speak a week in advance by asking a question or making a comment in class whenever possible. (You'll get used to hearing your own voice speak out loud.)
- Admit that giving oral reports is stressful for you. Tell yourself that you are *allowed* to experience stress at first. Realize that your body is simply reacting, and that the same body can adapt itself, too.
- Ask yourself how you might turn off your *"flight" response* and turn on your *"fight" response*. Make positive images in your mind of how you will use the energy from your stress reaction to "get into" and deliver your speech. Good public speakers know how to use the physical readiness caused by stress to improve their performance.

Sometimes stress is hard to spot. There are times when you feel the stress symptoms before you understand the cause of the stress. You should see a doctor about any physical symptoms that become too annoying or seem more serious than usual.

Learn something about relaxation. What is it that makes you relax? Perhaps it is one of these:

- a soft sofa and a good book
- an hour of jogging
- six of your favorite record albums
- a 20-minute catnap
- isometric exercises
- a chance to sit and daydream
- a long walk
- a phone call with a friend

The word *relaxation* reminds many people of the word *play*. Sometimes people use this association to dismiss their need to relax: "I can't relax today, I have too much to do." Relaxation can be enjoyable, but that does not mean that it is unnecessary.

When you relax the muscles in your body, you slow down the body's processes. When you use the muscles in your body forcefully, you reduce built-up body tension. Both of these acts provide physical and mental relief. From what you know about stress, you can see how relaxation can help prevent physical symptoms from building up. Relaxation helps you to stay healthy.

You may have noticed that relaxing after a stressful day feels even more refreshing than relaxing after a day when your stress load was low. After a stress situation, the relief you provide to your body feels particularly good. Can you think of some time when this has been true for you?

Some people find it difficult to relax. These people are often the ones who need relaxation the most in order to handle high stress loads. Relaxation is like any other physical activity you ask your body to perform—doing it improves with practice. By regularly giving your body a relaxation break, you will notice an improvement in your day-to-day performance. You will also notice an increase in your ability to adapt to sudden stress reactions.

These are only a few ways to cope with stress. You might have found that other ways work best for you. The important thing is to find a way to cope. You can't avoid all stress—and you would not want to. But you can learn how to handle the expected stress in your life and how to avoid unnecessary stress. This will make it easier for your body to adapt to those

Your body needs to relax for physical and mental relief. Relaxation helps you to stay healthy. What makes you relax?

stresses that you don't expect. By learning to cope with problems and pressures, you can keep your body from becoming ill or damaged by the effects of constant, unrelieved stress.

Something to think about . . .

How well are you able to handle the events that occur in your life? Why is it that some people are able to cope with an experience that would overwhelm someone else?

Some forces are known to affect one's ability to cope well. These include self-esteem, philosophy of life, relationships with other people, and successful handling of difficult situations in the past. Each event in your life offers a unique chance for emotional growth. Your failures as well as your successes offer you the potential for positive growth. It depends on how you view and handle the situation. Each crisis you are able to deal with makes your personality stronger.

One famous American faced many difficult situations in his lifetime. Many people believe that his successful handling of many crises added a great deal to his strength of character and his success later on.

In 1818, when he was nine years old, his mother died. In 1828, his sister died. In 1832, he lost his first job, joined the militia, and was defeated for the state legislature. In 1833, he failed in business. In 1835, a girl friend died. In 1838, four years after being elected to his state's legislature, he was defeated for speaker of the state house of representatives. In 1843 and again in 1844, he was defeated for nomination to Congress.

Elected to Congress in 1847, he did not seek reelection in 1848 because he knew he was too unpopular to win. In 1849, he was rejected for Land Officer. In 1850, his four-year-old son died. In 1854, he was defeated for the United States Senate. In 1856, he was defeated for nomination for Vice President. In 1858, he was again defeated for the United States Senate. HOWEVER, IN 1860, ABRAHAM LINCOLN WAS ELECTED PRESIDENT OF THE UNITED STATES OF AMERICA.

Main Ideas

1. Stress is the effect of physical and mental demands on the body.
2. A certain amount of stress is necessary for achievement.
3. Too much or too little stress may result in physical and mental illness.
4. Ongoing stress may have more effects on the body than the common stress symptoms show.
5. Keeping your body healthy and knowing how to make judgments about situations make you better able to adjust to stress.

Key Words

distress   "flight" response   stressor
"fight" response   stress

Apply Your Knowledge

1. When might your body produce a stress reaction? Give specific examples.
2. What happens when your body experiences a stress reaction and then cannot use the physical responses that result?
3. When could a certain amount of stress be helpful and even necessary? Give specific examples.
4. What is distress?
5. What are the common symptoms of stress?
6. Name some life changes that might involve stress.
7. What are some possible effects of ongoing stress?
8. Name some positive things you can do to cope with stress.
9. How would a good public speaker use the "physical readiness" caused by stress?
10. How can relaxation help you to stay healthy?

Extend Your Knowledge

1. Rate the following life changes according to how stressful you think they might be for you:
   a. graduating from high school
   b. writing a term paper
   c. starting or breaking up a relationship
   d. putting a dent in the family car
   e. getting a part-time job
2. Make a list of five healthy ways to relax that you have never tried before. Try out these new ways for one week. At the end of the week, report to the class about your experiences.
3. Find out about the work of Dr. Hans Selye, who did the original research on stress and who was responsible for the concept of the "stress syndrome."
4. Suicide is the third leading cause of death among young adults age 15 to 24. Many people misunderstand suicide. For instance, find out if the following statement is true or false: "People who threaten to commit suicide never really do." Research how stress is related to suicide.
5. What is biological feedback, or biofeedback? How does the current research in biofeedback relate to your knowledge of stress?

Unit 3

CHAPTERS:

7 Human Reproduction

8 Family Life

Human Sexuality

Chapter 7

Do you know . . .

- why some twins look alike and others do not?
- how some birth defects can be prevented?
- how cigarette smoking can affect an unborn baby?
- the function of the umbilical cord?

Human Reproduction

There are many different reasons why people become parents. Sometimes a baby is planned far in advance. At other times, the baby is not planned at all. Planned or unplanned, all human babies are formed by the joining of two cells. One cell comes from the mother and one comes from the father. The mother's egg cell, or *ovum,* is very small. It can hardly be seen by the human eye. The father's *sperm* cell is even smaller. It can be seen only through a microscope.

Sperm are made in two glands in the male called *testes,* or testicles. Ova (the plural of ovum) are made in two glands in the female called *ovaries.* In addition to sperm and ova, the testes and ovaries also produce hormones.

Puberty is the stage of life during which a person's reproductive system starts to work. For girls, puberty is the period when the ovaries begin to send out ova. For boys, puberty is the period when the testes start to make sperm.

The male reproductive system

For most boys, puberty is the period between the ages of 12 and 15. The outward signs of puberty are the development of *secondary sexual characteristics.* The boy's voice gets deeper. Hair begins to grow on the face, under the arms, and in the genital area. Arm, leg, and chest muscles become stronger and harder. The boy's skin becomes thicker and tougher, and his shoulders get wider. The development of these male sexual characteristics is controlled by a substance called *testosterone.* Testosterone is the male sex hormone. It is made by the testes.

Testes

The testes are formed in the abdomen. Shortly before birth, they usually move downward into a pouch of skin and connective tissue that hangs outside the body. This pouch is called the scrotum. In some cases, one or both testes do not move into the scrotum until after birth. Sometimes a doctor's help is needed to bring the testes into the scrotum.

As each testis passes through the lower wall of the abdomen, the passageway usually closes behind it. If the passageway does not close, a hernia may happen at this spot later in life. Such a hernia may be seen as a swelling in the groin that develops after lifting something heavy. Or it may feel like pressure from inside the abdomen. This kind of hernia can be fixed surgically without serious risk.

Sperm

Sperm are shaped somewhat like tadpoles. Each sperm has a head with a nucleus in it. The sperm also has a tail that waves back and forth, making the sperm move.

Sperm are found in tiny tubes in the testes called seminiferous tubules. Uncoiled, this network of tubes would be more than a mile long. After the sperm are made, they pass into the *epididymis.* This is a comma-shaped structure found on the back side of the testes. Here the sperm develop further. Then, helped by a wavelike movement, they pass into an inner duct called the *vas deferens.* This duct connects with the urethra, which opens to the outside of the body. The urethra is also the passage from the bladder to the outside of the body. But it does not carry urine and sperm at the same time.

The sperm are carried in secretions of special glands: the seminal vesicles, the prostate gland, and Cowper's glands. The seminal vesicles produce a fluid that mixes with the sperm. This fluid, with the sperm in it, is called *semen.* The semen picks up other substances from the prostate gland at the neck of the bladder and from Cowper's glands just below the prostate.

Semen is a thick, whitish fluid. Millions of sperm cells are carried in semen. Sperm and semen sometimes pass out of the body during sleep. This is called a nocturnal emission, or wet dream. It is a normal event.

The urethra passes through the penis, the outside reproductive organ of the male. The penis is a tubular organ made of spongy tissue containing many small blood vessels. When the blood vessels contain only a little blood, the penis is soft. When they are filled with blood, it becomes larger and erect, or stiff. At birth, the head of the penis, or glans, is covered by a fold of tissue called the foreskin. Often the foreskin is removed shortly after birth. The removal is called circumcision. This may be done for religious or health reasons.

The ability to reproduce: the mother's sex cell is called the ovum (left); the father's sex cell is called the sperm (right).

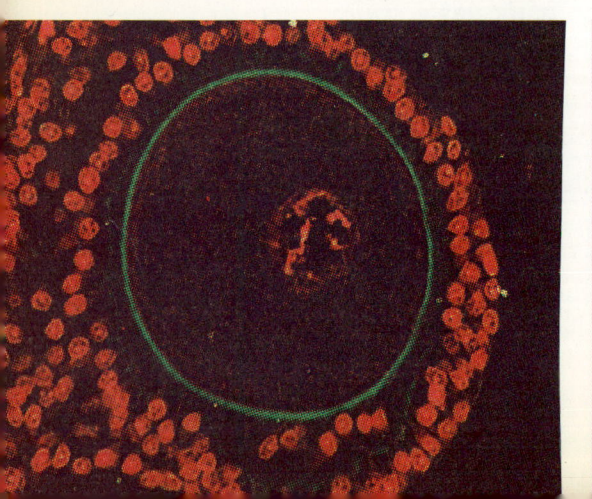

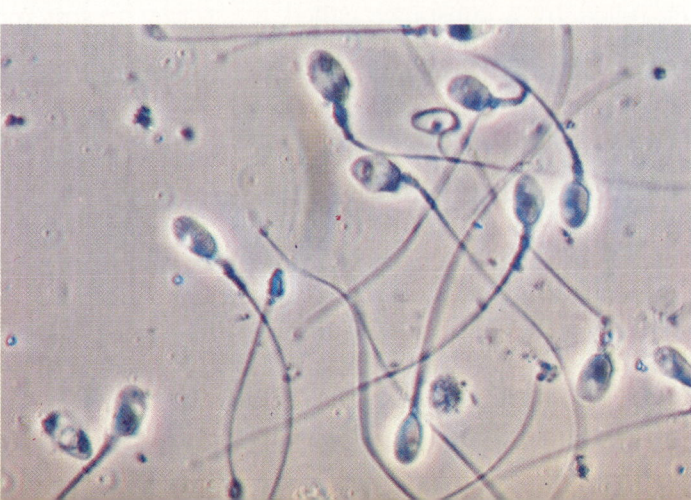

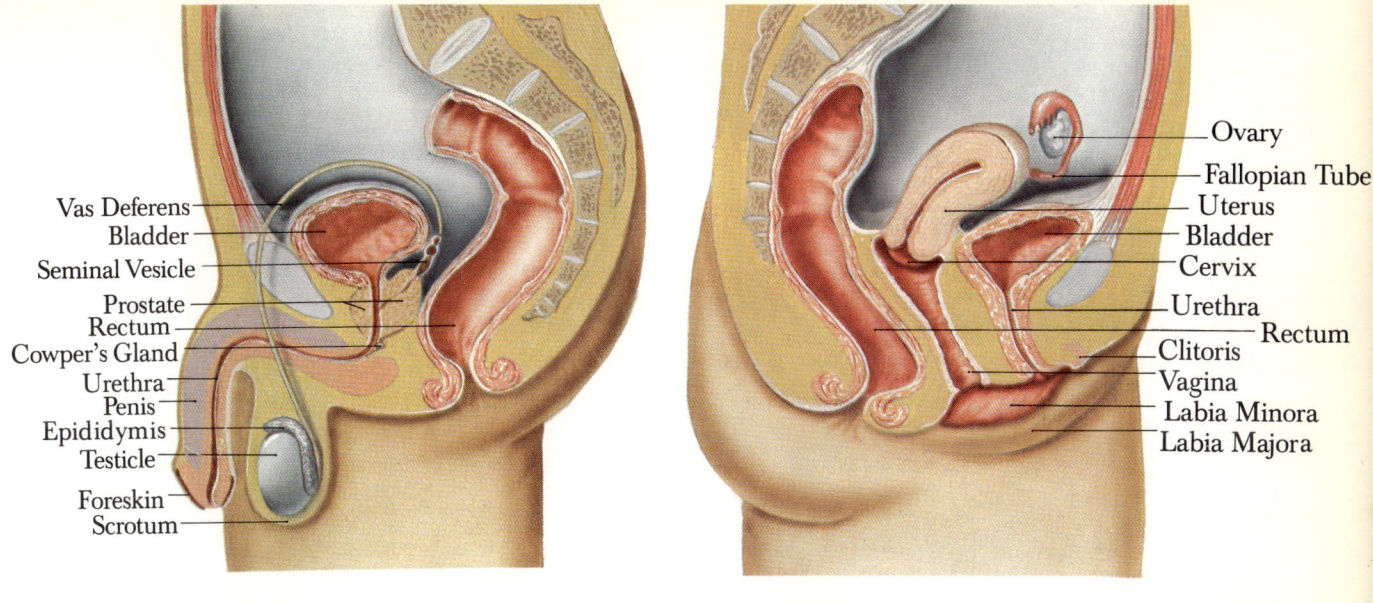

(left) At puberty, the testes of the male begin to make sperm.

(right) At puberty, the ovaries of the female begin to send out the ova that have been present since birth.

The female reproductive system

For most girls, puberty is the period between the ages of 11 and 14. The ovaries begin to send out ova at puberty, and secondary sexual characteristics appear as outward signs of puberty. The breasts develop, the hips get broader, and other parts of the body become more rounded. Hair begins to grow under the arms and in the genital area. The girl's skin becomes softer and smoother. *Estrogen* is the female sex hormone. It is made by the ovaries. Estrogen causes the female secondary sexual characteristics to develop.

Ovaries

The ovaries are formed before birth. They are in the lower part of the abdomen. All of the egg cells, or ova, are present in the ovaries at birth. Beginning at puberty, the ova mature and are released by the ovaries. Usually only one ovum matures and is released each month.

The monthly release, ejection, and movement of a mature ovum from the ovary is called *ovulation*. Ovulation happens at about the same time every month. It usually continues on a monthly basis for about 30 or 40 years. The time when the release of ova stops is called the *menopause*. The menopause usually comes when a woman is around 50 years of age.

Ova

An ovum is round and cannot move by itself. Gravity and gentle suction move it from the ovary to the open end of one of the oviducts, or *Fallopian tubes*. A Fallopian tube carries the ovum to the *uterus*, or womb. The uterus is a muscular organ shaped something like a pear. It is about 7½ centimeters (3 inches) long and 5 centimeters (2 inches) wide at the top. The uterus narrows down to the *cervix*, or neck of the womb. The cervix is about 1 to 2½ centimeters (½ to 1 inch) in diameter.

81

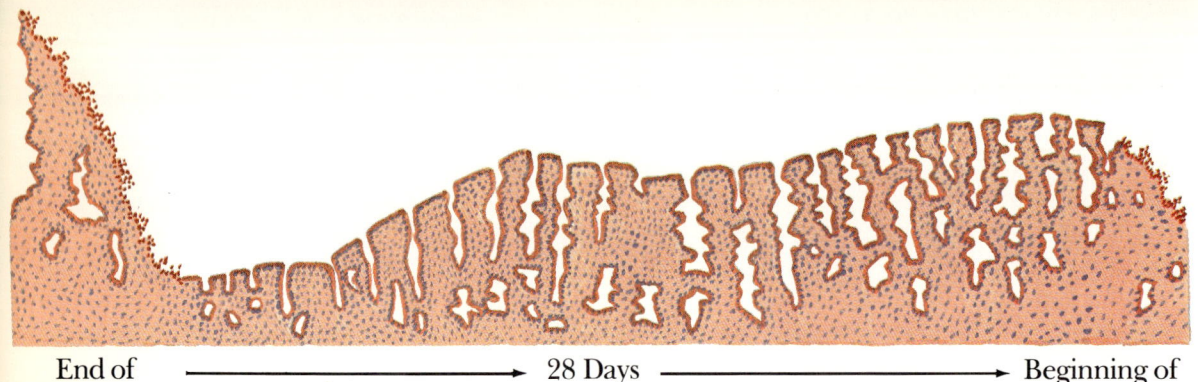

End of Menstruation → 28 Days → Beginning of Menstruation

During a period of about 28 days, the lining of the uterus builds up. If there is no pregnancy, the lining breaks down and leaves the body. This event is called menstruation.

Menstruation

The uterus is in the middle part of the abdomen. Its spongy lining is called the *endometrium*. This lining has many small blood vessels. Ten days to two weeks after ovulation, if there is no pregnancy, the blood vessels in the endometrium break down. The lining then comes away from the walls of the uterus. Along with the disintegrated ovum, the lining is passed out of the body through the vagina. The vagina is the tube that connects the uterus to the outside of the body. The loss of the endometrium is known as *menstruation*. It usually takes place once each month. Menstruation may last from three to seven days. Right after menstruation, the uterus begins to form a new lining.

The ovulation and menstruation cycles take about 28 days. But the cycles do not begin at the same time. Ovulation usually takes place 14 days before menstruation begins.

The outer female genital organs include the labia minora, the labia majora, and the clitoris. The labia minora are two small folds of skin that cover the openings to the vagina and urethra. The labia majora are two larger folds of skin that cover the labia minora. The clitoris is a small, very sensitive organ just above the urinary opening. The term vulva is used to mean all of the outer female sex organs.

The beginning of life

Semen can be discharged, or ejaculated, into the vagina. The millions of sperm that are in the semen move through the vagina toward the uterus. The sperm continue through the uterus to the Fallopian tubes.

Fertilization, or *conception*, can happen only when an ovum and a sperm join. An ovum can be fertilized for only a few days after ovulation. If no sperm is present during those few days, fertilization cannot take place. If there is an ovum in one of the Fallopian tubes, it is likely that it will be joined by a sperm. When this happens, changes take place in the cell membranes of the fertilized ovum that stop other sperm from joining with it.

During the next three to four days, the fertilized ovum starts to divide. It moves down the Fallopian tube to the uterus, where the embryo will grow. *Embryo* is the term used for the developing cluster of cells during these early stages. The blood vessels in the endometrium have a rich supply of blood to support growth.

Once an embryo has started to grow in the uterus, no more ova are released for the next nine months. This is the amount of time needed for the development of a baby. During this period, the endometrium does not break down. Menstruation does not occur until after the baby is born.

Cell division

After the ovum and sperm join together, the fertilized ovum divides into 2 cells. Then each of these cells divides, making 4. Cell division continues, making 8 cells, then 16, then 32, then 64, and so on. A great number of cells are formed in this way. The dividing process is rapid and gets more complex with each division.

Cell differentiation

Cells of many different shapes are formed. Some are flat. Others grow long and spindle-shaped. Some are six-sided. Others are irregular in shape. The many kinds of cells have different jobs in the human body. Each will join with others like it to form parts of the body. The flat cells will become skin cells. The spindle-shaped cells will become muscle cells. The six-sided cells will become liver cells. The irregular cells will form bone. This process is called *cell differentiation*.

As the cells grow, the embryo gets longer. A bulge appears on one end. Little buds form near the top and bottom. The bulge becomes the head. The buds become arms and legs. After the second month, the embryo is more than 2 to 3 centimeters (1 inch) long. The body, head, eyes, nose, mouth, arms, and legs have begun to form. The embryo is now called a *fetus*.

Needs of the fetus

As the fetus grows in size, the uterus gets larger. The walls of the uterus stretch so that there is enough room for growth. More room inside

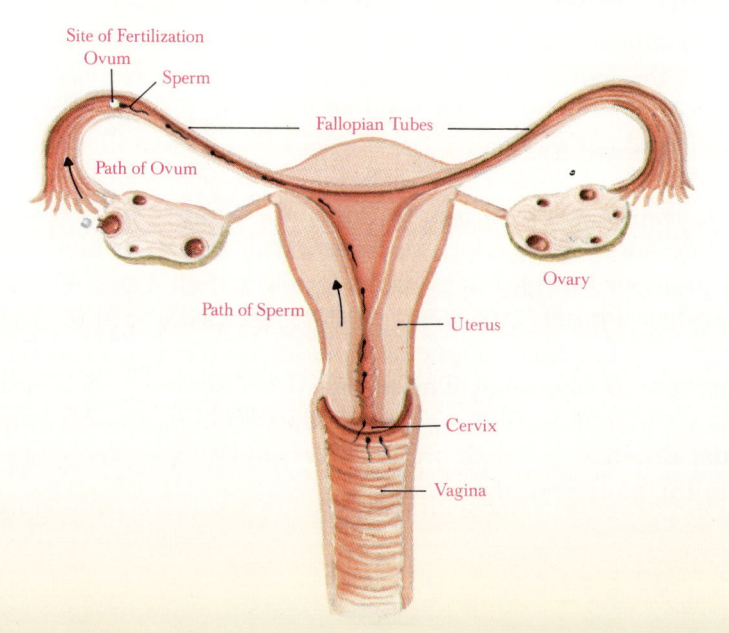

Sperm travel up through the uterus and into the Fallopian tubes. If sperm are present when an ovum moves out of an ovary, fertilization can take place.

the mother's abdomen is taken up by the uterus. So other organs are pushed aside, and the abdomen sticks out.

The needs of the growing fetus are like those of other living beings. It must have oxygen, water, and other nutrients. The organ that supplies these needs is the *placenta*. It forms along the wall of the uterus and is joined to the fetus by the *umbilical cord*. Through the placenta and umbilical cord, oxygen and nutrients pass from the mother's blood into the blood of the fetus. Also, waste products from the fetus pass into the mother's blood to be given off from the body.

Birth

Usually, a baby grows and develops inside the uterus for about nine months. However, in some cases, pregnancy lasts longer than nine months. In other cases, babies are premature. They are born before they have reached their full development, and they usually weigh less than 2.25 kilograms (5 pounds) at birth. With extra care during the first few weeks of life, many premature babies survive. A birth that takes place before the fetus is developed enough to live is called a *miscarriage*.

Labor

When the fetus is a fully developed baby, the muscles in the walls of the uterus start to contract. This puts pressure on the baby inside the uterus. The muscles begin to contract and relax. At first, the contractions are mild. As time goes on, the contractions become stronger and happen more often. They force the baby down into the lower part of the uterus. The contractions are painful and are called labor pains. The lower uterus and the birth canal stretch as the pressure pushes the baby along. The time from the start of the contractions until the baby is completely out of the birth canal is called labor.

In the birth of a woman's first baby, the muscles of the uterus may be hard to stretch. Labor may last longer than it does in the birth of the second or third child.

Birth process

Usually a baby is born head first. The head is the largest and heaviest part of the fetus. It moves to the lower part of the uterus many weeks before birth. The baby's head helps to dilate, or enlarge, the lower part of the uterus and the vagina.

Sometimes a breech birth happens. In a breech birth, the baby is not born head first. The feet or buttocks are at the lower end of the uterus. More time and skillful efforts are needed to deliver babies who are in a breech position. Breech births occur in fewer than 4 percent of all births.

When normal birth is not possible, the doctor can remove the baby by surgery. An opening is made in the mother's abdominal wall and uterus, and the baby is lifted out. This is called a Caesarean section. Caesarean sections are becoming more common today. New equipment helps the doctor to decide when the birth process is becoming too difficult and is causing harm to the mother or the child.

3 Months   6 Months   9 Months

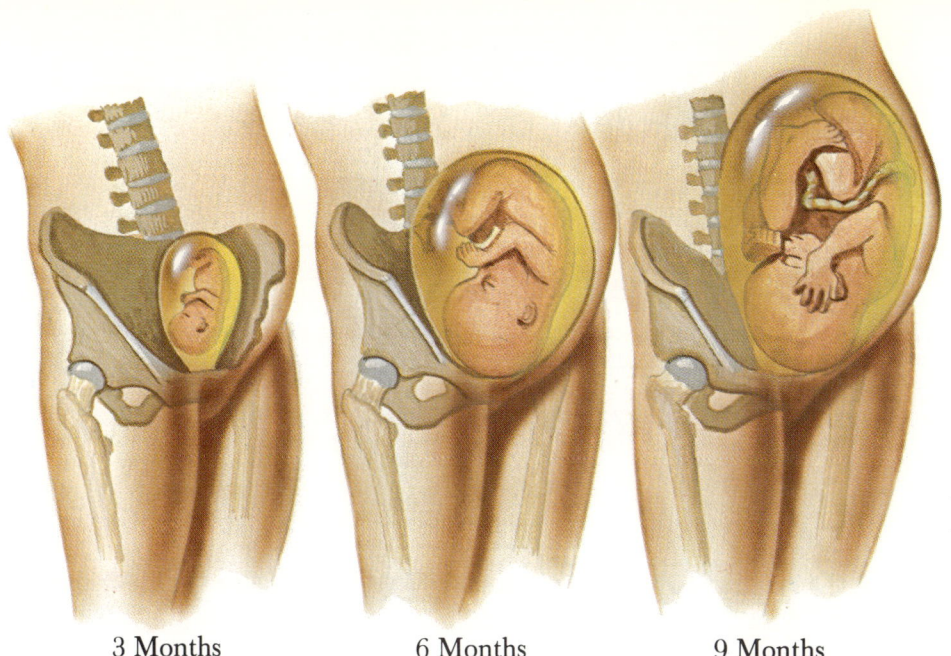

As the fetus grows, the walls of the uterus stretch to make room for it. After about nine months of growth, a baby is ready to be born.

Completion of birth

The umbilical cord connecting the baby to the placenta stays attached during birth. The doctor puts a clamp around the cord and cuts it soon after the baby is born. The baby is now ready to carry on life processes outside the mother's body. Within a few days, only the navel, or *umbilicus,* is left to mark the point where the umbilical cord was attached.

After the birth of the baby is over, the uterus continues to contract. These contractions push the placenta out of the mother's body. At this stage, the placenta is called the afterbirth.

During the next six weeks, the uterus contracts until it is back to normal size. After a period of rest, the endometrium begins to grow again. The ovaries release an ovum, and the menstrual cycle starts again.

Feeding the baby

In the later months of pregnancy, hormones in the mother's blood cause the breasts, or mammary glands, to develop. These glands get larger. Shortly after the birth, they begin to produce milk. It is natural, and it is usually desirable, for a mother to breast-feed the baby. If the mother cannot breast-feed, the child is given feedings of cow's milk, the milk of other animals, or specially prepared formulas.

Multiple births

A multiple birth is one in which more than one baby is born. The possibility of multiple births is thought to be:

           twins: 1 in 90 births
         triplets: 1 in 8000 births
    quadruplets: 1 in 500,000 births
    quintuplets: 1 in 54 million births

There are two kinds of twins—identical and fraternal. Identical twins are the same sex. Such characteristics as color of hair and eyes, facial

(left) Fraternal twins grow from two separate fertilized eggs. (right) Identical twins grow from the same egg.

Fraternal Twins   Identical Twins

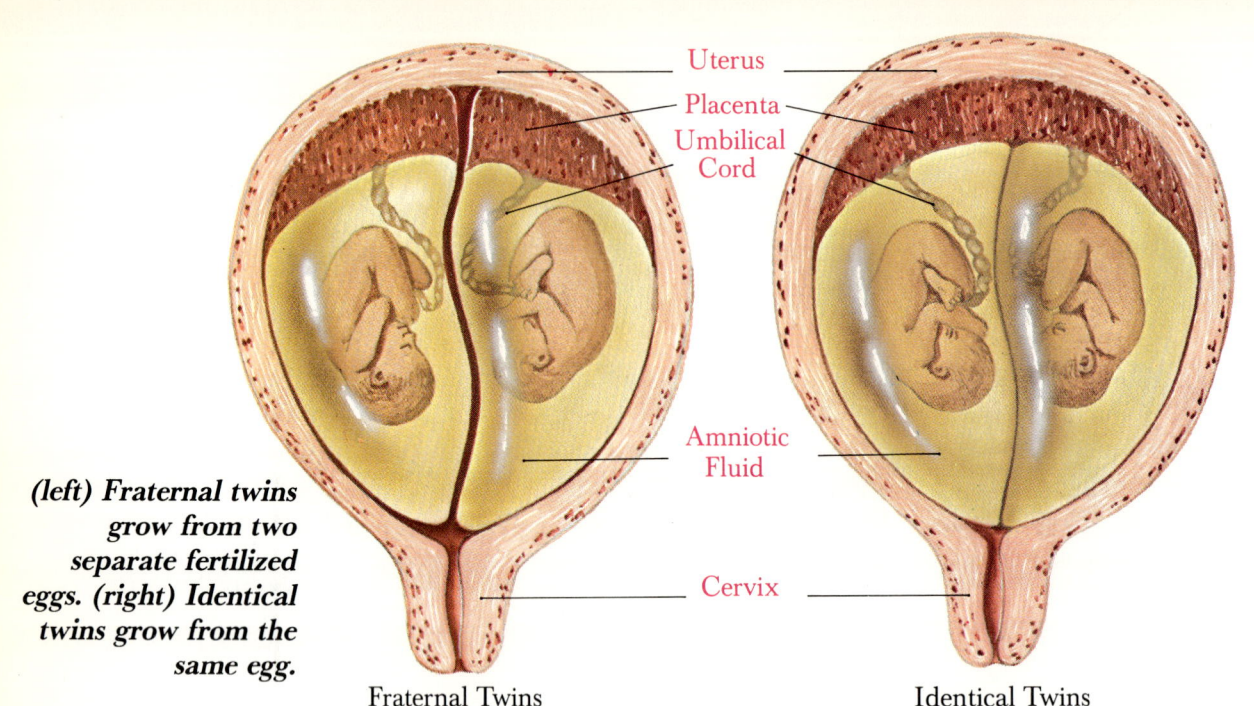

features, and size are the same. Not all fraternal twins are of the same sex. They are no more alike than ordinary brothers and sisters are.

Identical twins

Identical twins begin as one fertilized ovum. At one of the very early stages of cell division, something causes the cluster of cells to separate into two clusters. Then each set continues to divide. In this way, two embryos develop. Because both develop from the same ovum and sperm, they have the same genes. If another complete separation happens early in the cell division, identical triplets will be born. More separations are rare but could lead to four or more identical babies. When more than one embryo develops from a single fertilized ovum, all are attached to one placenta. However, each embryo has a separate umbilical cord.

Identical twins whose bodies are joined together are called Siamese twins. (In 1811, one famous pair of such twins was born in Thailand, which was then called Siam.) Siamese twins may be joined in any area of the body. The joining comes from incomplete separation of cells during the early stages of cell division. The joined place may include only skin and muscle. Or it may involve many tissues or vital organs. Sometimes, Siamese twins can be separated by surgery. In other cases, separation is not possible.

Fraternal twins

Sometimes an ovary releases two ova at or very near the same time. Or both ovaries release an ovum at the same time instead of alternating, as is usual. If both ova are fertilized by sperm, normal development then follows. This leads to the birth of fraternal twins. Each twin comes from a separate sperm and ovum. If three or more ova are released and each is fertilized by a sperm, three or more babies will be born at the same time. All are fraternal, because each one comes from a different ovum and sperm. Each will have a separate placenta and umbilical cord.

Prenatal care

It is important for a woman who might be pregnant to find out as soon as possible whether or not she is carrying a child. This is necessary so that the baby can get the best possible start in life. It is also important for the mother's health. The medical care given to a pregnant woman is called *prenatal care*.

Pregnancy testing

An early sign of pregnancy is missing an expected menstrual period. Other signs that may mean pregnancy include enlarged breasts, nausea, frequent urination, a tired feeling, and a need for more sleep.

When a menstrual period is two weeks late, a woman should have a pregnancy test. This test is simple and inexpensive. Chemicals are added to a sample of the woman's urine. The solution shows whether the woman is pregnant. This test can be done in a doctor's office, a hospital, or a clinic. Someone who is not sure about how much the test costs or where it is available can telephone the local public health department. Information is also available from "hot lines," and most communities have set up centers that give special, and often free, health services.

Nutrition

An expectant mother should begin to follow a doctor's advice about diet, vitamins, and exercise as soon as possible. During pregnancy, the developing baby depends on its mother for all its needs. Therefore, the mother's health is very important to the baby. Children born to poorly nourished mothers usually weigh less. They are also more likely than other children to be born with a serious health problem.

The expectant mother should eat plenty of nourishing foods, especially proteins. All of the baby's organs and tissues are built from digested foods absorbed from the mother's blood. An expectant mother needs to drink extra milk for calcium and vitamin D. This will give the baby strong bones and teeth. Pregnancy is a time to eat as many natural foods as possible. Pregnant women should avoid processed foods. They should also stay away from fast-food restaurants, where foods often have many additives and limited nutritional value. If a woman already has good eating habits, following a nutritious diet during pregnancy is easy. But for those women who often eat at fast-food restaurants, or who eat mostly junk foods, getting the needed nutrients during pregnancy will take a special effort.

Disease and drugs

The mother-to-be should avoid being around people with communicable diseases. Some illnesses that are not serious for a grown woman may do great damage to a fetus in the first three months of pregnancy. German measles (rubella) is one such disease. A pregnant woman should take the best possible care of herself if she does become ill.

Anytime a pregnant woman takes a drug or medication without a physician's supervision, she may be harming the unborn child. The list of

A woman who might be pregnant should find out as soon as possible whether or not she is pregnant. A pregnant woman needs good medical care, called prenatal care, from the start of pregnancy. Medical problems must be discovered early. Many fathers want to be included from the beginning in the birth of their child.

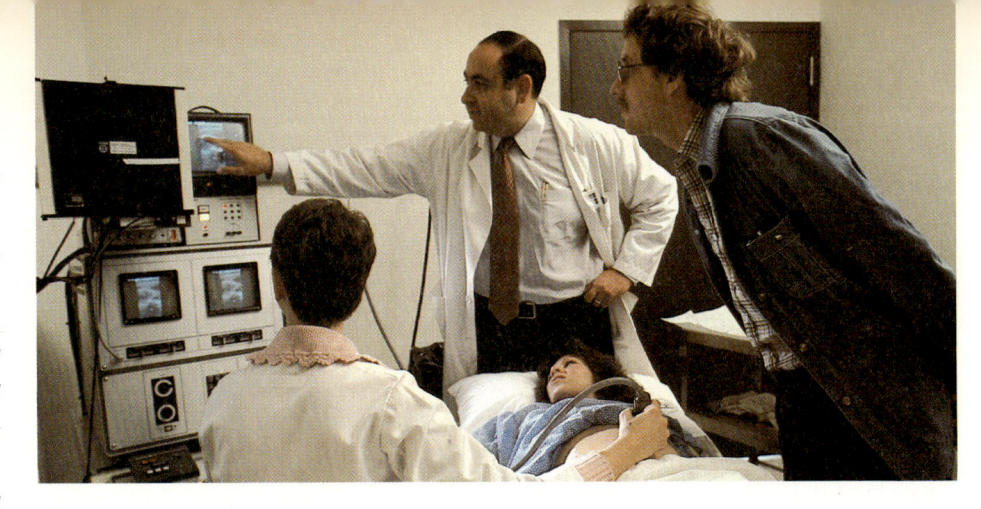

drugs that doctors believe may be harmful to a fetus gets longer every year. Effective in 1984, about 62,000 nonprescription drugs must carry the following FDA label, warning: "As with any drug, if you are pregnant or nursing a baby, seek the advice of a health professional before using this product." Some drugs have been found to be dangerous when taken at any time during pregnancy. Some seem to be dangerous only when taken in the early part of pregnancy. This is when the parts of the embryo are developing. Other drugs seem to be more harmful to the fetus when taken later in pregnancy. Some medications are thought to be safe when taken in small amounts but harmful in large amounts. Therefore, an expectant mother should use no drugs, except with her doctor's advice.

A pregnant woman who is addicted to hard drugs, such as heroin, runs a very high risk of seriously harming an unborn baby. Women who are drug addicts often give birth to babies who are addicted. Such babies may suffer withdrawal symptoms after birth. To avoid drug-related problems, an expectant mother who is addicted to drugs needs special treatment during pregnancy. Medical treatment and counseling have helped many expectant mothers to end or decrease their need for drugs. Birth defects in newborn babies that are the result of disease, drugs, or damage during pregnancy are called congenital defects.

Cigarettes and alcoholic beverages

Nicotine and alcohol are poisons. They may harm growing tissues. Nicotine and alcohol are absorbed into the blood and can pass through the placenta into a baby's body. A study of 7500 pregnancies showed that the number of miscarriages and premature births was nearly twice as great for smoking mothers as for nonsmoking mothers. A pregnant woman who regularly drinks a large amount of alcohol, or who drinks too much from time to time, also runs a high risk of harming an unborn baby. Research has found a very serious birth defect called fetal alcohol syndrome (FAS). Babies having FAS show a combination of symptoms, such as mental retardation, heart defects, or facial and other outer deformities. Babies of heavy drinkers also have other, more common health problems. These include low birth weight, crankiness, and sometimes alcohol addiction along with withdrawal symptoms. The exact amounts of nicotine and alcohol that may be harmful are not known.

Special problems

Sometimes special help is needed in handling a pregnancy. How much help is needed depends on many factors. These include the physical and emotional health of the expectant mother, whether or not the pregnancy was planned by both parents, the age of the parents, their relationship, their economic situation, and their plans for the future. In teenage pregnancy, most or all of the above factors often present a problem. For this reason, it is not unusual for a teenager who learns that she is pregnant to feel overwhelmed by the situation. Take the following story, for example.

Sue, age fifteen, had been dating Bob steadily for almost a year. Bob was seventeen. He had just started his last year of high school. They often talked of marriage and the future. When Sue learned that she was pregnant, she told Bob at once. Neither of them had planned on Sue's getting pregnant. Bob said that he wasn't ready to "settle down and get married." Bob also stated that he would try to help, but that he was "not going to pay for one mistake for the rest of my life." Sue was afraid to tell her parents about the pregnancy. She ran away from home. As a teenager, Sue ran a high risk of having health problems during her pregnancy. Also, as a teenage parent, she had a greater-than-average risk of having a child with health problems, including birth defects. (The younger the teenager, the greater the risk.) Sue needed special care and help. However, like many young people faced with an unwanted pregnancy, she was too desperate to think clearly about the situation.

According to present information, pregnancy is one of the main reasons why young people run away. Running away usually makes things worse for everyone involved. Teenagers can usually get more help from their parents than they realize. After the initial shock, most parents want to help their children. Also, free counseling and other professional services are available in most communities.

The challenge of parenthood

Nowadays, when you think about becoming a parent, you have many choices. You have the choice of

- whether or not to be a parent
- when to be a parent
- having the baby born in a hospital or at home
- having a medicated or a nonmedicated delivery
- having the father help during the delivery of the baby
- whether one or both parents will work outside the home.

Something to think about . . .

These are just some of the options that you have. How you decide on these and other important matters will affect you and the people around you. If you become a parent, your decisions will also affect the child. Some people willingly give up their right to make these personal decisions. That is, they let someone else make the decision for them. Or they let things happen by chance. But doesn't it seem logical that such important decisions should be made only after careful consideration and planning?

The fact that a person is biologically capable of being a parent does not mean that she or he is ready to be a good parent. Sometimes a child is conceived and brought into the world by people who are not prepared to be parents, or who have no wish to be parents. When this happens, many serious problems are likely to occur, for both the parents and the child. On the other hand, when two people plan and look forward to the birth of their baby, parenthood can be the beginning of some of life's most rewarding experiences.

Today there is a greater opportunity than ever before to enjoy being a parent. People have greater control over the timing of pregnancies. There are also many more options in family lifestyles and roles. Scientific research has made it possible to prevent many birth defects. And advances have been made in helping a child develop into a physically, socially, and emotionally healthy person.

Clearly, the opportunity exists for tomorrow's parents and children to be happier and healthier than ever before. But this can only happen if teenagers (tomorrow's parents) learn about the choices that they have. They can then carefully map out the route that will lead to health and happiness both for themselves and for those they love.

Main Ideas

1. Puberty is the period during which the ovaries start to release ova, or egg cells (in girls), and the testes start to produce sperm (in boys).

2. A human being starts as a single cell formed by the joining of one ovum and one sperm.

3. Normally, a baby grows and develops within the uterus for about nine months. During this time, oxygen and nutrients pass from the mother's blood into the blood of the fetus through the placenta and umbilical cord. Waste products from the fetus pass into the mother's blood to be given off from the body.

4. Identical twins are born if one fertilized egg divides into two embryos soon after the joining of egg and sperm. Fraternal twins are born if two ova are fertilized at about the same time.

5. The quality of nutrition a woman gets during pregnancy can affect the fetus.

6. A pregnant woman risks the health of her unborn baby any time she takes a drug without medical supervision.

7. Pregnancy during the teen years is likely to present special problems.

Key Words

cervix	menstruation	semen
conception	miscarriage	sperm
embryo	ovaries	testes
endometrium	ovum	testosterone
epididymis	placenta	umbilical cord
estrogen	prenatal care	umbilicus
Fallopian tubes	puberty	uterus
fetus	secondary sexual	vas deferens
menopause	characteristics	

Apply Your Knowledge

1. Describe how sperm pass from the testes to the outside of the body.
2. Describe menstruation.
3. What is fertilization? Where does it take place?
4. Illness or a drug can affect the ovulation cycle. Explain why a change in the ovulation cycle would change the time when fertilization could take place.
5. What is meant by cell differentiation?
6. How does a fetus get oxygen, water, and other nutrients?
7. Describe the birth process.
8. What is the main difference between fraternal and identical twins?
9. Discuss the importance of prenatal care.
10. What do you think an expectant mother should do when she has a headache?

Extend Your Knowledge

1. Look up the origin of the term *Caesarean section.* Report to the class.
2. If cell division is repeated 43 times between fertilization of an ovum and birth, what is the total number of cells in a newborn baby?
3. Investigate the services of a nearby prenatal clinic. How many patients does the clinic serve? How often are the patients supposed to visit the clinic? Do most of the patients follow the instructions they are given? Who pays the bills for those who cannot pay? Do you think the clinic provides adequate services? Why or why not?
4. Research the effects that cigarette smoking can have on an unborn baby. Report on effects other than those that are mentioned in this chapter.
5. What is your opinion on the question of when a person should become a parent? Be sure to include what you think the parents should be able to provide for the child.

Chapter 8

Do you know . . .

- how to get along with your family?
- what the advantages and disadvantages of going steady are?
- how to tell if a person is ready for marriage?

Family Life

The best start in life is to be part of a family where a baby is wanted and loved. The family gives a child its first chance to get love and protection. In the family, the child can learn how to receive praise and criticism, express anger, and take on responsibility. Gradually, the growing child also learns how to be independent. The way these and other basic human needs are handled within the family affects a person's attitudes and decisions all through life.

Family relationships

The family is the basic unit of society. But there are many different kinds of families. Some families have two parents. Others have one. Some families have two generations—parents and children. Others include grandparents or other relatives in the family unit. No matter what the family structure, the members of the family affect one another emotionally, socially, and economically. For example, when you are feeling really happy, the other members of your family probably know it. If you earn your own spending money, it may help the family budget. Sometimes you are not aware of the impact that you have on other family members. You may also not always realize the effect they have on you. But *relationships* within the family have a great deal to do with your moods, decisions, and ability to get along with other people.

Roles within the family

Every day, each of us plays many different roles. We behave differently in each role. Typical roles for a teenager might include those of child, student, friend, member of a group or team, babysitter, and newspaper deliverer.

It is often necessary to change roles in a matter of seconds. Sometimes you even have to play two roles at the same time. At home, for example, you may be a daughter or son to one family member and a sister or brother to another. At school, a classmate may see you as a friend, while your teacher sees you as a student. Each of these people expects different behavior from you. So it is no surprise that you sometimes respond in a way that is not appropriate. There are also bound to be times when you do not

It is important for family members to understand and accept their family roles. You play two roles with your parents at the same time: daughter or son, and friend. What other roles do you play in your family?

feel like playing a certain role at all. But the more roles you can handle, the more sure of yourself you are likely to be as you become an adult.

When a person plays a role in the wrong way, problems are likely to come about. For example, suppose a parent asks a teenager to be home by a certain time. But the teenager does not feel like playing the child role and snaps:

"I'm sixteen and old enough to take care of myself. Leave me alone." Of course it is true that a sixteen-year-old is able to accept a great deal of responsibility. But does such an answer to one's parent achieve anything? How do you think the parent should respond? That leads to a larger question. What is an acceptable relationship between a parent and a teenage child?

It is important for family members to understand and accept their family roles. As you mature, it becomes easier to change from one role to another when it is necessary. You also gain self-control, so that you can play a role even if you don't feel like it. For example, an adult may not always feel like playing a parenting role. But if the child needs the adult to play that role at a certain moment, the adult will nurture, comfort, guide, or support the child.

The role-playing skills you learn within the family are important, for you will continue to play many roles all through your life.

Responsibilities within the family

Each member of a family has responsibilities that fit his or her age, abilities, and relationship to others in the family. Parents are responsible for giving the kind of care that will help their child grow into a physically, emotionally, and socially healthy person. Children need to know that their parents will always try to care for them and protect them. They need to feel that their parents will go on loving them, even if they misbehave. When children do misbehave, it is very important for parents to show that they dislike the bad behavior, not the child.

Parents should have some knowledge about human growth and development. If they do, what they hope and expect for their child should be reasonable. They also need to be able and willing to help their child learn how to make good decisions. It is especially important for parents to realize how their own behavior can affect their children. Often, neither parents nor children are aware of the many ways in which the parents serve as models for the children.

Children are responsible for showing respect toward their parents and other family members. Children must also follow the standards that have been set up for their behavior. They are expected to do their share of the work in maintaining the home. And they may also be expected to help by earning some money on their own.

These responsibilities may seem "old-fashioned." Their purpose, however, is simple. Parents and children have to support each other.

Activities within the family

When is the last time you suggested an activity that involved all the members of the family? Naturally, each member of the family has different personal interests. And teenagers often want to spend their free time in peer-group activities with their friends. But family members can enjoy doing some things together. Eating meals together or sharing simple tasks around the home may give them a chance to share thoughts and feelings. If you take the time to let your family know how things are going with you, it will make it easier for them to understand you. Can you think of the last time you shared one of your problems with a family member? When was the last time someone in the family brought a problem to you?

Communication within the family

The quality of *communication* within the family is important. Communication is the way in which facts, ideas, and feelings are exchanged. It affects relationships within and outside the family.

For a young person, family life can be the training ground for learning how to communicate well. There is a great tendency for each of us to become emotional when talking about things that are very important to us. It takes practice to learn how to "keep cool" during this kind of discussion. It is hard to think clearly when we are feeling a strong emotion. It is also hard to concentrate on what is being said when someone (or worse, more than one person) is showing a strong emotion such as anger. Can you remember watching a very emotional discussion? Did you find it hard to concentrate on *what* the people were saying because of *how* they were saying it? Families can be very emotional groups of people. You learn how to handle emotions within your family.

It is not realistic to hope for total harmony in the family. Some disagreements are likely to happen in any group of human beings. *Conflicts* within a family are to be expected. Such conflicts may be about important matters, such as money, religion, choice of friends, drinking, or drugs. But often conflicts come up over small things, such as what television program to watch, or the length of time spent on the telephone. If the people involved are willing to talk about the problem and to listen to different points of view, many conflicts can be settled. But if family members waste time and energy simply in being angry with each other, or ignore each other's interests and welfare, serious family problems can develop.

A mature person will try hard to keep the lines of communication open within the family. Often another family member can help. But sometimes someone outside the family is needed. In the past few years, many special counseling services have been set up to help teenagers who are having a hard time with family life. People trained to help solve family problems include ministers, priests, rabbis, psychiatrists, psychologists, and social workers. Most communities offer free family counseling services for those unable to pay.

Dating

Dating is a widespread practice among high school students. Whether or not you date, the fact that so many people do has an effect on your life, your relationships with others, and your feelings about yourself.

Why date?

Young people have different reasons for deciding to date. Some teenagers say that they date to have fun and because their friends are dating. Others say that they date because they have romantic feelings for another person. Still others say that they are beginning to think about choosing a marriage partner. But some teenagers do not date at all. Some are more interested in other things. Some are shy and uncomfortable around members of the other sex. Others feel that they just "aren't ready." And the age at which dating actually begins does differ widely.

Take time to plan things that all the members of your family can do together. Let other members of your family share in what you are doing and feeling.

Dating practices

There are many different kinds of dating arrangements. Feelings about these arrangements are related to a person's physical, emotional, and social development. Cultural customs and peer-group practices also affect dating patterns.

When young people first begin to date, they often take part in group activities. Parties, dances, volleyball games, and other social or sports events offer them chances to be together in a relaxed and casual way. Being part of a group can help a young person feel more comfortable with members of the other sex. For this reason, many young people also enjoy double-dating with friends. Having a friend of the same sex present helps some teenagers feel more at ease. A date in which both people pay their own way can also help to ease financial and social pressure. This, too, can help create a more natural and relaxed atmosphere.

"Going steady," "going with" someone, or "steady dating" are ways of talking about an exclusive one-to-one dating arrangement. There are many different reasons for having such an arrangement. One of the reasons usually given is the security of always knowing that you have a date for social events. Other reasons people give include freedom from competition for dates and the dependable companionship that comes from a steady relationship. But there are disadvantages, too. Going steady may limit your chances to get to know many different people. Also, it may be difficult to "get back into circulation" if the steady relationship ends. What are some other advantages and disadvantages to going steady? How do you feel about the practice, yourself?

Each relationship you have with family members is important and different. Older family members can add much to the life of a family.

Everyone begins to date at a different age and for different reasons. Which kind of date do you feel most comfortable with? A single date? A group date?

Responsible dating

Mature teenagers accept and respect the responsibilities that come with dating. Their responsibility toward their parents includes letting the parents know where they plan to go and when they plan to get home. They are also responsible for getting home at the agreed-upon time. It is the parents' responsibility to make rules and set limits for their children's dating practices. If you and your parents don't agree on the limits, it can be helpful to talk about the reasons for the disagreement. Even if you don't reach an agreement, talking over the problem will help you understand each other's viewpoint.

Your sense of responsibility is very important in choosing a code of dating conduct. How much thoughtfulness and respect you show for your dating partner shows how mature you are.

Boys and girls share the responsibility for their sexual behavior. If you have a special affection for another person, it is easy to get carried away by your feelings. A physical attraction can be very strong. Think ahead about sensible limits to set in expressing affection. This will help you stay out of situations that could lead to uncomfortable feelings, unwanted pregnancy, or other serious problems. It is hard to make sound decisions on the spur of the moment. In the end, it is up to you to decide about sexual activity on a date. What do you consider responsible dating behavior?

Marriage

A sound marriage is a strong foundation for a happy family life. Today, because of available knowledge and resources, the chances for having a successful marriage should be greater than ever. But statistics show that there is also a very great likelihood that a marriage will end in divorce or separation. What are the ingredients of a successful marriage?

Preparation for marriage

"Getting married," said one young person, "is all that I've ever dreamed of doing." The first question is—why? What hopes does that person have? Are the hopes realistic? Does the person's intended partner know and share them? In fact, is the individual ready for marriage at all? These are just a few of the questions to be answered before getting married.

Marriage can be a rewarding experience. It can result in a special sense of belonging and fulfillment. But it is also a demanding relationship, even for people who are fully mature. When you make a commitment to another person, you are promising that you can be counted on. However, during the teen years, a young person's feelings and behavior are likely to be less steady, settled, and predictable than they will be later in life. How do you think the degree of consistency in a person's behavior would affect a marriage relationship?

Early marriage is seldom a dream come true. It usually means giving up comforts, conveniences, personal freedom, and sometimes educational opportunities. It also demands taking on responsibilities that most people are not emotionally or financially ready to accept. For these reasons, a high proportion of marriages between people who are from 15 to 19 years old end in divorce or separation.

Knowing whether to get married, or when to get married, is mainly a matter of self-examination. Because an early marriage is likely to present special problems, it is very important for a young couple to think carefully about their readiness for marriage. Both partners should be sure they understand and accept each other's habits, interests, religious beliefs, philosophy, and lifestyle. In addition, a young couple can discuss questions such as the following to determine their readiness for marriage:

- Have we both learned acceptable ways of meeting our physical and emotional needs?
- Have we planned a way for each of us to get the education necessary to realize our individual potentials?
- Have we planned a way to share the work and costs of maintaining a home?
- Are we able to afford the things that we think are important? Do we agree on what these things are?
- Would we be able to afford these things if we had to support a child?
- Do we have the same general goals in life?

What else do you think a person should think about before getting married? What do you think is a good time to get married?

A successful marriage

Marriage is an ongoing process. There is no one point or time at which a person can say, "I have a successful marriage. The task is complete." Marriage is a relationship that grows and changes over the years, just as the people who are married change and grow. Naturally, if a couple are well prepared for marriage, it will be easier for them to make their marriage work. But all marriages have strengths and weaknesses. The ones that succeed are the ones that build on the strengths and shore up the weaknesses. It takes practice. But learning to recognize a problem and being willing to work on it are two keys to marital success.

Sometimes a problem is all too easy to recognize. An event such as a serious illness, a long period of unemployment, a death in the family, or the birth of a handicapped child creates a situation that cannot be ignored. Learning to accept the challenges that life presents can be a painful part of the growth process in marriage. At such times, a couple's attitude becomes very important. If they believe that a good answer can be found, then they will probably succeed in overcoming the difficulty. Today there are also many community resources available to help couples with special problems.

Family planning

The birth of a baby is an important event. Many lives are touched when a baby is born. Just how the lives of the people involved are affected depends a great deal on whether or not the baby's birth was planned.

Scientific research has made family planning easier and safer. Today it is possible to prevent or postpone a pregnancy in a way that is in keeping with a person's religious beliefs, physical and emotional health, and financial situation. It is also possible to improve the likelihood of pregnancy if a child is wanted.

Birth control is also known as *contraception*. Contraception literally means the prevention of conception. A method is used to stop the union of a sperm and egg cell so that no pregnancy takes place. There are many different methods of contraception. Some methods include the use of a medication. Other involve the use of a mechanical device. Medications and devices that prevent conception are called *contraceptives*. Some contraceptives are reliable, and others are not. Also, some religions allow only certain methods of family planning and disapprove of other means.

A person trying to make a decision about contraception should think carefully about the matter. A doctor, hospital clinic, or family planning center can provide correct information and counseling. Such services are often available free of charge. Information is given in a private, confidential way.

Family planning also includes the decision to adopt children. Couples who are not able to have children, or who had previously decided not to, often adopt children. Couples who already have children sometimes choose to adopt also. And in some cases, a single person is allowed to adopt a child. Adoption agencies help people find a child that will benefit from becoming a member of their family.

Family planning makes it possible for parents to give their children economic advantages as well as more individual attention. Family planning also helps to slow down population growth. As the world's population increases, the need for food, energy, and other resources becomes greater. Some of these vital resources are limited. So family planning can affect not only the future of a family but also the quality of life in the world.

Abortion is different from contraception. Abortion means the ending of a pregnancy. If an abortion is done by a qualified physician, the health risk for the woman is small. But an abortion done by an unqualified person, or one brought on by the pregnant woman herself, is very dangerous to the woman's health and life. An abortion is a serious matter. Other factors, such as the psychological effects, should be carefully considered before any decision is made.

Any marriage changes as people grow and change. Learning to see a problem and being willing to work on it are two keys to a good marriage.

As you mature, changes take place both in your body and in your mind. Your attitudes and behavior change in many aspects of your life. Among the most important of these changes are the changes in *sexuality*.

You become aware of sexual desire and the emotions that come with sexual desire as you reach puberty. You may wonder what is normal, what is abnormal, what is acceptable, what is unacceptable.

Sexual attitudes and behaviors

Peer Pressure

There are two kinds of peer pressure. The most common kind is the pressure you put on yourself. When you are feeling unsure of yourself, it is easy to believe that other young people are more mature and have more exciting experiences than you. This is probably not true. Studies show that the majority of young people *do not* have sexual intercourse in their high school years. Most high school students are busy wondering about themselves and their future. Am I attractive to the opposite sex? When will I find someone to love?

The second kind of peer pressure is direct influence from others. Friends who try to talk you into doing something that you are not sure you want to do are robbing you of your personal freedom. You need to be free to find out who you are before making decisions that may have a lifelong effect. Direct peer pressure dulls your intentions and standards, while it sharpens feelings of inadequacy. Many young people are not aware of peer pressure while it is being applied. Looking back, they can spot it.

Homosexuality

As more is learned about the causes of behavior, there is a greater willingness to talk about and understand different kinds of sexual behavior. One kind of behavior that is widely discussed today is *homosexuality*. This word comes from the Greek root *homo*, meaning "same." Homosexuality is sexual attraction toward members of one's own sex. There are both male

As you mature, your sexual feelings and behavior change. Dealing with this change is a normal part of becoming an adult.

and female homosexuals. They usually look, speak, and act just like anyone else. Some homosexuals feel little or no sexual attraction toward members of the other sex. Others are *bisexual*. The root *bi* means "two." Bisexuals can be attracted to members of both sexes.

A person who is attracted to members of the other sex is called *heterosexual*. This word comes from the Greek root *hetero,* meaning "opposite." Heterosexuality is the normal and accepted condition.

Today, some believe that homosexuality is related to psychological confusion early in life about male and female roles. Some homosexuals who have a strong desire to change their sexual behavior have done so through psychotherapy.

It should be noted that there is a difference between being a homosexual and being curious about or attracted to the same sex for a limited period of time. Childhood and adolescent homosexual attractions, or games of curiosity such as "playing doctor," are common among both boys and girls. In most cases, these feelings are eventually replaced by heterosexual attractions.

Antisocial behavior

Unfortunately, sex can become linked with the most serious kinds of antisocial behavior. Sex linked with violence is totally unacceptable. Sexual violence may take the form of molestation or rape. Molestation means forcing one's attentions on another person. The unwilling person may be physically abused and sometimes injured. Rape is forced sexual intercourse. It is not an expression of sexual attraction but is a hostile crime of violence. Another kind of unacceptable sexual behavior is the seduction of very young people by older people.

People who commit sexual offenses are emotionally disturbed or mentally ill. They are also breaking the law. Growing public awareness about these criminal behaviors has led to new efforts to stop them from happening. Also, new and better ways are being found to help and treat the victims of sex-linked crime.

Abuse within the family: why does it happen?

A mother shakes her infant daughter because the baby won't stop crying. A father beats his two-year-old son so badly that the child has to be taken to the hospital. The parents try to hide the real cause of the injuries. They tell the doctor that the child fell down a flight of stairs.

A twenty-six-year-old married woman is very withdrawn and inhibited. Once again she phones to make an excuse for not being at an event that she had planned to attend. Why? Because she does not want her friends to see the swollen left eye and new bruise on her cheek. Her husband beat her the evening before—not a new experience for this young wife.

Why? Why would people treat a member of their own family this way? This is a question to which we are just beginning to find answers. More important, we are making greater efforts to prevent this kind of abuse.

Studies show that most of the people who abuse a spouse or a child are not mentally ill. Actually, the abusive person's behavior is normal most of the time. Most often the cause of the abuse is that the person feels extremely frustrated or angry at the moment. If the potential victim's behavior is annoying, the abuser strikes out impulsively. Often, the reason for abuse is that the abuser is under a great deal of ongoing stress. The person cannot cope with a difficult situation, so the helpless family member becomes the victim.

Another reason for child abuse is that often the parent does not know the difference between discipline and abuse. Studies have shown that many such parents were themselves brought up in homes where child beating was common. These parents have expressed the belief that "I can discipline my child any way that I want to. After all, it's my child!" Many child abusers look on a child as a possession or an annoyance, not as a human being with needs and rights.

In cases of abuse, both the victim and the abuser need help. The welfare of the victim has to be the first concern. An abused person may need to be in another environment for a time. In cases of child abuse, the child is often placed in a foster home. Many children have suffered, and some have even died, because they were taken out of foster homes and returned to abusive parents too soon.

Until recently, few attempts were made to rehabilitate abusive people. Obviously, these people need help. They must learn how to deal with their emotions and control their temper. The goal of treatment is to make it possible for family members to be reunited. Many kinds of programs now exist to provide therapy for abusive persons. One such program is Parents Anonymous, which works like Alcoholics Anonymous. The abusive parents voluntarily take part in group therapy. They learn how to help themselves and each other. The parents are able to call

Something to think about . . .

Pressures of life and anger can cause a person to lose control and to strike out without thinking. In cases of abuse, both the abuser and the victim need help.

other members of the group when they feel desperate. They can talk about their feelings and frustrations. This reduces the chance that the child will become the victim of the parent's emotions.

Child abuse in particular is a complicated problem. Each of us has the responsibility to report a suspected case of child abuse to the authorities at once. If suspected abuse is reported without delay, lives and family relationships can be saved. But the real solution to the problem is in the area of prevention. The more young people learn about good parenting, the less likely it is that future children will suffer abuse and neglect.

Main Ideas

1. Families are different in the number of members, the ages of the members, and the interests of the members.
2. Members of a family affect one another emotionally, socially, and economically.
3. Each member of a family has responsibilities that depend on age, capabilities, and relationship to other family members.
4. A mature person accepts responsibilities that come with dating.
5. People should think carefully about their readiness for marriage before getting married.
6. Marriage is a relationship that changes over the years.
7. Scientific research has made family planning easier and safer.
8. As you mature, changes take place in your sexuality.

Key Words

abortion
bisexual
communication
conflict
contraception
contraceptives
heterosexual
homosexuality
relationship
sexuality

Apply Your Knowledge

1. Why is the family considered the basic unit of society?
2. What are the advantages of group activities and double-dating?
3. What is peer pressure and how does it relate to dating?
4. What are some advantages and disadvantages of going steady?
5. What do you think the characteristics of a good dating partner are?
6. Explain why people who marry early are likely to have special problems.
7. When do you think a person is ready to get married?
8. What do you think are some of the advantages and disadvantages of being married?
9. Explain some of the advantages of family planning.
10. What would you say to a friend who had a serious family problem?

Extend Your Knowledge

1. Investigate the services available in your community to help solve family problems. How many different kinds of services are available?
2. Compare the family life of two cultures. State your opinion on some aspects of each culture's family living patterns.
3. What aspect of American family living patterns do you think would be most noticeable to an observer from another country?
4. Investigate the problem of family abuse. Explain how this kind of abuse can be prevented. What kinds of treatment are available for the abusive person? What ought to be done to protect the victim?
5. Communication and strong emotion can affect each other in opposite ways. Sometimes emotion can cloud communication. Sometimes it can make the message more effective. Watch a television news broadcast of your choice on three different days. Take notes on parts of the broadcast where a message is delivered with emotion:
    (a) Does emotion cloud the message or enhance it?
    (b) Which individual words seem to carry the most emotional impact?
    (c) What physical movements signalled the presence of emotion?
    (d) How might this message be stated showing no emotion? Would showing no emotion be appropriate?

Unit 4

CHAPTERS:

9 From Generation to Generation

10 Environmental Hazards

11 Cancer Prevention

Environment and Heredity

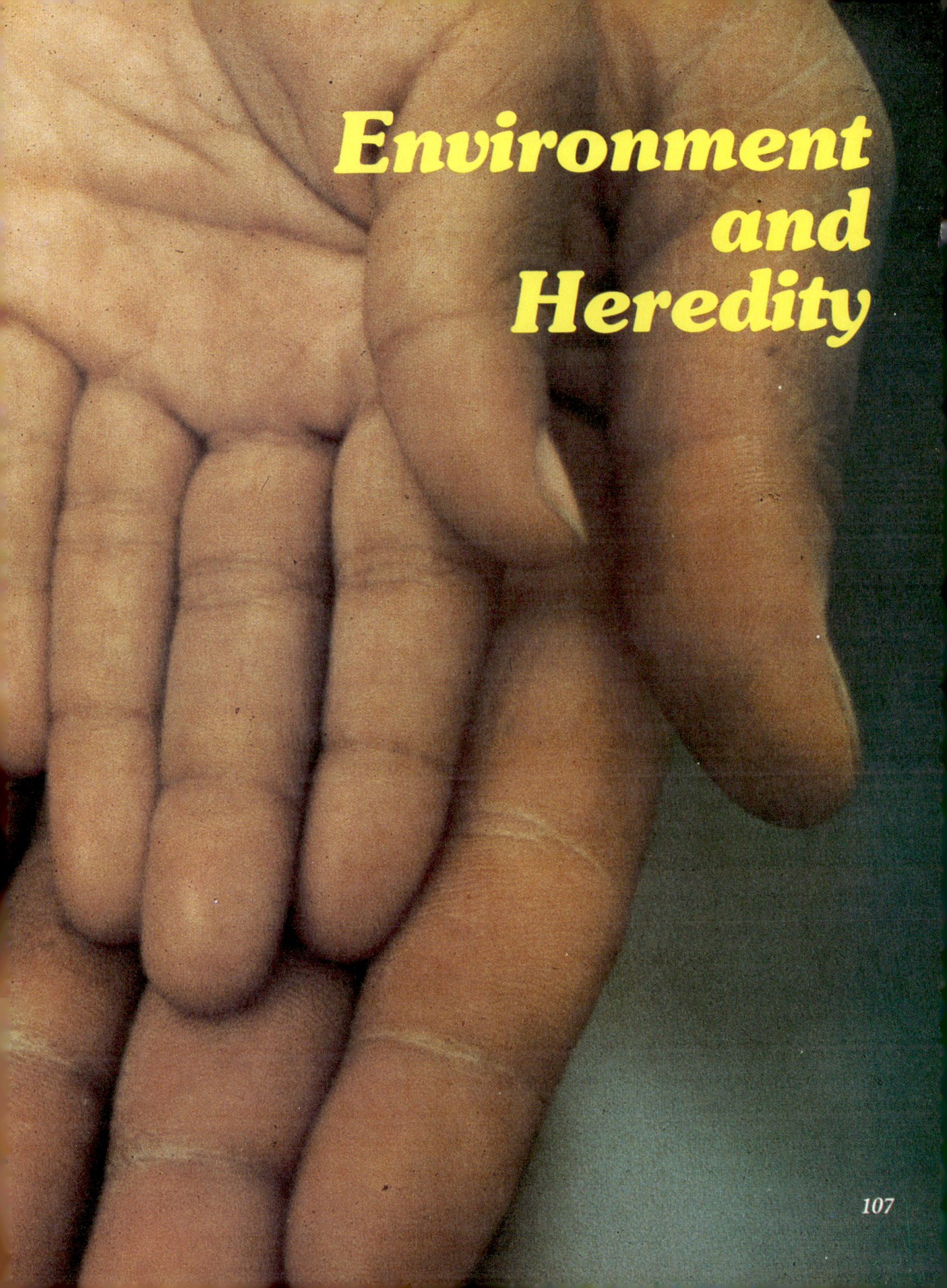

Chapter 9

Do you know . . .

- the job of a medical geneticist?
- that genetic counseling is a form of preventive medicine?
- how some genetic disorders can be found long before a child is born?
- whether or not sickle-cell trait is a disease?
- why there are more color-blind males than females?
- what happens when you have too many chromosomes?

From Generation to Generation

Have you ever heard the expressions "chip off the old block" and "it runs in the family"? If you have photographs of your ancestors, you can probably see some characteristics, such as hair or eye color, height, and facial appearance, that seem to appear in each generation. These characteristics are said to be *inherited.*

Heredity is the passing of traits or characteristics from parents to children. This process is carried out using complex structures called *genes.* Genes are the blueprint of your body. You have thousands of different genes neatly arranged on paired structures called **chromosomes.** There are 46 chromosomes inside the nucleus of almost every cell in your body. Only mature red blood cells that have no nucleus have no chromosomes. The sperm and egg cells have one-half the total number, or 23 chromosomes.

Although your characteristics depend upon your genes, your environment can greatly affect what you can become.

What are genes?

Genes are portions of a large molecule called deoxyribonucleic acid, or *DNA.* In 1953, Dr. James Watson and Dr. Francis Crick found that their model of DNA looked like a spiral staircase, or a twisted ladder. The sides of the ladder are long strands of DNA twisted around each other. The "rungs" of the ladder are made of chemical compounds called bases. The bases are found along the ladder in a special order. This order is a list of instructions that tells every cell in your body what to do. It is the "blueprint" we talked about earlier, and it is called the *genetic code.*

DNA instructs the cell. DNA causes the production of new cells. It also tells the cell to make proteins for its growth and development. Proteins are made of substances called *amino acids.* To make a certain protein, the right amino acids must be joined together in the right order. The arrangement of the DNA bases decides the order in which the amino acids are joined. When the amino acids are in the right order, they make the protein that the body needs.

DNA contains the master plan for forming all protein. Your skin, hair, muscles, and other body tissues are made up mostly of proteins. Proteins also control your body's activities. For example, hemoglobin, the oxygen-carrying substance in red blood cells, is a protein. Antibodies, the body's infection fighters, are proteins. Enzymes are proteins, and so are hormones. Without the DNA codon to specify the order of amino acids, your body could not make proteins correctly.

Genes at work

Genes work in pairs to develop each characteristic. One gene in each pair comes from one of the parents. The other comes from the other parent. Sometimes the two genes may not "agree" on what a characteristic will be. Then the trait is decided by the *dominant gene*. When this happens, the other gene, the *recessive* one, does not work.

Everyone has a pair of genes that decides eye color. Suppose that a person has one gene for blue eyes and one gene for brown eyes. This person will have brown eyes, because the gene for brown eyes is dominant. The gene for blue eyes is recessive. A person with two genes for brown eyes will also have brown eyes. A person with blue eyes must have two genes for blue eyes. If one gene is for brown eyes, the person will have brown eyes.

If you know the parents' genes for eye color, you can predict the eye colors of their children. For example, suppose one parent has two genes for brown eyes. Suppose the other parent has two genes for blue eyes. The child inherits one eye-color gene from each parent. The child can have only one possible combination of eye-color genes: one blue and one brown. In this case, the child will have brown eyes. (See Chart I.)

Let's take a more complicated example. Suppose that each parent has one gene for blue eyes and one for brown eyes. The child has equal chances of inheriting a gene for blue eyes or a gene for brown eyes from its father. It also may inherit either a gene for blue eyes or one for brown eyes from its mother. What are the possible pairs of eye-color genes the child could inherit? (See Chart II.)

Although genes are responsible for eye color, the amount of pigment, called *melanin*, may differ from one person to another. Blue eyes have little pigment. As pigment increases, the iris can be green, hazel, or brown. Some babies born with blue eyes may gradually develop more melanin in the front layer of the iris. Thus, their eyes may darken as they grow.

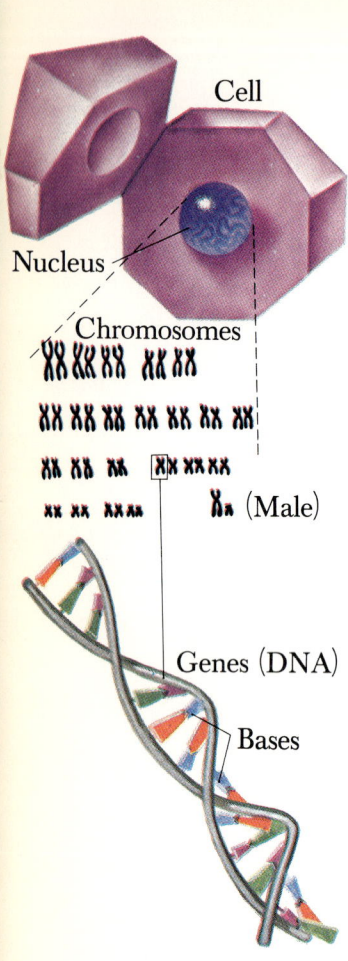

The nucleus of every cell contains chromosomes, which are made up of genes. The bases of the genes tell what a person will inherit.

Sex is determined by chromosomes X and Y.

You have already learned that 46 chromosomes are found in the nucleus of each cell. Two of the 46 chromosomes are sex chromosomes. If you are a female, you have the sex chromosomes known as *XX*. If you are a male, you have the chromosomes *XY*.

Before fertilization, every egg cell has one *X* chromosome. The sperm, however, can have either one *X* or one *Y* chromosome.

If the egg is fertilized by a sperm carrying an *X* chromosome, the baby will be a female with *XX* chromosomes. If the egg is fertilized by a sperm carrying a *Y* chromosome, the baby will be a boy with *XY* chromosomes. Thus, it is the father's sperm that determines the sex of the child.

Genetics in medicine

Brian and Jill Greene's first child seemed normal at birth. But by his first birthday, there were symptoms that showed he was mentally retarded and physically abnormal. The Greenes gave much tender loving care to this child. They also wanted very much to have a normal, healthy child. But they did not want to risk another pregnancy that might bring them a second retarded child. Financially and emotionally, the responsibility of raising two retarded children would be more than they could bear. Finally, they went to their family doctor. Their doctor suggested that they talk to a *medical geneticist*.

The Greenes had their second child. The baby was normal, as predicted by the medical geneticist. Brian and Jill had gotten good counseling from a specialist in genetics.

What is genetic counseling?

The study of heredity is called *genetics*. A knowledge of genetics has helped scientists understand many problems in medicine. Many diseases,

In Chart I, one parent has two dominant genes for brown eyes. The other parent has two recessive genes for blue eyes. Their child inherits one dominant gene and one recessive gene. With a dominant gene, the child's eyes must be brown.

Chart I

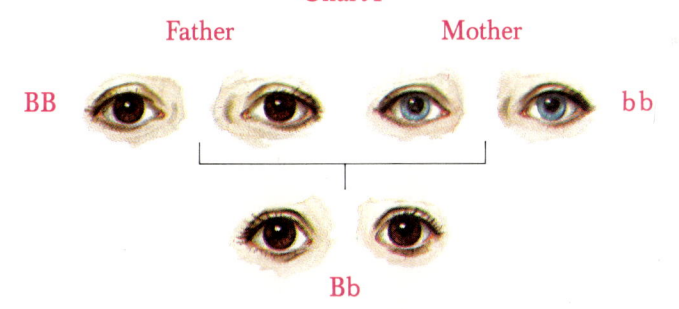

Father   Mother

BB   bb

Bb

In Chart II, each of the parents has one dominant gene for brown eyes and one recessive gene for blue. It is possible for a child to inherit two dominant genes, or one dominant and one recessive gene, or two recessive genes.

Chart II

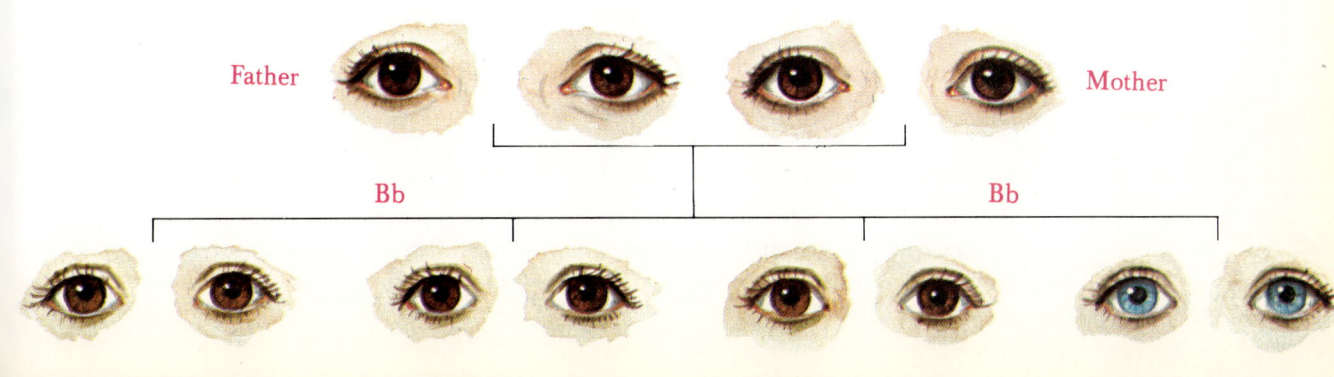

Father   Mother

Bb   Bb

BB   Bb   Bb   bb

for example, are hereditary. Some of these diseases show up at birth, causing birth defects. Other hereditary disorders, like those listed below, show up later in life:

- cystic fibrosis—birth to 6 months
- Tay-Sachs disease—birth to 6 months
- sickle-cell anemia—from 6 months on
- Duchenne muscular dystrophy—2 to 4 years
- Wilson's disease—8 to 20 years
- glaucoma—from late 30s on
- Huntington's disease—from late 30s on

The role of the medical geneticist is not an easy one. When a disease is caused by a chromosome or a gene, there is always a chance that it will appear in a family. The medical geneticist begins counseling by examining the affected child and others in the family. A family health history, called a *family pedigree,* can be an important key in unlocking the mystery of the disease.

There are over 2165 genetic disorders listed by medical geneticists. With the help of computers and a knowledge of mathematical probabilities, the medical geneticist helps the family understand all the facts about their genetic problem.

Can genetic diseases be prevented?

There is no way to prevent genetic diseases. But there are tests that can be given to *carriers*. Carriers are people who do not have the disease themselves. But carriers do have the gene or chromosome that might cause their children to be born with the disease or defect.

Prenatal (before-birth) tests, such as *amniocentesis,* can be performed in order to find possible defects caused by chromosome error. Amniocentesis is done after the fourteenth week of pregnancy. Amniotic fluid is the fluid in the uterus that is around the fetus. A small amount of this fluid is removed with a special needle placed through the walls of the mother's abdomen and uterus, into the amniotic cavity. The fluid has cells from the fetus. Using a complex method, the chromosomes of a cell are stained and photographed. The photograph is enlarged and the chromosomes are cut out like paper dolls. Next, they are arranged according to size. If a defect in a chromosome is found, the medical geneticist and the parents can lessen the damage through fast action at or before birth. When amniocentesis is done by a team of experienced geneticists, it has very little risk for mother

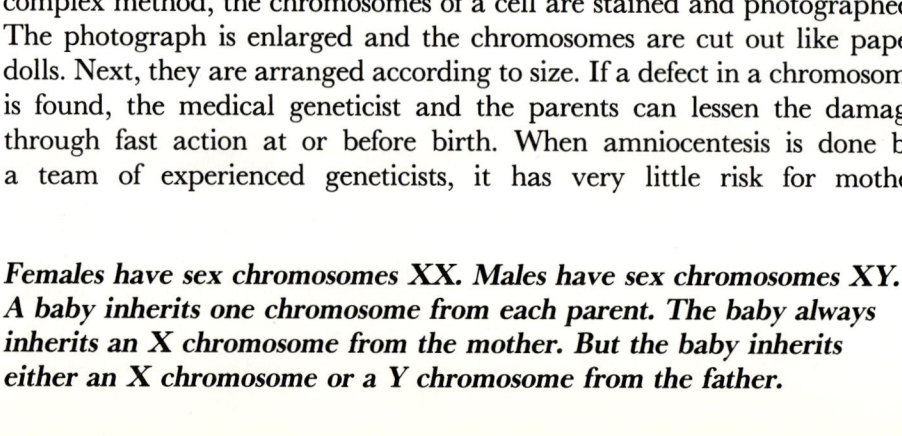

Females have sex chromosomes XX. Males have sex chromosomes XY. A baby inherits one chromosome from each parent. The baby always inherits an X chromosome from the mother. But the baby inherits either an X chromosome or a Y chromosome from the father.

and unborn child. However, not all birth defects can be found through prenatal testing.

What is a carrier test?

Rosalyn had volunteered to be tested for genetic disorders during the Health Fair held at her school. The test was very simple. Only two drops of blood from her finger were needed. Several days later, a genetic counselor called Rosalyn to the nurse's office. The counselor explained the results of the test to her. Rosalyn was told that she was a carrier of a sickle-cell gene. This condition is called *sickle-cell trait*. Sickle-cell trait is not a disease. It means that the carrier has inherited a sickle hemoglobin from one parent and a normal hemoglobin from another. The normal hemoglobin stops the cells in the body from growing into the sickle shape.

Sickle-cell trait does not usually produce symptoms. But in very rare cases, some people may have problems at very high altitudes. Others may sometimes have blood in their urine.

Amniocentesis is a test before birth to see if the unborn child has damaged, missing, or extra chromosomes.

What is sickle-cell anemia?

If a person inherits sickle-cell hemoglobin from both parents, the condition is called *sickle-cell anemia*. A person with sickle-cell anemia may

1. have serious infections;
2. become tired easily;
3. have slowed growth;
4. have slow-to-heal leg ulcers;
5. develop poor vision or blindness;
6. have strokes;
7. need blood transfusions;
8. have pain in any body part caused by sickle cells blocking small capillaries. This is called sickle-cell crisis.

If sickle-cell trait is not a disease, why should people be concerned? Sickle-cell trait is important because the condition is inherited. A person who has a sickle-cell gene may pass it on to his or her children. For example, suppose one parent has one sickle-cell gene and one normal gene. The other has two normal genes. Their child has a 50 percent chance of having sickle-cell trait. Suppose each parent has one sickle-cell gene and one normal gene. The child will have a 25 percent chance of being normal, a 50 percent chance of having sickle-cell trait, and a 25 percent chance of having sickle-cell anemia.

How did sickle-cell genes begin?

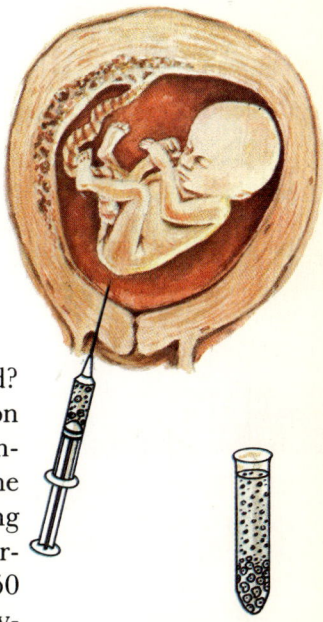

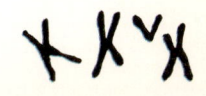

Many geneticists think that the sickle-cell gene may have been a helpful mutation. A *mutation* is a change in a gene. If the mutation takes place in a sperm or egg, it may be passed on to a child. Some mutations may be harmful. But others are believed to be useful. The sickle-cell gene may have been a useful gene. Scientific evidence shows that a person who has the gene is more resistant to malaria than a person who does not have the gene. The gene for sickle-cell anemia is much more common in parts of the world where malaria is widespread. In these areas, more people die of malaria who do not have the gene for sickle-cell trait. In some parts of Africa, where malaria is common, 40 percent of the Black population carries the gene. In the United States, where malaria is not common, only about 10 percent of the Black population has the gene.

Some genes are lethal.

Geneticists define *lethal genes* as genes that lead to death. *Tay-Sachs* disease is fatal brain damage found mostly in infants of East European Jewish ancestry. The lethal genes cause complete mental breakdown, blindness, muscular weakness, and eventually death. A person with Tay-Sachs disease is missing one enzyme. This enzyme prevents an important chemical process from taking place.

Tay-Sachs disease can be stopped by testing for carriers. Geneticists can measure the enzyme levels in blood to find out if the person is a carrier.

One person in twenty-five is a carrier of cystic fibrosis.

Cystic fibrosis is an inherited disorder of children. It is the most common genetic disease affecting the White population in the United States. The disease affects the mucous and sweat glands. It causes the mucous gland to secrete a thick and sticky mucus rather than a free-flowing secretion. The thick mucus blocks different pathways of the body, such as the pancreas, trachea, and digestive tract. Breathing becomes very hard when the mucus clogs the body's air sacs. The disease can be found early by checking the amount of salt in the perspiration of the patient. Unfortunately, there are no good carrier tests for cystic fibrosis.

What is recessive inheritance?

Sickle-cell anemia, Tay-Sachs, cystic fibrosis, and 943 other genetic diseases have one thing in common. They all have *recessive inheritance*. This means that two defective genes are needed to cause the disease. Both parents of the affected child may seem normal. But both parents may carry the same defective gene. The child who receives the harmful gene from both parents will inherit the birth defect.

When both parents are carriers of a recessive trait, each of their children will have a 25 percent chance of inheriting the disease. But each child born to the couple will also have a 25 percent chance of not inheriting the gene from either parent. And each child will have a 50–50 chance of getting only one defective gene. A child with one defective gene will become a carrier of the recessive trait.

What is dominant inheritance?

Over 1200 diseases have *dominant inheritance*. This means that only one defective gene is needed to cause the disease. Glaucoma (a disease of

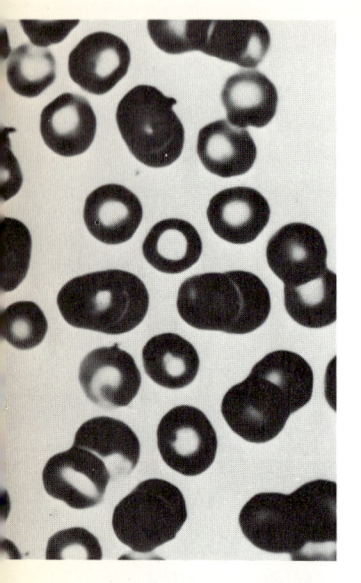

(top) Normal red blood cells are round in shape. (bottom) The red blood cells of someone with sickle-cell anemia are longer and are sometimes bent like sickles.

the eye), Huntington's disease (breakdown of the nervous system), polydactylism (extra fingers and toes), and achondroplasia (a form of dwarfism) are diseases caused by a dominant trait. The risk for a child with a parent having such a disease is 50-50. And there is an equal 50-50 chance that the child will not receive the abnormal gene. If the parent has two defective genes, then all children born will inherit one defective gene and be affected. Luckily, the chance of a person having two defective genes is very rare.

What is sex-linked inheritance?

Genes causing color blindness, hemophilia, and 172 other disorders are carried on the sex chromosome X. Normal females have two X chromosomes. Normal males have one X and one Y chromosome. In most cases of *sex-linked inheritance*, the mother carries the defective gene on one of her X chromosomes. Since her second X chromosome is normal, she is protected from the disorder. But each son born to her will have a 50-50 chance of inheriting the defective gene. If the son gets the defective gene on the X chromosome, he will automatically show the disorder because he does not have another X chromosome that is normal. His Y chromosome will not protect him.

(left) With recessive inheritance, two genes are needed to cause the trait to appear; (middle) with dominant inheritance, only one gene is needed; (right) with sex-linked inheritance, the gene causing the trait is usually carried on an X chromosome.

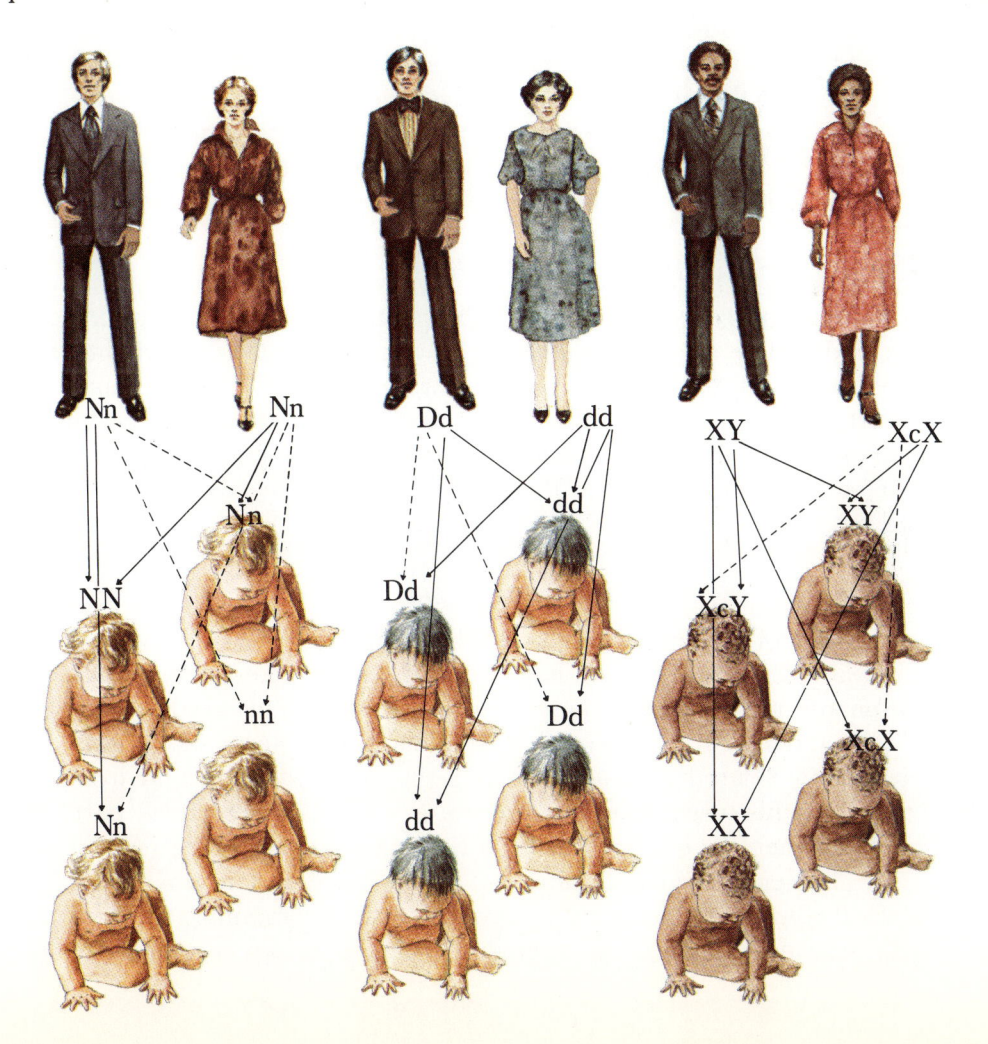

The daughters born to a carrier mother will have a 50-50 chance of being carriers, themselves. In turn, they may possibly pass the disorder on to their sons.

What will happen if there are too many chromosomes in the cells?

Down's syndrome, or trisomy 21, is the most common and best known of the chromosome errors. This disease is not caused by a gene but by a whole chromosome. Children with Down's syndrome have an extra chromosome. It is like the two which geneticists call the twenty-first pair. For this reason, the disease is also called trisomy (three-chromosome) 21. Symptoms include mental retardation, poor muscle tone, a large and protruding tongue, short and broad hands, and folding eyelids that give the eyes a slanting look.

The age of the mother seems to be important in the rate of Down's syndrome. The risk is one in 3000 if the mother is less than 29 years of age. It grows to one in 280 for mothers between the ages of 35 and 39. The risk becomes one in 70 after age 40.

Almost all children with Down's syndrome have 47 chromosomes instead of the normal 46. Researchers think that the extra chromosome is caused by poor splitting of the chromosome during cell division. Unlike the sperm cells of the male that are always being made, all the egg cells are formed and present in the female at birth. As the female grows older, so do the egg cells. Because the eggs are older, their chromosomes are more likely to divide incorrectly. And one egg cell may get an extra strand.

The importance of genetic research

Research is being done to see how genetic diseases can be controlled or cured. There are also other diseases and conditions that might be affected by heredity. Some forms of cancer, for example, happen more often in certain families. Heart disease also occurs more often in some populations or families than in others. It is not yet known, in both of these diseases, if heredity is more important than environment. Research is being done to find out what part genetics plays in these disorders.

Immune response and organ transplant

One of the newest benefits of the science of genetics is in the field of transplant surgery. Surgeons have learned how to take an organ from one person and put it into the body of another person. This needs a great deal of skill and much complicated equipment. Transplants have been done with many different organs, including the heart, kidneys, and liver. The benefits of this surgery are easily seen. It is like getting a new part for a machine when the old one has been damaged or worn out.

But even though doctors can put a new heart into a person who needs it, the operation is not always successful. Sometimes the body "rejects" the new organ. The rejection is caused by an immune response.

Color blindness is a sex-linked trait. In the most common kind of color blindness, red and green are hard to tell apart. Complete color blindness—not being able to see any color—is rare. These drawings are from a color-blindness test. People who are not color blind see certain numbers. People with color blindness see different numbers.

Ordinarily, this response is helpful because it protects the body from bacteria and other invaders. In transplant surgery, the new organ is rejected just as the bacteria would be. In that case, instead of helping the body, the immune response has done harm.

Genes control the immune response.

By studying the patient's genes before the transplant, doctors can find a kidney from a donor whose genetic makeup is like that of the person who needs the organ. Family members—brothers, sisters, and parents—are most often picked to be donors. Identical twins are the best donors for each other because they have the same genetic makeup. The closer the genetic makeup, the lower the risk of rejection. Maybe you have read that a heart patient was waiting for just the right donor to have transplant surgery. Choosing the "right" donor depends upon genetic knowledge.

In the whole area of biology, genetics has grown very quickly. It has given insight into basic life processes and has added to the control of disease.

The correction of defective genes seems almost impossible. Yet researchers are almost on the threshold of a new era in genetics. Geneticists have developed techniques to cut the threadlike molecules of DNA into tiny pieces with the help of enzymes. They then take the pieces of DNA of one species and combine them with pieces from another species. This structure, now called *recombinant-DNA,* is placed into suitable organisms that will make many copies of the foreign DNA.

Someday, the technique of recombinant-DNA may be used to correct genetically related diseases. If this ever happens, our society will gradually move

Something to think about . . .

Poor muscle tone, one of the symptoms of Down's syndrome, can be improved through exercise.

from the nuclear age into the age of genetic intervention. Future geneticists will have the awesome power and responsibility to intervene and correct people's defective genes. Cardiovascular (heart) problems, cancer, stroke, and sickle-cell anemia will all become diseases of the past. Unfortunately, there are also unknown dangers in research. Could new harmful organisms be created accidentally and released into the environment? Will genetic intervention fall into the hands of the wrong people and be used in warfare?

Guidelines regarding recombinant-DNA have been established by the National Institutes of Health. It is hoped that these guidelines will be followed by researchers all over the world.

Main Ideas

1. Genes and DNA are necessary parts of the chromosome.
2. The DNA controls the cell makeup and function.
3. The medical geneticist is a specialist in the area of genetic counseling.
4. Prenatal testing and carrier tests are very important methods of preventive medicine.
5. There is a relationship between the rate of Down's syndrome and the age of the mother.
6. Environment greatly affects genetic potential.
7. We are entering a new era of genetics in medicine.

Key Words

amino acids	family pedigree	recessive gene
amniocentesis	genes	recessive inheritance
carrier	genetic code	recombinant-DNA
chromosomes	genetics	sex-linked inheritance
cystic fibrosis	inherited	sickle-cell anemia
DNA	lethal genes	sickle-cell trait
dominant gene	medical geneticist	Tay-Sachs
dominant inheritance	melanin	
Down's syndrome	mutation	

Apply Your Knowledge

1. Which cells in your body do not have 46 chromosomes?
2. What is the difference between genes and chromosomes?
3. Will all genetic defects be seen at the time of birth? Explain.
4. How does DNA tell the cell to build protein?
5. Explain the job of a medical geneticist.
6. Explain the steps in amniocentesis.
7. What color are the eyes of a person who has two genes for blue eyes?
8. What color are the eyes of a person with one gene for blue eyes and one gene for brown eyes?
9. Why are carrier tests important?
10. What is the difference between sickle-cell trait and sickle-cell anemia?
11. List eight symptoms of sickle-cell anemia.
12. Is there any advantage for a person to have sickle-cell trait? Explain.
13. Explain recessive inheritance. Use Tay-Sachs disease as an example.
14. Explain dominant inheritance.
15. Explain sex-linked inheritance. Use color blindness as an example.
16. What is the difference between a normal hemoglobin and a sickle-cell hemoglobin?
17. Why is Down's syndrome more common in children of older mothers?
18. Name a disease that is caused by a person's lacking or not having enough of an enzyme.
19. Explain the problems caused by cystic fibrosis.
20. Describe the makeup of the DNA molecule.

Extend Your Knowledge

1. Explain how your environment has affected your growth and development.
2. Make a list of traits you have inherited from your mother and father. Are there any traits that they have which did not appear in you? What trait seems to "run in the family"?
3. Construct a DNA molecule using gum drops or other materials.
4. Construct a family pedigree chart to see how certain traits have been passed on to you.
5. Is there any sure way to tell the sex of an unborn child?
6. Contact your local medical center and interview a medical geneticist. Find out how many mothers have amniocentesis performed. What percent of the unborn babies are found to be normal?
7. Explain the advantages and disadvantages of recombinant-DNA.

Chapter 10

Do you know . . .

- what the number-one source of air pollution is?
- what causes a "killer smog"?
- the causes and effects of water pollution?
- whether or not a rock band can cause one kind of pollution?
- what radiation can do to the human body?

Environmental Hazards

Keeping the environment healthy is the responsibility of the government, society, and each individual. Today, many new problems must be solved in order to save our natural resources and to protect people from environmental dangers. The government has passed new laws to make our environment a safe and healthy one to live in. But there are still many dangers that may affect our health in the future. The success of laws to control these dangers depends on the cooperation of each individual.

All of us must have a knowledge of environmental problems. We must all do our part to make the world a safer place, not just for ourselves and our neighbors, but for future generations.

Air pollution

The air that you breathe contains gases such as oxygen, nitrogen, and carbon dioxide in certain amounts. But many people live in areas where the air contains pollutants that may be harmful to their health. Air pollution is a very common problem in cities of more than 100,000 people. Automobile exhaust and industrial wastes are often the cause of air pollution in cities. The five basic pollutants of air are carbon monoxide, sulfur oxide, nitrogen oxide, hydrocarbons (organic compounds made up of hydrogen and carbon), and small particles that float in the air.

Sources of air pollution

Carbon monoxide is a colorless and odorless gas that is poisonous in large amounts. Most of the carbon monoxide in the air comes from automobile exhausts. Nitrogen oxide and hydrocarbons are also produced as byproducts of engine combustion. The more vehicles there are on the road, the greater is the possibility of pollution. Unleaded gasoline and some antipollution automobile parts cut down the number of pollutants in the air. But transportation vehicles are still a major cause of air pollution.

Industry

Automobiles cause the greatest amount of air pollution. Industries are responsible for the second largest amount. Fuels that are used in some industries may give off large amounts of sulfur oxide, nitrogen oxide, and harmful particles of dust and ash *(particulates)*. Sulfur oxide is made when fuels containing sulfur, such as coal, are burned. Certain industrial pro-

The health of everyone living on earth is touched by the environment. Over time, our health, and even our ability to survive, will depend on the condition of the air, water, and land.

cesses may give off more of one pollutant than another. This depends on the kind of fuel used and the product that is being made.

Individuals

People pollute the air in many ways. Each time a person smokes a cigarette, the air is being polluted by cigarette smoke. When a person burns trash or drives a car with a poor exhaust system, air pollution is increased. More pollution is added when people burn wood in fireplaces or use soft coal in furnaces.

Effects of air pollution

Air pollution affects people directly and indirectly. It harms them directly by making them physically sick. And it harms them indirectly by spoiling the beauty of their surroundings and by being expensive to prevent.

Respiratory disorders

If you have breathed polluted air, you may remember how it affects you. The eyes may water; the nose may run; a cough may develop. Many serious illnesses are more likely to happen to people who have been exposed to polluted air for long periods of time. Chronic bronchitis, emphysema, and lung cancer are more common in air-polluted areas. In Chapter 11, you will learn that cigarette smoking is closely related to the development of lung cancer. Heart diseases, especially heart attacks, are found more often in places where there is a high level of carbon monoxide in the air.

Accidents

Automobile accidents happen more often in places where the air is polluted. These accidents may be caused by poor visibility in the polluted air. Or they may be caused by increased exposure to carbon monoxide. People with watery eyes, headaches, and breathing problems often find it hard to drive in air-polluted areas.

High economic cost

The federal government spends billions of dollars per year to control air pollution. The expense for medical treatment of diseases caused by air pollution is also enormous. Air pollution also can add to the rusting and corrosion of automobiles and machinery. This makes it necessary to repair or replace these items more often. Even farm crops may be harmed or stunted in growth by air pollution.

Although no place is completely free of air pollution, the amount of air pollution in an area depends on various factors. Some factors are weather conditions, geographic location, and type of industry found in the area. Certain heavily populated cities, such as Los Angeles and London, have an air-pollution problem referred to as *smog*. Smog originally meant the combination of smoke and fog. Now it refers to any area of polluted air in which the visibility is poor. In Los Angeles, the smog contains a large amount of gasoline vapors. At times it also contains *ozone*. Ozone is a very active form of oxygen that is produced by the action of sunlight on atmospheric impurities. Ozone may cause watering of the eyes and irritation of the nasal membranes. It also increases breathing problems associated with emphysema.

Normally, the polluted air near the Earth's surface is warmer than the air above it. The lighter, warmer air rises and carries the pollution away with it. But sometimes the polluted air close to the ground is cooler and heavier than the air above it. Then the cool, polluted air becomes trapped beneath the warmer, lighter air above. This is known as a *temperature inversion.*

Many people live in areas where the air is not healthy to breathe. Air pollution causes eye soreness and lung diseases. More heart attacks happen in places where the air is polluted.

Smog is a serious problem, especially in big cities. Automobiles cause the greatest amount of smog. Industries cause the second largest amount.

Sometimes there is not much wind flow, so the polluted air cannot rise and remove pollutants. This may cause a serious air-pollution problem called a "killer smog." Smog disasters have occurred in several major cities because of the weather conditions. In such cases, some people with respiratory problems have died, and many others have had to go to the hospital.

Prevention of air pollution

Everyone needs to care more about the problem of air pollution. Car exhausts and home-heating systems can be checked at regular times and kept in good working condition. Some home and trailer heaters, if not working properly, may give off harmful carbon monoxide. Automobiles should not be allowed to idle for more than a few minutes. Idling lets carbon monoxide escape into the air. Use of public transportation would lower the number of vehicles on the road. And strict laws about air pollution in industry must be enforced.

Water pollution

Water pollution was not a problem many years ago when the pioneers drank from clear streams. A farmer could easily dig a well and find water that was clean and free of harmful substances. Today, huge increases in population, with many people living close together, have added to the water-pollution problem. Human and industrial wastes are the largest water pollutants.

Human wastes may contain organisms that cause serious illnesses. Industrial wastes, such as chemicals, oils, and detergents, may also cause illnesses and poison wildlife. In some cases, small amounts of certain pollutants may even cause tumors, if taken into the body for long periods of time.

Sources of water pollution

Sewage is one source of water pollution. Sewage is made up of human wastes, food-processing wastes, and garbage. Many communities are unable to treat all the different kinds of sewage. This means that the wastes may increase the amount of water pollution in those communities. Some cities still dump large amounts of wastes into nearby rivers and seas. Bacteria harmful to fish in the water breed in the sewage decay. And the breakdown of the sewage often takes oxygen from the water. Because of this breakdown, fish cannot get enough oxygen to survive.

Chemicals are another source of water pollution. Detergents, fertilizers, and pesticides may be spilled or washed into water systems. These substances are often harmful to fish and other wildlife in the area. The long-range effects on people who eat the fish and drink the polluted water may be harmful. Some water pollutants, such as PCB (polychlorinated biphenyl), are now thought to be *carcinogenic,* or capable of causing cancer.

This "pollution board" in Tokyo tells people about the quality of the air and the level of noise in their area.

The effects of water pollution cannot always be measured and can last a lifetime. For example, did you know that when an oil tanker accidentally spills oil onto a beach, it takes the ocean over thirty years to clean its coastline? Water pollution can affect you physically and can also affect the environment in which you live.

Effects of water pollution

Serious illness

An *epidemic* is an outbreak of an infectious disease that affects a large number of people at the same time. Epidemics of hepatitis, typhoid fever, and different kinds of diarrhea have been traced to polluted water supplies. The long-term effects of chemical pollutants are not known for certain. But studies have shown larger numbers of tumors in fish that live in polluted waters.

Loss of recreational areas

Recreational areas are needed for exercise and relaxation to help keep people healthy. But many swimming beaches and fishing areas are lost each year because of pollution.

Because of the increase in population, many people now live close together. More lakes and rivers are polluted than ever before. Human waste and chemicals are the two major causes of water pollution.

Water shortages

To work properly, the human body needs to take in at least two liters (a little more than two quarts) of water each day. Water is also needed to bathe, shave, prepare foods, and flush toilets. Appliances, such as washing machines, automatic dishwashers, and garbage disposals, use large amounts of water.

Industries use a great deal of water to manufacture many products. Farmers need water for irrigation and for livestock. Cities use water for street cleaning, fire fighting, and sanitation purposes.

Many problems will develop if the supply of clean water is lowered because of water pollution. Pollution has become so bad in some countries that bottled drinking water must be bought.

Scientists are working to find better ways to get rid of sewage. Sewage treatment plants are being modernized. Laws are being made to stop the dumping of industrial wastes into waterways.

If you doubt that water is pure, boil the water before drinking it. Do not bathe in polluted water. This could lead to skin diseases or other infections. Avoid eating fish that have been caught in badly polluted rivers. When camping out of doors, do not dump human waste into waterways. Also, do not waste throwaway products. Instead, you can recycle many containers and other manufactured items. Everyone needs to be careful not to litter, especially in recreational areas.

Scientists test water samples to control water pollution. They now think some water pollutants cause cancer.

Noise pollution

Another type of pollution in our environment is noise pollution. *Noise pollution* refers to sounds that can damage the ears and other parts of the body. Noise is always with us. But most people are not aware of the growing amount of noise pollution in our society.

The loudness of sound is measured in *decibels*. A healthy ear may hear as low as one decibel. Normal conversation is usually in the 60-decibel range. Noise levels above 85 decibels may cause permanent hearing loss if

Sound Levels and Human Response

Sound Source	NOISE LEVEL	Human Response	Is As Loud As…
	150		
Carrier Deck Jet Operation	140	Painfully Loud	
	130		
Jet Takeoff (200 feet) Amplified Rock Music Auto Horn (3 feet)	120	Maximum Vocal Effort	
	110		
Riveting Machine Jet Takeoff (2,000 feet) Garbage Truck	100		Shouting at 2 ft. Shouting in ear
N.Y. Subway Station Heavy Truck (50 feet) Pneumatic Drill (50 feet)	90	Very Annoying Hearing Damage (After 8 Hours)	
Alarm Clock Freight Train (50 feet)	80	Annoying	Very Loud Conversation, 2 ft.
Freeway Traffic (50 feet)	70	Telephone Use Difficult	Loud Conversation, 2 ft.
Air Conditioning Unit (20 feet)	60	Intrusive	Loud Conversation, 4 ft.
Light Auto Traffic (100 feet)	50	Quiet	Normal Conversation, 12 ft.
Living Room Bedroom	40		
Library Soft Whisper (15 feet) Broadcasting Studio	30	Very Quiet	
	20		
	10	Just Audible	
	0	Threshold of Hearing	

one is exposed to them for too long. Very loud rock bands, motorcycles, some household appliances, and some industrial machines create familiar forms of noise pollution.

It is estimated that 10 million Americans are exposed to harmful levels of noise off the job. Long exposure to noise pollution may cause a gradual hearing loss. Sudden noises of very high intensity, such as dynamite explosions, may also damage hearing. Noise pollution may affect other parts of the body besides the ear. Noise may cause a lack of sleep. It may stop a person from relaxing, paying attention, or digesting food properly. Also, noise pollution may raise the blood pressure and add to emotional problems.

Effects of noise pollution

Environmental accidents can happen anywhere. What kinds of accidents are possible where you live? What could you and your community do if an accident happened in your environment?

Prevention of noise pollution

There are many ways to protect yourself against noise pollution. Know what noises are harmful to the ears. Whenever possible, stay away from loud ongoing noises. Don't be embarrassed to put your hands over your ears to protect them from a sudden, loud noise. If you must be near loud noises for a long period of time, wear earplugs or other devices that can help protect your hearing.

Read noise-level labels on appliances before you buy them. Similar products may make very different amounts of noise. Do not play the radio, TV, or stereo at a very high volume. It is also wise to sit far away from sound amplifiers at dances and athletic events.

Radiation pollution

Radiation pollution is a more recent kind of environmental danger. *Radiation* is an invisible form of energy that comes from the splitting of atoms. Atoms are tiny invisible particles that make up all matter. The most dangerous type of radiation is *gamma rays* that get into body tissues. Materials that give off radiation are *radioactive substances.* Radioactive substances are naturally available in small amounts in the earth's surface. (Radium and uranium are two such substances.) In tiny amounts, radioactive substances are harmless. In concentrated amounts, they destroy bone marrow and damage chromosomes.

The largest amount of radiation is given off into the environment by nuclear weapons, such as the atomic bomb. Many countries now have nuclear weapons that are able to produce very serious radiation dangers.

Getting rid of radioactive waste is also a major problem all over the world. Radioactive substances are used for positive purposes—in medical treatments and electrical power plants. Even those peaceful uses produce radioactive waste, which may take 70 to 80 years or longer to disintegrate. What would happen if such waste slowly leaked into the water supply?

People who come into contact with small amounts of radiation over a long period of time may develop health problems. X-ray machines, color televisions, and microwave ovens may give off small amounts of radiation. If these kinds of equipment work properly, there seems to be little danger from exposure. But overexposure to small amounts of radiation for long periods of time may cause serious medical problems, such as leukemia, certain tumors, and genetic disorders. Scientists do not know exactly how much radiation a human body can stand.

Radiation prevention

The federal government has taken many steps to prevent the dangers of radiation. Special safety precautions are taken in building radioactive substances and delivering them. Government agencies measure the amount of radiation from nuclear weapons testing and atomic power plants. Scientists from all over the world are working together to solve the problems of nuclear waste disposal.

X-ray machines are built to produce a large amount of radiation. Medical technicians who work near X-ray machines wear lead shields or operate the machine from behind a protective device. Such a device may be a wall made of lead. Pregnant women should avoid exposure to X-rays, particularly during the first three months of pregnancy.

Noise pollution can keep you from relaxing.

Your body doesn't get used to noise. Constant loud noise can lead to permanent hearing loss.

Something to think about . . .

If a balloon pops near you, you jump. But if you spend the afternoon in a motorboat or snowmobile, you seem to get used to the noise. Sound research shows, however, that your body doesn't really "get used to noise." Regular exposure to loud noise can cause many kinds of problems.

Constant loud noise can destroy the tiny hairs inside the ear and result in permanent loss of hearing. These hairs move when sound hits them, and nerves take the signal to the brain. When the hairs are damaged, they do not grow back. More and more young people have hearing as bad as people twice their age, most likely because they listen to very loud music. In Sweden, young sailors had trouble using submarine-tracking equipment because of bad hearing; and in Japan, students who listened to loud headphones for more than 24 hours a week lost a lot of their hearing.

Other physical damage can also occur. Even if you believe you are used to a noise, your body still reacts to it. To the body, noise means trouble is coming. Your heart beats faster, your blood pressure goes up, your muscles get tense. In the long run, these changes may lead to heart trouble, ulcers, less resistance to infection, and other problems.

Physical responses to noise may also cause social and psychological problems. Experiments suggest that people are less likely to help each other if there is a loud noise nearby. Also, people exposed to constant noise fight and argue more often. They feel tired and have more accidents. Noise may make it hard to learn, too. Other studies show that babies living in homes where the television is too loud don't learn as fast as other babies.

Main Ideas

1. Progress and the growing population have changed the environment and created many health hazards.
2. People can make the environment healthier to live in by solving and preventing pollution problems.
3. Natural resources are limited, and people must learn to use them wisely.
4. Keeping the environment clean and safe is the responsibility of the individual, the society, and the government.

Key Words

carcinogenic	ozone	sewage
decibel	particulates	smog
epidemic	radiation	temperature
gamma rays	radioactive substances	inversion

Apply Your Knowledge

1. What are the basic pollutants of air? Where do they come from?
2. What illnesses are connected with air pollution?
3. Describe some causes of water pollution.
4. How can water pollution be prevented?
5. Name some illnesses connected with polluted water.
6. Why do fish often starve for oxygen in a river used as a sewage dump?
7. What are the sources of noise pollution in our environment?
8. How can noise pollution be prevented?
9. What are some radiation hazards in the environment?
10. How has progress affected the natural resources of the environment?

Extend Your Knowledge

1. What happens to household wastes in your community? Find out how the sewage treatment facility works. What happens to garbage? Is there a recycling center?
2. Invite a local health officer to your school to discuss the laws in your community which control the various forms of pollution.
3. Explain the statement "Environmental control is everybody's business."
4. Once, a polluted river caught fire. Explain how this could happen.
5. Write to the Environmental Protection Agency for material concerning the latest pollution regulations.

Chapter 11

Six of every 24 people in the U.S. will have cancer at some time

cured

die from incurable cancer

dies because of late diagnosis

Do you know . . .

- what causes cancer?
- that many cancers can be prevented?
- what the warning signals of cancer are?
- how cancer is treated?

Cancer Prevention

About 1000 Americans die of cancer every day. In the United States, only heart disease causes more deaths than cancer. But many factors that add to the growth of cancer can be controlled. Many Americans have been successfully treated and cured of cancer. Others have gained extra years of life through treatment. Knowing how to prevent cancer and how to detect it early are two of the most important parts of health education.

What is cancer?

The word *cancer* causes many people to be fearful and to think of death. Cancer is often not understood because some people think all cancers are the same. Actually, there are more than 300 types of cancer. Some types grow and spread quickly and cause an early death. But other types may be completely cured. In all types of cancer, though, there is uncontrolled and irregular growth of abnormal cells. This growth can take place in any tissue or organ of the body.

Normal cells divide in an orderly way. One cell becomes two cells, two cells become four, four cells become eight, and so on. Through normal cell division body tissues and organs are formed. But cancer cells do not have order and control. When cancer cells divide, for example, one cell may become four or five. The four cells may become eleven cells, and these cells may continue to grow in a disorganized way. The cells are irregular in size and shape, and they no longer form useful tissues and organs. Cancer cells use nourishment needed by healthy cells. Also, the large mass of useless cancer cells crowds normal cells. This prevents healthy tissue from functioning.

What is a tumor?

A group of cells may grow together in a mass called a *tumor*. If the cells are normal and in an orderly pattern, the tumor is a *benign tumor*. Benign tumors grow inside a wall of tissue. They do not spread to other parts of the body or attack organs needed for life. A benign tumor usually does not cause serious medical problems. It may be removed by surgery.

If the cells in the tumor are not normal and grow in an irregular pattern, the tumor is a *malignant tumor*. Malignant tumors may break through the wall of tissue. They may spread to other parts of the body or attack body organs. Malignant tumors are cancers. The spreading of a disease from the place where it started to another part of the body is known as *metastasis*.

Research has led to important breakthroughs in the treatment of cancer. Some current research focuses on using the body's immune system (the system that defends the body against disease) to diagnose, treat, and even prevent cancer.

How does cancer spread?

Cancer cells may be carried to other parts of the body by the blood or lymph system. Cancer may also grow into the tissue next to it. There is no set rate of growth for cancers. Some types grow more in a few weeks than others grow in many years. It is very important to discover cancer at an early stage. In this way, it is sometimes possible to stop it from spreading.

What causes cancer?

There is no single cause of cancer. But a combination of environmental and biological factors is now known to affect the growth of different types of cancer.

Environmental factors

Carcinogens are substances that cause cancer. Different carcinogens cause different kinds of cancer. Exposure to asbestos for many years may cause a type of lung cancer. Heavy smokers have a much higher rate of lung, larynx, and esophageal cancer than nonsmokers do. Too much exposure to the sun can lead to skin cancers. Even dietary habits are related to some types of cancer. Cancer of the bowel is very common in the United States, but vegetarians rarely develop it. Too much exposure to radiation may also cause some form of cancer.

Biological factors

Some families have a "familial tendency" toward a certain type of cancer, such as breast or stomach cancer. This means that members of these families are more likely than other people to get a certain type of cancer. As you grow older, your chance of getting cancer will increase. For some unknown reason, cells that have been dividing normally for many years may suddenly begin to grow in a way that is not normal.

Prevention of cancer

Some types of cancer can be prevented. Lung cancer is the most common cancer in men. About one person dies from lung cancer every six minutes in the United States. People who smoke get lung cancer much more often than people who don't. More than 75 percent of all lung cancers could be prevented if people did not smoke.

Breast cancer is the most common type of cancer among women. As with most cancers, early detection increases the chance of cure. If breast cancer is found early, it can be cured 87 percent of the time. Most women discover lumps in their breasts themselves through monthly self-examination. Testicular cancer, the most common cancer in men aged 29 to 35, can also be detected through self-examination. The American Cancer Society has simple self-examination procedures which women and men can use.

Other types of cancer may be prevented by avoiding cancer-causing substances. The use of some industrial carcinogens is now being controlled by laws. Too much or unnecessary radiation should also be avoided. Following a proper diet can help, since diet seems to be related to the growth of some cancers of the intestine and rectum. Eating more fruits, vegetables, and other foods high in fiber seems to guard against bowel cancer. Avoiding foods with additives that are thought to be cancer-causing can also help. There is a clear link between heavy drinking of alcohol and cancer of the mouth, throat, esophagus, and liver.

A yearly physical checkup for anyone over the age of 30 may help to prevent or detect early cancer. Sometimes a cancer that causes no symptoms may be found. If a tumor is found, a doctor may suggest a *biopsy*. A biopsy is an operation to remove a small amount of tissue from the body so that a doctor can look for abnormal cells under a microscope.

Unfortunately, many types of cancer cannot yet be prevented. Therefore, finding these cancers early is very important. The chance of a cure is much greater when a cancer is found early. The American Cancer Society has issued a list of the warning signals of cancer. See a doctor if you notice any of these signs. These conditions do not always mean that cancer is present. But a doctor should examine you.

SEVEN WARNING SIGNALS OF CANCER*

a change in bowel or bladder habits
a sore that does not heal
any unusual bleeding or discharge
a thickening or lump in the breast or elsewhere
indigestion or difficulty in swallowing
an obvious change in a wart or mole
a nagging cough or hoarseness

* American Cancer Society

Early detection of cancer

(left) Normal cells are regular in size and shape. They divide, or grow, in a controlled way. (right) Cancer cells are not regular in size and shape. They divide in an uncontrolled way. They do not work as useful tissues and organs.

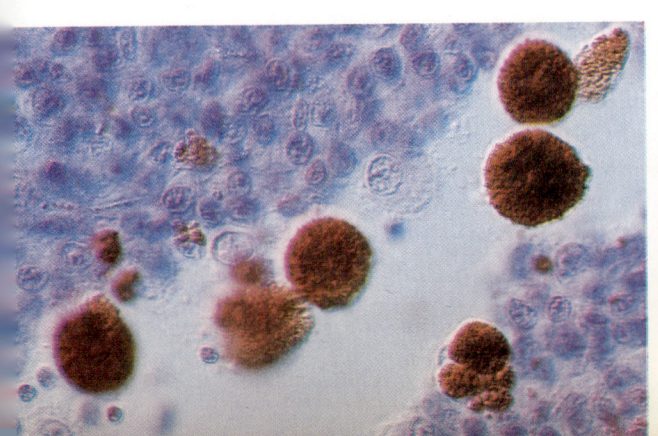

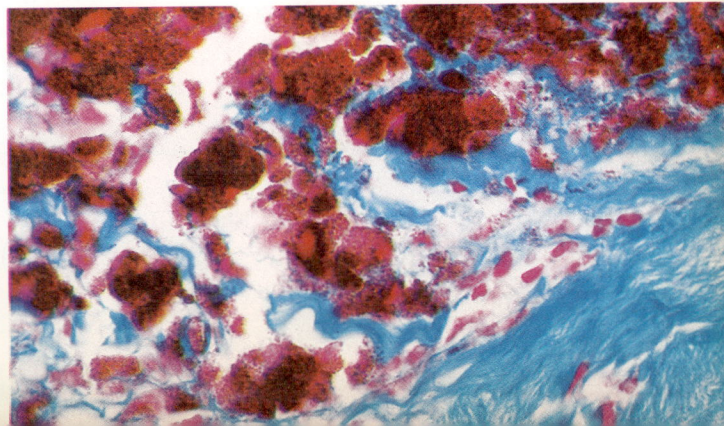

Treatment of cancer

The goal of cancer treatment is to destroy cancer cells or to remove them completely. Surgery, *chemotherapy,* and radiation therapy are the three standard ways of treating cancer. Any combination of these methods may be used. The method of treatment depends upon the location of the cancer, its size, and its type of growth. The effect of the treatment depends upon the type of cancer and how far it has spread.

The American Cancer Society arranges cancer-screening days at local health centers. If cancer is found early, the chance of a cure is much greater.

Surgery

Sometimes a surgeon may remove a tumor completely by operating. This type of treatment can be very successful. But it is limited to types of cancer that produce tumors which can be safely reached and removed.

Chemotherapy

Chemotherapy is the treatment of cancer with powerful chemicals. Certain malignancies, such as *lymphoma* (cancer of the lymph glands) and *leukemia* (cancer of the blood cells), may be treated in this way. But sometimes patients suffer serious side effects. Even so, chemotherapy has become a useful method of treating and sometimes curing many cancers.

Radiation therapy

In radiation therapy different kinds of radiation are aimed at cancer cells. The amount and direction of the radiation are controlled carefully. This is done to protect normal, healthy cells. Cancer cells are usually more sensitive to radiation than normal cells are. So the cancer cells are destroyed first.

Cancer quacks

Some cancer patients do not get well and may feel hopeless. Unfortunately, some turn to methods of treatment that have not been proven to work. They may waste large amounts of money on these worthless methods. People who sell unscientific methods of treating cancer are called "cancer quacks." Cancer quacks often do not want the patient to talk with doctors. The quacks may claim that the medical profession is against them. The

Research on Cancer Vaccines

Most children who start school have been given *vaccines* against several diseases like polio and measles. In vaccination, a few of the cells that cause the disease are injected or given orally. By fighting a little of the disease, the body learns to produce *antibodies* against it. Later, if the body is exposed to the disease, it remembers how to produce these antibodies quickly to fight the particular disease.

Because it is too dangerous to inject cancer cells into anyone, scientists once believed vaccination against cancer impossible. But a young scientist named Ariel Hollinshead got the idea to inject just the outside of cancer cells into hamsters. The hamsters did produce antibodies, and successfully fought off the same cancer when it was given to them later.

After more research, Dr. Hollinshead got permission from the Food and Drug Administration to begin a new experiment with humans. In 1982, she began a test with heavy smokers who had been exposed to asbestos. These people have a very high risk of lung cancer. After being injected with the outsides of lung-cancer cells, it is hoped that they will get fewer cancers. Then we will be a step closer to having cancer vaccines.

main danger with cancer quacks is that the patient may lose valuable time before getting proper treatment. This loss of time could lead to the patient's death.

The future

Medical scientists and doctors are now winning part of the battle against cancer. Important breakthroughs have been made in the treatment of cancer. But much more research needs to be done. Today, the prevention of cancer is the main aim of cancer research.

Would you rather not know these 7 warning signals?

1. Unusual bleeding or discharge.
2. A lump or thickening in the breast or elsewhere.
3. A sore that does not heal.
4. Change in bowel or bladder habits.
5. Hoarseness or cough.
6. Indigestion or difficulty in swallowing.
7. Change in size or color of a wart or mole.

If a signal persists for 2 weeks, see your doctor without delay. Because many cancers are curable if detected and treated early.

American Cancer Society
It's up to you, too.

See a doctor at once if you have any of the seven warning signals of cancer.

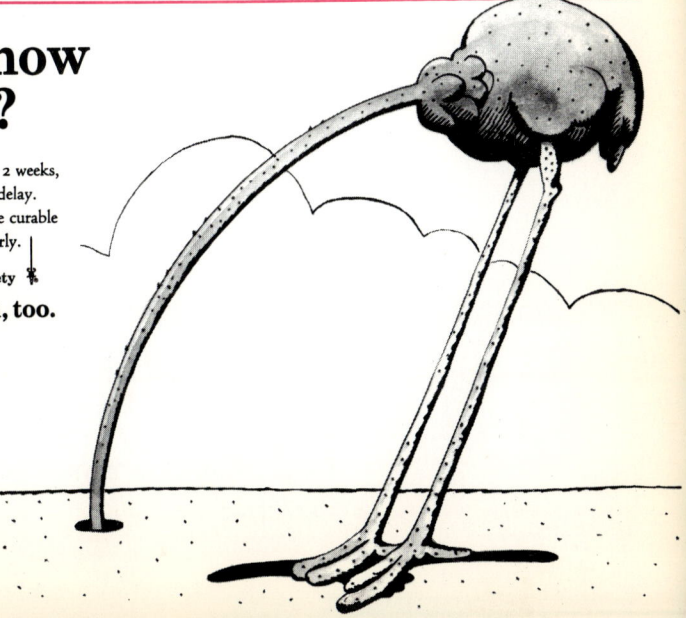

Cancer will always be a problem if people do not help to prevent it or to find it as early as possible. There is evidence that cigarette smoking can cause lung cancer. But many people continue to smoke. Many people also ignore the early warning signs of cancer. The government has passed some laws on smoking and carcinogens. But the real responsibility for cancer prevention and detection belongs to each person.

Radiation therapy is one way to treat cancer. Cancer cells are killed by radiation faster than normal cells.

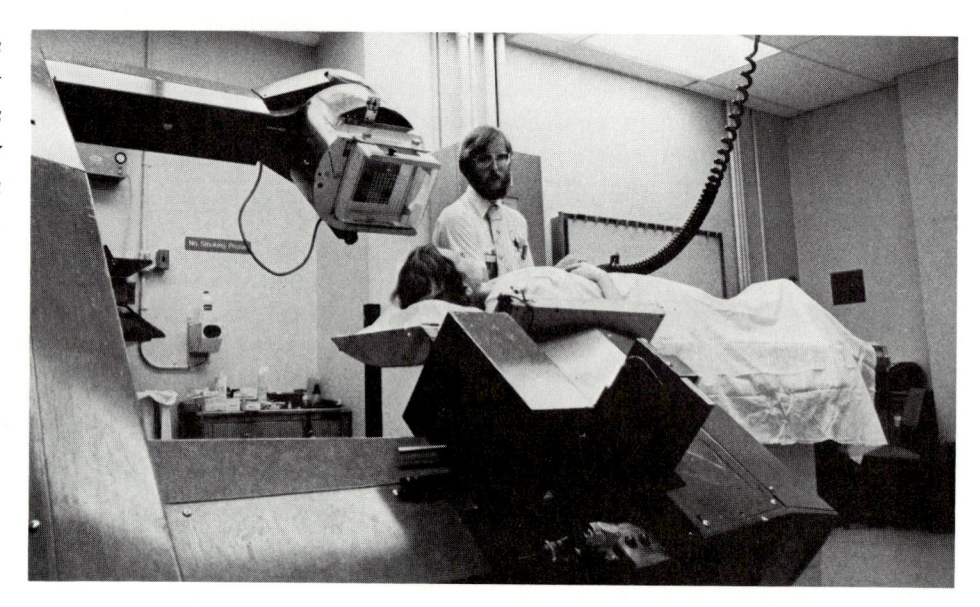

Something to think about . . .

Certain procedures are used to detect some of the more common types of cancer at an early stage. These procedures may be used as screening tests to check large groups of people for cancers before the cancers spread and become incurable.

The first sign of bowel cancer may be trace amounts of blood in the bowel movements. Small amounts of stool may be tested chemically for blood. If blood is found, the physician advises further studies. A proctoscope (a plastic tube with a light attached) is passed into the lower bowel to look for early tumors. An X ray of the large bowel is also taken. In this way, many bowel cancers may be detected early in the curable stage.

Screening tests have also been developed to detect breast and uterine cancer. Self-examination is the simplest screening test for early breast tumors. A pamphlet describing breast examination is available from the American Cancer Society. If a lump is noted during the self-examination, the advice of a physician should be sought.

An annual pelvic examination and a Pap test are recommended for detecting ovarian and uterine cancer. In a Pap test, cells are scraped from the lower part of the uterus and placed on a glass slide. The cells are viewed under a microscope to see if any are abnormal. In this way, cancer can be detected early, when a cure is very likely. The American Cancer Society recommends that all women have Pap tests regularly. A woman and her doctor can decide how often these tests are appropriate.

Main Ideas

1. Cancer is caused by a combination of biological and environmental factors.
2. Prevention and early detection and treatment are important factors in cancer cures.
3. There are seven warning signals that may point out the possibility of cancer.
4. Cancer can be treated by surgery, radiation therapy, and chemotherapy.
5. Everyone must take a role in the prevention and early detection of cancer in his or her own body.

Key Words

antibodies	carcinogen	malignant tumor
benign tumor	chemotherapy	metastasis
biopsy	leukemia	tumor
cancer	lymphoma	vaccine

Apply Your Knowledge

1. What is cancer?
2. How does cancer spread to other parts of the body?
3. What is the difference between a benign tumor and a malignant tumor?
4. Name some things in the environment that may cause cancer.
5. How can biological factors cause cancer?
6. What can be done to prevent certain types of cancer?
7. List the seven warning signals of cancer.
8. What is a biopsy? When does a doctor suggest having one done?
9. What are the three standard ways of treating cancer?
10. Why does radiation therapy kill cancer cells and not normal cells?

Extend Your Knowledge

1. Contact the local office of the American Cancer Society and obtain information on the prevention and early detection of cancer.
2. Invite a local doctor to discuss the current methods of detecting and treating cancer.
3. Report on controversies in the treatment of cancer, such as the use of laetrile or of special diets.

Unit 5

CHAPTERS:
12 Coordination and Control
13 Eye and Ear Care
14 Transport System
15 Respiration
16 Skin and Hair: Your Protective Covering
17 Regulators of Your Body
18 Healthy Teeth

Functioning Body

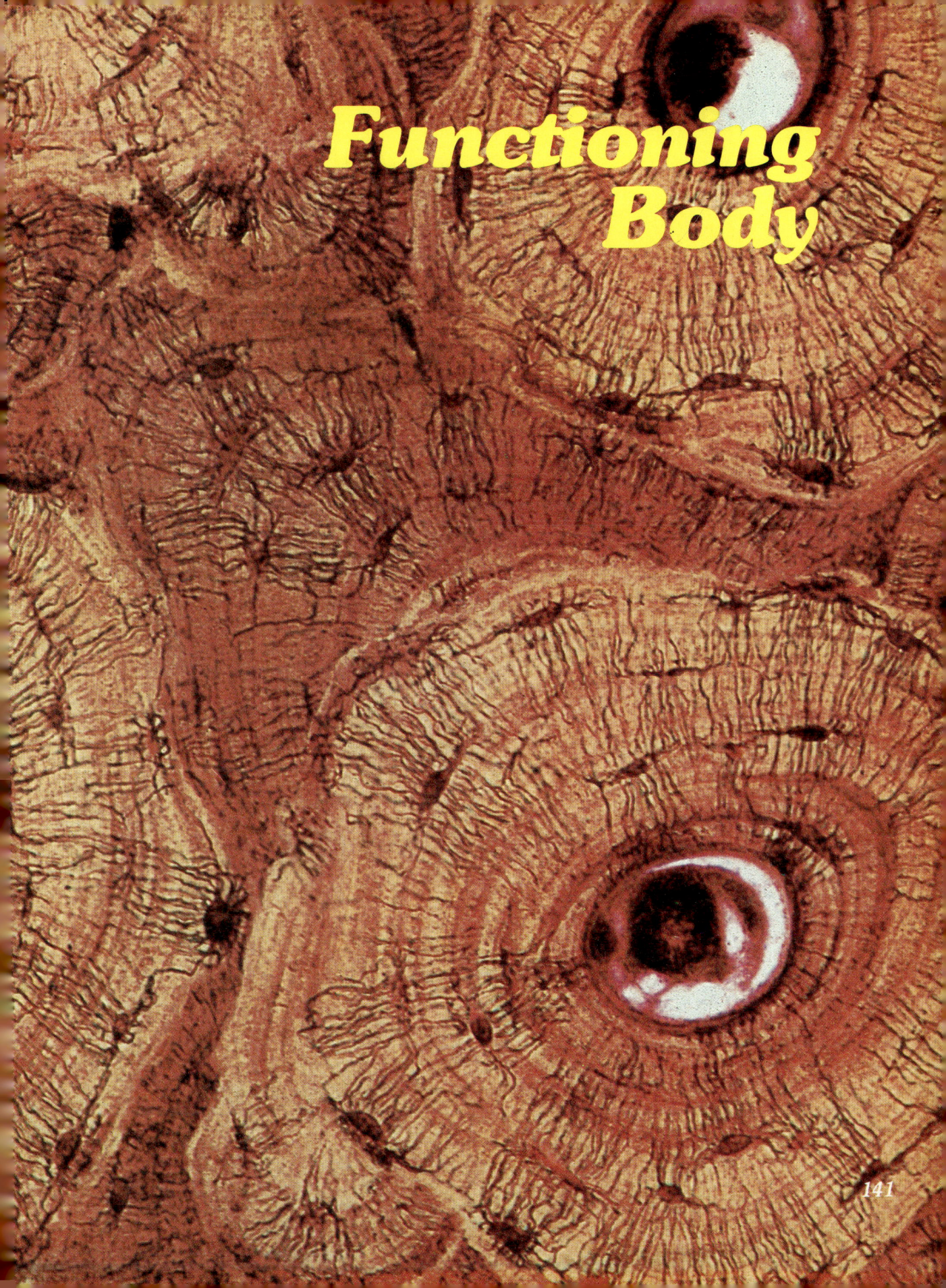

Chapter 12

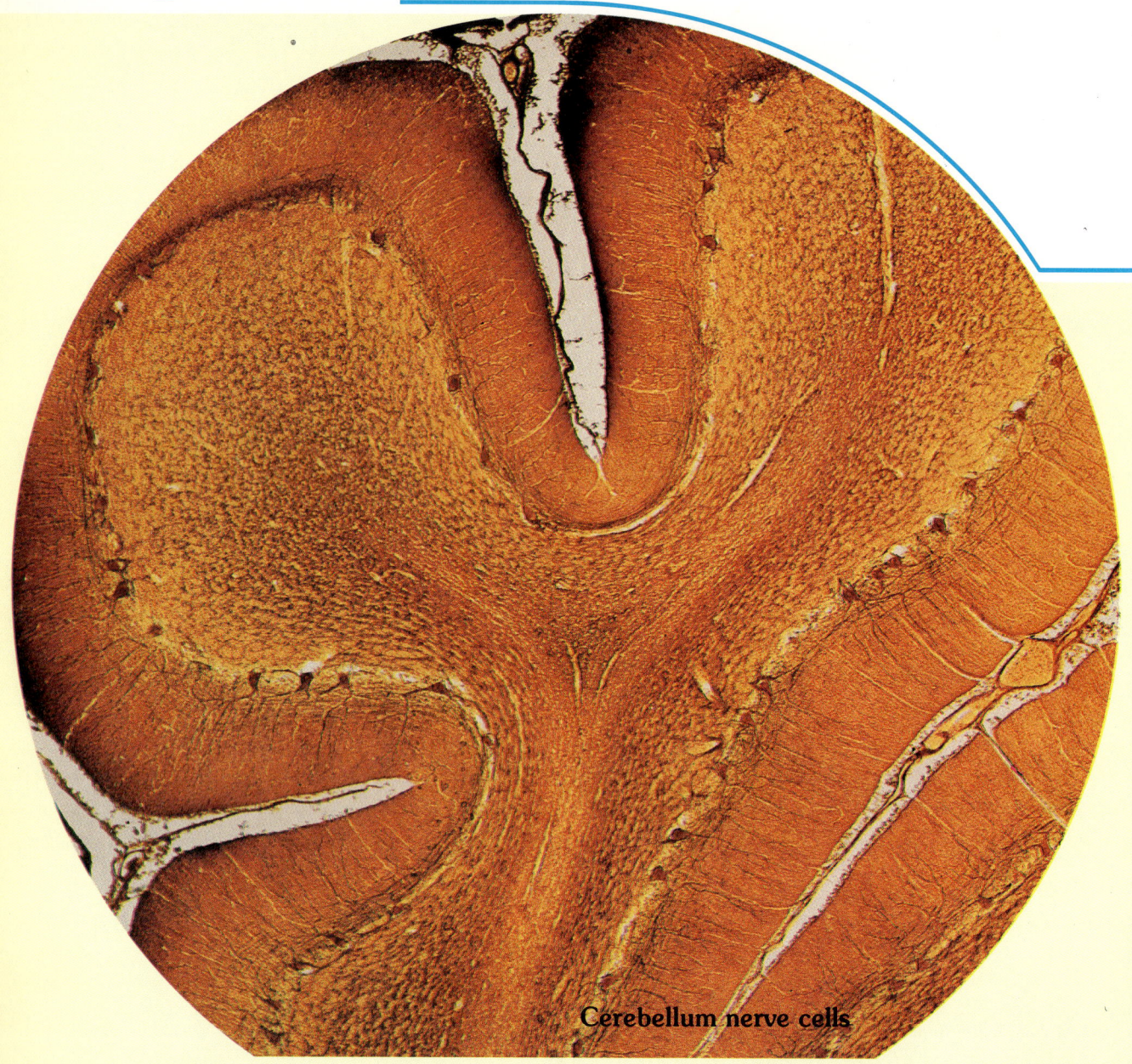

Cerebellum nerve cells

Do you know . . .

- what a cerebral vascular accident is?
- how messages travel from the nerve cells to the brain?
- what are the differences between a reflex and a habit?
- what part of the brain makes it possible for you to remember?
- how much rest you need to keep your nervous system working properly?

Coordination and Control

Your nervous system is always working to keep you aware of what is happening in the world around you. If you accidentally touch a hot stove, the nervous system helps you pull your hand away quickly to stop being burned. If you see a bright red apple, your stomach nerves tell your brain that you are hungry. Then, the brain tells your arm to reach out to take the apple. When you bite into it, nerves in your tongue called taste buds send a message to your brain—"Delicious!" The nervous system detects what is happening in your surroundings and then tells your body how to act.

Your nervous system

The nerves are the communication system of the body. They carry sensation, information, and orders from one part of the body to another. Information about the things that you see and do every day is stored in the nervous system, in the section of the brain you call "memory." This is why you do not have to touch a hot stove again and again to know that it is hot. You may also communicate this information about the stove to other people. The very high development of our nervous system is what makes human beings different from other living species.

The nervous system is made up of three smaller systems, all of which work together. These smaller networks are the *central* (in the center) *nervous system,* the *peripheral* (on the side) *nervous system,* and the *autonomic* (self-controlled) *nervous system.* The central nervous system is made up of the brain, and the *spinal cord* in the center of your back. The peripheral nervous system contains all the nerves that carry messages to the brain and spinal cord from both sides of your body. The autonomic nervous system is made up of nerves that regulate involuntary actions, such as digestion, heartbeat, respiration, blushing, and perspiration. Involuntary means that these physical events take place without any conscious help from you. For example, the autonomic nervous system makes the heart beat faster or more slowly. It also starts the waves of contraction in the digestive tract.

Transmitting a message

Twelve billion individual nerve cells, called *neurons,* carry messages, or impulses, along the nervous system. The neuron has a cell body with threadlike extensions that carry messages to and from the nerve cell. The extensions of the neurons that pick up impulses are called *dendrites.* The extensions that carry impulses away from the neurons are called *axons.*

Brain — Cerebrum

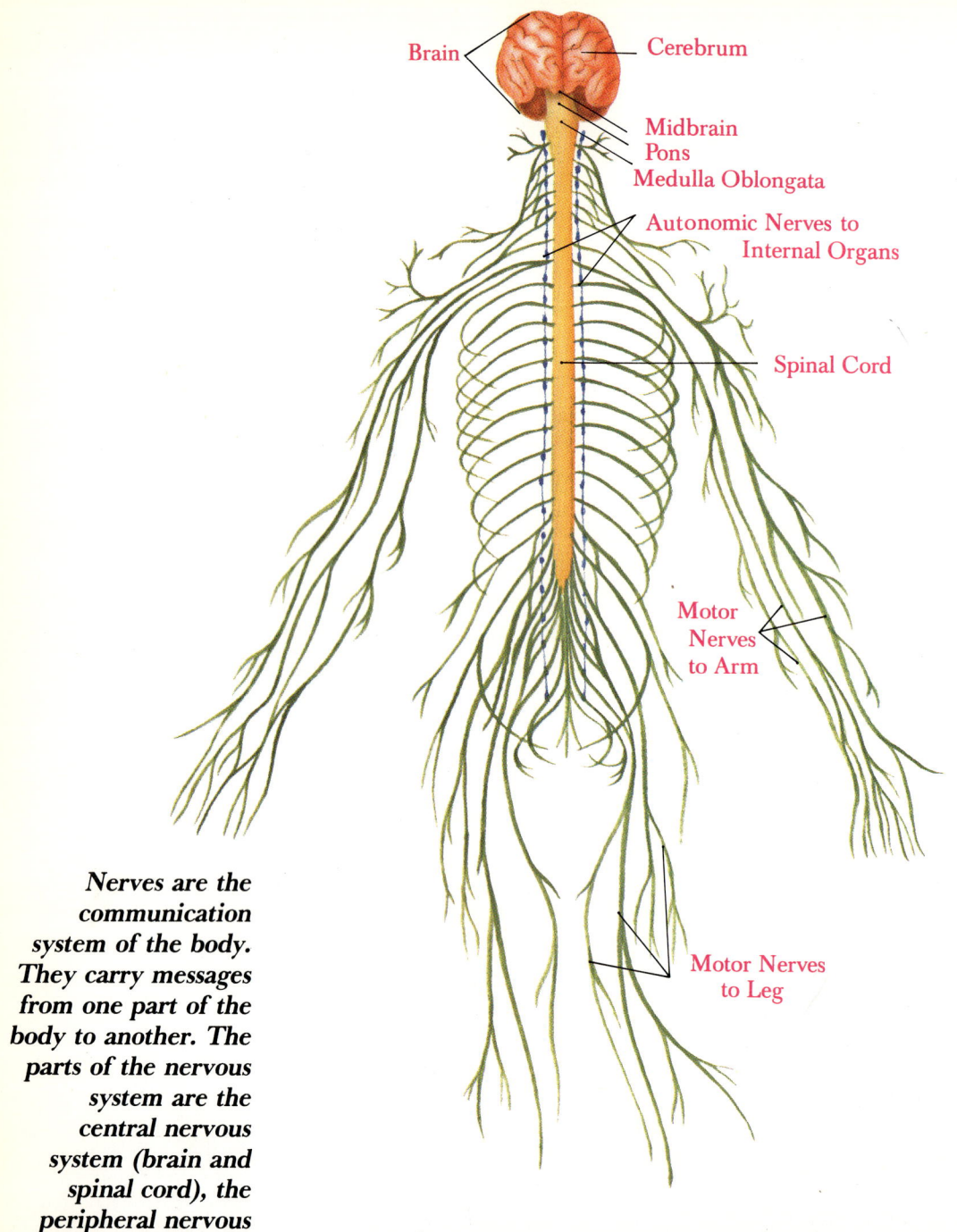

Midbrain
Pons
Medulla Oblongata

Autonomic Nerves to Internal Organs

Spinal Cord

Motor Nerves to Arm

Motor Nerves to Leg

Nerves are the communication system of the body. They carry messages from one part of the body to another. The parts of the nervous system are the central nervous system (brain and spinal cord), the peripheral nervous system (nerves on both sides of your body), and the autonomic nervous system (nerves your body controls without your help).

    A group of these threadlike projections from a nerve cell body form a *nerve fiber*. Nerve fibers are bound like single telephone wires. But entire nerves are like telephone cables that carry many wires. The thinnest nerve fibers (1/25,000 inch in diameter) carry impulses slowly—about one foot per second. Thicker nerves carry impulses at 450 feet per second. That's over 200 miles per hour!

    The body's five sense organs are the eyes, ears, nose, tongue, and skin. What your body feels through these five sense organs is carried by *sensory nerves* to the brain and spinal cord. The message is known as a *nerve impulse* because it is carried to the central nervous system.

Certain medications, such as *anesthetics,* may block nerve impulses as they travel over sensory nerves. A dentist who is going to pull one of your teeth may inject a *local anesthetic* in the area of the sensory nerves near the tooth. This lessens the pain of removing the tooth. Medications that block pain impulses act temporarily and usually wear off within a few hours.

Acting upon a message

When the nerve impulse reaches the central nervous system, orders are carried back through the body by means of the *motor nerves.* The motor nerves carry impulses away from the brain and spinal cord to the muscles and glands. These impulses cause the muscles to contract or relax. They also cause the glands to secrete or stop secreting their juices.

Reflexes and habits

When you touch a hot object, your hand instantly jerks away. This happens before you feel any pain. Such an action is called a *reflex*. A reflex is an automatic reaction directed by the spinal cord. Because the message is so urgent, the nerves tell the muscles to react before they carry the message to the brain. Blinking the eye when an insect flies near it is another example of a reflex.

Reflexes are designed to protect you, for the most part. You do not learn them. In fact, you do not even have to think about them. The nerve impulses travel over short pathways already set up in your nervous system. The pathway from the senses up to the brain and spinal cord, and back down to motor action, is called a *reflex arc*.

Habits of action

There are actions that you do not have to think about because you have done them many times. When nerve impulses have traveled over the same pathway a number of times, they tend to follow that pathway again. Such actions are *habits*.

Learning to ride a bicycle is an example of forming a series of habits. When you begin, you must think of every move. You think of how you get on the bicycle; where to place your hands on the handlebars; when to push with each foot; and how to turn, balance, stop, and get off.

After a while, you do not have to think about these things. You become alert to what is around you—traffic, signals, other people—and will probably do the right things quickly and skillfully. You no longer have to think about how to manage your bicycle as you did when you were learning to ride.

Habits are like reflexes because they do not demand constant thought. But they are different from reflexes because they must be learned. You can choose which habits you will develop, and you can change them if you wish.

Habits of feeling

In addition to habits of doing, there are habits of feeling. For example, a dog jumps on a small boy and frightens him. The next time the boy sees a dog, his nerve impulses will probably travel the same pathway, causing him to be frightened. This is a conditioned response.

Like habits of doing, habits of feeling can be changed. But this is not always easy. Often, though, you can change habits of fear. Fear of talking in front of the class or taking part in a play can be overcome by practicing until you are confident that you will perform well. When you practice, you are training your nerve impulses to travel over a different path. This helps you develop a new skill.

The central nervous system

The brain and spinal cord are protected against damage by a bony framework and protective membranes. The skull bone surrounds the brain. Membranes call *meninges* cover the spinal cord. The tissues of the brain and spinal cord are surrounded by a fluid called *cerebrospinal fluid* that adds further protection.

Brain

The brain has always been a mysterious link between mind and body. How does it work? Scientists are still looking for more clues about the way it stores and sends messages. A human brain is 1.5 kilograms (3 pounds) of spongy, pinkish-white tissue that is connected by a complex system of blood vessels. Its surface is wrinkled like a prune. The brain has several parts, and each controls different activities of the body. All areas of the brain work together through a two-way communication system that involves billions of small nerve cells. This is why you can do several things at one time and can think about and have feelings about what you are doing. Meanwhile, the actions of your glands and organs are being controlled automatically through the autonomic nervous system. It takes directions from the brain, too.

Cerebrum

The *cerebrum* is the large, upper part of the brain. It stores information and regulates memory, intelligence, and some emotions, such as appreciation of beauty. Specialized areas control the senses, such as vision, hearing, smell, and taste. In other words, you see and hear in the brain. Other areas control many other parts of the body. For example, if you think about moving your arm, the impulses travel from the arm center in your cerebrum to the arm muscles you wish to contract.

Motor areas in the left half of the cerebrum control movements of the right side of the body. Motor areas in the right half of the cerebrum control movements of the left side of the body. This is because the motor fibers from the cerebrum cross over to the opposite side as they enter the spinal cord. Ninety percent of all people are right-handed. The left side of the brain is dominant if you are right-handed. The right side is dominant if you are left-handed. By the time you were ten years old, one side had become dominant over the other.

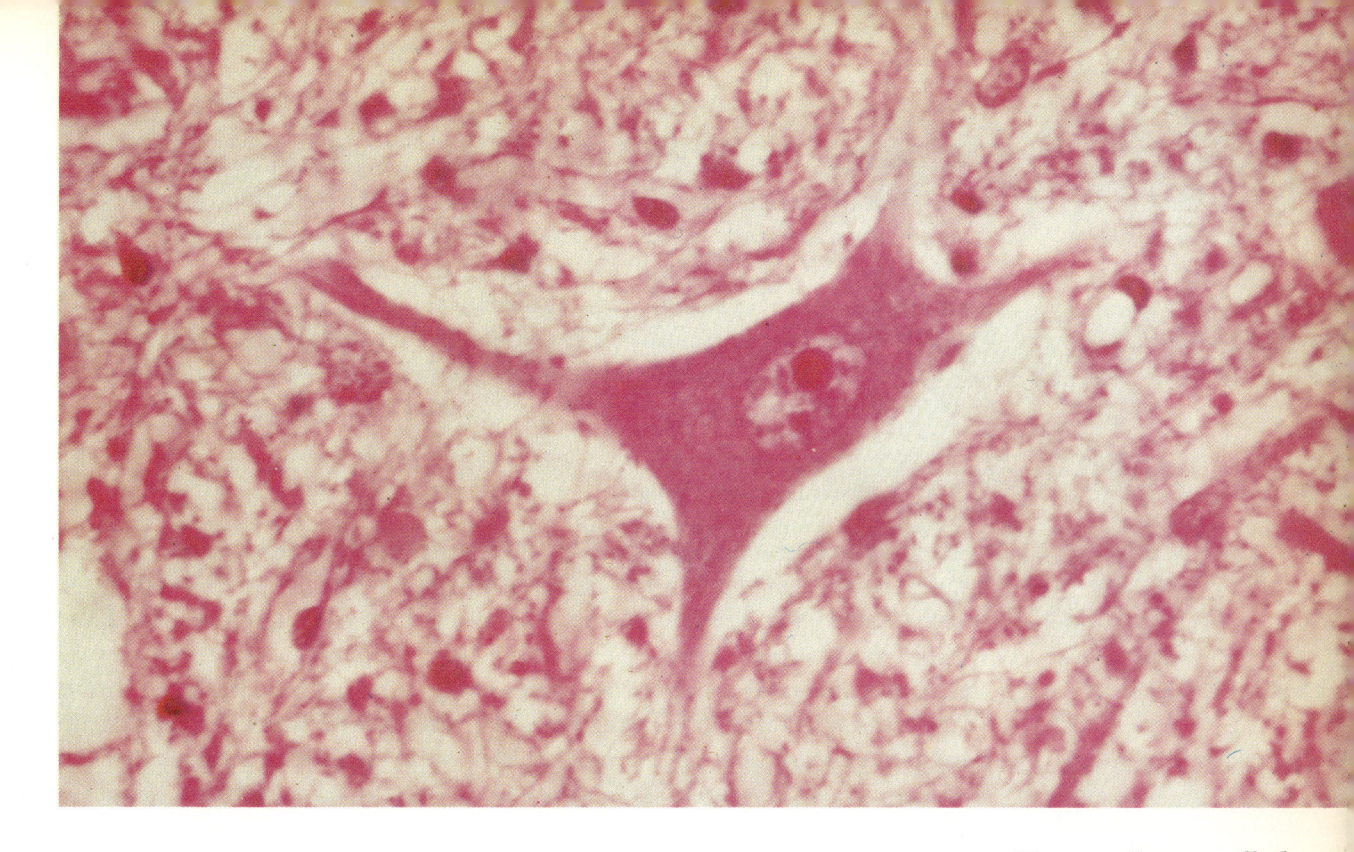

Cerebellum

Beneath the back part of the cerebrum lies the so-called "little brain," or *cerebellum*. The activities of the cerebellum are carried on below the level of consciousness. That is, you cannot choose the responses that the cerebellum will make. It coordinates muscle movements so that posture and balance can be maintained.

Midbrain and pons

Two smaller parts of the brain connect the spinal cord with the other areas of the brain. These two parts are called the midbrain and the pons.

Medulla oblongata

The medulla oblongata is the lowest portion of the brain. It tapers off into the spinal cord. The medulla oblongata regulates such important actions as breathing, heart action, and blood circulation. Nerve fibers from the upper brain pass through the medulla into the spinal cord.

The organs of the nervous system are well-protected against outside injury. But they are closely connected with all your other organs by the bloodstream. This makes it possible for infection to spread to the nervous system.

Nerve cells are called neurons. Each neuron has tiny "arms" that carry messages to and from the neuron.

Disorders of the nervous system

Epilepsy

Epileptic attacks, or seizures, are caused by irritation of nerve cells in the brain. In mild cases, a person briefly loses consciousness or has a blank stare for a few seconds. In severe cases, convulsions occur.

Anyone who suffers from epilepsy should be under a doctor's care. With good medical treatment, a patient may remain free from seizures. People with epilepsy look and feel normal between attacks. Since attacks can now be controlled, a person with epilepsy can lead a normal life.

Stroke

Strokes, or cerebral vascular accidents, are the third most frequent cause of death in the United States. Only heart disease and cancer cause more deaths. Strokes are rare in the young, but they often disable older people. Most people who have strokes have had high blood pressure. A study has shown that, in women between 45 and 54 years of age, strokes happen twice as often to cigarette smokers as to nonsmokers. A stroke occurs when the blood flow to an area of the brain is suddenly blocked. This blockage is usually caused by formation of a clot in a small blood vessel. As a result, the part of the body controlled by that area of the brain is partly or completely paralyzed. Frequently, speech is also affected. And, if the stroke is severe, it may cause unconsciousness or even death.

Nerves stretch from the top of the brain, out to the finger tips, and down to the toes. The nervous system makes one unbroken pathway to pick up and send information.

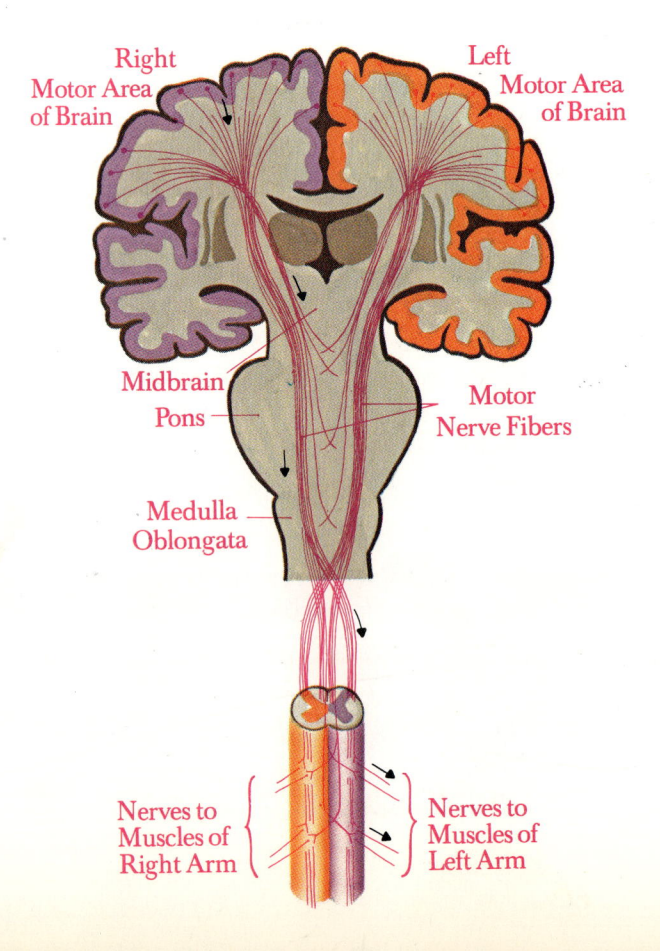

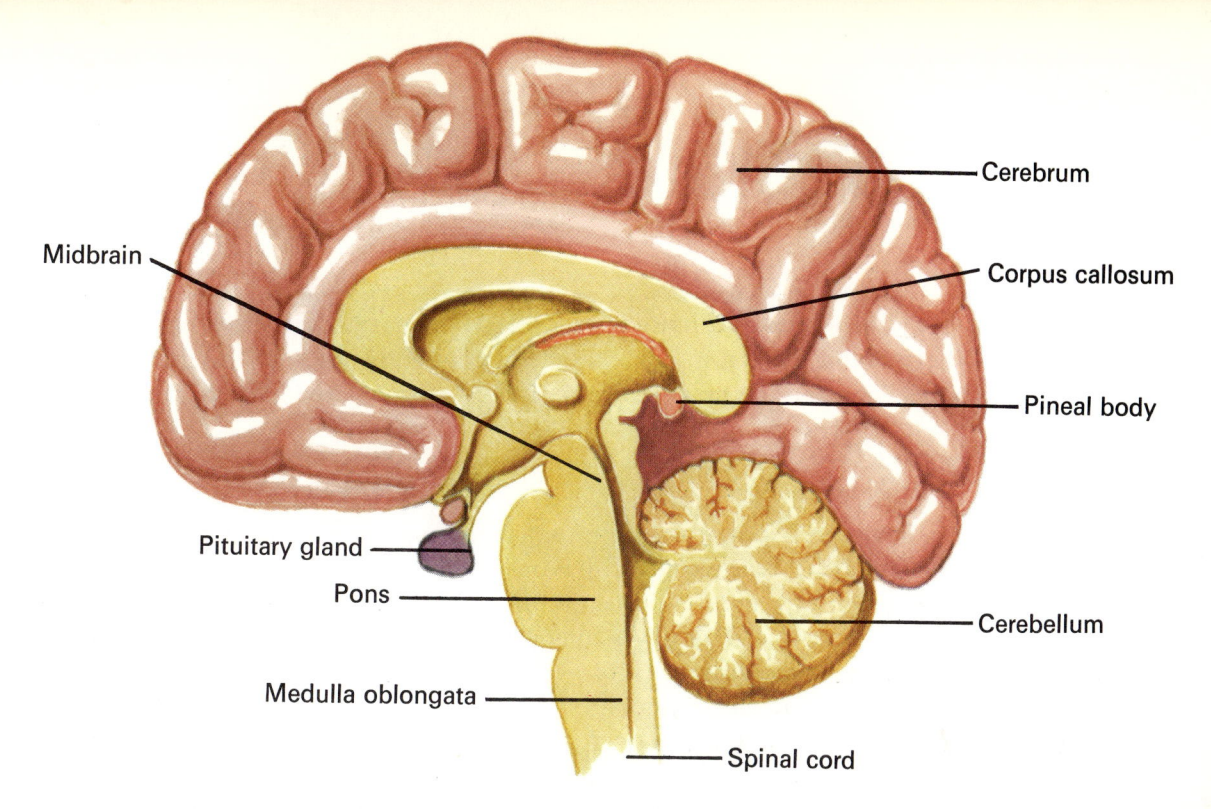

Brain diagram labels: Cerebrum, Corpus callosum, Pineal body, Cerebellum, Spinal cord, Medulla oblongata, Pons, Pituitary gland, Midbrain

Prompt medical treatment and physical therapy can greatly improve the condition of the stroke patient. Understanding and assistance from members of the family are also essential.

Meningitis

Meningitis is the inflammation of the membranes that surround the brain and spinal cord. Usually the inflammation is caused by a viral or bacterial infection. Meningitis is often a serious illness, and certain types are extremely contagious.

Multiple sclerosis

In multiple sclerosis, the covering that surrounds the nerves is destroyed. The symptoms depend on which nerves are damaged by the disease. Some cases may show loss of control of arm or leg movement. Other cases may show loss of vision or an unusual pattern of numbness. Multiple sclerosis may be caused by a slow-growing virus in the central nervous system.

Poliomyelitis

Poliomyelitis is caused by a virus that attacks nerve cells which control various groups of muscles. The result is paralysis of those muscles. Vaccinations to protect against polio have been developed in the past twenty years. Because so many people were successfully vaccinated, the once dreaded, crippling disease is now under control in the United States. However, not all children are being vaccinated against polio now. So there is always the chance of another epidemic. It has been estimated that over 15

Each part of the brain controls a different activity. The cerebrum controls movement. The left half of the cerebrum controls the movements of the right side of the body. The right half of the cerebrum controls the movements of the left side of the body.

149

million children are not protected from polio because they have not been vaccinated. Now some school systems are not allowing children to enter school until they have had all the vaccinations they need.

Taking care of your nervous system

Anything that happens anywhere in your body is likely to influence your nervous system in one way or another. Likewise, anything that influences your nervous system affects the rest of your body.

Protection

Nerve tissue is soft and can be damaged. Most nerve tissue is protected behind bones or within muscles. Extra care must be taken to prevent serious injuries to the central nervous system. Many head injuries in automobile accidents can be prevented if seat belts are worn and headrests are kept up. Spinal-cord injuries may happen in driving accidents or careless football tackling. Improper use of skateboards and trampolines may also cause permanent nerve injuries.

Food

A well-balanced diet should provide enough thiamine (Vitamin B) for the nervous system to function properly.

Oxygen

In order for you to think and act normally, the brain depends on the blood to provide it with a certain level of oxygen. The brain uses 25 percent of the oxygen you breathe in. Every minute, a pint of blood flows through your brain to carry in oxygen and food and to carry out wastes.

If the level of oxygen in the brain drops, a person may become confused and dizzy. If oxygen is not available for just half a minute (30 seconds) the person may lose consciousness. Eventually, the person may go into a coma or deep sleep. If the oxygen supply carried by the blood is cut off for five minutes, permanent brain damage results. For this reason, artificial respiration must be given immediately if someone stops breathing.

Drugs and poisons

Nerve cells are more sensitive to certain drugs and poisons than other body cells are. Alcohol and morphine, for example, act on the cells of the central nervous system. Other drugs relieve pain by blocking the path of the pain impulse to the brain.

Lead and arsenic may be poisonous to the central nervous system if large amounts are taken into the body. Young children who chew on objects that are covered with paint containing lead may develop permanent brain damage.

Rest and sleep

Since the nervous system must be working nonstop, a period of rest makes it work better. If you are worried or under emotional strain, the

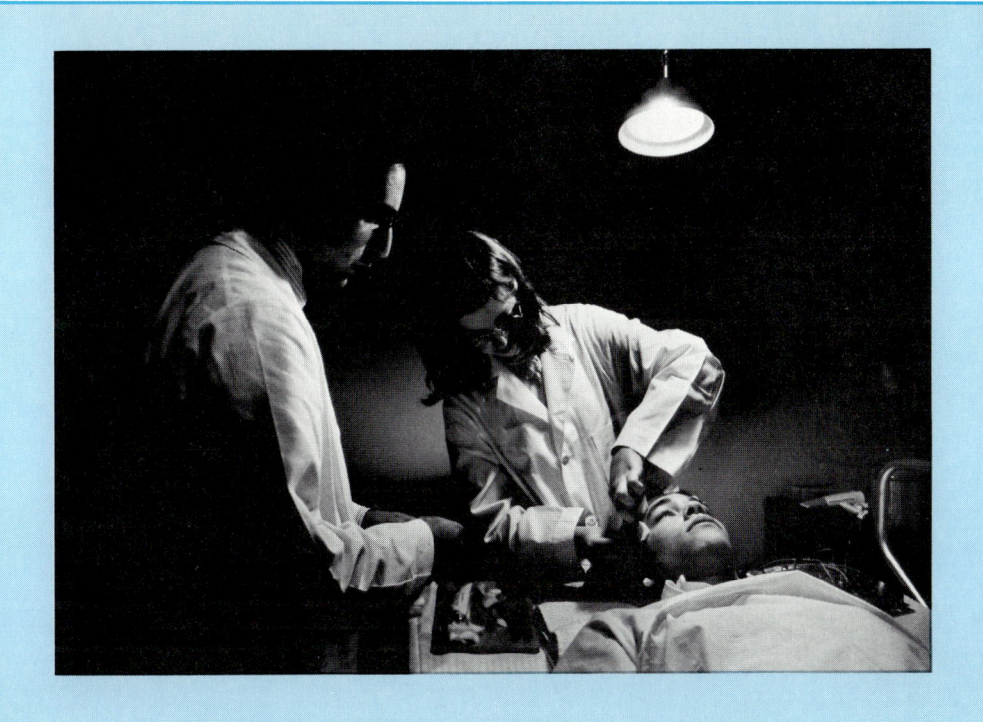

The Electroencephalograph and the EEG

The many neurons in your brain are constantly carrying impulses, so your nervous system is always working at a high level. These impulses may be recorded by a machine called an *electroencephalograph.* The electroencephalograph is used to record "brain waves" in a test called an *electroencephalogram,* or EEG. Small receivers attached to the machine are placed on the patient's scalp.

The EEG is a quick, painless test that can give a great deal of information to the doctor. Epilepsy is often discovered with the help of the EEG. The brain activity of someone in a severe coma can also be detected with an EEG. The EEG can be used to measure brain death in cases where the other functions of the body are being artificially supported.

extra nerve impulses may cause a feeling of tiredness. Boredom, excitement, extra weight, poor diet, and some illnesses may cause you to feel more tired than normal, too. People need a good night's sleep for their bodies to work properly. Sleep is such an important body activity that you will spend 30 percent of your life sleeping.

Your own body will help determine how much sleep you need. The amount of needed sleep and the patterns of sleep vary from person to person. Generally, eight hours a night are recommended. Many people do fine with less, but some people need more.

Did you ever notice that on the morning of a "special day" you may

Using the electroencephalograph, researchers have divided sleep into five stages. Dreaming takes place in the final stage, the "rapid eye movement" stage, called REM sleep.

get up earlier than usual and not feel that your sleep was cut off? Do you find yourself sleeping longer on the weekends? These are ways that your nervous system helps your body adapt. Did you ever have trouble waking up and then roll out of bed promising yourself that you'd get to bed early that night? That's a danger signal that you are shortchanging your body on the sleep it needs.

During the day, two opposite physical processes can relieve a feeling of tiredness: rest or exercise. Rest is more relaxing after physical activity. After a tense or confining situation—an examination, for example—jogging, a bicycle ride, a long walk, or other physical exercise would probably relax you.

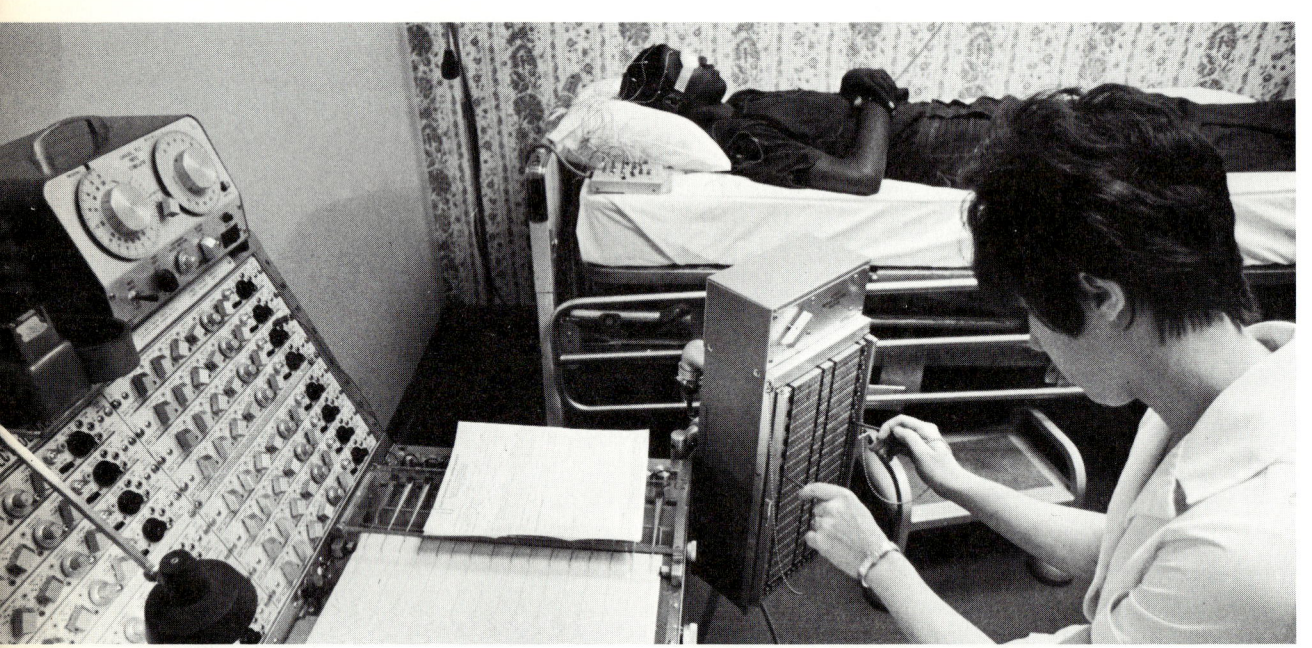

Something to think about . . .

Sleep is far more complex than people realize. With the aid of the electroencephalograph researchers have been able to divide sleep into five stages:

Stage 1. The muscles of the body begin to relax. Eyelids droop and the eyes roll from side to side.

Stage 2. Eye movement stops, but the muscle tone of the body remains.

Stages 3 and 4. Deep sleep goes on and there seems to be no dreaming.

Stage 5. Muscle tension increases in the jaw. But the rest of the body contracts strongly and then completely relaxes. Because the eyes move very rapidly, this stage is referred to as "rapid eye movement" sleep, or the REM stage. The movement of the eyes is thought to be related to the way you see your dreams. Because it is the time when you dream, the REM stage is thought to be very important for your health. When researchers repeatedly awakened sleepers just before they entered the REM stage, the sleepers became anxious and irritable.

The average person will go through the five different stages of sleep at least four to six times during the night.

Main Ideas

1. The nervous system is the communication network for the body. Through this network, the body acts on the mind and the mind acts on the body.
2. The nervous system also makes communication possible between human beings.
3. Reflexes and habits are similar. But habits are learned and reflexes are not.
4. Rest and sleep are important for your nervous system.

Key Words

anesthetic
autonomic nervous system
central nervous system
cerebellum
cerebrum
epilepsy
habit
meningitis
peripheral nervous system
reflex
spinal cord
stroke

Apply Your Knowledge

1. Explain how motor nerves are different from sensory nerves.
2. How do nerve cells carry information?
3. Explain how our reflexes protect us.
4. List four diseases that affect the nervous system.
5. If you are right-handed, which side of the brain is dominant? Explain why.
6. Give two examples of how the body structure protects the central nervous system.
7. Why is pain considered a warning?
8. Explain why constant tension and anxiety may be harmful to your nervous system.
9. Describe the actions of each area of the brain.

Extend Your Knowledge

1. How may a stroke be prevented?
2. Give some examples of drugs that may interfere with the activity of your nervous system.
3. Describe how a driver or passenger in a car may injure the central nervous system by not wearing a seat belt and not raising the headrest.
4. List some common reflexes that are used by athletes during sports activities.

Chapter 13

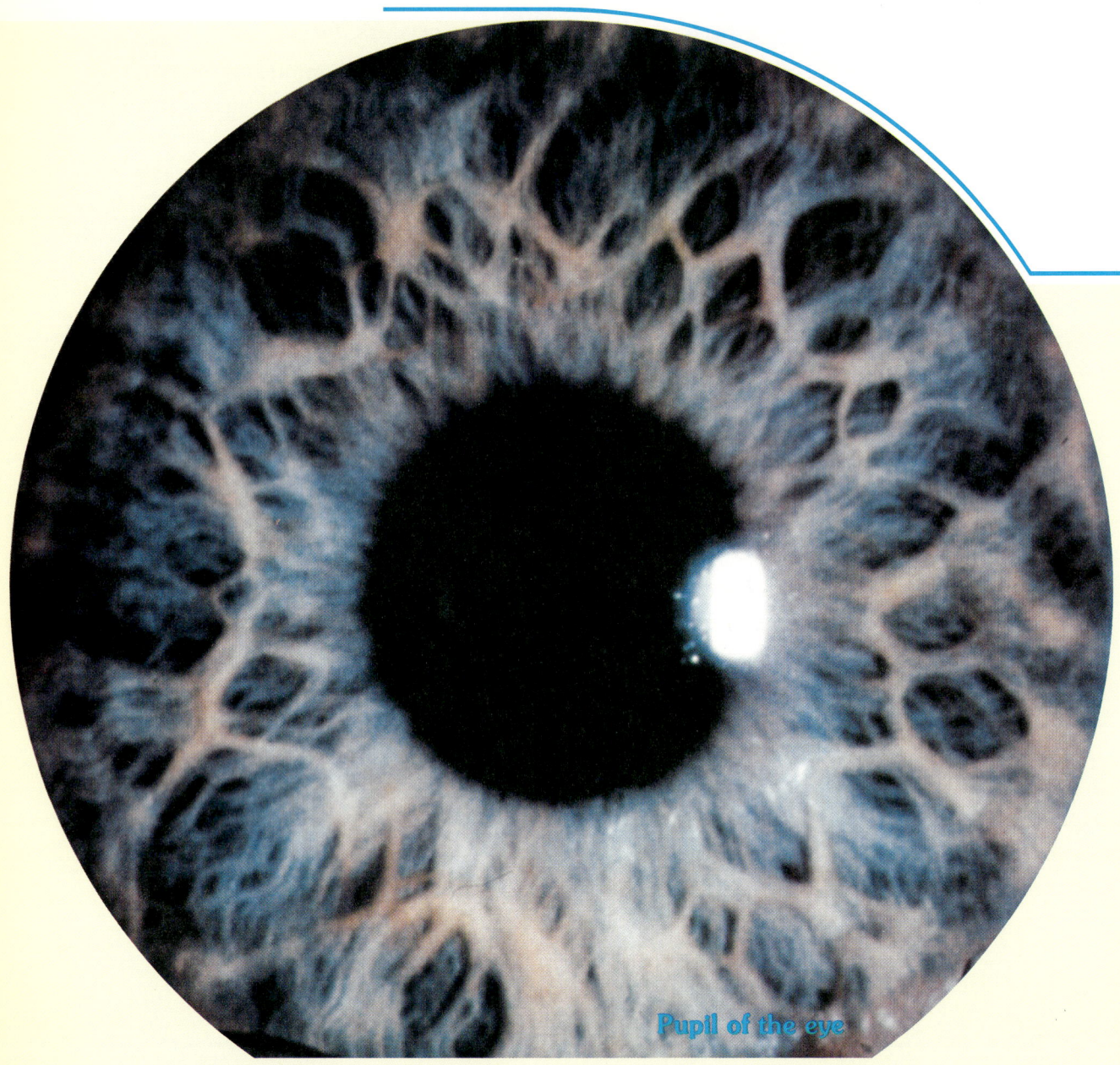

Pupil of the eye

Do you know . . .
- that your tears contain bactericide?
- the many advantages of contact lenses?
- why your eyes become tired?
- that you have a pathway from your throat to your ears?
- what causes hearing problems?
- which hearing disorders can be corrected?
- that the inner ear is also responsible for balance?

Eye and Ear Care

Your eyes and ears are the windows of the nervous system. Almost everything you know about the world you learn through your eyes and ears. Just consider how many things you have seen and heard since you got up this morning. Knowing more about your eyes and ears will help you take proper care of these important sense organs.

Structure and protection of the eye

The eyes are protected by seven bones in the face and skull. Each eye is also cushioned in a heavy padding of fat. The eyelids help to keep particles out of the eyes. Eyebrows shade the eyes and keep the flow of perspiration away.

The tear gland is about the size of an almond. It is found just above and toward the outer edge of the eye. Tears flow across the eye and drain through an opening near the corner of each eye. Then the tears flow into a duct in the nose where most of them evaporate. Tears contain bactericide, a fluid that kills bacteria and protects the eye against infection.

The six-million-dollar "camera"

The tough, white part of your eye is called the *sclera*. It gives the eyeball its shape. It is also the place where the muscles that move the eyeball are attached. The front part of the eyeball is called the *cornea*. It is transparent and lets light enter the eye. Many blood vessels beneath the sclera nourish the tissues of the eye. The *ciliary muscle* also lies beneath the sclera. It helps to change the shape of the lens in order to let you see things that are close to you. In front of the ciliary muscle is the colored *iris*. It controls the amount of light that enters the eye.

In bright light, the iris contracts, or gets smaller. This makes the round opening of the eye, called the *pupil,* get smaller. In dim light, the pupil becomes larger. Behind the iris is the clear *lens* that curves outward in front and in back. The lens bends the light rays so that they focus, or come together, on the inside lining of the eye called the *retina.* The retina has sensitive nerve cells that change the light rays into nerve impulses. These impulses are passed along the *optic nerve* to the brain centers that control vision.

The cornea and the lens bend light.

Light rays that come into the eye must be bent in just the right amounts to make a clear image on the retina. The lens is the most impor-

155

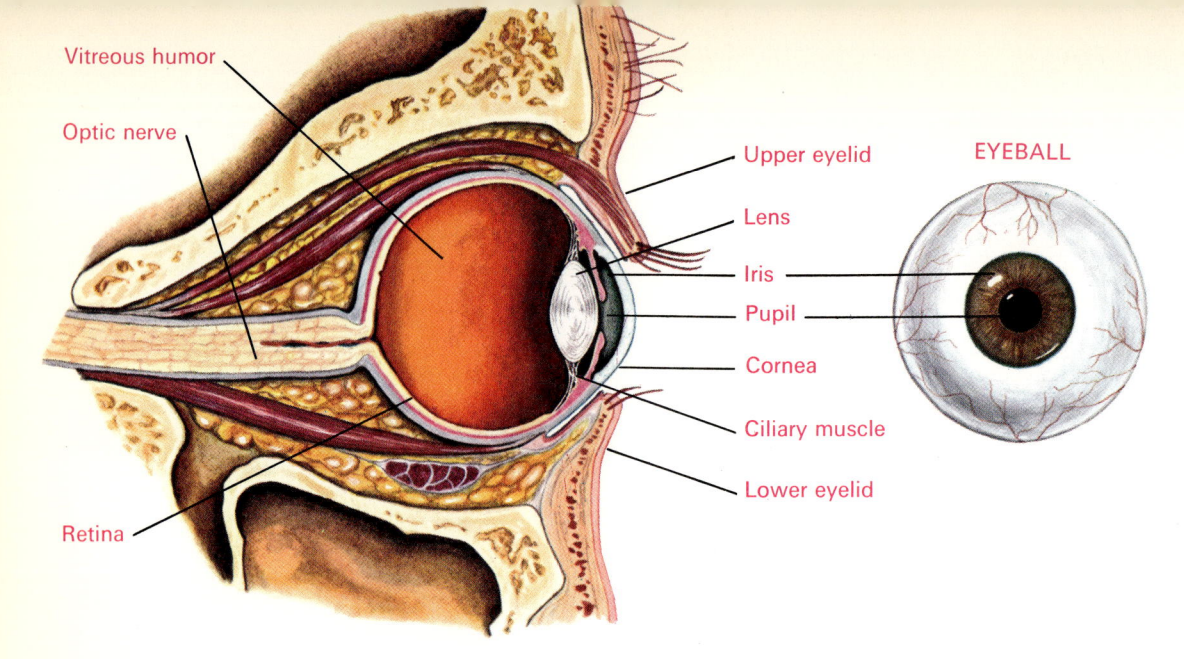

The eyelids and the bones around the eye protect the eye. Light goes into the eye through the pupil. Images are formed on the retina and are carried to the brain.

Visual problems

tant part of the eye for this work. The lens is attached to the eyeball by small muscles and ligaments.

When these muscles work, the lens becomes thicker or thinner as needed to make the light rays come together on the retina. This is called *accommodation*. Changes in the shape of the lens depend on how far an object is from the eye.

Visual problems may be caused by inherited defects in the shape of the eye. They may also be caused by disease, injury, or weakness of the eye muscles.

How can the shape of the eye cause normal or poor sight?

Most defective vision is caused by an eyeball that is not regular in shape. The retina may be too close or too far from the lens for light rays to focus on it. Or the lens or cornea may not be curved properly. This keeps the light rays from focusing in the right place.

If the eyeball is too long from front to back, the retina is too far from the lens. So objects from far away are blurred because the light rays from them focus in front of the retina instead of on it. Changes in the muscles of the eyes do not clear the blurred vision. But objects very close to the eyes can be seen clearly. This condition is called nearsightedness, or *myopia*. If the eyeball is too short from front to back, the retina is too close to the lens. Then objects nearby are blurred because light rays from them focus behind the retina. But far-off objects can be seen clearly. This condition is called farsightedness, or *hyperopia*.

In some people, the curved surfaces of the cornea and the lens are not regularly shaped. Light rays are not bent the same amount, so they do not form a clear image on the retina. This condition is called *astigmatism*.

Strabismus is caused by muscles that do not work together well.

Three pairs of muscles make each eyeball move. Usually, the muscles of both eyes work together. Sometimes, however, a defect in one muscle makes it pull harder than another. When this happens, one eye is pulled in one direction more than the other eye so that both eyes do not focus on the same object. This condition is a form of *strabismus* called crossed eyes. Crossed eyes cause double vision, or *diplopia*. After a time, the brain ignores the picture from one eye. If the picture from one eye is always ignored, that eye weakens. It then begins to lose its ability to see. This condition is called *amblyopia*, or dim vision. To make this eye see again, a patch is sometimes put over the good eye.

When one eye is more farsighted than the other, it must work harder to produce clear vision. If the strain is too great, the muscles that correct the farsightedness may stop working. Then the eye will not focus on a book or on other nearby objects. This may lead to strabismus. Strabismus seems to happen more often when a person is tired.

Strabismus should be corrected as early as possible to stop the loss of clear vision. Exercises, glasses, and surgery are all used to treat the condition.

A cataract is a cloudiness of the lens.

In older people, the lens of the eye sometimes becomes cloudy, causing blurred vision. This is called a *cataract*. Cataracts can be due to disease or radiation, but usually they are just due to aging. If the cataract interferes too much with seeing, the lens can be surgically removed. Afterward, contact lenses glasses can be worn, or a plastic lens can be put into the eye to replace the damaged lens. Cataract surgery is not considered to be very dangerous, and it usually works well in restoring vision.

Glaucoma is a dangerous eye disease that can be stopped.

If it is not found in its early stages, *glaucoma* can lead to total blindness. It is thought that about 2 million people in the United States have glaucoma. More than 67,000 people are legally blind because of it. Glaucoma is thought to be a disease of older people because its symptoms are often not seen until a person is older. However, the disease may begin early in life and get worse as one grows older.

Aqueous humor is the fluid that feeds the lens and cornea. In glaucoma, the tiny openings that let the aqueous humor flow out of the eyes are closed. This makes fluid pressure build up. The pressure causes damage to the optic nerve. Finally, the nerve is destroyed and vision is lost.

Glaucoma can be treated if it is found in its early stages. A doctor can give a treatment that lowers the pressure in the eye.

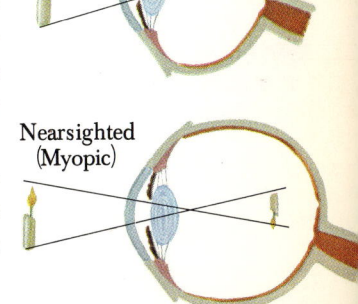

Normal

Farsighted (Hyperopic)

Nearsighted (Myopic)

With normal sight, the image of what you see forms directly on the retina. With farsightedness, the shape of the eyeball is too short. The image forms behind the retina and looks blurred. With nearsightedness, the shape of the eyeball is too long. The image forms in front of the retina and looks blurred.

Prevent Eye Strain

The muscles on the inside of the eyes and the outside of the eyeballs are always being used. This makes them tired.

1. When you read, write, sew, or do any kind of close work, make sure that you have plenty of light. Do not use a glaring light. The wrong kind of light can be as tiring as too little light.
2. If you read in bed, hold the book 36 to 42 centimeters (14 to 16 inches) in front of your eyes.
3. Don't read too much on a moving car or bus. Your eye muscles must always adjust to the motion.
4. When you read or study for a long time, rest your eyes often by looking at an object far away.
5. If you have eyeglasses—wear them!
6. If you notice any blurring of vision or foggy vision, tell your doctor.

Glasses or contact lenses?

If you wear glasses, it is important to keep them clean. Every bit of dirt on the lenses keeps out needed light. The frames also need care. Crooked frames may put the lenses out of line. It is very important for people with astigmatism to keep their glasses in top condition.

In the past, people chose to wear contact lenses to improve their appearance. But today, many people also use soft or hard contact lenses for better eyesight. The small, light contact lenses rest on the tear layer of the cornea. They do not change the size of the object being looked at. They also make it easier to see out of the sides of the eye. And they do not fog up with changes in the temperature outside. Contact lenses are used to improve eye problems such as astigmatism. People who have had cataracts are given contact lenses to correct farsightedness after surgery.

What will contact lenses of the future offer?

People who wear contact lenses want them to be more comfortable. They also want to be able to wear them longer. Today, new kinds of contact lenses are being developed. Some experimental lenses are made to be worn for many days without taking them out. New lenses made of silicone or special plastic are also being tested. These lenses allow the greatest possible amount of oxygen exchange with the cornea.

Avoid injuries to your eyes.

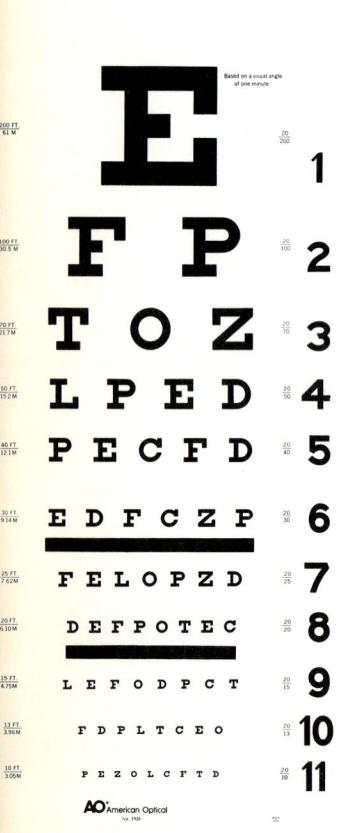

Any part of the eye may be injured. But the danger is greatest for the cornea. If you rub your eyes when you have particles in them, you may scratch the cornea. This could leave scars on the cornea. It is now possible to replace a scarred or cloudy cornea with a healthy cornea from another person's eye. This medical operation is called a corneal transplant. Sometimes people make wills leaving their corneas to medical science. They want to help others to see after they are gone. Sometimes, too, when people die suddenly in accidents, their families donate their corneas as a living memorial to them. Corneas that are donated are kept in eyebanks in some large cities. They are then ready for use when they are needed.

Damage to the retina is usually caused by changes inside the body. For example, people with high blood pressure or diabetes may have small blood vessels in the retina that bleed and blur their sight. Looking directly at the sun can also burn the retina and injure sight for life.

The use of sharp sticks, stones, and pointed toys by children can lead to serious eye injuries, or even blindness. Firecrackers sometimes cause loss of sight as well as painful body burns. Careless use of rifles, shotguns, and air rifles causes many cases of blindness in one or both eyes.

Little pieces of metal that are being filed, sawed, or ground may fly into the cornea, injuring it and causing scars. They may also damage the retina. Injuries can be prevented by wearing goggles or using protective screens while doing this kind of work.

Guard against chemical injuries to the eye.

Many household products, such as ammonia, liquid bleach, and cleaning agents, can cause serious damage to the eyes. Strong acid or alkali may cause lifelong harm. Before you use an aerosol spray, make sure the nozzle is pointed away from your eyes. If you should get any chemical in your eyes, wash your eyes again and again with water. As for any eye injury, get medical help as fast as possible.

Some substances, when taken into the body, may lead to blindness. Methyl alcohol, called wood alcohol, is one example. It should never be swallowed.

Remember: half of all blindness that occurs is preventable.

Infections can cause damage to the eyes.

Different parts of the eyes may become infected. Rubbing the eyes with dirty hands may put infectious organisms into them.

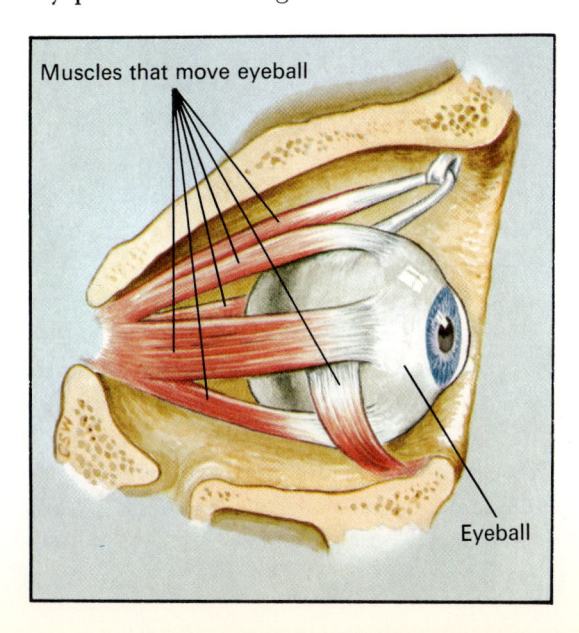

The action of three pairs of muscles moves the eye.

Swelling of the eyelid, or *blepharitis,* is caused by bacteria. The edges of the eyelids become swollen and scaly. The infected parts also may cause itching and burning. A doctor's attention is needed.

Another name for pinkeye is *conjunctivitis.* The conjunctiva is the mucous membrane that covers the front part of the eyeball and the inside surface of the eyelid. Conjunctivitis is an infection that causes the membrane to become red and to itch and burn. The eye also waters a great deal. Usually both eyes become infected. The upper and lower eyelids are often stuck together in the morning. Different bacteria, and sometimes viruses or allergies, cause conjunctivitis. When caused by bacteria or viruses, the infection may be contagious. Fast attention by a doctor is needed.

Tiny glands along the edge of the eyelids sometimes become infected. This causes a *sty.* Sties can be very painful. Redness, swelling, and pus that shows as a small yellow or white spot are common symptoms. Sties cannot be passed from one person to another. They usually take a week to go away.

Prevent Infections

1. Use only your own washcloths and towels.
2. Do not touch the area around your eyes with dirty hands.
3. Insert, remove, and clean contact lenses as directed. Wet contacts with the proper solution, not saliva.
4. Stop using eye cosmetics that cause irritation or redness. Make sure applicators for eye cosmetics are clean.

Have you had your eyes examined recently?

An eye examination includes both the examination of the eyes and a vision test. The vision test most often used is one in which the person stands 20 feet (6 meters) from an eye chart. On the chart are lines of letters in different sizes. If someone can read the letters that most people can read at 20 feet, the person is said to have 20/20 vision. If at 20 feet a person can read only the letters that people with normal vision can read at 40 feet (12 meters), the person has 20/40 vision. One use of a vision test is to find out if a person needs a complete eye examination. Some people may need eye examinations every few months. But others need them only every few years. People over age 35 should have an eye examination every year.

A doctor who specializes in the care and diseases of the eye is called an *ophthalmologist.* Ophthalmologists can give their patients medical treatment and prescribe glasses or contact lenses. The prescriptions for glasses or contact lenses are filled by an *optician.* The optician grinds the lenses and makes the glasses.

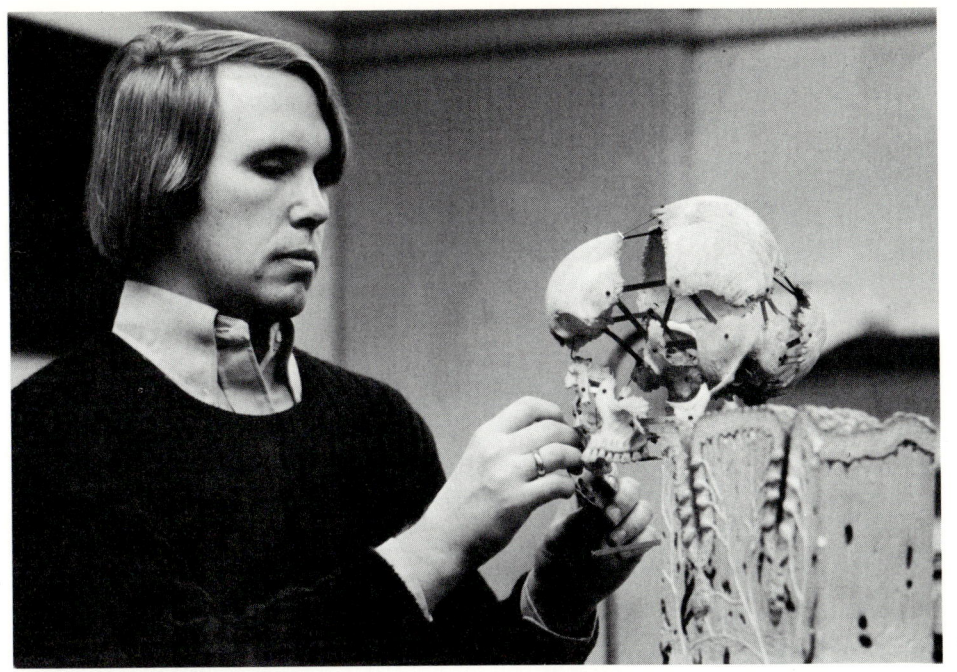

On May 27, 1976, 26-year-old David Hartman received a doctorate in medicine from Temple University in Philadelphia, Pa. Dr. Hartman, blinded by glaucoma when he was 8, was the first sightless person to graduate from an American medical school since 1872.

Education of blind and visually handicapped people

Other specialists who give eye examinations are called *optometrists*. They are not medical doctors, but they have been trained to make measurements and to fit glasses and contact lenses. When eye disease or injury is suspected, patients should be referred to an ophthalmologist.

In the United States, there are about 500,000 legally blind people. There are also more than 11 million others who are visually handicapped. Students who have a sight problem may join a class directed by a teacher who is specially trained. They may also take part in regular classes for some subjects. Or they may enroll in a regular class and get extra help from a special teacher.

Students with sight problems often use textbooks printed in large type. Books that do not come in large type may be listened to on records or tapes. People who have serious sight problems are often taught touch typing. Also, their listening skills are trained so that they depend less upon their eyes for learning.

Blind people are often taught to read and write in Braille. Braille is a language that is read by touch. Paper is punched with sharp instruments into patterns of raised dots. The dots stand for the letters of the alphabet. Blind people read by moving their fingers over these patterns. Many textbooks are translated into Braille to be used by blind students.

With the learning resources available today, blind students can do most of the things their sighted friends can do. Often their other senses are much sharper. They may also have a strong will to achieve and to become fully independent. These assets can lead them to overcome obstacles and to succeed in a wide range of careers.

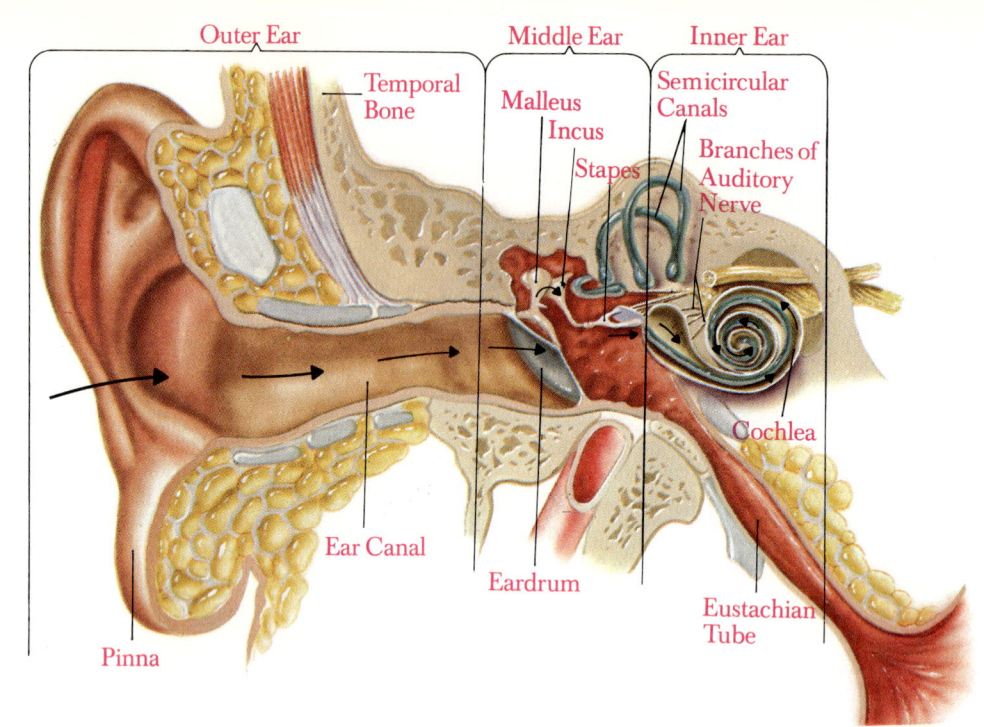

The outer ear picks up sound waves and sends them across the middle ear and into the inner ear. Nerve endings in the inner ear pick up the sound waves as nerve impulses and carry them to the brain. In the brain, the impulses are understood as sounds. The ear not only allows you to hear, it helps you keep your balance as well.

Protection and structure of the ear

Do you like listening to music? Can you imagine what your life would be like if you could not hear any sound? Your hearing plays an important role in helping you to adjust to your surroundings. Sounds let you judge the distances of objects and warn you of any danger. Of all the senses of the body, hearing is the last to disappear when you fall asleep. It is also the first sense to be aroused when you wake up.

Besides carrying or moving sound, the inner part of the ear controls balance, or equilibrium.

The ear is organized into three parts: the external (or outer) ear, the middle ear, and the inner ear.

The external ear picks up sound waves.

Cats, horses, and other lower animals can move their outer ears enough to direct sound waves into the ear canal. Humans, however, cannot move their ears in this way. The external auditory (ear) canal is S-shaped and goes about 2.5 centimeters (1 inch) into the temporal bone. This auditory canal has many wax-producing glands. The wax and the many hairs that line the canal stop foreign objects from getting into the deeper part of the auditory canal.

The thin skin that lines the external auditory canal also lines the eardrum. Therefore, an infection of the auditory canal can spread easily to the eardrum. Do not use any hard instruments, such as match sticks or hairpins, to clean wax out of the ears. The wax can be removed from the ear with a damp cloth. Too much wax buildup should be removed by a doctor.

The middle ear sends sounds into the inner ear.

The middle ear is a small, drumlike cavity in the skull. It is found just inside the external auditory canal. The membrane that separates the middle ear from the outer ear is called the *eardrum*. Three tiny, movable bones go across the middle-ear cavity. They are named according to their shape: the hammer (*malleus*), anvil (*incus*), and stirrup (*stapes*). These bones amplify vibrations, or sound waves, as they travel from the eardrum to the oval window of the inner ear.

The *eustachian tube* connects the middle ear with the back of the nose and throat. The tube opens into the middle ear and lets air into it. This balances the air pressure on both sides of the eardrum. When you swallow, the eustachian tubes open and adjust the air pressure in the middle ear. Riding in a fast elevator may cause an unpleasant feeling in the ears. This feeling is caused by the sudden change in pressure on the outside of your eardrums. Swallowing or yawning opens the eustachian tubes and lets the pressure inside the ears become the same as the pressure outside.

Most hearing defects in young people are caused by infections that reach the middle ear through the eustachian tubes. Swelling in the middle ear interferes with hearing by keeping the bones from moving. Many infections of the middle ear may thicken the membranes and lower their ability to carry sound waves.

If an abscess (a buildup of pus) forms in the ear and breaks the eardrum, hearing may be harmed seriously. But if the break is small and on one side, the eardrum may still be able to move when sound waves strike it.

Often, you can stop ear infections from becoming big problems by quickly getting medical help. A doctor can prescribe antibiotics (drugs that kill infectious organisms) or make an opening in the eardrum to drain the infectious fluids. This can greatly reduce the potential damage done by middle-ear infections.

The inner ear is made up of the cochlea, vestibule, and semicircular canals.

The inner ear lies in the solid bone of the skull. It is located behind the top of the nose. The *cochlea*, which looks like a snail shell, is filled with liquid. It contains nerve endings from the auditory nerve. When sound waves strike the eardrum, the three bones of the middle ear move. The stapes rocks back and forth against the membrane of the oval window of the inner ear. This starts waves of motion in the cochlea. These waves then start impulses that are transmitted by the auditory nerve to the brain. In the brain, the nerve impulses are understood as sounds.

Sound waves may also reach the inner ear through the bones of the skull. If you were to put the handle of a vibrating tuning fork between your teeth, the sound would be carried through the bones of the skull.

The *vestibule* is found between the cochlea and the semicircular canals. When the head is held to one side, gravity causes tiny solid particles inside the vestibule to touch nerve cells. These nerve cells carry impulses to the brain. The impulses let you figure out the position of your head in relation to gravity.

The *semicircular canals* control balance. These three small canals lie at right angles to each other. Each canal is filled with fluid and has nerve endings that connect to a part of the auditory nerve. Changing the position of the head changes the pressure of the fluid in the canals. This sets up the nerve impulses that tell you how to keep your balance.

Unusual disturbance of the fluids in the semicircular canals causes dizziness. Seasickness, car sickness, and air sickness are mostly caused by the effect of motion upon the semicircular canals.

Hearing disorders

More than 16 million people in the United States have hearing disorders. Most people can hear a wide variety of sounds, from high to low and from soft to loud. The sounds used in everyday speech are not very high or very low. The loudness of any sound is measured in decibels. Normal hearing means being able to hear speech sounds as low as 15 decibels (whispering). Unfortunately, there are over 3 million children who cannot hear even a loud conversation.

An instrument called an audiometer is used to measure a person's ability to hear. With an audiometer, a trained person can find out how loud a sound must be before the person being tested can hear it. People who have hearing problems should see an ear specialist to find the cause. An *audiologist* can test your ears for hearing problems. An *otologist* is a doctor who specializes in the care of the ears.

Hearing disorders are grouped into three major types: conductive loss, nerve loss, and central loss.

Conductive loss is caused by any block to the passage of sound waves through the outer or middle ear. Some causes are these:

1. too much wax or an infection in the external auditory canal;
2. an eardrum that is torn or inflamed;
3. broken or joined malleus, incus, or stapes, which stops movement;
4. thick fluid in the middle ear.

One of the most common causes of conductive loss in young adults is *otosclerosis* (*oto* = ear / *sclerosis* = hardening). In this disease, the stapes becomes joined to the oval window by a spongy growth of bone. Then the stapes cannot rock back and forth against the membrane of the oval window. When this happens, sound cannot be transmitted well.

Most deaf people are not totally deaf. They can hear loud sounds and can understand what people say when people speak slowly and clearly. In such cases, hearing aids that make sounds louder can be useful.

Medical operations for correcting and repairing torn eardrums, joined bones, and other causes of conductive loss have improved. More people now are able to get back their hearing through operations.

Nerve loss is caused by damage to the special sensory cells in the cochlea. The cells can be damaged in many ways:

1. allergic reaction to drugs, such as antibiotics;
2. loud environmental noises;
3. rubella virus, or German measles, caught from the mother by the unborn child;
4. infection spreading from the middle ear to the area near the cochlea.

Once a sensory cell is damaged in the cochlea, no medical operation can correct it. Hearing aids help many people with nerve loss. An otologist can discover the person's problem and a hearing health professional can fit the right kind of hearing aid.

Central loss is caused by damage to the auditory nerve that leads to the brain from the cochlea. It is also caused by damage to the brain center for hearing. If the brain center is injured, no matter how well the sound is carried by the eardrum, bones, and sensory cells, the brain cannot figure it out. Luckily, central loss is rare.

Will aging affect hearing?

As people grow older, changes take place in their inner ears. These changes make it impossible for older people to hear as well as they did when they were younger. The ability to hear high tones is the type of hearing most affected by age. Many people who have poor hearing do not know that they cannot hear well. Others may not admit that they have a hard time hearing. In either case, serious problems can develop when people feel left out of what is happening around them. Older people who cannot hear

The American Humane Association has come to the aid of people with hearing problems. The solution: a hearing ear dog. After three months of special training, a dog of any size, breed, or mix can alert its owner to noises that the person is unable to hear.

well may also have a harder time taking care of their basic needs. Hearing aids can often help them to communicate better.

How to protect your valuable ears

The major cause of defective hearing in young people is infection that travels up the eustachian tubes into the middle ears. Therefore, it is important to protect yourself against diseases that enter through the nose and throat. Learn to blow your nose gently so that tiny organisms will not be forced up into your ears. When you swim, keep from getting water into your nose. If you have a cold, do not go swimming. If you have a damaged eardrum or other ear problems, ask your doctor's advice about swimming or traveling in an airplane. Have your doctor remove any extra wax in the ears. And don't put anything smaller than your elbows into your ears.

Noisy surroundings may damage your ears. The risk can be lowered by taking a "quiet break" from a noisy environment every 30 minutes. Try wearing ear plugs when such breaks are not possible.

Something can be done about most cases of defective hearing if they are discovered early. Have your hearing tested regularly. If a defect is found, get the best possible medical help at once.

Most cases of defective hearing can be helped if they are discovered early. Have your hearing checked regularly.

Education of the deaf

Most people learn to speak by imitating the way other people sound. Deaf people cannot hear others talk. They also can't hear the sound of their own voices. Despite this fact, people with little or no hearing can learn to speak well enough to be understood. Deaf people can also commu-

If you use a portable radio or tape player with headphones, be careful not to play it too loud. Some doctors believe that headphones can cause permanent hearing loss if played at 90 decibels for more than 4 hours a day. Also, be aware that wearing headphones can make you dangerously inattentive to your environment.

nicate by using a hand alphabet. They can understand and speak to others in a language that spells out words or phrases with fingers and hands. Certain positions of the fingers and hands stand for letters, words, or ideas. Deaf people can also learn to understand the speech of others by watching lip movements. The study of speech reading should be started early. Mothers and fathers of deaf babies can learn to teach speech reading to their children while they are very young.

Rubella is the scientific name for German measles. It is a mild disease, caused by a virus that produces symptoms of fever and rashes. The rash first appears on the face and scalp, then spreads to the arms and body. The rash gradually disappears after two or three days.

Fortunately, the rubella virus causes little discomfort and few complications. Many people do not even realize that they have the disease. But rubella can be very dangerous for a pregnant woman. The virus can easily enter her bloodstream and pass through the placenta. It can then disrupt the growth process of the developing embryo or fetus.

Although the virus is potentially dangerous at all stages of an unborn child's development, the danger is greatest during the first trimester (three months) of pregnancy. The virus can attack many developing organs, such as the heart, eyes, and brain. If, by chance, the virus attacks the embryo at the time when the ears are forming, there is a high risk that the child will be born deaf.

Something to think about . . .

To reduce the chance that susceptible pregnant women may be exposed to rubella, a greater effort is required by all parents to have their children immunized. But the rubella vaccine virus, itself, may have an adverse effect on the developing fetus. So the vaccine is never given to pregnant women or to women who may become pregnant within two months of vaccination. However, a simple blood test can tell a woman whether or not she has already had rubella. People who have had rubella are naturally immune to the disease.

Main Ideas

1. In order to see well, the eyes must be in perfect working order, or corrective lenses should be used.
2. Visual problems may be caused by disease or by defects.
3. Most eye injuries are caused by carelessness and neglect.
4. The ear is an important organ for balance as well as for hearing.
5. Most middle-ear infections happen when bacteria travel through the eustachian tube.
6. Unlike conductive loss, nerve loss cannot be corrected by a medical operation.
7. Regular hearing tests may help in preventing serious hearing defects.

Key Words

accommodation	diplopia	optic nerve
amblyopia	eardrum	optometrist
aqueous humor	eustachian tube	otologist
astigmatism	glaucoma	otosclerosis
audiologist	hyperopia	pupil
blepharitis	incus	retina
cataract	iris	rubella
central loss	lens	sclera
ciliary muscle	malleus	semicircular canals
cochlea	myopia	stapes
conductive loss	nerve loss	strabismus
conjunctivitis	ophthalmologist	sty
cornea	optician	vestibule

Apply Your Knowledge

1. What is the job of the ciliary muscles? How can you rest these muscles?
2. What is the job of the muscles on the surface of the sclera?
3. List five structures that help to protect the eyes.
4. Explain why tears are important. Trace the flow of tears from the tear gland.
5. How does the lens change for near and far vision?
6. What does 20/70 on a vision test mean?
7. What is the shape of the eyeball in farsightedness? What is its shape in nearsightedness? How do lenses help to correct these defects?
8. Explain the work of an ophthalmologist, an optometrist, and an optician.
9. How is myopia different from astigmatism?
10. Explain what happens in glaucoma.
11. What is the major difference between a sty and conjunctivitis?
12. Describe the path of sound waves from the time they enter the ear until they become nerve impulses that reach the brain.
13. How is the eustachian tube related to deafness?
14. What is the job of the semicircular canals?
15. What is the major difference between conductive loss and nerve loss?
16. Explain how deaf people communicate.
17. Discuss how you can prevent hearing problems.

Extend Your Knowledge

1. If the aqueous humor is not secreted in large enough amounts, what do you think can happen to the eye?
2. If you had to choose between losing your vision or losing your hearing, which would you choose? Why?
3. Learn how to use Braille or the hand alphabet, and show your class how the method works.
4. Obtain a decibel meter from your local health department. Check the decibel levels of the sounds in your school.
5. An insect has entered your external auditory canal. What should you do?
6. If your eustachian tube is blocked and you decide to go skiing, explain some of the problems you may have.
7. Stand on your toes, stretch out your arms in front of you, and then close your eyes. Can you stand in this position without moving for 30 seconds? Try it!

Chapter 14

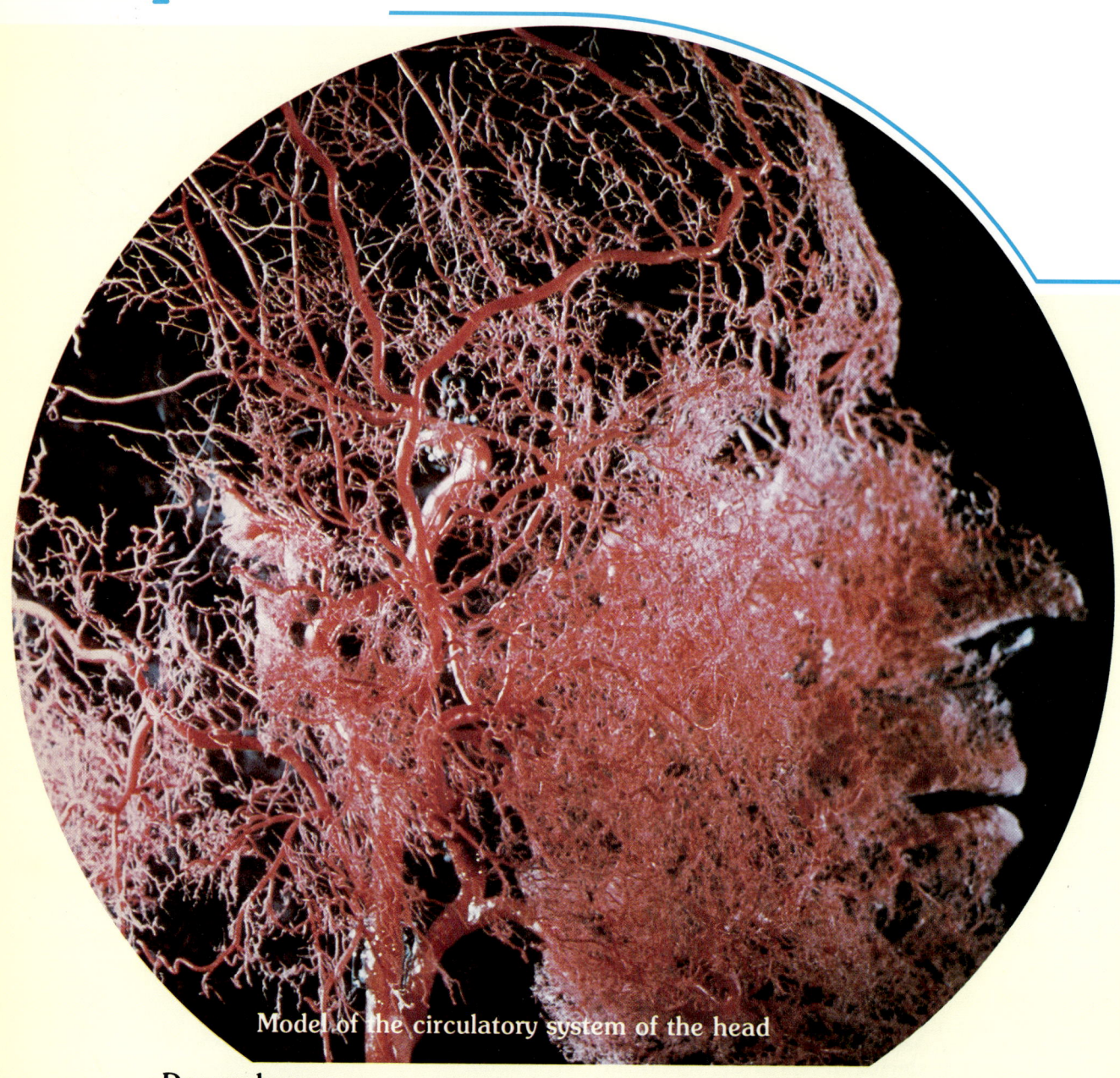

Model of the circulatory system of the head

Do you know . . .
- what makes blood red?
- why high blood pressure is dangerous?
- what is the leading cause of death in the United States?
- how people can lower their chances of getting a heart attack?
- how many times the heart beats in 24 hours?

Transport System

Blood is the transport system of your body. Blood is a fluid tissue made up of plasma, red blood cells, white blood cells, and colorless cells called platelets. *Plasma* is the liquid part of blood. It is 91 percent water mixed with salts and proteins. The red blood cells, white blood cells, and platelets float inside the plasma. The average adult has about 6 liters (6 quarts) of blood in the circulatory system. When the human body is at rest, blood travels around it once every minute.

The pumping action of the heart keeps the blood moving throughout your whole body. With it, blood carries all the things your body needs to live. For example, blood carries digested food from the digestive tract. It carries oxygen from the lungs to all parts of the body. It carries waste products back from body cells to the kidneys, the lungs, and the skin. Blood also sends hormones to different parts of the body. And it helps fight infections by clotting when you are injured. Clotting stops the loss of too much blood. In addition to these functions, blood carries heat to all parts of your body, to warm you. And it carries any medicine you take to the part of your body that needs it.

Red cells

Your blood

The blood in a human body has about 30 trillion red blood cells. Placed side by side, these cells could cover an area about as large as a football field.

Red blood cells are the oxygen carriers in blood. They contain a substance called *hemoglobin* which picks up oxygen in the lungs and carries it to all parts of the body. The red color of blood is caused by the hemoglobin. When hemoglobin is carrying oxygen inside the red blood cells, the blood becomes bright red. When blood reaches the tissues of the body, hemoglobin lets go of the oxygen and gives it to the cells to use. Then the hemoglobin changes back to a bluish-red color. Blood that has a lot of oxygen is red. Blood with less oxygen is bluish.

Red blood cells are always being formed in the bone marrow—the soft, inner part of bone. Red blood cells live only about four months. Worn-out cells are destroyed in the spleen and the liver. In the time that it takes you to read this sentence, about 15 million red blood cells in your body will die. And about 15 million new ones will be formed.

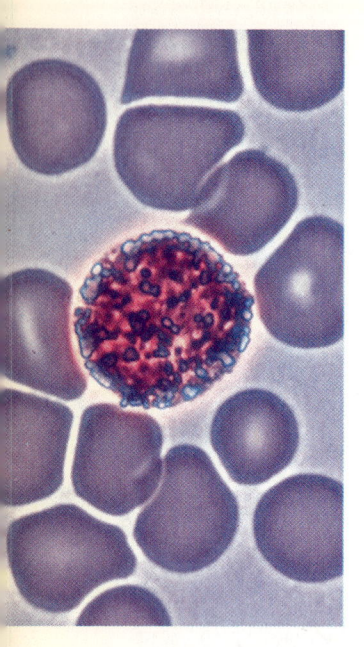

The large cell is a white blood cell. The smaller cells are red blood cells. All are magnified 400 times.

White cells

White blood cells are also made in the bone marrow. They are larger than red cells, but there are fewer of them. White blood cells work to fight infection. These white cells squeeze between the cells in the walls of the tiniest blood vessels, or capillaries, and enter the body's tissues. When bacteria or viruses enter the body, white cells collect in large numbers around them. White cells surround the disease organisms and eat them up. They also can take in polluted particles that stick to the lungs and can even slowly break up splinters. But if a white cell takes in more disease organisms than it can handle, it dies. The yellow pus found in some infections is really a mixture of dead white cells, active white cells, and disease organisms.

A doctor can often tell whether or not someone has an infection by counting the number of white blood cells in a tiny drop of the patient's blood. When there is an infection in the body, the bone marrow makes more white blood cells to fight against the infection.

Some infections, especially virus infections, lower the number of white blood cells instead of increasing them. Certain drugs may also lower the number of white cells in a person who is sensitive to these drugs. When such a person takes the drugs, many white cells may be killed off. Because of this reaction, it is hard for the person to fight infection. Then, any minor illness, even a sore throat, could be deadly. That is why drugs should never be taken without the direct order of a doctor.

Platelets

Platelets are smaller than red blood cells, and there are fewer of them in the blood. When you bleed, platelets help to form a clot that stops the bleeding. The clot then hardens into a scab that covers the wound. This covering helps prevent infection.

Anemia

Anemia is a disease that is present when the blood lacks either hemoglobin, red blood cells, or both. This means the body cells of an anemic person do not get enough oxygen. Less oxygen causes someone with anemia to get tired very quickly. It also causes an anemic person to get out of breath easily.

The main cause of anemia is not enough hemoglobin. Another cause is a diet without enough iron, the mineral needed to make hemoglobin. Infections may cause anemia and may stop the body from making hemoglobin. Loss of blood from a wound can cause a drop in plasma and red blood cells for a time. This can also result in anemia. When this happens, a person becomes thirsty and drinks a lot of liquid to make up for the fluid that was lost. The bone marrow also forms new blood cells to replace those that were lost. Loss of blood from internal bleeding may be another cause of anemia. One sign of bleeding inside the body could be dark or black bowel movements. Iron capsules taken to treat anemia may also cause dark or black bowel movements temporarily.

Leukemia

A white blood cell is called a *leukocyte*. When there is a great increase in the number of white blood cells, the disease called *leukemia* may be present. Sometimes, white blood cells may grow to ten or more times the usual number. The cause of leukemia is not known. But scientists think the disease is a cancer of the white blood cells. This disease is mostly found in young people and causes many deaths each year.

Researchers are trying to develop a cure for leukemia. The use of certain drugs, X-ray treatments, or both can slow down the growth of the disease. When the disease is slowed down, life lasts longer. With the right treatment, more than 75 percent of the people who have leukemia live through the first year of the sickness. And some people with leukemia now live for five years or longer.

Some kinds of leukemia are less serious than others. Some people live for a long time with chronic leukemia. Scientists are making an ongoing study to find treatments that will control or cure leukemia.

Hemophilia

Some diseases make the blood clot too slowly or not at all. One such disease is *hemophilia*. A person with hemophilia can bleed to death very easily. The slightest bump or scrape can cause a dangerous problem for anyone who has this disease.

People with hemophilia sometimes bleed inside the body, especially into the joints. And even a small operation may be serious for a person who has a clotting problem. This is why every patient's blood is tested for clotting before operations are done.

Hemophilia is an inherited disease, passed on to children by their parents. Hemophilia is found mostly in males. But luckily, it is not a common disease. If a hemophiliac is hurt, a clotting factor (a medicine that causes blood to clot) is given to help stop the bleeding.

Blood types

Human blood falls into four major classes, or blood types: A, B, AB, and O. About 4 percent of Americans have type AB; 10 percent have type B; and about 45 percent have type O and 41 percent type A. The same types of blood are found in both sexes and in all races of humans. Blood of one type will mix safely with blood of the same type. And some blood types may mix with two or three other types. For example, type O has been known as the "universal donor" blood. Type O can be given to people with almost any of the other blood types. It used to be thought that AB could mix with blood of any other type. But problems were discovered.

Today, before a doctor transfers blood from one person to another, the kinds of blood that will mix safely must be determined through testing. If a wrong blood type is given, the blood cells in the donated blood clump

A white blood cell acts quickly. It can attack and kill a germ in 70 seconds or less.

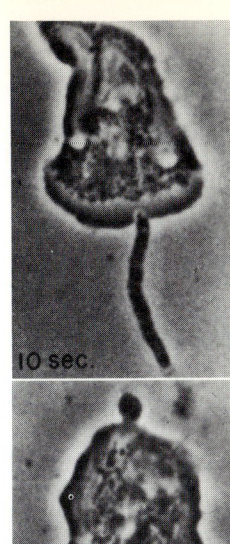

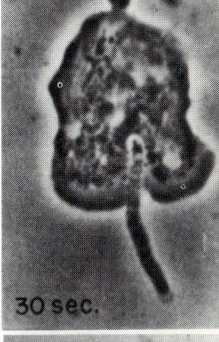

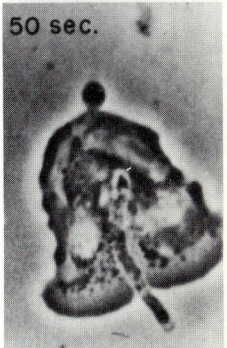

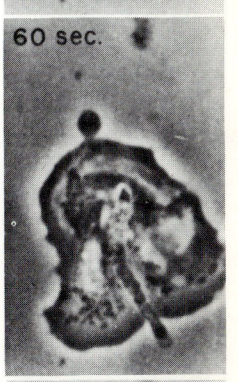

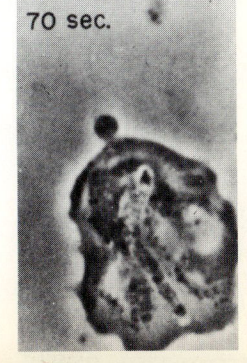

together. When this happens, the person getting the new blood becomes very ill—and sometimes dies.

Rh factor

Many people have a substance called the Rh factor in their red blood cells. Blood that has the Rh factor is called Rh-positive. Blood that does not have the Rh factor is called Rh-negative. About 85 percent of the population has Rh-positive blood, while 15 percent has Rh-negative. Rh-positive blood should not be given in a tranfusion to a person who has Rh-negative blood. The Rh-negative blood may react against the new blood.

The Rh factor sometimes becomes very important during pregnancy. When the first baby is expected, both parents should have a blood test for the Rh factor. A newborn baby with Rh-positive blood may have a blood reaction with an Rh-negative mother.

During the delivery, the baby's blood and the mother's blood may mix slightly. Since the mother does not carry any Rh factor, the baby's Rh factor is foreign to her. So the mother will develop antibodies to fight against the foreign substance. These antibodies do not hurt the first Rh-positive child that an Rh-negative mother has. But they do begin to destroy the blood of the second child. If a doctor thinks there is an Rh problem, the doctor may take steps to protect the baby.

Luckily, there is a medicine an Rh-negative mother can take after her first pregnancy that will stop her from forming antibodies against the baby's blood. But the mother must take the drug after every pregnancy, whether or not the pregnancy ends with the birth of a baby.

Blood banks

There are blood banks in most cities. Blood of all types is collected from healthy donors and stored under refrigeration. Blood banks store whole blood, that is, the plasma and blood cells. Whole blood can be kept for only a few weeks under ordinary refrigeration. But it may be kept for much longer if it is frozen.

Whole blood may be divided into parts that can be given separately in transfusions. Plasma, packed red blood cells, platelets, and gamma globulin (a protein in blood plasma) are the main parts of blood that are used in transfusions.

A blood transfusion is the transfer of blood from the blood vessels of one person into those of another. Someone who gives blood is called a *donor*. The blood received by the patient in a transfusion takes the place of blood that has been lost. It gives the person red cells to carry oxygen. The donor's blood stays in the body of the person who gets it for only a few days. By then, the person is usually able to make new blood.

The role of lymph

Lymph is the clear, liquid part of the blood that washes all the cells of the body. It comes mostly from blood plasma that has passed through the capillary walls. Lymph moves along the lymph vessels as it is squeezed and pushed by contractions of muscles and blood vessels around it. Valves in the lymph vessels keep the lymph from flowing backward.

Everything that the cells need for their work is carried by the lymph from the bloodstream. Digested foods, vitamins, and minerals picked up from the small intestine, oxygen from the lungs, and hormones from the endocrine glands are all brought by the lymph to the cells. Wastes from the body cells are carried by the lymph to the veins. Then the blood in the veins carries the wastes to organs in the body that excrete, or get rid of, them.

Lymph nodes

Along the lymph vessels are small structures called *lymph nodes.* The lymph nodes form some of the white blood cells in the blood. The lymph nodes also kill off disease organisms that enter the lymph vessels. When an infection starts in the body, the nearest lymph nodes act as filters to take out and destroy the disease organism. In doing so, the lymph nodes sometimes become bigger and feel sore. Infection in the leg causes swelling of the lymph nodes in the groin, the area where the legs join the trunk. Infection in the arm causes swelling of the nodes in the armpit. Infection at the root of the teeth, or in the nose and throat, causes swelling of the lymph nodes in the neck.

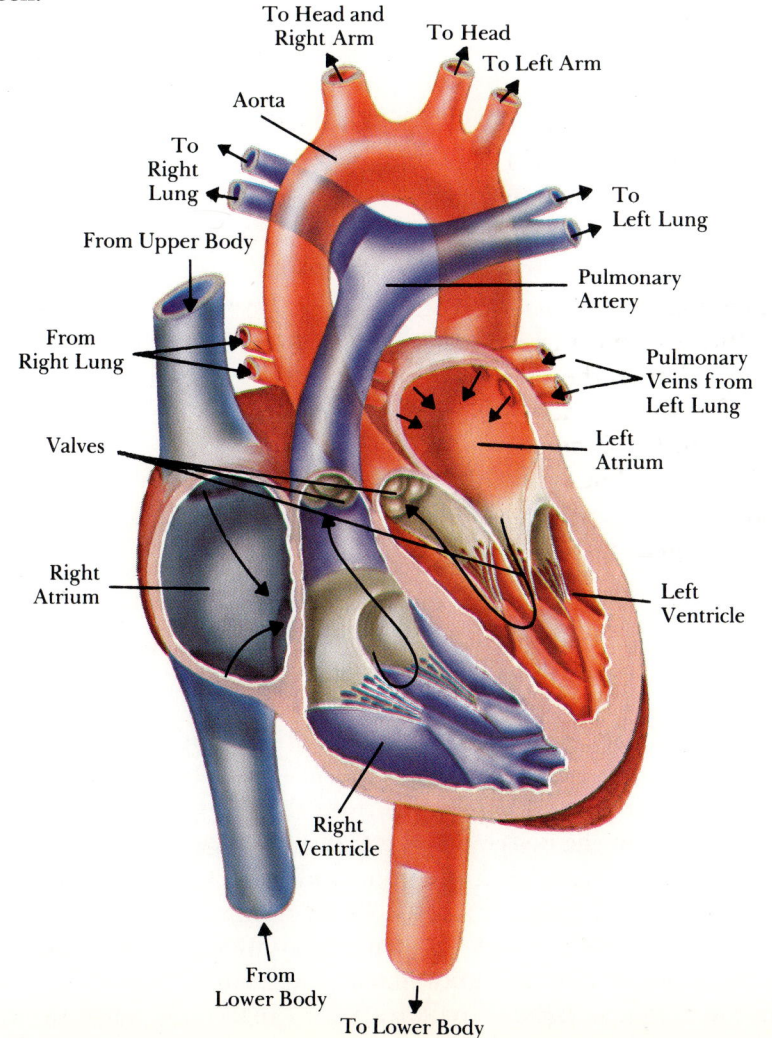

Oxygen-rich blood from the lungs moves into the left atrium of the heart. It is pumped into the aorta, the largest blood vessel in the body. The aorta and its branches, called arteries, carry blood to all the organs of the body. The blood gives up its oxygen to all parts of the body. Then the blood is carried back to the heart by the veins. It enters the right atrium, then the right ventricle. The right ventricle pumps the blood to the lungs, where it gets a new supply of oxygen.

175

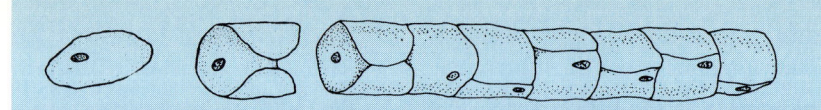

Capillaries are one cell layer thick. This drawing shows how the cells are arranged. Oxygen and digested food leak out of a capillary through the spaces between the cells. This is how nearby cells receive oxygen and food.

Your heart

The heart pumps blood to all parts of the body. If you are somewhat active, 5 to 8 liters (about 5 to 8 quarts) of blood are pumped through the heart each minute. In 24 hours, after about 100,000 heartbeats, more than 7500 liters (2000 gallons)—or about 4400 kilograms (10 tons)—of blood are pumped through the heart of an average human being.

Contraction of the heart squeezes blood out of the heart into the *arteries*. These are blood vessels that carry blood away from the heart. Arteries branch again and again to form smaller and smaller arteries. Finally, the smallest arteries branch to form tiny *capillaries*. Most of the material that leaves the blood does so through the thin walls of the capillaries. Materials that enter the blood from the cells also pass through the capillary walls. The capillaries join to form small veins that then form larger veins. It is the *veins* that carry blood back to the heart.

Four chambers of the heart

The heart is a pear-shaped hollow organ made of muscle. A wall of muscle divides the heart into two sides. The heart works like two pumps that act together. Each side of the heart—each pump—is divided into an upper part and a lower part. The upper part of each side is called the *atrium*, or auricle. And the lower part is called the *ventricle*. The heart, therefore, has four chambers.

Circulation of the blood

The blood in the veins from all over the body (venous blood) enters the right atrium. This blood has given up much of its oxygen to the tissues. It also has taken on carbon dioxide and other waste materials from the tissues. Then the blood flows from the right ventricle to the *pulmonary artery*. This artery carries the blood out of the heart to the lungs. The blood loses carbon dioxide in the lungs and picks up a fresh supply of oxygen.

The blood is carried back to the heart by the *pulmonary vein* and enters the left ventricle. It is pumped from the left ventricle into the *aorta*, the largest artery in the body. The aorta and its branches carry blood to the kidneys. Two other branches, the coronary arteries, carry blood to the heart muscle, itself.

If all the blood vessels in your body could be stretched out and measured, they would probably cover more than 160,000 kilometers (100,000 miles). The blood circulates very quickly. It flows all the way around your body in about one minute. Blood passes through the heart in only 1 or 2 seconds. It goes from the heart to the lungs and back to the heart in 10 to 15 seconds. It also goes from the heart to the brain and back to the heart in 10 to 15 seconds. Blood travels to the toes and back to the heart in about 20 to 25 seconds.

Valves of the heart

There is a set of *valves* between the atrium and ventricle of each side of the heart. The pressure of the blood as it collects in each atrium causes the atrium to contract. The contraction of each atrium opens these valves and lets blood flow into the ventricles. When the ventricles contract, the pressure of the blood forces these valves closed. In this way, blood cannot flow backwards into each atrium. There is another set of valves at the opening to each of the arteries that gets the blood from the ventricles. When the ventricles contract, these valves open to let blood pump into the arteries. When the ventricles relax, the pressure of the blood in the arteries closes the valves. The blood now cannot flow backwards into the ventricles.

Infections sometimes damage heart valves so that they cannot close tightly. Blood leaks back through the damaged valves with each heartbeat. When leakage occurs, the heart must work harder. If the damage is very great, the heart may not be able to keep enough blood moving through the body.

As the heart valves close, they make sounds. If a valve does not close completely, or if it is smaller than normal, a blowing or swishing noise is made by the blood passing through the defective valve. This noise may be heard with an instrument called a stethoscope. The sound is known as a *heart murmur*. A heart murmur needs medical attention by a doctor. Some-

An electrocardiograph is a machine that records heart action. Wires are attached to the patient's body. Heart action is passed over these wires and traced on a chart. The electrocardiograph can show if a person has heart disease.

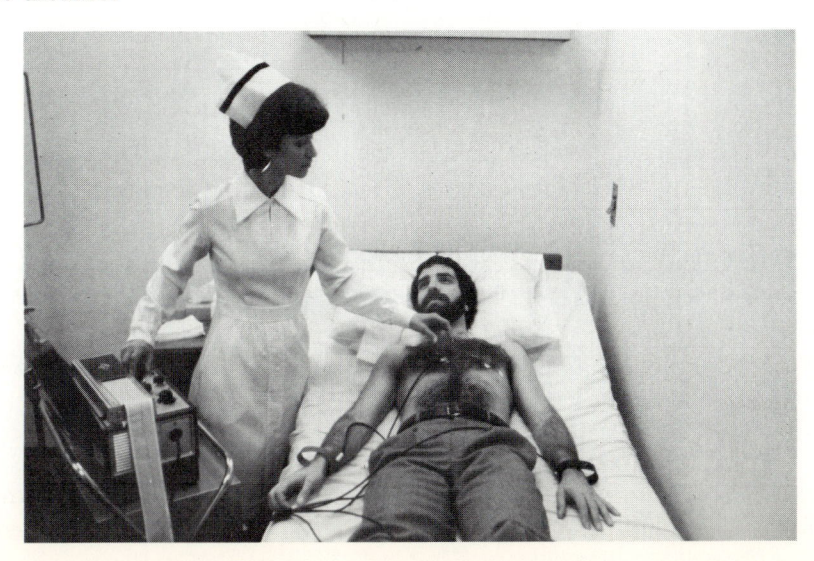

times the murmurs come and go. Some murmurs may tell a doctor that heart disease is present. Other murmurs might be found in a normal heart and do not mean heart damage. These are called innocent murmurs.

Diastole and systole

The heart rests between beats. During the period when the blood is flowing between the two atria (plural of atrium) and the two ventricles, the heart is relaxed. This resting time is called *diastole*. The contraction of the heart is called *systole*. Diastole lasts a little longer than systole. Out of 24 hours each day, the heart rests about 15 hours.

Pulse

When the heart beats, a wave of blood starts out from the heart and moves through the arteries. When you count your pulse, you are counting a series of these waves. The pulse rate is the number of times the heart beats each minute. It is usually counted by putting the second and third

This team of surgeons is performing an operation on a human heart. New methods of surgery of the heart and blood vessels have saved thousands of lives.

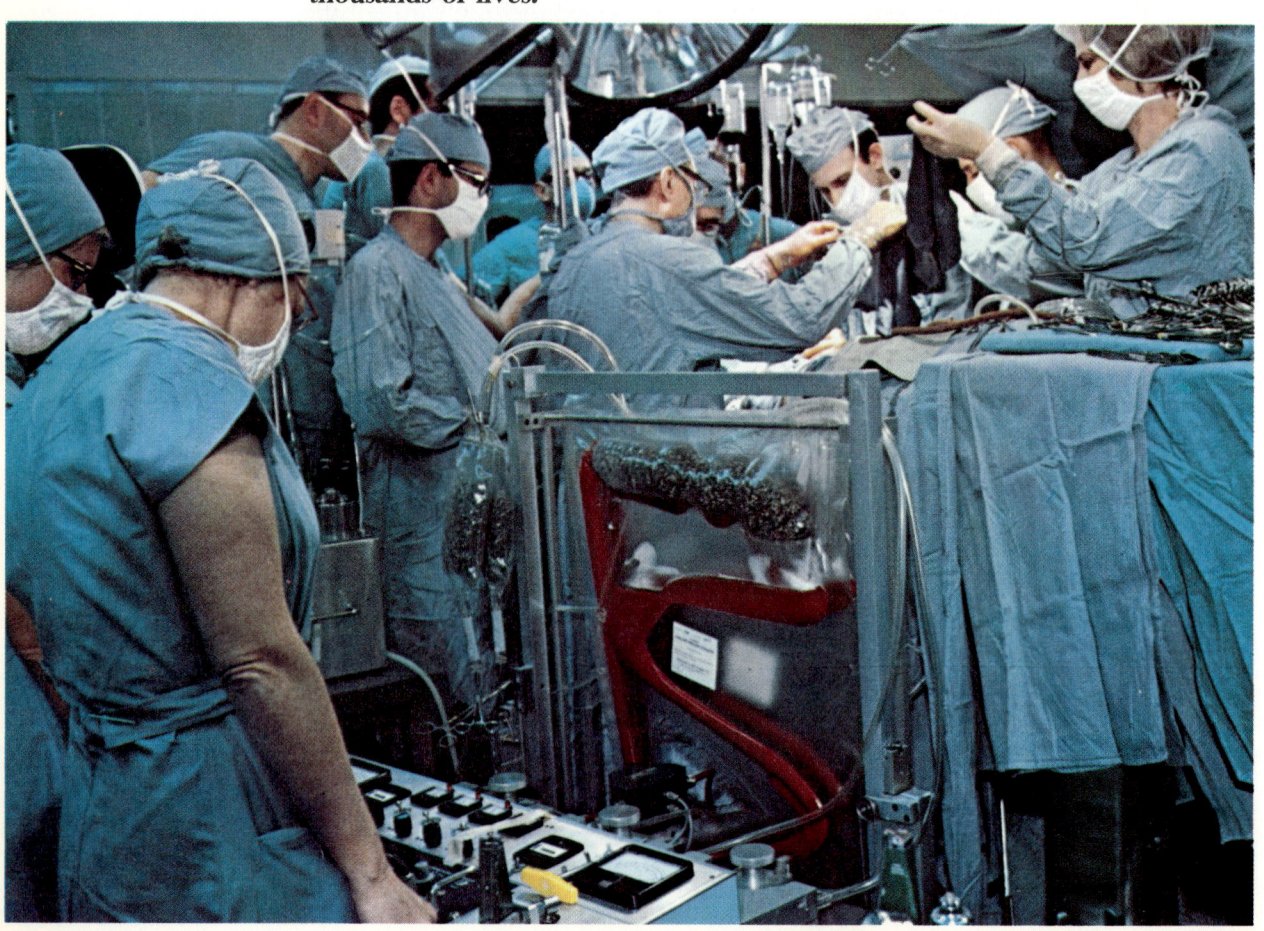

fingers on the wrist near the base of the thumb. The pulse rate can also be found along the neck. Pulse rate is the same as heart rate.

The heart of a human infant beats about 130 times a minute. This rate gets slower with age, until the adult rate is reached. This usually happens in the late teens. The pulse rate then averages about 80 beats per minute in women and 72 beats per minute in men. Athletic training and good physical condition seem to lower the pulse rate. It is increased by exercise, excitement, tobacco, fever, and some diseases.

Return of blood to the heart

The blood from the legs must travel a long distance against gravity to get back to the heart. The walls of the veins are thinner than those of the arteries. They put little pressure on the blood. Blood from the lower part of the body moves upward mostly because the muscles used in walking and running squeeze the blood along as they contract. Valves in the veins keep the blood from dropping back again.

Sometimes the walls of the veins stretch, and blood collects in the veins above the valves. This condition is known as varicose veins. Varicose veins can cause discomfort. They may also be dangerous if enough blood collects to break the walls of the veins. Resting with the feet raised or wearing elastic stockings may help varicose veins in the legs. Sometimes an operation is necessary.

Changes in circulation

Your blood circulates night and day, all through your life. Sometimes your heart beats very fast. Sometimes it beats slowly. When you eat, more blood is sent to your digestive tract. When you exercise, more blood goes to the muscles. In a healthy person, the heart usually sends the different parts of the body as much blood as they need.

There are nerves in the heart and the blood vessels. But you cannot control the impulses that travel over these nerves. Nerve impulses are started by the need for food or oxygen somewhere in the body, or the piling up of waste materials. These impulses speed up or slow down the rate of the heart. Other nerve impulses cause some of the small arteries to contract and push the blood to other arteries. Or some impulses will cause arteries to get larger so that more blood goes through them.

Fainting may happen when the brain does not get enough blood. A person may faint when emotionally upset, ill, or very tired. Bending or lying down with the head lowered lets blood run down into the brain. This eases the feeling of faintness.

Changes in the circulation may be caused by emotions. When you become excited, your heart beats faster. When you are embarrassed, the blood vessels in your face and neck get larger and let more blood flow to these areas. This makes you blush. Being sad may make your heart beat more slowly. When you are frightened, the blood vessels in your skin may become smaller. This removes blood from the surface of your skin and makes your face paler.

Blood pressure

Blood pressure is the pressure of blood against the walls of the arteries. The walls of the arteries are elastic, or stretchable, and contain involuntary muscles. There is usually enough blood in the arteries to keep them more or less always stretched. The pressure of the walls keeps the blood flowing into the smaller arteries and capillaries. When the heart beats, more blood is forced into the arteries, making the pressure greater.

A healthy person's blood pressure goes up when the person stands, runs, or becomes excited. But when the blood pressure stays high all or most of the time, it is said to be abnormal. This condition is called *hypertension*, or high blood pressure.

High blood pressure may be dangerous. The pressure in the arteries may become so high that the heart wears itself out trying to pump blood into the aorta. Some of the small arteries may break and let the blood escape into the tissue and clot there. When clotting happens in the brain, the parts of the brain affected by the clot cannot work properly. This can cause a stroke. A stroke is most likely to happen when there is hardening of the arteries, or *arteriosclerosis*. Small clots are usually absorbed. Then the person's brain works normally again. Arteriosclerosis decreases the flow of blood and may interfere with the work of the kidneys.

The causes of high blood pressure are not all known. Heredity, overweight, and emotional tension are related to high blood pressure. Too much salt in the diet may cause hypertension in some people.

Hypertension may begin at an early age. For that reason, blood pressure should be checked regularly in children and teenagers. With drugs and the right kind of diet, hypertension may be cured if discovered at an early age. It is only in later stages that it cannot be cured but can only be controlled.

Heart disease

The leading cause of death in the United States is heart disease. This may be because today the average life span is longer in this country than it was years ago. There are more older people today, and therefore, many cases of heart disease. The time to begin to guard against diseases of the heart is in adolescence or young adulthood. Although heart disease occurs in some young people, it usually happens in middle and old age.

Causes of heart disease

Heart disease includes almost any condition that weakens the heart or gets in the way of its proper work. Any infection that gets into the bloodstream may affect the heart by causing heart disease. Diphtheria, scarlet fever, syphilis, and many other diseases may harm the heart. Proper care during a recovery from these diseases helps to prevent heart damage.

Congenital heart disease

A child may be born with abnormal heart valves or other defects in heart structure. Heart disease that has been present since birth is known as *congenital heart disease*. Some types of congenital heart disease are very serious. Other types may cause only minor problems. Many congenital heart defects can be corrected by heart surgery. The *heart-lung machine* lets surgeons open the heart. While doctors work on the heart, the flow of blood is bypassed around it through this special machine.

Rheumatic heart disease

Children and young adults may get a type of heart condition called *rheumatic heart disease*. Rheumatic heart disease is the lifelong damage that

(top) Normal arteries are smooth and have no fatty deposits on the walls. (middle) In early atherosclerosis, fatty deposits collect on the walls of the artery. The artery begins to narrow. (bottom) In advanced atherosclerosis, the artery is almost completely blocked. At this point, a heart attack can take place.

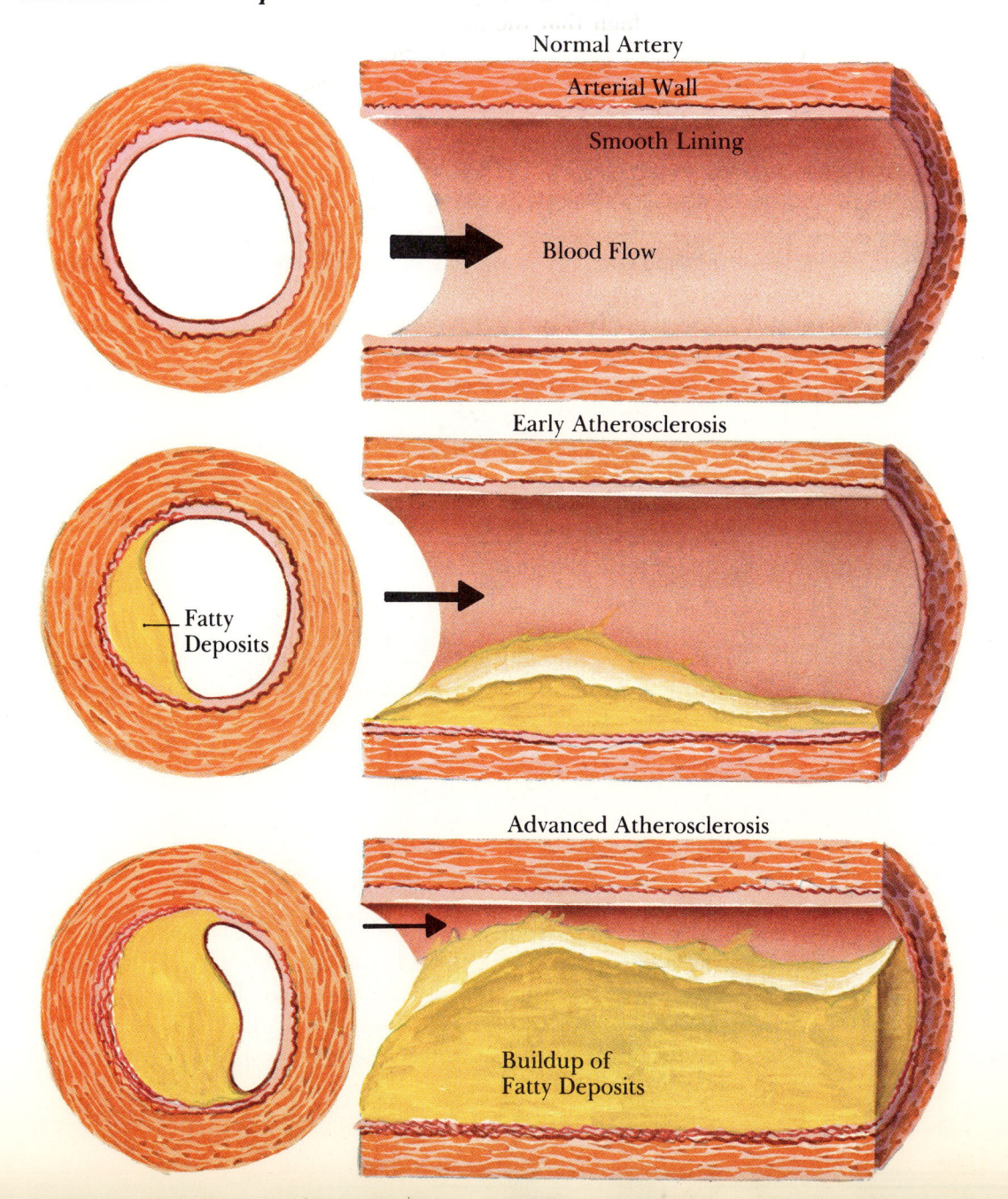

Normal Artery
Arterial Wall
Smooth Lining
Blood Flow

Fatty Deposits

Early Atherosclerosis

Advanced Atherosclerosis

Buildup of Fatty Deposits

181

comes from *rheumatic fever.* Rheumatic fever may develop two to six weeks after a throat infection from a type of bacteria called streptococcus. A person usually has fever and swelling in the bone joints. Swelling could start in the heart muscle and on the heart valves. This could cause scars to form. Scarring in these places is the permanent damage called rheumatic heart disease.

Not all sore throats are caused by streptococcal bacteria. But those that are should be treated with antibiotics to prevent rheumatic fever. When a child or young adult has a sore throat, a doctor may take a *throat culture.* A throat culture is done by rubbing a sterile cotton swab on the throat and then onto a culture plate. If there are streptococcal bacteria present, they will grow on the culture plate. Since doctors have been using throat cultures and antibiotics such as penicillin, there have been fewer cases of rheumatic heart disease.

Coronary artery disease

The vessels that carry blood to the heart muscle are *coronary arteries.* One common form of heart disease involves the coronary arteries. As people become older, deposits of fatty material, or cholesterol, collect on the walls of these arteries. This produces *atherosclerosis,* a condition in which the arteries become narrower. The hardening of the walls of the arteries is known as *arteriosclerosis.* Hardening of the arteries is a slow process that takes many years to develop. A human heart must work harder to pump blood through vessels with atherosclerosis or arteriosclerosis.

If a vessel carrying blood to the heart muscle becomes blocked, the heart muscle may be damaged. If the heart cannot get enough blood, a *heart attack* may develop. Usually, a person feels severe chest pain with nausea and sweating during a heart attack.

Many times people have symptoms such as mild chest pain before they have a severe heart attack. A doctor should be called when chest pain is first noticed. Many people survive heart attacks if help is gotten quickly. It is very important to get a heart-attack victim to a medical treatment center as soon as symptoms are felt.

Many people who have narrow arteries from coronary artery disease do not have heart attacks. Instead, these people develop chest pain whenever they try to exercise or when they are under stress. This chest pain is called *angina pectoris.* It happens when the heart muscle does not get as much blood as it needs. This pain is usually relieved by rest or by medicine placed under the tongue.

Angina pectoris is often a warning that medical treatment is needed. Patients with angina pectoris may have a dye injected into the coronary arteries. Using X rays, doctors can trace the dye as it goes through the circulatory system to see if anything is blocking the coronary arteries. If a blockage is seen in one of the three main coronary arteries, the patient may be advised to have cardiac surgery. In this type of surgery, the blocked artery is bypassed with another blood vessel from the leg. Years ago, such surgery was very dangerous. But today this *coronary bypass surgery* increases blood flow to the heart muscle.

Your circulatory system needs some exercise each day to keep it fit. Regular exercise, such as swimming, helps increase endurance and protect against circulatory disorders.

There are many reasons for the increase in coronary heart disease in the United States. The conditions that make the chance of a heart attack greater are called *risk factors.*

People who smoke cigarettes or have untreated hypertension have a greater than normal chance of having a heart attack. Lack of exercise, overweight, and too much stress also may increase the chances of heart disease. High blood levels of cholesterol and sugar are two more risk factors.

Circulatory disorders, such as heart disease and strokes, often cause disability and death. These illnesses happen mostly in adults, especially in older people. But studies show that prevention must begin at a much earlier age. The process of atherosclerosis takes many years to develop into a complete blood-vessel blockage. There are many things you can do to decrease your chances of someday having a serious circulatory problem.

Taking care of your circulatory system

Get enough exercise.

Many jobs do not require physical activity. Most people no longer walk long distances every day. Your circulatory system needs some exercise each day to keep it fit. Exercises such as walking, swimming, and jogging can be helpful to the circulatory system.

Choose a proper diet.

High blood levels of cholesterol are thought to lead to a higher rate of heart attacks. The average American diet has much more cholesterol and other fats than the body needs. The amounts of these substances should be limited. (See Unit Eight). Too much weight could also overwork the circulatory system. A diet that keeps body weight at normal limits should be followed.

Maintain normal blood pressure.

The circulatory system works best under normal conditions. High blood pressure is a serious disorder that should be treated with medications. Blood pressure can be checked easily with a blood pressure cuff. If there is a history of strokes, heart attacks, or high blood pressure in someone's family, the person's blood pressure should be checked at least once a year.

Avoid cigarette smoking.

Many more heart attacks happen to heavy smokers than to people who don't smoke. Just one cigarette speeds up the heartbeat and increases the blood pressure. Smoking interferes with the blood's ability to give oxygen to the tissues. In addition, smoking may be harmful to any one of the blood vessels in the circulatory system.

The more cigarettes a person smokes, the more likely that person is to have a heart or blood-vessel disease. But a person who stops smoking immediately begins to lower the risk of having a serious health problem. Even so, it takes years for a heavy smoker to lower the risk factor to that of a person who never smoked at all.

Something to think about . . .

A sphygmomanometer is the instrument used to measure your blood pressure. Though it has a rather complicated Greek name, it is a remarkably simple piece of equipment. An inflatable, baglike unit is linked to a tube which is connected to a measuring device. The measuring device contains a column of liquid mercury called a barometer.

If you have ever watched as the doctor or nurse took your blood pressure, a part of the process is probably familiar. But do you know how the sphygmomanometer functions? And do you know specifically what is being measured?

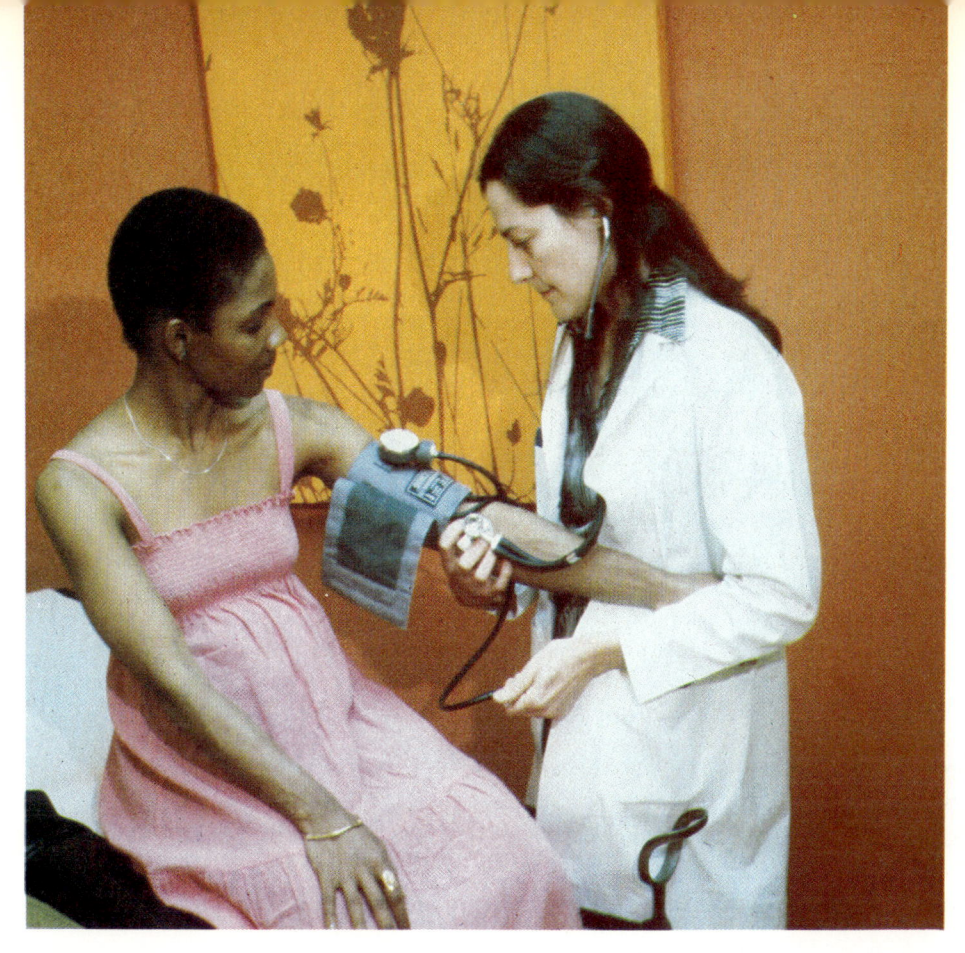

Blood pressure can be checked easily with a machine known as a blood pressure cuff. High blood pressure is serious and should be treated by a doctor. Have your blood pressure checked regularly.

First, the baglike unit, or cuff, is wrapped around the arm above the elbow and is inflated with air. This creates a kind of clamp that squeezes tightly about your arm and shuts off the flow of blood in the main artery. Inflating the cuff also causes the liquid mercury to climb to the top of the barometer.

Next, the stethoscope is placed over the artery as the cuff is slowly deflated. While watching the mercury in the barometer fall, the doctor or nurse is listening for the first sound of blood rushing through the artery. This sound indicates the systolic pressure—the maximum pressure in the artery when the heart is contracting, or squeezing out the blood. When the first pulse sound is heard, the doctor or nurse records the point to which the mercury has fallen. For an adult with normal blood pressure, this systolic reading ranges from 110 to 140.

As the cuff continues to deflate and the mercury falls, the doctor or nurse is listening for the moment when the pulse sound disappears. This point is read on the barometer as your diastolic pressure. Diastolic pressure is the minimum pressure maintained in the arteries between heartbeats, when your heart is relaxed and filling back up with blood. Normal adult diastolic pressure ranges from 65 to 85.

The final reading is the ratio of systolic pressure over diastolic pressure. Normally, it ranges from 90/60 to 140/90. But an estimated 37 million Americans have high blood pressure, with readings above 140/90. Only half of these people are aware of their condition. High blood pressure for long periods of time can damage the cardiovascular system.

Main Ideas

1. The heart is a pump. It keeps blood circulating through arteries, capillaries, and veins.
2. The blood carries everything the body tissues need—oxygen, digested food, water, hormones, and other substances. These substances pass from the bloodstream through the lymph to the cells.
3. Waste products from the cells are carried back through the lymph and the blood vessels to the skin, the lungs, and the kidneys, where they are excreted.
4. Plasma carries food and other materials dissolved in it. Red blood cells carry oxygen. White blood cells fight infection. Platelets help in clotting blood.
5. The heart and the blood vessels automatically increase or lessen the rate of flow of the blood. In this way, they adjust to the changing needs of the body.
6. Heart disease is the leading cause of death in the United States. Certain things can be done to help reduce the chances of having a heart attack.

Key Words

anemia	diastole	lymph nodes
angina pectoris	donor	plasma
aorta	heart attack	pulmonary artery
arteriosclerosis	heart-lung machine	pulmonary vein
artery	heart murmur	rheumatic fever
atherosclerosis	heart valve	rheumatic heart disease
atrium	hemoglobin	risk factors
blood pressure	hemophilia	systole
capillary	hypertension	throat culture
congenital heart disease	leukemia	vein
coronary arteries	leukocyte	ventricle

Apply Your Knowledge

1. What is the main job of plasma, red blood cells, white blood cells, and platelets?
2. What are blood types? Why is it important to know what your blood type is? What is the Rh factor?
3. Without looking at the diagram of the heart, make a sketch showing the four chambers and the valves. Use arrows to show the direction of the blood flow through the heart. From which side is the blood pumped to the lungs? From which side is it pumped to the rest of the body?
4. How do capillaries, veins, and arteries work together? In what direction does the blood flow through these vessels?
5. What are the dangers of high blood pressure?
6. What are some of the causes of heart disease? How can they be avoided?
7. What is rheumatic fever?
8. Why is it important to discover high blood pressure in young adults?
9. What foods may lead to circulatory disorders if you use too much of them?
10. What happens to the arteries of a person who has arteriosclerosis?

Extend Your Knowledge

1. Look at a drop of blood under the microscope. The next time you cut your finger, notice how long the blood takes to clot.
2. Ask the Red Cross about the blood-donor service in your community. Who can give blood? How is it collected? How is it stored? What use is made of it?
3. Get a sheep, beef, or pig heart from the meat market. Find each atrium, ventricle, and valve. Squeeze water through the heart. Can you see the valves close? Point out the major parts of the heart.
4. Contact the local branch of the American Heart Association for pamphlets on preventing heart disease. What added information do these pamphlets contain? What other services does the American Heart Association provide?
5. Check your pulse rate per minute by placing your second and third fingers over the artery at the base of your thumb and wrist joint. Now jump in place for two minutes. Check your pulse rate again. How does exercise affect your pulse rate?
6. Record the pulse rate of a cigarette smoker before and immediately after a cigarette is smoked. How many extra times does that individual's heart beat because of cigarette smoking?

Chapter 15

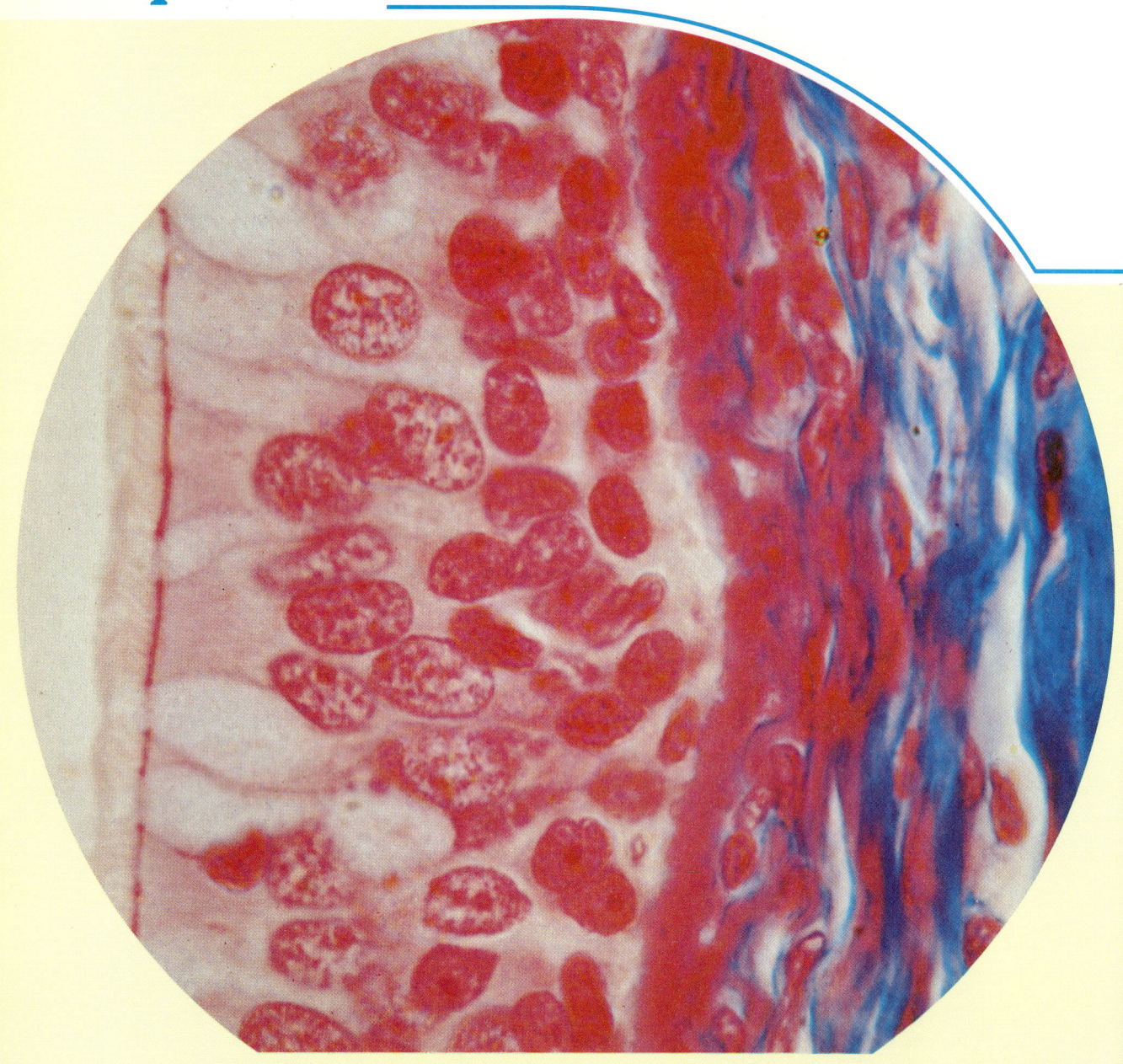

Lung cells

Do you know . . .

- why you can hold your breath for only a few moments?
- how to stop hiccups?
- what causes asthma?
- how air pressure affects breathing?
- what emphysema is?

Respiration

You can live for several days without water and for weeks without food. But you can live only a few minutes without air. Air is a mixture of gases. It contains about 78 percent nitrogen, 21 percent oxygen, 0.4 percent carbon dioxide, and traces of water vapor and other gases. But the most important part of air, of course, is oxygen.

Without oxygen, the body cannot make enough energy to work. Each cell of the body is a chemical machine that produces energy from food, with the help of oxygen. This process is called oxidation. And it happens every time you take a breath. In the lungs, oxygen you breathe in from the air passes into the blood. Then oxidation occurs. Waste gases, such as carbon dioxide, are given off by the blood and pass into the lungs again. You release these wastes back into the air every time you breathe out.

Respiratory tract

Air usually enters the body through the nose. From the nose, air passes back into the body's air passages. Air that is breathed in moves into the pharynx, down through the larynx (or voice box) and into the trachea (or windpipe).

The *larynx* is often called the Adam's apple. It is larger and shows more in men than in women. The vocal cords inside the larynx are also larger in men than in women. The larger size of the vocal cords gives the male voice its deeper pitch.

Trachea

The *trachea* is a tube in the upper part of the chest that branches down into two large tubes, called *bronchi*. Each of the bronchi divides and divides again into smaller tubes, ending in tiny air sacs called *alveoli*. The alveoli make up most of the lungs. The walls of the trachea are made mostly of involuntary muscle and cartilage. The larynx, trachea, and bronchi are kept from collapsing by rings of cartilage, or gristle.

All the upper parts of the air passages are lined with membranes that produce mucus. These membranes are covered with small, hairlike parts called cilia. The mucus and the cilia take out most of the bacteria, dust, and other harmful particles in air before the air gets to the lungs.

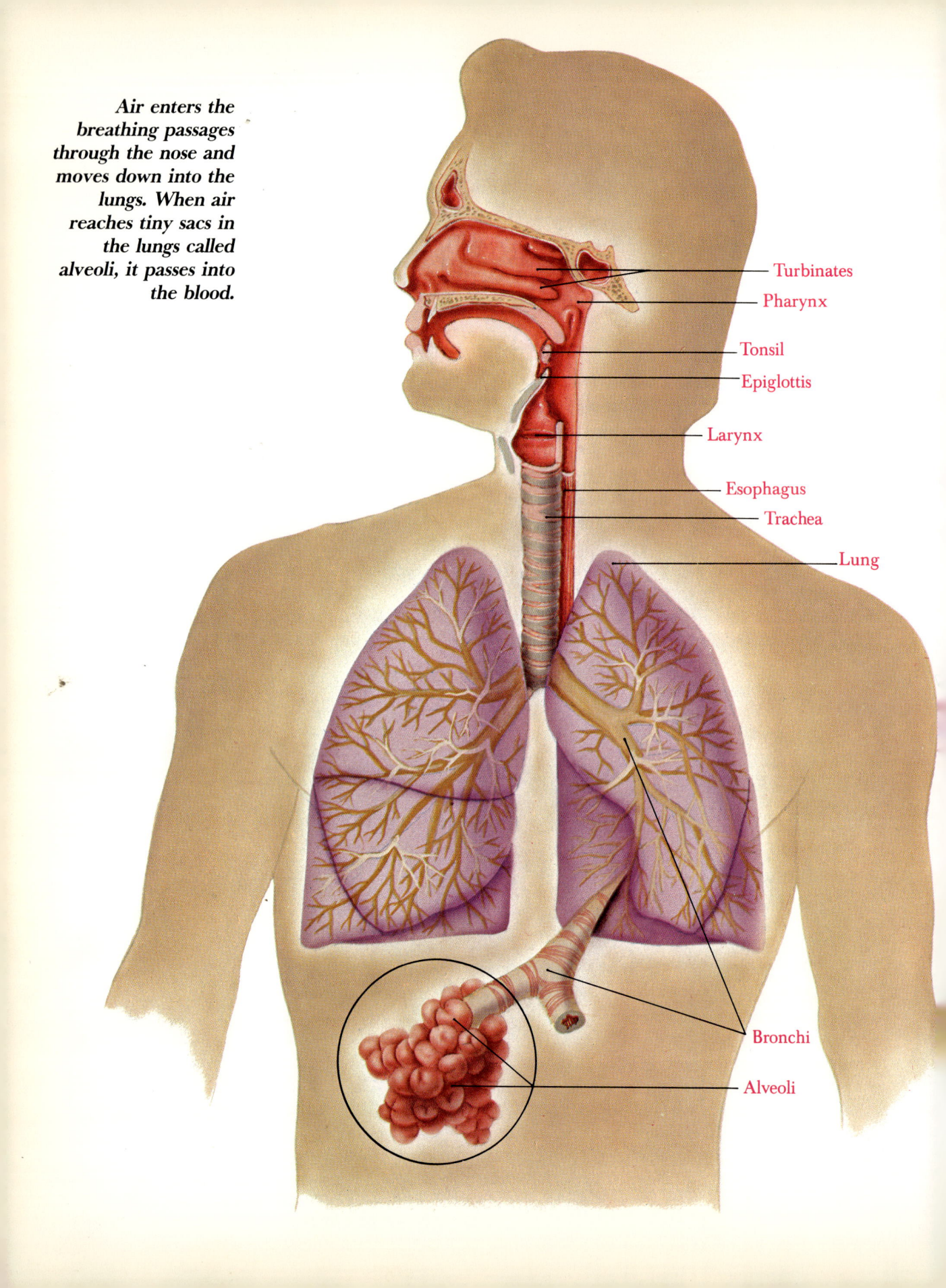

Air enters the breathing passages through the nose and moves down into the lungs. When air reaches tiny sacs in the lungs called alveoli, it passes into the blood.

- Turbinates
- Pharynx
- Tonsil
- Epiglottis
- Larynx
- Esophagus
- Trachea
- Lung
- Bronchi
- Alveoli

Lungs

The two lungs hang in the chest cavity, on the right and on the left. The chest cavity is completely enclosed and airtight. The walls of the chest cavity are made up of the ribs, the muscles between the ribs, and the breastbone. The floor of the chest cavity is formed by the *diaphragm*. This is a large sheet of muscle that separates the abdominal cavity from the chest.

The outside of the lungs and the inside of the chest cavity are covered with smooth, moist membranes called the *pleura*. The pleura let the lungs and the chest walls move easily. Sometimes infection or injury makes the pleura rough and sticky. This condition is called *pleurisy*. It makes breathing difficult and painful.

Lung capacity. During quiet, normal breathing, an adult takes in about 0.48 liter (1 pint) of air with each breath. This amount of air is only about one-eighth of what the lungs can hold. A person who runs or does hard work takes deep gulps of air and fills the lungs.

People have more lung space than they need for ordinary breathing. The extra lung space is very important when some injuries or diseases are present. Healthy parts of the lungs can usually carry on the needed exchange of air while the injured parts are healing. In fact, part of a lung, or even a whole lung, can be removed from the body. For example, one lung may be removed when cancer is present. If the other lung is healthy, the person may live a long, comfortable, and useful life.

Breathing and respiration

Breathing is the way we get air into and out of our lungs. Inhaling—also called *inspiration*—is the process of taking air into the lungs. Exhaling—also called *expiration*—is the process of forcing air out of the lungs.

Respiration is more than breathing. It includes outer and inner respiration. Outer respiration is what you do when you breathe in air from your surroundings and breathe out carbon dioxide from your lungs. Inner respiration is what all the cells of your body do when they take in oxygen from the blood and release carbon dioxide back into the blood.

Breathing habits

When they breathe, some people keep the diaphragm still and use only the rib muscles. Other people use only the diaphragm for most of their breathing. Either of these habits cuts down the amount of oxygen taken in. Also, the amount of lung space really exposed to fresh air is lowered. People should use all the muscles that are made to help them breathe. In that way, fresh air will get to all parts of the lungs.

Control of breathing

Breathing is controlled mostly by a nerve center in the brain called the *respiratory center*. This nerve center is affected by how much carbon dioxide there is in the blood. You can change your rate of breathing if you wish, but only for a short time. When you hold your breath, more and more carbon dioxide piles up in the blood. The added amount of carbon dioxide makes the respiratory center send out strong nerve impulses to the muscles used for breathing. These nerve impulses make you take a deep breath whether you want to or not. Breathing then gets quicker for a time, until the carbon dioxide in the blood is lowered to the usual amount.

If you breathe in oxygen deeply and quickly for a minute or two, the amount of carbon dioxide in the blood is cut down. Quickly exhaling too much carbon dioxide causes dizziness and even fainting. This is called *hyperventilation*. When this happens, the respiratory center sends out fewer impulses to the muscles used for breathing. This causes breathing to slow down until the level of carbon dioxide in the blood goes back to normal.

Sometimes the nerve center that controls breathing is harmed or destroyed. A machine called an artificial respirator may then be used to force air into and out of the lungs. People with very bad lung disease can also use a respirator to help them until they can breathe by themselves. For several months at a time, artificial respirators may do the work of breathing for some patients.

Changes in breathing

An adult at rest breathes 15 to 20 times per minute. Children breathe faster. Exercise makes a person breathe more quickly than usual. Some illnesses also cause breathing to speed up. But other illnesses slow down breathing. People breathe in many different ways at different times. Talking, for example, requires many changes in breathing. And when you laugh or cry, you inhale deeply and exhale in many short breaths.

Yawning is inhaling deeply with the mouth wide open. Did you know that you may yawn even when you are not tired? Sometimes, yawning is really your lungs' way of taking in more needed air. For example, when you are in a hot, stuffy room with little air, you may not take in enough oxygen by breathing normally. This causes the carbon dioxide in your blood to build up. To get rid of this waste, the respiratory center may signal the body to inhale deeply by yawning.

Breathing dust or bits of food into the trachea, or windpipe, makes you cough and sneeze to blow them out. Since sneezes usually get rid of unwanted matter, they should never be blocked. Don't be a "polite" sneezer. Stopping a sneeze could cause nosebleeds, ringing in the ears, and even sinus trouble.

Hiccuping is caused by jerky movements of the diaphragm that end with a click caused by the sudden closing of the vocal cords. You can usually control hiccups by holding your breath, by sipping water, or by trying hard to breathe slowly and regularly.

All of these kinds of breathing changes are very small. They are reactions to many different causes: to smoke, dust, and gas in the air you breathe; to the amount of oxygen and carbon dioxide in your blood and muscles; and to the way you feel. You have very little control over these changes in breathing. But your body's ability to breathe to fit your needs

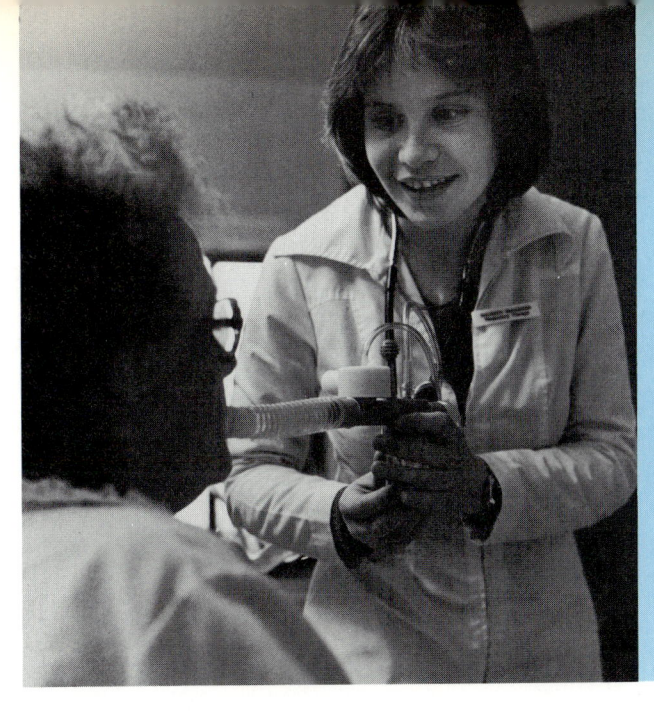

This woman is having her lung capacity tested. Did you know that your lungs can hold about eight times more air than you normally breathe in?

and feelings is an example of how your body works as a unit—a total organism.

Air pressure and oxygen

At sea level, air pushes down with a pressure of about 10,000 newtons per square meter (15 pounds per square inch). The higher you go above sea level, the thinner the air. Also, as you go higher above sea level, the lower the air pressure and the less the amount of oxygen in the air. At 3000 meters (10,000 feet) above sea level, many people feel light-headed and dizzy from not enough oxygen.

The human body can get used to small changes in the supply of oxygen. People who go on trips to high mountains breathe more quickly for a time. Their hearts also beat faster than normal before they adjust. Then the number of red blood cells increases so that more oxygen can be carried in the bloodstream. This adjustment happens over a period of several weeks. People who live at high altitudes become permanently used to having less oxygen in the air.

Athletes who are used to sea-level air pressure cannot compete at high altitudes. A team that is not used to the high altitudes of a scheduled playing location sometimes arrives there a week before the game to give the players' bodies time to make extra red blood cells.

Air travel

Many airplanes fly at heights where there is not enough oxygen for human needs. When the body cells do not get enough oxygen, the brain is affected. A feeling of light-headedness and stimulation occurs. This is followed by dizziness and confusion, and finally by unconsciousness. For this reason, all commercial airplanes and other high-flying airplanes are pressurized. This means that their cabins are airtight and air is pumped in to keep the level of air pressure higher than it really is at those heights. The lungs can then take in enough oxygen to keep a person comfortable and breathing normally. Extra tanks of oxygen are carried in airplanes in case

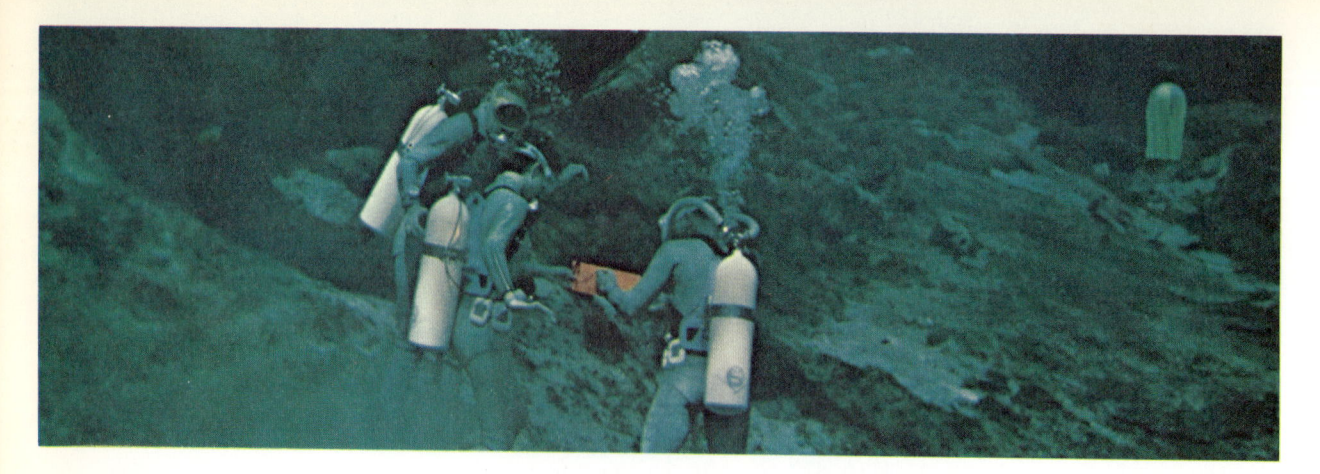

Underwater, the air pressure is so strong that a gas called nitrogen, which is in the air inside a diver's tank, may be forced into a diver's lungs. A diver must return to the surface slowly to stop the nitrogen from forming bubbles in the blood. If bubbles form, a painful condition called the bends happens.

there is a sudden loss of cabin air pressure. In such an emergency, the pilots and passengers can breathe through masks hooked up to the extra oxygen supply.

Breathing underwater

Divers may get air through hoses kept on the water's surface. Or they may carry air tanks underwater on their backs. Carrying tanks with them lets them swim freely over a wider area. The tanks may hold compressed air. In special cases, they may carry oxygen mixed with other gases. Such a tank, together with its other needed parts, is called a *scuba* (the word stands for *s*elf-*c*ontained *u*nderwater *b*reathing *a*pparatus). Air is usually exhaled right into the water. This is why you see bubbles rising up in pictures of scuba divers.

Air-pressure changes

The human body adjusts easily to small changes in air pressure. However, some safety tips must be followed when a person goes into an area where the air pressure is very different from normal air pressure. People building a tunnel deep underwater often work in a caisson. Caissons are large, watertight chambers in which the air pressure is kept very high. The air pressure inside the caisson equals the pressure of the water outside. It is important to keep the air pressure high to stop water from rushing into the caisson. Before going into the caisson, workers must spend some time in another chamber called an air lock. In this chamber, the air pressure first equals that at sea level. Then the air pressure in the lock gets higher at small intervals until it is equal to the pressure of the caisson in which the people will be working. After this slow adjustment, the workers may safely enter the caisson. When they leave the caisson, the workers must pass through the air lock again, and the process is reversed. The air pressure is slowly lowered from the high pressure of the caisson to sea-level pressure.

A large and quick change in air pressure affects the body. When a person goes into a high-pressure area, the higher pressure forces more air into the person's lungs. Nitrogen in the air, a gas that is usually not absorbed by the lungs, is forced into the blood by the added pressure. This causes no problem as long as the person stays in the high-pressure area. But if the person goes back to a lower-pressure area without letting the body adjust to the change, he or she may have problems. The nitrogen forms bubbles in the blood. The bubbles can block some of the small blood vessels and cause painful muscle cramps, dizziness, and nausea. These are symptoms of *the bends,* or caisson disease. In very serious cases, paralysis and death may result. But slow *decompression* can keep people from getting the bends. Decompression is returning to the low-pressure area slowly, to give the nitrogen time to pass out of the blood without forming bubbles. Nitrogen then goes back into the lungs and out of the body.

Respiratory disorders

The air passages of the body are always exposed to bacteria, viruses, and other irritating particles, as air travels into and out of the lungs. Cilia and mucus protect the lining of the upper air passages. Coughing also helps to get rid of irritating substances in the air passages. But the upper respiratory tract can easily get many illnesses, especially during the winter months. Viral infections, such as colds and influenza (the "flu"), are spread through coughing, spitting, sneezing, and talking.

Bronchitis

Acute *bronchitis* is swelling of the bronchi. It often comes with a viral infection and may last as long as two weeks. Chronic bronchitis may come from an infection that lasts a long time. It may also come from a long period of cigarette smoking. Coughing is the main symptom of bronchitis. But treatment for bronchitis should not be limited to the cough. If smoking is the cause of the bronchitis, then the smoking habit should be changed. Sometimes, the only way to cure chronic bronchitis is to break the cigarette habit.

Emphysema

Coughing and having trouble breathing are symptoms of *emphysema.* The alveoli, or air sacs, lose their elasticity. First they become enlarged. Later, they are permanently destroyed. Waste air that has carbon dioxide in it cannot be forced out of the lungs to let in fresh air. The result is that less oxygen is available for the blood. The person gasps for breath, and the heart beats faster and more strongly than it does normally.

As a cause of crippling disability, emphysema ranks second only to heart disease. In recent years, deaths from emphysema have increased even more rapidly than those from lung cancer. Tobacco smoking seems to be the chief factor contributing to emphysema (see Chapter 19). Infections and irritations of the lungs and air pollution are also thought to be likely causes.

Fast treatment of bronchitis, asthma, and sinus infections may help to prevent emphysema. To treat emphysema, ways must be found to help air pass out of and into the lungs. Some patients learn to use their extra lung capacity. Oxygen alone, or oxygen mixed in compressed air, may be given to some patients. It is also possible to reduce or remove the mucus that forms in the bronchial tubes.

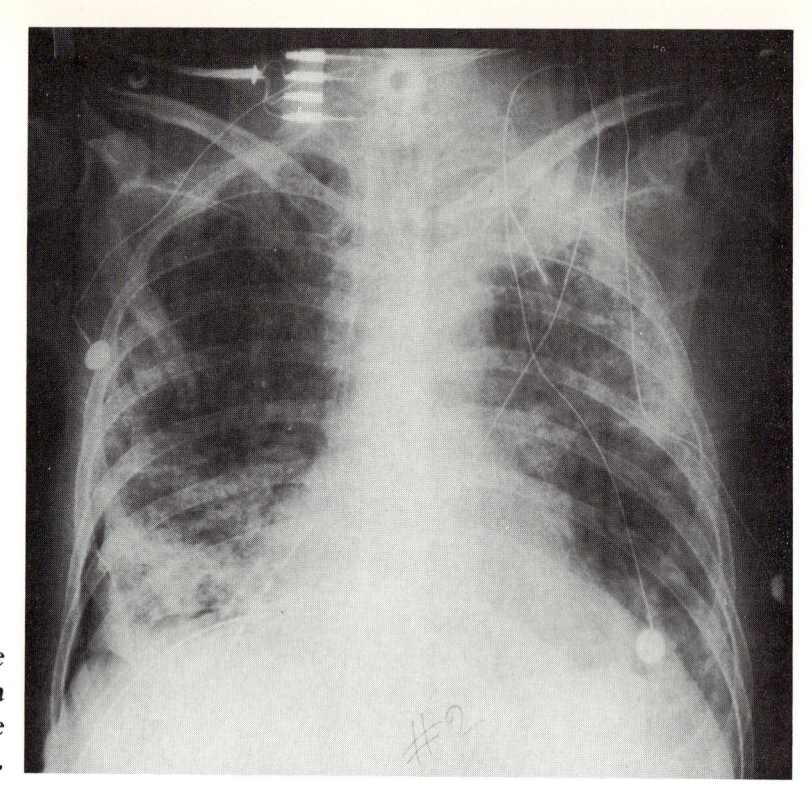

In this X ray of the lungs, pneumonia shows up as the white area.

Asthma

Asthma causes the mucous membranes of the bronchi to become irritated and to swell. This swelling narrows the openings of the tubes. The muscles of the walls of the bronchi contract, making the air passages even narrower. Thus, less than the normal amount of air gets through to the lungs. Too much mucus forms on the membrane, causing a wheezing sound and making breathing very hard. Untreated, asthma may develop into emphysema.

Asthma has many causes. One of these may be an allergy to something in the environment. Dust, molds, pollen, feathers, and certain foods are the most common substances that may cause an allergy. A doctor may use skin tests to find out which substances are the cause. Mental stress and too much exercise sometimes make the symptoms of asthma seem more serious than usual. Asthma can be a very serious illness. Treatment should be under a doctor's care. Using too many home cures or over-the-counter medicines may be harmful.

Pneumonia

Pneumonia is an infection of the lung tissue. The infection may cause fluid to build up in the lungs. Breathing then becomes difficult. Cough and fever are the main symptoms of pneumonia. By listening to a person's chest, or by taking a chest X ray, a doctor can tell if a person has pneumonia. The treatment given depends on the kind of infection the person has. Antibiotics are often needed, along with rest and plenty of liquids.

Scientists are always looking for ways to cure pneumonia. In 1977, a vaccine for one type of pneumonia was developed. It is currently being used with elderly people, who suffer the greatest number of deaths from this disease.

Taking care of your respiratory system

The respiratory system warms and adds moisture to the air you breathe. During the winter months, the air may be very cold. It is not healthy to expose your air passages to very cold air for too long a time. Sometimes the air you breathe may be too dry. Adding moisture to the air of a room with a humidifier may be helpful.

Avoid things that may irritate the respiratory tract.

Industrial gases, cigarette smoke, and certain fumes may be very irritating to the upper respiratory tract. Such irritants can cause harm to the mucous membranes and cilia. Asbestos and coal dust may cause lung disease if you are exposed to them for many years. Try to keep away from polluted air whenever possible.

Do not smoke cigarettes.

Cigarette smoking does more harm to the respiratory system than all the other irritating substances put together. Cancer of the lungs and larynx, chronic bronchitis, and emphysema are all linked to cigarette smoking. The harmful substances in cigarette smoke may destroy the cilia, the mucous lining, and the bronchi. Then there is little to safeguard the person against respiratory infection. This often happens in people who have chronic bronchitis. In emphysema, the small air sacs are destroyed by cigarette smoking, making it hard to breathe. Most victims of lung cancer would never have gotten the disease if they had not smoked. But in spite of the many warnings that cigarette smoking is harmful to health, some people continue to damage their respiratory systems through this habit.

A study done by the Department of Transportation showed that bicycling in hot, polluted air may have no short-term ill effects on health.

Something to think about . . .

Every day Allen bicycles to his law office in the city, even though summer weather in Washington, D.C., is often hot and muggy. Allen wonders if he should ride home with a friend in his car on days when the pollution levels are high. He worries about the effects of bicycling in hot, polluted air.

A Department of Transportation study indicates that bicycling in these conditions may have no adverse short-term effects on health. Ten healthy men between the ages of 23 and 39 were assigned to ride bicycles or ride in air-conditioned cars during the evening rush hours in the spring and summer. Their routes ranged from one with dense traffic and tall buildings (where pollution is supposedly heaviest) to one with low buildings and little traffic. The three men in cars and the seven bicyclists traveled to the Health Center of George Washington University, where they were given blood tests, tests of pulmonary function, exercise tests, and checks of coughs, wheezes, headaches, and eye irritation.

Bicyclists reported symptoms of fatigue, sore throat, and irritation of the larynx and the eyes more than motorists. Two of these symptoms may not have resulted directly from the heat and pollution. Because the bicyclists were instructed to breathe through their mouths, the sore throats they reported may have been dry throats. And some of the eye irritations they reported were caused by particles in the bicyclists' eyes. All the symptoms were most common when the bicyclists traveled routes with high concentrations of nitrates. Nitrates were as likely to be present on routes with little traffic as on those with dense traffic.

Motorists in air-conditioned cars tended to have *more* carbon monoxide in their blood than the bicyclists did. Perhaps long waits in traffic jams accounted for this carbon monoxide accumulation. Bicyclists were able to avoid the accumulation because they were able to move out of stalled traffic. In the exercise tests, tests of cardiovascular function, and tests of pulmonary function, neither motorists nor bicyclists had impaired performance. The minor symptoms such as "sore" throats reported by these subjects tended to disappear quickly.

The people associated with the study were surprised that the short-term effects of heat and pollution seem to be so harmless. But the researchers stressed that the study was limited and used only a small sample. A study of long-term health risks of bicycling in traffic has been recommended.

Main Ideas

1. The intake of oxygen and the release of carbon dioxide by the body are processes needed for life.
2. Outer respiration is what you do when you breathe air into your lungs and breathe carbon dioxide back into the surroundings.
3. Inner respiration is what your cells do when they breathe in oxygen from the blood and breathe out carbon dioxide back into the blood.
4. Breathing adjusts automatically depending upon the need for oxygen.
5. A person's lung capacity is about eight times greater than is usually needed. This helps the body get oxygen in emergency situations.
6. Cigarette smoking is harmful to the respiratory system.

Key Words

alveoli	diaphragm	pleura
asthma	emphysema	pleurisy
the bends	expiration	pneumonia
bronchi	hyperventilation	respiration
bronchitis	inspiration	respiratory center
decompression	larynx	trachea

Apply Your Knowledge

1. How does the body use oxygen?
2. Trace the passage of air from the nose to the alveoli. How is the air cleaned? What keeps the air passages from collapsing?
3. What is the difference between breathing and respiration? How is outer respiration different from inner respiration?
4. What muscles do we use in breathing? When these muscles contract, what happens to the size of the chest?
5. How is breathing controlled? Why can you hold your breath for only a few moments? Why is a mixture of oxygen and carbon dioxide given to a person who is suffocating? What would happen if only pure oxygen were given?
6. What happens when you hiccup, when you yawn, and when you cough?
7. What changes happen to air pressure at increasing heights above sea level? How does a person's body adjust to living at a high altitude?
8. What are common causes of asthma? Why does a person who has asthma find it hard to breathe?
9. What is bronchitis?
10. What is emphysema?

Extend Your Knowledge

1. Obtain the lungs of a sheep or a pig from the meat market. Find the trachea and bronchi. Put a glass tube into the trachea and try to blow up the lungs. Why do the lungs feel spongy?
2. Look at a model or dissection of the lungs of a small mammal. Find the ribs and the muscles between the ribs, the diaphragm, and the pleura.
3. Experiment with your own breathing. How slowly can you breathe? How fast can you breathe? (Be careful not to make yourself dizzy!) What happens when you cough? Keep your ribs still, and use your diaphragm for breathing. Keep your diaphragm still, and use your ribs for breathing.
4. Ask a physical education instructor or biology teacher to demonstrate the use of a spirometer. For a few members of the class, find the amount of air they breathe out in a normal expiration. Then find the amount of air they breathe out in a forced expiration. Find the amount they breathe out after a forced expiration and a forced inspiration.
5. Report on the special systems that provide air for space travelers and for people who live underwater for days or for weeks.

Chapter 16

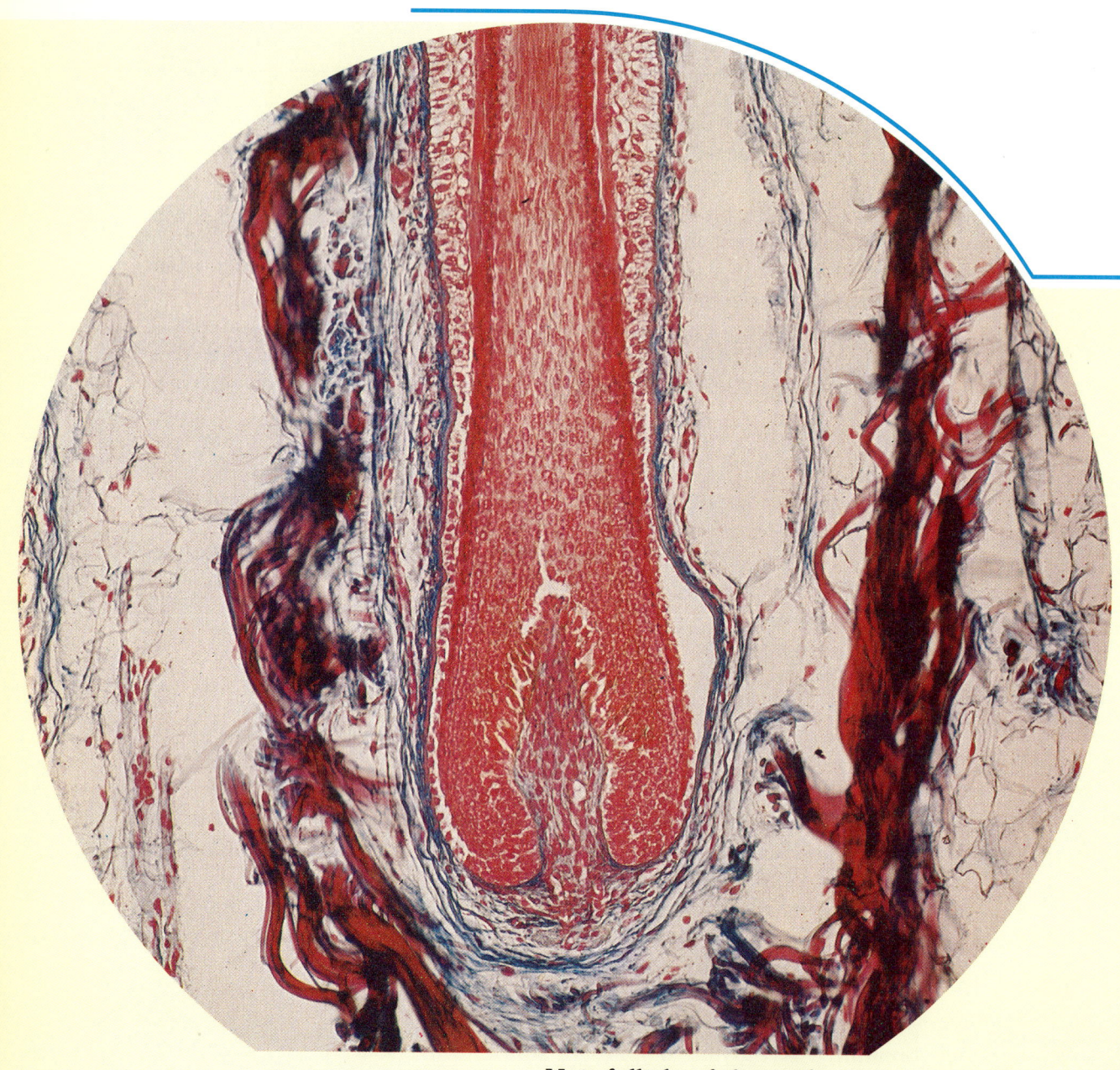

Hair follicle of the scalp

Do you know . . .

- why you don't feel pain when your nails and hair are cut?
- how many meters of skin are needed to cover the body of an adult?
- that your skin is constantly shedding?
- that some people can get poison ivy without actually touching the plant?

Skin and Hair: Your Protective Covering

The skin is the largest organ of the human body. Skin covers about 1.6 square meters (17 square feet) of body surface in adults. Your skin may look like a simple covering. But it is really a complex organ with many functions. Its most important function is to serve as a watertight container. Everything inside your body is wet—or at least moist. Your skin prevents the air around you from drying up your body's systems.

Skin structure

The skin has two main layers. The *epidermis* is the outer portion of the skin. The *dermis* is the under layer of skin. The dermis gives the skin its strength and elasticity, or ability to stretch.

Epidermis

The epidermis is a thin layer of cells. Along the inner surface of the epidermis, new cells grow and push the older cells to the outer surface of the skin. The skin cells that reach the surface are no longer alive. Millions of these cells are rubbed off onto clothing and towels each day. New cells replace the dead cells and constantly make a new outer covering. The thickest epidermis is on the soles of your feet. The thinnest epidermis is on your eyelids.

The inner portion of the epidermis contains cells that produce a skin coloring called *pigment*. Tanning of the skin is really an increased production of pigment, triggered by the sun. *Pores* are tiny openings in the epidermis that lead to sweat and oil glands in the dermis.

Dermis

The dermis is a network of connective tissue and fatty tissue. It is thicker than the epidermis. The dermis contains blood vessels, nerves, and glands. The sweat glands, oil glands, and hair roots are in the dermis.

Functions of the skin

Your skin performs many functions for you throughout the day. It protects you, keeps you warm, tells you about your environment through touching, and helps you express your feelings to others.

Protection

The skin is your main defense against the entry of disease organisms.

201

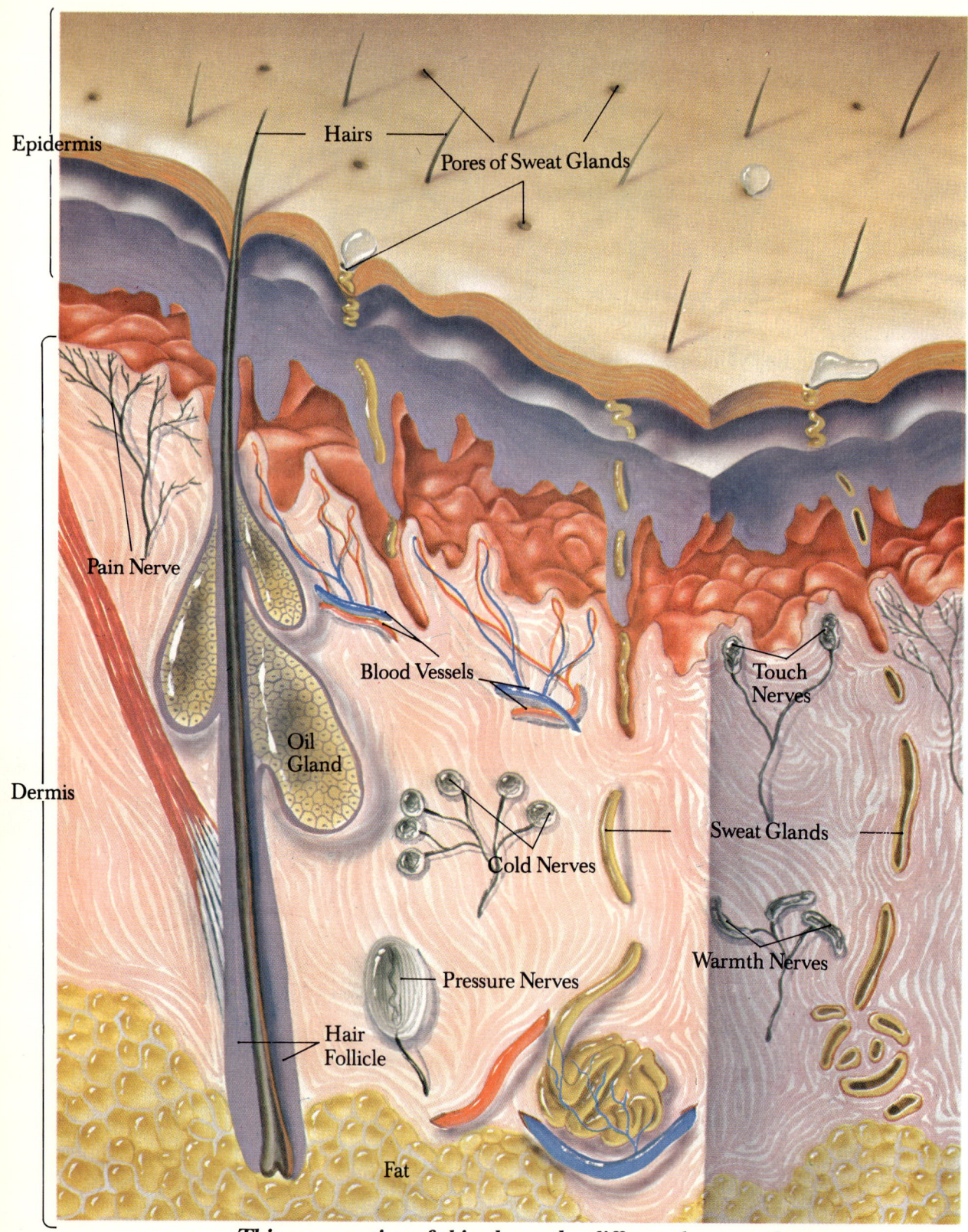

This cross section of skin shows the different layers and parts.

An infection usually cannot get started unless there is a break in the skin. As long as the skin is clean, it quickly gets rid of infectious organisms that may touch its surface.

The skin also acts as a cushion for bumps and a covering for delicate inner tissue. A suntan is your skin's way of protecting your body, too. The skin releases pigment to protect you against injury from too much sunlight.

The pigment that is made in the inner layers of the epidermis is called *melanin*. Melanin acts as a protection against the ultraviolet rays of the sun. It gives color to the hair, skin, and eyes. Some people have *freckles*. Freckles are small areas of the skin with many cells that produce melanin when exposed to the sun.

Dark-skinned people have more melanin in their skin than light-skinned people do. People who have no melanin in their skin at all are called *albinos*. Albinos are very rare. Sometimes, they are blind. It is not safe for them to be in the sunlight for long periods of time.

A *mole* is a growth in the pigmented layer of the skin. Moles may be found anywhere on the body surface. Usually they begin during the early years of life. Most moles are harmless. But some types of moles may develop into cancer. If a mole gets larger, changes color, or is constantly irritated, see a doctor. If the cells that produce melanin begin to grow rapidly and in an abnormal pattern, a tumor called a *malignant melanoma* may develop. This is a rare type of cancer that usually can be treated if discovered early.

Regulation of body temperature

When the body starts to heat up, the flow of blood increases in the tiny blood vessels of the dermis. This causes the skin to get red, especially on the face. Redness is a sign that heat has been carried by the blood to the surface of the body and is escaping through the skin.

As the body heats up, the pores release perspiration. Perspiration comes from the 2 to 3 million sweat glands in the human body. On a hot summer day, 2 to 3 liters (about 2 to 3 quarts) of perspiration must be released through the pores to keep the body from overheating. Perspiration is made up of water, salt, and body wastes. The water evaporates from the skin's surface. This evaporation helps the body cool down.

The skin holds in body heat when the environment is cold. The dermis contains a large amount of fat (adipose) tissue that may act as an insulation to help contain body heat. In addition, the blood vessels and nerves in the dermis help to control body temperature.

Sensation

You receive information about the environment from a network of nerve endings in the dermis. The sense of touch helps you to know the texture, shape, and weight of objects. Pain, cold, and warmth are sensations that warn you against possible dangers that might occur.

As the body heats up, pores, or openings, in the skin release perspiration. Perspiration is made up of water, salt, and body wastes. The water changes to a vapor on the top of the skin and cools the body.

Learning what causes skin problems will help you to avoid them.

Expression

Your skin tells you and others a lot about yourself. The look on your face will often tell others if you are angry or happy. Excess sweating on the forehead and palms may show that you are worried or nervous. Blushing of the skin may show that you are embarrassed. Well-cared-for skin, hair, and nails are often evidence of a healthy person who cares about personal appearance.

Skin problems

Skin problems, even small ones, may cause unneeded discomfort and worry. It is often easy to prevent these problems if you understand what causes them.

Contact dermatitis

Certain substances may irritate the skin and cause *dermatitis,* or inflammation of the skin. The redness and blisters of the skin that develop after contact with one of these substances are symptoms of contact dermatitis. Several plants, such as poison ivy, poison oak, and poison sumac, cause contact dermatitis in many people. The oils on such plants irritate the skin of sensitive people. This may happen either through direct contact with the plant or by touching something that has touched the plant, such as a ball or a dog. People who are sensitive to these plants should learn to recognize and avoid them.

Allergic dermatitis

Hives are small lumps on the skin that look like insect bites. In serious cases of hives, the lips, eyelids, hands, and other parts of the body may swell. Itching is usually severe.

Hives may be caused by a reaction to some substance the body is allergic to. Some people are sensitive to certain pollens, chemicals, drugs, or foods. To keep from getting hives, a person should find out what causes this allergic reaction and should avoid those substances. Treatment with medicines ordered by a doctor usually gives relief.

Sunburn

If you try to get a tan too fast, your skin cannot produce enough melanin to protect itself. Thus your skin may be injured and become red or blistered. Overexposure to the sun may cause a very serious burn that needs medical treatment. Careless use of sunlamps may also cause serious burns of the skin.

The proper way to get a suntan is to limit exposure at first. Then, slowly increase the time spent in the sunlight. Try a brief exposure of 20 minutes the first day. Then add on a few minutes each day, and let the suntan develop over 2 to 3 weeks. This gives the skin time to produce the melanin needed to protect the skin and develop a tan.

Some people, especially those with fair skin, may be more sensitive to sunlight than others. If you do not tan easily and your skin is sun-sensitive, you should take special safety measures to avoid overexposure to the sun. The harmful ultraviolet rays in sunlight are strongest at noon. So you should avoid that "peak burning" time. Severe sunburn is less likely before 10 A.M. and after 2 P.M. (standard time).

Sunscreens are substances that are put on the skin to protect it from the sun's rays. Sunscreens are used about 15 minutes before going out into the sun. They have no effect when used after sunbathing. The best commercial sunscreen preparations contain PABA (para-aminobenzoic acid) or other forms of this substance. Suntan lotions are also helpful in getting a tan. But suntan lotions may not always protect the skin from the sun.

Fungal infections

Ringworm and *athlete's foot* are common skin infections. Both are caused by a *fungus*. A fungus is a form of plant life that lives best in dark, warm, moist areas. Ringworm (*Tinea capitis*) causes itching and sores of the scalp. These sores tend to heal in the center and to spread outward. The ringlike appearance gives this infection its name. It is not really caused by a worm at all. Ringworm is very hard to treat at home. If you suspect you have ringworm, you should see a doctor.

Athlete's foot (*Tinea pedis*) usually begins with a slight itching, redness, and cracking of the skin between the toes. People often pick up the infection in shower rooms or on swimming-pool decks. The term athlete's foot is not really correct. Many people who are not athletes get this disease.

To prevent athlete's foot, wash your feet carefully with soap. It is very important to wash between the toes and to dry the feet thoroughly. Always use your own towel. Avoid footwear that causes your feet to perspire. If you think you have athlete's foot, you should see a doctor for proper diagnosis and treatment.

Boils

Boils are skin infections that often begin in a hair root. An area of swelling and redness with a center of pus may be seen on the skin's surface. The bacteria that cause this infection may spread to other people. For this

Some plants cause redness and blisters of the skin in many people. These are signs of contact dermatitis. Poison ivy (top), poison oak (middle), and poison sumac (bottom) may cause contact dermatitis.

Hair

Oil Gland

Hair Follicle

Normal

Epidermis

Dermis

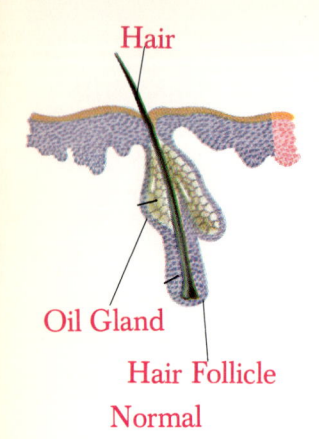

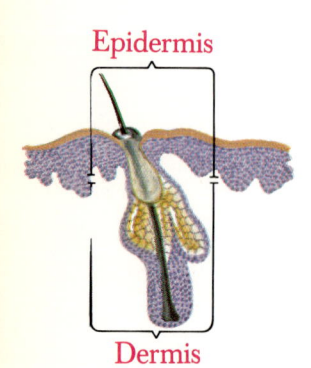

Whitehead

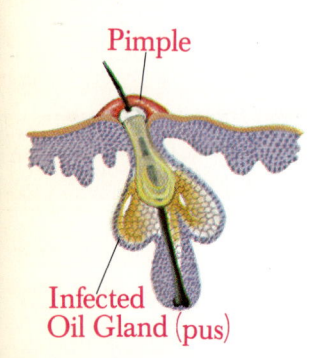

Pimple

Infected Oil Gland (pus)

Blackhead

Acne is a skin infection caused by bacteria that enter blocked pores. To prevent acne, wash often with soap and water and eat a well-balanced diet.

reason, people with boils should not prepare or serve food. Boils should not be squeezed or pinched. This may cause the infection to spread to other parts of the body. Boils may become a serious infection and should be treated by a doctor. (A carbuncle is a number of boils close together. A sty is a small boil on the eyelid.)

The best way to prevent boils is by washing daily to keep the skin clean.

Acne

Acne is most often a skin infection caused by an oily secretion called *sebum*. If the face is not washed with soap daily, the sebum is not removed. Sebum provides an ideal area for bacteria to grow.

When a pore becomes clogged, it appears as a blackhead. If bacteria enter the clogged pore, a yellow-white core develops that is most often called a pimple. Do not squeeze blackheads and pimples. The infection may be forced inward. Also, squeezing may cause permanent damage to the skin surface.

Acne is no longer considered a dietary disease. But some doctors still tell their patients not to eat fats, fried foods, chocolate, and candy. Reactions to foods vary with different people. If you find that certain foods cause skin blemishes to appear, don't eat those foods for a while. Substitute another food from that basic food group. Eating from the four basic food groups is necessary for good health. And good health is needed for clear skin.

To prevent acne and preserve a healthy complexion, follow the skin-care rules below. If your skin does not clear up after you follow these suggestions for a few weeks, see your doctor. The doctor may decide to treat your acne with antibiotics.

1. Wash the affected skin area with soap and warm water every morning and night. Also wash in the afternoon after school. Dry the skin with a towel. This helps to free the pores of dead cells and to remove some of the excess oils.
2. Avoid greasy creams and oily preparations. There is already too much oil on the skin.
3. Eat a well-balanced diet. Avoid any foods that seem to make acne worse.
4. Get enough rest and exercise.

Acne often improves during the summer months. This is due to the drying action of sunlight that prevents the buildup of oily material in the pores. For this reason, exposure to sunlight may be very helpful for some people.

Your hair and nails

Hair and nails are outgrowths of the epidermis layer of the skin. Each hair grows from a hair root in the dermis. It grows through a hair follicle (the tissue around the hair) to become a hair on the skin. Living cells in the follicle push upward as they grow together and harden into a surface hair. The hair above the skin's surface is made up of layers of dead cells that contain protein. The amount of pigment in these cells determines the color of your hair. As a person becomes older, the amount of pigment decreases. The hair may turn gray and then white.

Your nails grow out of the skin beneath them and out of the *cuticle*. The cuticle is the nonliving epidermis that surrounds the edges of fingernails and toenails. When your hair and nails are cut, you do not feel any pain. That is because the hair and nails do not contain nerve endings. But pulling the hair and nails does cause pain. This is because the force of the pull reaches into the dermis, where the nerve endings are.

Care of the hair

Healthy hair improves your personal appearance. Anyone can have healthy hair by taking care of it regularly.

Brushing

Brushing the hair increases the circulation in the scalp. It stops the buildup of dirt. It also spreads the natural oil evenly over the hairs. The oil makes the hair soft and glossy. Brushing the hair once or twice daily is usually enough. Brushing too often may cause hair loss because hair is slowly pulled and lifted from its roots.

Shampooing

You should wash your hair at least once a week with shampoo to keep the scalp and hair clean. If your hair is oily, you might want to wash it every day.

Dandruff

Ordinary dandruff is made up of dead cells. These come off the scalp in the same way that cells come off the epidermis all over your body. Sometimes the scalp is too oily. The oil causes the dead cells to clump together and become noticeable. Regular shampooing and brushing usually prevent dandruff. But sometimes a special shampoo may be needed. If most of the dandruff does not disappear with good hair care, see your doctor for treatment. Dandruff can be one cause of hair loss.

Regular shampooing can help prevent dandruff.

Hair dressings and sprays

Hair dressings and sprays may help keep hair in place. But, if you use them, wash your hair frequently. Dirt may cling to these substances. Some people are allergic to hair sprays. They wheeze and cough when using them. If this happens to you, do not use hair spray.

Hair coloring

There are different ways to change the color of hair. One way is to add color. With this method, dyes darken the natural color of the hair. Another way is to "strip" or bleach out the hair's natural color. Depending on how much color-removing chemical is used, the hair may be lightly or completely bleached. After bleaching, or stripping, a new color is sometimes added. A natural brunet, for example, may become a blond after stripping out hair color and then adding blonding chemicals.

Hair bleaches and dyes are harmful to some people. Some scientists think that frequent use of dyes may cause cancer. Care should be taken before any such process is used. Always test for an allergic reaction first.

Something to think about . . .

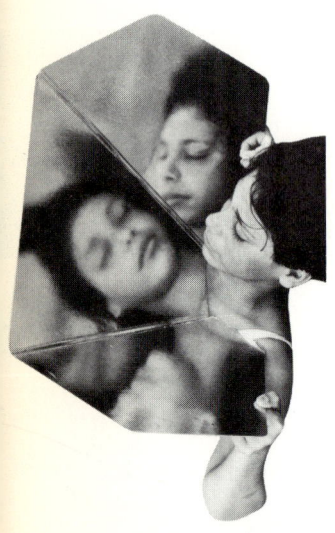

It is tempting to believe that once you have a tan, your skin is safe from the burning rays of the sun. Though the skin does try to protect itself by producing melanin, the resulting change in skin color can only block out 50 percent of the sun's ultraviolet rays.

Many people expect to get somewhat sunburned during the summer. But once the redness of sunburn goes away, does the skin return to normal? Many doctors would answer "no." They believe that the effects of frequent sunburns are cumulative (add up) and are irreversible (permanent).

After the sunburn cells peel off and the redness changes to brown, your skin still has not healed completely. If the sunburn was very bad, it probably damaged the cellular genetic material called deoxyribonucleic acid, or DNA.

Sun-damaged skin can look normal for some time—even for 20 years. But that is because the damage is underneath, in the dermis of the skin. Beneath the tanned epidermis, degenerative changes in the collagen (the connective tissue that gives the body its structure) are taking place. This decay leads to extreme tissue disorganization. All this is taking place beneath a summer tan.

Eventually, these changes beneath the surface may begin to affect the skin's outer appearance. The skin on the face may become wrinkled and leathery. The hands may develop brownish, flat "sun spots." This is called solar aging. Such skin changes are not usually seen in areas of the skin that have not been exposed to sunlight.

The next time you are planning to spend a day in the sun, think about the effects of the sun's light on your skin, and bring along an effective sunscreen.

The effects of many sunburns on the skin add up and are long-lasting.

Main Ideas

1. The epidermis and the dermis are the two main layers of the skin.
2. The skin keeps the body moist, protects the body, helps to control body temperature, and serves as an organ of sensation and expression.
3. To function properly, the skin needs to be kept clean. Proper care can prevent many skin problems.
4. Hair and nails grow from the upper layer of the skin. Proper care keeps hair healthy.

5. There are two types of dermatitis: contact dermatitis and allergic dermatitis. Both cause the skin to break out in a rash and to become inflamed.
6. Most moles are harmless. But if a mole gets larger, changes color, or is constantly irritated, see a doctor.

Key Words

acne	dermis	melanin
albino	epidermis	mole
athlete's foot	freckles	pigment
boils	fungus	pores
cuticle	hives	ringworm
dermatitis	malignant melanoma	sebum

Apply Your Knowledge

1. How is the dermis different from the epidermis?
2. What are the four general functions of the skin?
3. How does the process of perspiration help regulate your body temperature?
4. Give some examples of contact dermatitis.
5. What is the proper way to get a suntan? How can you keep from getting a sunburn?
6. How can athlete's foot be prevented?
7. How do pimples and blackheads form? Describe what can be done to help prevent the development of acne.
8. What determines the color of your hair? Why do some older people have gray hair?
9. Name some common skin problems that can usually be prevented with good personal habits.
10. When are moles harmful?

Extend Your Knowledge

1. Explain why you must drink more fluids on a hot summer day than on a cold winter day.
2. Make a list of cosmetics that claim to help your skin. Do you think they are all needed for proper skin care?
3. Which skin disorders are likely to be transferred to others if special precautions are not taken?

Chapter 17

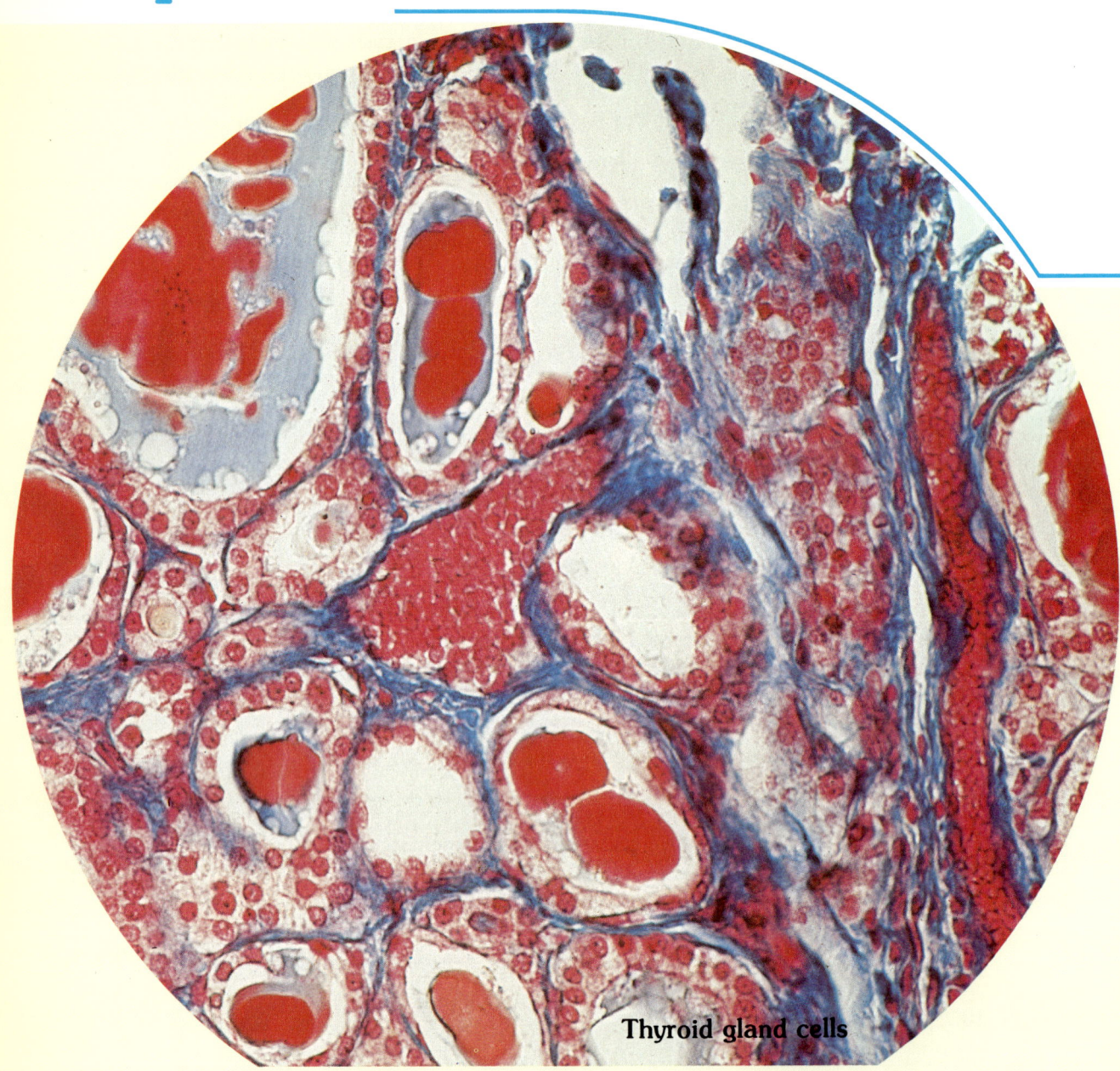

Thyroid gland cells

Do you know...

- how the endocrine glands are different from other glands?
- why the pituitary gland is sometimes called the "master" gland?
- what gland is the thermostat for your body temperature and function?
- what diabetes is and how it can be controlled?

Regulators of Your Body

Hormones are chemicals that act as the body's messengers. They travel throughout the body to "tell" various organs to speed up or slow down their activity. Hormones regulate the many systems in the body so that they work together. Thanks to your hormones, you function as a single living being, not just as a set of unrelated organs and body parts.

Hormones are produced by the *endocrine glands*. The endocrine glands are located in the head, neck, and trunk. These glands are different from other glands in the body. They do not have ducts, or tubes, that lead out to other parts of the body. Instead, the hormones produced pass directly from the cells of the gland into the bloodstream. Then they pass into the fluid that surrounds the cells of the organ they will act on. For this reason, the endocrine glands are called glands of internal secretion, or *ductless glands.*

Pituitary gland

The *pituitary gland* is located deep inside the brain. Of all the endocrine glands, it is thought to have the most influence on the others. In fact, it is sometimes called the "master" gland. One pituitary hormone is called the *thyroid-stimulating hormone.* This hormone causes the thyroid to produce its hormone. Another hormone produced by the pituitary is called *ACTH* (the adrenocorticotrophic hormone). This hormone makes the adrenal glands produce their hormones. Other pituitary hormones may make the ovaries and testes work.

The pituitary gland also produces the hormones that control body growth. Too much of these hormones may cause bones to grow unusually large and long. This causes giantism. Too few growth hormones may lead to dwarfism.

The pituitary gland is thought to control the temperature of the human body. Some scientists feel that the *hypothalamus,* a part of the brain located above the pituitary gland, sends hormones to the pituitary. These hormones from the hypothalamus may regulate body temperature.

Thyroid gland

The *thyroid gland* is located in the neck. It is perhaps the best known endocrine gland. The thyroid produces the hormone *thyroxin.* Thyroxin controls the rate of metabolism in all the cells of the body. *Metabolism* means the chemical change that goes on in cells to support life. If too much thyroxin is produced, cell metabolism is speeded up. People with too much thyroxin in their blood remain thin no matter how much they eat. They feel warm even in cool weather, and they are easily excited and too active. They change quickly from one activity to another.

On the other hand, too little thyroxin in the blood slows down cell metabolism. People with too little thyroxin in their blood become overweight, even if they eat very little. They may feel cold even in a warm room. Most food is stored instead of being used.

Iodine and the thyroid gland

The thyroid gland needs iodine to work properly. If the body does not get enough iodine, the cells of the thyroid must work harder to produce thyroxin. The thyroid gets larger in order to perform the extra work. This swelling in the neck is called a goiter.

We usually get iodine from our food and water. Because sea water contains iodine salts, people who eat seafood usually get the iodine they need. In places where the soil has iodine in it, the food and water will naturally supply enough iodine. But some soils, especially in places once covered by glaciers, have no iodine. In these areas, people are more likely to have goiters.

In places where there is little iodine in food and drinking water, iodized salt is a good source of iodine. Iodized salt is ordinary table salt to which iodine has been added.

Thyroxin and cretinism

A baby who has much too little thyroxin grows slowly. The skin becomes thick. The hair is dry and dull. The child is usually overweight and has trouble keeping warm. The baby is also slow in acting and thinking. These are symptoms of *cretinism*. Cretinism can lead to physical and mental retardation. But today, cretinism is rare because iodized salt is widely used. Early symptoms of cretinism can also be helped with thyroxin treatment.

Parathyroid glands

There are four *parathyroid glands*. These important glands are located in the neck, within the thyroid gland. Secretions from the parathyroids are needed for the metabolism of calcium and phosphorus. Calcium and phosphorus are needed to build all body tissues, especially the bones and teeth. Calcium is also needed to clot blood. A balance of calcium and other substances in the blood is necessary for the healthy working of muscles and nerves.

Years ago it was not known that the parathyroid glands were located within the thyroid gland. Doctors sometimes removed thyroid glands

- Pituitary Gland
- Thyroid Gland
- Parathyroids
- Islands of Langerhans in Pancreas
- Adrenal Glands
- Ovaries in Female
- Testes in Male

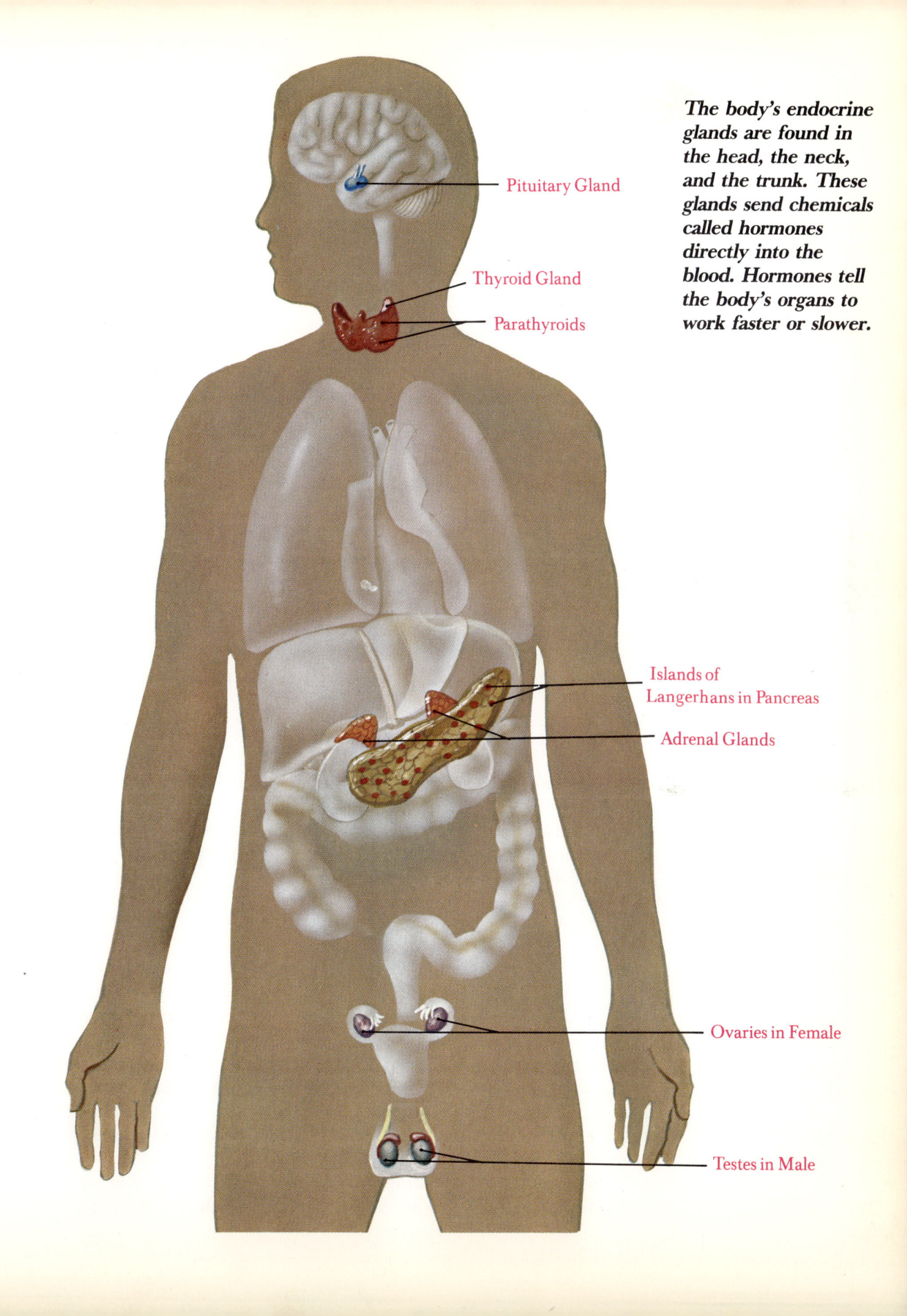

The body's endocrine glands are found in the head, the neck, and the trunk. These glands send chemicals called hormones directly into the blood. Hormones tell the body's organs to work faster or slower.

Adrenal Glands

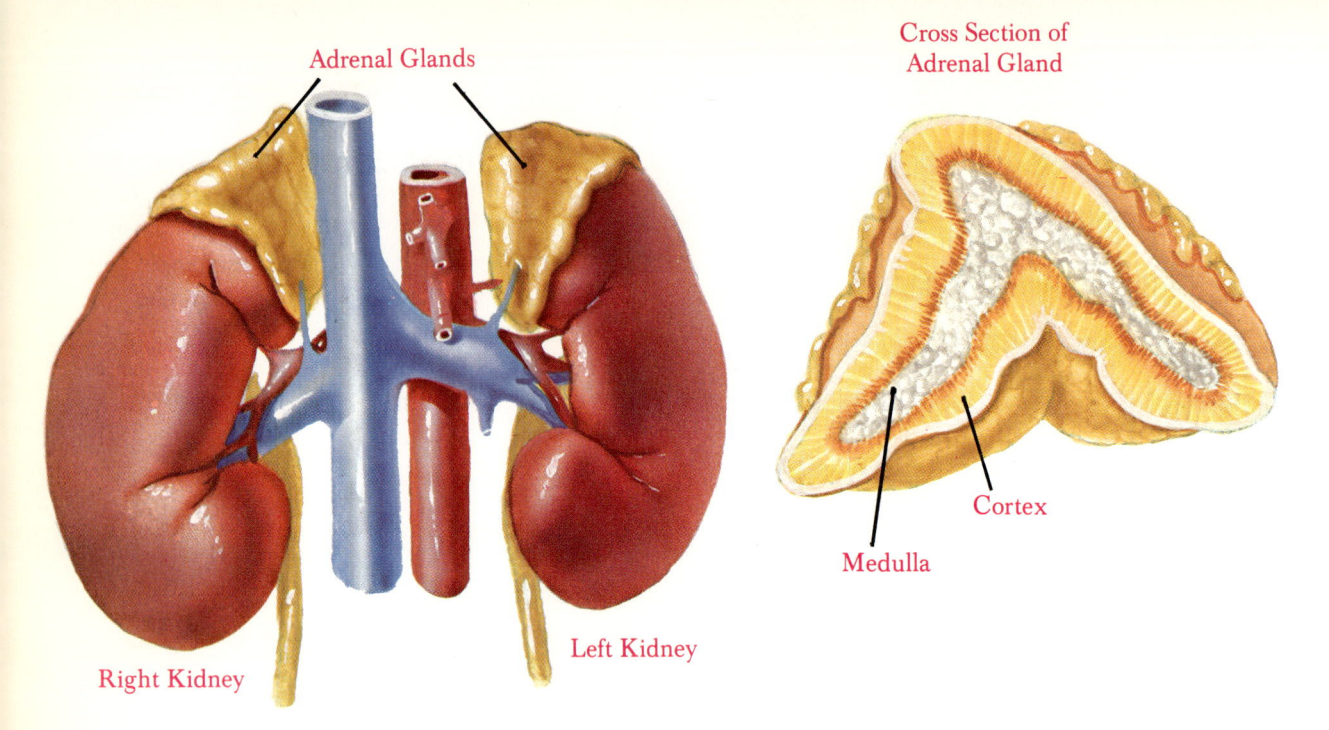

Cross Section of Adrenal Gland

Right Kidney

Left Kidney

Cortex

Medulla

The two adrenal glands are found one above each kidney. The medulla, or inner part of each gland, produces the hormone adrenalin.

that were secreting too much thyroxin. Then the patients had severe muscle spasms and died. Fortunately, doctors were able to discover that there are two different endocrine glands in one—the parathyroids within the thyroid. Since this discovery, doctors are careful not to remove the parathyroids.

Islands of Langerhans

The *islands of Langerhans* are tiny clusters of gland tissue found in the pancreas, which is located near the stomach. The islands of Langerhans produce the hormone *insulin*, a very important substance. Insulin is needed for breaking down sugar so that it can be used by body cells. If the islands of Langerhans do not produce enough insulin, a serious disease called *diabetes* develops.

Diabetes

Leslie's first symptom of diabetes was thirst. She was thirsty all the time. She waited anxiously for each class period to end so she could get a drink of water. After school, she drank several cans of soda. After a while, her terrible thirst was joined by a tremendous appetite. She began to eat often throughout the day. Despite the huge amount of food she ate, she did not gain weight. Before long, Leslie began to feel very tired. She sometimes lacked the energy even to talk with her friends.

Leslie's symptoms were signs of diabetes mellitus, the most common form of diabetes. The islands of Langerhans in her pancreas had stopped secreting insulin. She was eating plenty of food, which meant that there was more than enough sugar in her bloodstream. But without insulin, her body could not break down the sugar to use for energy. So Leslie's cells were starving.

Leslie's kidneys needed large amounts of water to remove the extra sugar in her blood. So Leslie was always thirsty, and she had to urinate frequently. She finally went to a doctor, who gave her a blood test and urinalysis. The above-normal amounts of sugar in her urine and in her blood showed that Leslie had diabetes.

Most cases of diabetes mellitus appear in persons over the age of 40. Only about 10 percent of all diabetics show symptoms before the age of 15. People who are obese have a greater than normal chance of developing diabetes later in life.

Today, most people who have diabetes are able to lead normal lives. They eat fewer carbohydrates and fats, they exercise regularly, and they take insulin to make up for the amount not produced by their glands. Insulin must be taken by injection. Taking insulin does not cure diabetes, but it controls the disease.

If too much insulin is injected, the diabetic may have an insulin reaction. The symptoms of insulin reaction are these:

1. **pale, cold, and clammy skin;**
2. **shallow breathing;**
3. **nervousness;**
4. **possible loss of consciousness if not treated.**

People with diabetes learn how to tell when they are having an insulin reaction. They can quickly restore the proper blood-sugar level by eating a sugary food.

Hypoglycemia

When the body produces too much insulin, the amount of sugar in the blood falls below normal. This condition is called *hypoglycemia*, which means low blood sugar. Nervousness, weakness, and other symptoms result because the cells do not get enough sugar to meet their needs. People who have hypoglycemia must watch their diet very carefully.

Adrenal glands

Your two *adrenal glands* are located in the trunk of your body, one above each kidney. They are 2.5 to 5 centimeters (1 to 2 inches) long. Each adrenal gland has an inner part and an outer part. Each part secretes a different hormone.

Adrenalin

Adrenalin is one of the hormones secreted by the inner part of the adrenal glands, or medulla. Adrenalin makes the heart beat faster and more strongly. It increases muscle tone in the skeletal muscles, and it slows down activity in the digestive tract. These changes make the body ready for action—fighting, running away, or perhaps doing something that the per-

Adrenalin is the body's "emergency hormone." It makes the heart beat faster and makes the muscles ready to do work. With adrenalin, the body can do things it would not be able to do under normal conditions. For example, people have been known to lift up cars in order to release someone who is trapped.

son would not have the strength to do under normal conditions. When a person is frightened or angry, for example, more adrenalin is produced.

Adrenalin can be made in laboratories. It is used in treating many disorders. Sometimes it is given to people who are having severe attacks of asthma. It can be used to speed up the circulation of the blood of a person suffering from shock or suffocation. In some cases, an injection of adrenalin into a heart that has stopped beating will cause the heart to start beating again.

Cortisone

The outer part of the adrenal glands is also known as the cortex. It produces a hormone called *cortisone*. Cortisone lessens swelling and helps the body react to stress. Cortisone is also used to treat kidney disease, arthritis, and other disorders. Cortisone should be used only under the watchful eye of a doctor, because it can have harmful side effects. Hormones from the cortex also control the body's use of salts, fats, and glucose (one form of sugar).

Gonads

The *gonads*, or sex glands, are organs that produce reproductive cells. In females, the gonads are the ovaries, which lie in the lower part of the abdomen. They release mature egg cells and produce several sex hormones. The most important female hormone is *estrogen*. In males, the gonads are the testes, which are in a small outer pouch below the abdomen. The testes produce sperm and the hormone *testosterone*. Scientists have learned that the ovaries secrete a small amount of testosterone and the testes secrete a small amount of estrogen.

Both the ovaries and the testes develop before birth. They produce sex hormones in small amounts during childhood. They begin to produce greater amounts of the sex hormones in most girls between the ages of 11 and 14, and in most boys a year or two later. The sex hormones cause the secondary sexual characteristics to develop in young men and young women.

Pineal and thymus glands

Two other endocrine glands, the *pineal gland* and the *thymus gland,* are now being studied by researchers. Much less is known about these glands than is known about the other endocrine glands.

The pineal gland, located in the center of the brain, plays a role in regulating daily rhythms. It seems sensitive to light and darkness. It also works with other endocrine organs.

The thymus gland is located in the upper chest. It is somewhat large at birth but seems to decrease in size thereafter. By the time one becomes an adult, it is very small. The thymus is believed to produce substances helpful in fighting infections.

Taking care of your endocrine system

The endocrine system usually takes care of its own chemical balance. If the system is not working well, a person usually has symptoms such as unusual thirst, unexplained weight change, extreme tiredness or nervousness, or signs of abnormal growth and development. Such symptoms signal the need for a doctor's care. Blood tests can be used to check the way the glands are working. For example, blood tests can quickly show if you have a thyroid disorder or diabetes.

Sometimes the body does not make enough of the hormone insulin. When this happens, too much sugar stays in the blood and then is passed out of the body in the urine. This serious disease is called diabetes. The materials shown here make testing for the amount of sugar in the urine easy for the diabetic.

Something to think about . . .

Why do placebos, sugar pills, or other inert "medications" sometimes produce dramatic relief from pain in certain patients? This mysterious phenomenon has been partially explained in a recent experiment. Subconsciously, some patients are able to activate their bodies' production of endorphins when they expect relief from a particular treatment. Endorphins are proteins released by the brain and pituitary gland. They modify signals between nerve cells, and are reported to be two hundred times more powerful than morphine. The name *endorphin* literally means "the morphine within."

Placebos have probably always been effective with certain people, even before medicine became a scientific discipline. Several decades ago, scientific research determined that a remarkably constant fraction of patients experienced a reduction of pain when they were treated with placebos. About a third of all patients are affected in this way.

Researchers first thought that the pain itself did not change, but that the patient's perception of the pain was altered by his or her belief in the effectiveness of the drug. But researchers found physiological changes in these patients as well. For example, stomach ulcers improved. Research was begun to determine whether placebos actually triggered some internal mechanisms for curing physiological conditions and reducing pain. When pain-suppressant proteins produced by the brain and pituitary gland were discovered, scientists were better able to explore the placebo effect. Through research, scientists have concluded that endorphins are produced in response to treatment with placebos. Experimental results suggest that variations in the amount of endorphin activity in different individuals may account for variations in the amount of pain they report for a specific illness or medical procedure. Further research in this area is planned. An understanding of the body's internal mechanisms for suppressing pain may result in more effective medical treatment—treatment for pain that combines methods which work psychologically and physiologically.

Main Ideas

1. The endocrine glands secrete hormones that are carried by the blood and that control various activities of the body.
2. Too much or too little secretion of hormones from one or more of the endocrine glands may cause a disturbance in the working of the body.
3. In many cases, modern scientific knowledge has made it possible to control disorders caused by too much or too little secretion of hormones.

Key Words

ACTH	estrogen	parathyroid glands
adrenal glands	gonads	pineal gland
adrenalin	hormone	pituitary gland
cortisone	hypoglycemia	testosterone
cretinism	hypothalamus	thymus gland
diabetes	insulin	thyroid gland
ductless glands	islands of Langerhans	thyroid-stimulating hormone
endocrine glands	metabolism	thyroxin

Apply Your Knowledge

1. Name the glands that make up the endocrine system.
2. Which gland is sometimes called the "master" gland? Why?
3. What is another name for an enlarged thyroid gland? What causes an enlarged thyroid to develop?
4. Explain what cretinism is. How has this disorder been controlled?
5. Explain how producing too much or too little insulin can cause disorders.
6. Which hormone helps to prepare the body for action or stress? How?
7. What hormones are produced in the ovaries? Which are produced in the testes?
8. What gland secretes cortisone? What does cortisone do in the body?
9. Which glands in the body secrete hormones that are needed to help use calcium and phosphorus?
10. List the functions of the pituitary gland.

Extend Your Knowledge

1. Locate the endocrine glands on a chart of the human body or on an anatomical model.
2. Do some research on the discovery of insulin. Report your findings to the class.
3. Ask a pharmacist which hormones are now synthetically made by drug companies. Synthetic hormones are available to help people whose glands do not work in the normal way.
4. Collect articles in newspapers and magazines about research on hormones and on the endocrine glands. Report your findings to your class.
5. Describe the blood tests that are used to find out whether or not the glands are working normally.

Chapter 18

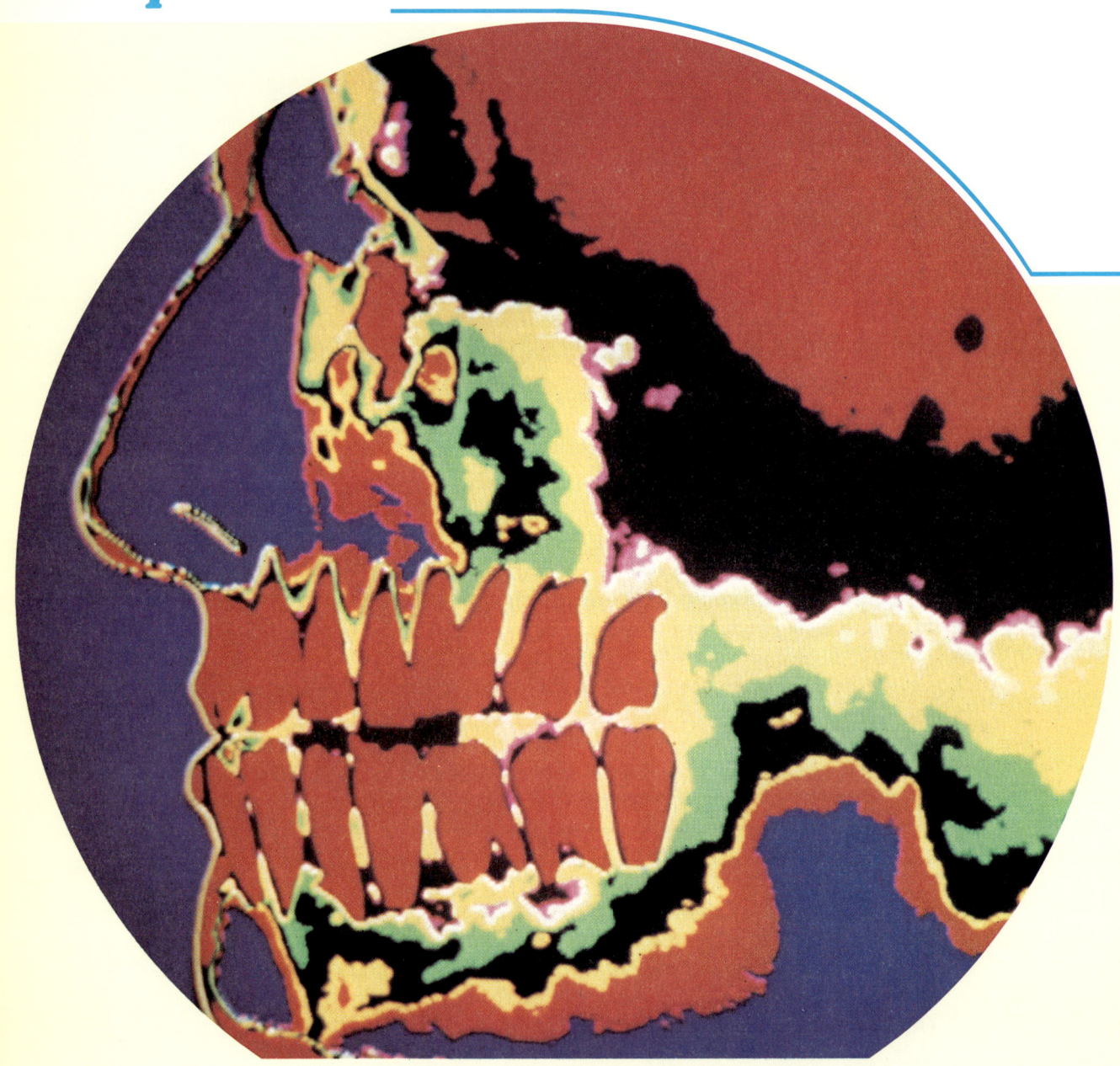

Heat-sensitive photo of the jaw and teeth

Do you know . . .

- why crooked teeth should be straightened?
- what causes bad breath?
- how to use dental floss?
- how to prevent gum disease?

Healthy Teeth

Your teeth are an important part of how you look. They are also important to good nutrition, proper digestion, and the overall health of your body. However, teeth may also cause many problems. Dental disease is thought to be the most common health problem in the United States. Most dental problems can be prevented or controlled by knowing how to care for your teeth.

Your teeth

Your teeth are powerful tools for cutting, tearing, crushing, and grinding food. Teeth help to prepare food for digestion. They break up solid food so that digestive juices can mix with it easily. The first of these digestive juices is the saliva in the mouth. Saliva adds fluid to food and begins the digestion of starches. When you chew food thoroughly, saliva can act upon it more effectively. So thorough chewing is important for good digestion.

Structure

Each tooth is made up of three parts. The *crown* is the part that can be seen above the gums. The *neck* is the thinner part of the tooth that is surrounded by the gums. The *roots* are firmly planted in the jawbone.

The inside of each tooth is made up mostly of a type of bone tissue called dentin. The dentin in the crown of a tooth is covered by a layer of hard *enamel*. Enamel is the hardest substance made by your body. The inside of the tooth is called the pulp cavity. This cavity holds nerves, blood vessels, and lymph vessels. These nerves and vessels enter the tooth through the root canal that goes from the tip of the roots to the pulp cavity.

Except for the enamel, the teeth are alive. Chewing causes blood to circulate in the gums and teeth. Cell metabolism in the teeth, gums, and jawbone is going on all the time.

Functions

The names of the different teeth tell what the teeth do. The 8 sharp teeth in front are called *incisors*. They cut, or incise, food. Next to the incisors are the 4 *cuspids,* or canines. These fanglike teeth are used for

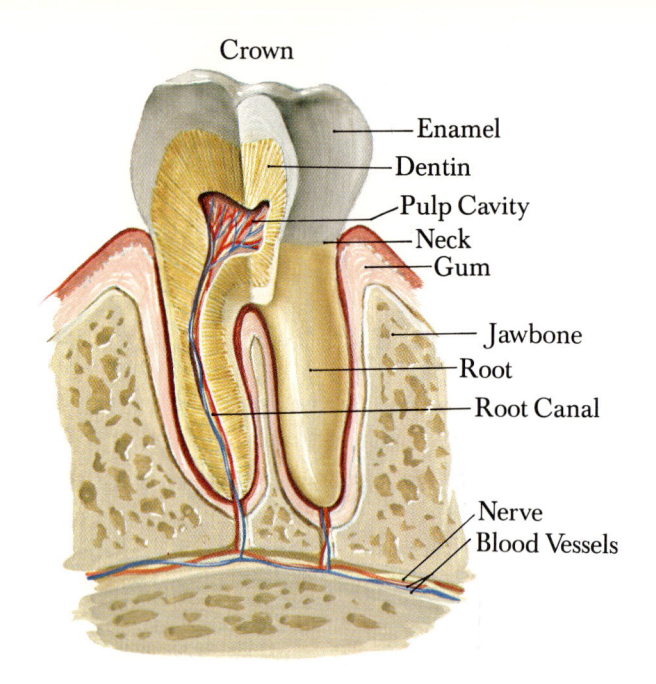

This cross section shows the parts and the position of a tooth. Except for the enamel, the teeth are alive. Cell activity in the teeth, gums, and jawbone is going on all the time.

tearing food. Behind the cuspids are the 8 *premolars* and the 12 *molars* that crush and grind food.

Development

Most people have 32 permanent teeth: 16 in the upper jaw and 16 in the lower jaw. But a few people have less than the usual number of teeth. And some people have more.

When a baby is born, all the primary teeth and some permanent teeth are already formed in the jawbones. There are 20 primary teeth: 10 in the lower jaw and 10 in the upper jaw. These primary teeth, or "baby teeth," will be replaced later by permanent teeth.

When a child is about six years old, the permanent teeth begin to push through the gums. The first permanent teeth to appear are the 4 first molars. When the child is about twelve, the second molars push up behind the first molars.

The third and last molars are called the wisdom teeth. They usually come in after the age of sixteen. Sometimes the wisdom teeth come in at the wrong angle and press against the second molars. Then they are called "impacted" wisdom teeth. If this happens, the impacted wisdom teeth may have to be removed. A dentist may extract, or pull out, the problem teeth after giving the patient a local anesthetic, such as Novocain. A local anesthetic temporarily deadens the nerves in the tooth and surrounding gum so that the patient will not feel pain. Sometimes, though, it is necessary for a dental surgeon to cut through gum tissue to remove impacted wisdom teeth. In such a case, a patient may be given a general anesthetic to put her or him to sleep during the extraction.

Care of the teeth

As the primary teeth, or "baby teeth," come in, a child should be taught to brush them. Visits to the dentist should start early, at the age of three or four. Not taking care of primary teeth may cause dental problems for the child later on. An infection at the roots of the primary teeth may affect the permanent teeth below them. Also, if a primary tooth decays so badly that it has to be removed, the space may close up before the permanent tooth comes in. This often causes crowded, irregular, or crooked permanent teeth.

Diet

To build good teeth and to keep them strong and healthy, the body needs foods with vitamin D and the minerals calcium and phosphorus. Foods with a great deal of sugar—such as candy, cake, cookies, pies, and sweet drinks—add to tooth decay. People who eat many sugar-rich foods often have more tooth decay than those who eat less of these foods. Bacteria in the mouth mix with the sugar. This forms an acid that may dissolve the hard enamel covering the tooth and start internal tooth decay. Most damage is done within 20 minutes after having sweet foods or drinks. So for snacks between meals, it is better to have foods such as raw fruits, celery or carrot sticks, and unsweetened drinks or milk.

Chemicals called fluorides make tooth enamel harder and better able to hold up against decay. Toothpastes that have fluorides which are known to fight decay carry the seal of the American Dental Association (ADA).

Fluorides

Some years ago, researchers found that there was less tooth decay in communities where fluorides were found naturally in the drinking water supply. Since then, adding the chemical *sodium fluoride* to drinking water has lowered the average amount of tooth decay by about 60 percent. Fluorides seem to make tooth enamel harder and better able to resist decay.

If your water supply is fluoridated, you probably have enough fluoride for strong, healthy teeth. If you are not sure about fluoridation in your community, ask your dentist. If your water is not fluoridated, your dentist may use a fluoride solution on your teeth. Or the dentist may suggest that you take fluoride tablets or drops at home. Fluorides in toothpaste may also be helpful. Toothpastes which contain fluorides that have been proven effective carry the seal of the American Dental Association.

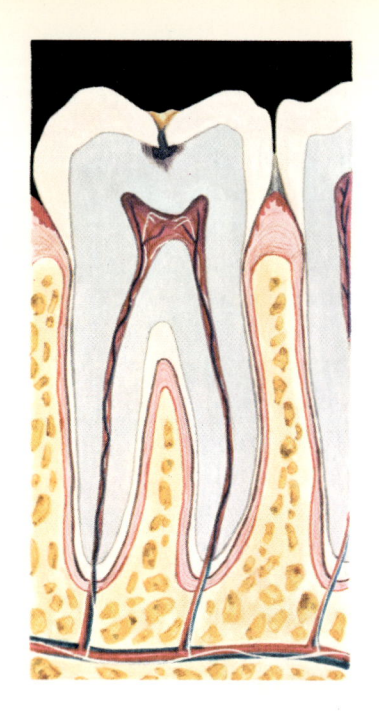

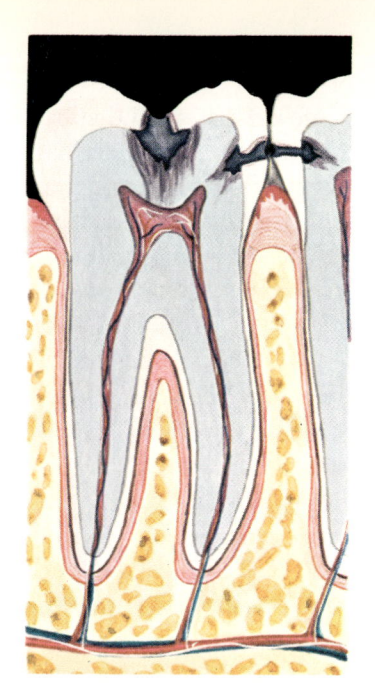

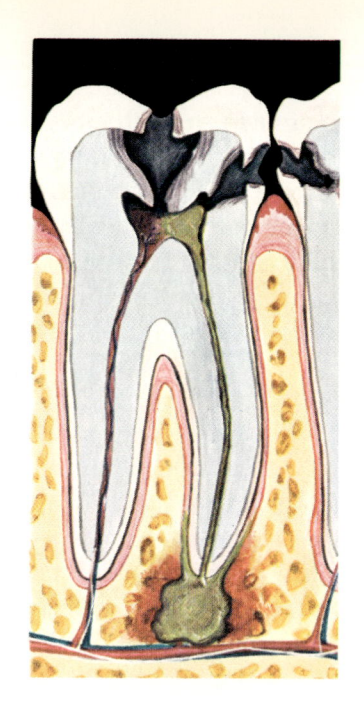

When tooth enamel breaks, tooth decay begins and moves inside the tooth. On the left, there is a small break in the enamel. In the middle, decay has spread inside and a new break has taken place in the side of the tooth, and in the tooth next to it. At the right, the decay has spread to the root of the tooth and an infection has started.

Cleaning the teeth

Plaque is a sticky, colorless layer of bacteria that forms constantly in the mouth. When plaque interacts with sugar, it produces acid. Acid dissolves the enamel, producing tooth decay. It is important to remove plaque in order to prevent dental disease. Teeth should be brushed after each meal and at bedtime. Use a brush that has a flat brushing surface and soft bristles with rounded ends. Hold the brush at an angle against the gum line where the plaque forms. Move it back and forth, using a gentle, scrubbing motion. Remember to brush all the surfaces of the teeth—inner and outer. Replace your toothbrush when it begins to show signs of wear.

Dental floss, a special waxed or unwaxed thread, is also very helpful in fighting tooth decay. Dental floss will reach particles a toothbrush cannot get to. It can remove the plaque that is located in the spaces between your teeth and at the gum lines. The correct way to use dental floss can be learned with a little practice. For the floss to be effective, it must be used in the right way.

If you cannot brush your teeth after a meal, rinse your mouth thoroughly with water. This may help to remove food particles.

Visits to the dentist

In addition to cleaning your teeth at home, it is wise to visit your dentist about once every six months. If you do this, dental problems can be treated before they become serious.

The dentist carefully cleans and examines the teeth and gums. The teeth and gums should be X-rayed to find small cavities, root abscesses, or other hidden problems. If cavities are found, the dentist prepares them for filling by first removing any decay. This stops the decay from spreading down into the pulp of the tooth. The filling then must be fitted carefully into the tooth so that it will not become loose. Also, a careful fit cuts down the chances for decay to start around the filling's edges.

Dental problems

Regular and careful care of your teeth can keep dental problems from happening. When such problems do arise, though, they should be treated without delay. They can affect not only your mouth but also your appearance and the health of other parts of your body.

Dental caries

The scientific name for tooth decay is *dental caries*. Dental caries is a common problem. About 95 out of every 100 Americans have some tooth decay. Even an infant may get tooth decay if often put to bed with a bottle filled with liquid containing sugar. Many people in their late teens have a high rate of tooth decay. A proper diet, fluorides, regular cleaning with toothbrush and dental floss, and professional dental care can prevent most cavities.

Root abscesses

If decay has spread to the root of the tooth, bacteria may cause an infection, or *abscess*. A root abscess is usually painful. Toxins (poisons produced by the bacteria)—and even the bacteria, themselves—may spread to other parts of the body. An abscess in the upper jaw may go directly to one of the sinuses and cause a serious sinus infection.

The painful swelling of the gums shown below is known as periodontal disease. If not treated, it can result in loss of teeth. Regular brushing and proper use of dental floss often stop swelling of the gums. Healthy gums are firm and pink, as shown on the next page.

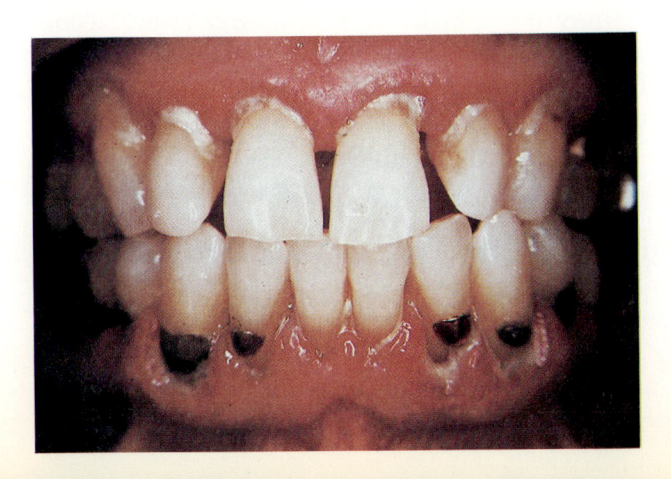

Malocclusion

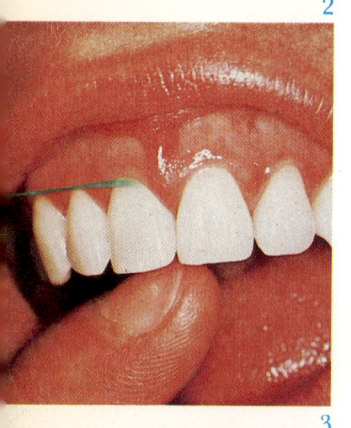

Irregular, or "crooked," teeth make it impossible for the teeth of the upper jaw to bite normally on those of the lower jaw. The result is *malocclusion,* or improper bite. Malocclusion sometimes causes people to breathe through their mouths. It may also interfere with speech and make a person look less attractive. Care of the primary teeth and of the six-year molars is helpful in stopping malocclusion. Proper care includes filling cavities, and either replacing lost primary teeth or putting in retainers that keep the spaces open until the permanent teeth grow in.

The treatment of malocclusion is known as *orthodontics.* A dentist who gives this treatment is called an *orthodontist.* Usually, orthodontics includes the use of braces that gently move the teeth into place. This process of moving, or "straightening," teeth may take months or even years to complete.

Gum problems

Teeth cannot be fully healthy without healthy gums. Healthy gums are firm. They are either pink or light red in color. Biting and chewing help to keep gums healthy by improving the circulation of blood.

Unhealthy gums become bright red or purplish, soft, and swollen. They bleed easily. This swelling of the gums is called *gingivitis.* Gingivitis is usually caused by poor care of the mouth and teeth. If a toothbrush or dental floss is not used properly, the gums may be injured and may swell. But regular brushing done in the right way and proper use of dental floss often stop swelling of the gums. A well-balanced diet with enough vitamin C may also help to stop gingivitis.

When plaque is not removed, it hardens to form a limelike layer on the teeth, especially near the tooth necks. This limelike layer is called *calculus,* or tartar. The only way to remove it is by a professional cleaning called a *prophylaxis.* Prophylaxis is done by a dentist or dental hygienist who scrapes away the calculus. This helps to prevent gingivitis, since a buildup of calculus irritates the gum tissue.

Gingivitis may not be easily spotted at an early stage because there is no pain or discomfort. But if your gums begin to bleed when you brush your teeth, contact your dentist. A *periodontal membrane* surrounds the tooth and holds it in place. If the gingivitis is severe and involves the periodontal membrane, it may result in the loosening and eventual loss of teeth. The advanced stage of gingivitis is known as periodontal disease. A *periodontist* is a dentist who specializes in the treatment of periodontal disorders. Peri-

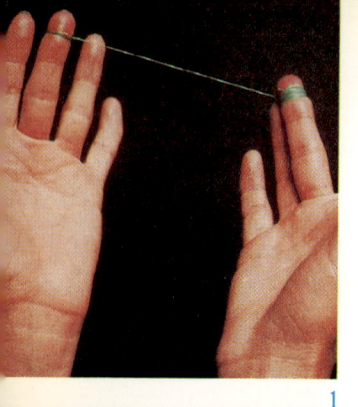

1. To floss your teeth, break off a piece of floss 18 inches long. 2. Wrap all but 3 inches around the middle fingers of each hand. 3. Guide the floss between two teeth with the thumb and forefingers, and bend it against the side of one tooth. 4. Holding the floss tightly, scrape the floss up and down against the side of the tooth. 5. Repeat these steps on the rest of your teeth.

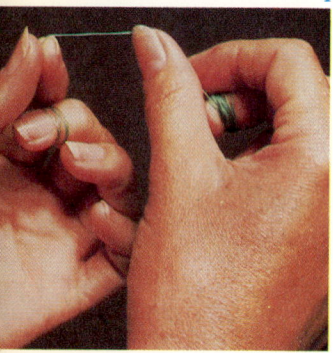

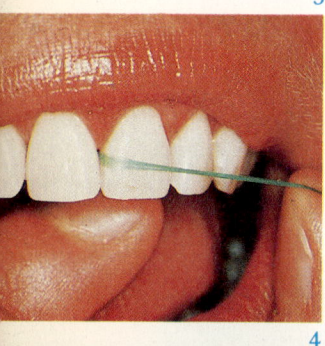

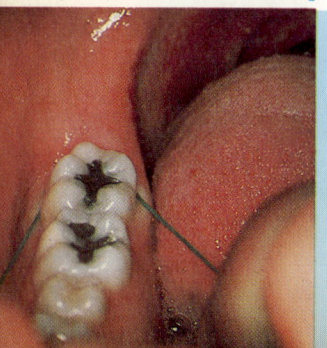

odontal disease usually affects those over twenty-five years of age. It is the chief cause for loss of teeth. For this reason, prevention should begin early in life, with proper brushing and use of dental floss.

Bad breath

Halitosis is another name for bad breath. Most people who take good care of their teeth do not have the problem of bad breath, since most mouth odors are caused by tooth decay and periodontal disease. Sometimes, infections of the nose, tonsils, or sinuses can cause bad breath. Also, substances in the air breathed out by the lungs can be the cause. Getting rid of the causes of bad breath is better than simply freshening the breath with a mouthwash. A mouthwash has only a short-lived effect.

Dental health

Good oral hygiene is your own personal job. You should choose foods that do not add to dental decay. Avoid snacks that have too much sugar.

Brush your teeth after eating and before going to bed. Clean your teeth with dental floss when necessary. Visit your dentist twice a year for checkups. And, if your water supply is not fluoridated, ask your dentist for another way to get fluoride. If you take proper care of your mouth and teeth, most dental problems can be stopped or controlled.

Something to think about . . .

How many dental caries does a chocolate bar cause? We know the number of calories in a chocolate bar (approximately 150 in a 1-oz. bar), but we do not have a clear measurement of the potential of certain foods to produce dental caries, or tooth decay. Studies are being done on this question, but there have been problems at each level of research.

Test-tube experiments have focused primarily on the composition of foods, especially carbohydrates, and the effects of different forms of food on the body. Experiments have also examined the chemical nature of food that is mixed with water and saliva. And experiments have revealed the ability of certain foods to buffer the acidity in other foods. The information produced by all these tests, however, may not be relevant to development of caries in humans.

Animal experiments have compared the effects on rats of foods with normal and altered sugar content. Rats were chosen as research subjects because they get caries, just as humans do, and they respond to diet and to microorganisms in a way that is similar to human response. But unfortunately, the results of the experiments on rats may also not be applicable to human beings.

There are several serious difficulties with clinical research on human subjects. Committees on human studies are reluctant to use refined carbohydrates on members of a control group. They are also unwilling to feed people a single substance for a prolonged period of time. And it is impossible to isolate the caries-producing potential of a single food in a varied diet.

When these research problems are solved, there may be a way to measure the caries-producing potential of different foods. Your dentist will then be able to advise you to go on a "low-caries" diet!

Main Ideas

1. **Daily mouth care is important to dental health.**
2. **Dental care is important in keeping a healthy and attractive appearance.**
3. **Proper diet, cleanliness, fluoridation, and regular visits to the dentist are the best ways to protect your teeth.**
4. **Most dental caries can be prevented.**
5. **Teeth that have begun to decay should be found early and filled. This keeps the decay from spreading.**
6. **Malocclusion can be treated by an orthodontist.**
7. **Diseases of the teeth and gums should be treated by a dentist.**

Key Words

abscess	gingivitis	orthodontist
calculus	halitosis	periodontal membrane
crown	incisor	periodontist
cuspid	malocclusion	plaque
dental caries	molar	premolar
enamel	neck	prophylaxis
fluoride	orthodontics	root

Apply Your Knowledge

1. Draw a picture of a tooth. Label the crown, neck, roots, dentin, enamel, pulp cavity, and root canal.
2. What is the function of teeth?
3. Diet is important in the formation of teeth and in stopping tooth decay. What kinds of foods should be included in the diet? Which foods should be eaten in small amounts? Which foods make good snacks?
4. What is plaque, and how can you remove it?
5. How is sodium fluoride used to stop tooth decay?
6. Why is it important to have cavities filled while they are small? How often should you go to the dentist?
7. Discuss ways to stop malocclusion.
8. Describe the way the mouth looks if a person has gingivitis.
9. Why is care of the gums important? In what ways can you keep your gums healthy?
10. Imagine that you have just sat down in the dentist's chair. List some of the things you expect the dentist to do to your teeth.

Extend Your Knowledge

1. If sodium fluoride is added to drinking water in your community, find out when this practice was started. What was the rate of dental caries before fluoridation? How much sodium fluoride is being used in the water? What, if any, results have been found so far? Make a report to the class.
2. Visit a dentist's office or a dental clinic. Ask the dentist to explain the use of some of the instruments and the X-ray machine. Ask to be shown X-ray photos of the following: primary teeth, with the permanent teeth ready to push through; dead teeth; root abscesses; and dental caries.
3. Discuss the advantages and disadvantages of electric toothbrushes, dental floss, and water irrigators.
4. Compare all the ingredients of five different mouthwashes sold in stores. Which ones contain sugar? How much sugar do they contain? If all the ingredients are not listed, write to the manufacturer and ask for a list.

Unit 6

CHAPTERS:

19 Use of Tobacco
20 Use of Alcohol
21 Drugs: Use and Abuse

Social Drugs

Chapter 19

Do you know . . .

- why many smokers find it difficult to stop?
- if there is such a thing as a "safe" cigarette?
- how "second-hand" smoke affects the nonsmoker?
- if most people automatically gain weight when they quit smoking?

Use of Tobacco

Medical and scientific knowledge leaves no doubt about the harmful effects of tobacco smoking. In fact, the Surgeon General of the United States Public Health Service has stated, ". . . cigarette smoking is the major preventable cause of illness, disability, and premature death in this country."

Smokers and nonsmokers alike share the high cost of smoking. Each year in the United States, accidents and diseases related to smoking cost billions of dollars in added health care expenses and lost work output. Especially tragic are the many home fires caused by smoking.

Tobacco smoke consists of more than 3000 components. It is a mixture of gases, vapors, and tiny suspended particles. Each cubic centimeter of the tobacco smoke that enters the mouth contains millions of these particles. One of the harmful gases in this smoke is carbon monoxide. Carbon monoxide reduces the oxygen-carrying capacity of the blood. It is believed to be responsible for the reduced wind (or shortness of breath) of smokers. There is often several hundred times as much carbon monoxide in tobacco smoke as is thought to be safe. The particles in smoke also contain *nicotine* and *tar*.

Substances in tobacco smoke

Nicotine

The nicotine in tobacco smoke is a powerful, colorless poison. When absorbed into the bloodstream, nicotine affects the nervous system. A drop of pure nicotine injected into the body would cause death in a few minutes.

Every smoker absorbs some of the nicotine in tobacco smoke. Heavy cigarette smokers who inhale absorb enough nicotine each day to kill instantly if it were injected directly into the blood. The reason a person does not die after smoking is that the amount of nicotine absorbed at any one time is less than a fatal dose.

The beginning smoker often has symptoms of mild nicotine poisoning. Even regular smokers sometimes show the same effects. These symptoms include dizziness, faintness, rapid pulse, clammy skin, and sometimes nausea, vomiting, and diarrhea.

Nicotine seems to be responsible for tobacco addiction and for many diseases of the heart and blood vessels.

Tobacco tars

The tars in tobacco smoke contain a large number of chemicals. Some of these, called carcinogens, produce cancer if applied to the skin of animals. Others, called co-carcinogens, act with other chemicals to cause cancer. Tars are also responsible for bronchitis, emphysema, and other diseases of the respiratory tract associated with smoking. However, smokers who switch to low-tar, low-nicotine cigarettes may be fooling themselves. They often smoke more cigarettes, inhale more deeply, or puff more often. The reason appears to be an addiction to nicotine. Also, additives have been included in the newer brands, and the nature and amounts of the additives are not known. For these and other reasons, the U.S. Surgeon General has stressed that there is no "safe" cigarette.

Effects of smoking on the body

In most people, smoking dulls the senses of taste and smell. Tobacco tars cause unattractive brown stains on the teeth and fingers of cigarette smokers, and both nicotine and tobacco tars are irritating to the respiratory tract. Smoking is also responsible for bad breath and the likelihood of developing facial wrinkles as one grows older.

The heart rate increases after smoking. In one group of young people studied, the average increase after a single cigarette was 21 beats per minute. Occasionally, the heartbeat becomes irregular, and there is pain in the chest. Smoking also causes the small arteries to contract, or become smaller. This cuts down the flow of blood through them. Decreased blood flow lowers the temperature of the skin. This is often accompanied by an increase in blood pressure.

Smoking and disease

Experts estimate that each year 340,000 Americans die early from the effects of smoking. Smoking is also one of the causes of long-lasting and uncomfortable minor ailments.

Coronary heart disease

Smoking puts a strain on the heart and blood vessels. It also reduces blood flow through the lungs. And it causes the lungs to absorb less oxygen. These effects cause shortness of breath. They also keep the heart from getting enough oxygen. There are many more deaths from coronary heart disease among cigarette smokers than among nonsmokers.

Cancer

According to the American Cancer Society, cigarette smoking is responsible for one in every five cancer deaths. Smoking has been linked to cancer of the lung, larynx, pharynx, oral cavity, esophagus, pancreas, and bladder. In a recent year, about 111,000 persons in the United States died of lung cancer. Of these deaths, it is thought that more than 75 percent were due to cigarette smoking.

The chances of developing lung cancer depend upon a number of factors: the age at which smoking begins, the number of cigarettes smoked each day, how deeply the smoke is inhaled, the total number of years of smoking, and the total number of cigarettes smoked over those years. Among men, lung cancer continues to be the leading cause of cancer deaths, and if present trends continue, it will soon be the leading cause of cancer deaths among women. Although the proportion of adults who smoke has been declining, present smokers (especially women) are smoking more heavily.

Researchers have also reported the damaging effects that cigarette smoking has on certain kinds of workers. Asbestos workers who smoke have 60 times as great a chance of developing lung cancer as do nonsmoking asbestos workers. Industrial workers are especially susceptible to lung diseases, due to the combined effects of cigarette smoking and exposure to toxic industrial substances.

Pipe and cigar smokers usually do not inhale as much as cigarette smokers do. Therefore, their risk of developing lung cancer is not as great as that for cigarette smokers. But it is still a greater risk than for nonsmokers. Also, smoke exposure in the upper respiratory tract is approximately the same for all smokers. Therefore, the chances of developing cancer of the pharynx, larynx, mouth, and esophagus are as great for pipe and cigar smokers as for cigarette smokers. Pipe smokers have the added risk of developing lip cancer.

Chronic bronchitis and emphysema

Heavy smokers often have a chronic cough. It is caused by irritation of the linings of the nose, throat, and lungs. In time, this irritation may be followed by chronic bronchitis and emphysema (see Chapter 15). Emphysema may begin with a slight difficulty in breathing at times. Later, an activity such as a short walk may result in breathlessness. After a time, emphysema reaches a point where the individual is unable to perform

You may think smoking makes you look mature. But it's not mature to do something you know is unhealthy. Smokers have a much greater chance of suffering from heart disease than nonsmokers. And smokers have a much better chance of getting chronic bronchitis, emphysema, and lung cancer, too.

normal activities. About 80 percent of all cases of emphysema are related to smoking.

Involuntary smoking

Ann Casey is a 24-year-old artist. She likes movies, plays, concerts, sports events, and eating out in restaurants. But only recently has she been able to enjoy some of these activities. Ann is allergic to tobacco smoke. This past year, her community established no-smoking areas in all public facilities. So Ann is now able to enjoy activities that she once thought she would never be able to attend.

People who have asthma, emphysema, or heart ailments cannot be in a smoky environment. Many of them are not as fortunate as Ann. They live in cities or towns that have not yet established smoking regulations. Such regulations guarantee smoke-free areas at restaurants, public meetings, and entertainment facilities.

Involuntary smoking occurs when a nonsmoker unwillingly inhales smoke from a burning cigarette, cigar, or pipe. In a smoky environment, the nonsmoker breathes many of the same particles in tobacco smoke that a smoker inhales. The chemical components in smoke-filled surroundings come from two sources—mainstream and sidestream smoke. *Mainstream smoke* is the smoke inhaled and then exhaled by the smoker. *Sidestream smoke* is the smoke that goes directly into the air from the burning end of a cigarette, cigar, or pipe. Sidestream smoke can be seen, for example, when a cigarette is burning in an ashtray. The sidestream smoke is not filtered in any way. So many substances, including nicotine and carbon monoxide, are found in much higher concentrations in sidestream smoke than in mainstream smoke. In smoke-filled environments, there may be more carbon monoxide and other pollutants in the air than there are during air-pollution emergencies! Many people—especially those suffering from chronic heart or lung diseases—are seriously affected by severe air pollu-

Estimates of the percentage of current, regular cigarette smokers, teenagers, aged 12 to 18, United States, 1970-1979.

Year	Ages 12-14 Male	Ages 12-14 Female	Ages 15-16 Male	Ages 15-16 Female	Ages 17-18 Male	Ages 17-18 Female	Ages 12-18 Male	Ages 12-18 Female
1970	5.7%	3.0%	19.5%	14.4%	37.3%	22.8%	18.5%	11.9%
1972	4.6%	2.8%	17.8%	16.3%	30.2%	25.3%	15.7%	13.3%
1974	4.2%	4.9%	18.1%	20.2%	31.0%	25.9%	15.8%	15.3%
1979	3.2%	4.3%	13.5%	11.8%	19.3%	26.2%	10.7%	12.7%

Note: Current regular smoker includes respondent who smokes cigarettes at least weekly.
SOURCE: Office on Smoking and Health.

Question: What's wrong with this picture?

Answer: One of the mouths is smoking.

American Cancer Society

AREN'T YOU A LITTLE OLD TO BE SMOKING?

tion. Many others experience discomforts such as stinging eyes, headache, nausea, or nose and throat irritation. Some people have a serious allergic reaction to the chemicals in tobacco smoke.

Effects on babies and children

Studies have shown that a pregnant woman harms her unborn baby when she smokes cigarettes. Infants born to smoking mothers weigh less and are more likely to have impaired growth and development.

Children have more respiratory infections than most adults have. Children are also more likely to be sensitive to the effects of "second-hand" smoke. Studies have shown that children whose parents smoke at home have twice as many respiratory illnesses as do children with nonsmoking parents. Children who have asthma suffer a great deal if they live in a household where people smoke. Asthma attacks can even be brought on by cigarette smoking.

"I knew smoking could become a habit. But I never planned on smoking that long."

"I never thought I'd have trouble stopping when I wanted to. I guess everybody feels that way."

A person may start smoking for any one of many reasons. The person then keeps smoking because a habit has been formed. Smoking leads to a strong dependence on tobacco which is very hard to overcome.

You look like you're old enough to read. And if you're old enough to read, why don't you sit down and read that pack of cigarettes. Especially the warning.

AMERICAN CANCER SOCIETY

237

Think once, twice, twelve times before you smoke.

12 THINGS TO DO INSTEAD OF SMOKING CIGARETTES.

Jump. Swim. Smell. Play. Dance. Ride. Listen. Talk. Sing. Jog. Draw. Nothing.

American Cancer Society

The smoking habit

Mistaken reasons for smoking

Some people think that tobacco relieves tiredness. This may be because the nicotine in the smoke causes a temporary increase of sugar in the blood. More sugar means more fuel for the muscles. After a brief time, though, the fuel is gone and the tiredness is greater than before. Some say that smoking relaxes them and eases nervous tension. This may be true for regular smokers who crave tobacco. A cigarette gives them temporary relief. But the feeling of relief from tension may simply result from the fact that smoking gives smokers something to do with their hands. There is no evidence that cigarette smoking has any other soothing or calming effects.

238

When people start smoking, they never think they will become addicted to cigarettes. Or they think they will always be able to quit. Many smokers dislike their habit and want to quit, but they need help. Now there are many smoking clinics around the country to help smokers "kick the habit."

Quitting the habit

Convincing evidence of the harmful effects of smoking has caused many people to stop smoking. Others go on smoking out of habit, because they do not make a strong effort to stop. Willpower, time, and discomfort are involved in breaking a well-established habit such as smoking.

Many cigarette smokers who would like to stop smoking are concerned about gaining weight when they quit. According to a report from the U.S. Department of Health and Human Services, the facts are these:

1/3 gain weight	These are people who substitute eating for smoking when they first quit.
1/3 lose weight	These are people who start a general physical-fitness program at the same time that they stop smoking. They burn up calories by exercising and therefore lose weight.
1/3 do not gain or lose	These people do not change their life-style or eating habits at all when they quit smoking.

The benefits of breaking the smoking habit are worth the effort. People who quit smoking have a better chance of living long and healthy lives. If there is no disease present, as soon as someone stops smoking, the body begins to repair the damage that smoking caused. The person will cough less, breathe more easily, and enjoy a general feeling of well-being. Many programs are now available to help people stop smoking.

Smokeless tobacco: a testimonial

I tried "dipping" snuff and chewing tobacco for a while before I decided to stop. Although my smokeless tobacco habits were the cause of many arguments with my parents and girlfriend, it was my dental hygienist, Garth, who really got

Something to think about . . .

Snuff and chewing tobacco came into use before cigarettes. Today, some people think that smokeless tobacco is a safe bet. But frequent use of snuff or chewing tobacco will harm the body.

me to think seriously about what I was doing. Garth's interest caused me to think about what effect this habit could have.

Snuff is a finely ground mixture of tobacco leaves and stems. The word *snuff* comes from the fact that people inhale or "snuff" this ground tobacco. Chewing tobacco is made from different kinds of low-grade tobacco. Garth explained about the harmful effects of these tobacco products on the body. He showed me photographs of people who were long-term users of snuff, chewing tobacco, or both. I thought he was just trying to scare me, and I tried to forget about the matter. However, I finally became curious and decided to find out for myself. After reading several articles in medical and public health journals, I learned that there is a lot more to "dipping and chewing" than just keeping up a macho image.

One article discussed leukoplakia, a precursor of cancer. Leukoplakia appears as a white patch on the soft tissues of the mouth. It is often the result of irritation of the tissues from a tobacco product. Chewing tobacco or rubbing snuff against the soft mouth tissues can cause leukoplakia, or even cancer of the mouth and tongue. There is also an increased risk of cancer of the pharynx, larynx, and esophagus.

Fortunately, I did not have leukoplakia or any of the other severe problems the dental hygienist warned me about. However, I did have more than the usual amount of cavities (caries) on the side where I sucked on my chaw. Since most chewing tobacco contains sugar, the incidence of caries increases among chewers. The nicotine caused my heart to beat faster and my blood pressure to rise. This is because nicotine is a stimulant. I also learned that I could develop a dependence on nicotine, bad breath, discolored teeth, decreased ability to taste, and receding gums as a result of my tobacco habits.

I was grateful to Garth for warning me about the hazards of oral tobacco. The rest was up to me.

Brad, Age 16

Main Ideas

1. Tobacco smoke consists of nicotine, tars, and other harmful substances.
2. There is no "safe" cigarette.
3. Cigarette smoking is a major cause of heart disease, cancer, chronic bronchitis, emphysema, and several other diseases.
4. Involuntary smoking occurs when a nonsmoker unwillingly inhales smoke from a burning cigarette, cigar, or pipe.
5. Tobacco smoke can harm nonsmokers as well as smokers. In an environment filled with tobacco smoke, there may be as much air pollution as there is during an air-pollution emergency.
6. Smokers and nonsmokers share the high cost of smoking that results from accidents, health care expenses, and lost work output.
7. The smoking habit is hard to break.

Key Words

(handwritten: passive smoking, emphysema, Lung cancer, bronchitis, carcinogens, Leukoplakia)

involuntary smoking   nicotine   tar
mainstream smoke   sidestream smoke   carbon monoxide

Apply Your Knowledge

1. Why does the carbon monoxide in tobacco smoke cause shortness of breath in smokers?
2. What is the effect of smoking on the mouth and teeth?
3. What effect does tobacco smoking have on the temperature of the skin, on the heart rate, and on the blood pressure?
4. What are some of the symptoms of mild nicotine poisoning?
5. What effects do tobacco tars have on the body?
6. Explain the difference between mainstream smoke and sidestream smoke.
7. Does tobacco relieve tiredness? Explain.
8. List the facts unfavorable to smoking.
9. What are some of the smoking regulations in your community?
10. What do you think the smoking regulations should be in:
    (*a*) hospitals?
    (*b*) restaurants?
    (*c*) transportation facilities (airplanes, buses, trains)?
    (*d*) high schools?

Extend Your Knowledge

1. Investigate the smoking regulations that have been established in some cities and states. Which city or state do you think has the best smoking policy? Give your reasons.
2. Studies have shown that smoking affects the way in which the body uses many different drugs. Report on the results of some of these studies.
3. Throughout the country, recently, individuals have been bringing lawsuits to secure a smoke-free environment, and courts have been upholding their rights. Investigate some of these cases. Are you in agreement with the courts' rulings? Give your reasons.
4. What is the history of the use of tobacco in the United States? What are some of the early laws pertaining to smoking?
5. The social trend in America today is not to tolerate tobacco smoking in indoor environments. Predict the attitude toward tobacco smoking twenty years from now. State the reasons for your predictions.

Chapter 20

Do you know . . .

- why people's behavior may change when they drink alcoholic beverages?
- how many calories there are in beer?
- how the blood alcohol level affects a person's ability to drive?
- why a person who passes out from drinking too much alcohol needs medical attention right away?
- what the clues are that tell if a person has a drinking problem?

Use of Alcohol

There are many reasons why people drink alcoholic beverages. Some people drink because they like the taste of alcoholic beverages. Others drink because they think it is a sophisticated thing to do. Some drink because alcohol seems to relax them and ease their worries for a time. Others drink to escape feelings of insecurity and inferiority. Still others drink to forget disappointments and failures. It is important for people to know why they drink alcoholic beverages. There may be other, better ways to reach the same goal.

Alcoholic beverages

Light wines and beers have been used since the earliest times. Both wine and beer are made by *fermentation*. Fermentation is caused by the action of certain yeasts on the sugars found in fruit and grain. In ancient times, fermented drinks were less likely to have disease-causing germs than was most drinking water. So in those days, people tended to drink more alcoholic beverages than water.

Light wines are from 8 to 16 percent alcohol. There is less alcohol in beer than in wine. But beer is usually drunk in larger amounts than wine is. Stronger alcoholic beverages, such as brandy, whiskey, gin, and rum, are made by *distillation*. This is a process of purifying liquids by heating them until they become gases. Then they are cooled back to liquid form again. Stronger alcoholic beverages contain from 40 to 50 percent alcohol.

Alcohol is high in calories. But alcohol does not have important nutrients such as proteins, vitamins, and minerals. People who drink a lot of alcohol and eat little food often suffer from malnutrition. Because alcohol is high in calories, it is also fattening. One serving of beer (360 milliliters, or 12 fluid ounces) has about 150 calories.

Effects on the body

Alcohol is picked up by the blood from the stomach and small intestine. Your blood picks up alcohol most quickly when you drink it on an empty stomach. Your blood picks it up more slowly when you drink it with food. The alcohol in your blood reaches all the organs in the body. It has some effect on most of them. But its greatest effect is on the brain.

Do you know that the amount of alcohol in 12 ounces of beer, 5 ounces of wine, and 1½ ounces of 80-proof liquor is the same?

12 oz.   **5 oz.**   **1½ oz.**

Alcohol is a powerful drug. Because of the widespread use of alcoholic beverages, many people do not realize that alcohol is a drug. Specifically, alcohol is a depressant. It dulls the nerve centers of the brain that control judgment, attention, memory, and self-control. A person who has been drinking acts more on feeling than on thought and judgment. The drinker may feel overconfident and act on impulse. This is very true when the person is active and in the company of other people. A person who drinks while alone is likely to be made depressed and sleepy by the alcohol. Typically, these effects begin to appear after a person has drunk about 10 milliliters (⅓ ounce) of alcohol. This is the amount of alcohol contained in 20 milliliters (⅔ ounce) of whiskey. A bottle of beer, a highball, or a cocktail has more than this amount.

Alcohol is used up, or metabolized, very quickly in the body. Therefore, a given amount of alcohol drunk over several hours will have less effect on a person than the same amount taken over a short period of time.

Drinking a large amount of alcohol—30 milliliters (1 ounce) or more—may make a person loud, talkative, affectionate, or quarrelsome. The drinker may not consider what other people think of this conduct. The alcohol is also likely to make the person dizzy and lightheaded. Movements become slow, and muscular coordination is upset. This causes an unsteady walk and slurred, mixed-up speech. A person in such a condition is said to be *intoxicated*. After many drinks, a person may pass out. Upon waking, the person usually feels uncomfortable and irritable. He or she is usually very thirsty, has a headache, is dizzy, and may suffer from nausea and vomiting.

The blood vessels of the skin get larger after the use of alcohol. This causes the face to flush and gives a false feeling of warmth. The rise in blood flow through the skin really causes the body to lose heat, not save it. So the idea of drinking an alcoholic beverage to keep warm is incorrect.

The regular intake of large amounts of alcohol may lead to indigestion and loss of appetite. The heart, liver, and kidneys may be badly damaged. Heavy drinking over a long period of time can lead to early death from heart or liver disease. And drinking large amounts of alcohol at one time may lead to paralysis of one nerve center in the brain after another.

Finally, the nerve centers that control the actions of the heart and lungs may become paralyzed. The result is death from alcohol poisoning. For this reason, "drinking contests" sometimes end in tragedy for the winner.

Automobile accidents

A safe driver must be in full control, with alert reflexes. He or she must make correct decisions and act quickly. A person who has been drinking is a menace on the highway because alcohol weakens the person's judgment and self-control. The drinker also often feels a false confidence about being able to drive.

The amount of alcohol in a person's blood is called the BAL, or *blood alcohol level*. It is usually expressed in terms of percent. A blood alcohol level of 0.06 percent alcohol usually results from drinking 60 to 90 milliliters (2 to 3 ounces) of whiskey or other distilled liquor, or 850 milliliters (2 to 3 12-ounce bottles) of beer. A driver with a BAL of 0.06 is twice as likely to have an accident as a driver who has not been drinking. If the alcohol level in the person's blood is 0.1 percent, the person's risk of having an automobile accident is 7 times as great as that of a nondrinking driver.

People who have been drinking are involved in automobile accidents that cause thousands of deaths each year. A study of 1134 fatally injured drivers in one state showed that 65 percent of the drivers who were

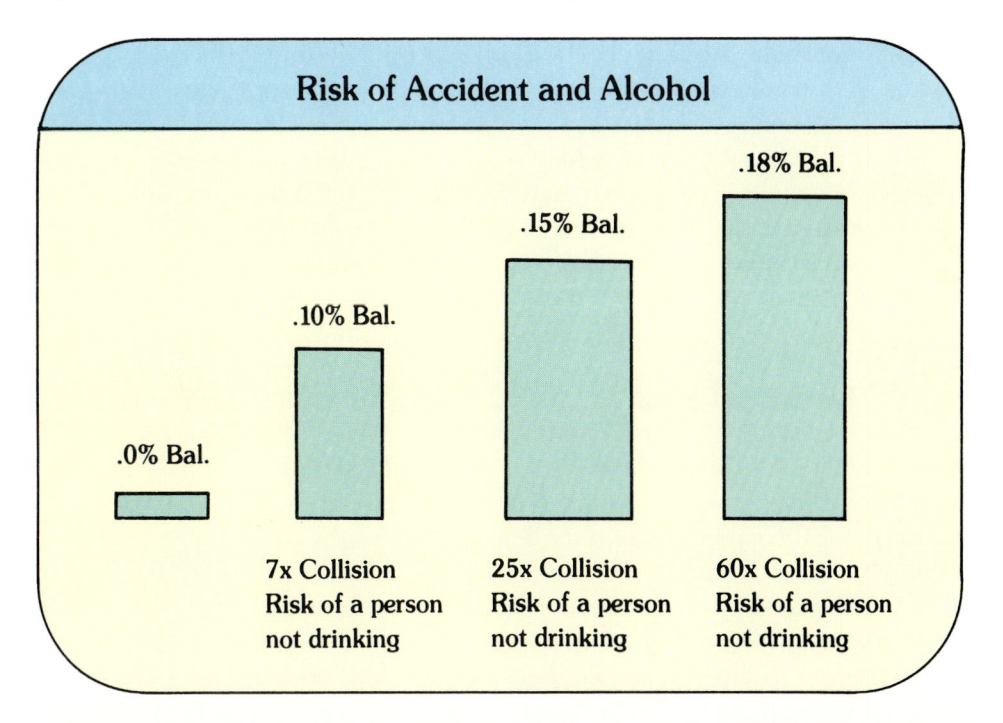

Risk of Accident and Alcohol

.0% Bal.

.10% Bal.
7x Collision
Risk of a person
not drinking

.15% Bal.
25x Collision
Risk of a person
not drinking

.18% Bal.
60x Collision
Risk of a person
not drinking

responsible for the accidents had been drinking. And of 353 fatally injured pedestrians, 59 percent of the ones under 65 years of age had been drinking. In another state, in a single year, it was reported that 6 out of 10 drivers and pedestrians killed in traffic accidents had been drinking. More than half of those who were killed had drunk enough to be intoxicated.

Over half of the automobile accidents that result in death in the United States involve alcohol. In some cases, the driver has been drinking. In other cases, a person walking has been drinking.

Misuse of alcohol

Every so often, many people enjoy alcoholic beverages in small or moderate amounts. But alcohol can be habit-forming, or addictive, if moderate use leads to heavy drinking. Alcohol addiction is a serious illness known as *alcoholism*.

As with many of the "abuse" problems of our times—whether the object of the abuse is food or alcohol or other drugs—the experts find the cause of the problem to be biological, social, or psychological. For example, some studies indicate an inherited tendency toward alcohol abuse. Other studies have shown that the way alcohol is handled socially in a particular country can make a difference. Still other people become heavy drinkers to escape from conflicts or emotional problems they have not learned to handle.

It is impossible to tell which moderate drinkers will become alcoholics. Most alcoholics began with an occasional drink. This is why it is important to recognize that alcohol is a drug that may cause addiction. There are more than 13 million alcoholics in the United States. About one-third of them are in their teens. And almost as many women as men are alcoholics.

Effects on mental health

The effects of alcohol on mental health are even more striking than its effects on physical health. The personality of the alcoholic goes through many changes. Alcoholics lower their standards of conduct. They lose self-respect and the respect of others. Sometimes they are not reliable as workers and lose their jobs. They may begin to care only about themselves and their problems. Their biggest worry may be where to get the next drink.

Teenagers who use alcohol to help solve problems may slow down their progress in learning how to manage their lives. Adolescence is thought of as the time when a person changes in mind and body from a child to an adult. But when a teenager chooses to use a drug to help solve problems, mental growth (maturity) may be slowed down. Using a drug to escape problems, instead of using the mind to solve them, can keep a teenager from developing into a true adult.

Parents who are alcoholics may affect the physical and mental health of their children. An alcoholic parent cannot be relied on. So the children of such a parent may feel insecure. They may also often be embarrassed by the parent's behavior. In more serious cases, a parent may spend money on alcohol instead of providing the family with the proper food, clothing, housing, and medical care. In extreme cases, an alcoholic parent may become violent. Broken homes, lost jobs, serious accidents, child neglect, poverty, and sometimes crime may be caused by the use of too much alcohol.

Help for the problem drinker

On a typical Friday or Saturday night, Brian drank five or six beers with friends. One Friday evening, Brian drank until he lost consciousness. His friends were worried about him. They wondered what to do.

Any person who is unconscious needs medical help. In this case, Brian could die from alcohol poisoning if he had drunk too much alcohol in too short a time. His life might also be in danger if he had taken another drug before or while he drank the beer. Some drugs can cause death when mixed with even a little alcohol. Or, if simply left to "sleep it off," Brian could choke to death on his own vomit. His life might depend on how much his friends knew about the dangers of drinking too much alcohol and on how fast they acted to get help for him.

If someone you are with loses consciousness from drinking too much alcohol, call a doctor or an ambulance immediately. Then, while waiting for help, place the person on his or her side, keep the air passages open, and remove any food or gum from the mouth. If the person's breathing stops, give mouth-to-mouth resuscitation, if you know how. When the doctor or ambulance arrives, tell the doctor or trained ambulance driver what the person drank and how much.

If someone you are with has drunk far too much and might lose consciousness, stay with the person and send for medical help.

Early identification

Sometimes a person with an alcohol problem is a "hidden alcoholic." Some alcoholics may be successful in hiding the problem not only

Life can be very unhappy for alcoholics and their families. Helping a person with an alcohol problem is hard to do. The person must first see that there is a problem. Then, many community organizations can help with the treatment program.

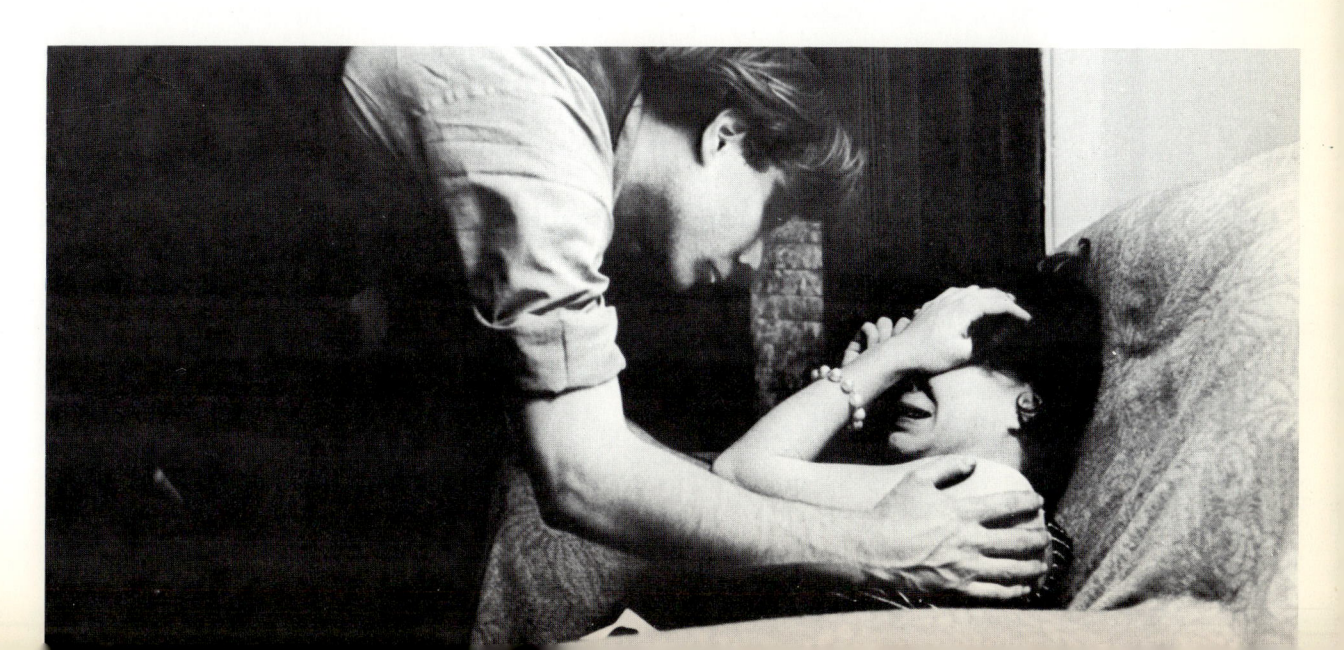

GETTING DRUNK DOESN'T MAKE YOU... TALL...
RICH... STRONG... HANDSOME...
SMART... WITTY... SOPHISTICATED...
OR SEXY... ...JUST DRUNK
IN FACT IT DOESN'T DO A THING FOR YOU — EXCEPT GET YOU DRUNK.

It is important for people to know why they drink alcoholic beverages. Then they can think about better ways to reach the same goal.

from their families and friends, but even from their own conscious minds. Admitting that you have any kind of problem is not easy. Admitting an alcohol problem is very hard to do.

What are some of the signs that a person has an alcohol problem?

According to the Department of Health and Human Services:

- Anyone who drinks in order to get to work, or to perform his or her job, has an alcohol problem.
- Anyone who is intoxicated and drives a motor vehicle has an alcohol problem.
- Anyone who does something under the influence of alcohol that she or he would not have done without alcohol has an alcohol problem.
- Anyone who becomes injured seriously enough to need medical attention, as a result of using alcohol, has an alcohol problem.
- Anyone who comes into conflict with the law as a result of being intoxicated has an alcohol problem.
- Anyone who has been intoxicated four times in a year has an alcohol problem.

Can you think of any other clues? Do you disagree with any of these statements? If so, share your opinion with teachers, school counselors, or counselors at an alcohol rehabilitation center. They would probably be glad to discuss the statement with you.

Helping a person with an alcohol problem is hard to do. It is often impossible, unless that person sees that there is a problem. Just as important, the person must want help in solving the problem. A person may have to go into a hospital or other facility for *detoxification*, or withdrawal from the drug. But if the person gets early treatment for the alcohol problem, entering a hospital is not usually needed. Once a person decides to get help, there are many different community organizations, such as churches, health centers, and family service agencies, to help with the treatment program. There are also many facilities to help teenagers cope with an alcoholic in the home or with their own alcohol problem.

Alcoholics Anonymous

Many alcoholics get help from an organization called *Alcoholics Anonymous* (AA). All AA members are former alcoholics. They try to help each other during times of crisis. They give one another extra strength to overcome the physical and psychological need for alcohol. This is done on a day-to-day basis. The AA member makes no promise to reform. But every day, the person pledges not to take a drink that day. Over a period of years, the alcoholic may be able to break the habit and to get back a feeling of self-respect and usefulness.

Alateen

A high school boy in Pasadena, California, whose father was an alcoholic, talked with some friends who had the same problems. Their discussion later included a counselor. It led to the development of *Alateen,* an organization for the children of alcoholics. There are now about 2000 chapters all over the United States. Local Alateen chapters are listed in the telephone book.

The purpose of Alateen is to help members cope with problems that come up in homes where one or both parents drink too much. Meetings are informal, with frank, sincere, and honest discussions. Members do not criticize alcoholics or look for sympathy. Instead, they try to understand their own problems. This helps them to overcome feelings of inferiority and hopelessness. It also helps them to face and adjust to their situations objectively and realistically. They report that they find it helpful to talk with other young people who have similar problems.

An important decision

The use of alcoholic beverages is widespread in the United States. More young people become addicted to alcohol than to any other drug or intoxicant. Many people, young and old, do not realize how easy it is to become addicted. Also, few people know how hard it is to return to normal life after a period of alcohol addiction. For these reasons, whether or not to use alcohol is an important adult decision.

Something to think about . . .

FAS, or *fetal alcohol syndrome,* is the name for a group of birth defects caused when a pregnant woman drinks. FAS has a wide range of severity. Infants may be born with abnormally small heads, mental retardation, and deformities of the heart, limbs, or face. Typically, FAS children with facial deformities have slitlike eyes; protruding foreheads; short, turned-up noses; cleft palates or short upper lips; receding chins; and deformed ears. They may have extra or missing fingers and toes.

One study indicates that a mother who drinks six or more drinks of any alcoholic beverage per day increases the risk of FAS for her child to nearly 75 percent. Among women who drank only one or two drinks per day, another study showed a 14 percent rate of birth defects. And even drinking heavily one time at one of the many crucial periods in fetal development can cause deformities or brain damage. Alcohol, or some product of alcohol metabolism, is probably the cause of these defects, but the exact way in which these malformations occur is not clearly understood.

Researchers at the University of North Carolina studied FAS in mice that were 7 days pregnant. They say that this is about the same as 3 weeks of pregnancy in humans—a time when most women do not even realize that they are pregnant. The researchers found that ethanol, which is in all alcoholic beverages, caused the brains of fetal mice to be abnormally small and narrow. This led to facial distortion and other FAS symptoms.

The National Council on Alcoholism advises that the only safe decision for an expectant mother is total abstinence from alcohol during the pregnancy.

Main Ideas

1. It is important for people to understand the reasons why they want to drink alcoholic beverages.
2. Alcohol is a dangerous, habit-forming drug.
3. Drinking too many alcoholic beverages can lead to serious mental and physical health problems.
4. Many automobile accidents and other tragedies among high school students are caused by the use of alcohol.
5. There are definite signs that a person has an alcohol problem.
6. A person who loses consciousness from drinking too much alcohol needs medical attention immediately.
7. There are many community organizations available to help the problem drinker and the drinker's family.

Key Words

Alateen
Alcoholics Anonymous
alcoholism
blood alcohol level
detoxification
distillation
fermentation
fetal alcohol syndrome
intoxicated

Apply Your Knowledge

1. List four reasons why a person may drink alcoholic beverages. For each reason, give another action that might serve the same purpose.
2. Alcohol is a depressant. Explain what this means.
3. Why does a certain amount of alcohol taken in over a long period of time have less effect on a person than the same amount of alcohol taken in during a short period?
4. What are the effects of alcohol on the nervous system?
5. List some ways in which drinking too much alcohol affects a person physically.
6. What is meant by *blood alcohol level*?
7. What are some reasons for getting medical help for a person who loses consciousness from drinking too much? What are some things you can do before help arrives?
8. What are some signs that a person may have an alcohol problem?
9. What do you think is meant by the statement "Alcohol is sometimes used as a form of self-medication"?
10. What advice would you give to someone whose parent was a problem drinker? Be as specific as possible about factual information that could help the drinker's child.

Extend Your Knowledge

1. Find out what laws your state has to control the sale of alcohol.
2. Find out how many automobile accidents happened in your state last year. What age group was most often involved? How many accidents involved someone who had been drinking?
3. What is your definition of the responsible use of alcohol? What is the irresponsible use of alcohol?
4. What resources exist in your community to help the problem drinker and the drinker's family? Do you think your community has enough resources? Do you think these resources are well publicized? Can you think of any other means of publicizing them?

Chapter 21

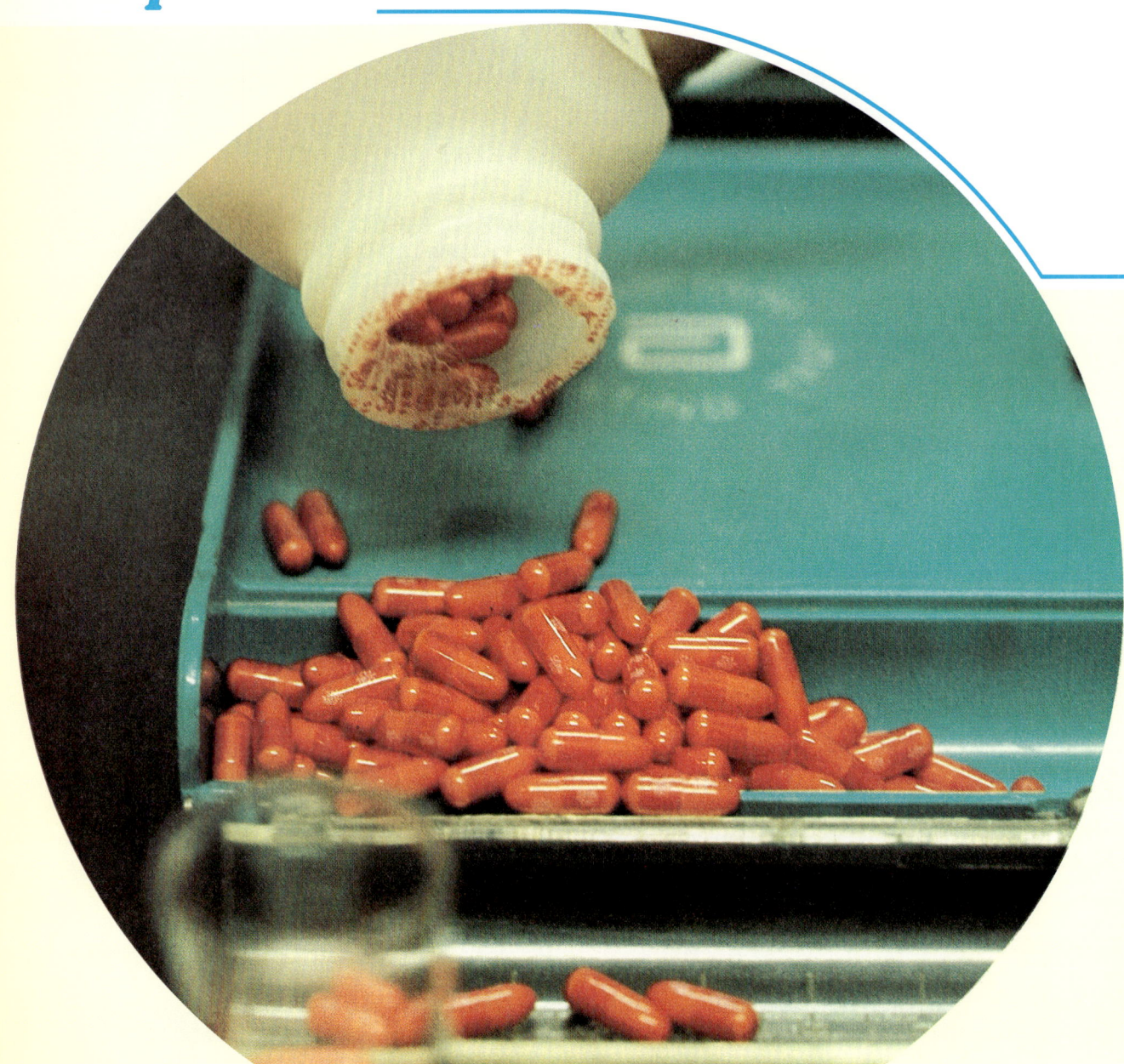

Do you know . . .

- why leftover prescription drugs should be thrown out?
- what is the most widely used drug?
- why certain drugs are likely to be abused?
- which commonly abused drugs are addictive?

Drugs: Use and Abuse

The next time you are watching television or reading a magazine, notice how often drugs are mentioned. The United States has been called the most drug-ridden society in history. People take pills for waking up and pills for sleeping, pills for losing weight and pills for gaining it. Many people take drugs into their bodies without even thinking about it when they smoke, drink coffee, or eat a bar of chocolate.

You can buy many kinds of drugs without prescriptions. These drugs are sold over-the-counter and are sometimes called *OTC drugs*. It is important to remember that every drug has its limited function and its risks, whether it is a common OTC drug or a prescription. Because of widespread advertising and popular attitudes toward drugs, many people believe there is a drug to solve every health problem. This is not true. These guidelines will help you to use drugs wisely:

1. Follow recommended dosages carefully. Do not take more or less than the recommended amount of any drug. Remember that more of a drug is not necessarily better.
2. Do not take drugs that have been prescribed for someone else. Even though your symptoms may be like a friend's, his or her drug and dosage may not be right for you.
3. Taking more than one drug at a time can be dangerous. The combined effects of more than one drug may be very different from the effects of each drug taken alone. When taking any medication, remember that alcoholic beverages are drugs, too.
4. The Drug Regulation Reform Act of 1978 requires that patients be given more information about drugs prescribed for them. Read all the information that is provided with both prescription and OTC drugs. If any information or warnings concern you, discuss them with your physician.
5. Do not save prescription drugs. The chemicals in them may change over a period of time, so they should not be used for another illness.

Drugs for health

Most drugs are used to restore or maintain health. Certain drugs actually prevent disease. For example, in 1967, 20 million people had smallpox. The World Health Organization organized a campaign against the disease. As a result of this, smallpox has been completely eliminated. *Vaccines,* like the one used against smallpox, help the body to fight germs that can cause disease. *Antibiotics* and other drugs fight infections that have already developed in the body. Penicillin has been used successfully to treat many diseases, including some sexually transmitted diseases. Still other drugs are useful in controlling those diseases that cannot be cured. Epilepsy and diabetes mellitus are examples of two diseases that can be controlled with medication.

Many different kinds of drugs are used to relieve pain. *Analgesics,* such as aspirin, allow people to be comfortable while they recover from illness or injury. Aspirin is probably the most widely used drug. Besides relieving pain, aspirin can reduce fever and inflammation. *Anesthetics,* such as Novocain or sodium pentothal, cause numbness or insensitivity to pain. With these drugs, physicians can perform surgery or other medical procedures that would otherwise be too painful for their patients.

Pharmaceutical companies, or drug manufacturers, also produce many drugs to relieve serious psychological problems. Such drugs have helped many people to deal with stressful situations. These medications are called *psychoactive drugs.* Psychoactive drugs seem to change a person's mood or behavior.

In many cultures psychoactive drugs have been used for pleasure, escape, and relaxation, as well as for treatment of disease. In certain native American societies, such drugs have been used for religious and mystical experiences. But psychoactive drugs can also be used destructively. In the United States, it is thought that hundreds of thousands of people are physically or psychologically dependent on drugs.

Some reasons why people use psychoactive drugs

Many people believe that the social environment is a very important cause of drug use and abuse. Because many drugs are easy to get and people now are more aware of them than before, drug use has increased. Popular attitudes toward drugs are important too. Some people claim that drug advertising is too widespread. They feel that advertising has made Americans believe that drugs can change anything—even their lives. Dissatisfaction and frustration may also lead people to use psychoactive drugs.

People in troubled emotional states are more likely to use drugs than happier people. People who are anxious, depressed, or bored may use drugs. They may return to the use of drugs again and again in order to feel comfortable. Peer-group pressure also influences many young people's experimentation with drugs. Using drugs again and again may seem to be a way to keep one's membership in certain social groups.

Some drugs are more likely to be abused than others because of the way they act in the body. A drug's capacity to produce tolerance and dependence may cause a person to use it again and again. *Tolerance* means that a person's body becomes used to the effects of a drug that is taken regularly. Larger and larger doses are needed to produce the effect. For example, half a glass of wine or liquor might make an inexperienced drinker "high." Later on, that same drinker might need half a bottle to produce the same effect. An expensive drug that produces tolerance may become extremely costly to a user.

Physical dependence takes time to develop. It may take six or more weeks for a person's body to become used to a drug. Then the person must have regular doses of it. If a person who is physically dependent on a drug does not get the amount of the drug that the body has come to need, that person suffers *withdrawal symptoms*. Trembling, hallucinations, nausea, and vomiting are some of the symptoms of withdrawal. Sometimes sudden withdrawal from a drug can even be fatal.

It is important to realize that not all psychoactive drugs cause physical dependence, or *addiction*. However, regular users develop another kind of dependence on these drugs, called *psychological dependence*. This kind of dependence results from a mental or emotional need, not a physical one. The problems produced by psychological dependence are similar to those caused by physical dependence.

What effects do psychoactive drugs have on a person's body? Which drugs produce tolerance? Which drugs are likely to cause physical dependence? Don't depend on friends and classmates for answers to these questions. The facts provided in this chapter are only part of the information that is available to you. Study as much of the current literature on drugs as you can. Your life, or the life of someone you know, may depend on how much you know about the effects of drugs.

Commonly abused drugs

Most of the commonly abused drugs can be divided into four major categories: depressants, narcotics, stimulants, and hallucinogens.

Depressants

Depressants slow down the activity of certain areas of the brain and spinal cord. These drugs cause muscles to relax and rates of breathing and heartbeat to slow down. Alcohol is the most widely used drug in this group. It is discussed separately in Chapter 20. The effects of alcohol are very similar to the effects of other depressants. Keep this in mind as you read about them.

Next to alcohol, *barbiturates* are the most widely used kind of depressant. Barbiturates slow down a person's reaction time, just as alcohol does. They also produce drowsiness and possibly slurred speech. They may reduce anxiety but they also decrease mental functioning and memory. And high doses of barbiturates may result in coma and death.

Barbiturates are extremely dangerous when they are taken with alcohol. Taken together in doses that would not be fatal by themselves, barbiturates and alcohol depress brain and nervous system functioning so much that they can actually stop a person's breathing. Many accidental deaths have been caused when people who had been drinking alcoholic beverages took what would have been an otherwise safe amount of sleeping pills.

Tolerance to barbiturates develops quickly. These drugs tend to produce both strong psychological and strong physical dependence. Sudden withdrawal from them can be dangerous or even fatal. Medically supervised, gradual withdrawal from barbiturates is safer and less painful for someone dependent on them.

Tranquilizers are depressants that help to calm a person's emotions without interfering with the person's alertness or ability to think clearly. Tranquilizers are less likely to cause dependence than barbiturates. But using tranquilizers in large doses over a long period of time can cause tolerance and dependence.

Narcotics

Some abused *narcotics* are opium, heroin, morphine, and codeine. All of these drugs are derived from the opium poppy flower. *Morphine,* a drug extracted from opium, is one of the best pain relievers known to medicine. *Codeine* is a weaker pain reliever than morphine and is used especially in prescription cough medicines. *Heroin* is made by heating morphine in the presence of acetic acid. Heroin has the same effects as morphine but is about twenty times more powerful than morphine. In the United States, heroin is illegal, even for doctors to prescribe, because it is so addictive. Heroin users in America usually become involved in crime and illegal trade to pay for their habit. Users take the risk of dying from an overdose of heroin. Overdoses usually happen because users cannot be sure of the strength of the black-market heroin they are buying. Overdoses also occur because of changes in individual tolerance levels.

Opium-based drugs are highly addictive, and physical dependence develops quickly. Withdrawal symptoms include runny nose and eyes, weakness, depression, nausea, vomiting, diarrhea, and muscle cramps. These symptoms reach their peak within 24 hours and are usually over in about 48 hours. Complete withdrawal, however, may take as long as 6 months. But the sickness caused by withdrawing from heroin or morphine is actually less severe than withdrawal from alcohol or barbiturates.

Methadone is a synthetic drug made in chemical laboratories. Since the 1950s, it has been offered to heroin addicts as a legal substitute for heroin in drug programs in the United States. Methadone has also been used as a painkiller in both Europe and the United States since World War II. It relieves addicts from their cravings and helps them to function in everyday society. But, like heroin, methadone is addictive. By itself, methadone has little mood-altering effect. However, it is especially dangerous to combine this drug with other depressants. Deaths from overdoses have occurred when methadone was used in combination with alcohol, barbiturates, or heroin.

Methadone can be an effective part of a withdrawal program for heroin addicts. Usually such a program includes psychological counseling and general health care. Heroin addicts must be helped to confront their own psychological dependence on drugs. Most drug abusers build their lives around obtaining and using a drug. This is especially true of people using illegal substances. Changing an entire lifestyle is difficult, but it must be done if addicts want to break their drug habit successfully.

There are other medical problems associated with narcotics abuse. Serious infections may result from injections with needles that are not sterile. Malnutrition is also common. Drug abusers often neglect the other needs of their bodies.

Each year, many babies are already addicted to heroin at birth. These infants need medical care to help them withdraw gradually from narcotics. Drugs such as heroin, tranquilizers, barbiturates, alcohol, and even aspirin, pass from a mother's bloodstream, through the placenta, to the unborn child.

Thus, pregnant women must be especially thoughtful and careful about drug use. It has been found that many drugs affect the normal development of unborn babies. This is true even when the drugs are used in commonly prescribed doses.

Stimulants

Stimulants speed up the body's processes. They cause the heart to beat faster, the circulation and respiration to increase, and the blood pressure to rise. Some of the stronger drugs in this group cause *euphoria,* or strong feelings of well-being. Nicotine is a harmful stimulant; it is discussed in Chapter 19, on tobacco and smoking.

Caffeine is the most widely used psychoactive drug in America. It is used by people of all ages. Caffeine can be found in beverages such as coffee, tea, cocoa, and cola drinks. It is also present in chocolate and in over-the-counter drugs used for overcoming tiredness. The use of caffeine is socially accepted and even supported in the United States. Products containing this drug are easy to buy and relatively inexpensive. A normal dose of caffeine, such as the amount in a cup of coffee or tea, can relieve drowsiness and muscle fatigue for a while by increasing the pulse rate. Caffeine also increases urination and may speed up movement of the small intestine.

Caffeine can be abused if too much of the substances that contain caffeine are consumed. Drinking five or more cups of coffee a day usually causes physical dependence. Physical effects of caffeine abuse include nervousness and insomnia. Excessive stimulation of the heart can produce palpitations (rapid heartbeat) and other problems. Caffeine can also complicate the health problems of people with high blood pressure and peptic ulcers.

Amphetamines are synthetic stimulants. Methamphetamine, or "speed," is a commonly abused drug in this group. Medically, amphetamines have been used to treat depression, overweight, and uncontrolled and excessive sleeping. They have also been used to treat overactive children. The immediate effects of amphetamines include a quick elevation of mood and a sudden feeling of power or energy. Users report that they are able to concentrate intensely and that tiredness is reduced. Abusers of these drugs often become thin, nervous, and aggressive. They suffer from lack of appetite, poor nutrition, and lack of sleep. They may also experience delusions (false ideas about themselves) and other emotional disorders.

Psychological dependence and tolerance develop very quickly with these drugs. People who use amphetamines depend on these substances in order to feel happy. Physical dependence and withdrawal symptoms do not appear to be problems with amphetamines.

The Food and Drug Administration and the Bureau of Narcotics and Dangerous Drugs have begun to control more tightly the illegal manufacture and trade of amphetamines. Since this control, cocaine has become a more popular drug in the United States. But, to some extent, the use of cocaine is limited because of its very high cost. *Cocaine* is a substance that

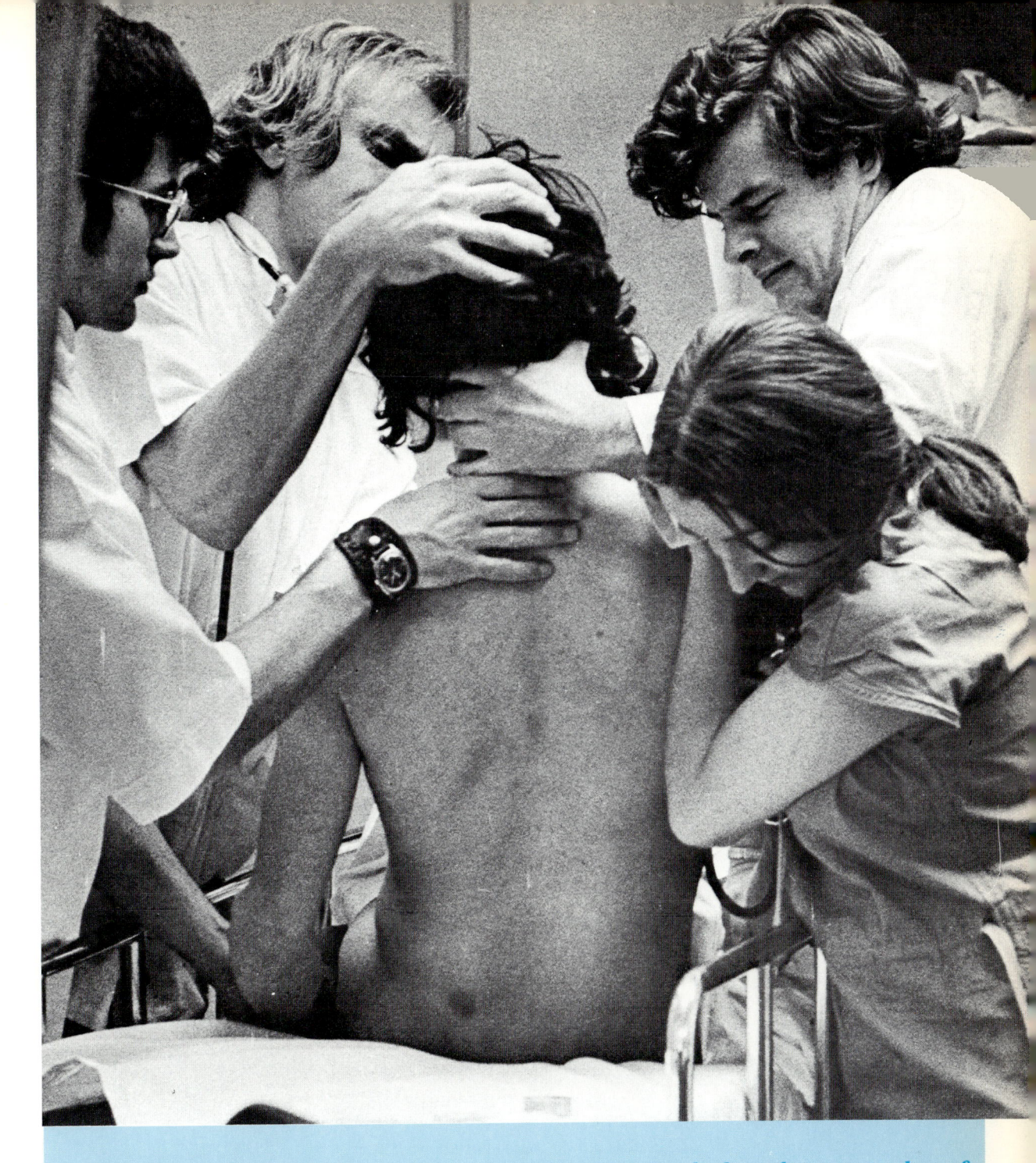

Workers in an emergency room try to save the life of someone who has taken an overdose of drugs. One emergency treatment is pumping a patient's stomach to remove some of the drugs before they enter the bloodstream.

comes from the leaves of the coca bush. Cocaine causes a quick, intense euphoria, or "high." Like the other stimulants, it increases heart rate, blood pressure, and body temperature. Users experience psychological dependence, and are often deeply depressed when they withdraw from cocaine.

Pure cocaine has been used as a local anesthetic for surgery of the eyes, ears, nose, and throat.

Hallucinogens

"Hallucinogen" is a drug classification under Schedule I of the Controlled Substances Act. Possession of nearly all of the drugs in this group is illegal in the United States. *Hallucinogens* include drugs like *LSD* (lysergic acid diethylamide), mescaline, and psilocybin. These drugs are usually swallowed, and they are psychologically addictive. As the name of these substances suggests, they cause hallucinations, or sense distortions, in the user. Mescaline, peyote, and psilocybin are obtained from plants. Mescaline and peyote come from the peyote cactus. Psilocybin is obtained from certain mushrooms found in Mexico. Other hallucinogens, such as LSD, are produced in chemical laboratories.

The effects of these drugs depend on the mental state of the individual user and on the surrounding environment. Some users may experience intense mood swings, from complete joy to utter depression or terror. Though tolerance can develop with frequent use, hallucinogens cause little psychological dependence and no physical dependence.

PCP (phencyclohexylpiperidine) has qualities of both depressant and hallucinogenic drugs. It is an extremely dangerous drug that, when used in combination with other drugs, intensifies their effects. Medical personnel in emergency rooms are often baffled by cases of acute PCP intoxication. The effects of this drug vary widely from one individual to another. "Angel dust," as PCP is sometimes called, produces either depression or stimulation of the central nervous system, depending upon the dosage and

Hallucinogens are drugs that affect the senses and the emotions. Some users may have strong mood swings, from joy to strong sadness and fear. When might such an effect not be harmful to a person?

the route of administration. Low doses produce an effect like alcohol intoxication. Higher doses may produce acute psychosis, convulsions, coma, and even death. At certain times, PCP may produce extreme agitation, hallucinations, and psychotic behavior, including such violent acts as homicide, suicide, or self-mutilation. At other times, PCP may produce a "sensory blockade," in which users are awake but unresponsive to people trying to communicate with them. PCP has been used successfully as an anesthetic for animals, but it is thought to be too dangerous for use as a medication for humans.

Marijuana is a common weed plant. Its dried tops and leaves are smoked or eaten to produce a relaxed mood and some changes in sense perceptions. *Hashish,* or "hash," is the resin produced in the tops of the marijuana plant. This dark brown, incense-like substance contains a more powerful dose of the same active chemical found in marijuana leaves.

Marijuana does not fit neatly into any of the four established drug categories. It acts partly like a depressant and partly like a stimulant. Marijuana increases the heart rate and blood pressure and decreases the body temperature. It causes the blood vessels around the eyes to become enlarged, so it makes the eyes look red and irritated. Unlike people who use other drugs that produce tolerance, regular users of marijuana may require less of the drug to get "high" than first-time users would need.

Marijuana produces mood changes, as well as distortions in a person's ability to judge time and space. Users experience a wide variety of effects. It seems that these effects depend upon one's expectations about the drug and previous experience with it. Because of this, people who smoke marijuana and drive cars face the very real danger of accidents.

Marijuana is a drug few people agree about. Some people argue that it is relatively harmless when it is used in small amounts. Other people are concerned about the possibly dangerous effects of long-term, regular use. There is no evidence that marijuana causes physical dependence. But it is possible to become psychologically dependent on this drug.

Physicians and other people studying the effects of this popular drug express concern over its abuse by young people. Any drug that becomes central in a young person's life can prevent him or her from facing problems and developing a strong, healthy personality. There is some evidence that certain changes in mood or perception may become permanent for regular users. Also, bronchitis and respiratory problems may develop in people who regularly smoke marijuana.

Something to think about . . .

Many young people today are finding that vigorous exercise, such as jogging, aerobic dancing, and other recreational sports, can be the source of a drug-free high. Some researchers feel that chemicals in the brain may be partly responsible for what has been called "the runner's high." Runners describe this as a sense of exhilaration that makes them feel they can run forever. Researchers are looking into the link between this sense of euphoria and the production of chemicals called *endorphins* in the brain. Various endorphins are produced by the brain and pituitary gland. Studies have shown that endorphins are produced in response to physical stress such as strenuous exercise.

Generally, intense stress causes an increase in blood pressure, heart rate, and metabolism. The resulting flow of adrenalin is valuable in emergency situations. It can become a problem in situations that call for a nonphysical response, such as giving an oral report in class. Scientists have found that psychological stress can also prompt the release of endorphins. This counters the adrenalin-triggered reactions. Endorphins lower breathing rate and blood pressure, and calm motor activity throughout the body. More research is needed to determine what goes on in the brain during vigorous exercise, but endorphins may play a part in the good feeling that comes following an after-school run around the track.

Main Ideas

1. More drugs are taken in the United States than in any other country.
2. Drugs are not the answer to every health problem.
3. Analgesics are drugs which relieve pain.
4. Psychoactive drugs alter a person's behavior and are the most commonly abused drugs.
5. People in troubled emotional states are more likely to use drugs than happier people.

Key Words

addiction	endorphin	OTC drugs
amphetamine	euphoria	PCP
analgesic	hallucinogen	physical dependence
anesthetic	hashish	psychoactive drug
antibiotic	heroin	psychological dependence
barbiturate	LSD	stimulant
caffeine	marijuana	tolerance
cocaine	methadone	tranquilizer
codeine	morphine	vaccine
depressant	narcotic	withdrawal symptom

Apply Your Knowledge

1. Name three things people can do to improve their use of prescription and OTC drugs.
2. Describe the function of vaccines and antibiotics.
3. Explain some of the ways in which a social environment can influence drug use and abuse.
4. What is the difference between physical and psychological drug dependence?
5. Compare the general effects of depressants and stimulants on the human body.
6. Define the term *psychoactive drugs.* Describe some of their effects.
7. What is tolerance? What effect does tolerance have on a drug user?
8. Why should pregnant women avoid taking drugs?
9. Why is the Drug Regulation Reform Act of 1978 important to consumers?
10. What are the medical uses for morphine, cocaine, and amphetamines?
11. What can happen when barbiturates and alcohol are used together?
12. What is methadone? What are some of its uses?
13. What are the physical and psychological effects of cocaine?
14. What may be some of the dangers of using marijuana?
15. Why should leftover prescription drugs be thrown out?

Extend Your Knowledge

1. Are there any medical or legitimate uses of hallucinogens or marijuana?
2. Write a report on the abuse of volatile chemicals, such as glue, aerosol propellant, and paint thinner. Find out what effects these chemicals have and what dangers they present.
3. Write to the General Accounting Office, Drug Enforcement Administration, 441 G Street, N.W., Washington, D.C. 20548, for information on the newest steps being taken to stop international drug traffic.
4. How would you feel if you found out that your younger brother or sister was using marijuana regularly? What might you say to him or her?
5. Collect as many current articles on drugs and drug abuse as possible. Try to evaluate the opinions of the author and the accuracy of reporting in each one. Write a monthly article for your school newspaper, or publish a newsletter to inform other students.
6. Visit one or more drug rehabilitation centers. Interview some staff members and some former drug abusers.

Unit 7

CHAPTERS:

22 Sexually Transmitted Diseases
23 The Common Cold and Other Miseries
24 Immunizations

Preventing Communicable Diseases

Chapter 22

Do you know . . .

- how sexually transmitted diseases are spread?
- the symptoms of gonorrhea, syphilis, and genital herpes?
- how sexually transmitted diseases can be prevented?
- how sexually transmitted diseases are treated?

Sexually Transmitted Diseases

Sexually transmitted diseases, or *STDs,* are communicable diseases that are spread from an infected person to another person through sexual contact. They are sometimes called venereal diseases. Today, most communicable diseases have been occurring less often than before. But STDs continue to spread. They threaten the health of many people, particularly young adults.

Types of STDs

Gonorrhea and syphilis are two sexually transmitted diseases that continue to cause epidemics all over the United States. They are different diseases caused by different organisms. These diseases are spread directly by an infected person during sexual intercourse or direct bodily contact involving the sex organs. Because many victims do not know that they are infected, they spread the disease to others without knowing it.

Genital herpes is caused by a virus that is introduced into the body mainly through sexual contact. Herpes infections can appear again after treatment. The reappearance is not always caused by sexual contact.

If these diseases are to be controlled, all young people must learn about them. A person should learn what the symptoms are and should feel free to talk about the diseases with doctors, nurses, parents, health teachers, and others. Most important of all, a person who has an STD must tell his or her sexual partner so that the partner can get medical help.

Gonorrhea

Gonorrhea is the most commonly reported STD. It is also a common communicable disease. It is about ten times more common than syphilis and more than five times as common as chicken pox. More than one million cases of gonorrhea were reported in 1980, and not all cases were reported. In a recent year, $770 million was spent to treat this disease.

Gonorrhea is caused by rod-shaped bacteria called *gonococci* that show up in pairs. The symptoms of gonorrhea begin 2 to 10 days after sexual contact with an infected person. The male usually has pain and burning when he urinates. There may also be a puslike discharge from the penis. The female may have a vaginal discharge, but often she has no symptoms at all. After a while, both male and female symptoms may disappear, and the person thinks the disease is cured. But the bacteria continue to live in the inner mucous membranes. In this way, a person may become a carrier of the infection without knowing it. Medical advice should be sought whenever exposure to the disease is suspected. A physician can take samples of fluids from the cervix, the vagina, and the urethra to find out if there is a gonococcal infection. Gonorrhea organisms in the fluids may be seen in the laboratory under a microscope, or may be grown in a culture bottle.

Gonorrhea infections can usually be treated successfully with antibiotics, such as penicillin. However, having the symptoms disappear does not mean the disease is cured. So a follow-up visit to the doctor is often needed to make sure that the infection is gone. If the infection is not treated, many other serious problems, such as crippling arthritis or sterility, may develop. Also, a pregnant woman may pass the infection to her newborn infant, sometimes causing blindness.

Syphilis

Syphilis is caused by spiral-shaped bacteria called *spirochetes*. The bacteria enter the body through a small break in the skin or through mucous membranes. They travel throughout the bloodstream. The bacteria can be picked up through open sores. But they cannot be picked up from toilet seats or towels, since they cannot live outside the body.

The first, or *primary*, stage of the disease includes a painless open sore called a *chancre*. The chancre usually appears 2 to 6 weeks after contact. It is very infectious. The male may see an open sore on his penis. The female may not have any outside sores. The sore may disappear without treatment. So the person may mistakenly think there is no longer a problem.

If the patient is not treated, a skin rash and mouth sores may appear about 6 weeks later. The rash is often on the palms of the hands and soles of the feet. Mild, flulike symptoms may occur. This is the *secondary stage* of the disease. The rash and other symptoms may disappear. But spirochetes will stay in the bloodstream unless proper treatment is obtained.

For many years, there may be no symptoms while the spirochetes attack other parts of the body, such as the heart and the brain. This is known as the *latent stage*. After many years, *late syphilis,* the final stage, may cause heart failure, mental illness, or blindness. For this reason, it is very important to treat syphilis at an early stage. A doctor may take a blood test or may examine a piece of the sore under a microscope to make the diagnosis. Syphilis can be treated and cured with penicillin.

A pregnant woman may pass the syphilis infection to her unborn baby. Therefore, a blood test is often done early in pregnancy to diagnose and treat syphilis before it can cause deformities in the newborn.

Genital herpes

Genital herpes is caused by the herpes simplex II virus. Herpes simplex I virus usually causes cold sores and fever blisters in the mouth. Herpes simplex II infections usually appear in the genital area. Herpes II virus is introduced into the body mainly by sexual contact. Cases of genital herpes

It's a fact of life... VD gets around

are rapidly increasing in number. Each year, about 500,000 people are infected with this virus for the first time.

The first symptoms of genital herpes are usually noticed 2 to 12 days after sexual contact. The first symptom is often pain in the genital area. A small skin lesion called a *vesicle* may then appear in the genital area. A vesicle is a blisterlike elevation on the skin. It can be as small as a pinhead or as large as a pea. It contains clear fluid. When a vesicle breaks, the area underneath it swells and becomes sore. Muscle aches, fever, and headache, symptoms usually associated with colds or the flu, may be associated with the herpes infection.

It is important to let the doctor decide if the vesicles are herpes or another disease. If genital herpes is diagnosed, one should avoid sexual contact during the time of active infection to keep from spreading the infection. There is no known cure for herpes. Even after treatment, herpes infections may appear again and again. In some people, this reappearance can be triggered by changes in the temperature of the environment or by emotional stress. The disease is easily spread any time the blisters are present, so contact should be avoided at that time.

In women, there are two other serious problems that may develop which would require further treatment. Pregnant women with genital herpes may give the infection to their newborn infants during childbirth if proper safety measures are not taken. Women who have repeated herpes also appear to have more abnormal Pap smears, and possible development of cancer, than do other women. All women should have Pap smears done every year. This is particularly important for women who have had genital herpes infections.

Preventing STDs

An individual must be responsible for her or his own social actions. Gonorrhea, syphilis, and genital herpes are prevented by not having sexual contact with infected people. The surest prevention is to not have sexual intercourse.

These diseases do not go away on their own. There is no self-medication to treat them. Anyone who notices symptoms of an STD should go to a doctor or health clinic for expert diagnosis and treatment. A toll-free referral service (1-800-227-8922) gives information on medical facilities in your area that treat STDs. There are also sexually spread diseases other than gonorrhea, syphilis, and genital herpes. Therefore, any sore, ulcer, or discharge involving the sexual organs should be diagnosed and treated by a doctor.

Also, there are diseases with similar symptoms that may *not* be transmitted sexually. (See the "Something to think about" that follows.) A physician should diagnose and treat these diseases as well.

People with an STD must tell their sexual partners so that the partners can also be examined. Those with a sexually transmitted disease must stop sexual activity until cured, so as not to infect others. Finally, it is important to know that a person who has had an STD and has been cured can catch the same disease again.

Something to think about . . .

Microorganisms are constantly present in the human body. Most are harmless, and some serve useful purposes in the functioning of the body. Two such organisms are a one-celled animal called *trichomonad* and a one-celled plant called *monilia.* They are present in both men and women.

Occasionally, these microorganisms may multiply rapidly in a woman's vagina. The resulting irritation, called *vaginitis,* is characterized by vaginal itching, redness, and discharge—symptoms that frequently indicate a sexually transmitted disease. While vaginitis, itself, is *not* an STD, an immediate visit to the doctor is necessary in order to diagnose the symptoms and eliminate the possibility of a sexually transmitted disease.

Vaginitis should be treated early to ease discomfort and to prevent symptoms from becoming even more pronounced. While treatment of vaginitis will depend on the agent causing it, proper hygiene is often helpful in preventing recurrences.

In the case of vaginitis caused by trichomonads, medication must be taken by the patient and her sexual partner, if there is one. The partner might reintroduce the organisms through sexual intercourse, making it difficult for vaginitis to be eliminated through treatment.

Main Ideas

1. Sexually transmitted diseases are infectious diseases that are spread from person to person through sexual contact.
2. Gonorrhea and syphilis are serious health problems.
3. Genital herpes can reappear in a victim without repeated sexual contact.
4. Gonorrhea and syphilis can be prevented and cured.

Key Words

chancre	latent stage	STD
genital herpes	primary stage	syphilis
gonorrhea	secondary stage	vaginitis
late syphilis	spirochetes	vesicle

Apply Your Knowledge

1. How are sexually transmitted diseases spread?
2. What are the symptoms of gonorrhea? Does every person with a gonorrhea infection have symptoms?
3. How does a physician find out if a person has gonorrhea?
4. How does a physician find out if a person has syphilis?
5. What are the four stages of syphilis?
6. How can STDs be prevented?
7. Why should a person with an STD tell a sexual partner?
8. If gonorrhea is left untreated, what other serious problems may develop?
9. Why can't a person get syphilis from towels or toilet seats?
10. Why do doctors often give pregnant women a blood test for syphilis?

Extend Your Knowledge

1. Make a list of the similarities and differences between gonorrhea and syphilis. Could a person be infected with both diseases at the same time?
2. Explain why it is possible for a person to have gonorrhea or syphilis, especially latent syphilis, without knowing it.
3. Visit your local health clinic and obtain information on the number of cases of STDs in your city, county, or state.
4. What ideas do you have on how to prevent sexually transmitted diseases among teenagers?

Chapter 23

Do you know . . .

- how your body defends itself against infections?
- how infections spread to others?
- if there is a cure for the common cold?
- if hepatitis is contagious?

The Common Cold and Other Miseries

History books tell us about great armies that were defeated, but not in battle. They were defeated by diseases such as smallpox and typhoid fever. These diseases spread quickly among the troops and killed large numbers of soldiers. In this way, these diseases changed history.

A few hundred years ago, the causes of disease were not understood. Some thought sickness was caused by "evil spirits." Others believed it was due to an improper balance of blood and other fluids in the body. Until the 17th century, microorganisms were unknown. They were first discovered by Anton van Leeuwenhoek, a Dutch cloth merchant. Leeuwenhoek ground special glass lenses to examine his yard goods more closely. Looking through these lenses, he was amazed to discover many living things that no one had ever seen before. Some of the "wee beasties" and "animalcules" that he described were *pathogens,* or disease-causing microorganisms.

Pathogens

The most common pathogens are bacteria and viruses. Bacteria have a cell wall around them. They are too small for you to see with the naked eye. But you can see them under a microscope. Viruses are smaller than bacteria. They cannot be seen under an ordinary microscope. However, many of them can be seen under the more powerful electron microscope.

Fungi (small, plantlike organisms) and protozoa (small, animallike organisms) may also cause disease.

Infectious diseases

The diseases caused by pathogens or their products are called *infectious diseases*. Once-feared infectious diseases such as polio and whooping cough rarely occur today. This is due to important advances in preventive medicine. When people are exposed to fewer infectious diseases, more people can live longer and healthier lives. However, there are still many other infectious diseases that can cause serious illness or even death.

Infectious diseases are also called *communicable diseases* or *contagious diseases*. They are diseases that can be passed from one person or animal to another. Some people can give a disease to others, even though they do not have the disease, themselves. These people are called *carriers*.

The plague (both bubonic and other forms) was one of the biggest killers in history. In ancient Rome, about 5000 people died daily during the plague. One outbreak of plague in the 1300s is thought to have killed more than half the population of Europe and Asia. The microorganism that causes plague is spread to humans by fleas from infected rats. Rat control, waste and garbage control, and separating infected patients from other patients in hospitals are important methods of stopping the spread of the disease. The plague still occurs in some parts of the world.

Sources of infection

Most of the pathogens that cause infectious diseases can live and reproduce only inside the human body or the body of an animal. These pathogens can spread from one person or animal to another in a number of ways. Some pathogens spread directly from person to person. For example, the mucus released in sneezing, speaking, or coughing can spread pathogens. So can direct contact with saliva. Colds and flu are often passed in these ways. Direct contact with open skin sores may also spread some bacteria and viruses.

Pathogens can also be spread indirectly, such as by handling the silverware or clothing of an infected person. Food may carry pathogens. Pathogens in the air may land on food. Or, pathogens may be carried directly to the food by the person preparing it. Some intestinal infections, such as typhoid and dysentery, are caused by pathogens in food that was eaten raw. Water polluted by sewage may also carry pathogens that cause intestinal diseases. Rats, houseflies, and mosquitoes frequently carry pathogens from such sources as garbage or sewage. Still other pathogens live on damp surfaces and can be carried on toothbrushes or towels.

Actions of pathogens in the body

Pathogens enter a human body in a number of ways: through the digestive or respiratory tracts, through breaks in the skin, or through the mucous membranes. After entering the body, the pathogens multiply. At first, they cause no symptoms of the disease. This period of time is called the *incubation period*. The incubation period of most infectious diseases may last from a few hours to several days. The pathogens continue to multiply. They spread into nearby tissues. Blood and lymph may carry them to all parts of the body. Once this happens, the symptoms of the disease appear, and you know you are sick.

Defenses against infection

You are always coming into contact with many pathogens. Yet, you are not always ill. This is because your body has an amazing system of defenses. This ability of the body to fight off infection is known as *resistance*.

Resistance to infection depends on several factors. A healthy person is usually able to resist many infectious diseases. Poor nutrition, chronic illness, too much alcohol, and smoking lower resistance. So does emotional stress. Age also affects resistance. The elderly and the newborn are more likely to get certain infections.

Your body has some natural barriers to infection. Healthy, unbroken skin provides one barrier. Hairs in the nose and cilia in the throat help to screen out pathogens from the air we breathe. Stomach acid destroys some pathogens after they enter the body.

Your body's best methods of defense are certain blood cells and substances made in the blood that help to kill some pathogens.

Leukocytes, or white blood cells, surround, kill, and digest invading organisms. Someone who has too few white blood cells is very open to infections. Some medications may lower the number of white blood cells in the body.

Antibodies are protein substances made by white blood cells. Antibodies circulate in the bloodstream and attack pathogens. Eating enough protein helps to make sure that your body will have the material it needs to make antibodies.

Antitoxins are substances your body sometimes produces to neutralize (make inactive) harmful toxins (poisons) that pathogens sometimes produce.

Common infectious diseases

The common cold, influenza, hepatitis, and mononucleosis are some of the common infectious diseases that affect people every year. Unfortunately, there are no cures for these diseases. But understanding something about their causes can help you to keep from getting them.

The common cold

Every year, people miss many days of school and work because of the common cold. The average person may have three or four colds a year. A heavy smoker may have six or more. Many different viruses cause colds. Each cold you get may be caused by a different virus.

The incubation period of a cold is very short—only about 18 to 48 hours. The cold, itself, usually lasts from 2 to 7 days. Runny nose, sneezing, sore throat, and slight headache are some of the symptoms.

Water fountains and public telephones often carry pathogens—bacteria and viruses that cause communicable disease. How else are these microorganisms spread?

There is no medication that will cure a cold. Most of the medicines you can buy without a doctor's prescription will not help you. Some may even harm you. For example, decongestants are sometimes used to dry up the mucous membranes in the nose. Unfortunately, they may dry them up too much. Then these membranes cannot defend the body against harmful bacteria.

It is very important to keep a cold from turning into a more serious disease. Rest, plenty of liquids, and perhaps some aspirin will help. They will also make you feel more comfortable while you have a cold. Breathing in moistened or humidified air is often a very helpful way to clear the passages in the nose. If you have a very sore throat or a high fever, or if your cold lasts longer than a week, you should see a physician.

Try to prevent colds. Enough rest, good nutrition, and proper clothing will help keep up your resistance. A cold is most contagious in the first few days of symptoms. Stay away from someone who has a "new cold," if you can. Try to stay away from crowds during the "cold" season. Do not pass your cold on to others. Practice good hygiene, such as covering your mouth and nose when you sneeze or cough.

Influenza

Influenza, commonly called the "flu," is a very contagious disease caused by a virus. There are only two main types of influenza virus—type A and type B. But there are many kinds of A virus and many kinds of B virus. In one way, these viruses act in a strange manner. They undergo *mutations* (changes in structure) very rapidly. Every few years, a new kind of influenza virus appears. When this happens, there is usually an epidemic. Many people "catch the flu." For example, in the late 1960s, the Hong Kong flu spread all over the world. In 1972, the London flu appeared, and in 1978 the Russian flu occurred. These flu epidemics often occur in the winter and spring.

Influenza usually has an incubation period of 1 to 3 days. The early symptoms are like the symptoms of the common cold. Fever, cough, weakness, and muscle aches are the most common symptoms. Sometimes a patient will also feel sad and depressed. Fluids, bed rest, and medications to ease pain are the best treatments. Influenza is contagious from the time just before symptoms appear to about a week later. The virus is usually spread by coughing and sneezing.

You are always coming into contact with people who carry pathogens. Most of the time, your resistance will keep you from becoming ill. Your resistance can increase or decrease in a short period. It is affected by nutrition, age, stress, and other diseases.

Some cases of influenza that occur during an epidemic can be rather severe. But the flu is usually not a serious disease. However, if complications such as pneumonia develop, the patient may become seriously ill. This is often a problem for pregnant women, elderly people, and people in poor health. Doctors often advise these people to be vaccinated each year. (See Chapter 24 for information about vaccinations.)

Hepatitis

Many different viruses may cause swelling of the liver, a condition called *hepatitis*. People with hepatitis usually have headache, nausea, vomiting, fever, and pain in the abdomen. They may also have jaundice (a yellow discoloration of the skin) and darkened urine. Hepatitis is a serious illness and may cause other severe problems.

There are several types of hepatitis. Hepatitis A, which is also called infectious hepatitis, is the most common type. The A virus is usually found in water or in food that has been contaminated by feces. It may also be found in uncooked clams and other shellfish. The hepatitis virus can spread through saliva, feces, semen, and vaginal secretions. A doctor may inject someone who has been exposed to the type A virus with a medication called gamma globulin. This helps to protect against the disease.

Hepatitis B, which is also called serum hepatitis, is the most dangerous type. The type B virus spreads through the blood. A person who carries this virus cannot give blood, because it would infect the person who received it. Drug users who share the same needles to inject drugs into the bloodstream often get hepatitis. Vaccines have been developed to protect people against hepatitis B.

You should take extra safety measures whenever you are close to someone who has hepatitis. Do not share cups and utensils. Avoid close contact with the infected person. Good personal hygiene helps prevent hepatitis. Always wash your hands before eating and after using the toilet.

Mononucleosis

Mononucleosis, better known as "mono," is a fairly common viral infection among high school and college students. In fact, the greatest number of cases of mononucleosis is found among young people 15 to 19 years old. This disease often occurs in places where there are large groups of young people, such as in schools, in colleges, and in the military services.

Mononucleosis is sometimes called the "kissing disease." This is because people thought it was spread by kissing. Actually, scientists are not sure how this disease spreads. It is caused by a virus that may be spread through the saliva. But the virus may be spread in other ways, too.

Patients with "mono" often complain of sore throat, nausea, chills, and fever. The lymph nodes and spleen may be enlarged. There are usually feelings of weakness and tiredness. These feelings can last for weeks, sometimes for months.

The symptoms of mononucleosis are like the symptoms of many other diseases. However, a physician can diagnose mononucleosis with a blood test. People with "mono" should be under the care of a doctor. They need plenty of rest and should avoid hard physical activity.

Preventing infectious diseases

Each individual must be responsible for disease prevention. Practice good personal hygiene, eat a nutritional diet with enough fresh vitamins and proteins, and get enough rest and exercise to help keep up your resistance against common infections.

If you think you have a communicable disease, get medical advice early. This stops other serious problems from developing. It also prevents the further spread of the illness to others. For most bacterial infections, the doctor may prescribe an antibiotic. However, most viruses cannot be killed with antibiotics.

Each day, new discoveries are being made in the control of infectious diseases. The prevention and control of communicable diseases have been major factors in creating longer, healthier lives.

Something to think about . . .

Is there help for the common cold?

For many years, both scientists and sneezing cold sufferers have hoped for a cure for the common cold. Since the 1960s, two substances have been suggested that may help some people keep from getting colds or lighten cold symptoms in others. The substance that seems to help prevent colds is called *interferon*. Interferon is a protein, made in the human body, that slows the growth of some kinds of viruses. While other animals make their own interferon, only human interferon will work in humans. For a long time after interferon was discovered, few experiments could be done because it was too hard to get enough interferon out of human cells. After the development of gene-splicing, however, scientists could make interferon by giving bacteria the instructions taken from human cells. At first, no one was sure if interferon made that way would work on cold viruses in humans. But in 1982, a British scientist, Dr. Geoffrey M. Scott, successfully used synthetic interferon to prevent a group of subjects from catching colds. In the future, we may be using interferon to prevent colds or slow them down.

In 1960, Dr. Linus Pauling (a Nobel Prize-winning physicist) recommended taking large doses of vitamin C two or three times a day to prevent or help cure the common cold. Later experiments suggest that Dr. Pauling's claims may have been exaggerated, but that the body really does need extra vitamin C in times of stress and illness. While Dr. Pauling suggested doses of 1000 milligrams of the vitamin, Dr. Terence Anderson, who did further research in this area, claims that 120 milligrams a day should be plenty of vitamin C for most people. That amount can be obtained by drinking a 6-ounce glass of fresh or frozen orange juice each day, or by eating fresh fruits and vegetables.

Main Ideas

1. Infectious diseases are caused by pathogens that are passed from an infected person or animal to others.
2. The human body has important natural defenses against disease: the skin, white blood cells, and antibodies.

3. Good nutrition, regular exercise, enough rest, and personal cleanliness may help prevent infectious diseases.
4. Infectious diseases may cause serious illnesses.

Key Words

antibodies	hepatitis	leukocytes
antitoxins	incubation period	mononucleosis
carriers	infectious diseases	mutations
communicable diseases	influenza	pathogens
contagious diseases	interferon	resistance

Apply Your Knowledge

1. What are some common types of pathogens that may cause infectious diseases?
2. Why does it help to know the incubation periods of common diseases?
3. How does your body protect itself against infection?
4. How do white blood cells kill invading organisms?
5. You have just breathed in a pathogen that causes the flu. What happens to that pathogen once it is inside your body?
6. How does the common cold or the influenza virus spread from one person to another?
7. What is the difference between viruses and bacteria?
8. How can you avoid contact with the hepatitis virus?
9. Name some common infectious diseases that teenagers may get. How can these diseases be prevented?
10. Name some of the factors that affect a person's ability to resist disease.

Extend Your Knowledge

1. Invite a doctor or public health official to talk to your class about the prevention of infectious diseases in your community.
2. Find out what influenza epidemics have occurred in the United States in the past 20 years.
3. Explain what is meant by "an ounce of prevention is worth a pound of cure."
4. Under a microscope, examine slides of different microorganisms, such as bacteria, that may cause disease.

Chapter 24

Do you know . . .

- how immunizations protect you from infectious diseases?
- which diseases can be prevented by immunizations?
- why epidemics of diseases such as measles and polio still happen today?

Immunizations

Less than a hundred years ago, many cases of diseases such as diphtheria, measles, polio, and whooping cough—called epidemics—were the leading causes of death among children. These diseases are communicable, or *infectious.* They are passed easily from one person to another. Scientists have found ways to stop the spread of some infectious diseases caused by pathogens. Now it is possible to stamp out many of them. But, to do it, people need to understand how the body's immunization system works.

When harmful microorganisms (pathogens) cause infection in the body, white blood cells make protein substances called *antibodies.* Antibodies and white blood cells attack the pathogens. Once the infection has been stopped, the number of antibodies in the body decreases because the antibodies are no longer needed. Sometimes the same pathogens enter the body a second time. Then some white blood cells with a kind of chemical "memory" rapidly produce more antibodies to kill the pathogens before the infection starts. This ability to form antibodies against pathogens before they can cause disease is called *active immunity.* All people are born with some immunity, called natural immunity. Immunity the body builds up after having a disease is called *acquired immunity.* In acquired immunity, the body actively produces substances to fight a certain disease. A person can have such diseases as diphtheria, scarlet fever, measles, mumps, or chicken pox only once. The active immunity that follows after recovery from these diseases lasts a long time.

Sometimes very few pathogens enter a person's body, and no disease symptoms appear. However, the white blood cells still produce antibodies against the pathogens. Immunity may be built up when the same pathogens enter the body in small numbers many times. In this case, a person may never seem to have the disease at all.

Scientists and physicians have found that the body can be "fooled" into making antibodies and active immunity. Vaccines, or *immunizations,* are made from weakened pathogens or from substances made by pathogens. They cause the body to make antibodies. Vaccines can be given to people by mouth or by injection. They are a safe way for the body to build up immunity against some diseases. Different types of vaccine build up immunity for different lengths of time. Measles or mumps vaccines, for example,

Active immunity

These harmful bacteria cause disease. The body makes protein substances called antibodies to fight against harmful bacteria. The body's ability to make these antibodies again and again is called acquired immunity.

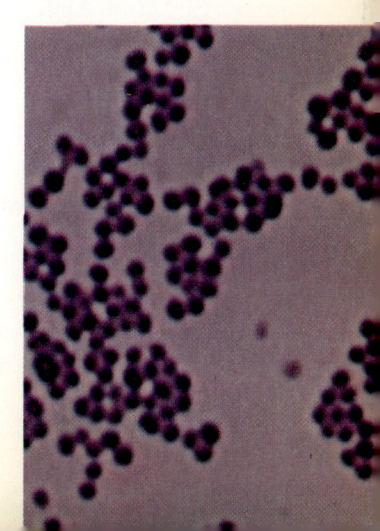

cause lifelong immunity. Vaccines against tetanus, however, last only a few years. Later doses of the vaccine, called boosters, must be taken to keep up the body's level of antibodies.

Passive immunity

Passive immunity lasts only a short time. With passive immunity, a person does not make antibodies but acquires them in some other way. For example, infants are born with passive immunity to some infections because they were given the antibodies by their mothers before birth. This protective immunity lasts for only a few months. Soon after birth, babies begin to build up their own antibodies against infection.

Another form of passive immunity occurs when a serum made from the blood of another person or animal is given to someone who has been exposed to an infectious disease. The serum contains antibodies and helps to protect the person against the disease-causing microorganisms. The protection lasts only a short time because the person getting the serum is not actively making antibodies.

Toxoids

Toxoids are another type of vaccine. They are made from the poisonous waste products of disease-causing microorganisms. These poisons are treated chemically to make them harmless. But they still can cause the body to make antibodies. Tetanus toxoid is one example.

Side effects of vaccines

Like many medicines, vaccines can cause side effects. However, these effects are usually mild and last only a short time. They may include a slight fever, a sore arm, or a mild rash. Very rarely a vaccine may cause a serious side effect. For this reason, vaccines should only be given under the direction of trained health professionals. The positive effects of immunization are much greater than the risks of vaccination. However, people with unusual diseases or allergies may not be able to get some vaccines.

Responsibility and immunity

You are responsible for keeping up your own immunity against disease. In this country, state laws require the immunization of children as they enter school for the first time. Diseases that have crippled or killed children in the past have been brought almost under control by immunization. But the pathogens that cause these diseases are still in the environment. Surveys show that millions of children in the United States have not been properly immunized against many common, preventable diseases, and epidemics can still happen.

Your doctor, school nurse, or parents may be keeping a record of your immunizations. You should keep a record, too. In order to be effective, tetanus immunizations must be kept up-to-date with booster shots. These boosters should continue about every ten years, even through adulthood.

Diphtheria, pertussis, and tetanus (DPT)

A combination DPT vaccine protects against three diseases. This vaccine has been available since the early 1950s. But today, almost 10 million children under age 12 are not properly immunized.

A series of three DPT shots should be given to healthy infants during the first 6 months of life. At 18 months, a fourth dose is given. Then the fifth dose is given before a child enters school. From then on, boosters for diphtheria and tetanus, given about every ten years, can keep the level of protection high.

Diphtheria is a serious infectious illness. In the late 1800s, 15 out of every 10,000 Americans died of diphtheria each year. The symptoms of this disease include sore throat and trouble with breathing and swallowing.

Pertussis is commonly called "whooping cough" because of the sounds many of these patients make as they fight to breathe in air. A major symptom of pertussis is very bad coughing spells. The disease often appears in children and is highly contagious. Pertussis can be fatal. Prevention of the disease is very important.

Tetanus appears in both children and adults. It is caused by pathogens that live in soil, dust, and manure. These germs often enter the body through small wounds or breaks in the skin. Once inside the body, tetanus germs make a poison that attacks the body's nervous system. This causes the muscles to lock in spasms, or abnormal contractions. Patients often have convulsions and may die from overtiredness and trouble with breathing. Because the muscles of the face are usually affected, many people call this disease "lockjaw." Even with the best medical treatment, about one-half of all tetanus cases are fatal. Immunizations are very important, especially for farmers and others who work near the soil.

Poliomyelitis

Poliomyelitis is a contagious disease that has been called infantile paralysis because it often affects young children. The disease can cause lifelong *paralysis,* a condition of not being able to move all or some parts of the body. Polio is fatal in about one out of every ten cases. Sometimes the breathing muscles are paralyzed and patients must be helped to breathe by machines. The widespread use of vaccines has made this disease rare.

All healthy infants and young people between the ages of 8 weeks and 18 years of age should have the polio vaccine.

Measles, mumps, and rubella

Measles is a serious childhood disease. It begins with a cough, a fever, and a red rash. Added problems such as pneumonia, blindness, or brain damage may follow.

Mumps often occurs in children, though it may appear in teenagers and adults. The first symptoms of this contagious disease are fever and painful, swollen glands under the jawbone. However, in severe cases, mumps can cause brain damage or sterility.

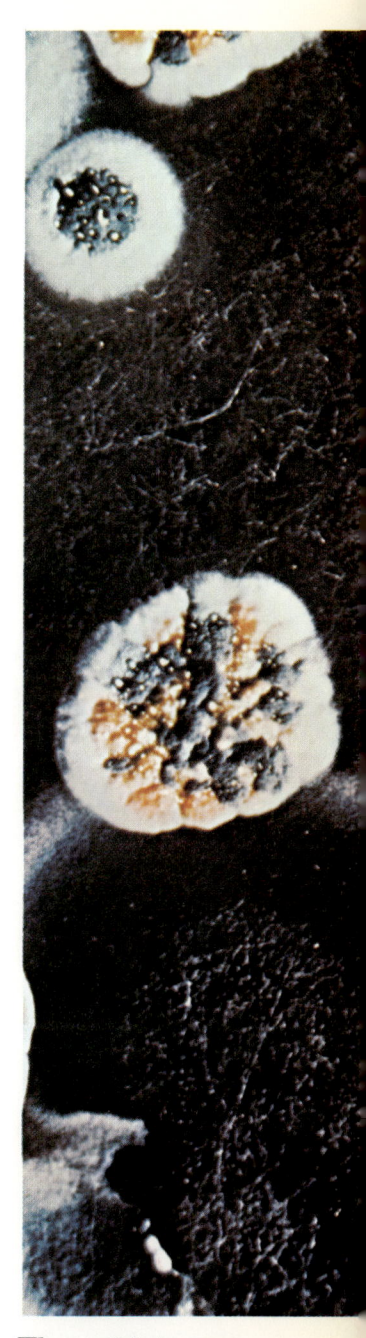

The mold shown here is grown in a laboratory. It produces an antibiotic drug. Antibiotic drugs are used to treat many diseases caused by bacteria.

Rubella is most dangerous to pregnant women. A woman infected by rubella virus early in pregnancy has almost one chance in four of giving birth to a deformed baby. Rubella is often called German measles, or three-day measles. Children should be immunized so that they do not catch this disease and spread it to pregnant women.

Knowledge of disease prevention

Scientists are developing new vaccines against many diseases. Knowing about the immunizations you and your family may need is important. By becoming immunized, you can protect yourself, your family, and your community from many serious diseases.

Something to think about . . .

In 1980, after a 13-year immunization campaign, the World Health Organization announced that smallpox had been completely eradicated from the earth. That made smallpox the first disease ever eliminated by medical science.

Smallpox was one of the oldest infectious diseases known to humankind. It seems to have been on the earth since before recorded history. The mummy of Egyptian Pharaoh Ramses V, who died about 1160 B.C., has lesions that may have been caused by smallpox sores. In 1967, when the immunization campaign began, smallpox was ever-present in more than 30 countries, and cases of it seemed to be "imported" regularly to about a dozen other countries. Immunization workers began to literally search countries, looking for people who had smallpox. The sick people were isolated and were sometimes even guarded 24 hours a day during the period in which they were infectious. All of the people in contact with known smallpox victims were located and vaccinated. Every effort was made to trace the chain of infection back to previously known outbreaks of the disease. This work demanded heroic effort in countries like Ethiopia, where terrain is rugged and more than half of the country's 28 million people live farther than a day's walk from any road.

In 1796, an English doctor named Edward Jenner gave a child the first smallpox vaccine. Before then, smallpox was a dangerous disease. Today, medical science has completely eliminated smallpox.

Today, as a result of the elimination of smallpox, vaccines against the disease are no longer needed. It is hoped that more widespread immunization against other infectious diseases, such as measles and polio, will eventually lead to their eradication.

Main Ideas

1. One of the recent achievements of medical science has been the control of many infectious diseases by immunization.
2. Immunization causes the body to defend itself against a certain disease.
3. When many children are not properly immunized, epidemics of preventable diseases may take place.
4. The good effects of immunization far outweigh the risks.

Key Words

acquired immunity	infectious	pertussis
active immunity	measles	poliomyelitis
antibodies	mumps	rubella
diphtheria	paralysis	tetanus
immunization	passive immunity	toxoids

Apply Your Knowledge

1. What is the difference between passive and active immunity?
2. Why should people be immunized even against diseases that are not common?
3. What is a vaccine?
4. Name seven diseases that may be prevented by immunizations.
5. Explain why epidemics of disease, such as measles, polio, and diphtheria, still happen today.

Extend Your Knowledge

1. Invite a local health official to your school to discuss the increase or decrease of preventable diseases in your state.
2. Plan an immunization schedule for a child from birth to age 16.
3. Ask your parents to list the childhood diseases that they had as a child. Are you protected from getting these diseases?

Unit 8

CHAPTERS:

25 Nutritional Needs
26 Snacks and Special Diets
27 Nutrition, Labels, and the Consumer
28 Digestion and Elimination

Food, Diet, and Digestion

Chapter 25

Do you know . . .

- if the foods you eat are the ones you need?
- how you can make "eating out" more nourishing?
- that large amounts of certain vitamins can be harmful?
- that water is a nutrient?
- why fiber is an important part of your diet, even though it cannot be fully digested?

Nutritional Needs

In one scientific experiment, rats are offered dishes of food that are the same in taste and smell, but not in nutritional value. The rats choose the more nutritious food. They choose by instinct, knowing automatically which foods are better.

You cannot count on such instincts when you walk into a supermarket that offers 10,000 or more food items. When you are hungry, your body craves food. But your body may not crave nutritious food. You must choose between nutritious foods and junk foods. So you must depend on common sense and what you have learned about nutrition.

Using the Daily Food Guide

What you eat is really your own business. You have likes and dislikes. But if you let your likes or tastes alone tell you what to eat every day, you might find that your body's need for nutrients is not being met. You can eat a lot of food and still be poorly nourished.

Nutrients are the substances in food that provide energy, build and repair cells, and regulate body processes. They aid in growth and development. Eating a lot of just one kind of food may not give your body enough nutrients. But if you eat a variety of foods, there is a good chance that your nutritional needs will be met.

One way to be sure you are getting enough of the right nutrients is to use a food guide when planning your meals and snacks. The U.S. Department of Agriculture recommends the Daily Food Guide shown on page 291. It classifies foods into groups based on the nutrients they contain. The groups are: (1) meat, poultry, fish, and beans; (2) milk and cheese; (3) vegetables and fruit; and (4) breads and cereals. Notice that for each food group, the guide gives the number of servings needed each day and the serving size; it also provides examples of the foods you can choose from.

For many years these were known as the four basic food groups. Now the Department of Agriculture recognizes a fifth food group—fats, sweets, and alcohol. This group includes foods and condiments such as cooking oils, salad dressings, catsup, jams and jellies, and pastries—foods that are meant to complement, not replace, foods from the other four groups. No servings from this fifth group are recommended in the Daily Food Guide, since these foods provide calories with few nutrients. They are called *empty-calorie foods*.

You can get a nutritious lunch in the school cafeteria or pack one at home for a picnic. Just refer to the Daily Food Guide when planning your meal.

A balanced meal provides between one-fourth and one-third of the nutrients you need daily. The meal contains a serving from each of the first four food groups. A Swiss cheese omelet served with steamed broccoli and French bread is an example of a balanced meal.

Take a minute to check your favorite meal against the Daily Food Guide. Make a list of each food in the meal. Are all four food groups included? If not, what other foods could you add to the meal to make it balanced nutritionally? Are there any empty-calorie foods that you could replace with more nutritious ones?

Get into the habit of mentally checking the nutritional value of the foods you are planning to eat against the Daily Food Guide. This will help you to make wise choices, whether you are preparing your meals at home or eating out in a restaurant.

Nutrients

Why is protein so important?

Protein is needed for the never-ending building and replacement of body cells. When you eat an omelet or a bowl of chili, you are taking in proteins of animals and plants. Inside your small intestine, these large protein molecules are broken down into smaller parts called amino acids. Then, like tiny building blocks, the amino acids are joined together to form specific proteins that your body needs.

The proteins in your body are made up of about twenty-three amino acids. Your body can make most of these amino acids from the proteins you digest. However, nine of the amino acids cannot be manufactured. These are called *essential amino acids*. They must be in the foods you eat.

Foods with high-quality protein contain the essential amino acids. The meat, poultry, fish, and beans group and the milk and cheese group are the best sources of such protein. Protein from the vegetable and fruit

Daily Food Guide

MEAT, POULTRY, FISH, AND BEANS GROUP

A Serving Is: 56 to 84 g (2 to 3 ounces) of cooked lean meat, poultry, or fish (not including bone).
Serving Daily: 2
Equivalents:
  1 egg
  120 to 180 mL (½ to ¾ cup) of cooked dry beans, peas, soybeans, or lentils
  30 mL (2 tablespoons) of peanut butter
  60 to 120 mL (¼ to ½ cup) of nuts, sesame seeds, or sunflower seeds

} = 28 g (1 ounce) meat, poultry, or fish

MILK AND CHEESE GROUP

Servings Daily:
  Children under 9   2 to 3
  Children 9 to 12   3
  Teenagers   4
  Adults   2
  Pregnant Women   3
  Nursing Mothers   4

A Serving Is: 240 mL (1 cup) of milk.
Equivalents (in calcium):
  240 mL (1 cup) plain yogurt = 240 mL (1 cup) milk
  120 mL (½ cup) cottage cheese = 60 mL (¼ cup) milk
  28 g (1 ounce) cheddar or Swiss cheese = 180 mL (¾ cup) milk
  120 mL (½ cup) ice cream = 80 mL (⅓ cup) milk

VEGETABLE AND FRUIT GROUP

Servings Daily: 4   Include 1 good vitamin C source every day and 1 good vitamin A source at least every other day.
A Serving Is: 120 mL (½ cup) of vegetable or fruit.
Equivalents:
  ½ medium grapefruit or cantaloupe
  1 medium orange, apple, or banana
  1 medium potato
  juice of 1 lemon

BREAD AND CEREAL GROUP

Servings Daily: 4   Select only whole-grain, enriched, or fortified products.
A Serving Is: 1 slice of bread.
Equivalents:
  120 to 180 mL (½ to ¾ cup) cooked cereal, cornmeal, grits, macaroni, noodles, rice, or spaghetti
  28 g (1 ounce) ready-to-eat cereal

---

group or the bread and cereal group does not have as many essential amino acids. It is low-quality protein. Vegetarians who eat only plant foods have a difficult time getting all the essential amino acids. Some vegetarians get a well-balanced assortment of amino acids by including dried legumes, milk, cheese, and eggs in their diets.

Carbohydrate is the body's main source of energy.

Starches and sugars are *carbohydrates*. There is plenty of carbohydrate in foods of the bread and cereal group. It can also be found in fruits, vegetables, and milk. Carbohydrate is the main source of energy for the body. The energy provided by carbohydrate is needed especially by the muscles and the brain. In Chapter 27 you will learn more about sugar.

If you eat more carbohydrate than your body needs, the excess is stored in the liver and muscles in the form of glycogen (stored sugar). If you eat more than can be stored in this way, the excess is changed to fat and stored in fat cells. Most overweight people blame carbohydrate for their weight problems. But overeating, not carbohydrate, is what causes people to gain weight.

Fat is concentrated fuel for the body.

Fat is found in many foods, such as nuts, meat, oils, eggs, chocolate, margarine, olives, avocadoes, and butter. Many people believe that fat is bad for them, so they avoid it as much as possible. It is true that eating large amounts of fat—more than 30 percent of your daily calories—can cause certain health problems. (These problems will be discussed at the end of this chapter.) But your body needs fat for several reasons. Gram for gram, fat supplies much more energy than carbohydrate or protein does. Fat is stored as a reserve source of energy. Fat also adds flavor to many foods and helps the body to absorb some vitamins.

Minerals are needed in small but steady supply.

Many *minerals* are needed to control the body's chemical processes. An example of the importance of minerals can be seen in a study of hemoglobin.

Iron is the mineral in hemoglobin that attracts oxygen. Without enough iron, your muscles do not get enough oxygen to contract properly and you feel tired or "washed out." This condition is known as *iron-deficiency anemia.* You can avoid iron-deficiency anemia by eating good sources of iron, such as meat (especially liver and kidney), dried beans, eggs, and enriched breads.

Calcium and phosphorus are minerals that are very important for strong bones and teeth. Calcium also helps blood to clot, muscles to contract, and nerves to send messages. Good sources of calcium include milk, hard cheese, yogurt, and dark-green leafy vegetables. Meat, fish, poultry, eggs, and milk are high in phosphorus.

Fluorine prevents tooth decay. The best source of fluorine is drinking water that has fluoride salts in it.

Iodine is needed for proper working of the thyroid gland. The body's need for iodine can be met by using iodized table salt.

Which foods are high in protein? In carbohydrate? In fat?

Many people think that taking large amounts of vitamins makes them healthy. This is not true. Unneeded amounts of vitamins B complex and C are removed from the body as waste. Overdoses of vitamins A, D, E, and K may be harmful to you.

Many other minerals are needed by the body. But if you include enough foods with iron, calcium, phosphorus, fluorine, and iodine in your diet, you will usually get all the other needed minerals along with them.

Getting the right amount of vitamins is important for health.

Vitamins are important to your body. They are substances that help regulate body processes.

Many people think that large amounts of vitamins will guarantee good health. Unfortunately, that is not really so. It is even possible to take in too much of certain vitamins. *Fat-soluble vitamins*—vitamins A, D, E, and K—are stored in your body until they are needed. Unneeded amounts are not removed as waste in the urine, so taking large amounts can be harmful. Excess *water-soluble vitamins*—vitamins B and C—cannot be stored and are removed as waste. You should know how much of each vitamin your body needs and eat to meet those needs.

Vitamin A is very important for the health of the skin and the eyes. It also helps keep the linings of the mouth, nose, throat, and digestive tract free from infection. A diet extremely low in vitamin A may lead to the development of dry, rough skin. Such a diet may also cause difficulty in adjusting the eyes to dim light.

Vitamin A is found in egg yolks, liver, butter, milk, and cheese. Fortified margarine contains vitamin A. The human body can also make vitamin A from carotene, a substance found in green and yellow vegetables and fruits. Usually, vitamin A is not destroyed by cooking. Large amounts of vitamin A taken continuously can cause liver damage.

Vitamin D is needed for growing strong bones and teeth. Because bones develop before birth, it is important for pregnant women to have plenty of calcium and vitamin D in their diets. A child with a serious lack of vitamin D may develop rickets, a condition in which the bones are poorly formed.

Vitamin D is found in fortified milk and in fish-liver oils. Vitamin D is also produced by the action of the ultraviolet rays in sunshine on certain oils in your skin. But in some environments, the hours of sunshine in a day are few, or heavy pollution lessens the full amount of sunlight. In these environments, fortified milk is important to the diet.

It is possible for human beings to get too much vitamin D by taking too many vitamin D pills. This causes kidney and liver damage and deformed bones. Concentrated forms of vitamin D should be used only in the exact amounts suggested by a doctor. For the most part, it is safer to get vitamin D from foods than from pills.

Vitamin E is not a miracle nutrient. Don't believe everything you hear about vitamin E. It cannot cure ulcers, arthritis, cancer, heart disease, or warts. It cannot make you a better athlete. This vitamin prevents vitamin A from being destroyed too quickly. It also strengthens the cell membranes of red blood cells.

Vitamin E can be found in salad oils, margarine, whole-grain cereals, and most fresh green leafy vegetables. The body will store excess vitamin E in tissues under the skin and in the ovaries or testes. Too much vitamin E intake, however, can interfere with the work of the glands and tissues.

Vitamin K plays an important role when you are bleeding from an injury. This vitamin helps the liver produce a protein that is needed for blood clotting.

Foods that are good sources of vitamin K are dark-green leafy vegetables and liver. If you eat well-balanced meals, you will not have to worry about getting the right amount of this vitamin. Your large intestine can also produce vitamin K.

Vitamin B is actually a group of vitamins. This group of vitamins is sometimes called the vitamin B complex. It includes thiamine, riboflavin, niacin, and vitamin B_{12}. The vitamin B complex is important for energy and growth.

Thiamine, or vitamin B_1, is needed by the nerves, muscles, and digestive system. With a serious lack of thiamine, nerve and muscle disorders can develop. A disease called beriberi, affecting the heart and the nervous system, can also develop. Pork, whole-grain and enriched cereals, lean meats, and dried legumes give the body thiamine.

Riboflavin, or vitamin B_2, and **niacin** are found in liver, cheese, leafy vegetables, beans, milk, eggs, and fish. Both of these vitamins are good for the skin, the digestion, and the nervous system. A serious lack of niacin causes dry and red patches to form on the skin. This is a disease called pellagra.

Vitamin B_{12} helps increase the number of red blood cells and helps

Without water, nutrients could not be carried from the intestine into the bloodstream, waste products could not be carried out of the body, and the body could not be kept at an even temperature.

the body use protein, fat, and carbohydrate. It is found in liver, leafy vegetables, milk, eggs, and cheese.

Vitamin C, or *ascorbic acid,* is found in citrus fruits, such as oranges, lemons, limes, and grapefruits. Tomatoes, potatoes, and cabbage are also good sources. A person who tires easily, whose skin bruises easily, or whose gums bleed may need more vitamin C.

Vitamin C cannot be stored in the body, so excess amounts are removed from the body as waste. But it is not a good idea to take extremely large doses of vitamin C, since this may cause diarrhea or kidney damage. There is also evidence that your body will begin to adjust to large amounts of vitamin C over a long period of time. Then, if you should decrease your vitamin C intake, minor symptoms of a disease called scurvy may appear.

Scurvy is caused by a severe lack of vitamin C. Long ago, sailors and others were cut off from supplies of fresh food for long periods of time. They suffered weakness, pain in their legs and joints, and severe bleeding from their gums. Sometimes they lost their teeth. These are symptoms of scurvy. This disease sometimes caused death. Sailors on long voyages did not develop scurvy if they had a little lime or lemon juice each day. In fact, the name "limey" for sailor comes from the days when British sailors drank lime juice each day to prevent scurvy.

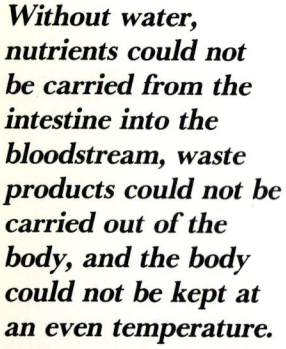

Water is also a nutrient.

Most people think that water is something to bathe in, swim in, and drink whenever they are thirsty. Actually, next to air, water is the most important element needed for life. At least 60 percent of your body is water. You can live for weeks without eating, but you can live only a few days without water.

Water is found in every cell of your body. Water has several important functions. It carries nutrients through the intestinal wall and into the bloodstream. It also helps to carry waste materials out of the body. The body's temperature-control system also needs water in order to work properly.

On an average day, 2 to 3 liters (about 2 to 3 quarts) of water can be lost through perspiration, urination, bowel movements, and breathing. If you exercise, you must replace the lost fluid; if you don't, your body may become dehydrated and malfunction, somewhat like a car with an overheated engine. The symptoms of dehydration are headache, fatigue, and a feverish feeling. You may also become dehydrated due to a fever, vomiting, or diarrhea.

The more dehydrated you are, the more likely you are to develop heatstroke. Heatstroke is the worst thing that can happen when fluids are not replaced in your body. In heatstroke, the pulse is fast and strong. The skin is hot and dry. Your body temperature may go as high as 40 to 41°C (105 to 107°F). You can even lose consciousness and die.

To make sure your body is getting the water it needs, you should drink 6 to 8 glasses of liquid daily. In addition to water, you can drink soup, milk, juice, tea, and other beverages. Many foods can also help you keep the delicate liquid balance in your body. Most of the foods you eat are over 50 percent water. Some fruits and vegetables are as much as 95 percent water. Even dry foods, such as bread, flour, and crackers, contain from 5 to 30 percent water. Water intake must increase when you exercise, have a fever, or lose fluid by vomiting or diarrhea.

If fiber cannot be digested, why do we need it?

For many years, nutritionists have recommended that we include more *fiber* in our diet. Lettuce and other vegetables, fruits, and whole-grain breads and cereals all provide fiber. Fiber is the "rough" part of the plant foods we eat. These unrefined carbohydrate substances are called *roughage*. Cell walls of the leaves, fruits, seeds, bulbs, and flowers of plants are made of cellulose. Cellulose is a complex carbohydrate that our intestines cannot fully break down.

Fiber is fairly soft once it reaches the intestines. Yet this roughage helps to "scrub out" materials left after digestion and absorption have occurred. The bulk formed by fiber helps the muscles of the large intestine to contract and push the waste products toward the rectum. If the diet does not have enough fiber, the waste materials in the large intestine travel slowly and allow bacteria more time to multiply. Present studies suggest that the contact with bacteria over a longer period of time increases the chance of intestinal cancer.

Fiber is the part of plant foods that the human body cannot fully digest. Fiber helps to clean out the materials in the intestine left behind after digestion has taken place. Whole-grain products have a high fiber content.

Breakfast, lunch, and dinner

It is not hard to give your body the right nutrients. Three balanced meals a day should do it. A balanced meal follows the Daily Food Guide, with a serving from each of the four food groups.

Breakfast is an important meal. For most people, it has been 12 to 14 hours since their last meal. People need a good supply of nutrients for energy to begin the day's activities. A breakfast of juice, cereal, eggs, and milk contains foods from the four food groups. It may provide about one-fourth of the day's nutrients. Some instant breakfasts are easy to prepare and may be useful at times. However, many of them lack the roughage that fruits and whole-grain cereals provide. Other important nutrients may be missing, too.

You should eat about one-third of the day's required nutrients at lunch. You can find foods from the four food groups in the school cafeteria or in a restaurant. Or you can carefully pack a lunch at home that includes something from each food group.

For many people, dinner is the biggest meal of the day. A dinner of meat, poultry, or fish, along with vegetables, salad, a roll or a slice of bread, and milk, represents all four food groups. Such a dinner provides about one-third of all the nutrients needed for the day.

You can plan healthful meals, even on a small budget. Learn as much as you can about the nutritional value of foods. Your own knowledge will help you to shop wisely and eat well. Remember that less-processed foods may be more nutritious than highly processed foods, such as canned or pre-prepared foods. You can get high-quality protein from inexpensive foods like eggs and cottage cheese. Certain foods, like rice and beans, combine to provide more high-quality protein than either food alone would. Combining foods to get the most protein value from them is called *protein complementarity*. Another hint to better eating on a small budget is that dark breads and other whole grain products contain more nutrients than foods made of white refined flour.

Basal metabolic rate

Nutrients such as carbohydrates, fats, and proteins provide energy. Energy is released in the cells. Your body uses and releases energy for breathing, circulation of the blood, and all physical activities that take even the slightest effort.

Your *basal metabolic rate* is the rate at which your body uses energy. Your basal metabolic rate is the amount of energy you use each hour, while resting, for each kilogram (2.2 pounds) of body weight. This rate tells something about how your body uses the energy in the food you eat.

Energy is measured in *calories*. A calorie is not a nutrient. It is not a substance found in foods. A calorie is a measure of energy. The number of calories in a food tells how much energy it provides.

All foods that supply fat, carbohydrate, and protein are sources of calories. When you take in more calories (energy) than you use, your body stores the extra amount. Each day, a moderately active young person uses about 45 to 55 calories per kilogram (20 to 25 calories per pound) of body weight. A very active person may need more calories per kilogram. Those who exercise very little may need as few as 40 calories per kilogram (17 calories per pound). Boys and men generally need more calories than girls and women do. Height, weight, and age—as well as the season of the year and climate of the area in which one lives—also affect the number of calories needed.

Most animal fats are "saturated" fats. They are believed to increase the amount of cholesterol deposits on the walls of blood vessels. This results in a higher risk of heart disease.

A high intake of fat is generally thought to be harmful because it may be related to cardiovascular disease (heart disease and circulation problems). Cholesterol, a fatlike substance, can be deposited on the inner lining of the arteries. The lumen, or the opening of the arteries, becomes narrow because of atheromas (fat deposits) on the inner lining of the arteries. This condition is called atherosclerosis. It can seriously decrease the circulation of blood and oxygen.

Most fats found in animal products—especially egg yolk, beef and pork, and organ meats, such as liver and kidney—are "saturated" fats; plant sources of food contain fewer saturated fats. Cholesterol is also found in many animal products. A person following a diet high in animal fat may be increasing the amount of cholesterol in the blood.

Something to think about . . .

Recently, researchers made an interesting discovery. They found that cholesterol is carried through the bloodstream in two ways. One way may be harmful, but the other may actually help prevent the formation of atheromas. Low-density lipoproteins (LDLs) carry the most cholesterol and may have a greater attraction for the artery walls; they can help form atheromas. But high-density lipoproteins (HDLs) may help carry cholesterol out of the arteries and back to the liver to be eliminated.

As a person becomes older, the ability to get rid of cholesterol decreases. The possibility of developing cardiovascular disease increases. To find out if a patient has a high potential for cardiovascular disease, doctors measure the level of cholesterol in the blood. To correct a dangerously high cholesterol level, a person can exercise more, consume less saturated fat (less meat), quit smoking, and reduce daily stress.

Main Ideas

1. Nutrients in food supply the body with energy, regulate body processes, and provide materials for building and repairing cells.
2. Carbohydrate and fat are the major energy sources for the body, while protein helps build and repair body cells.
3. Vitamins and minerals help regulate body processes. They are needed regularly in small amounts rather than in large amounts.
4. Water is also an important nutrient.
5. Fiber is important for good health, even though it is not fully digested.
6. The recommended daily servings of food from the Daily Food Guide provide a good diet for most people.

Key Words

ascorbic acid	fat-soluble vitamins	phosphorus
basal metabolic rate	fiber	protein
calcium	fluorine	protein
calories	iodine	complementarity
carbohydrate	iron	riboflavin
Daily Food Guide	iron deficiency	thiamine
empty-calorie foods	minerals	vitamins
essential amino acids	niacin	water-soluble
fat	nutrients	vitamins

Apply Your Knowledge

1. What is the difference between foods and nutrients?
2. Should you let your appetite choose the foods you eat? Why or why not?
3. Why is it important to have variety in your diet?
4. What can protein do for your body that fat and carbohydrate cannot?
5. Which food groups will give you the high-quality protein that your body needs?
6. Which nutrient is the main source of energy?
7. List three reasons why fat is important in your diet.
8. What is the function of iron in your body?
9. How can iron-deficiency anemia be avoided?
10. If you were not getting enough vitamin C, what symptoms would you have?

Extend Your Knowledge

1. Why must foods from the four food groups in the Daily Food Guide be eaten every day in order to maintain good health?
2. Using the Daily Food Guide on page 291, make up a meal plan for 1 day that includes three balanced meals.
3. Ask a classmate what his or her favorite meal is. Does it include foods from all four food groups? If not, go over the Daily Food Guide together and decide what other food or foods could be added to the meal to make it more nutritious.
4. Vegetarians who eat only plant foods must be especially careful to plan meals that provide high-quality protein. Interview a dietitian to find out how this is done. Report your findings to the class.

Chapter 26

Do you know . . .
- that snacking can be an important part of your diet?
- how thin people can gain weight?
- how to lose weight safely?
- whether athletes need special diets?
- that fad diets are not necessarily good diets?
- that in order for a vegetarian to remain healthy, the diet must be carefully planned?

Snacks and Special Diets

Now you know the nutrients your body needs. In this chapter, you will learn about snacking habits and the "how" and "why" of choosing nutritional snacks. You will also learn some good ways to maintain the weight you want.

Snacking

One of our favorite activities is snacking. Snacking has become a social custom in our country. For many people, it has become a part of their regular eating habits. Some schools stress nutritional snacking. And many schools offer nutritional breaks during the school day. They provide milk, fruits, and vegetables. Other schools are trying out automatic vending machines that stock many different kinds of foods. However, soft drinks and candy, though not the best snacking foods, are the most popular items sold by vending machines.

There is nothing wrong with snacking. You can eat as often as four or five times a day. However, you should eat a balanced daily diet without excess calories. Some nutritionists even suggest eating smaller amounts of food more often. In that way, you can use nutrients better. Snacks can help you get the nutrients that may be missing from your meals.

Not all snack foods are nutritious, however. Some foods do not fit into the traditional food groups. They are empty-calorie foods. The main thing they offer is calories. Carbohydrate and fat are the major nutrients in such snack foods as chips, candy, jam, and carbonated drinks. Compare the snacks in the chart on page 304.

What is your favorite snack?

Many people pick snacks according to how easy they are to get or to fix. It's much easier to slice a pie or to take a doughnut out of a package than to wash and slice a carrot or to peel an orange. If fruits and vegetables were washed and sliced and ready to eat, you might be more tempted to reach for them. So it's wise to place sliced carrots, cauliflower, or celery stalks in a glass of water and put them in the refrigerator. They will remain crisp there. Since most vegetables can be eaten raw, you might enjoy eating the crisp vegetables with dips made of yogurt, cheese, or other nutritious foods. Snacking can be more fun and better for you if you know just what

Some Snacks and Their Nutritional Values

	Carbonated beverage	Fresh orange juice	Raw carrot	Malted milk	Pizza	Chocolate bar
Amount=	1 cup	1 cup	6-8 strips	1 cup	1 medium slice	1.5 oz.
Calories=	96	110	20	245	185	160
Protein=	0	2 g	1 g	11 g	7 g	2 g
Calcium=	0	27 g	18 g	317 g	107 g	33 g
Iron=	0	.5 ml	.4 ml	.7 ml	.7 ml	.4 ml
Vitamin A=	0	500 IU	5500 IU	590 IU	290 IU	0
Thiamine=	0	.22 ml	.03 ml	.14 ml	.04 ml	.10 ml
Riboflavin=	0	.07 ml	.3 ml	.49 ml	.12 ml	.05 ml
Vitamin C=	0	12.4 ml	4 ml	2 ml	4 ml	0

Which of the above snack foods would you consider most nutritious?

The body needs a fresh supply of energy after a night's sleep. If you eat a good breakfast, your energy level is more likely to stay high all morning.

There is nothing wrong with snacking. But not all snacks are good for you. Some foods offer only empty calories and no nutrients.

you are eating. A large helping of apple pie with ice cream will not add ten pounds to your weight if you eat it only once in a while. But if the pie and ice cream are part of your daily snacking habit, there's a good chance that you will gain unwanted weight sooner or later.

How important is breakfast?

Many people eat a light breakfast or none at all. But breakfast is an important meal. By morning, your body has digested dinner from the night before. It has stored some extra carbohydrate in the liver. The extra carbohydrate is stored in the form of glycogen in an amount equal to about 600 calories.

However, about 350 to 400 calories are used up even when you are asleep. With more than half of the stored carbohydrate used up between dinner and breakfast, the need to renew your energy supply becomes important. If you eat breakfast, you are restoring calories you will need during the morning hours. But if you do not eat a good breakfast, your energy level may drop as the morning wears on. Then around 10 A.M., you may eat a high-carbohydrate snack, such as a candy bar or doughnut, to supply the missing energy. But you may not be getting all the nutrients your body needs, only calories.

It is very simple to talk about the importance of breakfast. Actually, eating a proper breakfast takes more planning when you have very little time. But remember, good breakfast habits can be learned. Try making a breakfast sandwich or mixing orange juice the night before to save you some time in the morning. The good eating habits you learn today will be a great help for the rest of your life.

Weight control

During childhood and adolescence, a healthy person usually gains regularly in height and weight. During the adolescent spurt of growth, however, you will gain at a fast rate for a few years. Then less rapid gains will be made until you reach your adult size.

Height-weight-age tables show weight ranges at different ages and heights. These tables are useful in a general way only. That is, they show average ranges. They do not show just what any one person should weigh. A person with a large frame would expect to weigh more than a person of the same age and height who has a smaller frame. The graphs on the next page show ranges in weight and height at different ages.

Diet for the underweight

Students who are underweight may be unhappy about the way they look. Some underweight students may worry not only about their looks but also about a lack of energy and more frequent sickness.

Why snack on potato chips or candy? Have a cold, delicious piece of fruit.

GIRLS' WEIGHT RANGE

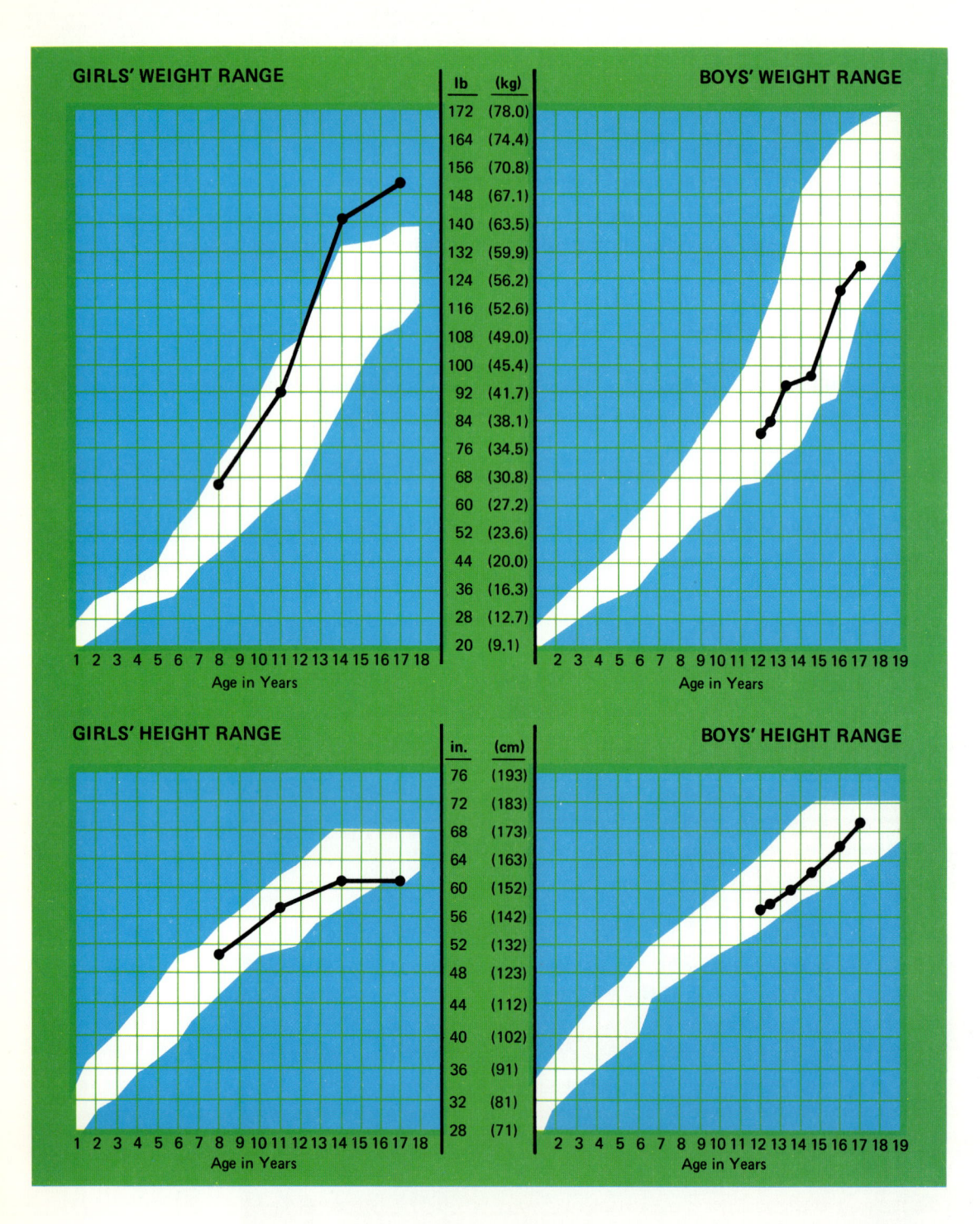

BOYS' WEIGHT RANGE

lb	(kg)
172	(78.0)
164	(74.4)
156	(70.8)
148	(67.1)
140	(63.5)
132	(59.9)
124	(56.2)
116	(52.6)
108	(49.0)
100	(45.4)
92	(41.7)
84	(38.1)
76	(34.5)
68	(30.8)
60	(27.2)
52	(23.6)
44	(20.0)
36	(16.3)
28	(12.7)
20	(9.1)

Age in Years

GIRLS' HEIGHT RANGE

BOYS' HEIGHT RANGE

in.	(cm)
76	(193)
72	(183)
68	(173)
64	(163)
60	(152)
56	(142)
52	(132)
48	(123)
44	(112)
40	(102)
36	(91)
32	(81)
28	(71)

Age in Years

The white areas in these charts show the average ranges of height and weight for girls and boys. The black lines show the growth patterns of one girl and one boy. What can you tell about the body build of each person?

Unusual thinness can be caused by a long-term illness. Infection, stress, or illness may interfere with appetite. If a person has a digestive disorder, the nutrients in food may not be absorbed in the right way. If there are physical problems, it is best to have a doctor prescribe the proper weight-gain diet.

Most often, underweight reflects lifestyle or a person's ideas about food in general. Some thin people pick at their food. They hesitate to try new or different foods. Overactive people may forget to eat. Too strict a weight-reduction diet may result in underweight. Sometimes the dining table may be the family battleground when one person is not willing to eat what is being served. Then eating becomes a chore, not a pleasure.

If you are underweight, examine yourself and your ideas and feelings about food. Think about why you might be underweight. When you are satisfied with the reasons, you might want to set some goals for yourself. Merely eating more food may not improve your health and appearance. Any new diet must have nutrients as well as calories.

If you really want to gain weight, you should get up early enough to have breakfast. Eat more of your favorite foods. Eat even if you aren't hungry. If your appetite is small, eat several smaller meals. Select nutritious but higher-calorie foods.

Eat snacks about two hours before the next meal. Snacking too close to mealtime raises the blood-sugar level (the amount of sugar in the blood). This may lessen your appetite.

Exercising also helps to stimulate the appetite. After school, eat a snack that is both nutritious and high in calories. Then, do some exercises for at least half an hour.

No one single food can help you to gain weight. So it is better to try a variety of foods to keep up your interest in eating. And remember this: gaining weight takes time. Don't try to fatten yourself up all in one week. Work slowly and carefully at changing your eating habits.

Diet for the overweight

No one gains 25 pounds all of a sudden. There is a gradual weight gain during your growth period. But some students gain more rapidly than they should. Weigh yourself regularly and look for bulges and flabbiness. Also compare your weight to your height and body type.

If you find a difference of 2 or 3 pounds in weight from one morning to the next, don't panic. There is no need to go on a diet. Some days your body tissue may hold more fluid than other days. On days when you exercise, you may lose these 2 or 3 unwanted pounds of fluid. Also, staying at your best weight and looking attractive does not mean staying extremely thin. Some people think they are overweight when they are not. As a result, they may not eat enough of the proper foods. So they may not get enough nutrients to stay healthy.

It is easier to take off a little extra weight than to go on a year-long diet to lose 10 to 15 pounds. Once you develop an eating habit that makes you gain weight, it becomes hard to break it. If you are gaining too much weight or gaining too quickly, try to figure out why. Sometimes problems at home, at school, or with friends may make you eat or snack too much. You may not even be aware of the total number of calories you are taking in.

An overweight person runs a greater risk of hypertension, diabetes, coronary heart disease, and other diseases of the circulatory system. If overweight prevents you from moving easily and freely, or if it affects your breathing or endurance, it can also be a problem in social life or in sports.

Before dieting, check with your doctor.

Hundreds of how-to-diet books are written by different people. But what may work for them may be harmful for you. You may not need professional advice to lose 2 to 3 pounds. But before you try to lose 10 pounds or more, check with your doctor. Your doctor can recommend a reducing diet that will suit you. Remember, no matter what you weigh, your body needs the nutrients from a balanced diet.

Overeating is one of the major causes of becoming overweight. The number of calories taken in is greater than the number of calories burned. The following eating rules will help you eat fewer calories than you burn:

People who weigh about 50 kilograms (110 pounds) use the number of calories per hour shown in the chart when they perform each different activity.

sleeping	sitting	walking	working	strenuous exercise	climbing stairs
40	120	220	350	440	700

Calories per Hour

BEYOND THE SUGAR BOWL

So you don't think you eat much sugar?

In the United States, every person eats over 100 pounds of sugar each year. Where does all that sugar come from?

1. Try to eat only when you are at the table, at mealtimes.
2. If you do snack, eat fruits or vegetables, not high-calorie foods.
3. Let everyone know that you will not have second helpings during a meal. Eat smaller helpings.
4. Instead of gulping down food, take small bites and rest between them. Put down your fork or spoon after each mouthful. During the course of the meal, pause for a few minutes, and slowly increase the time it takes you to eat your meals.
5. Substitute exercise for snacking. Compare your snacks to the amount of exercise you need in order to burn the calories you eat.

For example:

1 piece of apple pie (medium size)	=	55 minutes active exercise
1 medium-sized doughnut	=	24 minutes active exercise
1 medium slice of cake	=	32 minutes active exercise
1 18-ounce carbonated beverage	=	20 minutes active exercise

One pound of body fat equals 3500 calories. To lose 1 pound per week, then, just eat 500 calories per day less than you burn. To lose 2 pounds per week, eat 1000 calories per day less than your body uses for energy. You can either reduce the calories in meals and snacks or burn more calories through exercise. Examine the chart on page 308, and compare the number of calories used in various exercises.

Most fad diets are unbalanced in nutrients.

Fasting, high-carbohydrate diets, liquid-protein diets, high-fat diets, grapefruit diets, low-carbohydrate diets, and many more untested fad diets come and go. Many of the fad diets can harm the body's metabolism. One of the famous low-carbohydrate diets is known to cause feelings of tiredness. And it is high in fat and cholesterol. It also causes water loss, dizziness, and kidney trouble. Medical experts and nutritionists have all called the low-carbohydrate diet a dangerous one.

It takes time to gain extra weight. So it makes sense that it will take time to lose it. Fad diets that promise quick weight loss are useless and can be harmful. With them, you may lose weight in fluids. But real tissue weight will not be lost. Many are not nutritionally balanced. In the long run, fad diets won't help you take pounds off permanently.

Diet pills are risky.

Some people try to lose weight without dieting or exercising. They take diet pills. Some diet pills help reduce weight. But they do it by interfering with healthy body functions. Laxatives may speed food through the digestive tract so fast that it cannot be absorbed. Diuretics may increase urination, causing a loss of water and needed salts. Bulk fillers may swell in the stomach and reduce appetite. Other pills cause nervousness or drowsiness. Diet pills should never be taken except under a doctor's supervision.

A good weight-reducing group may help.

Several worthwhile organizations have been set up to help people lose weight. Members receive a medical examination when they join. A doctor or dietitian helps them to decide how much weight they should try to lose. A doctor also helps decide how quickly they should lose weight. Members go to regular meetings. At the start of each meeting, they are weighed. Awards are given to the members who reach their weight-loss goals. Members also help one another to keep from losing faith in their own goals.

Special diets

Because of activities they are involved in or because of their food preferences, some people follow special diets. But no matter what diet a person follows, it should be made up of foods that meet the body's needs for balanced nutrition.

Should athletes have special diets?

Do athletes need special amounts of vitamins, salt pills, or extra helpings of steak? Some athletes think so. Have you ever heard an athlete say that if you eat steak on the day of the game, you will be stronger because of added muscle growth? The athlete is partly right, but mostly wrong. Steak is high in protein. It does build new tissue, but not extra muscle cells. Only exercise can do that. And if the steak contains more protein than your body needs, it will be stored in your body as fat.

Do athletes need more vitamins than nonathletes?

All the vitamins an athlete's body needs can be found in the different foods eaten each day. Too much of vitamins A and D can harm the body. As mentioned before, vitamin E taken in large amounts will not improve an athlete's ability. If you are an athlete, you should make sure that you are getting enough rest and eating a nutritionally balanced diet. If you are active, you may need more calories. But as you eat more food to satisfy your hunger, you will probably be getting enough calories.

Athletes do not need increased amounts of vitamins or protein. There is no "superfood" to make you more active or give you more speed.

Avoid excess loss of weight.

Have you ever tried to lose 2.3 to 6.9 kilograms (5 to 15 pounds) of weight quickly to get on the good side of the coach, or to make the gymnastic team, or to qualify for a lower weight class in judo or wrestling? The advice from coaches, nutrition experts, physical education authorities, and doctors is "don't." Your performance will be poor if you are dehydrated and low in energy. You may make the team. But endurance and power depend on a good diet, so you may not be able to compete week after week. Maintain competition weight instead of constantly gaining and losing.

Remember, the nutritional needs of athletes are really no different from those of nonathletes, except for calories. There is no "superfood" that can make you more active or give you speed. You are better off eating a balanced diet made up of foods from the four food groups in the Daily Food Guide.

How long before exercising should you eat?

For top performance during a game, it is best to eat at least 3 hours before you play. Nutritious meals that are easy to digest will help you to keep up strength and endurance without upsetting your stomach. Many coaches even suggest eating five light meals instead of three large ones during the sports season. It takes a full meal about 2 to 4 hours to leave the stomach and enter the small intestine. If food is still in the stomach by game time, you may have cramping, nausea, and even vomiting. Fatty foods should not be eaten before a sports event. They take much longer to digest. Try to include 2 to 3 cups of water during the meal. If you eat 3 to 4 hours before the game, drink another cup of liquid 1½ hours before the event. Don't take salt tablets. A normal diet will supply enough salt.

Will special drinks and candy bars before a game give extra energy?

The candy bar, like other foods, must be digested. After digestion, which may take several hours, glucose is ready for use by the cells. Most of the reserve energy that you need for the event is formed several days ahead. Eating large amounts of glucose, cubes of sugar, hard candy, and dextrose pills may cause the intestinal tract to draw extra fluids from your body tissues. This will add to your dehydration problem during physical activity. Nutrition experts say that an athlete should drink water in small amounts at frequent intervals during the event. For prolonged activity, noncarbonated soft drinks and fruit juices provide an additional energy source and replace fluids.

Vegetarian diets must be carefully planned.

Vegetarian is a term that includes those people who do not eat meat. Most vegetarians will include eggs and milk in their diet. They are called *lacto-ovo-vegetarians* (*lacto*=milk/*ovo*=egg). Others use only dairy products such as milk, cheese, and butter. They are known as *lacto-vegetarians*. The few who eat only nuts, fruits, grains, and vegetables are called pure vegetarians.

Nutritionists do not recommend a pure vegetarian diet for most people. Without the meat, poultry, fish, and beans group or the milk and cheese group, your body may find it hard to get needed amino acids, iron, and vitamin B_{12}. Pure vegetarians, especially, must be very careful to combine plant foods in order to get all the important amino acids in adequate amounts.

When soybeans are added to foods such as cereals, a high-quality protein is made. Throughout the world, many people who eat a great deal of plant foods and little meat rely on soybeans and cereals such as rice for their protein.

Vegetarians are people who do not eat meat. They must plan their diets carefully to get all the protein their bodies need. Their protein comes from milk products, eggs, or the right mixture of grains and vegetables.

Often, instead of getting their ideas about weight from doctors and nutritionists, people get them from advertising. Today, it is fashionable to be extremely slim. Being very thin might be necessary for people who earn their living as models or movie stars. But, for most people, extreme thinness is not always healthy or even physically attractive.

In an effort to conform to society's weight standards, some young people who think they are overweight begin to diet. They are then unable to stop dieting, and their weight may drop well below 100 pounds. These people may suffer from a psychological illness called *anorexia nervosa*. The word *anorexia* means "lack or loss of appetite for food." Appetite is psychological and is dependent on the memory of past experiences. Hunger is physiological and is caused by the body's need for food. In the condition called anorexia nervosa, there is a loss of appetite resulting from fear, depression, anger, or other emotional states of mind. If people are suffering from anorexia, nothing can convince them that they are thin enough. Also, by

Something to think about . . .

strictly controlling their intake of food, they have a false sense that they are controlling their lives. If parents or friends encourage and even force them to eat more food, they may do so to avoid arguments, but often they will afterwards go to the bathroom and induce vomiting.

Approximately 90 percent of anorexia patients are girls and women. Their condition may be connected with an unwillingness to progress from childhood to adulthood. The unnatural thinness caused by anorexia can be a means of clinging to a child's body. The malnutrition associated with it can lead to serious physical illness and even death.

Another eating behavior related to the fear of getting fat is called *bulimia*. Bulimics eat huge quantities of food (binge) and then rid themselves of the food (purge) by making themselves vomit. They may also use laxatives, hoping to lose more weight. Some anorexics are also bulimics.

Anorexia and bulimia are self-destructive emotional disturbances and are symptoms of other life problems. For these reasons, psychiatric counseling is an important part of the patient's therapy. Since each patient responds differently, there is no universal cure. Various types of therapy are used, ranging from behavior modification to hospitalization.

Main Ideas

1. Nutritious snacks should be chosen.
2. Eating a nutritious breakfast will lower the chance of midmorning tiredness.
3. An overweight person is more likely to develop heart disease, high blood pressure, and diabetes than is a person of normal weight.
4. Your input of calories must equal your output of exercise if you are going to maintain your desired weight.
5. Many fad diets are nutritionally unbalanced, ineffective, and potentially dangerous to health.
6. Athletes do not need special diets, but pregame meals should include additional fluids.
7. Vegetarian diets need careful planning to provide high-quality protein and iron.

Key Words

anorexia nervosa
bulimia
lacto-ovo-vegetarian
lacto-vegetarian
vegetarian

Apply Your Knowledge

1. Why are jam, candy, and carbonated beverages called empty-calorie foods?
2. Examine the chart on page 304 and find out which snack is the best source of each of these nutrients:
   (a) vitamin C
   (b) calcium
   (c) vitamin A
   (d) riboflavin
3. Why is breakfast an important meal?
4. What is the best way to gain weight if you are underweight?
5. Discuss several safe ways to lose weight.
6. Using the chart on page 308, estimate how many calories you will use if you do the following:
   (a) walk for 20 minutes
   (b) clean your room for 15 minutes
   (c) sit and watch television for 1 hour
   (d) play volleyball for 1 hour
7. Why are diet pills dangerous?
8. What would happen if an athlete ate a large steak just before game time?
9. Should athletes eat high-energy foods just before a game? Should they drink any fluids during a game? Why, or why not?
10. What is the difference between the diets of pure vegetarians and lacto-ovo-vegetarians?

Extend Your Knowledge

1. Peanut à la celery is a nutritious snack. It is made of peanut butter spread on celery sticks. Invent another nutritious snack. Prepare it and eat it. Calculate the nutrients and describe the taste.
2. Discuss some current diet fads, including the pros and cons of each diet.
3. You know that a low-carbohydrate diet is dangerous. What might a high-carbohydrate diet do to your body?
4. If you were to take in 600 extra calories per week for 1 year, how many pounds would you gain during that time?
5. Find out what five or six members of the class ate for breakfast. Suggest lunches, dinners, and snacks that, along with these breakfasts, would make an adequate diet for the whole day.
6. Find out what the typical diet is of someone in another country. Compare the diet with your own, using the Daily Food Guide on page 291.
7. What advice would you give to help a friend lose weight?

Chapter 27

Do you know . . .

- how to read the nutrition information on packaged foods?
- if all the additives included in your foods are necessary?
- that sugar (sucrose) is not one of the requirements in your diet?
- if health foods are really nutritious?
- how additives are used to prevent food poisoning?

Nutrition, Labels, and the Consumer

You may know the nutritional values of certain foods and the kinds of nutrients that you need daily. But do you always know what to buy in the supermarket? With about 10,000 items on display, each supermarket attracts us through special sales, trading stamps, or various games with prizes. As we enter a supermarket, we see many shelves of foods. All are carefully arranged to encourage us to buy on impulse. Our eyes first notice the brands of foods most often advertised in magazines or on television. Food manufacturers spend large amounts of money designing packages. They want us to think that the foods inside are just as tasty and exciting as the pictures on the packages. We are not allowed to look inside the packages or to sample the foods by tasting them. So knowing what to buy depends a great deal on knowing about food labeling.

Food labeling

The nutritional information on a package should include the serving sizes and the number of servings per container. Calories and nutrients are usually listed. The consumer also wants to know the ingredients in the food—what's in it. Some products also list information about sodium, cholesterol, and unsaturated fat.

What is the U.S. Recommended Daily Allowance?

The dietary standards of the United States are established by the Food and Nutrition Board of the National Research Council, National Academy of Sciences. The diet specialists on the Nutrition Board are well qualified to set up the *Recommended Daily Allowance* of all nutrients. The U.S. RDA gives the amount of each nutrient needed by most people in the United States. The term "U.S. RDA" was adopted to ensure proper nutrition labeling. The recommended allowances are at least twice what most people need to avoid diseases that once plagued the United States.

Are the U.S. RDAs the same for everyone?

Our daily needs for various nutrients will differ according to sex, age, body size, and activity. The RDAs are a guide for the general population. Both age and sex are considered in each recommendation. Revisions to the recommendations are made about every 5 years.

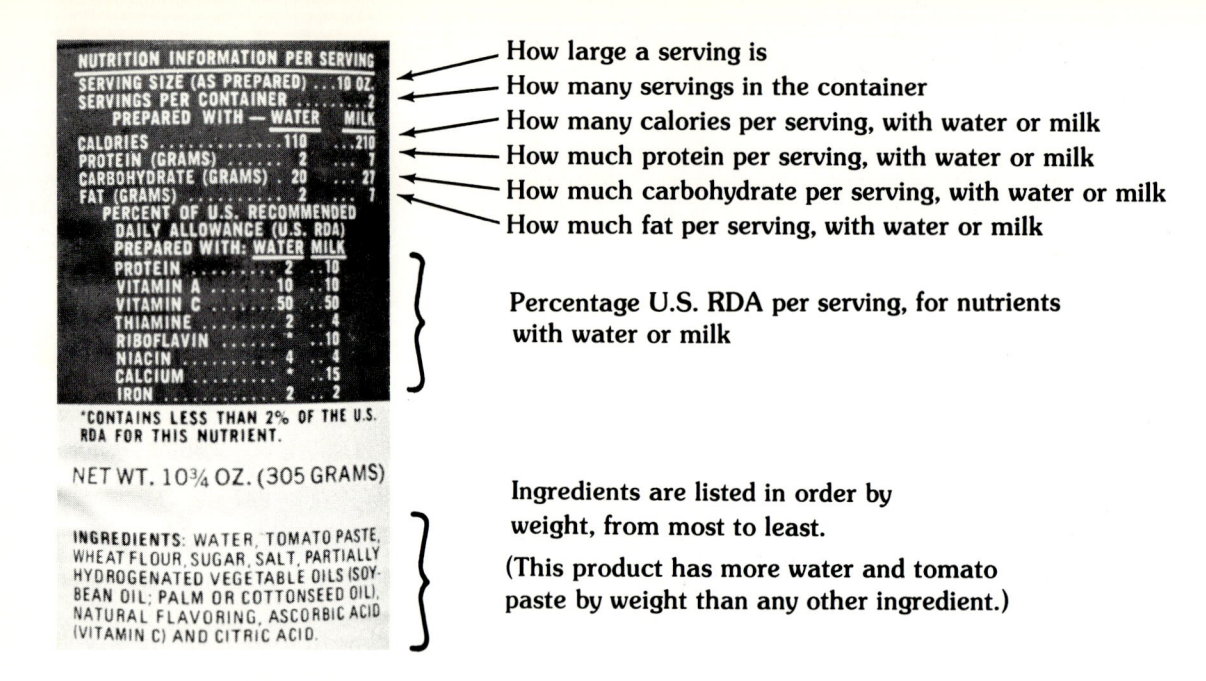

How large a serving is
How many servings in the container
How many calories per serving, with water or milk
How much protein per serving, with water or milk
How much carbohydrate per serving, with water or milk
How much fat per serving, with water or milk

Percentage U.S. RDA per serving, for nutrients with water or milk

Ingredients are listed in order by weight, from most to least.

(This product has more water and tomato paste by weight than any other ingredient.)

If you have a general idea of how many calories and nutrients you need each day, you can keep track of how many servings of each food you eat. Based on the amounts you eat, you can easily figure out what percentage of each of your U.S. RDAs is satisfied.

Ingredients—what's in food

If you check many product labels, you will generally find an ingredients list. Any of the following terms, for example, may be used to indicate ingredients: *made from, prepared from, contains,* and *content.* These terms refer to the same thing: what makes up the food.

On a certain cereal box, you might see a long list of ingredients, beginning with milled corn, sugar, oat and wheat flour, and rice. The first item listed is milled corn. This means that there is more milled corn by weight in the food than any other ingredient. The ingredient present in the second largest amount is sugar. Oat and wheat flour are third, and rice is fourth. *Additives* used in the food must be listed, too. Additives are substances added to food in small amounts that are meant to improve the food in some way or to increase shelf life.

Food additives: Are they all necessary?

Some foods lack nutrients. Others lose much of their nutritional qualities during processing treatments such as steaming, skinning, crushing, or deep frying. To put back some of the nutrients, food-processing plants add vitamins and minerals to packaged foods. Such products are said to be *enriched,* or fortified.

Preservatives are additives that keep bacteria, molds, and fungi from spoiling food. Our ancestors preserved their foods with sugar or salt, or used drying or smoking methods. Salt and sugar are still being used as preservatives today, along with nitrites, sulfur dioxide, calcium propionate, and others.

Antioxidants, such as vitamin C (ascorbic acid) and vitamin E (tocopherols), attract oxygen. This oxygen attraction prevents stored foods, especially fats, from changing in color, taste, and smell. Also used are synthetic antioxidants called BHA and BHT.

Acids and bases keep jams and jellies from hardening. They also put effervescence, or "fizz," into soft drinks.

Gelling agents, stabilizers, and emulsifiers keep oil and water mixed. They also keep ice cream "creamy."

Taste enhancers, such as monosodium glutamate and salt, enhance, or "bring out," the flavors in certain foods. They are not necessary food ingredients. The National Research Council has recommended that monosodium glutamate be dropped from baby foods. The council thinks that babies should eat bland foods as long as they can, so they are not taught to crave certain tastes when they are older. Many manufacturers are decreasing the salt content of other foods, too, since the high sodium content of the diet relates to hypertension. Other food enhancers include cloves, ginger, and citrus oils to add "spice" to foods.

Coloring agents make foods look better. About 90 percent of these agents are artificial and have no nutritional value. One food coloring, Red Dye No. 2, is thought to cause cancer. It was ordered off the market by the Food and Drug Administration (FDA).

Flavoring agents are a mixture of 10 to 15 different ingredients. It is the effect of these additives that most concerns researchers. Flavoring agents include over 1200 natural and synthetic flavors.

Improving agents include meat tenderizers and compounds for putting a glaze, or shine, on baked goods.

In packaged foods, preservatives and antioxidants are needed. They prolong freshness and keep bacteria from multiplying. In this way, we can store foods for use when we need them. They also stop the forming of *toxins* (poisonous substances) produced by chemical changes in spoiled foods. And enrichment and restoration are important, since foods that are refined and processed lose some of their food value.

Using additives also lets us have foods that are grown far away from our homes. The foods don't spoil on the way to our communities. Such foods can also be sold at any time of the year, not just during a special season. Thus, prices can be kept lower.

But some additives may be harmful. Nutritionists believe that some additives in our food are unnecessary. Many additives are dangerous except in small amounts. One such group of preservatives is called *nitrites*. Nitrites are added to hot dogs, bacon, and sausages to prevent the deadly bacterium called *botulinum* from growing. Botulinum causes *botulism*, a severe form of food poisoning that can kill. Unfortunately, nitrites are also capable

	1 OZ.	WITH ½ CUP WHOLE MILK
CALORIES	110	190
PROTEIN	1 g	6 g
CARBOHYDRATES	26 g	32 g
FAT	0 g	4 g

PERCENTAGE OF U.S. RECOMMENDED DAILY ALLOWANCE (U.S. RDA)

SUGAR FROSTED FLAKES

	1 OZ.	WITH ½ CUP WHOLE MILK
PROTEIN	2	10
VITAMIN A	25	30
VITAMIN C	25	25
THIAMIN	25	25
RIBOFLAVIN	25	35
NIACIN	25	25
CALCIUM	*	15
IRON	10	10
VITAMIN D	10	25
VITAMIN B₆	25	25
FOLIC ACID	25	25
PHOSPHORUS	*	10
MAGNESIUM	*	4

*CONTAINS LESS THAN 2 PERCENT OF THE U.S. RDA OF THESE NUTRIENTS.

INGREDIENTS: MILLED CORN, SUGAR, SALT, MALT FLAVORING, SODIUM ASCORBATE (C), VITAMIN A PALMITATE, NIACINAMIDE, ASCORBIC ACID (C), REDUCED IRON, PYRIDOXINE HYDROCHLORIDE (B₆), RIBOFLAVIN (B₂), THIAMIN HYDROCHLORIDE (B₁), FOLIC ACID AND VITAMIN D₂. BHA ADDED TO PRESERVE PRODUCT FRESHNESS.

Food-product labels must list the ingredients, or what makes up the foods. The largest ingredient by weight is given first. The other ingredients are listed by weight in decreasing order.

One of the best ways to lower your intake of additives is to eat fresh foods.

of producing cancer-causing agents. But botulism is a greater, more immediate threat to us than cancer. So nitrites are still being used in very small amounts in meats until researchers discover a safer preservative that can be used instead.

Commercially canned foods cooked at high temperatures are not likely to contain botulinum toxin. The high temperatures destroy the bacteria. However, if a can bulges or leaks, or if the food has an unusual odor, it should not be used. The can and its contents should be returned to the store or discarded.

As a consumer, you should read food labels in order to make good choices. You might write to food manufacturers or to your legislator about the additives in food.

The best way to lower your intake of food additives is to eat fresh foods and a varied diet. The greater variety in your diet, the less the likelihood of your consuming large amounts of any one additive. With so many packaged foods on the market, perhaps consumers have become lazy about taking the time to prepare and cook fresh vegetables, meat, fish, and fruit. By changing food-preparation habits, many people can improve the quality of what they eat.

Do we need sugar in our diet?

Can you think of any foods that contain no sugar? The sugar content in one popular dry cereal, for example, is 68 percent by weight. It has been estimated that each of us consumes more than 45.5 kilograms (100 pounds) of sugar a year in the form of cookies, soft drinks, doughnuts, and dry cereals.

Yet sugar has no nutritive value other than carbohydrate. And this sweetener is suspected of contributing to overweight, diabetes, tooth decay, and even heart disease. Starch, a carbohydrate in our diet, is broken down into the simple sugar our body needs for energy. We consume sugar, and foods containing sugar, only to satisfy our "sweet tooth."

Hidden Sugar

The approximate sugar content of popular foods expressed in teaspoons:
100 grams sugar = 20 teaspoons = ½ cup = 3½ oz. = 400 calories

Cakes and cookies

	tsp. sugar
Chocolate Cake .... 1/12 cake *(2-layer iced)*	15
Angel food cake .... 1/12 of large cake	6
Sponge cake .... 1/10 of average cake	6
Cream puff (iced) .... **1 average, custard-filled**	5
Doughnut, plain .... 3″ diameter	4
Macaroons .... 1 large or 2 small	3
Gingersnaps .... 1 medium	1
Molasses cookies .... 3½″ diameter	2
Brownies .... 2″ x 2″ x ¾″	3

Spreads and sauces

	tsp. sugar
Jam .... 1 level tbs.	3
Jelly .... 1 level tbs.	2½
Marmalade .... 1 level tbs.	3
Syrup, maple .... 1 level tbs.	2½
Honey .... 1 level tbs.	3
Chocolate sauce (thick) .... 1 tbs.	4½

Pie

	tsp. sugar
Apple .... 1/6 med. pie	12
Cherry .... 1/6 med. pie	14
Raisin .... 1/6 med. pie	13
Pumpkin .... 1/6 med. pie	10

Milk drinks

	tsp. sugar
Chocolate .... 1 cup, 5 oz. milk	6
Cocoa .... 1 cup, 5 oz. milk	4
Eggnog .... 1 glass, 8 oz. milk	4½

Soft drinks

	tsp. sugar
Sweet carbonated beverage .... 1 bottle, 6 oz.	4 1/3
Ginger ale .... 6 oz. glass	3 1/3

Ice cream

	tsp. sugar
Ice cream .... 1/8 quart (½ cup)	5-6
Sherbet .... 1/8 quart (½ cup)	6-8

Fruits and fruit juices

	tsp. sugar
Fruit cocktail .... ½ cup, scant	5
Orange juice .... ½ cup, scant	2
Pineapple juice, unsweetened .... ½ cup, scant	2 3/5
Grapefruit juice, unsweetened .... ½ cup, scant	2 1/5
Grapefruit, commercial .... ½ cup, scant	3 2/3

Candy

	tsp. sugar
Chocolate bar .... 1 average size	7
Chocolate cream .... 1 average size	2
Chocolate fudge .... ½″ sq.	4
Chocolate mints .... 1 medium	3
Marshmallow .... 1 average	1½
Chewing gum .... 1 stick	½

Cooked fruits

	tsp. sugar
Peaches, canned in syrup .... 2 halves, 1 tbs. syrup	3½
Rhubarb, stewed, sweetened .... ½ cup	8
Apple sauce (unsweetened) .... ½ cup, scant	2
Prunes, stewed, sweetened .... 4 to 5 med., 2 tbs. juice	8

Dried fruits

	tsp. sugar
Apricots, dried .... 4 to 6 halves	4
Prunes, dried .... 3 to 4 medium	4
Dates, dried .... 3 to 4 stoned	4½
Figs, dried .... 1½ to 2 small	4
Raisins .... ¼ cup	4

*Candy is 75 to 85% sugar. Popular candy bars are likely to weigh from 1 to 5 oz. and may contain 5 to 20 teaspoons of sugar. Adapted from current publications on food values. Courtesy of Dr. Herman Becks, University of California.

American Dental Association   211 E. Chicago Avenue, Chicago, Ill. 60611

It would be hard to stop eating sugar altogether. Many foods, such as catsup, canned pinto beans, and even tomato soup, contain some sugar. The best way to cut down on sugar intake is by adding less sugar to foods such as breakfast cereal and by avoiding the "hidden sugar" in sweet snacks and desserts.

Do we have too much salt in our food?

Doctors recommend that people who have high blood pressure or migraine headaches use less salt. They also advise people who tend to retain water in the body to lower their salt intake. People on salt-free diets are careful not to use salt when they cook or flavor their food. But many of the foods we buy have salt already added. For example, popcorn, pretzels, potato chips, French fries, and catsup are high in salt content.

Are health foods nourishing?

Many people believe in eating "health foods," such as granola cereals or organic honey. However, people disagree on just what health foods are. There is no definition of health foods that satisfies everyone. A food that one person thinks of as healthy, another person might think of as harmful. Although honey does contain very small amounts of vitamins and minerals (enough for a bee), it is still very similar to white sugar. Granola cereals are made with whole grains, but these cereals are high in sugar. You should be careful when you buy foods that are sold as health foods. Some may be no more nutritious than traditional foods.

Are organic foods possible in our environment?

Foods grown without the use of synthetic fertilizers, pesticides (insect killers), or herbicides (weed killers) are called *organic foods*. Natural substances, such as manure or compost, are used to fertilize the soil. Natural methods of insect control are also being tried. For example, praying mantis eggs may be scattered around a field after a crop is sowed or planted. The eggs hatch in the spring at about the same time that the plants start to grow. New mantises eat other insects but do not harm plants. Another way to control insects is to grow plants that repel insects naturally. These plants

Customers of health food stores are often shopping for organic foods. Organic foods are grown without the use of human-made fertilizers, insect killers, or weed killers.

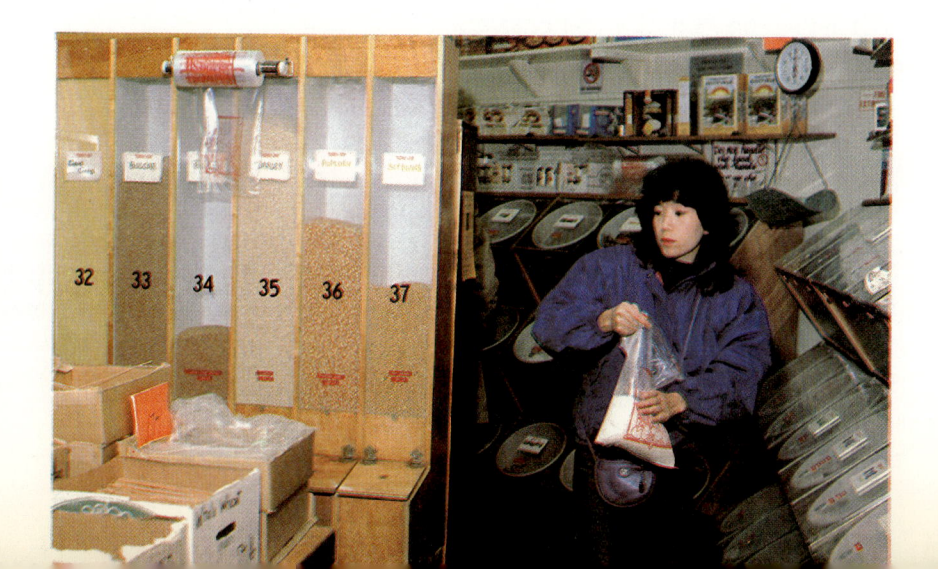

are often placed between the rows of food crops. Where meats are concerned, organically raised animals are given only organically grown feed. When raised for use as food, such animals are not given hormones or antibiotics to promote growth or prevent disease.

Much that is sold as organic food is not organically grown. Buyers are often getting the chemical fertilizers, pesticides, and herbicides they are trying to avoid in food. But organic foods are generally more expensive, since they are more costly to produce. These foods are no different in nutritional value from those grown with synthetic fertilizers.

Many preservatives are added to our foods. Even so, some foods will spoil or lose their flavor in a short period of time. *Open dating* helps consumers identify fresh food. However, different dates may have different meanings. Food manufacturers stamp packages with dates that tell when products should be removed from the shelves, when the food was packaged, or the latest date by which the food should be used. Consumers need to learn what the dates mean. Some foods have a shelf life of two to three years. Others must be consumed within several days.

Different brands of food on supermarket shelves are often packaged in containers of different sizes and weights. *Unit pricing* is a method of showing the cost per unit of weight, regardless of the size of the container or the weight of the contents. Unit prices are posted on supermarket shelves. Using this information, you can quickly compare the costs of two different-sized packages of raisins by reading and comparing their costs per unit of weight. Unfortunately, the unit pricing cannot give us additional information about the products, such as which brand tastes better.

During the past century, the diet of people in the United States has changed dramatically. We eat less fresh vegetables and fruits, whole grains, cereals, and dried legumes than our ancestors did. We eat more protein, fat, refined sugar and other sweeteners, and salt, and less complex carbohydrate (starch). Our diets are highly processed; as a result, our foods have less fiber and more sugar and salt. These dietary patterns are associated with many health problems: hypertension, heart disease, diabetes, stroke, and obesity.

What are open dating and unit pricing?

Some foods spoil or lose their flavor in a short time. Dates stamped on food packages help us identify fresh foods. This practice is called open dating. Open dating allows the buyer to feel sure that foods sold in stores are safe to eat.

Something to think about . . .

In 1980, the United States government set up "Dietary Guidelines for Americans" to help consumers select a healthier diet. These guidelines should be used along with the Daily Food Guide shown on page 291.

- Eat a variety of foods.
- Maintain ideal weight.
- Avoid too much fat, saturated fat, and cholesterol.
- Eat foods with adequate starch and fiber.
- Avoid too much sugar.
- Avoid too much salt.

Main Ideas

1. Food labeling helps us to "see" what is inside a package.
2. The Recommended Dietary Allowances tell us the kinds and amounts of nutrients we need. The U.S. RDA used on nutrient labels is based on the RDA.
3. Additives that keep food from spoiling allow us to ship foods for thousands of miles and to enjoy them out of season. Other additives improve the nutritional value of food.
4. Most additives are safe if only small amounts are consumed.
5. Health foods may not satisfy consumer needs.
6. Open dating and unit pricing help consumers make wise choices.

Key Words

additives	nitrites	RDA
antioxidants	open dating	toxins
botulinum	organic foods	unit pricing
botulism	preservatives	U.S. RDA
enriched		

Apply Your Knowledge

1. Refer to the picture on page 318 and answer the following questions:
    (a) Is this food a good source of calcium? Why, or why not?
    (b) How many servings are in this container?
    (c) How large is each serving?
    (d) Can you classify this food according to the Daily Food Guide? Which food groups are represented?
    (e) Is there a great difference in vitamin C content when this food is prepared with milk instead of water?
2. Check your cupboard for any food items that contain sugar. List them. Did you find any without added sugar? Would you add sugar to those foods? Why, or why not?
3. Why was monosodium glutamate dropped from baby food?
4. What are antioxidants? Are they necessary in your foods? Why, or why not?
5. How can nitrites be both helpful and harmful?
6. Does your body need sugar? Explain.
7. Why are some people interested in health foods?

Extend Your Knowledge

1. Check several soup cans to see what percentage of the U.S. RDA is given for the various nutrients.
2. Refer to the illustration on page 319 to find out how much protein you get from the breakfast cereal.
3. Explain how our eating habits would be affected if there were no preservatives.
4. Next time you are at the supermarket, check to see which items on the shelves have open dating. Make a list of those that are dated, and find out what the dates mean.
5. Find out who prepares the menus at your school. Check to see how foods are purchased and prepared for large numbers of students.
6. How might your family's shopping habits change if all mass media influences were absent?
7. Eat two samples of the same kind of food, one with additives and one without. Compare the taste.
8. Go to a supermarket and watch people shop. List poor shopping habits that you can discuss in class later on. Explain why such habits are poor ones.

Chapter 28

Do you know . . .

- why the liver is considered to be a part of the digestive system?
- why the villi of the small intestine are important?
- how emotions can affect the digestive process?
- where the major part of digestion occurs?

Digestion and Elimination

Before your body can make use of the food you eat, it must break down the food into simpler chemical substances. Then the food must go through several more hours of "processing" called digestion. This takes place in your digestive tract.

The digestive tract

The digestive tract is made up of a series of organs that move food through the body. The tract starts at the mouth and ends at the anus. The anus is the opening from the large intestine to the outside of the body.

The whole digestive tract is called the *alimentary canal*. It is about 10 meters (30 feet) long. Most of its length is curled back and forth within the abdomen.

Throughout the digestive process, important work is done by *enzymes*. These enzymes are in digestive juices produced by many different glands throughout the body. Digestive enzymes are chemicals that break down food into simpler compounds. These simpler substances are then absorbed into the bloodstream. The substances that are not absorbed into the bloodstream gather in the large intestine and are finally pushed out as waste, or feces.

Secretion of digestive juices and the movement of food through the digestive tract are involuntary. They are not under your control.

Digestion begins in the mouth.

The digestive tract starts with the mouth. The tongue, the teeth, and the mouth fluids prepare food for the later stages of digestion.

The tongue is an important tool. As food enters the mouth, the tongue guides it between the teeth. The food is then cut and ground by the teeth. This mechanical breakdown of food, or chewing, is called *mastication*.

The surface of the tongue is dotted with tiny, fingerlike projections called *papillae*. The papillae help the tongue "hold onto" food and move it. For example, without papillae it would be hard to lick an ice cream cone. Cats and dogs have many papillae. They use their raspy tongues to lap up food and fluids. Tiny taste buds are located along the sides of the papillae. You have four different kinds of taste buds—sweet, salty, sour, and bitter. Each group is located on a different part of the tongue's surface.

Epiglottis

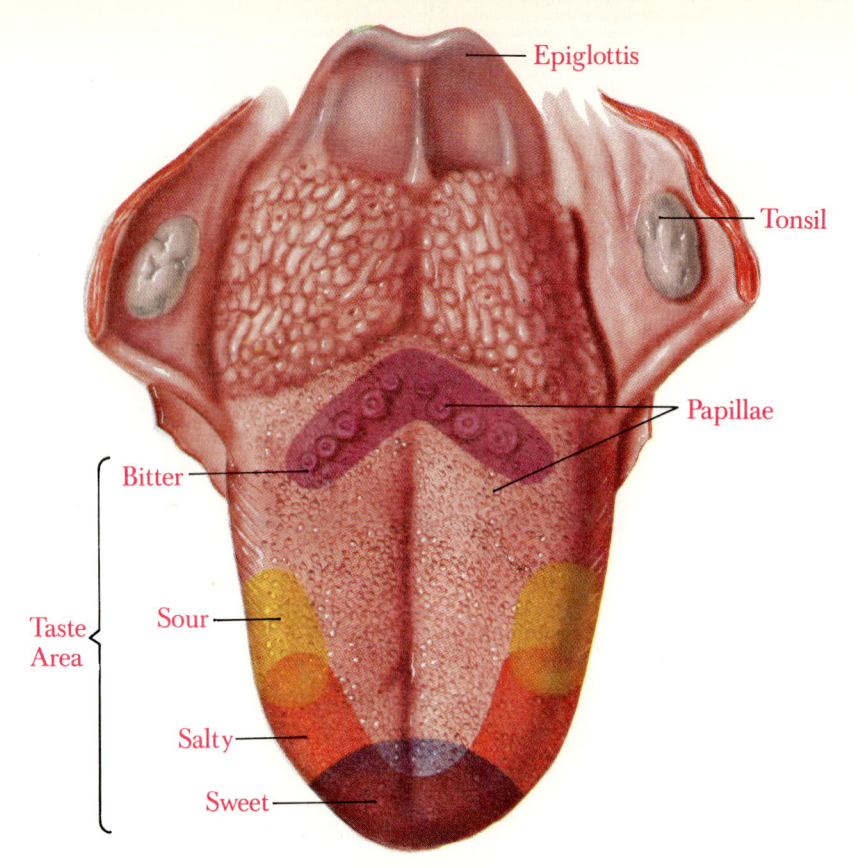

Tonsil

Papillae

Bitter

Sour

Taste Area

Salty

Sweet

Digestion begins in the mouth. When food enters the mouth, tiny taste buds in the tongue tell whether the food tastes bitter, sour, salty, or sweet. Then the tongue, the teeth, and the mouth fluids break up the food for the later stages of digestion.

Three pairs of *salivary glands* secrete saliva, the liquid that pours into the mouth. Saliva moistens and softens food. It contains the enzyme called salivary *amylase*. This enzyme breaks down starch into a form of sugar called maltose.

A "ball" of food that has been chewed and is ready to be swallowed is called a *bolus*. The tongue pushes the bolus back toward the pharynx (throat). The involuntary swallowing reflex then takes over. The *uvula* and the soft palate close the nasal opening. The epiglottis covers the trachea (windpipe). These actions stop food from entering the air passages. The bolus is now on its way to the stomach and intestines.

The pathway to the stomach

After food is chewed and swallowed, it is moved along the *esophagus*, a tube that connects the mouth to the stomach. The esophagus is about 25 centimeters (10 inches) long. It passes down through the thorax (upper trunk of the body) until it reaches the diaphragm. There it enters the abdominal cavity and connects to the stomach. The esophagus does not digest food, but it does secrete mucus that mixes with and moistens the food.

In the walls of the esophagus are rings of muscle that contract, one after the other. These waves of contractions are called *peristaltic waves*. These movements push the food along the digestive tract. Peristaltic waves are involuntary. You can't decide to stop or start them. Even if you were standing on your head, food would still be pushed or moved along the alimentary canal.

The stomach is a temporary storage place.

The stomach is a pouch that has digestive glands in it. The stomach works mostly as a temporary storage place for food during digestion. It gets larger as the body gets larger.

Glands in the walls of the stomach produce *gastric juice.* This juice contains the enzymes pepsin and rennin, which are needed for the digestion of proteins. Gastric juice also contains hydrochloric acid. This acid makes it possible for the pepsin to act. It also kills some of the microorganisms that enter the stomach in food. The stomach expands and contracts, mixing the food with the gastric juice. The food then becomes a thin, soupy liquid called *chyme.*

It takes three to four hours for the stomach to empty after an ordinary meal. Fatty foods stay in the stomach longer than other foods. Liquids may pass through the stomach in ten minutes or less.

Many people think that the stomach is the most important organ of the digestive system. Actually, very little food is absorbed directly into the bloodstream from the stomach. A person could even live comfortably without a stomach, as long as meals were small and taken frequently.

The major part of digestion occurs in the small intestine.

The small intestine is a very important part of the digestive tract. It is a coiled tube about 6 to 8 meters (20 to 25 feet) long and about 4 centimeters (1.5 inches) wide when filled. The most important part of the digestive tract is the *duodenum,* the first section of the small intestine. Most of the digestive process is carried on in the duodenum. Secretions from glands in the walls of the duodenum, from the pancreas, and from the liver act upon the bolus as it passes through the duodenum.

The liver is part of the digestive system.

The liver is a large organ on the right side of the upper part of the abdomen. It is one of the most important organs in the body. The liver carries out many functions needed for digestion and other body processes.

Bile is a fluid secreted by the liver. It aids in the digestion of fat. Bile is stored in the gall bladder, a small sac under the liver. During digestion, the gall bladder contracts. This causes bile to flow through the *bile duct* to the duodenum.

Worn-out red blood cells are destroyed in the liver. Pigments from these cells give a dark yellowish-green color to the bile. These pigments also give feces their yellowish-brown color.

The pancreas aids in digestion and helps the cells use sugar.

The pancreas is a gland that lies along the lower side of the stomach. It is about 8 to 10 centimeters (3 to 4 inches) long. The pancreas is both an endocrine gland and a gland of external secretion. It produces two kinds of secretions: pancreatic juice and a hormone called insulin.

Insulin is an internal secretion. It passes from gland cells in the pancreas right into the bloodstream. Insulin helps the body cells use sugar.

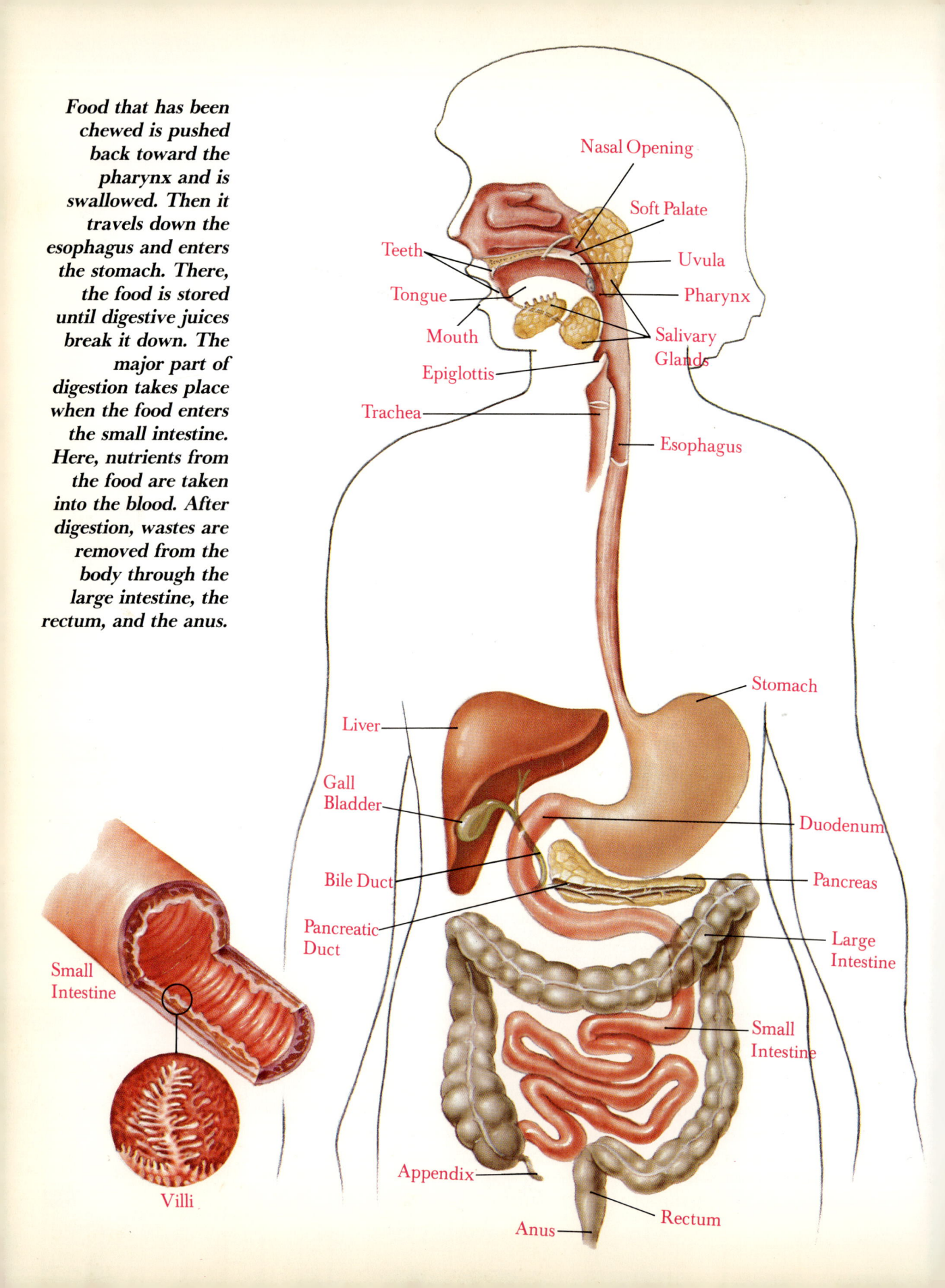

Food that has been chewed is pushed back toward the pharynx and is swallowed. Then it travels down the esophagus and enters the stomach. There, the food is stored until digestive juices break it down. The major part of digestion takes place when the food enters the small intestine. Here, nutrients from the food are taken into the blood. After digestion, wastes are removed from the body through the large intestine, the rectum, and the anus.

Pancreatic juice is an external secretion. It flows from the pancreas to the duodenum through a duct called the pancreatic duct. The pancreatic duct joins the bile duct so that pancreatic juice and bile go into the duodenum through the same opening. Enzymes in the intestinal and pancreatic juices finish the digestion of fat, carbohydrate, and protein. They change fat to glycerol and fatty acids, carbohydrate to simple sugars, and protein to amino acids.

Digestion is completed in the small intestine. The food has been broken down and is ready to be absorbed by the bloodstream or removed as waste. Nutrients enter the bloodstream, and wastes are passed to the large intestine.

The villi of the small intestine absorb nutrients.

The inner lining of the small intestine has millions of tiny, fingerlike projections called *villi* (singular: villus). The villi greatly add to the surface area of the lining of the intestine. Nutrients are absorbed through this large surface area.

Each tiny villus has a network of small blood vessels and a lymph vessel. Lymph is a colorless fluid found in all body tissues. It carries substances between body cells and the bloodstream. The walls separating the blood and lymph from the materials in the small intestine are very thin. Digested food substances can easily pass through these walls. Water, amino acids, simple sugars, mineral salts, and some vitamins enter the blood vessels. Digested fat and some vitamins enter the lymph vessel. From there, they enter the bloodstream. Nutrients absorbed into the blood go first to the liver, where some nutrients are stored for use later on.

Elimination of wastes

Some of the body's wastes are carried by the lymph to the veins. Then the wastes are carried by blood in the veins to other organs that excrete, or remove, them from the body. Carbon dioxide and water are breathed out through the lungs. Water and salts pass out through the skin as perspiration. Among the most important organs that remove wastes are the large intestine and the kidneys.

The large intestine reabsorbs water and removes wastes.

Undigested food, bacteria, and dead cells from the lining of the small intestine are not absorbed by the villi. Instead, these substances pass into the large intestine. The substances are now in a highly fluid state. They are mixed with many digestive juices and contain much water. The walls of the large intestine absorb most of the water and return it to the bloodstream. This is one of the most important functions of the large intestine.

Many bacteria live in the large intestine. Most of them are harmless. Some serve a useful purpose by breaking down waste materials.

Peristalsis along the large intestine is slow. It takes 12 to 20 hours for materials to pass through the large intestine. Feces (waste) are finally passed out of the body as a bowel movement.

The urinary system purifies the blood.

The urinary system consists of two kidneys, two ureters (tubes from the kidneys to the bladder), a bladder, and the urethra (passage to the outside of the body).

What is the function of the kidneys?

All of the blood in the body circulates through the kidneys. Extra water, salts, and wastes containing nitrogen are filtered out of the blood into small tubes within the kidneys. The wastes then flow through the ureters to the bladder. These liquid wastes, called urine, are stored in the bladder until they are excreted.

The kidneys remove waste from the blood. Then the liquid waste, called urine, flows through the ureters to the bladder. Urine is stored in the bladder until it is removed from the body. Infection or poison in the blood may damage the kidneys.

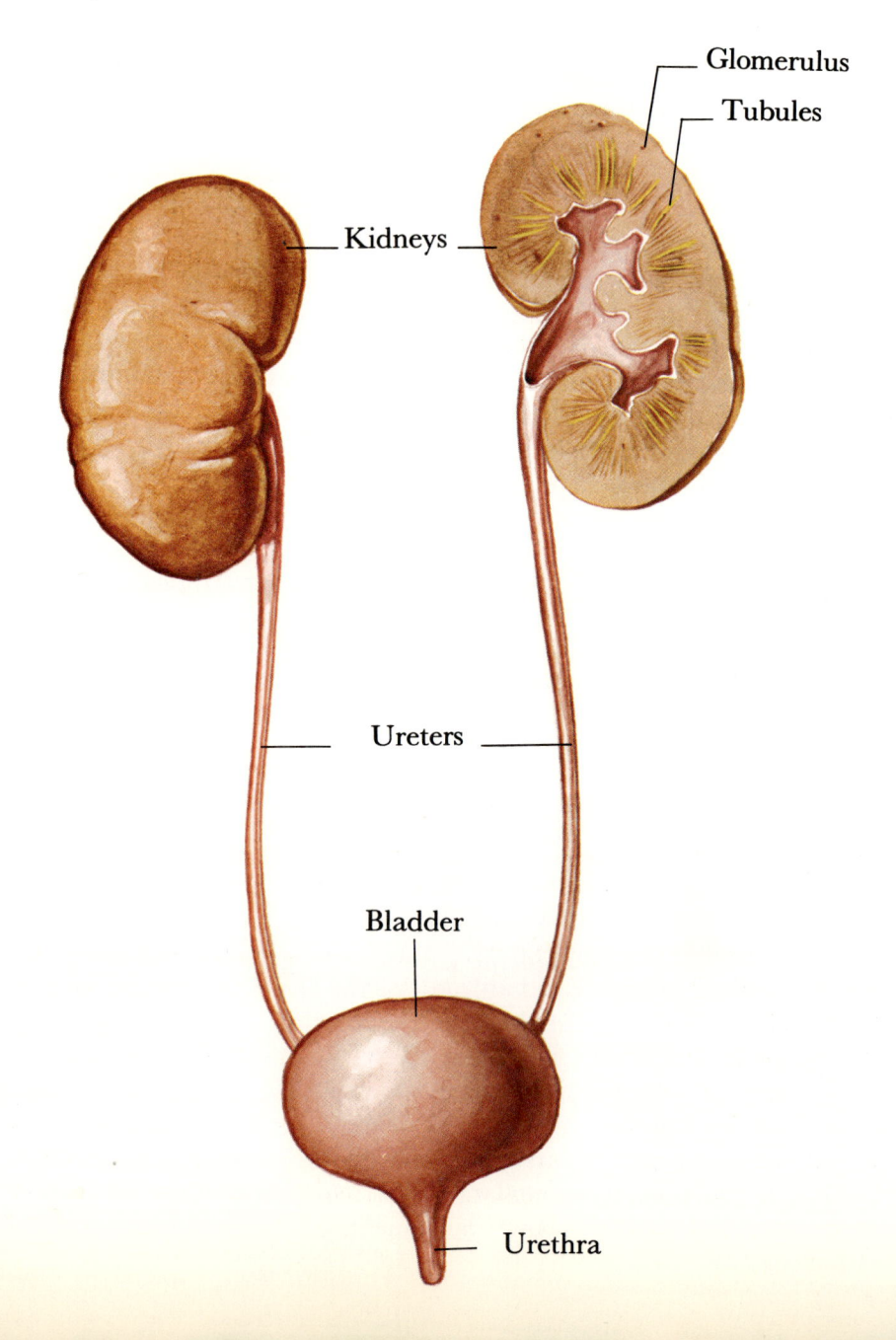

Glomerulus
Tubules
Kidneys
Ureters
Bladder
Urethra

Formation of urine takes place all the time. An average adult excretes from 1 to 2 liters (1 to 2 quarts) of urine every 24 hours. Usually urine is yellow. The color is lighter when there is a good deal of water in the urine and darker when there is less water.

Many kinds of wastes leave the body in the urine. Some of them change its color and odor. For example, a distinctive odor may be noted in the urine after eating asparagus. Even vitamins or certain drugs may change the color of urine.

Elimination of urine

When the bladder is full, pressure starts nerve impulses that cause release of urine. A person can stop the bladder from emptying by contracting the muscles in the wall of the urethra. Usually, children learn to control urination when they are 18 to 30 months old. Control is easiest when the child is awake. Bedwetting, called *enuresis,* is common in preschool children. But sometimes it occurs in schoolchildren and adults as well. Usually this is caused by strain, extra excitement, or illness. If bedwetting happens often in an older child or adult, a physician should be consulted.

What will happen if the filtration system breaks down?

Any infection or poison carried in the blood may damage the kidneys. Salts from the urine may form hard masses, or stones, and lodge in the kidneys, ureters, or bladder. Small stones may pass out of the body with urine. Larger stones usually must be removed by surgery. The kidneys can also be damaged by poisons such as mercury, or by large amounts of harmful substances such as caffeine or alcohol.

A person can get along very well with only one kidney, or even part of one kidney. If one kidney is removed, the remaining one can enlarge to twice its original size. It can do the work of two kidneys. However, if there is total damage to both kidneys, waste materials will collect in the blood. This can cause poisoning and even death. Artificial kidney machines have saved many lives. Blood travels from the patient's artery through tubes into the kidney machine. Waste materials in the blood are filtered out by special artificial membranes in the machine. The clean blood then returns to the patient through a vein.

Surgeons now perform operations that transplant a healthy kidney from a donor into another person whose kidneys are damaged or diseased.

More about the digestive system

A person has good digestion when peristaltic movement goes on smoothly and all of the digestive juices are secreted in the right amounts. The muscles and glands of the digestive tract have nerves that are part of the autonomic (involuntary) nervous system. Messages from the brain that travel over these nerves are not under your control.

Poor digestion is sometimes called indigestion. Indigestion may cause a loss of appetite, a bad taste in the mouth, a pain in the abdomen, vomiting, or diarrhea. Emotional strain can cause indigestion. Other causes

Being worried and tense at mealtime can upset digestion. Cheerful, clean surroundings and good company at mealtime help digestion and allow everyone to enjoy the food. Relax and eat slowly.

include appendicitis, gallstones, or ulcers in the stomach or intestines. Any long-lasting digestive problem should be checked by a doctor.

How do emotions affect digestion?

Strong emotions, such as fear, anger, resentment, embarrassment, or excitement, can affect the digestive system. Messages sent by the nerves can cause problems with peristaltic waves and gland secretion. The mouth may become dry. A dry mouth means that the salivary glands are not producing saliva. At the same time, the stomach and intestines may be "dry" because other digestive glands are not working well. This is not a good time to eat a large meal.

On the other hand, pleasant thoughts about eating may aid digestion. The smell, taste, sight, and even the thought of food can make the mouth "water" (produce saliva). The other digestive glands also start to secrete. The muscles of the digestive system contract, sometimes making the stomach and intestines "growl" or "rumble."

Good eating habits help digestion.

Pleasant, clean surroundings and good company at mealtime aid digestion. It is best to eat slowly. Nagging, arguing, or worrying out loud at the table creates tension. This upsets digestion. A calm, relaxed atmosphere helps everyone to enjoy the food.

Many people wonder if they should drink water with meals. Small amounts of water between swallows of food help the work of the enzymes. However, it is not a good idea to use water to wash large bites of food down the throat. When people do this instead of chewing thoroughly, they make it harder for good digestion to take place. Drinking ice water with a meal may also interfere with the digestive process.

What causes vomiting?

Vomiting is caused by backward, or reverse, peristaltic waves in the stomach and esophagus. It comes with strong contractions of the abdominal and chest muscles. Nausea, a feeling of faintness and weakness, yawning, and extra secretion of saliva usually occur before vomiting.

The center that controls vomiting is not in the stomach, but in the brain. Nerve impulses can travel to this center from many places in the body. Vomiting is always a sign of some kind of disturbance. Unpleasant sights, sounds, or even thoughts can stimulate the vomiting center. It is more easily stimulated in children than in adults.

Vomiting may be a symptom of a dangerous illness. Irritation in the stomach may start messages traveling over nerves that lead to the vomiting center. Irritations in the abdomen, caused by appendicitis, gall bladder disease, injuries to the abdomen, or intestinal infection may also send messages of distress to the vomiting center. The same is true for some illnesses that do not seem related to the digestive tract, such as pneumonia, scarlet fever, and some kinds of heart disease.

Some people become nauseated when they travel by car, ship, or airplane. This is known as motion sickness. In such cases, nerve messages go to the vomiting center from the eyes and the semicircular canals of the ears. Lying down and closing the eyes can help someone with motion sickness to feel better. Medications are used very successfully to treat motion sickness.

Diarrhea can lead to dehydration.

Diarrhea is a symptom of disturbance in the digestive tract or elsewhere in the body. In diarrhea, the feces are watery. Bowel movements also happen more often than usual. So large quantities of water are lost from body tissues. This may result in dehydration (water loss). If diarrhea is very bad and continues for some time, its cause should be discovered and treated. It is especially dangerous in infants and young children.

Common causes of diarrhea are nervous upsets, eating food to which the person is allergic, and the presence of microorganisms in food or drink. A simple way to prevent many microorganisms from getting into food is by washing the hands before eating, cooking, or serving food.

Constipation and its problems

Constipation is a common condition in which the feces are hard and bowel movements are difficult. Most people have a bowel movement once a day. Some people have one only every two or three days. Others have two or three bowel movements in one day. The number and frequency of bowel movements is not as important as the regularity.

The usual reason for constipation is a diet that does not include enough roughage and bulk to cause peristaltic waves. Roughage, or fiber, is nondigestible material. It stimulates the muscles of the digestive tract. Sometimes the muscles in the wall of the intestines contract, but do not relax. This stops the peristaltic waves. Another cause of constipation is lack of exercise. In this case, the muscles of the abdomen become too relaxed to be useful in bowel action.

Enemas are treatments sometimes used to relieve constipation. An enema usually is made up of warm water that has a little salt in it. The enema is put into the anus with a tube. The liquid goes into the lower part of the large intestine. It stretches the walls of the intestine. Then the walls contract and force out both the water solution and the wastes. An enema does not act on the whole digestive tract. This is an important difference between enemas and laxatives.

Laxatives can be dangerous.

Laxatives act in different ways to stimulate muscles of the digestive tract. They act upon the body in a way that causes a bowel movement. It is dangerous to take laxatives often and regularly. Laxative-taking can become a habit. As time passes, larger doses or stronger laxatives will be needed to produce a bowel movement. As a result, muscles of the intestine may become overworked and suffer damage. It is best to take laxatives only on the advice of a physician.

Ulcers can form in the stomach or duodenum.

Ulcers are eroded, or worn, spots in the digestive lining. Ulcers are usually in the stomach or in the duodenum. They may bleed or may "eat through" the wall of the digestive tract. In addition, they are usually very painful. Not all causes of ulcers are known. But they are often caused by an increase in acid in the digestive tract. Nervous tension is also an important factor in the formation of ulcers. So is cigarette smoking. Ulcers of the stomach are five times more frequent in cigarette smokers than in nonsmokers. Special diets, medications, and ways to ease tension are important in the treatment of ulcers. In some very serious cases, surgery may be needed to correct the problem.

Swelling of the appendix is called appendicitis.

The appendix is a small organ near the beginning of the large intestine. Its function is unknown. A condition called *appendicitis* occurs when the appendix becomes infected and swollen. The first symptom of appendicitis is usually pain. The pain may be sudden and very bad, or it may be mild. Later symptoms include nausea, vomiting, constipation, fever, and soreness in the lower abdomen. If these symptoms occur, call a doctor. In the meantime, remain quiet and eat nothing. Do not take a laxative. Do not use a hot water bag or electric heating pad. Heat or a laxative can cause an infected appendix to rupture, or break. This spreads infection throughout the abdominal cavity. Keep in mind that most of the deaths resulting from appendicitis today could have been prevented with proper medical treatment.

What causes hemorrhoids?

Sometimes veins around the anus or in the rectum become swollen with blood. Such a swollen mass of veins is called a hemorrhoid. Hemorrhoids may bulge out near the anus. A blood clot may form in a hemorrhoid, producing a painful lump. Sometimes hemorrhoids rupture and bleed.

Constipation, straining during bowel movements, physical exertion, inherited tendencies, and pregnancy are all thought to be causes of hemorrhoids. Proper diet and controlled exercise can help a person who has hemorrhoids. In very serious cases, surgery may be needed to correct this condition.

Gas in the intestinal tract

Having gas (*flatus*) in the stomach or in the intestine is a normal condition. Sometimes it can be uncomfortable. The extra gas puts pressure on the wall of the intestine. Divers and astronauts, who go through fast changes in atmospheric pressure, may get severe pains from gas as it expands in the digestive tract.

Gas is formed when you swallow air. Much of this gas will be belched from the stomach. A small amount can find its way into the large intestine. The bacteria in the large intestine can form other gases such as hydrogen and methane.

To prevent too much flatus from forming, stay away from foods that you know are "gas forming." People react in different ways to different kinds of food. Cabbage or beans, for example, may produce gas in some people but may have no effect on others.

How common are intestinal infections?

Until recent years, worms of different kinds were found in the digestive tracts of many people. Such worms included ascaris, hookworm, tapeworm, and pinworm. For several reasons, infestations with worms are now much less common in the United States. People who handle, cook, and serve food are instructed to wash their hands often. They do this to protect themselves and others from the spread of worms and other organisms. Modern buildings and sewage disposal have lowered the number of breeding places for flies. Because few people go barefoot, hookworm is now rare. Meat inspection gives protection against some infections. And we now know that thorough cooking kills harmful organisms in food.

In many places throughout the world, intestinal infections and infestations are still common. Travelers should find out if the drinking water in places they visit is free of contamination. They should also find out if it is safe to eat raw fruits and vegetables and how carefully food is cooked and served.

Why the stomach does not digest itself

Approximately two quarts of hydrochloric acid are secreted by the stomach every day. Hydrochloric acid is a very strong acid. It would cause severe burns if you spilled any on your skin. However, the strong acid does not "digest" your stomach lining. Protective safeguards keep this from happening.

The entire digestive system is lined with epithelial cells. Among these cells are goblet-shaped cells that secrete mucus. This mucus is slightly alkaline and forms a thick layer over the surface of the stomach and other parts of the digestive system. It serves as a chemical barrier between the acid in the stomach cavity and the delicate cells lining the stomach. Also, the mucus cells lining the wall undergo cell division every other day. A constant supply of new cells replaces damaged cells.

Thus, the mucus layer and the rapid cell division contribute to maintaining a barrier between the powerful acid and the delicate tissue underneath.

Something to think about . . .

Main Ideas

1. Good health depends partly on how well the digestive system does its work. Eating habits, foods, emotions, disease-producing organisms, exercise, and rest can affect digestion.
2. The tongue helps in tasting, chewing, and swallowing. Taste buds are found along the sides of papillae on the tongue.
3. Enzymes are chemicals in digestive juices that break down food into simpler compounds.
4. The salivary glands secrete saliva. Saliva moistens food and has an enzyme called amylase that breaks down sugar into maltose.
5. Food is pushed through the digestive tract by muscular contractions called peristaltic waves.
6. The major part of digestion takes place in the small intestine rather than in the stomach.
7. Bile from the liver is important in digesting fats.
   Nutrients are absorbed through the villi in the small intestine.
9. The danger in appendicitis is that the swollen appendix can burst. If that happens, infection can spread throughout the body.
10. A person can live a normal life with one kidney.

Key Words

alimentary canal	duodenum	mastication
amylase	enuresis	papillae
appendicitis	enzymes	peristaltic waves
bile duct	esophagus	salivary glands
bolus	flatus	uvula
chyme	gastric juice	villi

(handwritten notes: Bile, uvula, Palate, Colon, digestive juice)

Apply Your Knowledge

1. Put the following into the order in which they work in the digestive system: uvula, rectum, pharynx, duodenum, stomach, esophagus, tongue, large intestine.
2. List three functions of the tongue.
3. What is the function of the enzyme found in saliva?
4. What happens to food in the mouth? In the stomach? In the small intestine?

5. How do emotions affect digestion? Describe a school lunch scene that would be good for digestion.
6. What are common causes of constipation and diarrhea?
7. List two functions of hydrochloric acid in the digestive system.
8. Why is it unwise to make a habit of taking laxatives?
9. How can diarrhea be dangerous?
10. How does gastric juice help in the digestive process?
11. How can constipation be prevented?
12. How does flatus (gas) form in the digestive system?
13. Explain the work of the kidneys.
14. How are intestinal infections and infestations spread?
15. Describe the symptoms of appendicitis.
16. What should a person with appendicitis symptoms do until a doctor is reached? What kinds of treatment are dangerous?
17. Name the two types of secretions from the pancreas.
18. What are the functions of the liver and bile?
19. What is the function of the ureters?
20. How could a person function without a stomach?

Extend Your Knowledge

1. Explain which organs of the digestive system are absolutely needed for life.
2. Allow a dog or cat to lick your hand. How does it feel? What causes the roughness? Explain the purpose of the texture of the tongue. (Don't forget to wash your hands afterwards.)
3. Make a list of things in your own environment that may affect your digestion.
4. Visit the nearest medical center and find out how a dialysis machine (artificial kidney) works.
5. Ask a radiologist to show you X rays of a stomach and intestines. Explain how these X rays are made.
6. Study how thinking about foods affects you. Does thinking about certain foods cause you to salivate? Which foods make your salivary glands secrete the most saliva?
7. Smell some foods. Does smelling or thinking about foods cause more saliva to flow?
8. Hold your nose and look at some food. Does looking at foods affect your salivary glands? Does being hungry make a difference?
9. It is fun to do some experiments with taste and smell. Blindfold yourself. While holding your nose, bite into a slice of apple, onion, and potato, one at a time. Were you able to tell the difference between these foods?
10. Find the taste buds for sweet, sour, bitter, and salty on your tongue.

Unit 9

CHAPTERS:

29 Personal Safety
30 Basic First Aid
31 Cardiopulmonary Resuscitation (CPR)

Safety and Emergency Care

Chapter 29

Do you know . . .

- what causes the most deaths among people of high school age?
- why insurance companies charge higher rates for teenage drivers?
- why many accidents happen in the home?

Personal Safety

The main cause of death each year in the United States among people of high school age is *accidents.* A recent study showed that about 24,000 deaths of young people aged 15 to 24 were due to accidents. In almost every case, accidents result from carelessness. A strong sense of responsibility is one of the best safeguards against accidents.

Accidents are often a serious health problem among older people, too. Older people tend to be much more careful. But sometimes they do not react to danger as quickly as younger people do. Also, people who are older often do not recover from injuries as easily.

Automobile accidents

About 22 percent of all drivers are less than 25 years old. These young drivers usually see and hear better than older drivers. They also react more quickly. So you might think they would be good drivers. Yet drivers under 25 have more accidents per licensed driver than any other age group. They are in about one-third of the automobile accidents in the United States. At this rate, 1 out of every 3 people who are now 15 years old will be hurt in an automobile accident. About 1 out of every 100 will die.

Why do you think young people have more accidents? What do you think could be done to lower the high accident rate among young drivers?

Causes of Automobile Accidents

1. Unsafe driving practices: driving over the speed limit; passing on a hill or a curve; cutting in ahead of other cars; turning without signaling; *tailgating* (following the car ahead too closely).
2. Unsafe drivers: drivers under the influence of alcohol or other drugs; drivers who are sleepy, impatient, angry, or upset; drivers distracted by riders; drivers with poor and uncorrected vision or hearing.
3. Automobiles that are not safe: faulty brakes; worn tires; broken lights; various mechanical problems; overloading.
4. Dangerous driving conditions: stormy weather; narrow roads; slippery road surfaces; darkness; fog; headlight glare; heavy traffic.

A motorcyclist is five times more likely to be killed in an accident than an automobile driver. What special safety measures should be required for people riding motorcycles?

Motorcycle accidents

Many young people drive motorcycles and mopeds. Based on the number of miles driven, the chances of a cyclist being killed are about five times greater than those of an automobile driver. The chances of motorcycle passengers being killed are also higher than those of automobile passengers. Both drivers and passengers on motorcycles and mopeds are unprotected against the forces of a collision.

Because of the danger of serious accidents, do you think that special safety measures should be required for people riding motorcycles? For example, do you think crash helmets should be required?

Causes of Motorcycle Accidents

1. **Unsafe driving practices:** not obeying traffic rules; carrying people on the front of the motorcycle, or in other unsafe ways; *trick riding,* or stunting; weaving around cars; riding too close to cars; pulling out from driveways and between parked cars without looking.

2. **Unsafe drivers:** untrained or inexperienced cyclists; cyclists under the influence of alcohol or drugs; cyclists who are trying to show off.

3. **Motorcycles that are not safe:** poor headlights; faulty brakes; lack of safety equipment, such as crash helmet, goggles, and heavy gloves.

4. **Dangerous driving conditions:** wet, slippery roads; darkness; fog; roads with bumps and ruts; headlight glare; heavy traffic.

Bicycle accidents

Riding bicycles, for pleasure and for healthful exercise, is very popular. You probably know about some of the dangers of driving an automobile or a motorcycle. But riding a bicycle can be very dangerous, too. In fact, bicycles are involved in more injuries than any other product.

Bicycle riders should obey the same traffic rules that automobile drivers and motorcyclists follow. Ride on the right side of the road. Obey traffic signs and lights. Signal when you are about to stop or turn. Careless riders can harm others as well as themselves.

> **Causes of Bicycle Accidents**
>
> 1. Loss of control: difficulty in braking; riding too large a bike; riding double on "banana" seats, rear fenders, handlebars, or the horizontal top tube on a bike; *trick riding,* or stunting; hitting a rut, bump, or obstacle.
> 2. Mechanical and structural problems: brake failure; wobbling or loosening of the wheel or steering parts; difficulty in shifting gears; chain slippage; pedals falling off; spoke breakage.
> 3. Entangling one's hands, feet, or clothing in the bicycle.
> 4. Foot slipping from the pedal.
> 5. Collision with a car or another bicycle.

Accident prevention

Do you follow safety rules for the hobbies, sports, or jobs that you take part in? Are you careful not to drive, work, or play athletic games when you are tired? When you are working with equipment or driving, do you give your full attention to what you are doing?

Water safety

About 6000 people drown every year in the United States. Most drownings happen among young people while they are swimming, fishing, boating, waterskiing, skin diving, and surfing. How many of these water sports do you enjoy? Do you know how to enjoy them safely?

Even members of the Olympic teams, the best swimmers in the world, must follow safety rules in their swimming. Less expert swimmers have a greater need for safety rules. The American Red Cross makes the following suggestions:

> **Rules for Safe Swimming**
>
> 1. Learn to swim well.
> 2. Swim out-of-doors only when the water temperature will not chill your body.
> 3. Pick a place to swim where you know the depth and current of the water. This place should be free from weeds that may trap you. Swim where a lifeguard is present. Never swim alone.
> 4. Know how well you can swim, and do not take chances.
> 5. Know how long you are able to swim. Stop before you get chilled or overtired.
> 6. Do not swim long distances unless someone in a boat accompanies you.
> 7. Do not swim out to a drowning person unless you have had special training in lifesaving. Throw the person something that will float, such as an oar or a life belt.

8. Learn how to handle a boat or a canoe correctly. Wear a life jacket.

9. Use boats that are in good condition. Do not overload them.

10. Do not skate on ice that is less than 10 centimeters (4 inches) thick.

11. Be careful when wading in streams. Slippery rocks and a fast current can cause anyone to slip and fall.

12. Do not attempt to swim long distances underwater without coming up for air. Otherwise, you may lose consciousness and drown.

Home safety

About 21,000 people in the United States die every year from *home accidents.* More than 3 million people are injured. Many accidents happen at home because people tend to pay less attention to possible dangers in familiar surroundings. When is the last time you, or another member of your family, checked *your* home for possible safety hazards?

Most home accidents can be avoided by following these safety measures:

Rules for Safety in the Home

1. Light stairways well. Provide handrails for stairways. Do not leave toys or other objects on stairs.
2. Keep ice and snow off porches, steps, and sidewalks.
3. Use a stepladder to reach high places. Be sure that the ladder is steady.
4. Be careful when walking on waxed floors or loose rugs.
5. Keep electric cords in good condition. Do not use electrical appliances in places where they may be dangerous. For example, don't use a hair dryer next to the bathtub.
6. Keep knives, garden tools, broken glass, boiling water, matches, household chemicals, and medicines out of the reach of children.
7. Keep poisons in plainly marked containers and out of the reach of children.
8. Be careful of swinging doors.
9. Be alert for gas leaks around gas appliances.
10. Put out burning matches or cigarettes carefully.
11. Do not use gasoline or flammable cleaning fluids indoors.
12. Do not start an automobile in a closed garage.
13. Be sure that guns are unloaded and out of reach.
14. Arrange bedclothes so that babies cannot get blankets and pillows over their noses and mouths. Keep plastic bags out of the reach of children. Do not use plastic bags as slipcovers for pillows or mattresses.

Many accidents happen at home because people pay less attention to dangers in everyday surroundings. When is the last time you and your family checked your home for possible dangers?

15. Keep small objects that might be swallowed or that might stick in windpipes away from babies.

16. Place window guards on upper-story windows in homes where there are small children.

17. Securely lock or remove any large container, such as an empty refrigerator, in which a child could suffocate.

18. Use caution when working with power tools. Power lawn mowers are very dangerous.

19. Do not leave small children alone even for a few minutes.

20. Know what to do if fire strikes. Practice *Exit Drills In The Home* (EDITH).

Safety on the job

Each year, more than 12,000 people in the United States die in accidents related to their jobs. Some *work-related accidents* are caused by the workers themselves. So it is important for workers to know safe work habits. Other work-related accidents are caused by unsafe buildings, tools, and equipment and by the lack of proper safety equipment. It is important for owners to provide a safe workplace for the workers. The Occupational Safety and Health Administration (OSHA) is a government agency that sets standards for safety in the workplace. OSHA inspectors check to see if employers are meeting these standards.

Many accidents happen around machines. The most common unsafe practice is not turning off a machine before adjusting, repairing, or cleaning it. Lack of safety guards or poor use of safety guards causes a large number of accidents with saws. In the use of grinding wheels, eye protection and proper adjustment of the tool rest are important safety measures.

Accidents in industry are not spread evenly through the day. They reach a peak between 10 and 11 A.M. and again between 3 and 4 P.M. However, fewer accidents happen in the afternoon than in the morning. It

Accidental Deaths In A Recent Year

Years of age	Motor vehicle	Falls	Drowning	Fires, burns	Poisoning by solids, liquids	Suffocation —ingested object	Firearms	Poisoning by gases, vapors	Other	Total accidents
under 5	33 %	3 %	16 %	17 %	2 %	9 %	2 %	1 %	17 %	100 %
5 - 14	50 %	2 %	16 %	8 %	1 %	1 %	7 %	2 %	13 %	
15 - 24	68 %	2 %	9 %	3 %	5 %	1 %	3 %	1 %	8 %	
25 - 44	55 %	4 %	8%	4%	8 %	2 %	3 %	2 %	14%	
45 - 64	40 %	12 %	6 %	8 %	6 %	4 %	2 %	2 %	20 %	
65 - 74	35 %	24 %	3 %	9 %	2 %	5 %	1 %	1 %	20 %	
Over 74	18 %	53 %	2 %	5 %	2 %	3 %	1 %	1 %	15 %	

*National Safety Council

has been discovered that workers must be allowed rest periods. Rest periods relieve the workers' tiredness and cut down the number of accidents.

In many places, nuclear energy is replacing present sources of energy. This means that more and more workers will have jobs in which radiation will be a danger.

Farming is becoming a more dangerous occupation. More than one-third of the accidental deaths on farms involve machinery. Powerful machinery should not be operated without training. Careless driving of tractors is the major cause of farm accidents.

Something to think about . . .

Almost every day, newspapers carry stories about fires and families who are left without a home or who have lost everything. These accounts should start you thinking about how you can protect your life and home in case of fire.

One important step you can take is to buy and install a smoke alarm. This simple device sounds a warning buzzer when a room begins to fill with smoke. Smoke detector alarms operate on a 9-volt battery. There are two kinds—ionization and photoelectric.

Ionization smoke detectors react more quickly to the thin, wispy smoke produced by fast-burning paper or wood fires. Photoelectric detectors are better at sensing the dense smoke given off by a slow, smoldering fire. A typical slow-burning fire would be one caused by a cigarette dropped on a mattress or a piece of upholstered furniture.

You cannot predict whether a potential household fire will be a fast-burning one or a slow-burning one, so it is safest to install one photoelectric and one ionization detector. The ionization detector should be placed in the middle of the ceiling in the room or hallway next to the bedrooms. Then it will be easy to hear during the night if it sounds in response to the racing smoke of a fast-burning fire. The photoelectric detector should go in the living room or den to alert the family to smoke form a slow-burning rug or couch.

Main Ideas

1. Accidents are the leading cause of injury and death among people of high school age.
2. Most accidents can be prevented.
3. A strong sense of responsibility is one of the best safeguards against accidents.
4. Doing things safely may seem to take longer than doing things carelessly, but the extra time taken is worth it.

Key Words

EDITH
home accidents
tailgating

trick riding
work-related accidents

Apply Your Knowledge

1. State the main causes of death among young people.
2. Name four driving conditions you would consider very dangerous.
3. Watch pedestrians and automobile drivers for 30 minutes or longer. Make lists of the things they do that are related to safety.
4. Study the driving rules of your state and city. Ask the police to explain any rules that you do not understand or do not agree with.
5. Why do you think young drivers are involved in more automobile accidents than older drivers? What do you think could be done to lower the high accident rate among young drivers?
6. List three rules that are very important in preventing water accidents.
7. List some safety measures for stopping accidents in the home that could apply to your own home.
8. What are some safeguards that should be taken when working around machinery?
9. Collect newspaper articles about accidents. Discuss how some of these accidents could have been prevented.
10. What general rule is most important in preventing accidents?

Extend Your Knowledge

1. Imagine that a state official placed you in charge of lowering the number of injuries and deaths that occur in the high-school-age population in your state. Describe your plan for doing this. What percent of deaths and injuries do you think would be prevented if your plan were followed.
2. Write a report or lead a class discussion on the topic of high school driver education courses. Include such facts as these: why some states require high schools to offer driver education courses; why other states are in the process of ending these courses; the cost of such courses, and who you think should pay for them. Be sure to state your point of view and the reasons for it.
3. Find out the number, location, and type of accidents that happened in your school last year. Explain how some of these accidents could have been prevented. Have any safety measures been added as a result of these accidents? If so, have these safety measures helped to lower the number of accidents? Why or why not?
4. Find out whether or not your community has enough bicycle paths and special lanes for bicyclists on heavily traveled roads. What person or group in your community is responsible for carrying out bicycle safety measures? What needs to be done to improve bicycle safety on the road?
5. Give a report on federal regulations that set safety standards for automobiles.

Chapter 30

Do you know . . .
- what to do in an emergency?
- how to stop the bleeding from a wound?
- how to help someone who has taken poison?
- what are the differences between first-, second-, and third-degree burns?

Basic First Aid

First aid is emergency treatment given to a person who is injured or ill. First aid takes place before medical or surgical care arrives. Fire and police departments in many communities have first-aid equipment and trained personnel to help in emergencies.

The term *first aid* may also be used to describe caring for small cuts, bruises, and other minor injuries. Proper care may keep a minor injury or sickness from becoming serious.

An *emergency* is a situation that needs very fast action. It is not always possible to tell which emergencies are serious and which are not. However, certain conditions, such as severe bleeding, failure to breathe, heart attack, and poisoning, must be spotted and cared for at once. General rules to follow are these:

1. If there is more than one injured person, care for the most seriously injured first.
2. Keep calm and act quickly and quietly. Speak in a normal tone of voice. Try not to worry the victim.
3. Find out if the injured person is bleeding. Serious bleeding must be stopped as quickly as possible.
4. Check for breathing. Make sure that the victim has an open air passage. If the victim is not breathing, start artificial respiration at once.
5. Check for the victim's pulse. If there is no pulse, cardiopulmonary resuscitation (CPR) must be started. (Note: Information on cardiopulmonary resuscitation (CPR) and choking can be found in Chapter 31.)
6. If there are signs of poisoning or drug use, begin the right treatment at once.
7. Do not move an injured person unless you must for the person's safety. Moving an injured person the wrong way may harm the person even more. Do not let the person sit up or stand until you know how bad the injury is. It is best to let trained people (medical workers, police officers, or trained rescue workers) tell how serious an injury is.
8. Get trained medical help fast. However, do not leave the victim in order to get help, unless you have no other choice.

First aid

Control of bleeding

Controlled bleeding can help a wound to clean itself. But bleeding that is out of control can lead to death. If bleeding is not very serious, let it continue for a short while. Then wash the area very carefully with soap and water. Do not apply iodine or other antiseptics. Finally, cover the area with a clean dressing, such as sterile gauze.

It is possible for a person who is bleeding very heavily to bleed to death in just a few minutes. If there is very serious bleeding, or *hemorrhage*, the bleeding must be stopped at once. Place a clean cloth over the wound and press down firmly. A sterile bandage is best. But any clean cloth, such as a clean handkerchief or part of a clean shirt or slip, will do. If no cloth is available, press your hand directly on the wound. Firm pressure will usually stop the bleeding. If bleeding starts again when you release the pressure, keep pressing until medical help comes. Do not keep lifting your hand and looking at the wound to see if the bleeding has stopped. In addition to applying pressure to the wound, raise the injured part of the body, if no bones are broken. This will help to slow down the loss of blood from the wound.

To help stop bleeding, you can also apply pressure to the artery leading to the wound. The illustration on this page shows the different places on the body where pressure can be applied to arteries.

If pressure and raising the injured part of the body do not stop the bleeding, a *tourniquet* can be used, but *only as a last resort*. A tourniquet is a band of cloth or any other material that is pulled tightly around an arm or leg. The tourniquet is placed above the wound (between the wound and the heart). A tourniquet is dangerous, because it cuts off the supply of blood to the tissues of the limb. The decision to apply a tourniquet is really a decision to risk a limb in order to save a life. A tourniquet should be at least 2 inches wide to stop added injury to tissue when it is tightened. Once applied, the tourniquet should be released only by a doctor.

A person with a tourniquet should be given fast medical attention. Be sure to point out the tourniquet to the doctor. It may be hidden from view by clothing or some other covering.

Poisoning

If the poisoning victim is conscious, dilute the poison by giving the person several glassfuls of water or milk to drink. Try to identify the poison before giving any other treatment. The label of the container will probably tell you the name of the poison and the antidote. An *antidote* is a substance that works against the poison. Unfortunately, many labels contain incorrect, outdated information. For example, labels on some lye products still recommend drinking vinegar or a citrus juice to neutralize the poison. The chemical reaction that results can cause further damage to internal tissues. Other labels advise the use of oils as an antidote. Oils are of no proven value in the treatment of poisoning and could get into the lungs and cause a form of pneumonia.

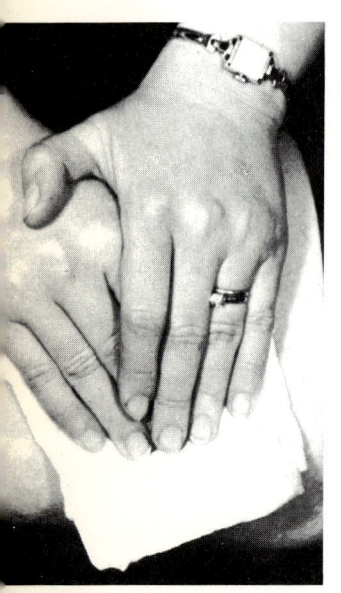

(top) The large dots show points where pressure can be applied to arteries to stop bleeding. (bottom) In most cases, however, firm pressure on the wound itself will stop the bleeding.

The safest thing to do is to call a poison center or the emergency room of a nearby hospital and ask for specific instructions. The toll-free number for your state's Poison Control Center can probably be found in the front of your local telephone book. (It may be listed under *Poison Center* or *Poison Information Center*.) If you are unable to reach either one, call the police or the fire department.

Keep on hand epsom salts to act as a laxative and syrup of ipecac to induce vomiting. You may be instructed to use 1 tablespoon of syrup of ipecac to make the person vomit. Sometimes, however, vomiting should not be induced. Vomiting a strong acid or alkali, for example, can cause further damage. If the poisoning victim is unconscious, keep the air passage open; do not induce vomiting. If needed, give artificial respiration or cardiopulmonary resuscitation. Do not give liquids to an unconscious person.

Get the victim to medical help as fast as you can. If possible, take along the poison container or a sample of the victim's vomit. Tell the specialist what poison has been taken and how much.

Treatment of shock

Very serious injury, bleeding, or burns often cause *shock*. Shock is a serious condition and must be treated quickly. Shock means that a person's blood is not circulating as it should. A shock victim usually feels faint, weak, cold, and often nauseated. The victim's skin may look pale or blue. It will feel cold and clammy. Breathing is not regular. The pulse is weak and fast.

The blood of a person in shock is not moving through the body as it should. It is important to keep the victim from losing body heat. Use only enough blankets to keep the body temperature about normal.

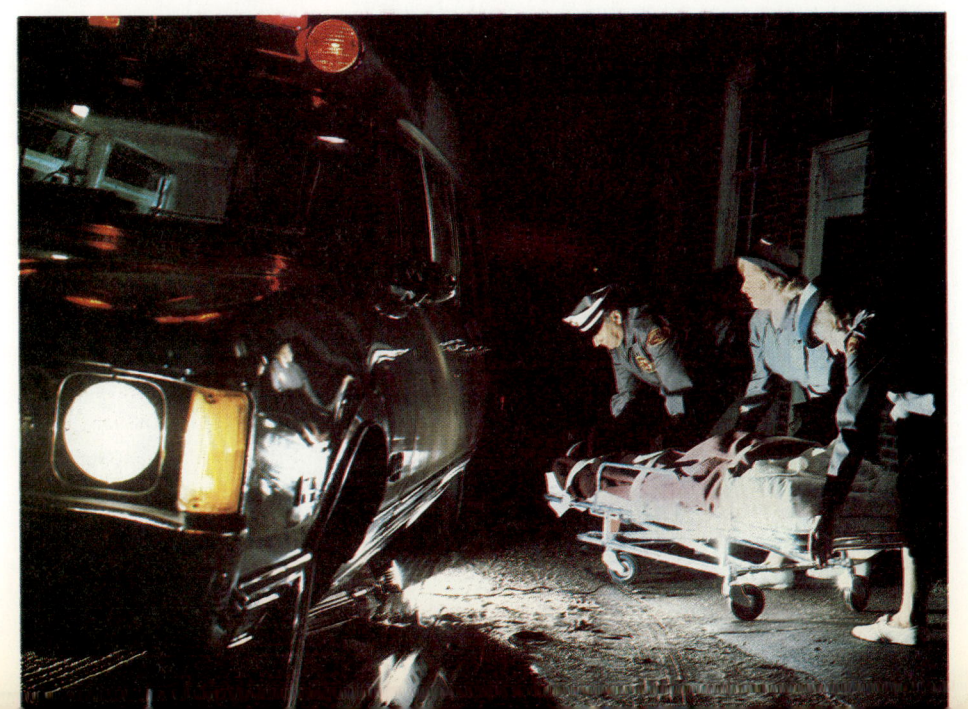

The label on a poison bottle may contain incorrect, outdated information. The safest thing to do for a poisoning victim is to call a poison center or the emergency room of a nearby hospital. Ask for specific instructions.

353

The most important factor in preventing and treating shock is to keep the victim from losing body heat. Cover the person only enough to keep the body temperature about normal. Place the person flat on the back, with the feet slightly raised. Control bleeding if any is present. Make sure the breathing passages are clear. Loosen all tight clothing. Do not move the person more than is needed. Do not give the person anything by mouth. Reassure the victim and get medical help at once.

Fractures

A break in a bone is called a *fracture*. Usually there is pain at the point of fracture. The victim finds it hard to move the injured part. It may be bent out of shape, and swelling may occur very quickly. In a closed fracture, the skin is not broken. In an open fracture, the broken bone comes through the skin, or a wound reaches from the surface of the skin to the break in the bone. There is danger that infection may enter the wound. When you think that someone may have a fractured bone, send for medical help. Make the injured person lie down. Give care for shock. Control any bleeding. It is more dangerous to move a person who has a fracture than to wait for medical help. If you must move the person, try to keep the injured part from moving.

Fractures of the neck or the back can be made worse by moving the injured person. Wrong movements can lead to injury of the spinal cord. This can cause permanent paralysis or death.

Dislocations and sprains

When a bone gets out of place at a joint, the condition is called a *dislocation*. When the ligaments, tendons, or muscles around a joint are torn or bruised, the condition is called a *sprain*. Swelling and pain occur very quickly. Without an X-ray examination, even a physician may not be able to tell whether the injury is a sprain, a dislocation, or a fracture.

The best first aid for a sprain is to wrap the injured area tightly, apply ice to it, elevate it above the heart, and then rest it. The tight wrap limits swelling, and ice shrinks the blood vessels. Elevating the injured area helps to drain the fluid, and resting will prevent further damage. If the victim of a sprain or a dislocation is in shock, treat the shock in the proper way. But remember, only a doctor should try to put a dislocated bone "back in place."

Burns

Burns can be caused by fire, sunlight, electricity, and chemicals. In the case of fire burns, if the burned area is large, send for medical help fast. While waiting for help, treat the person for shock. If the burned area is small, follow these general rules:

1. **Cut clothing from around the burned part. Do not pull it.**
2. **If there are blisters, do not break them.**
3. **Do not use any substance, such as grease, soda, or salve, on the burned area.**

Do not *use any* substance, such as butter or salve, on burned areas.

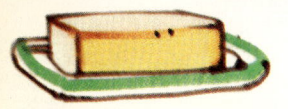

First-degree burns. In a first-degree burn, the skin is not broken, but it may be reddened. Cold water is soothing if applied at once. If needed, apply a dry dressing.

Second-degree burns. In a second-degree burn, the skin is blistered. Cover a small burn area completely with cold water until the pain is gone. A large area should be treated as an open wound. Remove loose clothing, but do not try to remove material that sticks to the skin. If needed, apply several layers of gauze or clean towels. Second-degree burn victims sometimes suffer from shock. This calls for fast attention.

Third-degree burns. In third-degree burns, the burns are deep and the skin is destroyed. Third-degree burns are always serious. First-aid care should include treating the shock that usually follows such burns. Use a clean dressing, just as you would for second-degree burns. Do not apply water or any medicine. Get medical help as soon as possible.

Chemical burns. When burns are caused by chemicals, flood the burned areas with large amounts of water as quickly as possible. Do this until the chemical is removed. Cut away all clothing with scissors. Then treat the injury like any other burn.

Give careful attention to eye burns caused by chemicals. Flood the eye with large amounts of water for at least 15 minutes. Do this before worrying about calling for help. Cover the eye until the injured person can get to a physician.

Fire. Fast action may keep a person whose clothing is on fire from being badly burned. Place the person on the floor or ground, and smother the flames by rolling the person over. If possible, wrap the person in a heavy material, such as a rug, a coat, or a blanket.

Do apply cold water to first-degree burns.

Exposure to heat or cold

Too much heat or cold can cause illness or injury that needs medical attention. Overexposure to heat can cause *heatstroke*. The skin is hot and dry. The pulse is fast and strong. Unconsciousness and convulsions may follow. Move the victim to a cool place and apply wet cloths or ice to the victim's skin or place the person in a tub of water. Get medical help as quickly as possible.

Heat exhaustion comes from the body's loss of large amounts of water and salt in perspiration. The skin is cold and clammy. Breathing is shallow and the pulse is weak. The victim may faint. To treat heat exhaustion, move the victim to a cool place. Then give the person salt water to sip. Use 2 teaspoons of salt in .475 liter (1 pint) of water.

Too much cold may injure body tissues. This condition is called *frostbite*. The affected part of the body loses feeling. The skin may look pale and shiny. To treat frostbite, bring the person indoors. Warm the frostbitten part as gently as possible. Put it in warm water or apply cloths soaked in warm water. Do not use strong heat. Do not rub with snow or anything else.

Snakebite

Get medical help as soon as possible. Even if the bite is from a nonpoisonous snake, a tetanus shot may be needed.

Symptoms of a poisonous snakebite are swelling and pain. The snake venom, or poison, spreads slowly through the body. Keep the victim as quiet as possible. Movements increase circulation and make the venom spread faster. Keep the bitten limb still, and keep it at or below the level of the heart. If symptoms develop and you will have medical help within an hour, apply a tight band about 2 inches above the bite. Do not cut off circulation. Leave enough slack so that a finger may be put under the constriction band.

If severe symptoms develop and help is more than an hour away, cut through the skin over the bite. Suck the venom out of the wound with a suction cup or with your mouth. Snake venom is not a stomach poison. But it can be dangerous to the person giving first aid if that person has an open sore in the mouth. Always rinse your mouth well.

Electric shock

Rescuing an unconscious person from a live electrical wire is always dangerous. The rescuer may be killed by electricity from touching the body of the victim. If the switch is near, turn off the current. Otherwise, use a dry stick, dry clothing, dry rope, or some other dry material—not metal—to move the victim from the wire. Start artificial respiration or cardiopulmonary resuscitation if needed. Send for help.

Convulsions

A *convulsion* is a strong attack of involuntary muscle contractions. Some causes of convulsion are epilepsy, serious head injuries, some kinds of poisoning, and different illnesses. In some types of convulsions, the person's body stiffens. In other types, the arms, legs, trunk, and neck go through violent muscular contractions.

First-aid treatment for convulsions usually means protecting the person who may be thrashing about from getting hurt. Do not restrict the person's movements. Put a folded blanket under the person's head, if possible. But be careful. The movements of a person having a convulsion can be very powerful. The person cannot control them. You may be hurt while trying to help. After the seizure, place the victim on his or her side. Check to see if the air passage is open. Be sure that breathing is normal.

Children sometimes have convulsions when they have a fever. This may be the beginning of a serious illness. Call a physician at once.

Everyday emergencies

You may never have to take care of people who are seriously hurt. However, you may have to take care of yourself or someone else in a minor emergency. Be sure to keep the following points in mind:

1. **What looks like a small injury may turn out to be serious. Look for a hidden or severe injury.**
2. **Give treatment for shock, if necessary. Keep the person quiet and the body temperature about normal.**

3. **Whenever the skin is broken even slightly, there is a danger of infection. Clean the wound and cover it with a sterile bandage.**

Bruises. When the skin is bruised but not broken, apply cold, wet cloths or ice to the areas for 30 minutes or longer. This relieves pain and lessens swelling and black-and-blue marks. If a bruise is not treated until the next day, use warm, wet cloths. Bruise marks mean that blood vessels under the skin are broken. It may take days or even weeks for the blood to be reabsorbed into the blood vessels. A black eye is an example of such an injury.

Nosebleeds. Hold the bleeding nostril closed with slight pressure on one side of the nose. Apply continuous pressure for 10 minutes. Most nosebleeds can be stopped this way. A person with a nosebleed should sit up but should not move about. If bleeding continues, get medical attention.

Blisters. Cover a blister with a sterile dressing. In most cases, leave it alone, and do not break it. The liquid will be absorbed back into the surrounding body tissue. But the blister may be on the foot or some other place where it may accidentally break. Then, wash the area thoroughly with soap and water.

Animal bites. Because of the chance of infection, wash any animal bite thoroughly with soap and water. Call a physician. If possible, the animal should be caught immediately. Notify the police or the local health department. An expert should find out if the animal has rabies. If the animal is not rabid, the victim does not need antirabies vaccinations.

Insect bites. Stings from bees, wasps, hornets, and yellow jackets are usually not serious. However, a person with an allergic reaction may die from the sting of one of these insects. Check the affected area carefully for any stinger that may need to be removed. To ease pain and lessen swelling, apply cold cloths or ice. Then apply a soothing lotion, such as calamine. If the swelling and pain do not lessen quickly, or if the person has had an allergic reaction to an insect bite in the past, get medical help right away.

Something to think about . . .

Rachel, age 16, was studying at home. Both of her parents were still away at work. David, her 12-year-old brother, was playing basketball on the rear patio with his friend, Mark.

Suddenly, Rachel heard a loud crashing noise. Mark had lost his balance while reaching for the basketball and had plunged his right arm through the patio window.

Rachel rushed to the patio and found that Mark had cut himself severely on the shattered glass. Mark appeared alarmed at the sight of the many bleeding cuts on his right arm, especially the large gash above his wrist. Rachel had taken a first-aid course about a year ago. Now she tried to remember what she should do. She recalled how important it was to remain calm and to act quickly. First, she told Mark to lie down. Almost at the same time, she was asking David for his shirt. She began to use it as a pad to apply direct pressure on the deep gash above Mark's wrist. Rachel sent David to call the rescue squad. She raised Mark's arm and continued to apply pressure to the wound. To get emergency medical help in their community, David only had to dial 911.

Soon Rachel realized that direct pressure to Mark's wound was not going to stop the hemorrhaging. Carefully, Rachel found the brachial artery on Mark's upper right arm and pressed the artery against the underlying bone, about midway between the elbow and armpit. Gradually, the bleeding began to stop. Rachel sighed a breath of relief, as she told Mark, "You're going to be all right. Just lie still." In a few moments, Rachel released the pressure from the brachial artery and found that she needed only to continue to apply direct pressure to the wound to keep it from bleeding. Now Rachel noticed that Mark appeared to have the symptoms of a person in shock. She sent David to get some blankets from one of the bedrooms. Then she placed a blanket under Mark to conserve his body heat. She used another blanket to raise Mark's feet. After what seemed like a long time, but in fact was only 14 minutes from the time the accident happened, the rescue squad arrived.

Later, Rachel learned that Mark needed nearly 40 stitches to repair the gash and other cuts on his arm. She also was told that the fast and efficient first aid she had administered probably saved Mark's life.

Main Ideas

1. Proper first aid can prevent additional medical problems and may save a life.
2. Certain emergency conditions must be recognized and treated at once. Such conditions are severe bleeding, failure to breathe, heart attack, and poisoning.
3. The most important factor in preventing and treating shock is to keep the victim from losing body heat.
4. Whenever the skin is broken even slightly, there is a danger of infection.

Key Words

antidote
convulsion
dislocation
emergency
first aid

fracture
frostbite
heat exhaustion
heatstroke
hemorrhage

shock
sprain
tourniquet

Apply Your Knowledge

1. Is there any emergency situation in which you would hesitate to give first aid? Why, or why not?
2. Describe how to control bleeding.
3. Why is a tourniquet dangerous to use?
4. What is the location and telephone number of the closest poison center? Where in your home would be a good place to keep this information?
5. If a poisoning victim is conscious, how can you help? How can you help an unconscious victim?
6. Explain how you can help prevent shock.
7. How are a closed fracture and an open fracture different?
8. How can you tell whether or not a person is suffering from heatstroke or from heat exhaustion? What is the treatment for each?
9. Find out where the first-aid kits are in your school. Look in the gymnasium, science laboratories, and shops. Do you think your school has enough first-aid supplies?
10. Collect newspaper clippings about accidents. Discuss the first aid that should be given in each case.

Extend Your Knowledge

1. If you were teaching a first-aid course, what advice would you give to the students to help keep them from panicking in an emergency situation?
2. Are there disaster centers in your community? What supplies are provided in them? Where else in the community are there supplies for first aid? Do you think your community is adequately prepared for the emergencies that are likely to occur?
3. Ask your local Red Cross about classes in first aid and how to qualify for a first-aid certificate.
4. Investigate the policies of an ambulance service in your community. What are the policies regarding the following:
   (a) required training for the ambulance drivers?
   (b) use of warning devices such as lights or siren?
   (c) transporting minors when a legal guardian is not available to give consent?
   Do you agree with all of the policies? Why, or why not?
5. Fire departments often have information on preventing fires. Does the fire department in your community offer this service?

Chapter 31

Do you know . . .

- what cardiopulmonary resuscitation is?
- the early warning signals of a heart attack?
- how to make the distress signal for choking?
- what a "café coronary" is?

Cardiopulmonary Resuscitation (CPR)*

*Special appreciation is extended to the American Heart Association for the information and pictures contained in this portion of the text.

It was Friday afternoon and there were long lines at the bank. Bob Davis, age forty-two, was one of the many people waiting to see a teller. Suddenly, for no apparent reason, Bob fell to the floor. For a second, everyone seemed to "freeze." Then the bank manager and six other people hurriedly gathered around him. Bob was unconscious and had stopped breathing. A few moments later, it was also determined that he had no pulse. Only one person, fifteen-year-old Nancy Martelli, knew what to do. She had completed a course in the lifesaving technique called CPR *(cardiopulmonary resuscitation)*. She immediately began the procedure. If she had not been there, Bob Davis would have died.

Each year, many thousands of Americans die suddenly. The most common cause of these deaths is heart attack. In a recent year, more than 566,000 people died as a result of heart attacks. Other causes of sudden death include choking, drowning, poisoning, suffocation, electrocution, and smoke inhalation. A large number of these sudden deaths can be prevented. Since more than half the victims die before they reach the hospital, the person's life may be in the hands of those who happen to be nearby. Many more lives would be saved if more people were trained to use CPR.

Prevention of sudden death

Who can perform cardiopulmonary resuscitation? CPR should be performed only by a person who has successfully completed a CPR course, and who has passed the CPR tests of knowledge and performance. CPR courses are offered throughout the country by the American Heart Association and the American Red Cross.

Cardiopulmonary resuscitation combines artificial respiration with artificial circulation. How does CPR work?

1. The rescuer makes sure that the victim's airway is open and unblocked.

361

2. The rescuer gives the victim oxygen by breathing air into the victim's lungs. Air exhaled by the rescuer contains enough oxygen to keep life processes working in a person who is not breathing.
3. The rescuer forces the victim's heart to pump blood by applying pressure to the victim's chest. The heart lies behind the breastbone and against the backbone. Pressure on the breastbone squeezes the heart and forces blood out. Releasing the pressure allows the heart to fill with blood.

The most frequent cause of sudden death is heart attack. Everyone should know the early warning signs of a heart attack.

The most common signal is this:

- uncomfortable pressure, fullness, squeezing, or pain in the center of the chest lasting 2 minutes or more. Pain may spread to the shoulders, neck, or arms.

Other signals may be these:

- sweating
- nausea
- shortness of breath
- a feeling of weakness

Sometimes these symptoms seem to become less severe. Then they return again. They can occur in anyone, even in a young person, at any time and in any place, for no apparent reason.

There are two important phases of emergency care—*basic life support* and *advanced life support*.

Basic life support. A rescuer who provides basic life support has been trained to recognize

- a blocked airway
- absence of breathing (called *respiratory arrest*)
- absence of a heartbeat or pulse (called *cardiac arrest*; *cardium* = heart/*arrest* = stopping)

The rescuer can then provide the correct method of CPR.

Advanced life support. A rescuer who provides advanced life support has been trained to give basic life support. In addition, such a rescuer knows how to operate medical equipment and to use other techniques to keep the person alive. Advanced life support includes the kinds of emergency care started by an ambulance paramedic, a nurse, or a doctor.

Would you know how to get care for a person in need of advanced life support? Advanced life support can usually be obtained by calling a community's *emergency medical services (EMS) system*. You should know the telephone number to reach your community's EMS system. In most of the United States, the emergency number is 911. This number may be dialed at a pay phone without depositing money. In case the EMS system is not available, you should also know the location of the nearest hospital emergency room that provides 24-hour emergency care.

A community's emergency care system might provide a fast response and expert service. Even so, the person who is with the victim at the beginning of the emergency can make the difference between life and death. If that person can provide basic life support, the victim will have a better chance of surviving.

CPR is a simple procedure, as simple as A-B-C: Airway = Breathing = Circulation.

Airway

If you find a collapsed person, first determine if the victim is conscious by shaking the person's shoulder and shouting, "Are you all right?" If there is no response, call out for help.

Next, open the victim's airway. If the victim is not already lying flat on the back, roll the victim over, moving the entire body at once as a total unit. To open the airway, lift up the neck or chin gently with one hand while pushing down on the forehead with the other to tilt the head back. Once the airway is open, place your ear close to the victim's mouth and

- **look** for the chest to rise and fall.
- **listen** for sounds of breathing.
- **feel** for breath on your cheek.

If none of these signs is present, the victim is not breathing.

If opening the airway does not cause the victim to begin to breathe, *rescue breathing* must be provided.

Breathing

The best way to provide rescue breathing is to use the mouth-to-mouth technique. The trained rescuer puts the palm of one hand on the victim's forehead and pinches the victim's nose shut. The heel of the hand is kept on the forehead to maintain head tilt. The other hand should remain under the victim's neck or chin, lifting it up. The rescuer's mouth is placed over the victim's mouth. Then the rescuer blows 4 quick, full breaths into the victim.

Circulation

The rescuer must next find out if the victim's heart is beating. This is done by feeling the carotid artery in the neck. The hand under the victim's neck moves to the voice box (Adam's apple). The tips of the index

Reproduced with permission © American Heart Association.

The A-B-C steps of cardiopulmonary resuscitation

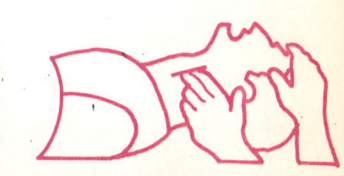

CPR
IN BASIC LIFE SUPPORT
Place victim flat on his back on a hard surface.
If unconscious, open airway.
Neck lift, head tilt **or** Chin lift, head tilt

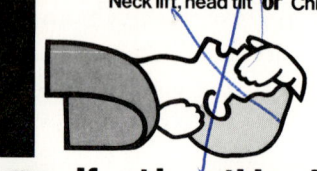

1

2 If not breathing, begin artificial breathing.
4 quick full breaths. If airway is blocked, try back blows, abdominal or chest thrusts and finger probe until airway is open.

3 Check carotid pulse.

4 If pulse absent, begin artificial circulation. Depress sternum 1½" to 2".

One Rescuer	Two Rescuers
15 compressions	5 compressions
rate 80 per min.	rate ~~60~~ per min. 80-100
2 ~~quick~~ slow breaths	1 breath

CONTINUE UNINTERRUPTED UNTIL ADVANCED LIFE SUPPORT IS AVAILABLE

AMERICAN HEART ASSOCIATION
7320 GREENVILLE AVENUE, DALLAS, TEXAS 75231

77-006-AREV
77-50M
9-77 50M
© 1977 American Heart Association

and middle fingers slide into the groove beside the voice box to feel for the pulse. If there is no breathing, and no pulse in the carotid artery in the neck, the victim is suffering cardiac arrest.

If there is no pulse, artificial circulation must be attempted, along with rescue breathing. Artificial circulation is provided by external pressure on the breastbone. This is known as *external cardiac compression*. The rescuer kneels at the victim's side near the chest. Pressure is applied just above the notch at the lowest portion of the breastbone. The rescuer places the heel of one hand on the breastbone 4 to 5 centimeters (1 1/2 to 2 inches) above the notch. The other hand is placed on top of the first. The fingers should be kept off the chest wall. This is easier to do if the fingers are interlocked.

The rescuer's shoulders are moved directly over the victim's chest as the hands press downward. Arms must be kept straight. On an adult victim, the breastbone is pushed down about 4 to 5 centimeters (1 1/2 to 2 inches). Then the pressure is completely relaxed. This allows the victim's chest to return to its normal position. But the rescuer's hands are kept on the victim's chest, ready for the next push. Applying pressure and relaxing pressure should take equal lengths of time.

When there is only one rescuer, she or he must switch back and forth between rescue breathing and cardiac compression. The proper ratio is 15 chest presses to 2 quick breaths. The speed for chest presses should be 80 times per minute when a person is working alone.

When there are two rescuers, they kneel on opposite sides of the victim. One breathes into the victim's mouth during the relaxation after each fifth press. The other rescuer should press the chest 60 times per minute, or once per second.

Reproduced with permission © American Heart Association.

Rescuers	Ratio of Compressions to Breaths	Rate of Compressions
1	15:2	80 times/min.
2	5:1	60 times/min.

Neck injury. If the victim has possibly suffered a neck injury (in a diving or an automobile accident, for example), lift the chin alone, without pressing on the forehead. Do not move the victim's head.

CPR for infants and small children

Basic life support for infants and small children is similar to that for adults, with a few important differences.

Airway. When handling an infant, it is easy to tilt the head back too far. Backward tilting that is forceful might block breathing passages instead of opening them. So tilt the head back by placing one hand under the infant's upper shoulders.

Breathing. Instead of closing an infant's nose with the fingers, the rescuer covers both mouth and nose with his or her own mouth. Small breaths with less air are used to inflate the lungs—one small breath every three seconds.

Circulation. The pulse of an infant or small child is checked by placing the tips of the fingers over the brachial artery on the inside of the upper arm. This pulse can be felt midway between the elbow and the shoulder. The technique for cardiac compression is also different for infants and small children. Only one hand is used for compression. The other hand must be slipped under the infant to provide a firm support for the back.

For infants, only the tips of the index and middle fingers of one hand are used to compress the middle of the chest. The breastbone is pressed down only 1 to 2 1/2 centimeters (1/2 to 1 inch). The rate is faster—100 presses per minute.

For small children, the heel of one hand is used to press the chest. The breastbone can be pressed down 2 1/2 to 4 centimeters (1 to 1 1/2 inches), depending upon the size of the child. The rate should be 80 times per minute.

365

In the case of both infants and small children, breaths are given during the relaxation after every fifth chest compression.

	Part of Hand	Hand Position	How Much to Push	Number of Presses
INFANTS	tips of index and middle fingers	mid-breastbone	1 to 2 1/2 centimeters (1/2 to 1 inch)	100 per minute
CHILDREN	heel of hand	mid-breastbone	2 1/2 to 4 centimeters (1 to 1 1/2 inches)	80 per minute

Unless CPR is performed properly, artificial respiration and circulation are not effective.

Complications, such as rib fractures or fracture of the breastbone, may result from putting external pressure on a victim during CPR. But remember, the alternative to CPR might be death.

Choking

Choking on food or some other object causes many accidental deaths. Most of these deaths can be prevented.

How to avoid choking

In children:

1. Keep small articles that could be swallowed out of the reach of infants and small children.
2. Encourage children to stay seated and calm while eating. Food can easily become lodged in the throat if the child gets excited or trips while walking or running.
3. Remove all bones and shells from foods before giving them to a small child. Don't give nuts, candy containing nuts, or unchopped pieces of meat to small children.
4. Be certain that toys do not contain small parts (such as plastic eyes) that could be chewed or pulled off.

In adults:

1. Eat slowly. Watch for small bones, seeds, or pieces of shell.
2. Cut meat into small pieces.
3. Keep dentures in good repair. Do not wear ill-fitting or defective dentures when sleeping.
4. Be aware that alcoholic beverages decrease sensation in the mouth and lessen one's normal caution in eating. Thus, alcoholic drinks may increase the possibility of choking.

Reproduced with permission © American Heart Association.

How to save a choking victim

Immediate recognition and treatment of choking are necessary if the victim is to survive. The "universal distress signal for choking" is clutching the neck. (See the drawing on page 366.) But not everyone knows about this signal. This emergency is often mistaken for a heart attack. That is why fatal choking accidents in restaurants are sometimes referred to as "café coronaries."

A physician named Dr. Henry Heimlich has developed a simple procedure to save a choking victim. The Heimlich maneuver, as it is called, can be performed by almost anyone. It takes only a few seconds. When a person is choking, follow these steps. If the victim is conscious, and in a sitting or a standing position:

- Stand behind the victim and wrap your arms around the person's waist.
- Make a fist with one hand. Place the thumb side of the fist against the victim's abdomen between the breastbone and the navel.
- Grasp the fist tightly with your other hand.
- Press your fist into the victim's abdomen with a quick upward thrust. Give 4 of these fist thrusts. Repeat abdominal thrusts until the food or other object is forced out or the person becomes unconscious.

Another procedure for saving a choking victim is shown below. It is recommended by both the American Red Cross and the American Heart Association.

FIRST AID FOR CHOKING

CONSCIOUS VICTIM

1. If the victim can speak, cough or breathe, do not interfere.
2. If the victim cannot speak, cough or breathe, give 4 quick back blows.
3. If unsuccessful, give 4 upward abdominal thrusts, or 4 backward chest thrusts.

Repeat above sequence. Be persistent. Continue uninterrupted until advanced life support is available. Call for help #_____

IF VICTIM BECOMES UNCONSCIOUS

1. Open airway and try to ventilate.
2. If unsuccessful, give 4 quick back blows.
3. If unsuccessful, give 4 abdominal or chest thrusts.
4. If unsuccessful, try finger probe.

Repeat above sequence. Be persistent. Continue uninterrupted until advanced life support is available.

AMERICAN HEART ASSOCIATION

The American Heart Association and the American Red Cross recommend this maneuver for an unconscious victim:

- Place the victim on his or her back.
- Roll the victim toward you, using your thigh for support.
- Give 4 forceful and rapidly delivered blows to the back between the shoulder blades.
- Return the victim to his or her back.
- Facing the victim, kneel and straddle the victim's legs.
- Place the heel of one hand on the victim's abdomen between the breastbone and the navel.
- Cover this hand with the other hand and press into the victim's abdomen with 4 quick upward thrusts.
- If the victim does not recover, probe the victim's mouth with hooked finger and then attempt to give rescue breathing.
- If the victim does not begin to breathe, repeat the above steps. BE PERSISTENT.

Infants and small children. To dislodge an object in the airway of a conscious infant, turn the infant upside down over one arm and deliver 4 blows on the back between the shoulder blades.

Main Ideas

1. Many sudden deaths could be prevented if more people knew how to perform cardiopulmonary resuscitation (CPR).
2. CPR is a combination of artificial respiration and artificial circulation.
3. Everyone should know how to contact the emergency medical services system in the community.
4. The universal distress signal for choking is clutching the neck.
5. To save a choking victim, you must know how to recognize and treat the problem quickly.

Key Words

advanced life support
basic life support
cardiac arrest
cardiopulmonary resuscitation

emergency medical services system
external cardiac compression
rescue breathing
respiratory arrest

Apply Your Knowledge

1. Name six unexpected events that could result in a sudden death.
2. In your own words, explain how CPR saves a person's life.
3. List four early warning signs of a heart attack.
4. Explain the difference between basic life support and advanced life support.
5. Do you think your community has an effective emergency medical services (EMS) system? Why, or why not?
6. State four preventive measures that should be used with children to avoid choking.
7. Describe the distress signal for choking.
8. What is a "café coronary"?
9. Suppose you were in a restaurant and someone eating at a nearby table suddenly collapsed. Describe the steps that you (or someone else) should take to help that person.
10. What civic groups or individuals in your community could organize CPR classes so that more people could become trained to perform this procedure?

Extend Your Knowledge

1. What person or group in your community would be responsible for carrying out an effective emergency medical services system? If a community did not have the 911 emergency telephone number, how might the residents obtain this valuable service?
2. What steps would you take to motivate people to take the lifesaving CPR course?
3. In discussing the physiology of death, the terms *clinical death* and *biological death* are frequently used. Explain the relationship of each of these terms to the performance of CPR.
4. Good Samaritan laws protect lay people from liability suits resulting from an injury that a victim might sustain during a rescue effort. Does your community have these laws? Do you think these laws are adequate?
5. Often there are psychological problems related to performing CPR. Discuss one or more of the following concerns that a rescuer may have:
    (a) fear of taking responsibility for someone else's life;
    (b) mouth-to-mouth contact with a possibly dead or dying person;
    (c) risk of "catching something";
    (d) inability to perform when others are watching or when anxious and under pressure.

Unit 10

CHAPTERS:

32 Selecting Health Care
33 Self-care and the Health Consumer
34 Health in the United States
35 Health Careers for You

Health Careers and Services

Chapter 32

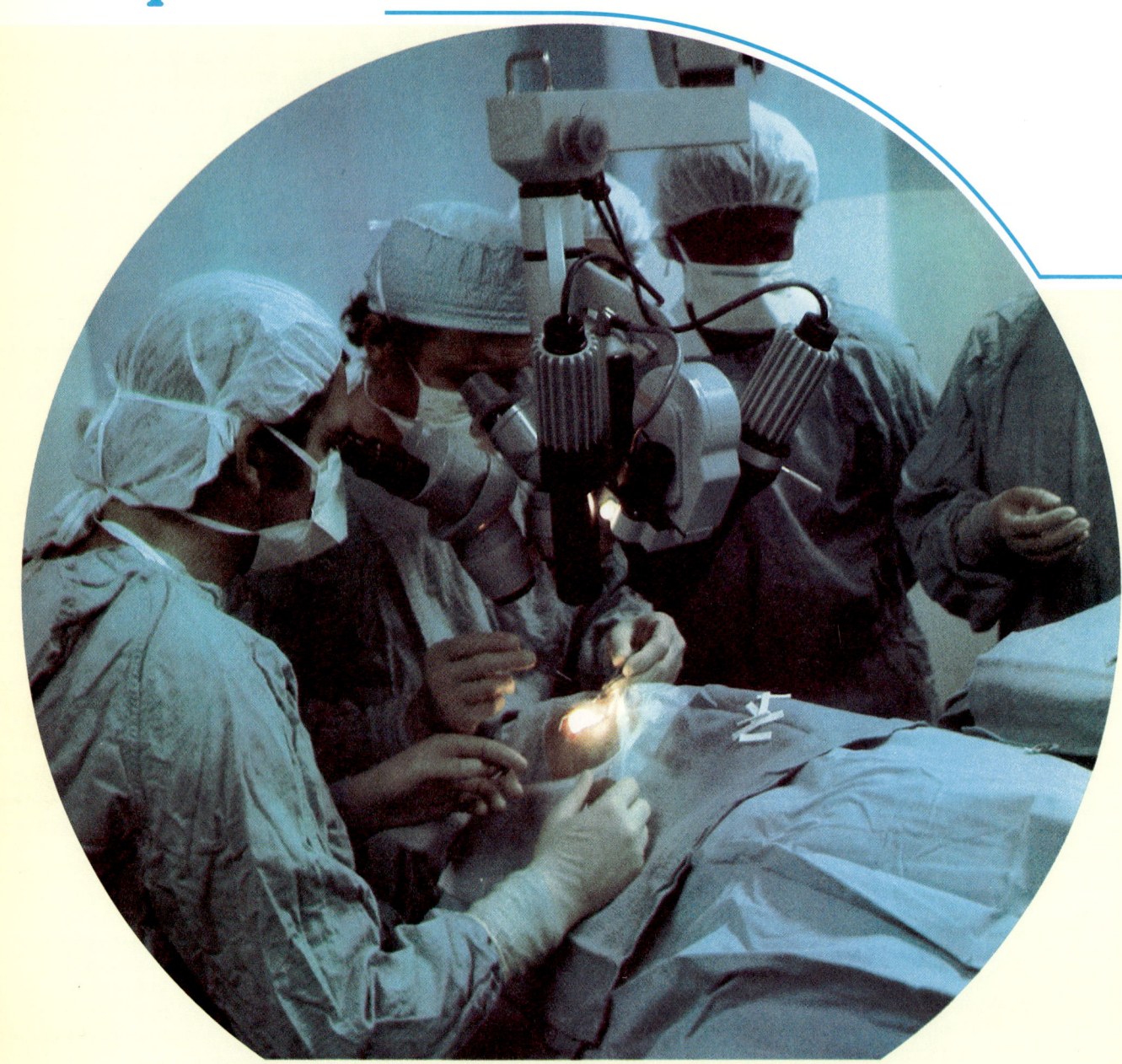

Do you know . . .

- when to call your family doctor?
- when to go to a medical specialist?
- how to talk with your doctor?
- how to spot a medical "quack"?
- about your own medical health history?
- what an internist is?
- what a family doctor is?

Selecting Health Care

Medical care

It is very important to know who can give you the very best medical care during emergencies. But good medical care is also important when you are in good health and trying to prevent disease. You have to trust your doctor with your most valuable possession—your health. Be sure that your doctor is worthy of your confidence.

A doctor should have a license to practice medicine in the state where he or she works. If the doctor specializes in one field of medicine, certificates of training for the specialty should be on view in the doctor's office. Your medical doctor should be a member of the staff of at least one government-approved hospital.

Doctors may be general practitioners or specialists.

Many family doctors are general practitioners. A person studying to become a general practitioner spends three or four years in college and four years in medical school. Next, up to three years is spent as a resident in an approved hospital. This residency is a time of advanced training. After training, doctors must pass a state board examination before receiving a license to practice medicine.

Medical science has grown so quickly that it would be impossible for one person to learn enough to treat all illnesses. Instead, more and more doctors are *specialists.* Specialists spend years studying one system of the human body to learn the most advanced skills in diagnosis and treatment for that field. Special fields a doctor may choose include, for example, brain surgery, medical care for children, treatment of eye disorders, or treatment of skin disease.

Family doctors can recommend a medical specialist to you if they find that you need special attention.

Internists, or diagnosticians, are specialists. They are skilled in diagnosing, or finding out, what illnesses people have. They specialize in internal medicine (medical care for the inside of the human body). Internists must have three years of advanced training in diagnosis and in the care of internal disorders. After training, they must take a special examination to be certified.

The following is a list of some other medical specialists and what they do:

Allergist ... diagnoses and treats patients for asthma, hay fever, hives, and other allergies.

Anesthesiologist ... gives anesthetics (drugs that ease pain) during surgery; checks the condition of the patients before and after surgery.

Cardiologist ... diagnoses and treats heart diseases.

Dermatologist ... diagnoses and treats all forms of skin diseases.

Endocrinologist ... diagnoses and treats problems having to do with the endocrine glands.

Gastroenterologist ... treats gastrointestinal (stomach and intestine) disorders.

Gynecologist ... diagnoses and treats problems having to do with the reproductive organs of women.

Neurologist ... diagnoses and treats problems of the central and peripheral nervous systems.

Obstetrician ... specializes in all aspects of childbirth—care of the mother before, during, and after delivery.

Ophthalmologist ... cares for and corrects eye problems.

Orthopedic surgeon ... performs surgery on bones and joints.

Otolaryngologist ... treats nose, ear, and throat disorders.

Otologist ... treats ear problems.

Pathologist ... carries out laboratory tests of body tissues and fluids; studies the causes of death.

Pediatrician ... specializes in the medical care of children.

Plastic surgeon ... treats skin and soft-tissue deformities; performs surgery to improve external features.

> Psychiatrist... specializes in mental and emotional disorders.
>
> Radiologist... examines and treats patients using X-ray and radium therapy.
>
> Thoracic surgeon... performs surgery on the chest and lungs.
>
> Vascular surgeon... performs surgery on the heart and blood vessels.
>
> Urologist... treats disorders of the urinary tract (kidneys, ureters, urethra); also specializes in treatment of male reproductive organs.

When should you call your family doctor?

Jenny was looking forward to the district track meet. She was the top athlete in the 404.8-meter (440-yard) run and the 809.6-meter (880-yard) run. Two days before the track meet, she began to feel pains in her abdomen. She didn't pay much attention to them, because she had felt pains like these during spring training. The pains got worse and worse. Jenny was nauseated and felt like she was going to vomit. She took her own temperature and found out that she had a fever. She told her father about her symptoms. He reminded her that the flu was going around and suggested that she rest in bed. Jenny's father then called the family doctor to ask what could be done to speed up recovery in time for the track meet. The doctor recommended an examination right away. The examination showed that Jenny had appendicitis. The very next day her swollen appendix was taken out by a surgeon.

Jenny missed the track meet, but she was lucky to have quick medical care. If her father had put off calling the doctor and had given her remedies for the "flu," Jenny's appendix might have burst. Infection would then have spread throughout her abdomen. The result could have been a long, serious illness or even death.

Jenny's case shows a decision that people must often make. At what point should a doctor be called?

Most parents call the family doctor when their child has a fever over 38.5° C (102° F). They usually don't call a doctor if the child has just a runny nose, headache, or scraped knee. The decision is probably based on past experience and clear thinking.

Be aware of the most important warning signals. You should call a doctor at once if you or someone around you shows these signs:

1. pain is very bad and does not go away;
2. blood is coughed up or appears in the stool or urine;

3. diarrhea or vomiting does not stop;
4. fever is high—38.5° C (102° F) or over;
5. breathing is uneven, fast, or short;
6. heartbeat is very fast or not regular;
7. the person is unconscious;
8. there are injuries such as broken bones, cuts, or wounds;
9. the person is confused or in a dazed state; or
10. the person has been bitten by a strange animal.

How to talk with your doctor

When you visit a doctor, you should be able to explain as clearly as possible just what is bothering you. Doctors want you to tell them specifically about your real problems. They will ask questions such as these:

1. What is the major problem? The doctor is trying to find out what bothers you the most. Let's imagine that your main problem is ringing in your ear.

2. How long have you had the problem? The doctor wants to know when you first heard the ringing in your ear. Try to be exact and, if possible, give a date. You should know the answer to this question before you go to the office.

Many people do not understand the medical terms used by their doctor. Don't be afraid to ask. Also, it is your right to know about the cost of treatment and any possible side effects.

3. Have you ever had the problem before? The doctor wants to know about your past medical history. It is important to know if you have allergies, what medicines you may be taking, and what illnesses you have had. This kind of information may be a clue to the cause of the ringing in your ear.

4. Have you had problems with your eyes, nose, glands, digestion, lungs, etc.? The doctor is going over the systems of your body to make sure no information has been overlooked.

5. How do you like school? Do you smoke cigarettes or drink alcohol? Do you take part in sports? These questions have to do with your environment and social setting. Important clues to an illness may be found through questions about your social history. For example, the doctor may learn that you play in the school band and sit right in front of a trumpet player. This may have affected your ear. The doctor can then give certain tests or examine certain parts of the ear to find out the true cause of your problem.

Next step: physical examination

After learning your medical history, the doctor may give you a complete physical examination. This head-to-foot examination is very thorough. The doctor will use different kinds of equipment during the examination. A *tongue depressor* is a flat wooden stick used to press down the tongue to get a better view of the tonsils and throat area. An instrument called an *otoscope* shines a light into the outer ear canal and onto the eardrum. In order to see the retina of the inner eye, the doctor uses an *ophthalmoscope,* an instrument especially designed for this purpose. The doctor listens to the sounds made by your heart and lungs with a *stethoscope.* The *sphygmomanometer* measures blood pressure. To test reflexes, the doctor strikes the patella (knee cap) with a triangular rubber mallet.

The doctor will feel your thyroid and lymph glands, located under the jaw, the armpits, and in the groin region. The abdominal cavity will be checked for strange lumps and swollen organs. The reproductive organs and rectum will also be examined.

Laboratory analysis

The third stage of a medical checkup often includes a chest X ray, blood count, and urinalysis. There are many kinds of blood tests and other laboratory tests. Some special tests include the following:

- analysis of cerebrospinal fluid (fluid in the spinal cord),
- analysis of a throat culture for strep (a bacterial infection),
- analysis of a cervical smear in a PAP test (a test for cancer of the uterus),
- analysis of amniotic fluid in amniocentesis (a test to find out, before birth, whether any of a baby's chromosomes are abnormal).

You will not always be given as complete an examination as the one described above. The type of examination will differ depending upon your illness.

Patients' rights

Regardless of the length or type of checkup, always ask questions when you do not understand the medical terms used by your doctor. You have the right to ask, too, about the methods of treatment the doctor uses and whether they will be painful. If you must have an operation, you will want to ask what the risks are and how much time you will spend recovering.

Before you decide to have a particular treatment, you might want to ask the opinion of a second doctor. This is especially true if the problem is very serious or the treatment very risky.

When to get treatment for mental health problems

Psychiatrists and psychologists are specialists in the treatment of mental health problems. Many people still think these specialists only treat individuals who are "crazy." These people would be embarrassed to be treated for mental health problems. But attitudes toward these specialists are changing fast, as people's ideas about mental health are changing. Did you know that today psychologists and psychiatrists are helping large numbers of normal people?

Sometimes a crisis—breakup of a relationship, death of a close friend or family member, personal failure, overwork—can upset a normal person for a period of time. The person might even be unable to carry out daily activities for a while. Such a person may need the guidance of a psychiatrist or psychologist in order to get through the crisis. At other times, a person might want the advice of a psychologist or psychiatrist to help cope with problems before they develop into crises.

If you decide to seek the help of a psychiatrist or psychologist, don't be embarrassed. Try to relax and be as truthful as possible in answering the questions you are asked.

Oral surgeon ... performs surgery on the jaws and other parts of the mouth if they do not work properly or are injured.
Oral pathologist ... studies diseases of the oral cavity.
Orthodontist ... diagnoses and treats deformities of the teeth.
Endodontist ... diagnoses and treats diseases of the pulp chamber and root canals inside the teeth.
Periodontist ... diagnoses and treats problems of the gums and bones that support the teeth; uses braces to straighten crooked teeth.
Prosthodontist ... specializes in making supporting structures and artificial replacements, or dentures, for missing natural teeth.

Doctors of dental surgery

In addition to doctors of medicine, another group of practitioners is important to our health: doctors of dental surgery. A doctor of dental surgery (D.D.S.), or dentist, is qualified to treat the diseases of the gums, teeth, and jaws. Some get advanced training and specialize in a certain area. Check the list of dental specialists on the previous page.

The medicine show

Many years ago, there were more traveling medicine shows than medical doctors. The traveling medicine shows were popular. They entertained people with songs and comedy. And they convinced many people that sickness, aging, insomnia, and other illnesses could be cured quickly and simply with one of "nature's elixirs" (cure-alls).

Medicine shows were convincing because people were "planted" in the audience to tell how a certain elixir cured their illness. These people were paid by the shows. They often staged their stories with dramatic action. The sales pitch made many listeners think that the "plants," or storytellers, really felt better after taking the elixir. In modern medicine this effect of high expectations is called the *placebo effect*. In medical experiments, a placebo looks the same as a medicine that is being tested. The placebo itself usually has no medicine in it. It is given to patients to see how they react to the suggestion that they are taking medicine. The patient and even the physician may not know which is the real medicine and which is the placebo. Researchers have found that one-third of the patients taking a placebo will show improvement. This shows that medicine is often effective because of the placebo effect and not because of its chemical qualities.

Medicine shows are still around today, but they aren't on wagons pulled by horses from city to city. Instead, printed advertising has taken over. About 200 million people spend $2 billion each year to buy miracle cures for cancer, lifelong cures for arthritis, instant weight-reducers, devices claimed to be breast enlargers, so-called health foods, and vitamins that are not needed. The audience is larger than ever, but the pitch remains the same.

There are many reasons why some people think they are helped by devices and products that really have limited value. Just like the make-believe healers of years past, modern "quacks" use our deepest fears of disease, illness, pain, and death to sell their products. When family doctors and specialists cannot cure us or ease our pain, we sometimes become frightened. Worried people may be easily swayed by overstated claims because they want so much to find hope somewhere.

Many diseases are self-limited. The human body has many defense systems that fight illness. That means most patients recover from illness in time, whether or not they get proper treatment. A person may think a "miracle treatment" has brought about a cure when, in fact, the disease has simply run its course.

Other diseases are *chronic,* or ongoing. A person may seem to improve at times and become worse at other times. Arthritis, stomach ulcers, epilepsy, and some types of cancer are examples of chronic illnesses. A reliable doctor will tell the patient that there will be ups and downs. A good doctor will also explain that the patient can be helped but probably not cured. But a person or organization selling a "miracle cure" may take advantage of the situation. Treatment may be given and a cure claimed when improvement comes. Then, when a relapse occurs, the patient is told that treatments were stopped too soon. More treatment is prescribed.

Sometimes illness is caused by emotional problems. Because of the placebo effect, the patient may get better with any kind of treatment that takes the mind off of the problems. Such improvement is only short-lived. But this may not be explained. And when symptoms appear again, the patient may lose faith in the treatment. Then she or he may go from one kind of "sure-cure" to another, hoping for a magical cure.

Another kind of deception happens when "cures" are claimed for diseases that a person may not even have.

How to guard against "medical quackery"

The American Medical Association suggests that people use common sense to protect themselves from unreliable medical products and advisers. Be suspicious and report to your local Better Business Bureau when

- a person or company claims that it alone has a special formula or a newly invented machine that will cure a certain disease.
- a person or company guarantees that you will be cured very quickly. (In medicine there are no guarantees. Cases differ in many ways.)
- a product is sold by mail or door-to-door, especially when case histories and testimonials are stressed in the advertising.
- the person or organization claims that it is being mistreated by the medical profession because of fear of competition.
- the advertising demands use of the product for a "trial period" to test the treatment.
- you are encouraged to ignore medical advice you may have already received regarding surgery, X rays, or prescribed drugs.

Something to think about . . .

We live in an information explosion. Radio, television, newspapers, and magazines give up-to-the-minute reports on almost everything. But reports may conflict, and news may be inaccurate. It is imperative that we learn to evaluate news about drugs and medical procedures that may be critically important to our well-being.

How can you evaluate a story about a "miracle drug"? These questions may be helpful.

1. *What is the source of the story?* A national health institute, medical school, or major medical center is likely to release more significant news about a new drug than a pharmaceutical company or a single practitioner.
2. *What stage of research is reported?* Is the drug being tested in test tubes, in animals, or in human subjects? Clinical research involving human subjects will yield more meaningful results about drugs intended for human use.
3. *How valid were the clinical testing procedures?* Drug research may be influenced by the subject's desire to get well and the investigator's desire to have positive results. Medical research has found that a relatively constant one-third of all patients respond positively to any substance that they believe is medication (See "Something To Think About," Chapter 17). "Double-blind testing" neutralizes both patient and investigator influences. In such tests, one group of patients receives the drug being tested. A second, similar group receives placebos—inert "medications" that look, taste, and are administered exactly like the drug being tested. The two substances are coded by an independent person so that the patients, the people administering the substances, and the observers recording the results of the experiment do not know who received the real drug. The random selection of patients involved in such testing is also important.
4. *How extensive was the testing?* Tests with large sample populations, performed over fairly long periods of time, are likely to reveal results that are found to be valid in general practice. Follow-up studies that

Medicine shows are still around today, but they are not on wagons pulled by horses from city to city. Instead, printed advertising now sells us "miracle cures." The American Medical Association suggests that people use common sense to protect themselves against medical quackery.

look for the effects of prolonged use, or for possible later side effects, are also important.

5. *How completely are the results of the study reported?* An evaluation of the seriousness of the side effects and a comparison of the new drug or treatment with drugs or medical practices currently used are important elements in medical reporting.*

* Adapted from "How to Evaluate News About Miracles," *The Medicine Show,* Consumers Union of the U.S., Inc., Mt. Vernon, New York, 1976.

Main Ideas

1. The family doctor or general practitioner is often the first person to turn to during illness.
2. Medical history is important to the doctor in making a diagnosis.
3. It is important to know the main danger signals that tell you when to contact the family doctor.
4. A family doctor will recommend specialists for serious or complicated illnesses.
5. Many sick people spend large amounts of money on unreliable cures.
6. If you think you are a victim of a quack, contact the Better Business Bureau.

Key Words

allergist
chronic diseases
dermatologist
gynecologist
internist
medical quack
obstetrician
ophthalmoscope
otoscope
pediatrician
placebo effect
specialist
sphygmomanometer
stethoscope
tongue depressor
urologist

Apply Your Knowledge

1. List ten warning signals that mean you should call a doctor.
2. Describe what happens in the three stages of a medical checkup.
3. What are six ways of detecting a medical "quack?"
4. Give at least three reasons why people sometimes become victims of exaggerated or false medical claims.
5. How do internists differ from family doctors?
6. Describe the placebo effect.
7. Why are there many specialists in the medical field? What kinds of new specialists would you expect to see in the future?
8. How are gynecologists and obstetricians related?
9. What is an otoscope?
10. What does the abbreviation D.D.S. mean?

Extend Your Knowledge

1. If you were a cardiologist, what would you want to know from your patient? Make a list of questions you would ask the patient.
2. If you were a victim of medical quackery, what steps would you take to put the person or company out of business?
3. Make a list of 20 radio and television advertisements for medical or related products or services. Decide which are on the borderline of quackery. For each advertisement that you think is not true, explain your reasoning.
4. Write down, in detail, your medical history. Check with your parents about childhood diseases and immunizations.
5. Many medical terms come from Greek and Latin roots. For example, *cardiology* comes from *cardio-*, meaning "heart," and *-logy*, meaning "the study of." Using a dictionary that gives word histories, look up the following terms and list their literal meanings: *dermatology, gynecology, neurology, ophthalmology, otology, pathology, urology.*

Chapter 33

Do you know . . .
- what primary care is?
- what secondary care is?
- how much hospital care might cost?
- that self-care is preventive medicine?
- when tetanus shots are needed?
- what your doctor writes on a prescription?
- how to read labels on "over-the-counter" medical products?

Self-care and the Health Consumer

Self-care does not mean self-treatment or self-medication. Self-care means that you know enough to be responsible for your own health. The health goal that you set for yourself is self-care.

You don't need a family doctor to remind you that exercise is important for the heart. A specialist doesn't have to tell you that a proper diet must be followed if you want to stay in shape. And everyone knows smoking is harmful to both lungs and heart. You also know that alcohol can irritate the stomach lining and that drugs are not the answer to indigestion, cough, or every pain. Self-care is simply a commonsense way to practice preventive medicine.

Being an intelligent *health consumer* is part of self-care. Choosing the right medical treatment center, buying medicines, knowing the cost of health care, and investing in a medical insurance plan make up a total health care program.

The health consumer

If you are an informed consumer, you will be able to choose the best and the most economical products being sold.

What should you know about health insurance?

Can you afford to pay $200 or more each day you are in the hospital? Doctors' fees, the cost of medicine, and hospital charges are much higher now than they were a few years ago. Also, methods of diagnosis and treatment of illnesses have become more complex. Because the cost of good health care has increased greatly, few people today can afford to pay all the costs of a major illness themselves.

Many people in the United States have bought health insurance plans. Such plans help to pay the costs of medical bills. Other people, such as those with low incomes and older people on Social Security, are able to get government aid to pay for health care. *Medicare* is a program of health insurance available to those over 65. *Medicaid* is available to those who cannot afford private health insurance. Private health insurance plans are called *voluntary insurance*.

People who cannot get government aid and who do not have insurance must pay the full amount of health care themselves. In the case of a serious illness, these costs may be very high. It may be very hard, or even impossible, to pay them.

Many people belong to group health insurance plans at the places where they work. Other people buy insurance policies on their own. The costs of these insurance plans differ a great deal. So do their benefits. If you buy health insurance in the future, be sure that you fully understand the cost of the insurance policy and the amount of the benefits you can receive from it. You should also know exactly what health care your insurance will pay for.

Many insurance plans do not provide enough coverage. People find that they cannot plan their budgets to afford health insurance. And most people are not able to get government aid. These facts have caused political pressure for a standardized national health insurance program in the United States. Many other countries have plans like this. Those in favor of such a program stress that it would make proper health care available to everyone, rich or poor. People who are against it feel that a national health insurance plan would be costly to taxpayers. They also feel that medical care would not be as good as it is now.

Every health care center is different.

As a consumer, you should be careful to choose a family doctor who you know will send you to a good specialist when you need one. Your doctor should also be associated with the best medical center in your area. The following are terms you should know when choosing a medical center:

Primary care: treatment that is given by a doctor at a clinic, emergency room, or doctor's office. This care is also called "ambulatory" or "outpatient" care.

Secondary care: treatment that is given by specialists at a private or community hospital. This care is also referred to as "hospital" or "inpatient" care.

Tertiary care: treatment that is given by specialists at a hospital which is part of a university. Some types of operations, such as experimental heart surgery and organ transplants, can be done in these hospitals.

Medical centers have improved.

Less than a century ago, many people refused to go to a hospital for care. Conditions were not clean. Many attendants, if they had any training at all, were poorly trained. Patients with mental illness or contagious diseases often were confined without good care. Many patients died in hospitals. Some died of the diseases that they had when they entered the hospital. Others died of infections they got in the hospital.

Today's hospitals give good and total medical services. They also make the patient as comfortable as possible. Many kinds of medical treatment can be given only in a hospital. Laboratories, X-ray equipment, and operating rooms are important tools in diagnosing and treating disease. For example, one new development is the modern X-ray machine unit called the Computerized Tomographic Scanner (CTS). It can take tens of thousands of X-ray readings in less than five seconds. The scanner makes cross-sectional views of any part of the head or body. With this new tool, physicians are able to locate tumors and other internal problems. Now, surgery is not needed to discover such problems.

Greater resources in the hospital

In a medical center, such as a hospital, the family doctor and the medical specialist can work as a team. Trained registered and practical nurses, technicians, and many other hospital staff members are also part of the team.

Self-care

Staying healthy is your own responsibility. You decide what happens to your health by good self-care, or preventive medicine. Preventive medicine means working to keep yourself healthy and finding ways to keep from getting diseases. Choosing the best doctor, going to the best medical center, and having the most complete health insurance are good practices. Good self-care may mean that some of these measures may not be used. Preventive medicine may save you a good deal of money and time.

Good self-care includes using your common sense to avoid things that can be harmful to your health. For example, painful sunburn can be avoided simply by making sure that you don't expose yourself too long to the ultraviolet rays of the sun. Also, indigestion can be avoided by being careful about the amounts and types of food you eat. You may or may not have to see a doctor if either of these disorders affects you. It depends on your self-care. Do you know how to prevent illness or to avoid those things that may be harmful to you?

Taking your temperature is part of self-care. What would you do if your temperature were 101°?

Some people think self-care means never getting a doctor's help and never taking any medication. They think all drugs are harmful. These people abuse the responsibility of self-care by refusing medical treatment and drugs that could be helpful and even necessary. Don't be a fanatic about your own self-care. Instead, find out whether or not the risk of taking a drug is less than the risk of doing without it.

Immunization is preventive medicine.

Immunization is a way of using medicine that can keep you from getting certain diseases. Usually, injections or "shots" are given that put antidisease substances into the body. When you were a child, your parents probably had you immunized for diphtheria, pertussis (whooping cough), tetanus, polio, mumps, measles, and rubella (German measles). These diseases can be controlled, but today some parents are not having their children immunized. And, in recent years, cases of measles have become common. Many schools have closed their doors to children who have not been immunized.

If you have been immunized regularly, according to the schedules set up by pediatricians, you should be immune to the following diseases by age five: diphtheria, pertussis, tetanus, polio, measles, mumps, and rubella. To prevent getting diphtheria and tetanus, you should have a booster shot (added immunizing medicine) every ten years. If you got your last diphtheria and tetanus (DT) shots at age five, you should have another one at age fifteen. Have you had your boosters?

In addition to common sense and immunization, here are a few other preventive measures:

1. **Skin tests and chest X rays are good ways to check for tuberculosis.**
2. **Remember the early warning signs for cancer, and avoid the environmental dangers that can cause cancer.**
3. **Learn how to take your own blood pressure, and know how to avoid hypertension.**
4. **Breast self-examination, a way to check for suspicious lumps along the breast and armpits, is recommended for both males and females.**

Can some medicines be harmful to you?

Every year, people in the United States spend billions of dollars for drugs without the advice of a good doctor. Many of the drugs bought for self-treatment are of little or no value. Others may be harmful.

When you are ill, your family doctor uses tests and questions to decide what kind of medication is best for you. Let your doctor know if you are taking medication of any kind. If you are taking over-the-counter drugs (called OTC drugs) and your doctor prescribes a different drug, the mixing of the two could be dangerous.

Let your doctor know if you have any allergies. Also let the doctor know if you have ever been allergic to an antibiotic. If antibiotics or other drugs are prescribed for you to treat an illness, throw away leftover medications after you are well. Do not take them for another illness without seeing a doctor. Taking antibiotics without a doctor's advice can make you resistant to their effects. But do make sure you take all the doctor prescribes. Not taking an antibiotic for as long as you should may cure symptoms but not the disease. Later, the symptoms could return again.

What should a prescription say?

A prescription is a written note from your doctor to a pharmacist. It tells the pharmacist what kind of medicine you need and how often you should take it.

A prescription should have at least the following information: name of the medication, amount, dose (*dosage*), date when it is no longer good or useful (the "expiration" date), how long between doses, specific instructions, and your name. Specific information, such as "refrigerate," "take only on full stomach," or "shake well before using," is important to help the medicine work well.

Doctors and pharmacists can make mistakes when writing or preparing your prescription. It is your responsibility, as a consumer, to read the prescription and understand what you are taking. Don't be afraid to ask your doctor or pharmacist about your prescription.

If you are curious about the instructions written on the prescription by your doctor, you can use the following list to help figure out the information:

SPECIAL ABBREVIATIONS USED BY YOUR DOCTOR

ad lib.	as needed	q.2h	every 2 hours
agit. a. us.	shake before using	q.3h	every 3 hours
a.c.	before meals	q.4h	every 4 hours
b.i.d.	twice a day	q.i.d.	4 times a day
dieb. alt.	every other day	q.s.	as much as is needed
o.d.	every day	stat.	immediately
p.c.	after meals	t.i.d.	three times a day
q.h.	every hour	p.r.n.	when needed

Nonprescription or over-the-counter drugs

Labels and warnings on OTC drugs help to protect you against using them in the wrong way. They also protect you against possible harmful effects. A federal law requires all OTC drugs to have the following information on the labels:

Many drugs come in special tamperproof packaging. A few examples are shown below.

Bubble Pack

Shrink Wrap

Vacuum Seal

1. name of the product;
2. name and address of the manufacturer, packer, or distributor;
3. net content of the package;
4. active ingredients and the amount of certain ingredients;
5. name of any habit-forming drug contained in the prescription;
6. warnings and cautions needed for the protection of the user;
7. proper directions for safe and effective use.

Before buying any OTC drug, check to make sure that the package has not been opened. Most drugs now come in special tamperproof packaging. Do not buy any drug with a broken seal or wrap.

What do you have in your medicine cabinet?

If you checked your medicine cabinet, how many different kinds of drugs would you find? The medicine cabinet in an average home probably holds these drugs:

1. some kind of antiseptic, such as iodine or hydrogen peroxide;
2. decongestants, such as nose drops and spray for allergy;
3. cough syrups for sore throats and colds;
4. aspirin or aspirin substitutes for pain and fever;
5. antacid for stomach upsets.

Here are some important things you should know about these common OTC medications.

Antiseptics, such as hydrogen peroxide and iodine, may be good for cleaning wounds and for killing bacteria. Three percent hydrogen peroxide is good as a cleaning agent. But the peroxide used for bleaching hair is too strong. Remove all embedded dirt with soap and warm water or hydrogen peroxide from wounds that are small and can be treated at home. If the dirt cannot be removed, see a doctor.

Decongestants are drugs used primarily to ease congestion. The drugs cause the membrane in your nose to "shrink" in order to stop too much secretion. Two decongestants are ephedrine and phenylephrine. These drugs work only for several hours. When these drugs are used for several days, the membranes of the nose will again produce more secretions. See your doctor to find out the cause of an allergy or congestion. If antihistamines must be used, use only a small amount. Since some antihistamines cause drowsiness, do not take them if you must drive. Follow carefully the directions on the label.

Cough syrups can make you cough to help remove anything that is irritating the trachea. They can also help stop your cough. Cough syrups that help you produce sputum contain an *expectorant,* an ingredient that makes you cough more. Cough syrups that help to quiet the cough center contain an ingredient called an *antitussive.* Sometimes a dry, hacking cough may prevent sleep. In those cases, a cough syrup with dextromethorphan, an antitussive, may help. Most cough syrup labels suggest that you stop taking a cough syrup and contact your doctor if the cough does not go away in three days.

NAME OF PRODUCT

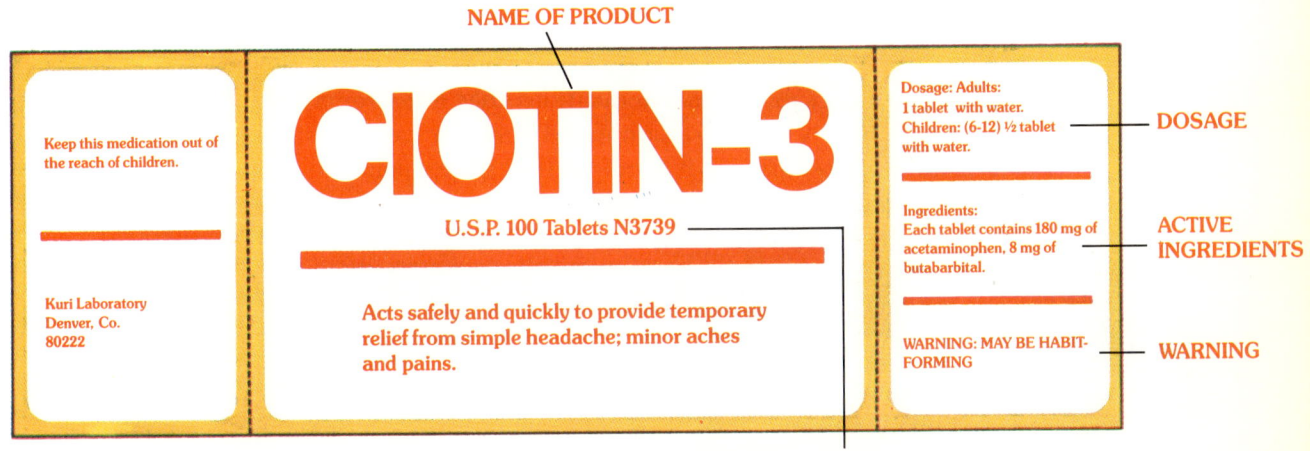

CIOTIN-3

U.S.P. 100 Tablets N3739

Keep this medication out of the reach of children.

Kuri Laboratory
Denver, Co.
80222

Acts safely and quickly to provide temporary relief from simple headache; minor aches and pains.

Dosage: Adults: 1 tablet with water. Children: (6-12) ½ tablet with water. — **DOSAGE**

Ingredients: Each tablet contains 180 mg of acetaminophen, 8 mg of butabarbital. — **ACTIVE INGREDIENTS**

WARNING: MAY BE HABIT-FORMING — **WARNING**

ACCEPTED STANDARDS AND NET CONTENT

Aspirin or aspirin substitutes are used for many illnesses. People with arthritis use aspirin to decrease swelling of the joints. Many people use aspirin to lower fever and ease pain. Although some people think aspirin may be effective, it cannot cure diseases. Aspirin only treats symptoms. Using too much aspirin may irritate the stomach or cause a ringing in the ears. If your bottle of aspirin has a vinegary odor, throw it away. You've kept it too long.

Antacids decrease acid in the stomach. One major type of antacid is called *systemic*. These popular and widely advertised antacids contain sodium bicarbonate that neutralizes or decreases hydrochloric acid quickly. However, it does not have a long-term neutralizing effect. The disadvantage of systemic antacids is that they dissolve and are absorbed into the bloodstream. Then the kidneys must work hard to keep the acid-and-base balance in the body.

The second major type of antacid is called *nonsystemic*. These antacids are not absorbed, or taken into the bloodstream. Some contain magnesium and make the feces soft. Others contain aluminum and make the feces hard. If you have stomach pains, *don't* take any antacids before seeing your doctor to find out the cause of the pain.

Clean your medicine cabinet.

How long have you had the drugs in your medicine cabinet? Do you still have the medicine from your last cold? Many of the OTC drugs have an expiration date. This date shows that the drug may no longer be useful. Most antibiotics lose their effectiveness over a period of time. The antibiotic tetracycline may even become poisonous after the expiration date.

If you leave your medicine cabinet open, the drugs inside will be exposed to the light. This may make the drugs lose their strength, or po-

Labels and warnings on over-the-counter drugs help to protect you against using them in the wrong way. Follow directions carefully!

tency. If you do not tightly screw the caps on medicine bottles, the moisture and warmth of the bathroom may make pills crumble. Other medications may decompose or break down into their chemical elements. Some medicines, such as iodine and cough syrups, are mixed with alcohol. If bottles are not properly closed, or if they are old, the alcohol will evaporate, leaving harmful substances. Medications that must remain sterile, such as eye drops, may become contaminated through careless storage. Bacteria will grow in the solution. Medications that have sugar may also grow bacteria if they are kept too long.

Many over-the-counter drugs have a date stamped on them which tells when they are no longer useful. How long have you had the drugs in your medicine cabinet?

Drugs no one knows much about

Many new drugs and chemical products are constantly being developed by researchers. These and other, older drugs and chemical products are being tested by new methods for their harmful effects. One government agency in Washington, D.C., which tests new and old products is the *Food and Drug Administration (FDA)*. The FDA makes sure all products meet government safety and health standards. If a certain product does not meet these standards, the FDA removes it from the market.

Drug manufacturers must get permission to put a new drug onto the market from the New Drugs Section of the FDA. Before the drug can be accepted, the manufacturer must submit a report of the studies made on the drug.

One job of the Food and Drug Administration (FDA) is to test old and new drug products. The FDA makes sure all products meet government health and safety levels.

The FDA is our public health defender. It gives us the latest scientific opinion on all kinds of products, from cold pills, lipsticks, and hair dyes, to food colorings. But the findings of the FDA do not always agree with the findings of other scientists in the United States and in other countries. Some people think that the FDA makes public health regulations very cautiously. For example, let's say that an artificial sweetener is thought to cause cancer in animals. The FDA wants to remove it from the market. But this drug is very important for people who suffer from diabetes and must not use real sugar in their diet. Sometimes the immediate useful effects of a drug must be weighed against the potential side effects.

How can you know for sure about the drugs and chemical products you use? How can you know about the latest findings of the FDA? Today, television and radio are the major voices of scientists and organizations like the FDA that constantly discover new facts about what we use. Make a habit of listening to the evening news to get the latest facts. Don't be uninformed about the products you use.

Would you rather pay a doctor for treating you when you are sick, or for helping you to keep from getting sick? Instead of making unexpected, high-cost payments for care when they are sick, many people in the United States are joining Health Maintenance Organizations (HMOs). These organizations offer round-the-clock health care. For some HMO members, there is a fixed monthly fee. For others, membership is paid for in part or in full by their employers, replacing traditional medical insurance.

Something to think about . . .

Physical examinations, including X rays, blood tests, cardiograms, and other specialized diagnostic tests, are available to HMO members at no additional cost. Care during illnesses or medical emergencies, including surgery and hospitalization, is also covered by the regular monthly payments. These payments, along with government support, create a fund that helps cover the costs of establishing and running a Health Maintenance Organization. The cost of treating patients is paid for out of the fund. HMOs attempt to keep medical costs low by promoting health measures and practicing preventive medicine.

HMOs keep medical costs down in other ways. Doctors always treat patients. But nurse specialists and physician's assistants administer routine health care. Also, prepayment for medical services encourages people to seek care early in the development of illnesses. With early medical care, possibly serious conditions can be detected when they are less difficult and less expensive to cure. Finally, HMOs eliminate the nuisance of health insurance claim forms and medical bills.

HMO physicians earn a fixed yearly salary, which is generally less than the amount that traditional fee-for-service doctors earn. However, group practice offers HMO doctors a number of advantages. Physicians working together benefit by sharing their knowledge and expertise. They are able to devote their time to the practice of medicine rather than to administrative and financial concerns. Group practice also allows physicians to take regular time off for enjoyment or for professional enrichment.

In 1982 there were 267 HMOs in the United States, with a membership of almost 11 million people. New HMOs are beginning to develop all over the country. Is there an HMO in your area?

Main Ideas

1. Self-care does not mean self-medication.
2. The cost of health care can be very high without medical insurance to help pay expenses.
3. Hospitals are equipped with the most modern testing and surgical equipment.
4. Good self-care means using your common sense to avoid those things that can be harmful to your health.
5. Immunization is one form of preventive medicine.
6. It is very important to read the labels on both prescribed and OTC drugs.
7. Your medicine cabinet may contain outdated medicine that may be harmful to you.

Key Words

antacid	expectorant	primary care
antihistamine	FDA	secondary care
antiseptic	immunization	self-care
antitussive	Medicaid	systemic
Computerized Tomographic Scanner	health consumer	tertiary care
decongestant	Medicare	voluntary insurance
dosage	nonsystemic	
	OTC drugs	

Apply Your Knowledge

1. What is the difference between self-care and self-medication?
2. Explain the total self-care concept.
3. Explain the difference between primary and secondary care.
4. List some of the ways you can practice self-care.
5. Make a list of all the diseases to which you are immune.
6. List four types of disease-preventive measures.
7. Name some OTC drugs that your family keeps in the medicine cabinet.
8. If you have to make an emergency visit to the hospital, why should you bring with you all medications you are taking?
9. List all of the information that must appear on all medicines sold over the counter.
10. List all of the information that physicians must include on a prescription.

Extend Your Knowledge

1. Assume that your city has five hospitals and each one purchases an expensive Computerized Tomographic Scanner. What effect will this have on health care costs? Do you think it is necessary for all hospitals to have the best equipment? Why?
2. Ask your pharmacist about "rebound effect" the next time you purchase any form of antihistamine.
3. Make a list of the medicines you think you should have in your medicine cabinet. Give a reason for each one.
4. Ask your parents if you can study the health insurance plan for your family. Check to see what medical expenses are covered by the insurance.
5. Examine several of the advertisements for medicine on television and in magazines. Check to see if there are any distortions or false claims.

Chapter 34

Do you know . . .

- that epidemics and plagues are still possible in the United States?
- what the term *public health* means?
- who is responsible for keeping our water clean and fit to drink?
- what a "disease detective" is?

Health in the United States

How healthy are people in the United States? How long can Americans expect to live? Will living in our environment become so harmful to our health that we will not live as long as we do now?

Experts believe that by the year 2000 people can expect their average life span to be 80 years. How healthy we will be then will depend a great deal on our eating and drinking habits. Our life span will also depend on preventive medicine, health care methods, and the state of our environment.

Today, we take it for granted that standards have been set up for pure water, clean air, safe food, and proper medications. We think that these standards make sure that the quality of the environment, of food, and of medicine is the same everywhere in the United States. However, these set standards can protect us only as long as they stay in effect. New problems keep coming up. Technology and government red tape can keep us from solving these problems quickly.

History of our healthy nation

People organized governments when they began to live in villages, towns, and cities. They made laws to control things that were important to them as a group. No one person could deal with these matters alone. Governments took care of police and fire protection, water supplies, disposal of wastes, and protection and improvement of *public health*. Public health means the health of everybody, not just certain individuals.

In the past, communicable or contagious diseases were the greatest health problem. Preventing the spread of these illnesses was the biggest health concern of governments. Quarantine and smallpox vaccination are examples of early methods that helped to stop the spread of communicable diseases. Later, it was discovered that communicable diseases are caused by microorganisms. Ways to kill these microorganisms were organized in society. They include making drinking water pure, disposing of sewage, and pasteurizing milk. Other methods of destroying these organisms are inspecting food supplies and killing off insects that spread disease. Modern cities could not exist without such services.

Little by little, many other health services have been added to the responsibilities of government. However, the government does not provide the only health services. Business and labor organizations and voluntary health associations also help to fight disease and to improve health.

Health services

Services provided by your city health department

Your city, county, or town health department is responsible for the following:

1. Keeping stray animals off the street. Have you ever been bitten by a stray dog? In many cities, dogs that are abandoned by owners run in packs. They become hunters and tip over trash cans, looking for food. Then rodents and flies eat the garbage. In this way, stray dogs add to the spread of diseases.
2. Inspecting kitchens in restaurants and hotels. Did you ever have stomach pains after eating out? If you did, you may have had food poisoning. Your city health department checks the cleanliness of eating places. It tries to make sure that food is prepared in a safe and clean way.
3. Removing wastes. We are a nation of "throw-aways." We throw away everything from paper diapers to plastic spoons. Your health board supervises how these solid wastes are collected and destroyed.
4. Examining the water supply. Clean water is needed for the survival of a city. The local health department makes sure that the minimum standards of water purity set by federal health agencies are followed.
5. Inspecting hotels, motels, and all public buildings. Are bed bugs, lice and other "critters" things of the past? No one sleeping in hotels or motels wants to find these pests. The local health department makes sure that buildings used by the public are sanitary.
6. Coordinating neighborhood health centers and clinics. These clinics give care to those who would have a hard time finding it elsewhere. The clinics usually deal with problems related to unwanted pregnancies, drug abuse, mental illness, and sexually transmitted diseases.
7. Collecting and analyzing *vital data* (needed information). Can you imagine a city the size of New York not keeping records of the marriages, births, and the health status of its people? Records are also kept of the number and causes of deaths. This kind of information is used to plan for future needs and to control health problems.

Information about the causes of death in a city can be fed into a computer for quick analysis. Public health officials can very quickly find out if an epidemic seems to be starting.

Every state has a department of health.

City and state departments of health have similar jobs. The state department of health usually deals with problems too large for local or city departments. Special health services, such as running large centers for mentally and physically handicapped people, are usually funded by state governments.

What you can expect from federal health services

The federal government is responsible for public health services that cross state boundaries. It gives a great deal of money to these state and local health services to carry out their programs. They must, however, meet government standards before receiving such help.

The *Department of Health and Human Services* (formerly the Department of Health, Education, and Welfare) includes the following agencies: the Public Health Service, the Food and Drug Administration, the National Institutes of Health, the Office of Human Development Services, the Office of Child Support Enforcement, the Office of Community Services, and the Social Security Administration.

City water supplies must be checked often for pollution. In this laboratory, special tests are made to find small amounts of detergent and other substances that sometimes get into drinking water.

The most important federal agency that takes care of public health is the Public Health Service: This agency:

1. supports research programs in all areas of health and disease. Many of these programs are carried out in universities, hospitals, and research institutes all over the United States.
2. investigates and controls serious outbreaks of communicable diseases anywhere in the United States.
3. prevents communicable diseases from entering the United States from other countries.
4. certifies the safety, quality, and usefulness of vaccines (serums that prevent or treat diseases).
5. gives information about the prevention and treatment of disease.

The Centers for Disease Control (CDC), in Atlanta, Georgia, is a branch of the Public Health Service. Some activities the CDC is concerned with are the control of communicable diseases, urban rat control, prevention of lead poisoning in children, and the safety of workers on their jobs. The CDC provides its services to people all over the world.

Epidemiologists, or "disease detectives," at the CDC track down the source of infection when an outbreak of infectious disease occurs. Then health officials try to stop the disease from spreading. CDC officials have tracked down the source of epidemics of typhoid, malaria, hepatitis, and sexually transmitted diseases throughout the United States. Sometimes these diseases can still be serious health hazards.

In 1977, the CDC helped to track down the carrier of the mysterious "legionnaires' disease." This previously unknown illness took the lives of a number of veterans who had met for a convention. After a long trial-and-error search, CDC officials found that the disease is a microorganism carried in the droppings of pigeons. The virus was spread by pigeon droppings in the air conditioners of hotel rooms where the veterans were staying.

Nongovernmental voluntary health agencies also work for public health.

Voluntary agencies do important work in medical research and health education. The American Heart Association, the Arthritis Foundation, the National Foundation-March of Dimes, and the National Association for Mental Health are examples of such voluntary agencies. Sometimes they show a community what can or should be done and then turn the work over to local agencies supported by taxes.

The American National Red Cross and the American Heart Association help to teach large numbers of people methods of saving lives. Still other agencies are interested in the needs of special groups. Such agencies work to help crippled children, the blind, the deaf, babies, the mentally retarded, and veterans, among others. There are visiting-nurse associations that provide health instruction and nursing care for patients in their own homes. Safety councils work to prevent accidents.

Voluntary health agencies do important work in medical research and in health education. The American National Red Cross teaches many people methods of saving lives.

Professional associations, such as the American Medical Association, the American Public Health Association, the American Dental Association, and the American Nurses Association, have added much to the knowledge of diseases. These groups also work to inform the public about ways to prevent disease and injury.

An important function of voluntary health agencies is the sharing of their information and expertise. On request they may provide free pamphlets, newsletters, and posters. You can write for this free information. Check the address list at the end of this chapter.

A special health organization

A special agency of the United Nations, the *World Health Organization (WHO)*, has its headquarters in Geneva, Switzerland. The goal of WHO is to improve the level of physical and mental health of all the world's people. This is one of the goals that can be reached only by worldwide cooperation.

The major activities of WHO are these:

1. to give new information about medical and health matters, such as epidemics and research results, to all countries;
2. to stop the illegal traffic of narcotic drugs;
3. to stop serious communicable diseases from spreading from country to country;

4. to give financial and technical help to countries that need help to control communicable diseases;
5. to give emergency aid to countries which must deal with epidemic diseases such as malaria, typhus fever, yellow fever, and tuberculosis; to help with special health problems, such as the care of refugees (needy people who must leave their homelands);
6. to get all people to use good methods of fighting water, soil, food, and air pollution; to spread information on family planning.

Toward better health for everyone

Today, health plays a large part in every community. Taxes support public health agencies that care about the health of all citizens. There are laws to protect your health. Different agencies work on special health problems. Millions of dollars are spent for medical research and for health care.

Still more information is needed about how to keep people healthy. It is also important to make full use of the knowledge we already have. Each person has the responsibility to keep as strong and healthy as possible. Everyone should work with the governmental and voluntary organizations that have been set up to protect and improve health.

Volunteers play an important part in protecting and improving the health of people in the United States. The work of volunteers is the backbone of many health organizations.

Have you ever experienced any side effects from medications? It is expected that people will react differently to various medicines. The Food and Drug Administration is responsible for the proper testing of drugs to protect you from harmful drugs. A dramatic example of how the FDA protects us took place in 1962.

A tranquilizer called *thalidomide* was made in Germany and sold in European countries during 1961 and 1962. Thalidomide was prescribed to many pregnant women to help them sleep and also to relax their nerves. When thalidomide arrived in the United States, Dr. Frances O. Kelsey, a research physician in the federal Food and Drug Administration, tested the drug. Dr. Kelsey did not give her approval. She was not thoroughly convinced that the drug would have no side effects. So the drug was not distributed.

Unfortunately, other countries soon found that large numbers of children with deformed arms and legs were being born to women who had used thalidomide. The drug passed through the placental barrier and caused an improper growth sequence in the developing embryo.

Dr. Kelsey was presented the highest civilian award for her thoroughness in research and prevention of a catastrophe in the United States.

Something to think about . . .

Main Ideas

1. Today's health standards may not meet our future health needs.
2. Public health means the well-being of everybody, rather than of individuals.
3. The local or city health department has the hard job of supervising everything from sanitation to keeping stray animals off the streets.
4. The World Health Organization (WHO) is a branch of the United Nations. It works to improve the health of all people.

Key Words

Department of Health and Human Services
public health
Public Health Service
thalidomide
vital data
World Health Organization

Apply Your Knowledge

1. Why is it necessary for city health departments to pick up stray dogs?
2. List five jobs your local health department does.
3. Why are vital data important to a city?
4. What are the jobs of the World Health Organization?
5. What are some of the services provided by the Public Health Service?
6. List five federal agencies that take care of public health.
7. What are some ways to kill microorganisms?
8. What is the role of the state health department?
9. How do voluntary health agencies work for public health?

Extend Your Knowledge

1. Find out how common chickenpox and measles are at your school each year.
2. Make a survey of your class to find the number of students who have immunity to tetanus, polio, diphtheria, and other diseases.
3. Visit your local heart association or the Red Cross and find out how you can be certified for cardiopulmonary resuscitation.
4. Ask your city or county health department about what kinds of health care are given to people who cannot pay for it. How does your community care for the handicapped?
5. Study the health program in your school. How are epidemics controlled? What responsibilities do the students have for the success of the health program?
6. Using the address list in this chapter, write to five voluntary health agencies for free public health information. Share with your class the information you receive.

Resource Guide

This resource guide was developed to assist you in obtaining information and materials on topics covered in the text.

Action on Smoking and Health (ASH)
2013 H Street, N.W.
Washington, D.C. 20006

*Alcoholics Anonymous
General Service Office
P.O. Box 459
Grand Central Station
New York, New York 10163

*Al-Anon Family Group Headquarters, Inc.
P.O. Box 182
Madison Square Garden
New York, New York 10010

*American Cancer Society
777 Third Avenue
New York, New York 10017

American Dental Association
211 East Chicago Avenue
Chicago, Illinois 60611

American Diabetes Association
2 Park Avenue
New York, New York 10020

American Dietetic Association
430 North Michigan Avenue
Chicago, Illinois 60611

*American Heart Association
7320 Greenville Avenue
Dallas, Texas 75231

*American Lung Association
1740 Broadway
New York, New York 10019

American Medical Association
535 North Dearborn Street
Chicago, Illinois 60610

*American National Red Cross
17th and D Streets, N.W.
Washington, D.C. 20006

Arthritis Foundation
221 Park Avenue South
New York, New York 10003

*Better Business Bureau of Metropolitan New York
257 Park Avenue South
New York, New York 10010

Cystic Fibrosis Foundation
60 East 42nd Street
New York, New York 10017

*Epilepsy Foundation of America
815 15th Street, N.W.
Washington, D.C. 20036

Family Service Association of America
44 East 23rd Street
New York, New York 10017

Group Against Smoker's Pollution (GASP)
9811 Lanham-Severn Road
College Park, Maryland 20740

National Council on Alcoholism, Inc.
733 Third Avenue
New York, New York 10017

*National Dairy Council
6300 River Road
Rosemont, Illinois 60018

National Fire Protection Association
470 Atlantic Avenue
Boston, Massachusetts 02210

National Hemophilia Foundation
19 West 34th Street
New York, New York 10001

*The National Foundation–March of Dimes
1275 Mamaroneck Avenue
White Plains, New York 10602

*National Kidney Foundation
2 Park Avenue
New York, New York 10016

*National Multiple Sclerosis Society
205 East 42nd Street
New York, New York 10017

National Safety Council
444 North Michigan Avenue
Chicago, Illinois 60611

National Society for the Prevention of Blindness, Inc.
79 Madison Avenue
New York, New York 10016

U.S. Consumer Product Safety Commission
Washington, D.C. 20207

U.S. Department of Agriculture
Washington, D.C. 20250

U.S. Department of Health and Human Services
Clearinghouse on Child Abuse and Neglect Information
P.O. Box 1182
Washington, D.C. 20013
Consumer Information Center
Pueblo, Colorado 81009
Food and Drug Administration
Office of Consumer Affairs, Public Inquiries
5600 Fishers Lane (HFE-88)
Rockville, Maryland 20857
National Clearinghouse for Alcohol Information
P.O. Box 2345
Rockville, Maryland 20852
National Clearinghouse for Drug Abuse Information
P.O. Box 416
Kensington, Maryland 20795
National Clearinghouse for Family Planning Information
P.O. Box 2225
Rockville, Maryland 20852
National Clearinghouse for Mental Health Information
Public Inquiries Section
Rm. 15C–17
5600 Fishers Lane
Rockville, Maryland 20857
National Institute on Aging
9000 Rockville Pike
Bldg. 31, Rm. 5C–36
Bethesda, Maryland 20205
Office on Smoking and Health
Technical Information Center
Park Bldg., Rm. 116
5600 Fishers Lane
Rockville, Maryland 20857

U.S. Department of Transportation
National Highway Traffic Safety Administration
Washington, D.C. 20590

*Contact local chapter

Chapter 35

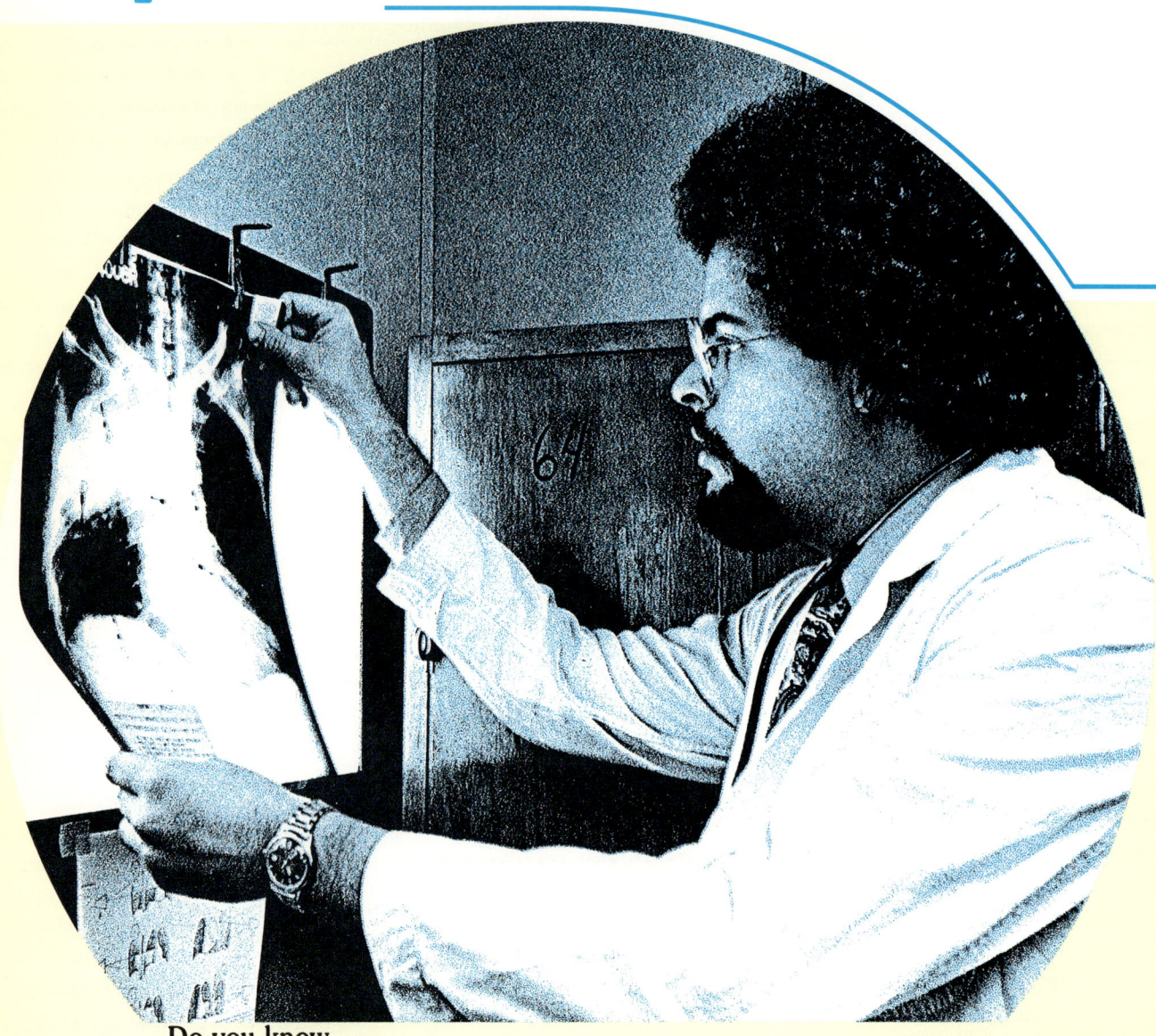

Do you know . . .

- that health careers are one of the fastest growing fields of employment?
- where you can get information about tuition and scholarships, education and training, or job descriptions and opportunities in the health area?
- how many years of education or training are needed to be an electrocardiograph (EKG) technician or a pediatric assistant?

Health Careers for You

Are you interested in following a health career? There are over 200 careers in health services waiting for you. The need for good health care has caused a rise in the need for highly trained health workers.

When most people think of big industry, they think of car manufacturing, transportation, steel, food production, or banking. People do not often think of health as a big industry. Actually, though, the health industry is one of the largest in the United States.

The advantages of health careers

Unlike some other large industries, the health industry is not found in only a few small areas of the country. Large cities, where many people live, need large numbers of health workers. But small towns and rural areas need health workers, too.

There are places in the United States where there are few people. In such places, small numbers of people may be spread out over a large area. There are also places where mountains or deserts as well as long distances make it hard for families to get to the towns where health services can be found. Fortunately, transportation and communication have improved. However, in order to give the best possible care, health service workers should be close to those they serve, even in places with few people.

Because of the need for good health services in all parts of the world, health workers can find jobs almost any place they choose. This is another fine feature of a job in the health field.

Many opportunities may be found in health careers.

The health-care industry has hundreds of different kinds of job openings. Some jobs call for many years of special training. But others require little special training. Still other jobs let you learn while you are working. There are some careers in which you can set up your own business. In other careers, you can work for someone else. Some jobs are very technical. They call for a solid scientific background. Other jobs do not demand such knowledge. But they do call for people who can work with their hands or who can get along well with other people.

Health service—one of the fastest growing areas of employment

Do you need help in getting money to start your own health career?

One of the biggest advantages of choosing and following a career in health services is the possibility of getting help to start. Because of the great need for good health care, government and nongovernment groups have programs to make it easier to begin a career in the health field. Several ways exist for students to get loans or grants. Scholarships and part-time employment opportunities are possible as well. The federal government has more than 150 programs to support training in the area of health. Hospitals, private industry, labor unions, and other organizations offer more help.

Technological advancements make new jobs.

Jobs in the field of health change all the time. Some jobs today didn't exist a few years ago. You are familiar with the discovery and the many uses of the X ray. Many jobs have come from this discovery. Today, the uses of X rays have also been advanced further. As a result, computerized *tomographic scanners* are providing new jobs. These scanners are X-ray machines that can take pictures of a section of the inside of the body without shadows from other sections interfering. Computers are now being used to study and interpret information from laboratories. Therefore, people who know about computers are also needed in the health field.

Your health career can be very rewarding.

Some health jobs are scientific. The work is done in a university or laboratory. Other health jobs are not technical at all. Many such jobs call for people who can get along well with others and who can work in places where there is a great deal of activity. A receptionist in a clinic is one example of such a job.

There are also opportunities for those who like to teach. What is known about health must be passed on to others if society is to get the most good from that knowledge.

How should you prepare for a health career?

There is no single answer to this question, because there are so many different careers. With a wide choice of careers, the length of time and place of preparation change.

There are some jobs in which a person can work and learn at the same time. This is called *on-the-job training*. Other jobs have a training period that begins after high school and lasts for several weeks or months. The health careers that require the least amount of formal education are called *entry-level careers*. Here are a few of these entry-level health careers:

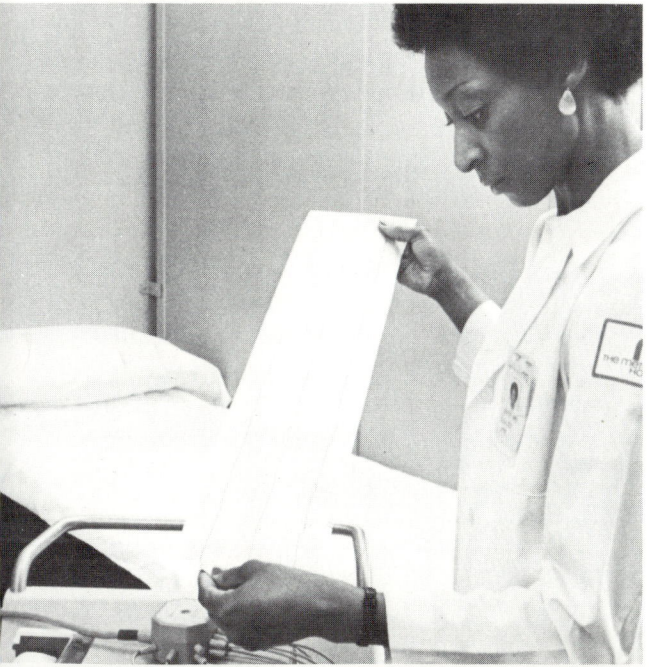

Certified laboratory assistant. The certified laboratory assistant works in the areas of bacteriology, chemistry, hematology, parasitology, serology, blood banking, and urinalysis. The job includes collecting blood specimens, grouping and typing blood, separating body fluids into their chemical parts, and examining urine, blood, and other body fluids through a microscope. These laboratory activities must be done under the direction of trained physicians or medical technologists. Graduation from an accredited high school, usually with extra work in science and mathematics, is needed to get into an accredited certified laboratory assistant (CLA) school. These schools are found mostly in hospitals. In some areas, they are located in vocational and technical schools, in community colleges, and on military bases. After twelve months of solid training, and after passing the Board of Registry examination, a person is eligible for national CLA certification. For further information, write to the American Society for Medical Technology, 612 Smith Street, Houston, Texas 77006.

Electrocardiograph technician. An electrocardiograph technician runs the electrocardiograph. This device records changes in the heartbeat of the patient. EKG technicians prepare the patients for treatment by placing electrodes on their arms, legs, and chests. Technicians watch for any electrocardiographic abnormalities. Usually six to twelve months of on-the-job training are needed, directed by experienced technicians or cardiologists in accredited hospitals. Because of the growing complexity of the equipment, educational plans are being developed for this field. For further information, write to the American Cardiology Technologists Association, 1 Bank Street, Suite 307, Gaithersburg, Maryland 20760.

Central service technician (hospital). The central service technicians in a hospital may perform duties such as cleaning and sterilizing equipment, instruments, and supplies. They may collect used materials from the nursing units, operating rooms, delivery rooms, laboratories, emergency units, and nurseries. They may assemble and process sterile and nonsterile treatment trays or packs. They may also operate and maintain different kinds of equipment, such as oxygen tents, ambulance equipment, wheelchairs, and traction setups. A high school diploma is necessary. Three to six months of on-the-job training are also needed, with stress on beginning chemistry, medical terminology, problem solving, and laboratory and hospital procedures. For further information, write to the American Hospital Association, 840 North Lake Shore Drive, Chicago, Illinois 60611.

Dietetic assistant. The dietetic assistant works with a dietitian or a dietetic technician at all times. The duties depend on the size and organization of the department of dietetics. The wide range of jobs might include food receiving, storage, preparation, cooking, and serving. Most of the training takes place on the job or in a supervised environment. For a postsecondary dietetic assistant certificate, 120 hours of study at an accredited vocational school are needed. For further information, write to the American Dietetic Association, 430 North Michigan Avenue, Chicago, Illinois 60611.

Operating room technician. Operating room technicians prepare equipment and supplies for the operating room. They also arrange instruments for operations, help the nurse or surgeon during operations, and wash and sterilize instruments and equipment. Nine months of training in a classroom and hospital are required. For further information, write to the Association of Operating Room Nurses, 10170 E. Mississippi Ave., Denver, Colorado 80231.

Ward clerk. The ward clerks do many of the routine tasks needed to make hospital patients comfortable. They receive visitors, answer telephones, put together records, post patients' charts, fix orders for special diets and supplies, and type and record doctors' orders. The ward clerks work in hospital nursing units under the direction of a registered nurse. Their job requires six to twelve weeks of approved courses, with on-the-job training. Some hospitals require six months of office experience. For further information, write to the Colorado Department of Health, 4210 East 11th Avenue, Denver, Colorado 80220.

Careers that require some formal college education

An associate degree, which can be earned in two years of college, is the next level of preparation for a health career. Since more preparation and training are necessary for *intermediate-level careers,* the pay is usually more than for entry-level jobs. The responsibilities are also greater. Some intermediate-level health careers are these:

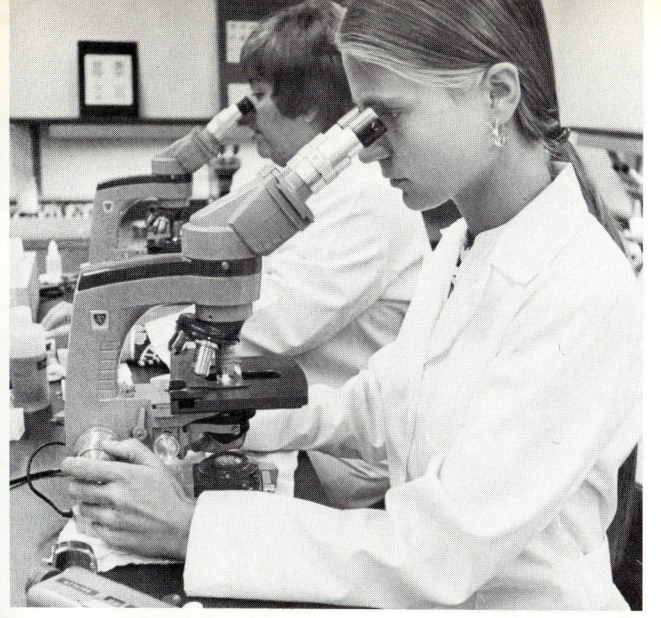

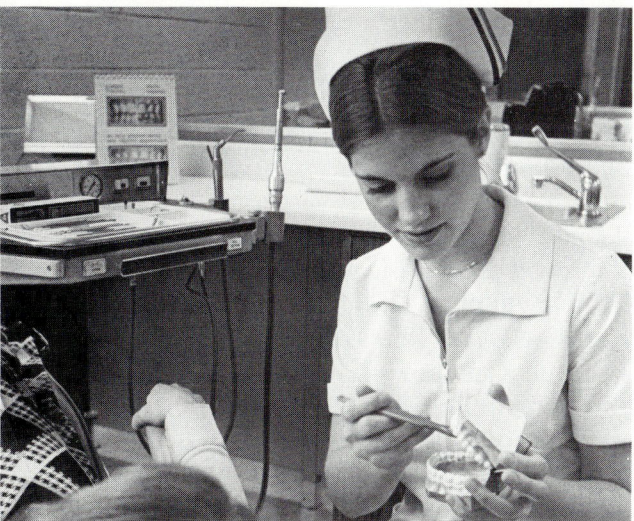

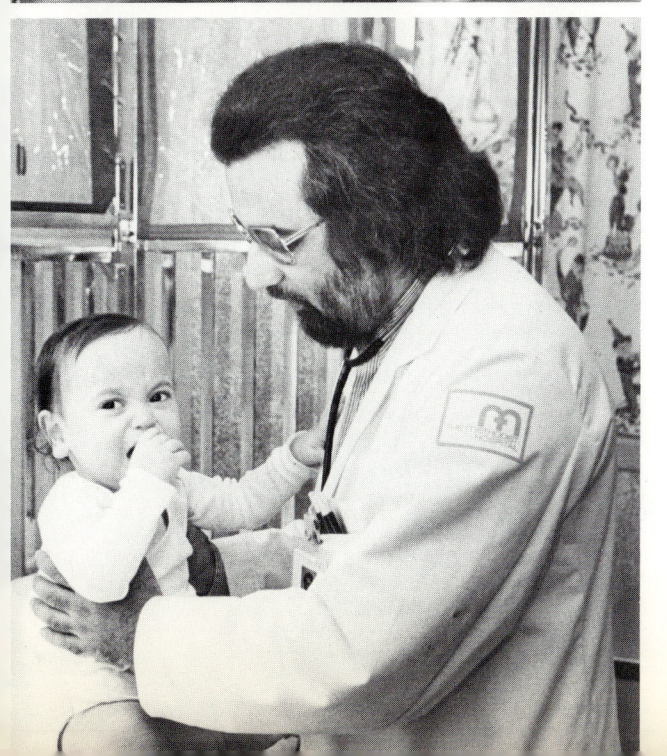

Cytotechnologist. The cytotechnologist is a trained medical laboratory technologist who works with a pathologist. The main job of the cytotechnologist is to examine, under the microscope, cells taken from different body areas, such as the cervix, mouth cavity, or any other body cavity that sheds cells. Using special staining techniques, the cytotechnologist picks out any abnormalities of the cell. These may be the first warning signs of cancer. Two years of college and one year of training in an accredited school of cytotechnology, approved by the American Society of Cytotechnology and the American Medical Association, are required. In order to be certified, you must pass the Board of Registry examination. For further information, write to the Board of Registry, American Society of Clinical Pathologists, 2100 West Harrison Street, Chicago, Illinois 60612.

Dental hygienist. The dental hygienist works under the direction of a dentist. The hygienist scales and polishes teeth, gives fluoride treatments to make teeth more resistant to decay, and promotes dental health by giving instructions for proper care of teeth. To qualify for clinical practice, the dental hygienist must go to an accredited school of dental hygiene for two years. He or she must complete the associate degree and be licensed by the state. The four-year bachelor's degree program in dental hygiene will allow you to look for jobs in public health or to become a teacher in dental health education programs. For further information, write to the American Dental Hygienists' Association, 444 North Michigan Avenue, Chicago, Illinois 60611.

Pediatric assistant. Pediatric assistants do both clerical and clinical jobs. They work as secretaries, prepare young patients for examination or treatments, take temperatures, measure height and weight, and sterilize instruments. The requirements include graduation from high school, two years' study of social and biological sciences, and typing skills. This preparation includes courses in anatomy and physiology, medical terminology, and medical law and ethics. The course of study also includes the growth and development of infants and children, methods of immunization, knowledge of infectious diseases, and experience in pediatric clinics. For further information, write to the American Association of Medical Assistants, One East Wacker Drive, Suite 2110, Chicago, Illinois 60601.

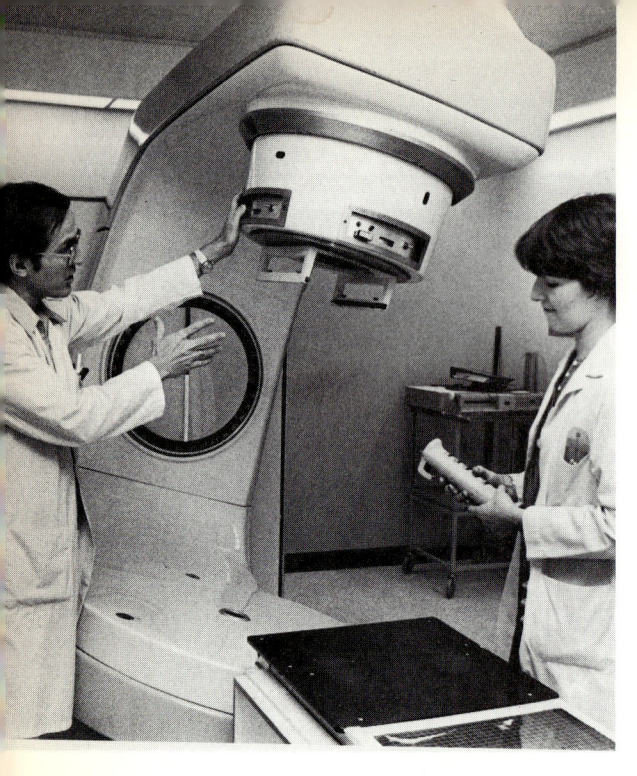

Radiation therapy technologist. Radiation therapy technologists work under the direction of a radiologist. They treat diseases by using X rays or other forms of ionizing radiation. Usually, the technologist works in a cancer-treatment center and has the following responsibilities:

1. to know the rules for radiation safety and to spot defects in equipment that could become a radiation hazard.
2. to provide care and comfort to the patient and be able to apply simple surgical dressings.
3. to check the physician's prescription and find any mathematical errors.

There are two types of programs for those who are interested in becoming radiation therapists. For the two-year program, the applicant must be a high school graduate with a background in the basic sciences and mathematics. The program includes entry-level study in the basic principles of using ionizing radiation and other basic sciences. For the one-year program, the applicant must be either a graduate of an approved educational program in radiologic technology, or a registered nurse with a background in radiation physics. For further information, write to the American Society of Radiologic Technologists, 55 East Jackson Blvd., Suite 1820, Chicago, Illinois 60604.

Careers needing four years of college and a bachelor's degree

There are many more health careers for college graduates. *Higher-level careers* are open to those who have many years of experience as well as a college degree.

Medical technologist. Medical technologists carry out chemical, serologic, and bacteriologic tests for the purpose of helping to diagnose and treat diseases. They are trained in microscopic studies and in operating many complex instruments. Requirements include a bachelor's degree and clinical experience in a hospital laboratory educational program. For further information, write to the American Society for Medical Technology, 612 Smith Street, Houston, Texas 77006.

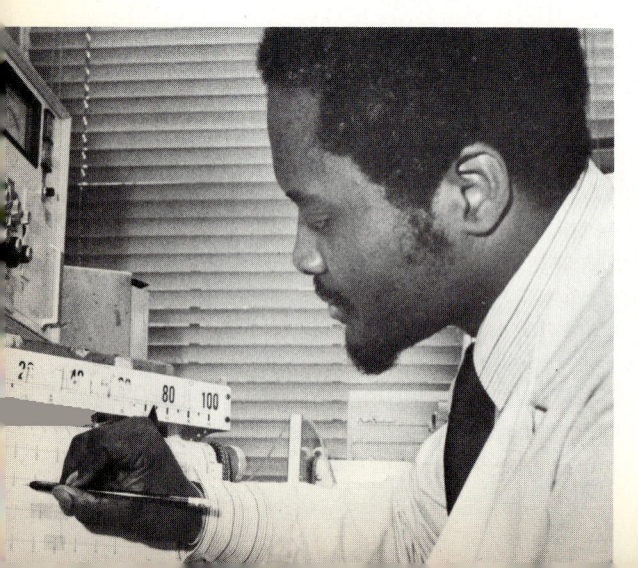

Therapeutic recreation specialist. Therapeutic recreation specialists are responsible for organizing, administering, and presenting therapeutic recreational activities. These activities help patients who have an illness, disability, or social problem. Therapeutic specialists look for new recreation and leisure programs for the ill, handicapped, and disabled in nonmedical settings. Such settings are special schools and community recreation agencies. A bachelor's degree is needed for this career. Many schools have a four-year program and a graduate program. For further information, write to the National Therapeutic Recreation Society, National Recreation and Park Association, 3101 Park Center Drive, Arlington, Virginia 22209.

Health careers such as veterinarian, speech pathologist, or medical doctor need the most education and training. The yearly income for these careers is very good, but there are also many responsibilities.

Speech pathologist. The speech pathologist rates the speech and language of children and adults. The speech pathologist also works to prevent speech, hearing, and language disorders. Speech pathologists work in public schools, universities, hospitals, private practice, and community organizations. A bachelor's degree with a major in speech is the minimum requirement. Standards set up by the American Speech and Hearing Association include successful completion of work towards a master's degree in speech pathology, good performance in a year's supervised clinical practice, and passing grades in a national examination. For further information, write to the American Speech and Hearing Association, 10801 Rockville Pike, Rockville, Maryland 20852.

Physician. The physician, in general, uses knowledge and skills to cure diseases of the human body and mind. Refer to Chapter 32 for a brief description of medical specialists. The requirements include three to four years of college in a premedical course, four years of medical school, one year of residency, and two to five years of extended residency in a special area of medicine. For further information, write to the American Medical Women's Association, 465 Grand Street, New York, N.Y. 10002, or the American Medical Association, 535 N. Dearborn Street, Chicago, Illinois 60610.

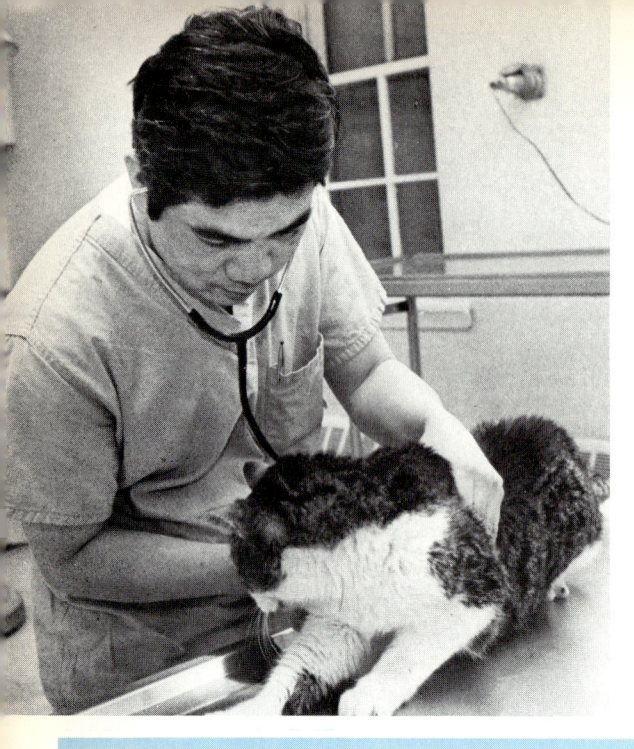

Veterinarian. Veterinarians guard our health by controlling diseases that can be given to humans by animals. They inspect meat, poultry, dairies, creameries, water plants, and animals imported from abroad. Requirements include two years of college in a preveterinary course, and four years at an accredited school of veterinary medicine. After receiving the degree of Doctor of Veterinary Medicine (D.V.M.), the graduate must pass the state board examination to be licensed to practice in any state. High school preparation should include courses in English, mathematics, general science, physics, and chemistry. For further information, write to the American Veterinary Medical Association, 930 N. Meacham Road, Schaumburg, Illinois 60196.

Some Other Careers in the Health Field

Career	Description of work	Preparation required
Biomedical equipment technician	Services, operates, and maintains medical machinery used in health care facilities	1 to 2 years of training after high school
Computer programmer	Writes programs (instructions) for computers for analyzing results of laboratory tests and other information	3 to 4 years of college
Dental laboratory technician	Makes and repairs dentures and other dental devices	1 to 3 years of training after high school
Dentist	General practice or one of the dental specialties, such as orthodontics or dental surgery	3 to 4 years of college; 4 years dental school
Dietitian (nutritionist)	Plans special diets; conducts research in foods; supervises food preparation in institutions	4 years of college
Dietetic technician	Plans meals and supervises food service staff in institutions	1 to 2 years of training after high school
Emergency medical technician	Gives first aid in emergencies; drives ambulance or attends the patient in the ambulance	Several weeks to 6 months of training after high school
Food technologist	Develops practical processing methods to produce new foods in commercial quantities and test new foods. Designs new packing techniques.	4 years of college and graduate work
Health educator	Health teaching in schools, colleges, public-health departments, special programs for the handicapped, and so on	4 to 5 years of college
Histologic technician	Prepares sections of body tissues for microscopic examination by freezing, cutting, mounting, and staining. Pathologist makes final diagnoses	12-month hospital course and graduate from AMA-accredited histologic technician program, plus Board of Registry examination
Industrial hygienist	Protects personnel from industrial health hazards, such as vibration, toxic chemicals, dust, gas, poor lighting, infectious diseases, and fatigue	4 years college and graduate work

Career	Description of work	Preparation required
Inhalation therapy technician	Assists physicians in operating equipment to supply oxygen to patients	1 to 3 years of training after high school
Medical laboratory technician	Makes special laboratory tests in hospitals, clinics, and physicians' offices	2 to 4 years of college
Medical librarian	Supervises medical libraries; supervises medical records in hospitals	4 to 5 years of college
Medical record technician	Prepares, codes, and preserves patients' records in clinics and hospitals	1 to 2 years of training after high school
Medical social worker	Assists families with economic and other problems related to medical care	4 years of college, 2 years of graduate work
Noise technician	Devises noise control programs for today and for the future	2-7 years of study; both on-the-job training and formal college education
Nurse, registered (RN)	Nursing care of the physically and mentally ill; public health; teaching and supervision	2 to 4 years of college or 3 years in a school of nursing
Nurse, licensed practical (LPN)	Routine nursing care under supervision	1 year in hospital training school
Nurse practitioner	Expanded nursing role, including some health care services that traditionally have been the responsibility of the physician	Training as a registered nurse plus advanced formal study
Nursing aide	Nonmedical duties to assist professional nurse	A few weeks of training in hospital (varies)
Occupational therapist	Works with patients to develop skills that will aid in recovery	4 years of college
Optician	Makes eyeglasses or contact lenses from an ophthalmologist's prescription	1 to 3 years of training after high school
Optometric technician	Assists the optometrist	1 to 2 years of training
Optometrist	Tests vision; prescribes glasses	3 to 4 years of college, 4 years of optometric school
Orthopterist	Assists ophthalmologist in teaching corrective eye exercises	2 or more years of college
Osteopath	General medical care with emphasis on manipulation and massage	2 years of college, 4 years of osteopathic college, 1 or more years of internship
Pharmacist	Preparation of drugs for treatment of illness; filling of prescriptions	4 to 5 years of college
Physical therapist	Uses heat, massage, exercise for rehabilitation of the disabled	4 years of college
Podiatrist (chiropodist)	Treats foot disorders; prescribes correct shoes	1 to 2 years of college, 4 years of school of podiatry
Prosthetist and orthotist	Designs, makes, and fits artificial limbs or braces	2 or more years of college
Psychologist, clinical	Mental testing; diagnosis and treatment of mental and emotional disorders	4 years of college, 3 or 4 years of graduate work in psychology, 1 or more years of internship
Public-health engineer	Specializes in environmental health	4 to 5 years of college

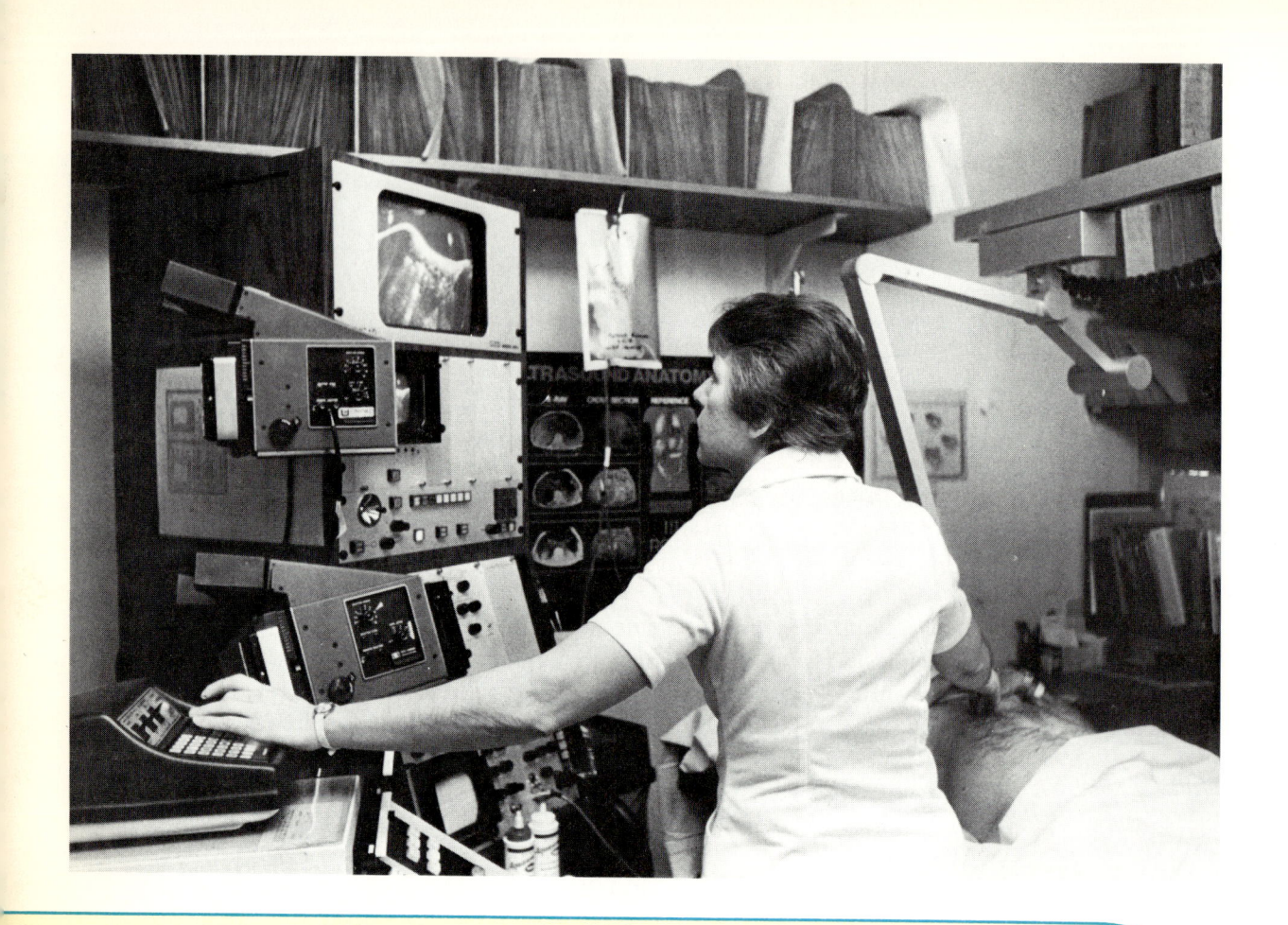

Main Ideas

1. Many opportunities exist in health careers.
2. Jobs for health workers are available in both rural and urban areas throughout the United States and the world.
3. Financial assistance is available in training for a health career.
4. Entry-level health careers allow you to start working right after high school.
5. With advances in technology, new careers in health services are possible.
6. Many interests or talents can be used in a career in health.
7. The amount of education and training needed for a health career will determine the salary and responsibilities.

Key Words

entry-level career
higher-level career
intermediate-level career
on-the-job training

Apply Your Knowledge

1. What are some of the reasons for the growing need for highly trained health personnel?
2. List five advantages of pursuing a health career.
3. Name five different health jobs that would be considered entry-level careers. What are three jobs that would be considered intermediate-level careers? Name two jobs that would be considered higher-level careers.
4. How have science and industry affected health careers?
5. What is the advantage of getting a college degree for a health career?
6. Name two kinds of jobs available today in the health field that were not available twenty years ago.
7. How might an art major in college find a career in a health field?
8. How are the two health careers in cytotechnology and certified laboratory assistance alike? How are they different?
9. Describe the role of the nurse practitioner.
10. Besides giving immunization shots to pets, what are other jobs of the veterinarian?

Extend Your Knowledge

1. Turn to the classified ads, or "want ads," in your local newspaper to see which health career has the most openings.
2. If methods to prevent and cure cancer are perfected, what new health careers would develop?
3. How would the cost of dental health care be affected if there were no careers such as dental hygienists or dental assistants?
4. What abilities or interests do you have that would be helpful to you in a health career? Name careers to which your abilities might apply. Share your information with the class.
5. Prepare a poster or exhibit based on what you have learned that will interest other students in a health career.

Glossary

abortion The ending of a pregnancy.

accommodation The change in the thickness of the lens of the eye that lets one see clearly at different distances.

acquired immunity (ih MYOO nuh tee) Immunity the body builds up after having a disease.

ACTH A hormone produced by the pituitary gland. It causes the adrenal glands to produce their hormones.

active immunity The ability to form antibodies against pathogens before they can cause disease.

addiction A condition in which a drug user must either have regular doses of the drug, or suffer painful or even fatal withdrawal symptoms.

adrenal (uh DREE nul) **glands** Two endocrine glands that lie above the kidneys. They produce adrenalin and cortisone.

adrenalin (uh DREN uh len) A hormone produced by the inner portion of the adrenal glands. It increases muscle tone in the skeletal muscles and slows down activity in the digestive tract.

advanced life support Emergency care that includes both basic life support techniques and the use of medical equipment and therapy.

alcoholism An illness characterized by regular, heavy drinking of alcoholic beverages and the inability to stop.

alimentary (AL uh MEN tuh ree) **canal** The series of organs that move food through the body.

alveoli (al VEE uh LY); singular, **alveolus** (al VEE uh lus) Tiny air sacs that make up the greater part of the lungs.

amblyopia (AM blee OH pee uh) Dim vision.

amino (uh MEE noh) **acids** The building blocks from which protein is made; the end products of the digestion of proteins.

amniocentesis (AM nee oh sen TEE sis) A test performed before birth to find possible defects in the fetus by examining the amniotic fluid.

amphetamine (am FET un MEEN) A synthetic drug that is used to treat depression, overweight, and excessive sleeping.

amylase (AM uh LAYS) An enzyme in saliva that breaks down starch into sugar.

analgesic (AN ul JEE zik) A drug used to relieve pain.

anemia (uh NE mee uh) A disease in which the blood lacks either hemoglobin or red blood cells, or both.

anesthetic (AN es THET ik) A drug that causes insensitivity to pain.

angina pectoris (an JY nuh PEK tuh ris) Chest pain that occurs when the heart muscle does not get as much blood as it needs.

antacid (ant ASS id) A substance that decreases the amount of acid in the stomach.

antibiotic (ANT ih by AH tik) A drug that can kill organisms that infect the body.

antibodies (ANT ih BAH deez) Substances, produced by the white blood cells, that attack disease organisms or their poisons.

antidote (ANT ih DOHT) A substance that works against a poison.

antiseptic Any substance that prevents the growth of bacteria.

antitoxins (ANT ih TAHK sinz) Substances produced by the body to destroy poisons produced by pathogens.

antitussive (ANT ih TUSS iv) A substance that helps quiet the cough center.

aorta (a OR tuh) The largest artery in the body. The aorta and its branches carry blood to the body.

aqueous humor (A kwee us HYOO mur) The fluid between the cornea and the lens of the eye.

arteriosclerosis (ahr TIR ee oh skluh ROH sis) A condition in which the walls of the arteries harden and become thick, making it hard for blood to circulate.

artery A blood vessel that carries blood away from the heart.

arthritis A condition in which joints become swollen and painful.

ascorbic (uh SKOR bik) **acid** Vitamin C.

asthma (AZ muh) A condition in which the muscles in the walls of the bronchi contract, making it hard to breathe.

astigmatism (uh STIG muh TIZ um) Faulty vision caused by irregularities in the curved surfaces of the cornea or lens.

atherosclerosis (ATH uh roh skluh RO sis) A condition in which the coronary arteries are narrowed by deposits of fatty material on the inner walls.

atrium (A tree um) The upper chamber of each side of the heart.

autonomic (AW tuh NAHM ik) **nervous system** The nerves that control involuntary body action, such as heartbeat, breathing, and digestion.

barbiturate (bahr BICH ur it) A drug that is used to relieve anxiety, but which can also

barbiturate (continued) be dangerous if used without proper medical supervision.

basal metabolic rate A measure of the amount of energy a person uses per hour, while resting.

basic life support Emergency care that uses the techniques of cardiopulmonary resuscitation (CPR) to restore heartbeat or breathing.

benign (bih NYN) **tumor** A tumor that is not harmful and does not spread.

bile duct A tube through which bile passes from the gall bladder to the duodenum. Bile helps the body digest fats.

biopsy (BY AHP see) A method of cancer detection in which body tissue is removed and examined under a microscope.

blepharitis (BLEF uh RY tis) Swelling of the eyelid.

blood alcohol level (BAL) The amount of alcohol in a person's blood.

blood pressure The pressure of the blood against the walls of the arteries. **Systolic** (sis TAH lik) **pressure** is the blood pressure at the time of the heartbeat (systole). **Diastolic** (DY uh STAH lik) **pressure** is the blood pressure between heartbeats (diastole).

bolus (BOH lus) A "ball" of food that has been chewed and is ready to be swallowed.

bone marrow Soft tissue found in the hollow area inside bones.

botulinum (BAHCH uh LY num) The bacterium that causes **botulism,** a severe form of food poisoning.

bronchi (BRAHN KY); singular, **bronchus** (BRAHN kus) The two large tubes that lead from the trachea to the lungs.

bronchitis (brahn KY tis) Swelling of the bronchi, usually caused by viral infection.

caffeine A mildly stimulating drug contained in tea, coffee, cocoa, chocolate, and cola drinks.

calcium A mineral that is needed for proper development of bones and teeth.

calculus (KAL kyuh lus) A hard, limelike layer that forms on the teeth when plaque is not removed.

calories Units in which energy is measured. Calories are used to measure the energy value of foods.

cancer An uncontrolled and irregular growth of abnormal cells.

capillary (KAP uh LEH ree) A tiny blood vessel. Capillaries connect arteries to veins.

carbohydrate (KAHR boh HY DRAYT) A nutrient that is the main source of energy for the body. Sugars and starches are carbohydrates.

carcinogen (kahr SIN uh jen) A substance that causes cancer.

carcinogenic (kahr SIN uh JEN ik) Able to cause cancer.

cardiac arrest Absence of a heartbeat or pulse.

cardiac muscle The heart muscle.

cardiopulmonary resuscitation (KAHR dee oh PUL muh ner ee ree SUSS uh TA shun) A lifesaving technique that combines artificial respiration and artificial circulation; also called CPR.

cartilage (KAHR tuh lij) Tough connective tissue that is softer than bone.

cataract (KAT uh RAKT) Cloudiness of an eye lens, causing blurred vision.

central loss A hearing disorder caused by damage to the auditory nerve that leads from the cochlea to the brain, or by damage to the brain center for hearing.

central nervous system The brain and spinal cord.

cerebellum (SER uh BEL um) The "little brain," located beneath the back part of the cerebrum. Its activities are below the level of consciousness.

cerebrum (suh REE brum) The large, upper part of the brain, considered the center of conscious mental activity.

cervix (SUR viks) The neck of the uterus.

chancre (SHANK ur) A painless open sore on the genital organs, occurring during the primary stage of syphilis.

charley horse An injury to the front part of the thigh in which the muscle, blood vessels, nerves, and other soft tissues are damaged.

chemotherapy (KEE moh THER uh pee) The treatment of disease, such as cancer, with chemicals.

chromosomes (KROH muh SOHMZ) Threadlike bodies found in the nuclei of cells. They contain the substances that pass along inherited characteristics.

chyme (KYM) The thin, soupy liquid that food becomes in the stomach when it mixes with gastric juices.

ciliary (SIL ee EHR ee) **muscle** A muscle in the eye that helps change the shape of the lens in order to focus.

cocaine A dangerous drug that is both a stimulant and a painkiller. Cocaine users experience strong psychological dependence on

419

cocaine (continued) the drug. This drug should not be used without medical supervision.

cochlea (KOHK lee uh) An organ of the inner ear that is filled with liquid and transmits impulses from the middle ear to the brain.

codeine (KOH DEEN) A narcotic, made from opium, that is used for relief of pain and congestion, particularly in cough medicines.

conception The uniting of an ovum and a sperm to form a fertilized ovum.

conditioning A planned program of exercise, rest, and eating that is followed in order to get, and stay, in top physical condition.

conductive loss A hearing disorder caused by any block to the passage of sound waves through the outer or middle ear.

congenital (kahn JEN uh tul) **heart disease** A heart defect present at birth.

conjunctivitis (kun JUNK ti VY tis) An infection that causes swelling, redness, and itchiness of the mucous membrane covering the front part of the eyeball and the inside surface of the eyelid.

contraception Prevention of conception. Also called **birth control**.

contraceptives Medications and devices that prevent conception.

convulsion A strong attack of involuntary muscle contractions.

cornea (KOR nee uh) The clear covering over the front part of the eyeball through which light enters the eye.

coronary arteries Vessels that carry blood to the heart muscle.

cortisone (KOR tuh ZOHN) A secretion from the outer part of the adrenal glands. Cortisone helps the body react to stress.

CPR See **cardiopulmonary resuscitation**

cranium (KRAY nee um) The eight flat bones of the head, not including the bones of the face and the lower jaw.

cretinism (KREE tun IZ um) A condition that occurs when the body does not produce enough thyroxin. It can lead to physical and mental retardation.

cystic fibrosis (SISS tik fy BROH sis) An inherited disease that affects the mucus and sweat glands of children.

Daily Food Guide A chart recommended by the U.S. Department of Agriculture for planning nutritious meals and snacks. It classifies foods into groups based on the nutrients they contain.

decalcification (dee KAL suh fuh KAY shun) Loss of calcium, which causes bones to weaken.

decibel (DESS uh BEL) The unit for measuring the loudness of sound.

decongestant Any drug that eases congestion in the nasal passages.

defense mechanisms Ways of behaving that help a person maintain a sense of security when experiencing certain kinds of emotional conflict.

dental caries (KAR eez) Tooth decay.

depressant A drug that causes the activity of certain areas of the brain and spinal cord to slow down.

dermatitis (DER muh TY tis) Inflammation of the skin.

dermis (DER mis) The under layer of the skin.

detoxification (dee TAHKS uh fuh KAY shun) Removal of a possible poison, such as alcohol, from the body.

diabetes (DY uh BEE teez) A disease in which the body cannot use sugar properly. It is caused by failure of the islands of Langerhans in the pancreas to produce enough insulin.

diaphragm (DY uh FRAM) The wall of muscle and connective tissue that separates the chest cavity from the abdominal cavity.

diastole (dy ASS tuh lee) The period of rest or relaxation of the heart.

diphtheria (dif THIR ee uh) A serious infectious illness caused by bacteria. The main symptoms are sore throat and difficulty in breathing and swallowing.

diplopia (di PLOH pee uh) Double vision.

dislocation Displacement of one or both bones at a joint; a painful injury that occurs when a bone is pushed out of its socket.

DNA The abbreviation for deoxyribonucleic acid, a molecule that is basic in cell production and heredity.

dominant gene (JEEN) A gene that determines which trait will appear in someone.

dominant inheritance The process of receiving at least one dominant gene for a trait from one parent. In dominant inheritance of genetic diseases, one parent has a single defective gene that is dominant over the normal recessive gene.

Down's syndrome An inherited disease in which a child receives 47 chromosomes instead of 46. The child is retarded. Also called trisomy 21.

ductless glands See **endocrine glands**

duodenum (DOO uh DEE num) The first section of the small intestine. Most of the digestive process occurs in the duodenum.

eardrum The membrane that separates the outer ear from the middle ear.

embryo (EM bree OH) In human reproduction, the cluster of dividing cells during the first two months of development in the uterus.

emergency medical services (EMS) system A system set up within a local community to provide fast action when emergencies take place.

emphysema (EM fuh ZEE muh) A condition of the lungs in which the alveoli become enlarged and inflexible, making it very hard for a person to breathe.

endocrine (EN duh krin) **glands** Glands that produce hormones and release them directly into the bloodstream; also called glands of internal secretion, or ductless glands.

endometrium (EN doh MEE tree um) The lining of the uterus, shed in menstruation.

enriched Having added vitamins and minerals.

enuresis (EN yoo REE sis) Bedwetting, or the involuntary discharge of urine.

enzymes (EN ZYMZ) Chemicals in digestive juices that break down food into simpler substances so that they can be absorbed into the bloodstream.

epidermis (EP uh DER mis) The protective outer layer of the skin.

epididymis (EP uh DID uh mis) A structure in the male connecting the testis with the vas deferens.

epilepsy (EP uh LEP see) A nervous disorder. It may cause a person to lose consciousness briefly or to go into convulsions.

equilibrium Balance.

esophagus (ih SAHF uh gus) The tube that connects the mouth to the stomach.

essential amino acid One of the nine amino acids that cannot be produced by the human body. They must be obtained in food.

estrogen (ESS truh jin) The hormone that stimulates the development of secondary sex characteristics in females.

eustachian (yoo STAY shun) **tube** A tube that connects the middle ear with the back of the nose and throat. It allows air to enter and leave the middle ear, which balances the air pressure on both sides of the eardrum.

expectorant (ik SPEK tuh runt) A substance that helps a person cough up and spit out matter that is irritating the lining of the trachea.

expiration The process of forcing air out of the lungs.

Fallopian (ful LOH pee un) **tubes** Two tubes in the human female through which ova pass from the ovaries to the uterus.

fasciculus (fah SIK yuh lus) A bundle of connected muscle fibers. A single muscle is made up of many fasciculi.

fat A nutrient in food that provides energy and helps the body absorb vitamins.

FDA The Food and Drug Administration, a U.S. government agency which makes sure that food and drug products meet safety and health standards.

fetus (FEE tus) In human reproduction, the developing individual after the second month in the uterus.

fiber The "rough" part of plant foods—the cell walls of leaves, fruits, seeds, bulbs, and flowers. Fiber is also known as "roughage."

"fight" response Positive, constructive use of the energy created by stress.

flatus (FLAY tus) Gas produced in the stomach or intestine.

"flight" response Response to stress which consists of destructive action or avoidance.

fluoride (FLOOR EYED) A salt of fluorine that is helpful in preventing tooth decay, often added to drinking water.

fontanel (FAHN tuh NEL) One of the soft areas between the bones of the cranium of a young infant. The spaces fill in with bone as the head grows.

fracture A break in a bone. In a closed fracture, the bone does not break through the skin. In an open fracture, the wound extends from the skin to the bone.

frostbite Injury to body tissues caused by extreme cold.

fungus (FUNG gus) A form of plant life that lives best in dark, warm, moist areas.

gamma rays The most dangerous type of radiation. Gamma rays can penetrate body tissues.

gastric juices Liquids secreted by glands in the walls of the stomach. They mix with food in the stomach and aid in digestion.

genes Small units of DNA in chromosomes that pass inherited characteristics from parent to child.

genetic code The order in which certain chemi-

genetic code (continued) cal compounds are arranged in DNA molecules; the "instructions" that tell the cells of the body what to do.

genital herpes (JEN uh tul HUR peez) A viral infection in the genital area.

genitals The external sexual organs.

gingivitis (JIN juh VY tis) A condition in which the gums become dark red and soft and swollen, and bleed easily.

glaucoma (glau KOH muh) A disease of the eye in which fluid is trapped between the cornea and the iris. Pressure builds up in the eyeball and injures the light-sensitive nerve cells.

gonads (GOH NADZ) Sex glands; the organs that produce ova or sperm and sex hormones. In females, the gonads are the ovaries. In males, the gonads are the testes.

gonorrhea (GAHN uh REE uh) A common sexually transmitted disease caused by rod-shaped bacteria called gonococci.

gynecologist (GYN uh KAHL uh jist) A physician who specializes in the functioning and disorders of women's reproductive organs.

halitosis (HAL uh TOH sis) Bad breath.

hallucinogen (huh LOO sin uh jen) A drug that causes visions and distortions of the other senses.

hashish The powerful resin produced in the tops of the marijuana plant.

heart attack A condition that occurs when the heart muscle does not receive enough blood. Usually a person feels severe chest pain, with nausea and sweating.

heart murmur A blowing or swishing noise caused by blood passing through a defective heart valve.

heart valve One of the structures between the atrium and the ventricle of each side of the heart. These valves open and close in a way that controls the direction of blood flow.

heat exhaustion An illness that occurs when the body loses large amounts of water and salt through sweating after exposure to heat.

hemoglobin (HEE muh GLOH bin) The substance in red blood cells that carries oxygen from the lungs to all parts of the body.

hemophilia (HEE muh FIL ee uh) A condition in which the blood clots slowly or not at all.

hemorrhage (HEM uh rij) Very heavy bleeding.

hepatitis (HEP uh TY tis) A condition in which the liver becomes swollen and inflamed. This serious condition is caused by a virus.

hernia (HER nee uh) The condition that occurs when any organ, or part of an organ, is pushed through the wall around it; also called a rupture.

heroin A dangerous, habit-forming narcotic drug, made from opium.

heterosexual (HET uh roh SEK shoo wal) Attracted to members of the other sex.

homosexual (HOH muh SEK shoo wal) Sexual attraction to members of one's own sex.

hormone A chemical produced by the endocrine glands and carried in the bloodstream. Hormones regulate the body's many systems so that the systems work together.

hydrocephalic (HY droh suh FAL ik) Having fluid trapped inside the brain, which causes the brain to enlarge and push against the skull.

hyperopia (HY puh ROH pee uh) Farsightedness; difficulty in seeing things that are close because the eyeball is too short from front to back.

hypertension (HY pur TEN shun) Continued high blood pressure.

hyperventilation (HY pur VEN tuh LAY shun) Breathing in too much oxygen, causing dizziness or fainting.

hypoglycemia (HY poh gly SEE mee uh) A disorder that occurs when the body produces too much insulin. The amount of sugar in the blood falls below normal.

hypothalamus (HY poh THAL uh mus) A part of the brain located above the pituitary gland. Some scientists believe the hypothalamus helps the pituitary gland regulate body temperature.

immunization (IM yuh nuh ZAY shun) Injecting into the body a substance that helps the body resist a disease.

incubation (ING kyuh BAY shun) **period** The time between the entrance of disease organisms into the body and the appearance of symptoms.

incus (ING kus) A tiny bone between the malleus and stapes in the middle ear. It is shaped like an anvil and helps amplify sound waves as they travel from eardrum to inner ear.

infectious (in FEK shus) Easily spread from one person to another, as a disease.

influenza (IN floo EN zuh) A highly contagious respiratory disease caused by a virus.

inspiration Taking air into the lungs.

insulin (IN suh lin) The hormone secreted by the islands of Langerhans in the pancreas. Insulin breaks down sugar so that it can be used by the body.

internist A physician with special training in diagnosing illness.

involuntary muscles Muscles that are not under a person's conscious control, such as stomach and heart muscles.

involuntary smoking Unwilling inhalation of smoke from someone else's burning cigarette, cigar, or pipe.

iodine (EYE uh DYN) A mineral needed for proper working of the thyroid gland.

iris (EYE ris) The round, colored muscle behind the cornea that controls the amount of light entering the eye.

iron A mineral that is important for proper muscle contraction. It is found in hemoglobin.

iron-deficiency anemia A condition in which a person feels tired because not enough iron is being taken into the body.

islands of Langerhans (LAHN gur HAHNZ) Tiny clusters of gland tissue in the pancreas that produce the hormone insulin.

joint A place where two or more bones are connected.

lactic acid A chemical that forms in muscles as they contract.

lacto-ovo-vegetarian (LAK toh OH voh vej uh TER ee un) A person who eats no meat, but does include eggs and milk in the diet.

lacto-vegetarian (LAK toh vej uh TER ee un) A person who eats no meat or eggs, but does include milk, cheese, and butter in the diet.

larynx (LAR inks) An organ in the upper part of the respiratory tract that contains the vocal cords. Also called the voice box or Adam's apple.

lens The oval, clear structure behind the pupil of the eye that bends light rays so that they focus on the retina.

lethal gene A gene that causes the death of the organism that inherits it.

leukemia (loo KEE mee uh) A cancer in which there is a great increase in the number of white blood cells (leukocytes).

leukocytes (LOO kuh SYTS) White blood cells. Leukocytes surround and destroy organisms that enter the body.

ligament (LIG uh munt) Tissue that connects two or more bones to each other at a joint.

LSD Lysergic acid diethylamide, a synthetic drug that causes unpredictable changes in sensations.

lymph nodes (LIMPF NOHDZ) Small structures along the lymph vessels that make some white blood cells and that kill pathogens.

lymphoma (lim FOH muh) Cancer of the lymph glands.

mainstream smoke The smoke inhaled and then exhaled by a smoker.

malignant melanoma (muh LIG nunt MEL uh NOH muh) A rare type of skin cancer.

malignant tumor A tumor that is made up of abnormal cells and grows in an irregular pattern; a cancer.

malleus (MAL ee us) A tiny hammer-shaped bone between the eardrum and incus in the middle ear. It helps amplify sound waves as they travel from eardrum to inner ear.

malocclusion (MAL uh KLOO zhun) Failure of the teeth to bite together properly due to irregular spacing or to the shape of the jaw.

marijuana A plant whose dried tops and leaves produce changes in one's mood and sense perceptions when they are smoked or eaten.

measles A serious childhood disease that begins with a cough, fever, and red rash. It can lead to pneumonia, blindness, or brain damage.

Medicaid A program of health insurance provided by the U.S. government to people who cannot afford private health insurance.

Medicare A program of health insurance provided by the U.S. government to persons over 65 years of age.

melanin (MEL uh nin) A pigment that gives color to the hair, skin, and eyes.

meningitis (MEN in JY tis) Inflammation of the membranes that surround the brain and spinal cord, usually caused by a viral or bacterial infection.

menopause (MEN uh PAWZ) In the female, the stage of life when the ovaries stop producing ova, usually around age 50.

menstruation (MEN stroo AY shun) Discharge of the endometrium from the uterus.

metabolism (muh TAB uh LIZ um) The chemical change that goes on in cells to support life.

metastasis (muh TAS tuh sis) The spreading of a disease, such as cancer, to another part of the body.

methadone (METH uh DOHN) A synthetic

methadone (continued) drug used as a painkiller and as a heroin substitute.

microcephalic (MY kroh suh FAL ik) Having a head much smaller than normal size.

minerals Nutrients needed to control the body's chemical processes.

miscarriage The birth of a fetus before it has developed enough to live outside the uterus.

mononucleosis (MAH noh NOO klee oh sis) A common viral infection among young adults. Symptoms include sore throat, fever, chills, and a tired feeling.

morphine (MOR FEEN) A narcotic drug, made from opium, that is used primarily for the relief of pain. It is dangerously habit-forming.

mumps A contagious disease that produces fever and painful swollen glands under the jawbone.

muscle lameness The condition that occurs when muscles are overused; the tearing of tiny muscle fibers that have been forced to contract under a heavy load or force.

mutation A change in a gene.

myoglobin (MY uh GLOH bin) A red-colored protein that supplies oxygen to muscle cells and is very much like hemoglobin.

myopia (my OH pee uh) Nearsightedness; difficulty in seeing things that are far away because the eyeball is too long from front to back.

narcotic (nahr KAH tik) Any of a group of drugs that relieve pain and bring on sleep.

nerve loss A hearing disorder caused by damage to the special sensory cells in the cochlea.

neurosis (noo ROH sis) A form of mental illness characterized by poor development of skills needed to meet basic emotional needs.

niacin (NY uh sin) An important B vitamin that is needed for healthy skin and for proper functioning of the nervous and digestive systems.

nicotine (NIK uh TEEN) A powerful, colorless poison in tobacco smoke.

nitrites (NY TRYTS) Chemical preservatives added to hot dogs, bacon, sausages, and other foods to prevent deadly botulinum from growing.

nocturnal emission (nahk TURN ul ee MISH un) A normal, involuntary discharge of semen during sleep; also called a wet dream.

nutrients Substances in food that provide energy, build and repair cells, and regulate body processes.

obstetrician (AHB stuh TRISH un) A physician who specializes in all aspects of childbirth.

open dating The practice by which food manufacturers stamp packages with dates that help the consumer identify fresh foods.

ophthalmologist (AHF THAL MAHL uh jist) A physician who specializes in the care and diseases of the eyes.

optic (AHP tik) **nerve** The nerve that carries impulses from the retina to the brain.

optician (ahp TISH un) A person trained to grind lenses and make eyeglasses.

optometrist (ahp TAHM uh trist) A person trained to give eye examinations and to prescribe and fit lenses or glasses.

organic foods Foods grown without the use of chemical fertilizers, insect killers, or weed killers.

orthodontics (OR thuh DAHN tiks) The treatment of malocclusion.

osteomyelitis (AHS tee oh MY uh LY tis) Bone infection.

OTC drugs Over-the-counter drugs; drugs that can be bought without a doctor's prescription.

otosclerosis (OH toh sklih RO sis) A condition in which too much bone forms where the stapes connects to the inner ear. The stapes cannot vibrate, and deafness results.

ovaries (OH vuh reez) Two organs in the lower part of the abdomen in the female. They produce ova (eggs) and hormones that cause the female secondary sexual characteristics to develop.

ovum (OH vum); plural, **ova** (OH vah) The female reproductive cell, made in the ovaries.

ozone (OH ZOHN) A very active form of oxygen produced by the action of sunlight on impurities in the atmosphere.

papillae (puh PIL EE) Tiny projections on the tongue that contain taste receptors and help the tongue "hold onto" food.

paralysis Inability to move all or some parts of the body.

parathyroid (PAR uh THY ROID) **glands** Small endocrine glands in the neck. Their secretions control the body's use of calcium and phosphorus.

particulates (par TIK yuh lits) Tiny harmful

particulates (continued) particles of dust and ash, especially those given off by burning fuels.

passive immunity Resistance to disease that lasts only a short time.

pathogen (PATH uh jin) A disease-causing microorganism.

periodontal (PER ee oh DAHNT ul) **membrane** A tissue that surrounds each tooth in the gum and holds it in place.

peripheral (puh RIF uh rul) **nervous system** The nerves that carry messages to the brain and spinal cord from other parts of the body.

peristaltic (PER uh STAWL tik) **waves** A series of contractions of the muscles making up the esophagus. Peristaltic waves push food down to the stomach.

pertussis (pur TUSS is) A highly contagious disease marked by very bad coughing spells. Also called whooping cough.

phosphorus (FAHS fuh rus) A mineral needed for proper development of bones and teeth.

pigment Matter in the cells of the epidermis that produces skin coloring.

pineal (PY nee ul) **gland** An endocrine gland located in the center of the brain. It produces substances that help to regulate the body's daily rhythms.

pituitary (pi TYOO uh TER ee) **gland** An endocrine gland located deep inside the brain. The pituitary gland regulates growth and influences the other endocrine glands.

placebo (plah SEE boh) **effect** Improvement in patients who have taken an inactive substance which they believe has a medicine in it but does not.

placenta (pluh SEN tuh) The organ by which the fetus is attached to the uterus and through which it is nourished.

plaque (PLAK) A sticky, colorless layer of bacteria that constantly forms on the teeth.

plasma (PLAZ muh) The pale yellow liquid part of the blood, as distinguished from the blood cells.

pleura (PLOOR uh) Smooth, moist membranes that cover the lungs and the inside of the chest cavity.

pleurisy (PLOOR uh see) A condition in which the pleura become rough and sticky and make breathing difficult and painful.

pneumonia (noo MOH nyuh) Inflammation of the lungs.

poliomyelitis (PO lee oh MY uh LY tis) A contagious viral disease that can cause nerve damage and result in permanent paralysis of muscles.

prenatal care A doctor's care of a pregnant woman.

primary care Treatment that is given by a doctor at a clinic, an emergency room, or a doctor's office.

prophylaxis (PROH fuh LAK sis) Thorough cleaning of the teeth by a dentist or a dental hygienist.

protein complementarity Combining foods to get the most protein value from them.

protein A nutrient needed for building and replacing cells. High-quality protein comes mostly from animal sources and contains all the amino acids needed by the human body. Low-quality protein comes from plant sources and contains some of the needed amino acids.

psychoactive (SY koh AK tiv) **drug** A drug used to change a person's mood or behavior.

psychoanalysis (SY koh uh NAL uh sis) A method of treating emotional and mental disorders in which patients are made aware of their psychological makeup.

psychosis (sy KOH sis) A mental disorder in which a person is out of touch with reality at least part of the time.

psychosomatic (SY koh suh MA tik) **disorder** A form of mental illness in which a real physical illness or symptom occurs as a result of an emotional disturbance.

psychotherapy (SY koh THER uh pee) The treatment of mental and emotional disturbances.

puberty (PYOO bur tee) The stage of life when a person's reproductive system starts to work. In girls, the ovaries begin to send out eggs. In boys, the testes start to make sperm.

pulmonary (PUL muh ner ee) **artery** A blood vessel that carries blood from the heart to the lungs.

pulmonary vein A blood vessel that carries blood from the lungs to the heart.

pupil The round opening of the eye through which light enters.

radiation An invisible form of energy that comes from the splitting of atoms.

radioactive substances Materials that give off radiation.

rape Forced sexual intercourse.

recessive (ri SESS iv) **gene** A gene or trait that has no effect when a dominant gene is present.

425

recessive inheritance The process of receiving two recessive genes for a trait, one from each parent. In recessive inheritance of genetic diseases, both parents are normal but each carries a "hidden," or recessive, gene.

reflex An automatic muscle action directed by the spinal cord rather than by the brain.

resistance (to infection) The body's ability to fight infection.

respiration The exchange of oxygen and carbon dioxide, including both outer and inner respiration. Outer respiration is the process of breathing in air through the lungs and breathing out carbon dioxide. Inner respiration is the process that takes place when the cells take in oxygen from the blood and release carbon dioxide back into the blood.

respiratory arrest Absence of breathing.

respiratory center The area of the brain that controls breathing.

retina (RET in uh) The lining of the back of the eyeball on which light rays focus. The light rays cause nerve impulses to travel from the retina along the optic nerve to the brain.

rheumatic (roo MA tik) **fever** An infectious disease that affects the joints and often causes damage to the heart.

rheumatic heart disease Lifelong damage that results from rheumatic fever.

riboflavin (RY buh FLAY vin) An important B vitamin needed for healthy skin and for proper functioning of the nervous and digestive systems.

ringworm A common fungal infection that causes itching and sores of the scalp.

root (of tooth) The part of the tooth that is set within the gum and jawbone.

rubella (roo BEL uh) A mild form of measles that is dangerous to the fetus of an infected pregnant woman. Also called German measles, or three-day measles.

salivary (SAL uh VER ee) **glands** The three pairs of glands that secrete saliva, the liquid that pours into the mouth to moisten and soften food.

sclera (SKLER uh) The tough, white part of the eye that gives the eye its shape.

sebum (SEE bum) An oily secretion of the skin.

secondary care Treatment that is given by specialists at a private or community hospital.

secondary sexual characteristics The different characteristics that develop at puberty in the two sexes. Secondary sexual characteristics are not directly related to human reproduction.

self-care The act of using common sense to prevent illness and injury and to avoid harming one's health.

semen (SEE mun) Fluid containing sperm that is made and discharged by the male reproductive organs.

semicircular (SEM ih SUR kyuh lur) **canals** The three small tubes in the inner ear that control the sense of balance.

sewage Waste that passes through sewers; mostly human waste and garbage.

sex-linked inheritance The process of receiving traits carried on the sex chromosomes. The X chromosome is usually the carrier. Since a male has only one X chromosome, a son will automatically show the trait if he receives the defective gene from the mother. If a daughter inherits the trait on one of her X chromosomes, the other X chromosome may dominate and the trait may not appear.

sexuality The condition of being male or female; the sum of the feelings, thoughts, behavior, and structure that make up males and females.

sexually transmitted disease A communicable disease spread from an infected person to others through sexual contact; also called an STD.

shinsplints A pain in the lower leg, in front of the shin, usually caused by running on a hard surface.

shock A condition, which often follows an injury, in which a person's blood is not circulating properly. Symptoms may include weakness, faintness, weak pulse, chills, nausea, and irregular breathing.

sickle-cell anemia A disease caused by an inherited gene which affects the shape of red blood cells and their ability to carry oxygen.

sickle-cell trait A condition in which a person carries one gene for sickle-cell anemia but does not suffer from the disease itself.

sidestream smoke The smoke that goes directly into the air from the burning end of a cigarette, cigar, or pipe.

specialist A doctor who has spent years studying one system of the human body to learn the most advanced skills in diagnosis and treatment for that field.

speed The ability to move the whole body, or parts of the body, quickly from one place to another.

sperm The male reproductive cell.

sphygmomanometer (SFIG moh muh NAHM uh tur) An instrument used to measure blood pressure.

spinal cord The part of the nervous system contained within the backbone.

spirochetes (SPY ruh KEETS) The spiral-shaped bacteria that cause syphilis.

sprain A painful injury to ligaments, tendons, or muscles near a joint.

stapes (STAY PEEZ) A tiny, stirrup-shaped bone between the incus in the middle ear and the inner ear. It helps amplify sound waves as they travel from the eardrum to the inner ear.

STD See **sexually transmitted disease.**

stethoscope (STETH uh SKOHP) An instrument used to listen to the sounds made by the heart and lungs.

stimulant A drug that speeds up the body's processes.

strabismus (struh BIZ mus) An abnormality of the eyes in which the two eyes do not focus on the same point.

stress The effect on the human body of physical and mental demands and pressures.

stressor Something that makes a demand on the body.

stroke A sudden blocking of blood flow to an area of the brain, usually caused by the formation of a blood clot in a small blood vessel.

sty An infection of glands along the edge of the eyelid.

synovial (su NOH vee ul) **fluid** A fluid surrounding the ends of bones. It keeps the joints moistened so that the bones can move freely.

syphilis (SIF uh lis) A sexually transmitted disease caused by spiral-shaped bacteria called spirochetes.

systole (SIS tuh lee) Contraction of the heart.

tar A black, sticky substance obtained from the burning of wood, coal, or dried plants such as tobacco.

Tay-Sachs (TAY SAKS) Fatal brain damage caused by a certain inherited gene found mostly in infants of East European Jewish ancestry.

temperature inversion An unusual situation in which warm air high above the Earth's surface traps cool air closer to the ground and prevents the cool air from rising. This is dangerous to humans when the cool trapped air is polluted.

tendon A tissue that joins muscles to bones.

tertiary (TUR shee EHR ee) **care** Treatment that is given by specialists at a university hospital.

testes (TES TEEZ); singular, **testis** (TES tis) Two glands in a pouch lying outside the abdomen in the male. They produce sperm and make hormones that influence the development of the male secondary sexual characteristics.

testosterone (tes TAHS tuh ROHN) The hormone that stimulates the development of secondary sexual characteristics in males.

tetanus (TET in us) A disease usually caused by bacteria that enter the body through a break in the skin. Tetanus causes the muscles to lock in abnormal contractions. Also called lockjaw.

thalidomide (thuh LID uh MYD) A tranquilizing drug that can cause deformities in children born to women who use the drug during pregnancy.

therapist A person trained in methods of helping a mentally ill person to recover.

thiamine (THY uh min) An important B vitamin that is needed by the nerves, muscles, and digestive system.

throat culture A test used to detect infection. A sterile cotton swab is rubbed on the throat and then onto a special plate to see what kinds of bacteria are present.

thymus (THY mus) **gland** An endocrine gland located in the upper chest. The thymus gland is believed to produce substances that help fight infection.

thyroid (THY roid) **gland** An endocrine gland in the neck that influences metabolism.

thyroid-stimulating hormone A hormone produced by the pituitary gland that causes the thyroid to produce its hormone.

thyroxine (thy RAHK SEEN) The hormone produced by the thyroid gland.

tolerance The ability of the body to take in a drug without feeling the expected effects.

tourniquet (TOOR nih kit) A band of cloth or other material pulled tightly around an arm or a leg to stop bleeding.

toxin (TAHK sin) A poisonous substance.

toxoid (TAHK soid) A type of vaccine made from poisonous waste products of disease-causing microorganisms.

trachea (TRAY kee uh) A tube in the upper part of the chest; the windpipe.

tranquilizer A drug that is used to calm a per-

tranquilizer (continued) son's emotions without interfering with alertness.

trick riding An unsafe driving practice, sometimes practiced by motorcycle drivers, in which the driver carries out stunts for pleasure.

tumor A group of cells forming a mass or lump.

umbilical (UM BIL ih kul) **cord** The cord that connects the fetus to the placenta. Oxygen, water, and other nutrients pass through the umbilical cord from the mother to the fetus. Wastes pass through it from the fetus to the mother.

umbilicus (UM bu LY kus) The navel; the small depression in the abdomen where the umbilical cord was attached to the fetus.

unit pricing The practice by which food merchants post signs that tell the cost of foods per unit of weight.

urologist (YOO RAHL uh jist) A physician who specializes in disorders of the urinary tract and reproductive organs of men.

U.S. RDA U.S. Recommended Daily Allowance, a list that tells the amount of nutrients and calories needed daily by most people in the United States.

uterus (YOO tuh rus) The organ in the female in which the fetus develops; womb.

uvula (YOO vyuh luh) A small, fleshy organ at the back of the roof of the mouth. It helps to close off the nasal opening when food is swallowed.

vaccine (vak SEEN) A substance used to increase the body's immunity to a certain disease.

vaginitis (VAJ uh NY tis) An irritation of the vagina caused by an excessive number of microorganisms that are normally harmless.

vas deferens (VAS DEF uh runz) Two sperm ducts in the male, leading from the epididymis to the urethra.

vegetarian A person who does not eat meat.

vein A vessel that carries blood to the heart.

ventricle (VEN tri kul) The lower chamber of each side of the heart.

vesicle (VES ih kul) A small, blisterlike elevation on the skin that is a symptom of genital herpes.

vestibule A structure between the cochlea and semicircular canals in the inner ear that helps one know about the position of the head in relation to gravity.

villi (VIL EYE); singular, **villus** (VIL us) Tiny, fingerlike projections in the inner lining of the small intestine. Villi contain blood vessels for absorption of nutrients into the blood and lymph vessels.

vitamins Nutrients that help regulate body processes.

voluntary muscles Muscles that can be purposely controlled. These muscles are attached to bones and are also called skeletal muscles or striated muscles.

withdrawal symptoms Undesirable side effects that occur when an individual stops taking certain drugs, including trembling, hallucinations, nausea, and vomiting.

work-related accidents Accidents that take place on the job or are related to one's job.

World Health Organization (WHO) A special agency of the United Nations that works to improve the physical and mental health of all the world's people.

Index

AA, *see* Alcoholics Anonymous
Abortion, 100
Abscess, 163, 225
Abuse within the family, 103-104
Accidents, 342-349; automobile, 5, 245, 343; bicycle, 344-345; at home, 346; motorcycle, 344; work-related, 347-348
Accommodation, 156
Achievement, personal, 44
Achondroplasia, 115
Acne, 206
Acquired immunity, 281
ACTH, 211
Active immunity, 281-282
Adam's apple, 189
Addiction, 256
Additives, food, 318-320
Adrenal glands, 215-216
Adrenalin, 215-216
Afterbirth, 85
Agility, 27, 28
Air, 189
Air pollution, 121-124, 197-198
Air pressure, 193-195
Air travel, 193-194
Alateen, 249
Albinos, 203
Alcoholic beverages, 243-249; and automobile accidents, 245; and effects on body, 88, 243-245, 333; and help for drinker, 246, 249; misuse of, 246-248
Alcoholics Anonymous, 249
Alcoholism, 246-248
Alimentary canal, 327
Allergen, 64
Allergies, 64
Allergist, 374
Alveoli, 189, 195
Amblyopia, 157
American Cancer Society, 138
American Heart Association, 368
American Red Cross, 368
Amino acids, 109, 290, 331
Amniocentesis, 112-113, 377
Amphetamines, 258
Amylase, 327
Analgesics, 254
Anderson, Dr. Terence, 278
Anemia, 172, 295
Anesthesiologist, 374
Anesthetics, 145, 254
Anger, 55-56
Angina pectoris, 182
Anorexia nervosa, 313-314
Antacids, 391
Antibiotics, 254
Antibodies, 109-110, 137, 275, 281
Antidote, 352-353
Antioxidants, 319
Antiseptics, 390
Antisocial behavior, 56, 102-103
Antitoxins, 275
Antitussive, 390
Anxiety, 57-58
Aorta, 176
Appendicitis, 334, 336, 375
Appendix, 336
Aqueous humor, 157
Arches, 13
Arteries, 176
Arteriosclerosis, 180, 182
Arthritis, 14-15, 70, 216, 379, 391
Artificial circulation, 362, 364-365; *see also* Cardiopulmonary resuscitation
Artificial respiration, 362, 363-364; *see also* Cardiopulmonary resuscitation
Ascaris, 337
Ascorbic acid, 296
Aspirin, 391
Asthma, 196
Astigmatism, 156
Atherosclerosis, 182, 183
Athlete's foot, 205
Atrium, 176
Audiologist, 164
Audiometer, 164
Auricle, 176
Automobile accidents, 5, 245, 343
Autonomic nervous system, 143, 333
Axons, 143

BAL, *see* Blood alcohol level
Backache, 70
Bacteria, 3, 4, 273
Balance, 25, 26, 27
Ball-and-socket joints, 12
Barbiturates, 256
Barometer, 184-185
Basal metabolic rate, 298-299
Bedwetting, 333
Bends, 195
Benign tumor, 133
Bicycle accidents, 344-345
Bile, 329, 331
Bile duct, 329
Biopsy, 135
Birth defects, 112
Birth process, 84-85; *see also* Reproduction
Bisexual, 102
Bladder, 332-333
Bleeding, 352
Blepharitis, 160
Blind people, education of, 161

429

Blindness, 157, 159, 294
Blisters, 357
Blood, 171-175; diseases, 172-173; lymph, 174-175; platelets, 172; red cells, 11, 171, 172; types, 173-174; white cells, 11, 172, 173
Blood alcohol level, 245
Blood banks, 174
Blood clotting, 295
Blood count, 377
Blood pressure, 180, 184-185, 377
Blood transfusion, 174
Boils, 205-206
Bolus, 328
Bone marrow, 11, 171, 172
Bone surgery, 15
Bones, 11-13, 21
Booster shot, 388
Botulism, 319-320
Braille, 161
Brain, 146-147
Breakfast, 298, 304-305
Breathing, 191-194; see also Respiration
Bronchi, 189
Bronchitis, 195, 197, 235
Bruises, 357
Bulimia, 314
Burns, 354-355

CPR, see Cardiopulmonary resuscitation
Caesarean section, 84
Caffeine, 258, 333
Caisson disease, 195
Calcium, 11, 12, 21, 212, 223, 293
Calculus, 226
Calories, 298-299, 303
Cancer, 4, 133-138, 379; causes of, 134, 234-235; research, 137-138; treatment of, 136-137; types of, 133-135, 203; warning signals, 135, 138

Capillaries, 12, 176
Car accidents, see Automobile accidents
Carbohydrate, 291-292, 303, 331
Carbon dioxide, 189, 192, 331
Carbon monoxide, 121
Carcinogenic, 125, 134
Cardiac arrest, 362, 364
Cardiac muscle, 17
Cardiologist, 374
Cardiopulmonary resuscitation, 351, 360-369
Carriers, 112, 113, 273
Cartilage, 12
Cataract, 157
Cavities, 225, 228
Cell differentiation, 83
Cell division, 83
Centers for Disease Control (CDC), 400
Central nervous system, 143, 146
Central service technician, 409
Cerebellum, 147
Cerebral allergies, 64
Cerebrospinal fluid, 13, 377
Cerebrum, 146-147
Certified laboratory assistant, 409
Cervix, 81
Chancre, 268
Charley horse, 33
Chemical burns, 355
Chemotherapy, 136
Chest X ray, 377
Chewing Tobacco, 239-240
Child abuse, see Abuse within the family
Choking, 366-368
Cholesterol, 182, 184, 299-300

Chromosomes, 109-111, 116
Chronic, 64, 379
Chyme, 329
Cigarettes, see Tobacco smoking
Cilia, 274
Ciliary muscle, 155
Circulatory system, 183-184; see also Blood; Heart
Circumcision, 80
Clinical psychologist, 62
Clitoris, 82
Clotting of blood, 11, 171, 172, 173, 295
Cocaine, 258-259
Cochlea, 163
Codeine, 257
Cold, 275-276
Colitis, 70
Color blindness, 115, 116
Communicable diseases, 273
Communication, 95-96
Compensation, 58
Computerized Tomographic Scanner (CTS), 386-387, 408
Conception, 82-83
Conductive loss, 164
Congenital heart disease, 180-181
Conjunctivitis, 160
Constipation, 335-336
Contact lenses, 158
Contagious diseases, 273
Contraception, 100
Conversion, 59
Convulsions, 356
Coordination, 26, 27
Cornea, 155, 158-159
Coronary arteries, 182
Coronary artery disease, 182-183, 234
Coronary bypass surgery, 182
Cortisone, 216
Cough syrup, 390

Cowper's glands, 80
Cranium, 13
Create, need to, 44-45
Cretinism, 212
Crick, Dr. Francis, 109
Crossed eyes, 157
Crown, 221
Cuspids, 221
Cuticle, 206
Cystic fibrosis, 112, 114
Cytotechnologist, 411

Daily Food Guide, 289-291
Dating, 96-98
Daydreaming, 59
Deaf, education of, 166-167
Death, causes of, 3-4, 148, 180
Decalcification, 13
Decibels, 126
Decision making, 48-49
Decompression, 195
Decongestants, 390
Defense mechanisms, 58-59
Dendrites, 143
Dental care, 378-379
Dental caries, 225, 228
Dental floss, 224
Dental hygienist, 411
Dentist, 379
Department of Health and Human Services, 399
Depressant, 244, 256
Depression, 57, 64
Dermatitis, 204
Dermatologist, 374
Dermis, 201
Detoxification, 249
Diabetes, 70, 157, 159, 214-215, 320
Diagnosticians, 373
Diaphragm, 191, 328
Diarrhea, 3, 335
Diastolic pressure, 178, 185
Diet, 302-314; breakfast, 304-305; and energy, 312; and exercise, 312; overeating, 308-309; and overweight, 307-308; and underweight, 305, 307; vegetarian, 291, 312-313; and weight loss, 309-310, 312-314
Dietary Guidelines for Americans, 324
Dietetic assistant, 410
Digestion, 327-331, 333-334
Dim vision, 157
Diphtheria, 281, 283, 388
Diplopia, 157
Disease, 273-274; *see also* specific disease
Dislocations, 34-35, 354
Distillation, 243
Distress, 69
Disturbed feelings, 43
DNA, 109-110, 117-118
Doctors, *see* Medical care
Dominant gene, 110
Dominant inheritance, 114-115
Double vision, 157
Down's syndrome, 116
Drug therapy, 62
Drugs, 252-263; abused, 256; depressants, 256; hallucinogens, 260-261; narcotics, 257-258; and pregnant women, 88; psychoactive, 254-256; stimulants, 258-260; use of, 253-254
Duchenne muscular distrophy, 112
Ductless glands, 211
Duodenum, 329, 331, 336
Dysentery, 274

EDITH (exit drills in the home), 347
EEG (electroencephalogram), 151
Eardrum, 163
Ears, 162-169; and aging, 165-166; care of, 166; hearing disorders, 164-165; parts of, 162-164
Electric shock, injury, 356; treatment, 62-63
Electrocardiograph, 177
Electrocardiograph technician, 409
Electroencephalograph, 151, 152
Elimination, 331-333
Embryo, 83
Emergency, 351
Emergency medical services (EMS) system, 362-363
Emotional needs, 43-45
Emotions, 55-59; and defense mechanisms, 58-59; and digestion, 334
Emphysema, 195, 197, 235-236
Endocrine glands, 211-217; adrenal, 215-216; gonads, 216-217; parathyroid, 212, 214; pineal, 217; pituitary, 211; thymus, 217; thyroid, 211-212
Endocrine system, 210-217; care of, 217; glands, 211-217; problems with, 214-215
Endocrinologist, 374
Endodontist, 378
Endometrium, 82
Endorphins, 218, 261-262
Endurance, 27, 30
Enemas, 335
Energy, 312
Enriched foods, 318
Enuresis, 333
Environmental hazards, 120-131; air pollution, 121-124; noise pollution, 126-128, 130; radiation pollution, 128-129; water pollution, 124-126

Enzymes, 110, 327
Ephedrine, 390
Epidemic, 125, 281
Epidermis, 201
Epididymis, 80
Epilepsy, 148, 151, 356, 379
Epithelial cells, 337
Epiglottis, 328
Equilibrium, 25, 26, 27
Escape, 57
Esophagus, 328
Estrogen, 216
Euphoria, 258
Eustachian tube, 163
Exercises, 24-39; agility, 27, 28; aging and, 29, 31; balance, 26-27; conditioning, 31; coordination, 26-27; eating and, 29, 312; endurance, 27, 30; flexibility, 26-27; and the heart, 27, 29; and injuries, 32-35, 37; speed, 27-28; strength, 27, 30; warm-up, 20, 25; and water and salt, 31-32
Expectorant, 390
Expiration, 191
External auditory canal, 162-163
External cardiac compression, 364
Eyes, 154-161; accommodation, 156; and blindness, 159; and contact lenses, 158; examination, 160-161; and glasses, 158; injuries to, 158-159; parts of, 155-156, 157, 160; problems with, 156-157, 159-160; and strain, 158

Fainting, 179
Fallopian tubes, 81
Family, 93-96; communication within, 95-96; and conflicts, 95-96; and personality, 43; relationships, 93; responsibilities within, 94-95; roles within, 93-94
Family pedigree, 112
Family planning, 100-101
Farsightedness, 156
Fasciculus, 16
Fatigue, chronic, 64
Fat, 292, 299-300
Fatty acids, 331
Fear, 57
Feces, 331
Feelings, "transferred," 43; understanding own, 46-47; see also Emotions
Fermentation, 243
Fertilization, 82-83
Fetal alcohol syndrome (FAS), 88, 250
Fetus, 83-84
Fiber, 297, 335
"Fight" response, 72
First aid, 350-359; for bleeding, 352, 357; for burns, 354-355; for choking, 366-368; for convulsions, 356; for electric shock, 356; for fractures, 354; for frostbite, 355; for heatstroke, 355; miscellaneous, 357; for poisoning, 352-353; for shock, 353-354; for snakebites, 355-356; for sprains, 354; see also Cardiopulmonary resuscitation
First-degree burns, 354-355
Flatus, 337
Flexibility, 26, 27
"Flight" response, 72
Flu, 3, 276-277
Fluorides, 223
Fluorine, 293
Fontanels, 13
Food additives, 318-320
Food and Drug Administration (FDA), 320, 392-393, 399, 403
Fortified foods, 318
Fractures, 354
Fraternal twins, 86
Freud, Anna, 52
Frostbite, 355
Fungal infections, 205
Fungi, 273
Fungus, 205

Gallbladder, 329
Gallstones, 334
Gamma globulin, 174
Gamma rays, 128
Gas, in intestinal tract, 337
Gastric juice, 329
General practitioner, 373
Genes, 109-110, 114, 117-118
Genetic code, 109
Genetic counseling, 111-112
Genetic diseases, 112-116
Genetic research, 116
Genetics, 109-118; carriers, 112-113, 114; chromosomes, 109, 110-111, 116; DNA, 109-110, 117-118; dominant inheritance, 114-115; mutation, 113; organ transplants, 116-117; recessive inheritance, 114; sex-linked inheritance, 115
Genital herpes, 267–268, 270
German measles (Rubella), 87, 167-168, 284, 388
Gingivitis, 226
Glaucoma, 112, 114-115, 157
Gliding joints, 11
Glucose, 312
Glycerol, 331
Glycogen, 292, 304
Goiter, 212
Gonads, 216
Gonococci, 267

Gonorrhea, 267-268
Gout, 14
Group therapy, 63
Guilt, 58
Gynecologist, 374

Habits, 145-146
Hair, 206-208
Halitosis, 227
Hallucinogens, 260-261
Hammer, 163
Hashish, 261
Health care center, 386
Health careers, 406-417
Health foods, 322
Health in the United States, 396-404; city health department, 398; federal health services, 399-400; history of, 397-398; state health department, 399; voluntary health agencies, 400-401
Health insurance, 385-386
Hearing, see Ears
Heart, 176-185; and blood pressure, 178, 180, 184-185; chambers, 176; and circulation of blood, 176-179; and exercise, 27, 29; and pulse, 178-179
Heart attack, 4, 70, 182, 362
Heart disease, 5, 180-184, 234, 320
Heart-lung machine, 181
Heart murmur, 177-178
Heatstroke, 32, 296, 355
Heimlich, Dr. Henry, 367
Hemoglobin, 109, 171, 172
Hemophilia, 115, 173
Hemorrhage, 352
Hemorrhoids, 336
Hepatitis, 277
Heredity, 109
Hernia, 20-21, 80
Heroin, 257

Herpes, 268-270
Heterosexual, 102
Hiccuping, 192
High blood pressure, 4, 70, 159, 180
Hinge joints, 11
Hives, 204
Hollinshead, Dr. Ariel, 137
Holmes, Dr. T. H., 70-71
Home accidents, 346
Home safety, 346-347
Homosexuality, 101-102
Hookworm, 337
Hormones, 211, 216-217
Hospitals, 386-387
Hostility, 55-56
Huntington's disease, 112, 115
Hydrocarbons, 121
Hydrocephalic, 13
Hydrochloric acid, 329, 337
Hydrogen peroxide, 390
Hyperopia, 156
Hypertension, 180
Hyperventilation, 192
Hypoglycemia, 215

Identical twins, 86
Identification, 59
Immune response, 116-117
Immunizations, 280-285, 388; active immunity, 281-282; acquired immunity, 281; childhood diseases, 283-284; influenza, 284-285; passive immunity, 282; toxoids, 282
Incisors, 221
Incubation period, 274
Incus, 163
Indigestion, 333-334
Individual therapy, 62
Infection, 273-275
Infectious diseases, 3, 273, 275-278, 281
Influenza, 3, 276-277
Inheritance, 114-115

Inherited characteristics, 109
Injuries, to muscles and bones, 31-35, 37
"Inpatient" care, 386
Insect bites, 357
Inspiration, 191
Insulin, 214, 331
Interferon, 278
Internal secretion, 211
Internists, 373
Intestines, and gas, 337; and infections, 337; large, 331; small, 329, 331; and ulcers, 334, 336
Intoxicated, 244
Involuntary muscles, 17
Iodine, 212, 293
Iris, 155
Iron, 172
Isherwood, 99
Islands of Langerhans, 214

Joints, 11-12

Kelsey, Dr. Frances O., 403
Kidneys, 216, 332-333

Labia majora, 82
Labia minora, 82
Labor, 84
Laboratory assistant, 409
Laboratory tests, 377
Lactic acid, 19
Lang, Prof. Frederick, 21
Large intestine, 331
Larynx, 189
Laxatives, 336
Lens, 155-156
Lethal genes, 114
Leukemia, 136, 173
Leukocytes, 173, 275
Life span, 397
Ligaments, 11
Lincoln, Abraham, 74
Liver, 329, 331

433

Local anesthetic, 145
Love, 43
Low blood sugar, 215
LSD, 260
Lung cancer, 5, 134, 138, 197, 234-235
Lungs, 191, 192
Lymph, 174-175, 331
Lymphoma, 136

Mainstream smoke, 236-237
Malaria, 114
Malignant tumor, 133
Malleus, 163
Malocclusion, 226
Maltose, 328
Marijuana, 261
Marriage, 98-100
Marrow, bone, 11
Mastication, 327
Maturity, 45-52
Meals, 298
Measles, 281, 283, 388; *see also* German measles
Medicaid, 385
Medical assistant, 412
Medical care, 373-379; dental care, 378-379; general practitioners, 373; mental health, 378; and patient's rights, 378; physical examination, 377-378; primary, 386; secondary, 386; specialists, 373-375; tertiary, 386
Medical centers, 386
Medical geneticist, 111
Medical quack, 379, 380
Medical specialists, 373-375
Medical technologist, 412
Medicine show, 379-380
Medicines, 388-392
Medulla oblongata, 147
Melanin, 203
Melanoma, 203
Meningitis, 149

Menopause, 81
Menstruation, 82
Mental health, 4-5, 8, 63-64
Mental illness, 59-63; causes of, 59-60; kinds of, 60-61; treating, 61-63, 378
Mercury poison, 333
Metabolism, 212, 298-299
Metastasis, 133
Methadone, 257
Microcephalic, 13
Microorganisms, 335
Midbrain, 147
Migraine headaches, 70
Minerals, 293-294
Miscarriage, 84
Molars, 222
Mole, 203
Monilia, 270
Mononucleosis, 277
Morphine, 257
Motor nerves, 145
Motorcycle accidents, 344
Mouth, and digestion, 327
Mouth-to-mouth breathing, 363
Multiple births, 85-86
Multiple sclerosis, 149
Mumps, 284, 388
Muscles, 16-21; and bones, 11; contraction of, 16; and exercise, 20, 25; and hernia, 20-21, 80; increasing size of, 19; injury to, 33-34; red and white, 18; soreness of, 19-20; types of, 17
Muscular dystrophy, 112
Mutations, 113, 276
Myoglobin, 17
Myopia, 156

Nails, 206-207, 208
Narcotics, 257-258
"Nature's elixirs," 379

Nearsightedness, 156
Neck injury, 365
Negativism, 58
Nerve loss, 165
Nerve fiber, 144
Nerve impulse, 145
Nervous system, 143-153; autonomic, 143; care of, 150-152; central, 143, 146-147; disorders of, 147-150; peripheral, 143; and reflex, 145; transmitting messages, 143-145
Neurologist, 374
Neurons, 143
Neurosis, 60
Neutralize, 275
Newbold, Dr. H.L., 64
Niacin, 295
Nicotine, 88, 233
Nitrites, 319
Nitrogen, 189
Nitrogen oxide, 121
Noise pollution, 126-128, 130
Nonsystemic, 391
Nosebleeds, 357
Nurse practitioner, 412
Nutrients, 289-292; absorption of, 331; carbohydrate, 291-292; fat, 292, 299-300; protein, 290-291; water, 296-297
Nutrition, 316-325; and food additives, 318-320; health foods, 322-323; and labeling, 317-318, 323; poor, 275; and salt, 322; and sugar, 320-322
Nutritional needs, 288-301; fiber, 297; food groups, 289-291; meals, 298; minerals, 293-294; nutrients, 289-292; for pregnant women, 87; vitamins, 294-296; water, 296-297

OTC drugs, see Over-the-counter drugs
Obstetrician, 374
Occupational therapist, 62
Open dating, 323
Operating room technician, 410
Ophthalmologist, 160, 374
Ophthalmoscope, 77
Optic nerve, 155
Optician, 160
Optometrists, 161
Oral pathologist, 378
Oral surgeon, 378
Organ transplants, 116-117
Organic foods, 322-323
Orthodontist, 226, 378
Orthopedic surgeon, 374
Osteomyelitis, 15
Otolaryngologist, 374
Otologist, 164, 374
Otosclerosis, 164-165
Otoscope, 377
Ova, 79, 81
Ovaries, 79, 81, 217
Over-the-counter (OTC) drugs, 253, 388-392
Overweight, 307-308
Ovulation, 81, 82
Ovum, 79, 82
Oxidation, 189, 193
Oxygen, 189
Ozone, 123

PCP, 260-261
Pancreas, 329, 331
Pap test, 138, 377
Papillae, 327
Paralysis, 283
Parathyroid gland, 212, 214
Parenthood, 89-90
Parents, and personality, 45
Parents Anonymous, 103-104
Particulates, 121
Passive immunity, 282
Patella, 377
Pathogens, 273-275, 281

Pathologist, 374
Pauling, Dr. Linus, 278
Pediatric assistant, 411
Pediatrician, 374
Penis, 80
Pepsin, 329
Periodontal disease, 226-7
Periodontist, 226, 378
Peripheral nervous system, 143
Peristalsis, 328, 331, 334
Pernicious anemia, 295
Personal achievement, 44
Personality, 45, 49-52
Perspiration, 331
Pertussis (whooping cough), 273-281, 283, 388
Pharmacist, 389
Pharynx, 328
Phencyclohexylpiperidine (PCP), 260-261
Phenylephrine, 390
Philosophy of life, 45
Phosphorus, 11, 21, 212, 223, 293
Physical dependency, on drugs, 255
Physical examination, 377-378
Physical well-being, 4, 5, 7-8
Physician, 413
Pigment, 201
Pineal gland, 217
Pinworm, 337
Pituitary gland, 211
Pivot joints, 12
Placebos, 218, 379, 380
Placenta, 84
Plaque, 224
Plasma, 171
Plastic surgeon, 374
Platelets, 11, 172
Pleura, 191
Pleurisy, 191
Pneumonia, 3, 197, 277
Poisoning, 352-353, 356

Polio, see Poliomyelitis
Poliomyelitis, 149, 273, 281, 283, 388
Pollution, 120-131; air, 121-124; noise, 126-128, 130; radiation, 128-129; water, 124-126
Polydactylism, 115
Pons, 147
Pores, 201
Posture, 16
Pregnancy testing, 87
Prenatal care, 87-89
Prescription drugs, 389
Preservatives, food, 318-319
Preventive medicine, 5, 385, 387-388
Primary care, 386
Prostate gland, 80
Prosthodontist, 378
Protein, 109-110, 290-291, 298, 331
Protein complementarity, 298
Protozoa, 273
Psychiatric nurse, 62
Psychiatric social worker, 62
Psychiatrist, 62, 375, 378
Psychoactive drugs, 254
Psychoanalysis, 62
Psychological dependency, on drugs, 256
Psychologist, 62, 378
Psychosis, 60-61, 62
Psychosomatic disorders, 61
Psychotherapy, 61
Puberty, 79, 81
Public health, 397
Public Health Service, 399-400
Pulmonary artery, 176
Pulmonary vein, 176
Pulse, 178-179
Pupil, 155
Pus, 172

"Quacks," 379, 380

435

REM, *see* Rapid eye movement
Radiation accidents, 348
Radiation pollution, 128-129
Radiation therapy, 136
Radioactive substances, 128
Radiologist, 375
Rapid eye movement (REM), 152
Rationalization, 58
Recessive gene, 110
Recessive inheritance, 114
Recombinant-DNA, 117-118
Recommended daily allowance, 317-318
Recreational therapist, 62
Red blood cells, 11, 109, 171
Reflex, 145
Regression, 59
Relaxation, 72-73
Repression, 57
Reproduction, 79-91; birth process, 84-85; cell differentiation, 83; cell division, 83; and female, 81-82; fertilization, 82-83; fetus, 83-84; and male, 79-80; multiple births, 85-86; parenthood, 89-90; pregnancy testing, 87; prenatal care, 87-88; teen-age pregnancy, 89
Rescue breathing, 363
Resistance to disease, 274
Resource guide, 405
Respiration, 189-199; and air-pressure changes, 193-195; breathing, 191-193; lungs, 191; respiratory tract, 189-191; trachea, 189
Respiratory arrest, 362
Respiratory center, 191-192
Respiratory disorders, 122, 195-197
Retina, 155
Rh factor, 174
Rheumatic fever, 182

Rheumatic heart disease, 181-182
Rheumatoid arthritis, 14
Riboflavin, 295
Rickets, 12, 295
Ringworm, 205
Role models, 45
Roughage, 297, 335
Rubella, 87, 167-168, 284, 388
STDs, *see* Sexually transmitted diseases
Safety, 345-348; home, 346-347; job, 347-348; water, 345-346
Saliva, 274, 328
Salivary glands, 328
Salt, 322
Schizophrenia, 64
Sclera, 155
Scurvy, 296
Sebum, 206
Second-degree burns, 355
Secondary care, 386
Secondary sexual characteristics, 79
Self-care, 385, 387-388
Self-concept, 44
Self-confidence, 48
Semen, 80
Semicircular canal, 164
Seminal vesicles, 80
Seminiferous tubules, 80
Sense organs, 144-145
Sensory nerves, 145
Sex-linked inheritance, 115
Sexually transmitted diseases, 266-271; genital herpes, 268-270; gonorrhea, 267-268; syphilis, 268
Shinsplints, 37
Shock, 353-354
Siamese twins, 86
Sickle-cell anemia, 112, 113-114
Sidestream smoke, 236-237

Skeleton, 13
Skin, 201-206, 208-209; problems with, 204-206; as protection, 201, 203; and sensation, 203; structure of, 201-202
Sleep, 150-152
Small intestine, 329, 331
Smallpox, 273, 284-285
Smog, 123-124
Smoke alarm, 348
Smokeless tobacco, 239-240
Smoking, *see* Tobacco smoking
Snacks, 302-304
Snakebite, 355-356
Snuff, 239-240
Social well-being, 4-5, 8
Specialists, dental, 378; medical, 373-375
Speech pathologist, 413
Sperm, 79-80
Sphygmomanometer, 184-185, 377
Spirochetes, 268
Sports, 36; concentration in, 37-38; and injuries, 32-35, 37; *see also* Exercises
Sprains, 34-35, 354
Stapes, 163
Stethoscope, 177, 377
Stimulants, 258
Stirrup, 163
Stomach, and digestion, 328-329, 337; ulcer, 334, 336, 379
Strabismus, 157
Strength, 27, 30
Stress, 67-74; coping with, 69-72; and health, 70-71, 275; and relaxation, 72-73; responses to, 67-69
Stressor, 68
Stroke, 4, 148-149, 180
Sty, 160
Sugar, 223, 320-322, 331; *see also* Diabetes

Sulfur oxide, 121-122
Sunburn, 205, 208
Suppression, 59
Synovial fluid, 11
Syphilis, 268
Systemic, 391
Systolic pressure, 178, 185

Tamperproof packaging, on OTC drugs, 390
Tapeworm, 337
Tar, 233
Tartar, 226
Taste buds, 327
Tay-Sachs disease, 112, 114
Teeth, 220-229; care of, 224-225, 227; and diet, 223; and fluorides, 223; problems with, 225-227; structure of, 221-222
Tel-Med, 9
Temperature inversion, 123
Tendons, 13, 16
Tertiary (medical) care, 386
Testes, 79-80, 217
Testicles, 79
Testicular cancer, 135
Testosterone, 19, 79, 216
Tetanus, 283, 388
Thalidomide, 403
Therapeutic recreation specialist, 413
Therapist, 61
Therapy, 62-63
Thiamine, 150, 295
Third-degree burns, 355
Thoracic surgeon, 375
Thorax, 328
Throat, and digestion, 328
Throat culture, 182
Thymus gland, 217
Thyroid gland, 211-212
Thyroxin, 212
Tobacco smoking, 232-241; as habit, 237-238; and health, 183, 184, 195, 197, 234-236, 275, 336; involuntary, 236-237; and lung cancer, 4, 134, 138, 197, 234-235; and pregnant women, 88, 237; substances in, 233-234
Tolerance, 254-255
Tomographic scanners, 386-387, 408
Tongue, and digestion, 327
Tongue depressor, 377
Tooth decay, 225, 228
Tourniquet, 352
Toxins, 275, 319
Toxoids, 282
Trachea, 189, 328
Tranquilizers, 256
"Transferred" feelings, 43
Transplant surgery, 116-117, 333
Trichomonad, 270
Tuberculosis, 3, 388
Tumors, 133
Twins, 86
Typhoid, 274

U.S. RDA, see Recommended daily allowance
Ulcers, 70, 334, 336, 379
Ultrasound, 408, 416
Umbilical cord, 84
Umbilicus, 85
Underweight, 305, 307
Unit pricing, 323
"Universal donor," 173
Ureters, 332, 333
Urethra, 80, 332, 333
Urinary system, 332-333
Urologist, 375
Uterus, 81, 82
Uvula, 328

Vaccines, 137, 254, 281-285
Vagina, 82
Vaginitis, 270
Valves, 177
van Leeuwenhoek, Anton, 273
Varicose veins, 179
Vas deferens, 80
Vascular surgeon, 375
Vegetarians, 291, 312-313
Veins, 176
Venereal disease, see Sexually transmitted diseases
Ventricle, 176
Vesicle, 269
Vestibule, 164
Veterinarian, 414
Villi, 331
Viruses, 3, 4, 273, 276
Vitamins, 294-296; A, 294; B, 150, 295; C, 278, 296; D, 12, 223, 295; E, 295; K, 295
Voluntary muscles, 17
Vomiting, 334-335

Wastes, elimination of, 331-333
Water, 296-297
Water pollution, 124-126
Water safety, 345-346
Watson, Dr. James, 109
Weight control, see Diet
Wellness, 4
White blood cells, 11, 172, 173, 275
Whooping cough, 273, 281, 283, 388
Wilson's disease, 112
Windpipe, 328
Withdrawal symptoms, 255
Womb, 81
World Health Organization (WHO), 401-402
Worms, 337
Worry, 57

X ray, chest, 377; equipment, 386-387, 408; for tuberculosis, 388

Yawning, 20, 192

Picture Credits

Frontispiece: L. T. Rhodes/Taurus; Dana Hyde/Photo Researchers; Hugh Rogers/Monkmeyer; Eric Knoll/Taurus; James H. Karales/Peter Arnold, Inc.; John Lei/Omni Photo Communications.

Unit Openers: Unit 1: Henry Deters/Monkmeyer; Unit 2: Bonnie Freer; Unit 3: The Bettmann Archives; Unit 4: William Hubbell/Woodfin Camp; Unit 5: Manfred Kage/Peter Arnold, Inc.; Unit 6: Owen Franken/Stock, Boston; Unit 7: Mieke Maas/The Image Bank; Unit 8: Bill Stanton/Magnum; Unit 9: Arthur Grace/Stock, Boston; Unit 10: Steve Niedorf/The Image Bank.

Page 2: Cary Wolinsky/Stock, Boston; 5: Wil Blanche/DPI; 8: Ted Tsumura; 15: George Hall/Woodfin Camp; 17: Manfred Kage/Peter Arnold, Inc.; 19, 20: Ted Tsumura; 21: Olivier Rebbott/Stock, Boston; 24: Stan Pantoric/Photo Researchers; 26, 28, 30: Ted Tsumura; 32: (left) John Dominus/Time-Life Picture Agency, (right) *Friends Magazine;* 33: (left) Sam Falk/Monkmeyer, (right) John Running/Stock, Boston; 34: (left) Tim Carlson/Stock, Boston, (right) Rick Smolan/Stock, Boston; 35: James H. Karales/Peter Arnold, Inc.; 38: Hugh Rogers/Monkmeyer; 42: Ann Hagen Griffiths/DPI; 44: Wayne Miller/Magnum; 45: National Educational Association; 46: Owen Franken/Stock, Boston; 49: Irene Fertig; 50: Suva/DPI; 54: Peter Menzel/Stock, Boston; 56: Peter Smallman/Taurus; 57: L.H. Jawitz/The Image Bank; 58: Gabe Palmer/The Image Bank; 59: Owen Franken/Stock, Boston; 61: Erika/Peter Arnold, Inc.; 66: Bernard Wolf/DPI; 68: Owen Franken/Stock, Boston; 69: Irene Fertig; 72: Paul Conklin/Monkmeyer; 73: National Educational Association; 78: Pam Hasagawa/Taurus; 80: Manfred Kage/Peter Arnold, Inc.; 88: Kenneth Garrett/Woodfin Camp; 92: Joan Menschenfreund/Taurus; 94: Owen Franken/Stock, Boston; 96: Rhoda Sidney/Monkmeyer; 97: Eric Anderson/Stock, Boston; 98: Owen Franken/Stock, Boston; 101: Mimi Forysth/Monkmeyer; 102: Ginger Chih/Peter Arnold, Inc.; 108: Mimi Forsyth/Monkmeyer; 110: (bottom) Fritz Goro/Time-Life Picture Agency; 114: Sickle Cell Disease Foundation; 117: Rick Winsor/Woodfin Camp; 120: Porterfield-Chickering/Photo Researchers; 122: Eric Anderson/Stock, Boston; 124: Leonard Lee Rue/Photo Researchers; 125: Sekai Bunka; 126: (top) Alan Roberts, (center) Eric Anderson/Stock, Boston; 128, 129: Tom McHugh/Photo Researchers; 130: Hugh Rogers/Monkmeyer; 134: Ira Berger/Woodfin Camp; 135: Manfred Kage/Peter Arnold, Inc.; 136: Guy Gillette/Memorial Sloan-Kettering Cancer Center; 137, 138: American Cancer Society; 142: Manfred Kage/Peter Arnold, Inc.; 147: Carroll Weiss/Camera MD; 151: James H. Karales/Peter Arnold, Inc.; 152: Hospital of the University of Pennsylvania; 154: Manfred Kage/Peter Arnold, Inc.; 161: Brian Payne/Medical World News; 165: Lou Niznik/DPI; 166: Martin M. Rotker/Taurus; 167: Mike Maple/Woodfin Camp; 170, 172: Manfred Kage/Peter Arnold, Inc.; 173: Dr. James G. Hirsch; 177: Robert J. Capece/McGraw-Hill; 178: Dow Corning; 183: Stan Pantovic/Photo Researchers; 185: Paul Conklin/Monkmeyer; 188: Manfred Kage/Peter Arnold, Inc.; 193: Richard Wood/Taurus; 194: Judy Joye/Oceanographic News Service; 196: Lawrence Frank; 197: Robert J. Capece/McGraw-Hill; 200: Manfred Kage/Peter Arnold, Inc.; 203: Mimi Forsyth/Monkmeyer; 204: William Hubbell/Woodfin Camp; 205: (top to bottom) W.H. Hodge/Peter Arnold, Inc.; John Bova/Photo Researchers, Alexander Lowry/Photo Researchers; 207: Michal Heron/Monkmeyer; 208: Burk Uzzle/Magnum; 210: Manfred Kage/Peter Arnold, Inc.; 216: Rhoda Sidney/Monkmeyer; 217: Robert J. Capece/McGraw-Hill; 220: Howard Sochurer/Woodfin Camp; 223, 225–227: American Dental Association; 235: Frank Siteman; 237–239: American Cancer Society; 240: Culver Pictures; 242: Larry Mulvehill/Photo Researchers; 246: Bob Hammon/Stock, Boston; 247: Lawrence Schiller/Magnum; 248: National Institute of Alcohol Abuse and Alcoholism; 252: Mimi Forsyth/Monkmeyer; 259: Adam Wolinsky/Stock, Boston; 260: Gill C. Kenny/The Image Bank; 266, 269: State of New York, Department of Health; 274: The Pierpont Morgan Library, m. 638, f.21v (detail from 13th-century French Manuscript depicting a Biblical account of a plague of mice visited on the Asotians by God); 275: Hugh Rogers/Monkmeyer; 276: Suva/DPI; 280: Steve Niedor/The Image Bank; 281: Manfred Kage/Peter Arnold, Inc.; 283: Dow Chemical/New York; 284: Culver Pictures; 288: (top left) Simon Cherpital/Magnum, (top right) Tana Hoban/DPI, (bottom left) Costa Manor/Magnum, (bottom right) Wil Blanche/DPI; 290: Clyde H. Smith/Peter Arnold, Inc.; 292–293: William Hubbell/Woodfin Camp; 297: Wil Blanche/DPI; 299: Jerry Cooke/Photo Researchers; 302: American Egg Board; 304: Paul Conklin/Monkmeyer; 305: Erich Hartmann/Magnum; 309: American Dental Association; 313: Paul Conklin/Monkmeyer; 316: Marvin Newman/Woodfin Camp; 320: California Table Grape Commission; 322: Robert J. Capece/McGraw-Hill; 326: James Holland/Stock, Boston; 334: Gabe Palmer/The Image Bank; 343: Harry Wilks/Stock, Boston; 344: Jon Bailey/Stock, Boston; 346: John Running/Stock, Boston; 350: Mottke Weismann/McGraw-Hill; 353: Francis Laping/DPI; 357: Mimi Forsyth/Monkmeyer; 360: Elizabeth Hamlin/Stock, Boston; 367: (left) Mimi Forsyth/Monkmeyer; 372: E.R. Squibb & Sons, Inc.; 376: Robert J. Capece/McGraw-Hill; 381: Culver Pictures; 384: Mimi Forsyth/Monkmeyer; 387: Michal Heron/Monkmeyer; 393: Robert J. Capece/McGraw-Hill; 393: Wide World; 396: Martin Rotker/Taurus; 399: Monsanto Company; 401: American Red Cross; 402: March of Dimes/Birth Defects Foundations; 414: Courtesy of Humane Society of New York.